"Spur Up Your Pegasus"

Salmon P. Chase with his daughters Nettie (b. 1847), left, and Kate
(b. 1840) in a photograph made at Matthew Brady's studio in
Washington, D.C., perhaps in the summer of 1857.

Courtesy of the Library of Congress.

"Spur Up Your Pegasus"

Family Letters of Salmon, Kate, and Nettie Chase,

1844–1873

Edited by

JAMES P. McCLURE,

PEG A. LAMPHIER,

and

ERIKA M. KREGER

The Kent State University Press

KENT, OHIO

© 2009 by The Kent State University Press, Kent, Ohio 44242
All rights reserved
Library of Congress Catalog Card Number 2009001439
ISBN 978-0-87338-988-4
Manufactured in the United States of America

Library of Congress Cataloging-in-Publication Data
"Spur up your Pegasus" : family letters of Salmon, Kate, and Nettie Chase, 1844–1873 /
edited by James P. McClure, Peg A. Lamphier, and Erika M. Kreger.
    p. cm.
Includes bibliographical references and index.
    ISBN 978-0-87338-988-4 (hardcover : alk. paper) ∞ 1. Chase, Salmon P. (Salmon
Portland), 1808–1873—Correspondence.   2. Sprague, Kate Chase, 1840–1899—
Correspondence.   3. Hoyt, Janet Ralston Chase, 1847–1925—Correspondence.
4. Fathers and daughters—United States—Correspondence.   5. Chase, Salmon P.
(Salmon Portland), 1808–1873—Family.   6. Judges—United States—Correspondence.
7. Chase family—Correspondence.   I. McClure, James P.   II. Lamphier, Peg A.
III. Kreger, Erika M.
    E199.R74A4   2009
    973.7092—dc22

                        2009001439

British Library Cataloging-in-Publication data are available.

                13 12 11 10 09   5 4 3 2 1

Publication of this volume has been supported by a grant from the
National Historical Publications and Records Commission.

Contents

Preface

THIS VOLUME contains letters of an American family during the middle decades of the nineteenth century. While the expected model for a middle-class household of that era might center on a married couple and their children—perhaps focusing especially on the role of the wife and mother—this family consisted, for most of the period documented in these pages, of a father and his two daughters. Salmon Portland Chase married three times, but his wives all died, one of infection and two of tuberculosis, none of the three surviving more than six years after her wedding. Four children of those marriages, all daughters, also died, all in infancy or early childhood. The daughters who survived, Kate (born in 1840) and Janet (called Nettie, born in 1847), were from Chase's second and third marriages. Chase and his daughters made their home in Ohio until just before the Civil War, when they moved to the nation's capital. An attorney and politician, Chase was frequently away from home as his daughters were growing up, and Kate and Nettie attended boarding schools in New York City and Pennsylvania. Letters exchanged by the three of them bridged the separations. This father sought to train his daughters to be not just competent letter writers but also accomplished participants in a culture of letters. Their involvement in that world began at an early age: Nettie dictated two of the letters in this book when she was three years old (both addressed to Kate, dated September 28, 1850, and January 9, 1851).

We have taken the book's title from a letter that Chase wrote to Nettie on June 18, 1866, in which he alluded to the mythical winged horse Pegasus as the carrier of a writer's inspiration. Medieval and Renaissance poets and writers drew on the classical myth to expand and develop the association of Pegasus with the Muses and to play on the image of a writer figuratively taken aloft by a flying steed. That symbolism was well established by the nineteenth century. Byron put it to use several times in *Don Juan* and in his satirical *English Bards and Scotch Reviewers* ("Each spurs his jaded Pegasus apace"). Keats employed the allusion in *The Cap and Bells* and jabbed, in *Sleep and Poetry,* at mundane poets who "sway'd about upon a rocking horse, / And thought it Pegasus." In his novel *Pendennis,*

William Makepeace Thackeray construed Pegasus as a cart horse, the symbol of writers who must earn a living by their pens (see Peter L. Shillingsburg, *Pegasus in Harness: Victorian Publishing and W. M. Thackeray* [Charlottesville: University of Virginia Press, 1992], xiv). Nathaniel Hawthorne—whose works Nettie Chase knew and with whom she was thrilled to have an acquaintance when she was thirteen—retold the Pegasus tale for young readers and also drew on the allegory of the winged horse as the imaginative writer's soaring steed. Nettie understood the imagery when her father, suggesting that her recent letters were not quite as good as her sister's, urged her: "Spur up your Pegasus, and make him keep step." Significantly, however, her father could not simply advise her to mount the fabled horse and let her creative spirit fly. She must never abandon control or leave discipline behind. "Let Pegasus use his wings," Chase offered, "but do you use the reins."

The letters printed in this volume range in date from 1844 to 1873. Most were written by Chase and his daughters, but we have also included some correspondence of Kate's and Nettie's mothers, teachers, and husbands. Collectively, the letters touch themes important to many American families of the nineteenth century. A parent's plans for his children's education; his prescriptions for their moral conduct and his wishes for their religious fulfillment; his concerns for their health, given the early deaths of both of their mothers and other members of the family; children's efforts to meet parental expectations; the social culture and educational curriculum of boarding schools; loneliness and homesickness; aspirations and hopes of achievement; bonds of family and friendship; home life and social customs; the changing relationship between parent and offspring during and after the children's maturation into adults; health problems of the aging parent—these topics and others appear in these letters, all relating to a world beyond the family sphere.

Yet in some respects, this trio was unlike other families. Salmon Chase was a U.S. senator from 1849 to 1855, governor of Ohio from 1856 to 1860, secretary of the Treasury from 1861 to 1864, and chief justice of the Supreme Court from 1864 to 1873. From the mid-1850s into the 1870s he was a potential presidential candidate. Kate Chase, moreover, was a preeminent public figure for a number of years, her prominent role in the world of high society charted by the popular press. That was not the same public realm as her father's, but their worlds overlapped, both involving forms of politics and power. The Chases were familiar to a vast newspaper-reading public in the middle of the nineteenth century. Their letters to one another, although personal and private communications within the family, mention major events of the era. Great topics of politics, law and justice, economic change, race, and war engaged the nation in that period. While the manuscripts presented here reflect themes universal to all families, elements in this correspondence do distinguish the Chases from many other families of their time.

This book is independent of the Salmon P. Chase Papers project that produced selective microfilm (forty-three reels, University Publications of America, 1987) and printed editions of Chase's papers (five volumes, published by the Kent State University Press from 1993 to 1998). However, each of the editors of the present volume worked on the Chase Papers in some capacity. We have benefitted from the original project's organization of S. P. Chase's papers, its system for maintaining control over annotation references, and the research files created in the course of annotating the Chase volumes. In many cases we drew on transcriptions and textual verifications made for that project. We thank Leigh Johnsen, who directed the closing phase of the Chase Papers and has been of great help in our work. We salute the late John Niven, who initiated the Chase Papers project, gave that edition its form, and directed it until his final illness. He also wrote a significant biography of Salmon P. Chase. Without him there would have been no Chase Papers, and the present work would not have come about.

We are deeply grateful to John Hubbell and Julia Morton, who long ago at the Kent State University Press made suggestions that set this project on foot. Special thanks to Will Underwood and Joanna H. Craig of the Press for staying with us on this journey, to Mary Young, and to all their colleagues and associates who helped bring the book to publication. This volume received the endorsement of the National Historical Publications and Records Commission (NHPRC) in 1996, and in 2007 the commission awarded the Press a subvention to support the volume's publication. We appreciate that certification and assistance and extend our thanks to Timothy Connelly of the commission's staff and three of his former colleagues who helped us: Nancy Sahli, Dane Hartgrove, and Kathryn Allamong Jacob.

Thanks also to the institutions having custody of most of the manuscripts printed in this volume: the Historical Society of Pennsylvania, the Manuscript Division of the Library of Congress, and Brown University. We also utilized the resources of the American Antiquarian Society, the Cincinnati Historical Society Library of the Cincinnati Museum Center, the Claremont Library of the County of Los Angeles Public Library, Honnold Library of the Claremont Colleges, the New-York Historical Society, the New York Public Library, the Ohio Historical Society, Princeton University Library, the Rhode Island Historical Society, the Rivera Library of the University of California at Riverside, and the A. K. Smiley Public Library of Redlands, California. Portions of our work were aided by research support extended to members of our editorial team by the Gilder Lehrman Institute of American History; the Interdisciplinary General Education Department, California State Polytechnic University, Pomona; the Department of English and the Humanities Institute of the University of California at Davis; San Jose State University; and the California State University System Research Funds. Edwin C. Hoyt graciously shared materials and ideas pertaining to his grandmother and great-grand-father. Mark Brown and Mary-Jo Kline, formerly of the John Hay Library at Brown, assisted us with that institution's collections. Betsy McClure aided us in the volume's later stages of preparation. Kathleen Dorman for the Papers of Joseph Henry, Paul Branch of Fort Macon State Park in North Carolina, and the Office of Public Records of the District of Columbia were very kind in answering research inquiries. Hend Gilli-Elewy and Scott McClure helped us decipher foreign-language phrases. Choon (David) Nguyen and Leo Burke assisted our fact checking. Mela-nie Bower, Museum of the City of New York; Rutha Beamon of the Still Pictures Branch, National Archives and Records Administration; Linda Bailey of the Cincinnati Historical Society Library; Leonora A. Gidlund, New York City Municipal Archives; and David J. Johnson of the Casemate Museum helped in our search for illustrative material. William M. Fer-raro suggested sources for us to consult. Barbara Oberg of the Papers of Thomas Jefferson has been an encouraging friend to this venture. We are grateful to all these individuals and institutions and to all others who have helped us along the way.

The three of us are deeply appreciative of our families' indulgence in allowing us to devote so much time to this other family, one that has demanded much attention over the course of many years. Thanks to our children, siblings, parents, other relatives, and stalwart good friends who have been so tolerant. In particular, Jim McClure thanks Betsy, Scott, and Kate McClure, Richard McClure, Gladys August, and Robert B. August; Peg Lamphier thanks Leo Burke, Emma Burke, and Jackie and Paul Lamphier; and Erika Kreger thanks Joanne Feit Deihl, Beth Anne Kreger, Rosa Sauter Kreger, David Mesher, and Linda Morris. We hope they understand why we believed this thing was—to borrow one piece of an aphorism that Chase imparted to both his daughters—"worth doing."

Editorial Method

SELECTION OF LETTERS

Some choosing is required to make the letters exchanged by Chase and his daughters fit into a single volume. The selection process, however, has primarily been a matter of deciding which of the father's letters should be selected, since the extant correspondence is preponderantly his. We are including in this volume every letter we could find from Kate or Nettie to their father and all correspondence between the sisters during their father's lifetime. To winnow the father's letters, we have tried to select those that feature him speaking as a parent. That requires the omission of letters that might be interesting in another context but do not say enough about relationships within the family. In the end, we are printing 155 letters from him to his daughters and omitting 128. Chase has not been slighted by this selectivity, for the majority of letters in the volume are still his, even with our filtering. Such is the nature of the extant correspondence in this case: we see more of the parent's side of the family's relationships than we do the daughters', and in many cases one must infer the daughters' perspective.

We have reached somewhat beyond the orbit of just the father and daughters. The first letter in the collection is one written by Kate's mother, Eliza (Lizzie). We have included ten letters from Chase to Nettie's mother, Belle, and two that Belle wrote to Kate in 1850. We are also printing some letters exchanged by Chase and Kate's husband, William Sprague. Nettie's husband, William Hoyt, was coauthor of a couple of the letters Nettie wrote to her father soon after her marriage in 1871. Finally, reflecting the quasi-parental roles of boarding-school headmistresses, there are a few letters in this volume between Chase and two of Nettie's school principals, Maria Eastman and Mary Macaulay.

The chronological coverage of the letters is not uniform. There were periods when this father and his daughters were not apart and therefore did not write to one another. Some gaps appear because we have not found letters that they did write. Conversely, in some periods the exchange of letters was relatively heavy. That chronological unevenness is

one of the features of this body of letters. There is, inevitably, some over-
lap between this volume and the five-volume *Salmon P. Chase Papers.*
Twenty-nine of the 214 letters printed in this volume also appear in the
Chase Papers edition (which was also selective).

RENDERING THE TEXT

A source note at the foot of each letter identifies the location of the original manuscript. If a letter is in a handwriting other than author's, we indicate that fact in the source note. Otherwise—which is to say in most
cases—the source note is silent on that subject, and the reader may presume that the letter is in the handwriting of, and signed by, the attributed
author.

In transcribing the letters, we have tried to show spelling, punctuation, abbreviations, and capitalization as they appear in the original
manuscripts. That policy may seem harsh with regard to the letters written by Nettie and Kate when they were young. However, their father's
insistence on perfection in letter writing is best seen in the context of
literal, uncorrected transcription of all their letters (including his). It
seems important also to see how the different writers—not just Kate and
Nettie at progressive stages, but their mothers, their teachers, and later,
their husbands—expressed themselves on paper, with a minimum of editorial intervention or judgment of what should constitute "correct"
usage.

We have not shown most changes made by the letter writers, such as
cancellations or interlineations. In that regard, our intent is to show each
letter as its writer left the text at the end of the composition process.
However, we do show, in our annotation, some alterations that are particularly informative. On occasion we have used a note to clarify some
point about the text.

Underlining in the original appears as italic type in the transcriptions.
Any text underlined with double strokes in the manuscript appears as
underscored italic type. We have brought superscripted text down to
the line and shown any mark underneath a superscription as a period
at the end of the word. Otherwise we have not inserted or altered any
punctuation. Sometimes a clause or sentence that ends at the edge of the
manuscript page seems to lack punctuation, due to damage, or because
the writer accidently made the mark off the page, or because the writer
was content to let the line break serve as "punctuation" of the break in
thought. In such cases, if readers might be confused by the lack of punctuation, we have inserted a slash mark to show the break.

If the reading of a word, passage, or part of a word is conjectural, we
have enclosed the text within square brackets, as in "remem[ber only]

our duty" at July 11, 1864. If the text cannot be read, we have inserted the notations "[*illeg.*]" (for text that is visible but illegible) or "[*torn*]" (for text missing due to damage). Such editorial notations appear as italic type within square brackets to distinguish them from conjectural readings of the manuscript, which are in roman type enclosed within brackets. In the example "exercises [contribute] [*illeg.*] [beautifi]cation" at February 26, 1864, illegible text appears between the conjectural readings "contribute" and "beautification."

For more than two dozen letters written by Chase beginning while he was secretary of the Treasury, the only manuscripts we have are letter-press copies. The letterpress process required the use of a device to roll or press a sheet of translucent paper against a freshly written letter. The copy paper picked up enough ink from the original to leave a facsimile of the written page. If a letter received by Kate or Nettie is now missing, a letterpress copy retained in Chase's files is the next best thing to the letter itself. The text of a pressed copy can be faint or blurred, however. A letterpress copy also might have a gap in the dateline if the letter was written on stationery paper on which the initial digits of the year were already imprinted. As a result, Chase's date at the top of a letter can look like "Aug 17,   3" (as is the case with his letter to Nettie of August 17, 1863). We have let those gaps stand. The letterpress copies in this volume date from August 12, 1863, to October 14, 1865. All are identified as press copies in their source notes.

ANNOTATION

Annotation appears as numbered notes at the end of the letter. It is impossible to make the contents of nineteenth-century letters as intelligible to a later reader as they would have been to their original recipients. Even when the references in a letter were not meant by the writer to be particularly subtle or cryptic, we cannot know or recover all of the information mutually understood by a letter's author and receiver. We have attempted, not always successfully, to identify subjects mentioned in the letters. If we have been unable to find useful information, we have in most cases let the reference stand without any note. Often for the sake of brevity we have not said much about broad historical, social, or political context of topics mentioned in the letters. Because many letters exchanged by our trio have not survived, we have not said anything in the annotation when the writer of a letter has referred to other correspondence that we have not found. In quoting biblical passages in the annotation, we have used the King James Version of the Bible.

The two largest collections of S. P. Chase's papers are in the Library of Congress and the Historical Society of Pennsylvania. We have abbreviated those repositories in our citations as LC and HSP, respectively. Printed works that appear in the notes with shortened citations are listed in the bibliography.

Members of the Chases' extended families who are mentioned in the letters are identified in the appendix, which allows us to group them according to family relationships. Other people are generally identified at their first appearance in the correspondence. In many cases we have not attempted to provide full biographical sketches. Often our identification of a person is brief, serving only to provide some context to the reference in the letter, and we have placed emphasis, when we could, on the person's relationship with the Chases.

IDENTITIES

Although Kate's and Nettie's names were officially Catharine and Janet, in this volume we use the names by which they were known in the family. Kate was properly Catharine Jane Chase, the namesake both of her father's first wife, Catharine Jane ("Kitty") Garniss, and of Chase's and Kitty's daughter, who died as a young child. When Kate was young, she was sometimes "C. J. Chase" in correspondence (see November 18, 1846). In his memoranda of family birth, death, and marriage information, her father spelled the name "Catharine," but Kate came to write it "Katharine." Within the family she was Kate, and even in the wider world she was known more by that name than by any version of Catharine (*Chase Papers*, 1:142, 227).

Nettie's full name was Janet Ralston Chase, after her paternal grandmother, who before she married was Jannette (or Janet) Ralston. In his listing of family data, Chase spelled Nettie's name "Janette," but later she and he both wrote it "Janet" (*Chase Papers*, 1:19, 223–24). The monograms of linked initials on her stationery and in her drawings always contained a *J*, not an *N*, and she seems to have been called Nettie only within an intimate circle. In the family, however, including her correspondence with her father and half-sister, she was always Nettie.

Their father presents a more difficult problem. To the wider world he was, and remains, a public figure called Salmon P. Chase. But to Kate and Nettie, and throughout their letters, he was "Father." Just as we pay heed to the two sisters' identities within the family, so we have tried to appreciate their father's, which is not the same identity he had as a public figure in his day or the one he has acquired as a subject of historical inquiry. To accommodate that duality, in this volume he appears by different labels in different situations. In the introduction to the volume, where we relate his historical persona to his life as a parent and where the discussion is removed from the family's correspondence, we have called him "Chase." Within the chapters containing the correspondence, however, we call him "Father," to match the identity he has in the letters.

Unfortunately we cannot easily refer to Kate's and Nettie's mothers by the identity that each of them had, in succession, in the family—that is, "Mother." Both Eliza and Belle Chase were, in turn, and in a way simultaneously, "Mother" to Kate. When Kate's father wrote to her on August 13, 1850, saying that "Your dear mother, was extremely solicitous that you should become a sincere, devoted christian," it seems likely that he meant Lizzie, who had died almost five years before. Yet in that same letter he went on to refer to Belle as Kate's "dear mother" in the present tense. To avoid that confusion, in our annotation, chapter introductions, and headings to the documents we refer to the two mothers by their first names. Since Eliza died in 1845 and Belle died early in 1852, neither of them appears as a writer or receiver of a letter after chapter 1.

Kate (in 1863) and Nettie (in 1871) each married a man named William. Members of the family tended to refer to Nettie's husband, William Hoyt, as "Will," and to Kate's husband, William Sprague, as "the Governor," an honorific that then, as now, commonly stayed with a politician after his service as governor of a state had concluded (in Sprague's case, he was called "Governor" even after he had been a major general and a U.S. senator). In our annotation and chapter introductions, "William" by itself means Sprague, "Will" means Hoyt, and "Willie" means Kate's and William Sprague's son, born in 1865.

Introduction

A letter written at Cincinnati, Ohio, in December 1848 captured a moment of a little girl's childhood. "All are well," the letter writer reported to his uncle, who was away from home on business: "after breakfast Nettie mounted the table and danced the Mazurka, in a very Old womanish manner, perfectly comical—while Aunt Belle hummed a tune for her."[1] Nettie, known more formally as Janet Ralston Chase, was fifteen months old when she pranced on that tabletop. Her father, Salmon Portland Chase, who at the time was an attorney in Cincinnati, was the recipient of the letter. He had gone to Columbus, the state capital, where he had court cases pending and he could monitor political developments that soon resulted in his election to the United States Senate.[2] It is significant that he experienced his daughter's spontaneous dance vicariously, reported to him in a letter. Chase, his older daughter Kate, who was eight years old in December 1848, and Nettie are the principal figures of this volume. A good portion of the time they were separated by distance but connected by letters, and this volume contains highlights of their correspondence from when Nettie and Kate were girls until the death of their father in 1873.

The three of them, father and daughters, were the survivors of a succession of overlapping families. Kate's mother, Eliza (Lizzie) Smith, married Chase in 1839, when she was seventeen and he was thirty-one. When he married her he had a child from a previous marriage, his first wife having died in 1835 soon after the baby's birth. That child, a lively girl with curly blonde hair and big blue eyes, was called Kate and was much adored by her father. She died of scarlet fever at the age of four, a few months after Lizzie and Salmon married.[3] Lizzie and Salmon had a child together, born in August 1840, and they called her Kate, like the lost daughter. They had two more children, both girls, who died in infancy. Then Lizzie died of tuberculosis in September 1845, at the age of twenty-three, just after Kate turned five. In November of the following year Chase married Belle Ludlow. They had Nettie in September 1847.

A younger sister, Josephine, was born in 1849 but died soon after her first birthday. Yet Belle, like Eliza, suffered from consumption. She died in January 1852, leaving Chase, Kate, and Nettie as the surviving nuclear family.[4]

Chase did not marry again after Belle's death, and even though he and his daughters could not always be in residence together, his influence as the girls' sole parent was apparent. He did not have great inherited wealth or the money of a powerful capitalist. He kept a good financial grounding but made his way as an attorney and holder of public office, accruing some real estate investments and stocks along the way. Perhaps never fully satisfied with what he accomplished, he could attribute what success he had in overcoming life's challenges to his professional skills, which were based overtly on his education, and he placed great emphasis on virtues centering on religious devotion and personal morality.

On that foundation he built, even before Kate and Nettie were born, the structure of their immediate world. His niece Eliza Whipple, who lived in the household for a time around 1838 to 1840, long remembered that the family "always had prayers before breakfast." Her uncle once sat up late on a Saturday night to be sure that she finished her sewing before midnight so as not to violate the Sabbath. Eliza described as "almost Puritanical" his strictures about conduct on Sundays, a day on which he allowed "no letter writing, no light reading," and "no gossiping." During the period she was in the Chase household, Eliza recalled years later, her uncle "abominated" card playing, forbade members of the family from going to the theater, and did his utmost to suppress the excited curiosity of Jenny Skinner, another of his nieces, about the local horse races. He "would let us dance a plain quadrille but never a waltz," Eliza noted.[5] Time did not soften that opinion. "My objection to your dancing was to the waltz, which I presume is the almost universal dance in Europe," he wrote to Nettie in 1866, when she and Kate traveled to Europe. "So I will withdraw it, & leave you to your own discretion. Exercise that however, & be careful to avoid persons and frivolities condemned by your own judgment & conscience." He wanted her "to be an ornament of Society," he declared, but "an ornament in the Christian sense." He also apparently chastised Kate for waltzing in 1857, when she was sixteen.[6]

When Belle Chase died early in 1852, her husband was in the middle of a six-year term as a U.S. senator that required him to spend much of his time in the nation's capital. Kate, eleven years old, was already at a boarding school. Belle had not been home consistently for some time, as she traveled to springs and hospitals in hopes of besting her tuberculosis. After her death, her sisters and other female relatives pleaded with Chase to let them care for Nettie, whom they adored—she was "an uncommonly lovely engaging little child," one of them said. Chase did leave Nettie with her relatives in the Cincinnati area when he was away from Ohio, and Evelina Chandler Ball, the wife of his law partner and a "dear friend," who had assisted Lizzie when Kate was born, also had a role in taking care of Nettie. A little later he boarded Nettie with other relatives from her mother's side, the Collins family in Hillsboro, Ohio.[7] The result was that, after Belle's death, no one woman had the role of mother for Kate and Nettie as they matured.

Long afterward, Nettie published her recollections of a time when they lived in Columbus—she was eight when her father was first inaugurated governor early in 1856 and thirteen when they left the state's capital city. "We lived in simple fashion," as she remembered, "and there was no governess to keep us in the schoolroom away from our elders."[8] Kate, seven years older than Nettie, could certainly play a supervisory role. At the age of seventeen Kate had considerable responsibility for furnishing their house in Columbus (see chapter 3), and, as shown by the letters that Nettie wrote from school in 1861, Kate functioned as something of a second parent for her younger sister (chapter 4).

In the absence of a governess, as Nettie recalled of the time in Columbus, she and Kate roamed the residence freely and their curiosity flourished. Nettie opened the graves of dead pet canaries to exhibit the skeletons in a makeshift "museum." With Kate or perhaps a cousin, she made a pretend fort to celebrate John Brown's attempt to rouse a slave rebellion at Harpers Ferry in October 1859—which earned her a firm rebuke from her father, who explained that no matter how appealing a cause might seem, the law must be obeyed.[9] She remembered that "in my father's library I had always a welcome corner 'if I kept quiet.'" His study connected to the rest of the house "in pretty straggling fashion" by what Nettie later referred to as the conservatory, a sunroom with a door and windows opening onto the garden. It was a favorite spot for the girls in winter and summer, and because it was the route to Chase's study from the main body of the house, callers coming to see the governor often encountered his daughters. Nettie and Kate became familiar with their father's political cronies and the issues of the day. In a family discussion in 1857, nine-year-old Nettie initially stood up for an expelled member of the state House of Representatives, then "abandoned him on learning he was proslavery." She later remembered James A. Garfield and Carl Schurz from the time in Ohio, and Charles Sumner as a frequent caller later, when the Chases lived in Washington. She once spoke up to Sumner but then failed to support her argument, and he teased her thereafter as "my little logician." She and Kate both admired Sumner terribly, and Nettie remembered her embarrassment when, at her first introduction to him, her father revealed that she had pictures of the famous senator in her room. In 1857, Kate had framed copies of the Lawrence, Kansas, *Herald of Freedom*, a free-state newspaper, hanging in her room, flanked by portraits of Sumner and her father.[10]

In Washington in 1861, thirteen-year-old Nettie had a brief friendship with Nathaniel Hawthorne, who was staying with friends across the hall from the rooms the Chases temporarily occupied in a family hotel. Nettie found the writer to be extraordinarily shy, a "gentle recluse" who seemed painfully uncomfortable at social gatherings. He was, however, "willing enough to make friends with a child," she remembered.[11]

She was eager to meet Hawthorne when the opportunity arose because she knew and loved his published stories. She and her sister grew up in a bookish household. Their father's personal library was not the grandest private collection of books of its day, but it was not small. He had a college education, valued learning, and owned and used books on a range of subjects. Recalling a time not long before Kate was born, Eliza Whipple remembered her Uncle Salmon as "a very close student" who, in addition to spending hours in his study, habitually went through two candles each night reading in bed. Books also played roles in his interactions with other people. Reminiscing about an early conversation with Kitty Garniss, the woman who became his first wife, Chase wrote that he could not remember "the subjects of conversation, but I believe we talked a little about books." On one occasion after calling on Kitty, the only physical detail of the scene that he recorded in his diary was that when he entered the room she was holding a copy of Bulwer-Lytton's *England and the English*. Once, after they married, when she claimed a present from him as her spoils in a game called "philopena," the gift he gave her was a book. Later, when he was a widower, it was a note from Lizzie Smith to Eliza Whipple about the loan of a book that first prompted him to pay notice to Lizzie.[12]

He had entered Dartmouth College as a junior in 1824, at the age of sixteen, presumably having demonstrated sufficient mastery of the Greek, Latin, algebra, trigonometry, Euclid, Horace, Cicero, history, and philosophy that made up the core of the curriculum for freshmen and sophomores. Coursework for the junior year included chemistry, natural philosophy (natural science), astronomy, conic sections, spherical trigonometry, and geometry, but much of the junior year and practically all of the last year were devoted to law and government, moral and political philosophy, and "natural theology." Exercises in composition and "declamation" provided training in writing and speaking.[13]

Later, in keeping with his work in law and politics, he was interested in books on government, political economy, and history, including Gibbon, Carlyle, Burke, Hume, Adam Smith, Jefferson, John Adams, and Tocqueville. He wanted Belle, Nettie's mother, to get a strong foundation in American history, and he pushed Kate, at the age of ten, to read European history. In addition to various works of travel and descriptions of foreign locales, the family owned the seventh edition of the *Encyclopaedia Britannica*, published in 1842. Chase also had a deep interest in works on religion or those illustrating good Christian conduct. In literature, he knew the English standards such as Shakespeare, Milton, and John Bunyan's *Pilgrim's Progress* but was also familiar with Le Sage's *Gil Blas* and the works of Voltaire, Racine, and Molière in French. His education also included Greek and Latin, and according to Nettie's later recollection he regretted not knowing Hebrew. When he urged Belle to read the "English Classics," he meant eighteenth- and nineteenth-century British essayists such as Samuel Johnson, Addison and Steele, and Charles Lamb. He sampled contemporary fiction, including novels by Bulwer-Lytton and Harriet Martineau and works not well known today, such as John Gibson Lockhart's *Valerius*, a tale of Christians in the Roman Empire. Kate and Nettie had access to the work of contemporary writers, including—along with Hawthorne—Charles Dickens, Washington Irving, James Fenimore Cooper, and James Russell Lowell. In the 1850s and 1860s their father read Victor Hugo's novels, in French.[14]

Chase was familiar with the poetry of Wordsworth, Southey, Keats, Byron, Dryden, Cowper, Samuel Butler, Burns, and Mark Akenside, as well as didactic verse on religious or moral themes by Coventry Patmore, Edward Young, and H. H. Milman. In a letter to Belle of March 16, 1850, printed in this volume, he rated Milton, Cowper, Alexander Pope, and "the like" as the "classics" of English poetry. In 1857, when he was governor of Ohio, he immersed himself in Edmund Spenser's *Faerie Queene*. Two years later, when a political supporter quoted Tennyson to express optimism for the future of their cause, Chase knew instantly that the line should be "faintly trust the larger hope," not simply "trust the larger hope."[15] In Columbus, Chase—and Kate—were social patrons to a young William Dean Howells, introducing him to the dinners, receptions, and entertainments of polite society in the state capital. Nettie later recalled hearing her father read aloud from Howells's and John J. Piatt's *Poems of Two Friends*.[16]

He also bought Kate and Nettie books of their own, even when they were quite young. In November 1845, he purchased a "series of little books for little Kate," who was then five. He had her read the Bible to him every day, along with poetry and one of her "little books." That reading may all have been devotional or moral in theme—"heard dear little Kate read verses, & bible, & pray: talked to her," he recorded in his diary. He also read to her, from the Book of Job: a meaningful choice, since Kate's mother had died only a couple of months earlier. Kate seemed to enjoy the "solemn" rhythm of those passages, even if, he thought, she did not comprehend all of their meaning.[17]

If Kate was reading in November 1845, she may have learned to do so at the age of four, and apparently Nettie followed a similar schedule. In May 1852, when Nettie was four months' shy of her fifth birthday, she was taking instruction from a relative, Miss C. C. Clopper, who was a governess and teacher. "Nettie spelled several words for me," one of Belle's cousins reported to Chase at that time, "and I think is learning rapidly." By the time Nettie was seven and a half, books were her "passion."[18]

We know nothing about Kate's earliest schooling, but it was apparently in 1849 that she entered Miss Henrietta B. Haines's school in New York City. That year Kate turned nine and her father entered the U.S. Senate. John Garniss, whose daughter Kitty had been Chase's first wife, reported from New York in January 1850 that Kate was "in excellent spirits and highly pleased with her situation" at the school. That report hints that she was in her first year there.[19] Henrietta Haines was from a New York merchant family with a strong record of achievement: her brother Daniel was governor of New Jersey in the 1840s and became a justice of the state supreme court in 1852, and a sister, Sarah Platt Haines Doremus, was a well-known philanthropist. Haines's school earned a significant reputation in the 1850s and 1860s. Julia Newberry, of the prominent Chicago family, yearned from the age of nine to attend Miss Haines's school. At first Julia was intimidated when, as a prospective student in her teens, she finally met Henrietta Haines in 1869. She soon found Miss Haines, whose "eyes twinkled," to be "*supremely* gracious." Jessie Benton Frémont believed that Haines was "so truly a lady that it is good to live in her atmosphere."[20]

The school occupied a townhouse completed in 1848 at 10 Gramercy Park, in one of the city's fine residential districts. The academic year began in mid-September.[21] In the early months of 1854, toward the end of Kate's time there, another student wrote letters to her family that described activity at the school. Catharine Beekman was a local girl, from a New York family of lengthy pedigree, but her parents left her at Haines's school while they and her brother went to Georgia to allow her mother to recuperate from an illness.[22] Born in 1841, Catharine was only slightly younger than Kate. She called her age category at the school the "betweens," older than the "little children" but younger than the oldest girls. In her correspondence she described a full daily and weekly schedule with a good bit of studying, a number of programmed activities, a modest amount of unstructured time on Saturdays, and "not much variety." The girls rose at 5:30 on school days and studied until 7:00, when they had prayers and breakfast. After breakfast they exited the school and walked through the Gramercy Park neighborhood, walking two abreast, each group of girls accompanied by a teacher. That ritual became a trademark of private girls' schools in the city.[23] Returning to the school, the students had classes until midafternoon, when it was time for another procession outdoors until a little after 3:00 P.M. The girls then sewed or studied until dinner was served at 4:00. After dinner, which was the major meal of the day, there was an hour of French conversation, a half-hour of study, then tea and prayers at 6:30 followed by more study until bedtime at 8:00. Tuesday evening was parlor evening for Catharine's (and likely Kate's) group. That night they could sit in the parlor to sew and did not go to bed until 9:00. One Tuesday they performed "tableaux"—live stagings of images from paintings or literature—for which some girls "sent to Boston for dresses" and spent "at least a month getting them up." The "betweens" and younger children all had singing on Saturdays, and for an additional fee Catharine took piano lessons at the school.[24]

As indicated by Catharine's schedule, the French language was a regular component of the curriculum at Miss Haines's. A French "mademoiselle" always had a prominent place on the staff. When Kate first arrived, that position was occupied by Henriette Deluzy Desportes, former governess to the children of the duc and duchesse de Praslin.[25] After she married an American in 1851 and left the school, her successor was Camille de Janon. When Janon and Henrietta Haines began to run the school in partnership in 1863, they advertised it as an "English and French Boarding and Day School for young ladies and children." They expected their students to speak French at dinner, between classes, and on the outdoor walks.[26]

In 1854, Catharine Beekman reported to her family that the girls had "parsing" in English every day, although she found that members of her class were poor spellers. She wrote a composition on "presence of mind," and Kate Chase, that same academic year, wrote one on "the Hand" (see her father's letter to her of July 5, 1854, in this volume). Catherine mentioned studying Oliver Goldsmith's poem *The Deserted Village*. Miss Haines also saw to it that her students had access to speakers or instructors on a variety of topics. While at the school in 1851, Kate heard the clergyman Stephen Tyng. In 1854, Swiss-born geologist Arnold Henry Guyot gave a series of lectures at Miss Haines's school on the subject of glaciers, a specialty of his. Although he joined the faculty at Princeton that year, he maintained a connection with the school and later married Haines's niece, the daughter of Daniel Haines. Also in 1854, Henrietta Haines's nephew, chemist Robert Odgen Doremus, offered an optional course at the school. At the time, he was a member of the faculty of both the New York College of Pharmacy and the Free Academy, which became the City College of New York.[27]

Miss Haines maintained strict control over the girls' time and activities. When Mrs. Vanderbilt—likely Maria Kissam Vanderbilt, wife of Commodore Vanderbilt's son William Henry—applied for leave to take Catharine Beekman out for a Saturday, Catharine was disappointed but not surprised when Haines said no.[28] In 1852, the headmistress denied Kate permission to spend Christmas with her father in Washington. Chase felt it was his "duty" to acquiesce to Haines, and Kate spent that Christmas in New York (see his letter to her of December 21, 1852). His journal entries show that he wrote Haines regularly, suggesting a close involvement in his daughter's education also illustrated by his letters to her printed in this volume, which mention specific topics he wished Kate to study as well as indicating the educational philosophies underlying those wishes. His admonitions underscore the same values reinforced by the many midcentury commentators who urged educators to help girls cultivate three primary traits: obedience, self-government, and altruism. Popular discourse emphasized not just that girls should obey but also that they should learn to take pleasure in obedience. As one midcentury commencement speaker for a female academy put it, "gratitude and obedience to your parents will characterize the truly educated lady," who "will find it even a pleasant thing to yield to authority." Taken in the context of this discourse, Chase's comments about Kate's duty to fulfill his wishes seem quite moderate, especially since the request under discussion was for her to write regularly, which reiterated his eagerness to hear from her. He echoed the sentiments of many tracts and sermons in his assertion that Kate would find happiness for herself by making others happy, and he encouraged her to be a positive influence on others, such as Nettie and the children of family friend Gamaliel Bailey.[29]

He not only wanted Kate to develop her own ability to be a positive influence but also wanted her to benefit from the "excellent advice" of her "kind guardian as well as instructress, Miss Haines." Given the great respect often accorded to school heads at the time and the growing cultural confidence in women's unique ability to mold children's character and morality, his confidence in Haines's opinion would not have been exceptional or unwarranted. He seems to have genuinely trusted in the counsel of the woman he considered to be, as he expressed it to Kate, "supplying the place of your sainted mother."[30] He had himself been a schoolteacher, during winter breaks as a college student and for a time in Washington before he became a lawyer, and he acknowledged to Kate that he had found it difficult to remain patient with his pupils. As governor of Ohio in 1857, in a letter to the state teachers' association, he declared of teachers that the "responsibility of their trust, the magnitude of their work, and the dignity of their calling must be acknowledged, and not coldly acknowledged only, but thoroughly appreciated."[31] Henrietta Haines read all the letters her students wrote, even to their families. Chase acknowledged that the educator's scrutiny gave Kate's letters an unfortunate "dryness." Her correspondence exhibited "a freer and more affectionate spirit," he thought, once she was no longer under Haines's supervision.[32]

Kate remained at the school through June 1854. She departed with a final academic performance report that did not meet all of her father's expectations. That September she entered another boarding school, a "seminary" for young ladies at Aston Ridge in southeastern Pennsylvania. B. S. Huntington, an Episcopal minister, had founded the institution in the mid-1840s. In 1850, when the census listing included, in addition to Huntington and his wife, half a dozen adults who may have been teachers and workers at the school and sixteen girls who were apparently the students in residence, aged ten to eighteen. Of those girls, the majority were born in Pennsylvania, three were from New Jersey, and one was from Maryland.[33] By the time Kate attended, Maria L. Eastman was the school's principal. She was from Concord, New Hampshire, where the Chases had relatives, and she was in her midthirties when Kate attended her school. Like Henrietta Haines, Eastman was a headmistress for many years and earned an excellent reputation as an educator. Ida Saxton of Ohio, who later married William McKinley, completed her education under "the beloved Miss Eastman" in the latter part of the 1860s. As indicated below, Nettie Chase also attended a school directed by Maria Eastman, a few years after Kate.[34]

Kate was at the Aston Ridge school for one academic year, from September 1854 to the spring of 1855, and it was her last experience with a boarding school. For at least part of the time during the Chases' residence in Columbus in the period from 1856 to 1860, she attended the Esther Institute, a "female seminary" in the city. She may have taken only some foreign language and music classes, not the school's academic or "collegiate" program—which perhaps offered nothing beyond what she had already received from Henrietta Haines and Maria Eastman. However, a brief entry in her father's diary in January 1857 hints that he attended a presentation by her of a "Report," and, while it is unclear what classes she took at the Esther Institute, she appears to have attended the school on a regular basis during that academic year.[35] Nettie also attended the institute, which was very likely her first encounter with formal education, at least at a school of much size. For a couple of years before the Chases moved to Columbus, Nettie was in Hillsboro much of the time with the Collinses. There Catharine Collins, a cousin of Belle Chase, gave Nettie instruction in art and French, and perhaps provided her other schooling as well. Prior to that, Nettie's education may have come entirely from Miss Clopper and Nettie's relatives in the Cincinnati area.[36]

The Esther Institute, in existence from 1852 to 1861, was the creation of a Columbus native, Lewis Heyl, who named the school after his mother. Heyl, whose father was a local baker and hotelier, was trained as a lawyer and had been clerk of courts and a prosecutor before opening his school (and later, when Chase was secretary of the Treasury and Heyl's school had closed, Chase appointed Heyl to a position in the Treasury Department). In 1854 a catalog of the Esther Institute listed Heyl and Miss Agnes Ward Beecher as principals. A faculty register indicates that the school offered instruction in mathematics, chemistry, modern languages, instrumental and vocal music, and drawing and painting. The school had an impressive assortment of teaching aids for instruction in anatomy, including a skeleton and a "full size natural anatomical preparation" of a dissected human body. There was a primary department for younger students, and the staff included a matron. Some students boarded at the school, although the majority of the pupils, at least in the period 1857–60, were from Columbus. A list of pupils from the 1859–60

school year includes Nettie (with seven other girls) in a division devoted
to "painting and drawing only." Earlier, however, she must have been en-
rolled in the school's regular academic curriculum: in 1857, for example,
her father jotted a reference to Nettie's "lesson," and she took Latin during that term.[37] Students at Heyl's school included daughters of some
influential men of the city and state, including newspaperman and politician Oran Follet; Congressman Samuel Galloway; the state auditor,
Francis M. Wright; A. P. Stone, a former congressman; jurist and politician Joseph R. Swan; newspaper publisher Allen M. Gangewer, who for a
time was Chase's secretary in Columbus; and William Dennison, Chase's
successor as governor.[38]

The family's relocation to Washington in 1861, when Chase became
secretary of the Treasury in the Lincoln administration, marked a significant transition in each of their lives. Nettie had not traveled outside Ohio
much since her mother's death when she was a small child.[39] She was thirteen when the family moved to the nation's capital during the stressful
and exciting secession winter. When she and Kate made a visit to New
York in April 1861, Nettie was in awe at her first encounter with "a great
city." The two of them were in New York when they first heard the "electric" news of the Confederates' firing on Fort Sumter. They witnessed the
proud, anxious mustering and departure of a New York City regiment,
and they attended a notable service at Henry Ward Beecher's Plymouth
Church in Brooklyn. There the famed preacher gave a long sermon that
began with the command of God to a hesitant Moses at the edge of the
Red Sea—"speak unto the children of Israel, that they go forward"—and
went on to exhort his listeners to march forward themselves, in the face
of unprecedented national crisis and civil war. Thirty years later Nettie
still remembered that invocation by Beecher of "the Lord God of Joshua
and of Gideon."[40]

When they moved to Washington, Kate was old enough to attend
official functions and take part in the city's society. Nettie was too young
for that role, but her father sometimes took her along on his official
calls. Apparently she stayed in the room with him during at least some of
those conferences. On one stop at William Seward's house, she later recalled, the secretary of state "courteously and kindly provided me with
a quantity of pictorial periodicals for my amusement before proceeding with his talk with my father." She remembered, too, her boredom
as her father discussed military strategy with Winfield Scott. On another
occasion, at a dinner, she attempted to choke down a highly seasoned
dish that was General Scott's own proud concoction. To her dismay he
boomed out for all to hear: "The little Chase does not like my salad."[41]

The family's move to Washington marked a different transition for
Kate, who had turned twenty in August 1860. She was an attractive young
woman situated within the closest circles of political power in wartime

Washington. She had taken on the role of her father's hostess in Columbus when he was governor, and in the national capital she continued in that capacity when he entertained guests. She accompanied him to receptions and other events and held a very high position in the social order of official Washington. "Pretty Katie," a beguiled John Hay, Lincoln's secretary, called her in his diary.[42] She acquired a reputation as a social leader and a beauty that reached well beyond Washington. Her marriage in November 1863 to a wealthy Rhode Island manufacturer and politician, William Sprague, was a great event, and for some years afterward she continued to draw attention as one of the preeminent women of American high society. According to an account published in 1869, Kate's "reign" over Washington society was "undisputed." "Queen of all the continent," journalist Whitelaw Reid called her in verse when she married. "She could make all the Astors look like fishwomen beside her," a contributor to the *Chicago News* exulted: "She had more the air of a great lady than any woman I ever saw." Mary Logan, the wife of the Illinois politician Gen. John A. Logan, called Kate's beauty "remarkable" and "incomparable."[43]

"Miss Grundy," the social reporter and commentator of the New York *World,* asserted in 1870 that everything she had heard said about Kate's beauty proved to be "but little exaggerated." But Gideon Welles, the secretary of the navy and a curmudgeonly diarist, made an important distinction when, after writing in his journal that Kate was "beautiful," he added: "or, more properly perhaps, interesting and impressive."[44] Observers noticed her eyes, her hair, and the contours of her figure and neck. "Her slender form became a rich and ornamented style of dress," wrote Elizabeth Fries Ellet in 1869, noting also that "her eyes, fringed with dark lashes, lighted her intellectual face with expression." Two years earlier Ellet wrote that Kate was "slender to fragility, with abundant brown hair and beautiful eyes, shadowed by long dark lashes." Miss Grundy submitted a similar description to the New York *World:* "Mrs. Sprague has fine eyes, a well-shaped head and a graceful figure, though perhaps she is a trifle too slender." Hamilton Gay Howard, the son of Senator Jacob M. Howard, recalled that Kate's "distinguishing physical features" were her "neck and poise of head," and she had "perhaps the most perfectly swanlike neck ever molded by the Divine Sculptor." Her "large and dove-like eyes" also made an impression on Howard.[45] "Her figure is tall and slight, but at the same time beautifully rounded," wrote an Englishwoman who met Kate in Ohio in 1858. Kate's neck was "long and graceful, with a sweet pretty brunette face. I seldom have seen such lovely eyes and dark eyelashes; she has rich dark hair in great profusion, but her style and dress were of the utmost simplicity and grace." The effect was such, joked the traveler, that she could "almost" forgive her husband, who seemed enchanted by the eighteen-year-old Kate Chase.[46]

Decades later, William Dean Howells looked back on a time when, during that same period in Columbus, Kate forced him to overcome his shyness and join a game of charades: "Nothing but the raillery glancing through the deep lashes of her brown eyes, which were very beautiful, could have brought me to the self-sacrifice involved."[47] Carl Schurz, the German-born political figure, also remembered, many years later, Kate's appearance in Columbus. Arriving at the governor's house one morning, where he had been invited to stay, Schurz was greeted by Chase.

> His daughter Kate, who presided over his household, he said, would be down presently. Soon she came, saluted me very kindly, and then let herself down upon her chair with the graceful lightness of a bird that, folding its wings, perches upon the branch of a tree. She was then about eighteen years old, tall and slender, and exceedingly well formed. Her features were not at all regularly beautiful according to the classic rule. Her little nose, somewhat audaciously tipped up, would perhaps not have passed muster with a severe critic, but it fitted pleasingly into her face with its large, languid but at the same time vivacious hazel eyes, shaded by long dark lashes, and arched over by proud eyebrows. The fine forehead was framed in waving gold-brown hair. She had something imperial in the pose of her head, and all her movements possessed an exquisite natural charm. No wonder that she came to be admired as a great beauty and broke many hearts.[48]

Around that time, when she was still a teenager in Ohio, Kate began to draw widespread attention. In March 1858, she went to the state penitentiary to deliver a pardon from her father, the governor, to an old Polish soldier who had been convicted of burglary. An unplanned newspaper report of the event, "with some embellishments," circulated widely and was noticed in New York State by Gerrit Smith, one of Chase's political associates.[49]

As Gideon Welles detected, Kate's captivating aura was less a matter of stunning physical beauty than a charismatic effect of several features of her appearance and personality. The word *grace* recurs in descriptions of her, beginning with the one in 1858. Not long after the end of the Civil War, the *New York Herald* referred to her "grace, tact and beauty" and her "great good taste." "She is a glorious girl," the capitalist Jay Cooke exclaimed to his brother in 1861.[50] The Englishwoman calling at the governor's residence in 1858 found both Kate and her father to be "full of intelligence." Elizabeth Fries Ellet noted Kate's "brilliant mental qualities," and Miss Grundy mentioned her "bright intellect."[51]

John Hay observed Kate's willingness to comment on issues related to the Lincoln administration's policies, and Mrs. Logan paired her "brilliant conversational powers" with an "inborn diplomacy." Kate had "a good deal of diplomatic capacity," readers of the New York *World* learned from Miss Grundy's reports. In 1868, when there was some prospect, ultimately fleeting, that Chase might get a presidential nomination from the Democratic Party, Kate took a lead role in reporting to her father and communicating with his supporters as the convention met in New York City. She married one politician—William Sprague, governor of Rhode Island and a U.S. senator—and formed her other great romantic attachment with another one—Roscoe Conkling of New York.[52] In 1863, when she and Sprague became engaged to marry, Welles reflected in his diary that although the prospective groom had inherited a privileged station in life, "Miss Kate has talents and ambition sufficient for both." One newspaper at the time of her wedding referred to her as an "accomplished," as well as a "lovely," bride. Mary Clemmer, another observer of the Washington scene, grouped Kate Chase with two famous statesmen's daughters of an earlier generation, Thomas Jefferson's daughter Martha and Aaron Burr's daughter Theodosia. All three women were, in Clemmer's opinion, "intellectual" as well as "beautiful" and "charming."[53]

When Hay called her "the statuesque Kate," as he did in a passage of his diary that he later deleted, he referred not to her physique but to the undemonstrative mien of a piece of statuary. He detected an uncharacteristic breach of Kate's guarded reserve when he caught her shedding a tear over a theatrical performance. On another occasion he referred to her "severity & formal stiffness of manner," which she seemed to have lost by the evening of her wedding reception. She then "seemed to think," Hay declared, that "she had *arrived*."[54]

Nettie's appearance drew far less notice than Kate's. As a teenager, she reported that she was often told she looked "like Father." Her father, as characterized by Howells, was "a large, handsome man, of a very Senatorial presence." Nettie wondered if she would "grow like him in character," since he was "so noble."[55] She seemed never to project her half-sister's intensity of personality. In his diary, Gideon Welles, who recorded strong opinions of Chase and Kate, failed even to mention Nettie. Hay noted her once in his journals, without elaboration, as "Miss N. Chase." After the war she made only a modest impression on Elizabeth Fries Ellet, who noted that Kate's "lovely sister, Miss Chase," helped to receive guests at Kate's glittering Washington receptions. Mrs. Logan took more notice, observing that "Mrs. Kate Chase Sprague and Miss Nettie Chase, both fascinating and brilliant women, presided over" events at their father's home "and made it one of the most attractive in the city." "There could not possibly have been sisters more unlike each other than were the Chase sisters," Logan declared, "not only in personal appearance but in disposition, talents, and characteristics. Nettie, though of a plainer face, was one of the most gentle, modest, retiring, and lovable characters that one could possibly imagine." According to Miss Grundy, "Miss Nettie Chase is, perhaps, more universally liked" than Kate—whom

Grundy considered to be "haughty." In the summer of 1863, Nettie had a running joke with Hay's friend John G. Nicolay: he claiming that he would send her a bison, she retorting that she would "have a cage fitted up in the parlor" for the beast.[56]

In 1865, Rutherford B. Hayes, who at the time was a thirty-three-year-old congressman from Ohio, described Nettie in dismissive terms. In a letter to his wife describing a call on Chase, Hayes growled: "His little daughter is not at all handsome, and no longer *little*, but she is natural and kindly, *perhaps* bright." Earlier that year, however, Nettie had made a much different impression on John Chipman Gray, a young graduate of Harvard Law School. After meeting the seventeen-year-old Nettie Chase when she traveled through Hilton Head, South Carolina, where he was the army's judge advocate, Gray confided to his mother that the young woman was "quite good looking."[57]

Upon Kate's marriage in the autumn of 1863, Nettie, who was sixteen, stepped into the role of "Miss Chase." She did so "charmingly," according to reports that came back to her father. Later, Miss Grundy of the New York *World* said that Nettie "does the honors of her father's house with much grace, and fills her position with the ease usually acquired only by long experience."[58] After the family's move to Washington, Nettie's education continued with one academic year at Maria Eastman's boarding school in Pennsylvania, from September 1861 to early July 1862. It was not, however, the same school that Kate had attended. Soon after Kate finished at Aston Ridge, Eastman left that institution to become the principal of the Brooke Hall Female Seminary, which was also in Delaware County. The new school opened in Media in 1856. Like the school at Aston Ridge, Brooke Hall had a founding connection to the Episcopal Church. It began under the patronage of Alonzo Potter, the Episcopal bishop of Pennsylvania, who was an energetic proponent of education and an admirer of Maria Eastman's abilities. H. Jones Brooke, a successful businessman, investor, and politician from the region, provided the money to establish the school. Brooke Hall acquired a reputation as "a most successful institution of higher learning for young ladies." Among "the best seminaries of its class" in Pennsylvania, it was a place where young women were "thoroughly instructed in all the useful and ornamental branches." In 1859, a Philadelphia publisher printed music for a "Brooke Hall Polka" that was "respectfully dedicated to Miss Maria L. Eastman."[59]

A private girls' school of the period could be thought of as "'the lengthened shadow' of its headmistress," according to a mid-twentieth-century work on women's education.[60] In Miss Eastman's case, a catalog of Brooke Hall from the early 1870s listed her not just as the principal but also as the school's teacher of physics and "mental and moral science." The faculty at that time had a dozen teachers, plus some additional instructors, such as a physician to teach physiology and some clergymen who taught "general literature." The curriculum included grammar, elocution, rhetoric, logic, penmanship, literature, and philosophy; geography and history; mathematics through algebra, geometry, and trigonometry; Latin, French, German, and Italian; and, in the sciences, natural philosophy plus geology, chemistry, botany, astronomy, and physiology. There were also teachers of piano, singing, drawing and painting, dancing, and calisthenics. By that time, however, Eastman and her staff probably thought of the school as a college: in 1875, Brooke Hall professed to award a dozen master's degrees, although the school had no accreditation from the state for that level of study. During Nettie's attendance in 1861–62, the institution must have been much smaller and its curriculum more restrained, although the curriculum of the 1870s may reflect some of the range and content of Eastman's program from the earlier period. In 1860, the census taker recorded "M. L. Eastman" and three other female teachers living at the same location. Eastman's age then was thirty-nine years old; her assistant, who like Eastman came from New Hampshire, was twenty-seven, and the two other teachers, who were from Pennsylvania and New York, were twenty-two and twenty-nine. They may have constituted the institution's entire full-time faculty at that time. The school probably grew considerably during the 1860s, as it had about sixty pupils in 1869.[61]

Like Kate, Nettie was at Miss Eastman's for one school year. Beginning in September 1862, Nettie spent two academic years at a boarding school in Manhattan, but not with Henrietta Haines. Instead, Nettie attended the "French and English Boarding and Day School" of Mary E. Macaulay at Madison Avenue and 40th Street. Mrs. Macaulay was, by Chase's description, an "elegant" widow. The "French and English" label under which she advertised her school indicates that she, like Haines, gave French a prominent role in the school's curriculum and culture (Nettie referred to a stern "Mademoiselle," who was probably both a teacher and a matron). The daily regime at Mrs. Macaulay's was similar to what Kate experienced under Miss Haines. Nettie rose early in the morning, had a modest breakfast at seven, and by eight was marching through the streets with her schoolmates for exercise and fresh air— along Fifth Avenue, in the case of Mrs. Macaulay's charges in February 1864. At night, a "terrible bell" tolled lights out and forced Nettie into what was, by her description, a very uncomfortable bed.[62]

Chase deferred to Mary Macaulay's supervision of his daughter, just as he had with Henrietta Haines's strict oversight of Kate. "I do not want to do anything concerning you while under her care except with the sanction of her judgment," he informed Nettie.[63] Both Maria Eastman and Mary Macaulay found Nettie wanting in self-discipline. Acknowledging that the girl had a "quick & comprehensive intellect," Eastman made plain that she thought Nettie was "deficient in mental discipline" and needed to keep working on "regularity" and "promptness." Macaulay's assessment was similar: Nettie was "full of talent," the headmistress stated, "but erratic—and must be *compell'd* to apply herself systematically."[64]

Despite the principals' lamentations, during Nettie's final term at Mrs. Macaulay's her father thought that she could become skilled enough, especially in French, to act as his "interpreter & Secretary" if he traveled to Europe.[65] But the aspect of Nettie's education that must have been of greatest importance to her was her art training. She studied drawing and painting in schools such as Heyl's Esther Institute in Columbus, but she had also been drawing at a young age under Catharine Collins's tutelage. She could have had little direct instruction from her mother, since Nettie was only four when Belle died. She must have been aware, however, that her mother had illustrated letters with sketches, a practice that Nettie herself came to employ (and like Belle, she sometimes included herself in the scenes she sketched, acting as both participant and observer). When she and Kate went to Europe in 1866, their father urged Nettie to "illustrate more freely" her correspondence: "Your pictures add life to your sketches" ("sketches" here meaning her anecdotes). The library at Edgewood, Chase's later residence in the District of Columbia, contained four works published by the critic and pedagogue John Ruskin in 1864 and 1865, which may indicate the direction Nettie's interest took in the period after she left Macaulay's school and before the European sojourn. On that trip, she stayed on in Dresden for some months to study art. Her father, as much as he enjoyed the drawings in her letters, pronounced himself "indifferent," at best, on the subject of her pursuit of art training in Germany. He thought little of the prospects of a woman making a career in art and wished that Nettie would spend her time overseas concentrating on languages instead.[66]

Yet according to Miss Grundy of the New York *World*, writing early in 1870, a person who had seen Nettie's drawings declared them to be "really miracles of their kind." Grundy opined that Nettie showed "great taste and ability as an artist" and should be "admired for her stylish appearance and ease of manner, but more for her mental acquirements."[67] The sketches that Miss Grundy had heard about may have been Nettie's illustrations of Mother Goose rhymes, which were published that year. Later she produced another children's book, *Janet et ses Amis* ("Janet and Her Friends"). Nettie wrote the book's text—prose and verse, all of it in French—and did several of the illustrations. Literary notices of the books called her work "sprightly" and filled with "humor and fancy." She "exhibited a positive talent for humorous drawing," the editors of *Harper's* declared, "which is so rare that the American public can not afford to have it confined to the entertainment of private personal friends." Her *Mother Goose* should be among "books for the parlor rather than for the nursery."[68] Nettie did not pursue a career as a professional artist, although she continued her creative work, especially in the decorative arts, and became a very active patron of art education.

We do not know much about the choices that lay behind Chase's and his daughters' decisions about their schooling and preparation for life as adults. Not long after her sister's wedding, Nettie, aged sixteen and cloistered within Mary Macaulay's school, wondered if her future might hold only "old maidism and forty cats."[69] In 1871 she married William S. Hoyt, who like her sister's husband was financially well off. She and Hoyt led a quieter existence than Kate and William Sprague, Nettie eschewing overt participation in politics while Kate involved herself in rivalries for power (including the social politics of high society). But apart from their differences, both were influential women. As they grew up they were prepared—by their education, their life outside school, and their father's earnest direction—not for an independence so complete that it would have cut them off from the frameworks of society, politics, and religion, but for a reliable and consequential self-sufficiency.

FATHER: SALMON PORTLAND CHASE

Salmon P. Chase was chief justice of the United States when he died in 1873. He had been secretary of the Treasury, a U.S. senator, governor of Ohio, and several times a prospective presidential candidate. But in the mid-1840s, when the earliest letters printed in this volume were written, he was none of those things, any notion of a political career having been stymied by a failure to win reelection after one term on the Cincinnati city council. He was, though, an attorney of growing success. Since his arrival in Ohio in 1830 as a new lawyer at the age of twenty-two, he had advanced his career by a series of strategic law partnerships and relationships with influential clients. He was the solicitor of the Lafayette Bank and of Cincinnati's branch of the Bank of the United States. He later represented telegraph entrepreneur Henry O'Reilly in a prolonged challenge to the Morse monopoly—litigation that came before the Supreme Court in 1852 and involved both mechanical patents and twisted skeins of franchise rights. Chase was legal counsel also for the estate of the deceased Israel Ludlow, who during Cincinnati's early years had acquired extensive landholdings. Chase supplemented his law income by investing in local commercial real estate, and his marriages reflected his attainment of position in the community. He first married Kitty Garniss, whose father co-owned a ferry service across the Ohio River. After her death in 1835, he wed Eliza Smith, whose family had connections on the Kentucky side of the river. She died from tuberculosis, and in 1846 Chase made his third and last marriage to Belle Ludlow, one of Israel Ludlow's grandchildren and heirs.

There was another aspect to Chase's law work, one that earned him attention beyond Ohio. In just a few years beginning in 1837, he became the preeminent courtroom defender of African Americans who escaped the bonds of slavery on the Kentucky side of the river, and the defender also of Ohioans who aided the fugitives. He came to be called the "attorney general of runaway slaves." In his first fugitive case he attempted to use a writ of habeas corpus to prevent the return of a woman named Matilda to slavery and then represented Matilda's employer, reformer James G. Birney, who was charged with harboring a fugitive slave. Chase's argument in Matilda's case was published, as was his brief to the U.S. Supreme Court in 1847 in defense of John Van Zandt, whose assistance to fugitives provided the model for a character in Harriet Beecher Stowe's *Uncle Tom's Cabin*.[1] Chase also drew up affidavits of freedom and consulted in cases in which he did not act as legal counsel. In 1845, Cincinnati's black community gave him an engraved silver pitcher in appreciation for his efforts on behalf of Samuel Watson, an Arkansas slave who tried to leave his master in the city. Chase actually lost Watson's case in court, as he did most of the fugitive cases, including those of Matilda, Birney, and Van Zandt. When he did succeed in preventing the extradition of Mary Townes to Kentucky in 1841, he did it by exploiting a technical defect in an affidavit. But it was a victory nonetheless. His goal was to challenge the incursion of slave catchers into the free polity of Ohio. His legal arguments articulated the notion that slavery was "local," not national: that human bondage might be sanctioned by some states' laws, but it effectively ceased to exist at their borders, and federal assistance to it by such means as fugitive slave statutes was illegitimate. According to one historian, Chase's "legal briefs and arguments against slavery were the most widely circulated in the country."[2]

Paralleling Chase's rise to notice as the fugitives' legal advocate was an equally rapid evolution in his political involvement. In 1840 he was modestly Whiggish in politics, partly because Whig positions on some issues appealed to him and partly from sympathy with anti-Jackson sentiments. Studying law in Washington under William Wirt in the close of John Quincy Adams's presidency and the beginning of Andrew Jackson's administration, the young Chase shared Wirt's distrust of Jackson and his popular democratic style. "I am not a politician," Chase informed a friend in August 1840, even though he had won a place on the Cincinnati city council, as a Whig, a few months before. In terms of national politics he claimed that his position was based less on allegiance to the Whigs than opposition to the Democrats, because he thought the latter, as the party in power, were "the most corrupt."[3] Well before the presidential election of 1840, Chase committed himself to William Henry Harrison, who lived not far from Cincinnati, and he gave Harrison measured support through the campaign. The reform-minded publicist Gamaliel

Bailey criticized Harrison's implicit support of slavery, but Chase only went so far as to advise the president-elect to avoid taking a position on the issue.[4]

At the time, Chase's politics lagged behind his work as a lawyer in fugitive slave cases. In 1840 Birney was the presidential candidate of the tiny and largely symbolic Liberty Party. One of his sons later asserted that it was Birney, founder of the antislavery newspaper the *Philanthropist,* who introduced Chase to the legal points on which the fugitive slave cases hinged.[5] Asked to sign a call for an antislavery convention in July 1840, Chase refused and cited "the impropriety of the step at the present time." But in January of the next year he helped call a Cincinnati meeting on the topic of slavery in Washington, D.C., and at that gathering—having prepared himself by reading Theodore Dwight Weld's *The Power of Congress over the District of Columbia*—he gave a speech. With that address, he became a public speaker for the antislavery cause. Soon he evolved into the primary or sole author of key Liberty Party position statements, including a "Liberty Man's Creed" published in 1844 and the *Address of the Southern and Western Liberty Convention* of the following year. He built relationships with influential antislavery publicists, such as Bailey, who succeeded Birney as the publisher of the *Philanthropist* in Cincinnati and then established the *National Era* in Washington. Chase made connections with like-minded attorneys and politicians, including William Seward of New York, his cocounsel in the Supreme Court phase of Van Zandt's case.[6]

Chase was not, by any of these actions, joining the ranks of what he called "Abolitionists proper." The most committed abolitionists, exemplified by such leaders as William Lloyd Garrison, might insist on the immediate eradication of slavery from every inch of American soil, denounce the Constitution for its condoning of slavery, and threaten to sever themselves from the Union if the moral wrong could not be immediately corrected; Chase could not abandon his legal training or evade his understanding of the bounds of law and Constitution. In his view, American chattel slavery had its basis in states' laws and would not be cast away by moral outrage. He also believed in the efficacy of political means. "The General Government has power to prohibit Slavery everywhere outside of slave states," he wrote in 1856. "A great majority of the people now accept this idea. Comparatively few adopt the suggestion that Congress can legislate abolition within slave-states." To use federal power in those circumstances in which it could be applied against slavery would be, he thought, "a great step." It would make slavery "*denationalized,*" enlisting the full power of the federal government "on the side of freedom" and giving "moral influence and wise action" a chance to operate. Chase "believed slave holding wrong," as he insisted during the Civil War, and he affirmed "that all responsible for the wrong should do what was possible for them, in their respective spheres, for its redress." But he was not of "that school which taught that there could never be a human duty superior to that of the instant and unconditional abolition of slavery."[7]

If he sidled into his involvement with antislavery, and then, after joining the cause, operated only within what he saw as legitimate political and constitutional channels, he nevertheless showed traits of a moral crusader. He was born in New Hampshire in 1808. When he was nine years old his father, who had quit farming and then failed in a glass-making venture, died and left the family in financial difficulty. In 1820 Salmon's mother sent the boy, the seventh of her ten children, to live with his uncle Philander Chase, who had recently been made the Episcopal bishop of Ohio. There the youth absorbed heavy doses of religion and moral stricture. The bishop's belief and commitment as a young man had been powerful enough not just to draw him away from his ancestral religious background of Congregationalism but to pull a fair portion of his extended family into the Episcopal Church with him. He was, in addition to being a religious leader, an unflinching disciplinarian, an administrator, and an energetic seeker of financial support for educational institutions that he established. After spending a few years in the household of that strong-willed clergyman and beginning his higher education at Cincinnati College, Salmon Chase returned to New England and entered Dartmouth College, which, in the months before his graduation in 1826, was swept by a religious revival. Initially reserved about that event—"I was not taught to believe much in the efficacy of such things," he confessed—he before long referred to "service" for Christ and declared that everyone "must be accountable to a higher tribunal than any earthly court" for the use to which we put "the talents entrusted to our care." Yearning perhaps for a calling, he may have considered a career in the ministry. Passing through New York City following his graduation from Dartmouth, on a single Sunday he attended services in three different churches—one Episcopalian, one Presbyterian, and one Dutch Reformed. He longed for encouragement "to fight more valiantly the good fight of faith."[8]

Unsure what to do with himself after college, he went to Washington, fell into an opportunity to teach school, and took up the study of law. He also found himself at the center of national politics, surrounded by its practitioners. Several of his pupils were sons of cabinet officers. He read law under Wirt, who was attorney general. Chase attended public receptions at the White House and encountered President John Quincy Adams and Jackson, Webster, Clay, Van Buren, and Calhoun.[9] But the slavery issue, which was presumed to have been abated by the Missouri Compromise of 1820, did not dominate the capital city at the end of that decade. Slavery was legal in the District of Columbia—a federal protection of the institution that Chase would later decry—but it did not intrude much on his thinking during his residence in Washington as a teacher and law student. He drafted a petition to Congress that called for gradual abolition in the District but did so in response to a request for his professional services rather than through any initiative of his own. Although he later recalled that he "complied cheerfully" with the request, he based the memorial on materials handed to him; he was uninvolved and largely uninterested once the draft left his hands, and the event seems to have represented no larger commitment on his part.[10]

It was more difficult to avoid the issue in Cincinnati. A commercial center separated from slavery only by the span of the Ohio River, the city was also the home of Lane Seminary, where intellectually engaged and energetic reformers such as Weld, Lyman Beecher, and Calvin Stowe taught. In 1834, students at the seminary walked out after the institution's trustees suppressed discussion of the slavery issue. The next year, activists in and around Cincinnati formed an antislavery society, and the year after that Birney began to publish the *Philanthropist.* Chase was uninvolved in those events, but moved in the same social and intellectual circles as the region's antislavery leadership. James C. Ludlow, whose daughter Chase married in 1846, provided a meeting place for the radical Lane students. Chase's strongest connection to the movement was through his sister Abigail, who had moved to Cincinnati from New Hampshire in 1832 with her husband, Dr. Isaac Colby. As Chase later phrased it, Colby was "one of the most worthy and respectable" members of the Cincinnati Anti-Slavery Society.[11]

If Chase early in his career had moral commitments other than a strong one to religious devotion, they centered on temperance, education, and Sunday schools. In May 1829 he attended a meeting to consider the founding of an "infant school." Also in Washington, he attended a temperance sermon and discussed that reform issue with the Wirt family. He took this interest with him to Ohio. Temperance and regulation of the sale of alcohol were core issues during his single term on the Cincinnati city council—a platform spurned by the majority of voters when they declined to elect him to a second term. In 1836 he joined the Western Board of Agency of the American Sunday School Union. And in 1845 he donated $100, a significant sum, to the construction of a Temperance Hall.[12]

The precise mechanism of his entry into the antislavery cause remains unclear, but there was a defining moment late in July 1836, when antiabolitionist mobs in Cincinnati went hunting for Birney, wrecked the printing office of the six-month-old *Philanthropist,* and attacked African American neighborhoods. Some prominent local businessmen and professionals, and members of their families, took leading roles in the mob action, and local government authorities intervened only late and mildly. Chase could not avoid being touched directly when a crowd singled out Colby as a target, almost burning the contents of the doctor's office in the middle of the street, and Chase's sister Abigail sought protection at his home. He quickly became involved, joining with others in an effort to organize meetings and to draft resolutions against the mobs. Most dramatically, he blocked a doorway to face down a malicious group searching for Birney, whom he did not yet know. "From this time on," Chase later asserted, he was in the antislavery movement, although in terms of politics his real participation started in the 1840s.[13]

Just as he believed that moral fervor could not trump law and Constitution, he saw practical limitations to what a purely moral position against slavery could accomplish, especially where he lived. Cincinnati had been the scene of a riot against African Americans in 1829, before Chase moved to the city, and in September 1841 mobs targeting abolitionists and blacks became even more violent than the crowds of 1836. Much of the white population of the Ohio Valley resented any signs of advancement by blacks and feared all varieties of "amalgamation" of the races. Harriet Beecher Stowe later wrote that some people in Cincinnati shunned Chase outright for his work in Matilda's case: "Many of the former patrons and friends of the rising young lawyer walked no more with him."[14] The call for the 1841 meeting to discuss slavery in the District of Columbia, written by Chase although not published over his signature, took care to praise "men who are not members of Abolition societies." And Chase, labeled an abolitionist despite any distinctions he might make for his own part, failed to win the nomination for a seat in the state senate. But his recognition of those political realities did not make him callous to the fundamentally ethical basis of the problem. Near the end of the nineteenth century, historian Albert Bushnell Hart said of Chase's motivation that the "testimony of those who came closest to him is that he took up the antislavery cause because he felt it to be a religious duty" and that Chase "believed slavery to be a dreadful moral wrong."[15]

Doubting that a small, single-issue political party could accomplish the goals of antislavery, Chase advocated the reform of one of the established national parties. Despite his first entry into local politics as a Whig and the early influence of mentors such as Wirt, who had departed Washington at the advent of the Jackson administration, Chase saw the Democratic Party as the best political means of opposing slavery. The Democrats, after all, gave ideological primacy to the states, which accorded with his views of the relationship between the Constitution and slavery. Moreover, by the 1840s, there was, in his own local political arena of southern Ohio, more chance of success with the Democrats than with the Whigs. The main body of the Democratic Party, though, did not align with Chase's views on slavery, so he and his political allies distinguished themselves as "True" or "Independent" Democrats. His insistence that the Democratic Party should be the device for effective political action put him at odds with antislavery leaders who worked from a Whig political base or were committed to a single-issue third party.[16] From Senator Thomas Morris of Ohio—who in 1838–39 dramatically changed the target of his intense zeal as a Jackson Democrat from banks and business monopolies to the threat of the "Slave Power"—Chase learned the necessity and the strategies of political action against slavery.[17]

Following the war with Mexico, the potential extension of slavery into new territories with federal sanction gave definition to the Free Soil political movement of the late 1840s and early 1850s. Events in Ohio beginning late in 1848 put Chase into politics at the national level. A Whig-sponsored apportionment law caused a deadlock over legislative representation for Hamilton County. Neither the mainstream Whigs nor their Democratic rivals held a majority in the legislature. Free Soil members were themselves divided, but they could, by cooperation with one party or the other, furnish the votes needed to form a majority. Chase and others brought Democratic Free Soilers into alliance with Democrats in a series of arrangements under which the coalition elected a speaker, resolved the apportionment issue, undertook the repeal of the "black laws" that had circumscribed rights of African Americans in the state, and elected Chase to the United States Senate. Whigs and some Whig Free Soilers decried the results as a brokered political deal, but Chase carefully asserted that it had been a matter of convincing people to ally for common benefit while allowing them to maintain their political convictions.[18]

Although there were antislavery Whigs and antislavery Democrats, each national party also had members who favored slavery and powerful leaders who were more than willing to compromise on the issue. When Chase entered the Senate in 1849, he united with William Seward and Charles Sumner in that chamber, with Ohio's Joshua Giddings in the House of Representatives, and with others to make up a Free Soil cadre. Collectively the group had both Whig and Democratic ties, but its members were isolated from real influence and received no meaningful committee assignments. Chase was able to make two big speeches on the great national issue. One, "Union and Freedom, without Compromise," opposed the package of bills that became the Compromise of 1850, which allowed slavery in part of the new western territory through popular sovereignty and which was passed in conjunction with a refurbished Fugitive Slave Act. Chase's other major speech in the Senate, which he titled "Maintain Plighted Faith," was against the legislation backed by Stephen A. Douglas that became the Kansas-Nebraska Act of 1854 and prospectively opened Kansas to slavery. Chase also engaged in debate on the Senate floor, tried to forestall or alter the compromise and the Kansas-Nebraska legislation, and assumed a critical role in creating and distributing the "Appeal of the Independent Democrats" of January 1854, an influential manifesto of Free Soil Democrats in the Senate and House.[19]

And so through the 1840s and into the 1850s, as he had built a reputation for his courtroom defense of fugitives, Chase assumed an increasingly conspicuous place within antislavery politics. Although he did not receive the Free Soil Party's presidential nomination in 1852, he was considered for it. He did not embrace the "fusion" movement in the mid-1850s, declaring that he could cooperate with Know Nothings but had no desire to "fuse" with them. He stressed "the importance of keeping the Anti-slavery idea paramount," making opposition to the Kansas-Nebraska Act his fundamental political test. He maintained his preference for the label "Independent Democrat," and in 1855 he thought that the prospects for the Republican Party, the new coalition with its denatured, as he thought, emphasis on the slavery question, were poor. He would work with the new party, however, as long as he felt he could maintain his principles, and that year the Republicans nominated him for the governorship of Ohio. He was elected and won a second two-year term in 1857. His election marked an early success for the party that joined Free Soilers, Know Nothing nativists, temperance reformers, and others who were frustrated with established Whig and Democratic politics.[20]

Appropriately for an attorney who had probed fugitive slave statutes for exploitable flaws, he placed emphasis on definitions and language. The title of his argument in the Van Zandt case referred not to fugitive slaves, since the word *slave* could give credence to the notion of a fixed caste, a status conferred by birth and supported by natural order. Instead, Chase's brief in the case referred to "fugitives from service." Later, at the close of the Civil War, he urged Edwin Stanton to abolish from the War Department such vocabulary as *contrabands* for former slaves and *corrals* for the places where groups of freed people had collected under the government's auspices. "Words are things," he observed, "& terms implying degradation help to degrade."[21]

He was not, though, without prejudice. Almost all white Americans of that era, including Abraham Lincoln, showed signs of racism even if they opposed slavery. In January 1849, Chase described a woman who came to ask for his professional assistance as "an old negress, grimy black, fat and squat & *odorous.*" He noted too that she said "'scription" for "subscription," "drefful" for "dreadful," and "abbitrerry" for "arbitrary." In the end, though, he was struck by the woman's initiative, goodness of soul, and forthrightness: she had purchased her own freedom with $250 of her earnings and was undertaking a subscription campaign to raise $350 (beginning with $2 from Chase) to buy her son's freedom rather than have him escape to Canada and be separated from her. A few months later Chase had a similar experience when Belle, following the birth of their daughter Josephine, sought a nurse. "Miss Townley," the preferred nurse, was occupied elsewhere, and they could find no one except "a fat colored woman." Chase quickly found himself "well pleased with her."[22]

While it is difficult to ascertain all of the details, it is certain that African Americans worked for him. Vina Lewis, employed in the Chase household in 1846, was apparently a runaway slave from Mississippi, and Catherine ("Cassie") Vaudry, Chase's housekeeper in Washington in the 1860s and 1870s, was a mulatto woman manumitted from slavery early in 1861.[23] William Joice, his valet and driver from near the end of the Civil War until Chase's death, was in all probability the person of that name who, as a seven-year-old black boy in the District of Columbia in 1841, had been apprenticed as a servant until he was twenty-one. A youth named David, who performed tasks in Chase's residence in 1836 and received tutoring from Chase, seems likely to have been African American. William Dean Howells remembered "a shining black butler" in Columbus, and there were other household employees through the decades about whom we know very little.[24]

He was far more progressive than most politicians in his advocacy of fundamental rights for African Americans. In his response to the presentation of the silver pitcher by Cincinnati's black residents in 1845, he stressed the importance of equality and lamented the state laws that barred black Ohioans from adequate schools and the right to vote.[25] In 1863, as a stockholder of the Washington and Georgetown Street Railroad (and on close terms with the Cooke family that controlled it), he protested the company's prohibition against blacks riding on its streetcars. He urged not only that people of color be allowed to ride but that they be given access to the same streetcars as whites—if the company would let blacks ride but insisted on segregation, he argued that the cars set aside for blacks should be "*better* than the others so as to compensate in some measure for exclusion from the others." During the Civil War he was well in front of Lincoln in asserting that blacks were entitled to serve as soldiers; vote, even in the South; and—contrary to the holding of the Supreme Court in the Dred Scott case—enjoy the benefits of citizenship. As early as July 1863 he looked ahead to Reconstruction and argued that the rebelling states should be readmitted to the federal union only if they embraced emancipation. In 1865, he was instrumental in the admission of John S. Rock as the first black attorney authorized to plead cases before the Supreme Court.[26] Chase's will included a provision for a substantial gift of $10,000 to Wilberforce University, the Ohio institution dedicated to the higher education of blacks. After his death, when his coffin lay in state in Washington, the *New York Times* noted that two of the four Capitol Police officers who formed the guard of honor were black. Thirteen years later, when his remains were moved to Ohio for reburial, the pallbearers were African Americans—five from Washington, plus two men who had worked for him as servants in Cincinnati.[27]

As governor of Ohio, Chase promoted and monitored bills in the general assembly, gave speeches on various occasions both within and outside the state, and had to deal with numerous applications for pardon. In terms of politics, he worked to tidy up the Republican cause in his state, using appointments to sort out satisfactory relationships among the different elements of the new coalition. In 1857, an election year in Ohio, he had to manage a fiscal and political crisis when it was revealed that a former state treasurer had lost a half-million dollars of state funds in private speculation—an episode followed closely by a nationwide financial panic.[28]

During his first year in office he considered setting in motion a plan to forcibly liberate free-state men who were being held prisoner in Kansas, and slavery continued to be a prominent issue within Ohio as well. Although the governor's office was not directly involved, interference by some Ohioans with federal officers executing the Fugitive Slave Act resulted in court cases that drew considerable attention.[29] Two weeks into his first term, Chase was confronted with the ugliest fugitive slave incident of his career. Margaret Garner, her husband, their four children, and her husband's parents fled from slavery in Kentucky; slave catchers cornered the family in Ohio, and Margaret, convinced that her children would be better off dead than enslaved, succeeded in killing her three-year-old daughter before their pursuers captured the family. Chase concurred in the indictment of Margaret for murder under state law, and of the other adults in her family as accomplices, as a device to keep them under the control of Ohio authorities and out of the slave catchers' hands. A federal judge intervened, however, and ordered the surrender of the family to a U.S. marshal, who took them back to Kentucky. Although he doubted that the tactic would work, Chase issued an extradition request. By the time his writ reached Kentucky, the Garners had been spirited away by their owners and could not be found. The awful affair had a persistent legacy. In a speech late in 1863, the abolitionist Wendell Phillips caustically rebuked Chase, accusing him of having done too little in Margaret Garner's case.[30]

Chase took a leading role in making the Republicans a national party by pushing for a national convention and presidential ticket in 1856. He was one of the potential candidates for the nomination but was too closely identified with the antislavery cause, and the party selected John C. Frémont.[31] Chase looked ahead to 1860, perhaps prompting the unidentified "vain imagining" that troubled him one day in 1857. In his assessments of the coming presidential contest, rivals such as William Seward and Edward Bates were on his mind.[32] But they were all outmaneuvered by Abraham Lincoln's skillful operatives when the Republican convention met in Chicago in May 1860. Chase and Lincoln had never met, but they had corresponded, and Chase had done more than just about any Republican from outside Illinois to speak for the cause during the 1854 and 1858 political campaigns in that state.[33]

Chase had also led the way in recasting the nation's history to favor the antislavery cause. He did that by advocating that Thomas Jefferson and other members of the founding generation had favored truly universal freedom and had wanted slavery to end. That argument focused on the seemingly unalloyed and unqualified statement of equality in the Declaration of Independence and pointed to the prohibition against slavery in the Northwest Territory. Such reasoning gave antislavery politicians a weapon to use against claims that the institution had legitimacy through the Constitution and long-established national law. Chase apparently got the premise from Birney, but amplified it, packaged it, and gave it currency, making it by the 1850s a primary component in the oratorical and rhetorical arsenal of speakers such as Charles Sumner and, notably, Lincoln.[34]

Lincoln appreciated Chase's political importance, and as the president-elect planned his administration he invited Chase to Springfield, Illinois, for a private conference in January 1861. Lincoln also polled Republican senators and found Chase to be their favorite for secretary of the Treasury. The Ohio legislature had named Chase to the U.S. Senate, and he had just taken his place in Washington for a special session of the Thirty-Seventh Congress in March 1861 when Lincoln appointed him to the Treasury position.[35]

In the spring of 1861 no one knew the eventual duration or magnitude of the civil conflict, and Chase as secretary of the Treasury initially sought to finance war expenditures by negotiating loans with associations of bankers in major cities. Six months into the war, though, demands on the Treasury exceeded a million dollars a day and the government owed $24 million for requisitions not yet paid. By February 1862 the Treasury was paying out almost $1.5 million a day on average, and Chase figured that the floating debt, in the form of obligations not yet paid, was more than $45 million. During his first eight months at the Treasury he cobbled together $175 million of borrowed gold and silver, but it was not enough as the demands of war expenditures grew and grew.[36] He extended the borrowing overseas and made Philadelphia banker and entrepreneur Jay Cooke the sole agent to sell interest-bearing bonds that Congress first authorized in 1862. Cooke was originally from Ohio, and his brother Henry, a newspaperman, claimed credit for getting Chase into Lincoln's cabinet. The relationship with the ambitious and ethically limber Jay Cooke caused the Treasury secretary some problems, but the financier was successful in promoting the government's bonds to a wider market. In 1862 also, the United States issued its first paper legal tender, the famous greenbacks. Chase's picture appeared on the $1 greenback bill, and he became popularly known by sobriquets such as "General Greenbacks."[37] In addition to the bonds and legal-tender currency, the United States issued a variety of interest-bearing notes, certificates of indebtedness, and, to stand in for coins of small denomination, postal and "fractional" currency notes. Congress approved a system of national banks to give some regulation to the money supply, increased excises and duties, and, for the first time, taxed personal income. One of Chase's successors as secretary of the Treasury, Hugh McCulloch, later wrote that to Chase, "more than to any other single man, always excepting Abraham Lincoln," were the American people "indebted for the preservation of the national unity."[38]

New measures demanded new means of implementation. To issue millions of dollars' worth of bonds, certificates, and legal tender, the government had to print those instruments and forestall counterfeiting. That required finding the correct paper, ink, plates, presses, and methods; implementing procedures to guard printing plates and finished currency; and creating investigative services to root out counterfeiters. Each interest payment coupon on a bond had to be signed. Each disbursement required handling by comptrollers' and auditors' clerks. This expansion of tasks required a huge increase in the number of jobs in Treasury bureaus, while the demand for soldiers eroded the supply of men available for civilian employment. As a result, although the Treasury was not the first federal agency to employ females, it was, during Chase's tenure as secretary, the first department to hire women in significant numbers. Hundreds of women spent the war signing bond coupons or cutting, counting, and sorting Treasury notes.[39]

To regulate trade on the margins of the rebelling states and to deal with confiscated property, Chase used special agents of the Treasury. Whereas before the war the department had appointed special agents on an occasional, ad hoc basis for investigations or other tasks, during the course of the conflict Chase formed a large, tiered bureaucracy of geographic districts. Although by the end of the war the War Department and its Freedmen's Bureau had oversight of former slaves, earlier it was Treasury agents who took leading roles in educational, social, and economic reforms meant to give some freed slaves a life after bondage. Edward L. Pierce, for example, a Massachusetts attorney and associate of Sumner, was the Treasury's agent on the Sea Islands of South Carolina and Georgia, a plantation district controlled by Federal forces through much of the war. Chase also received reports from the Reverend Mansfield French, who went to the Sea Islands not as a government employee but as the general agent of the National Freedmen's Relief Association.[40]

On matters of race and slavery, Chase was among the most progressive of officials in Lincoln's administration. He stayed ahead of the president, anticipating and urging emancipation, the use of black soldiers, and political rights for African Americans well before Lincoln advocated such measures. Lincoln was concerned about sentiment in border states such as Missouri and Maryland that allowed slaveholding but did not secede. He knew, too, the possible political consequences of appearing too forward to conservative voters in all states, who needed much cajoling to move from the cause of Union to a war against slavery. To Chase, while the Emancipation Proclamation was a huge step, its effects were terribly constrained by the exemptions and limitations that Lincoln wrote into the document.[41]

Within the administration Chase also had a distrustful relationship with William Seward, whom Lincoln had made secretary of state and who had long been more pragmatic on the slavery issue than Chase. In the cabinet, Chase and Seward each wanted his own influence to be robust and his rival's to be limited. More than once Lincoln found himself caught between them, and more than once Chase offered his resignation. Although content with Chase's direction of fiscal affairs, Lincoln disliked his seeming refusal to compromise on behalf of broader political factors, particularly in the selection of people for Treasury positions. In June 1864 one such instance gave Lincoln reason to accept the proffered resignation, and he abruptly removed Chase from the cabinet. An effort by some disgruntled politicians, unhappy with Lincoln, to promote Chase as a presidential candidate had flopped, so Lincoln could dismiss Chase from his administration without fear of setting loose a serious rival. Lincoln was confident enough to think that if Chase, who was still the favorite of some radicals, caused no trouble on his departure from the cabinet, he might qualify for an appointment to the Supreme Court or some other position. Chief Justice Roger B. Taney died in October 1864, and after some hesitation Lincoln named Chase, in December, to the vacancy.[42]

He had never held any judicial position. He immediately faced cases that dealt with the legality of wartime measures that he had helped to craft—his first decision, in the case of the ship *Circassian* in January 1865, concerned the legitimacy of the blockade at New Orleans. And not surprisingly, aspects of the war and its aftermath demanded the court's attention. The court dealt with wartime loyalty oaths in the cases of *Garesche v. Missouri, Cummings v. Missouri*, and *Ex parte Garland* and ruled on the trial of civilians by military tribunals in the *Milligan* and *McCardle* cases.[43] Supreme Court justices also sat with U.S. district judges to constitute the circuit courts. Chase's circuit originally included Maryland, Delaware, Virginia, West Virginia, and North Carolina. It later included South Carolina but not Delaware. When Jefferson Davis was indicted for treason in 1866, Chase refused to hear that case, or any other in the formerly rebellious states, until the regular court system reclaimed its full jurisdiction—that is, until the federal government ceased to use military commissions for trials and restored full access to the writ of habeas corpus. Chase was among the influential Northerners who did not favor the prosecution of Davis on treason charges, which was expected to be more divisive than productive. Attorneys on both sides delayed the case, even after Chase's objections regarding courts in the South were removed, and Davis was eventually covered by an amnesty from President Andrew Johnson.[44]

When cases that involved the status of greenbacks as legal tender for all obligations, even for debts contracted before Congress had authorized the paper money, came before the court, Chase confronted his own experience as a member of the executive branch. When the first legal-tender legislation had been under consideration early in 1862, Chase, reaffirming hard-money principles that he had long held, expressed "a great aversion" to making paper money legal tender. He conceded, however, that it was "inevitably necessary" to make U.S. notes legal tender during the war. As chief justice he led the court in ruling, in *Hepburn v. Griswold* in 1870, that greenbacks could not be substituted for gold or silver to pay a contract made before the wartime legal tender acts. The Supreme Court, following changes in its membership, overturned the *Hepburn* ruling the next year, but Chase continued to maintain that greenbacks should not be made the permanent equivalent of specie.[45]

In his most lasting statement as chief justice, writing for the majority in *Texas v. White* in 1869, he declared that secession had not irreversibly broken the relationship between states and union or demolished the continuity of government in the seceding states. The United States, he asserted, was "an indestructible Union, composed of indestructible States." Two years earlier the court had dismissed challenges to the Reconstruction Acts from Georgia and Mississippi, and the *Texas v. White* opinion affirmed the power of Congress over Reconstruction.[46]

On circuit in 1867, Chase in the case *In re Turner* ruled in favor of a young African American woman, striking down a Maryland law that had had the effect of continuing servitude for blacks under the guise of apprenticeship.[47] But as the postwar nation took shape, at least so far as the Supreme Court played a role in the process, the chief justice's views did not always align with those of his brethren on the bench. In particular, he dissented when the court refused to apply the Fourteenth Amendment, ratified in 1868, as a limitation on the powers of states against individuals. He was the only dissenter when the court turned down the appeal of Myra Colby Bradwell, a woman who sought admission as an attorney to the Illinois bar. He dissented again in the Slaughter-House Cases, a decision by the court that boded ill for African Americans hoping to use the Fourteenth Amendment against repressive measures by state governments. Those cases came before the court in 1873, as Chase's health failed, and in neither instance was he able to write an opinion to articulate his reasoning.[48]

For Chase, joining the court did not end his involvement in policy and politics. He tried to shape Lincoln's Reconstruction policies and wrote letters on the subject to the president in April 1865, days before Lincoln was assassinated. He tried, too, to advise Lincoln's successor as president, Andrew Johnson, but was frustrated in the effort.[49] When Johnson was impeached in 1868, Chase became the first chief justice to preside, as specified by the Constitution, over the Senate impeachment trial of a U.S. president, and he alienated many radical Republicans by his efforts to keep the trial a judicial proceeding and prevent any outright political gambit to remove the president. Later that year, as shown by correspondence in this volume, he hoped to gain the Democratic nomination for the presidency on what he hoped would be a reforming platform (he continued to advocate principles over party labels). In 1872 he was again spoken of as a presidential candidate, although his health and political circumstances prevented any real development of that prospect.

After suffering a stroke in 1870, he struggled to regain full participation in the court's business while his health declined. In the spring of 1873, he died after another stroke. For most of his daughters' lives he had been a political figure at the national level: Kate was only eight years old, and Nettie not yet two, when the Ohio legislature elected him a United States senator in 1849. Before Kate married and while Nettie was still in school, their father's picture embellished every one-dollar U.S. greenback note—an illustration of the public identity that ran parallel to the family relationships chronicled in this volume.

OBLIGATION AND FULFILLMENT

"May God give the child a good understanding that she may keep his commandments," Chase wrote in his journal right after Kate's birth.[1] Religious belief formed the core of his understanding of conduct, and in religion as in politics, his own devotion mattered more to him than unquestioned allegiance to a particular denomination for the public forms of ritual. His family was rooted in New England, but he matured in an Episcopalian rather than a Congregational religious culture. In Cincinnati, he became part of the Episcopal establishment, serving on Sunday school committees and as a vestryman of St. Paul's Episcopal Church. Like some other Episcopalians, however, he was distressed by the denomination's failure to take a firm position against slavery.[2] Nor did he feel bound exclusively to Episcopalian liturgy, although he did limit the range of his experimentation to other Protestant churches. At various times, prompted by politics, convenience, or curiosity, he attended Congregational, Unitarian, Presbyterian, Baptist, Quaker, Dutch Reformed, and African American churches.[3] Methodism in particular intrigued him. Once as a young man he attended a Methodist chapel when other churches were unavailable due to bad weather, and he found himself enthralled by the service. Later he obtained the *Works* of John Wesley and histories of Methodism by Abel Stevens for his library. Chase declared the story of Methodism to be "one of the grandest which the History of Christ's Church affords," and in the final decade of his life he frequently attended Methodist services in Washington and elsewhere.[4] In January 1872, when he felt ready to take communion again after having foregone the rite for several years, he did it in a Methodist church.[5] After his death, a Methodist Episcopal clergyman presided over the memorial service held in the U.S. Capitol. Chase's will contained only one bequest to an institution connected with religion: Wilberforce University, affiliated with the African Methodist Episcopal Church.[6]

Private devotion, family prayer, and reading of scripture were important elements of the daily household schedule when Nettie and Kate were young. Their father also placed emphasis on memorization of Bible passages.[7] That personalized spiritualism, emphasizing the individual and the close family, allowed some freedom but placed great responsibility on the person. "What a spectacle is such a creature as I am," Chase lamented in his diary in 1840: "loaded with benefits by a gracious Father and rendering such poor returns."[8] He found it difficult to meet his own standards. Time and again he excoriated himself for falling into "wandering thoughts" during sermons, for being insufficiently "christian" in attitude about someone who had done him wrong, for failing to grasp scripture with sufficient comprehension, for being too reserved in prayer. The turn of the new year prompted critical self-assessment, and he usually found his spiritual performance during the previous twelve months wanting.[9] If he failed to confront his responsibilities, the burden was compounded by guilt and shame: "I feel so little my sinfulness & so little my obligations for mercies recd. that I am distressed by it," he wrote in 1846.[10]

His early experience as a husband and father reinforced the necessity of individual spiritual duty and brought home, too, the connection of duty to the transience of life on earth. From December 1835 to January 1852, he lost three wives and four children. Two of his brothers and two sisters died within roughly the same period, from 1838 to the end of 1852. "Death has pursued me incessantly ever since I was twenty five," he wrote to Charles Sumner in 1850, apparently marking the start of that mournful period with his mother's death in 1832. He felt death's "Shadow" to be a constant presence.[11] With each loss, he despaired over the spiritual state of the dying person. When his first wife died, he grieved that he had not been "so faithful with her on the subject of religion as I should have been," leaving him "no certain assurance that she died in the faith." On her deathbed, asked by her father if she had "thought of God," Kitty Garniss Chase answered that she had done so "long and seriously." For her husband that was not enough. He lacked the "clear evidence of her salvation" that "might reasonably have been expected to result from more faithful & diligent efforts" on his part.[12]

According to Chase, his second wife, Kate's mother, was "a renewed child of God." Lizzie professed her faith and "died trusting in Jesus," but for her husband, comfort was still elusive. "I think I should not have felt so very wretched," he confided to a clergyman friend, Charles D. Cleveland, "if I could as it were have gone with her to the margin of the river, and heard her say as she entered it that all was well. Perhaps this was designed of God as a punishment for my want of fidelity to her as a Christian husband, which I acknowledge and deplore." He could always find room for doubt and attribute it to his own lack of spiritual "fidelity." He pronounced his efforts to help Lizzie achieve grace during her final illness "defective and insufficient."[13]

His spiritual obligation, then, extended beyond himself, but was still highly personal. Complete satisfaction that one had done all one could was unattainable. His letter of January 6, 1850, to Belle, Nettie's mother, which is printed in this volume, shows his constant yearning for assurance that he had done all he could, that he had not failed to help a loved one attain salvation. Each loss taught him how little time there was to prepare for the transit from mortal life on earth to everlasting life beyond, and to avoid guilt he must do everything possible to perform his role. The gnawing of obligation could never be fully sated. In his version of a Puritan psyche, the individual could never be sure if he or she was saved, but could certainly feel inadequacy.

A self-reflective and endless quest for grace pervaded his being, beyond the narrowly religious aspects of life. "How precious a treasure is time," he noted in his journal to mark his twenty-first birthday, "and how have I lavishly squandered it!" Years later, not long before he became governor of Ohio, he seemed no closer to self-appeasement when he "lamented" his "misapplication of time."[14] Each new year furnished occasion for a self-critical assessment of the twelvemonth just completed, in secular as well as religious terms, with the almost certain regret that he had done too little. Despite accomplishments and an application of effort that would have more than satisfied a person less driven than he was, he berated himself for frittering time, thought himself lacking in discipline, and keened that he was not reading and reflecting deeply enough. He was "ashamed" during a period when he thought that he was rising too late in the morning. For several weeks in 1840 he hoped to force "system" into his already highly structured life, reading *The Student's Manual* by John Todd and prescribing a detailed agenda for each day.[15]

It is no surprise that his correspondence with his daughters reflects his experience with loss and a many-layered sense of obligation that encompassed both his children's responsibilities and his own toward them. The deaths of family members taught him that all were vulnerable, and he worried about his daughters' health. His letters to Kate and Nettie imposed standards of conduct, hygiene, education, handwriting, spelling, and religion, exactly as he had enjoined the girls' mothers before them.[16]

He could not do otherwise and fulfill his notions of obligation and the necessity of striving for salvation and grace. "Our life is very short at the longest," he wrote to Kate when she was fourteen, "and after this life, there is a long life to come." As he expressed it to both daughters when they were young women, his love for them made him want them to be "perfect in these apparently small but really important matters." "Perfection will cost you labor & pains," he wrote, but Kate and Nettie should expect to make sacrifices for the benefit of their own "internal satisfaction" as well as for the "gratification" of their father's needs.[17]

A language of perfection runs forthrightly through the correspondence of this father and his daughters. Nettie, regularly admonished about her penmanship and spelling, was warned not to be satisfied with her letter writing "as long as any degree of perfection remains unattained." He reminded Kate, at the age of fourteen, of the importance of "perfect propriety of behavior." Nettie and Kate acquired the vocabulary, but tended to employ it for more workaday ends: Kate reported that she was "perfectly well"; Nettie could say that the seamstress mending her clothes did so "to perfection" and that she had experienced the "most perfect trip."[18] Their father's language made clear that he was interested in a higher—perhaps more perfect—category of perfection. "May your faith be perfected and your hope established in Christ," he told Nettie's mother. He explained to Kate that Christian belief demanded "perfect conformity" but offered in return "repentance and faith"—"perfect safety," as he said in another letter. Scripture was important "to the regulation of your life and the perfecting of your faith." He was a father, he assured his elder daughter, "who loves you beyond expression, and longs to see you perfect in every wifely & christian duty."[19]

Perfection promised, then, complete fulfillment and a final satisfaction of responsibilities: since perfect conduct, perfect duty, and perfect salvation were linked, there was a rationale behind the meticulously prescriptive parental correspondence. But obsession with minute responsibility and details of comportment could dominate the father's letters to the exclusion of other matters. See, for example, his letter to Kate of August 13, 1850, in which he held her accountable at some length for several matters, dealt rather brusquely with the death of the family's youngest child, baby Josephine, and took no notice of the fact that August 13 was Kate's tenth birthday. His letter stands in contrast to the more tender one that Kate's stepmother, Belle, wrote to her on August 29. It was a "pity," Chase rued to one of his sisters in 1864, "that we brothers and sisters were not more demonstrative. We ought not merely to have loved one another; but to have told one another of our love."[20]

Writing to Kate on April 13, 1855, Chase mistakenly attributed to Samuel Johnson the aphorism that anything worth doing at all is worth doing well. Johnson would have relished the irony of that error, for the maxim came in fact not from Johnson but from one of the letters that his contemporary, the earl of Chesterfield, had written to an illegitimate son. First published in the 1770s, those letters of advice from father to offspring were often viewed as impious and cynical, quite contrary to Chase's ideals of attainable perfection.[21] Yet one can draw parallels between Chesterfield's son and Chase's daughters—statesmen's children in each case, closely coached but seemingly prevented by birth from attaining the full measure of their fathers' power. However, while Chesterfield rarely lost sight of what was possible and necessary for his son to make his way in eighteenth-century English politics and society, Chase's goal was not the full empowerment of his daughters in the world they inhabited. His pedantry aimed at that ideal of Christian perfection, preparing his daughters by readying them for salvation rather than for achievement and success on earth.

Not all pious Protestant Christians were as concerned with the same details of their children's conduct and development as Chase was, or to the same degree. Nor was Chase's brand of religion a prerequisite for a controlling father. There were, of course, features of personality involved, attributes visible in some other detail-oriented, striving, and possibly insecure political figures. After Alexander Hamilton's son graduated from Columbia College and began to read law, Hamilton penned "Rules for *Mr Philip Hamilton*" that specified when the young man would rise in the mornings and exactly how he would spend his days—a structure similar to what Chase created for himself using Todd's *Manual*. Thomas Jefferson once proclaimed "a new law" by which he would only write to his adult daughters in answer to letters from them. In language not unlike what Chase used a couple of generations later, Jefferson manipulated his daughters' feelings by closing his letters with such admonitions as "continue to love me" and insisted that his daughters "remember how pleasing your letters will be to me."[22] Chase probably would have been just as compulsive with his daughters if he had not been the devoted Christian that he was. In his case, however, religion was the context in which his concerns about his family, and his efforts to prepare his daughters for the future, found expression.

He showed more respect for women's abilities than a great many men of his day. He could call his daughters' attention to the example of Annis Lee Furness, whose skill with languages particularly impressed him (see his letter to Kate of August 4, 1853). Susan Walker, with whom he had a lasting friendship, worked for a period in the Washington offices of the U.S. Coast Survey, where she performed mathematical calculations and computed the occurrence of eclipses. She earned higher pay than some men in the bureau, and later she taught freed slaves in the Sea Islands.[23] Writing to Elizabeth Smith Miller, the daughter of the reformer Gerrit Smith, in 1869, Chase declared that he was "heartily desirous of all things which will really improve the condition of woman," including "the increase of facilities for moral & intellectual culture; ample recognition & full protection to rights of property; and access to & perfect security in all employments for which she is qualified by strength, capacity & integrity." In 1872, when asked about the Treasury's employment of women during the war, Chase said that he had "always favored the enlargement of the sphere of woman's work and the payment of just compensation for it." A few months later, he tried to uphold Myra Bradwell's attempt to join the Illinois bar.[24] Writing to Kate in 1866, he remembered "the remark I once made in answer to some body who wanted to know my opinion on womans-rights, that I was for putting every thing in the hands of the women & letting them govern. Certainly I dont see but you & Nettie are as well qualified to take part in affairs as I was at your age."[25]

Earlier, before he first married and started a family, he saw examples of intelligent, able women in his sister Abigail, who learned several languages and thought purposefully about the role of education, and Elizabeth Washington Gamble Wirt, the matron of the Wirt household in Washington when Chase learned law from her husband. *Flora's Dictionary*, Mrs. Wirt's guide to the symbolism of flowers, had a feminine theme, but in 1829, when the book appeared, it was uncommon for a woman to bring her work to publication. She enlisted Chase, who as a young, unmarried man seemed to be at least as interested in her daughters as in her husband's legal instruction, to assist with the book, and apparently she intimidated the young swain. Although she was "religiously educated," which he surely admired, he found her aristocratic in demeanor and rather disconnected from the society around her.[26] In Washington in 1829 he became acquainted with Margaret Bayard Smith; he enjoyed her anecdotes of the capital's bygone political life and gave respectful but brief notice to her authorship of "several little works." At Mrs. Smith's house he met Martha Jefferson Randolph. He found the fifty-seven-year-old daughter of Thomas Jefferson so thoroughly "dignified" that he was quite willing to accept "on trust" the reputation that "she inherits much of her fathers intellect." Conversing "extremely well but sparingly," she gave him little opportunity to engage her intellect for himself. For "dignified propriety of manner" he also admired Letitia Porter, the wife of John Quincy Adams's secretary of war, and he marveled at the poise with which she matched her propriety with a talent for making others feel comfortable.[27]

During that period in Washington he used the word *intelligent* in his diary to describe a few of the young women of his own age, but he usually did not elaborate. On occasion he recorded a few hints of a young woman's ability as a conversationalist, her social manner, or some musical proficiency, but rarely anything that gives insight into what he meant by intellect. Significantly, religion held a primary place in his assessments of potential spouses. Captivated by Mary Maxcy, the daughter of the solicitor of the Treasury, he wrote not a word in his journal about her intellect but noted ruefully that he and she were terribly mismatched. She was a social butterfly, while he was not, and she was "disinclined to religion and it's duties; I value them more than any earthly possession." He hoped to find a wife who had the self-possession and graciousness of Mrs. Porter, with "the added and more precious ornament of pure religion."[28]

He was not always without reservation regarding females' power and independence. "I don't like argumentative ladies," he scrawled in his diary at the age of twenty-two after encountering a pair of "agreeable, intelligent" young women. The two "had read much, thought much and (perhaps) talked more. They made subtle distinctions with a skill worthy of old Aristotle" and "syllogized" like medieval scholastics. They aroused in him not admiration but disquiet. Clearly intimidated, he joked to himself uncomfortably that such women "have no right to encroach upon our privileges. And is it not settled by grayheaded prescription that the masculine is the more worthy gender and that we are entitled to an exclusive monopoly of all the wit, sense & learning in the world."[29] Jacob Schuckers, who during the Civil War worked closely with Chase in the Treasury, later wrote that "it was an inflexible rule with Mr. Chase never to transact business with ladies." Schooled to fear women's appeals as governor of Ohio, when a woman appeared on his doorstep with baggage and children in tow and vowed to remain until her husband received a pardon, Chase as secretary of the Treasury believed that "no amount of statement or explanation was sufficient to convince a woman that to grant any particular request was either inexpedient or impossible." On a couple of occasions when women by bluster or guile did manage to enter his office, his reaction was so harsh that one woman "retreated thoroughly frightened" and the other, an acquaintance who had boasted that she could circumvent the defenses of his office, fled in tears. He followed and spoke to her in the corridor, "but did *not* invite her into his office."[30] When asked about women's suffrage late in his life, in 1873, Chase declared that Susan B. Anthony moved "a little too fast." He thought that women might gain voting rights on a state-by-state basis and at a very measured pace, preferably after "education in the duties & responsibilities of citizenship." He had expressed a similar caution to Elizabeth Smith Miller in 1869. He said then that he favored having the "experiment" of voting rights for women "tried in one or more of the states, &, if found to work well, extended to all."[31]

The only formal training his daughters received outside their boarding-school education was some additional tutoring in languages. There were few options for women who might be interested in attending college in the middle of the nineteenth century, but there is no evidence that Chase or his daughters even considered the possibility. Nettie had aptitude and a strong interest in art but received no encouragement from her father to develop it as a career. In 1866, when she wanted to improve her skills in Europe, he declared that it would be a good opportunity to improve herself in foreign languages but thought little of the prospect that she might give serious attention to painting. He considered Nettie's drawing ability to be a useful accomplishment but believed it was practically impossible for a woman to assume "her proper part in Society" and also develop her art seriously.[32] He was of little help in exploring means by which Nettie might follow both paths, even though he thought that Edward Livingston's daughter Cora had done so, and it was apparently beyond consideration for Nettie to choose art over taking her "proper part" in the world.

"My ambition for you is the same as yours for yourself," Chase wrote to her on January 17, 1867, "that you may be a true christian and an accomplished woman." The word *ambition* and its cognates appear only a few times in the correspondence in this volume and always reflect a positive meaning: perfection was the end of ambition. On his twenty-first birthday Salmon Chase took stock of himself and left a chiding lamentation in his journal: "How precious a treasure is time and how have I lavishly squandered it! Oh that I could recall some of it from the abyss. Vain is the wish. Time lost can never be recalled or redeemed. Yet even now there is time if I will but resolve and resolutely act to do much. Knowledge may yet be gained and golden reputation. I may yet enjoy the consciousness of having lived not in vain. Future scenes of triumph may yet be mine. Let me awaken then to a just sense of my great deficiencies."[33] A few months after this call to action he faulted himself again for having insufficient "energy" and "industry." At the age of twenty-three he resolved to "try to excel in all things."[34]

During his public career, however, that striving brought reproach from his political enemies, who turned his ambition into an epithet. As the Ohio assembly set about choosing a U.S. senator in 1849, one Ohioan asserted that Chase was "as ambitious as Julius Caesar." Nathaniel Read, who as a lawyer was Chase's opponent in the Matilda and Birney cases and who became a judge before whom Chase argued other fugitive slave cases, remarked acidly that Chase was "a political vampire. No! He's a sort of moral bull-bitch." Benjamin Wade of Ohio, sometimes a cautious political ally but also without question a rival, was silent about his own formidable ambitions when he declared that "Chase is a good man, but his theology is unsound. He thinks there is a fourth Person in the Trinity, S. P. C."[35] The accusation came most often from those who had reason to consider him a rival, a political threat, or some impediment to their own aims. Some abolitionists, for example, scorned him for his willingness to engage in the political process.[36] Carl Schurz, depicting the scene long afterward, found himself taken aback by Chase's presumption that he might be a candidate for the presidency in 1860. Schurz in hindsight declared it to be a sign of the "high ambition" and a diseaselike "presidential fever" that afflicted Chase. But in 1860 Chase's claim on the nomination was at least as strong as that of William Seward, who before Lincoln's success at the Republican convention was Schurz's exclusive favorite among all potential candidates. At that moment, Chase's sin of ambition was that he dared to suggest an alternative to Schurz's (ultimately fleeting) fascination with Seward.[37]

Some of Chase's contemporaries (and some historians since) disparaged him because of his apparent lack of devotion to Lincoln. Presidential assistant John Hay, discomfited by the Treasury secretary's failure to accept all of Lincoln's decisions unquestioningly, wrote in his diary of "the unmanly conduct of Mr. C in trying to cut under"—then changed the phrase to say "the conduct of Mr. C in acting in the way he is doing." Secretary of the Navy Gideon Welles, primly secure in his own denial of personal aspiration, believed that Chase had "inordinate ambition," vanity, and "intense selfishness for official distinction." In 1863 another member of the cabinet, Attorney General Edward Bates, reacted with distaste to Chase's evident willingness to consider himself again a potential candidate for the presidency.[38]

Lincoln himself provided one of the most vivid characterizations of Chase as a grasping politician, saying that Chase's head was "full of Presidential *maggots*."[39] Lincoln also employed other mean-spirited, dehumanizing devices to make Chase seem contemptible and to undercut his standing as a rival. Lincoln declared that Chase was goaded by presidential aspirations like a plow horse molested by a biting fly. With regard to patronage, Lincoln claimed that Chase "will, like the blue-bottle fly, lay his eggs in every rotten spot he can find." Lincoln proclaimed Chase to be "a little insane" in terms of political desire.[40] But Father Abraham was no disinterested observer. Chase was the darling of some radical Republicans who grumbled that Lincoln did not move far enough, fast enough, on such critical matters as slavery and military policy. According to historian David Donald, Lincoln recognized that Chase "would probably make a very good President," and early in 1864 Lincoln's political helpers labored furiously to stop the movement for a Chase candidacy.[41] In the end, that dissent by some radicals proved to be no real threat to Lincoln's reelection in 1864. But Chase could be labeled (and dismissed) as ambitious, not because he considered himself as a potential candidate for the presidency in abstract terms but because he did so as a challenge to Lincoln.

Chase was not distinctively ambitious for his era, which was populated by unapologetically ambitious political figures in perpetual contention for power. In 1860 he had as much reason as anyone to be considered for the presidential nomination. There had also been a run of one-term presidents, and it was entirely "reasonable," to use Harold Hyman's term, for Chase to think in 1860–61 that he might be among those in contention for the office in 1864. That he did not discard that notion when the 1864 election drew closer, as other contenders of 1860 did, was motivated by his perception that Lincoln was not doing all that he should and that there was no one better qualified than Chase to take on the job.[42]

Not surprisingly, some politicians who committed their own fates to one of the major parties viewed with alarm Chase's seemingly fickle attachment to any one party. In 1869, Asa Fowler impatiently declared Chase "an ambitious, selfish man, who would sacrifice his party or his principles to obtain the Presidency."[43] Fulfillment of political ambition in nineteenth-century America, however, was more easily achieved from a partisan political base than by independent action. Chase could argue, too, that adherence to principles trumped affiliation to parties that went astray. According to biographer Albert Bushnell Hart, once Chase committed himself against slavery "nothing ever drew him aside," and he was "not at any time willing to change his opinions in order to win votes." Hyman has argued similarly, citing the "remarkable consistency" of Chase's views and declaring that he was no political opportunist. "I really think," Chase protested to Gerrit Smith in 1868, "that I am not half so ambitious of place as I am represented to be." He declared that in public affairs he "worked for ideas & principles & measures embodying them, . . . and was always quite willing to take place or be left out of place as the cause, in the judgment of its friends required."[44]

Certainly if he was driven by aspiration to attain high office for its own sake, he went about it the wrong way. In 1868, in her adulatory *Men of Our Times,* Harriet Beecher Stowe wrote that after Chase delivered his argument in Matilda's case an onlooker exclaimed, "There goes a fine young fellow who has just ruined himself."[45] Moderation and avoidance of issues that alienated voters would have been a much surer means of gaining popular approval and elective success than was Chase's early and persistent avowal of antislavery and his later advocacy of political rights for African Americans. In the Senate, his opposition to the compromise arrangements of 1850 and 1854 and his adoption of the "Independent Democrat" label were not avenues to political success at the national level. "To defend negroes," Hart wrote of Chase at the end of the nineteenth century, "to appear before the Supreme Court as their champion, to tell them that they ought to have a ballot, was to create against himself that social prejudice which was felt in equal measure by Charles Sumner."[46] According to Hyman, Chase's advocacy of legal and political rights for African Americans during the Civil War was "not shrewd" for anyone hoping to be president. Chase also never managed to build the kind of state-based political operation that was essential to the success of

Lincoln, Seward, and many others. Although his enemies feared that the Treasury's patronage would allow him to construct a political machine superior to the best state organizations, that did not happen. What did occur was corruption on the part of some Treasury officers that, while Chase was not himself involved, damaged his claims to moral authority and fed accusations of duplicity.[47]

He could not cultivate the image of a populist democratic politician. As Allan Nevins commented, too bluntly, Chase "almost totally lacked the arts of popular appeal."[48] What he projected, in Hart's assessment, was "an impression of strength, readiness, and power." When James A. Garfield first met Chase in August 1859 at a political event in Akron, Chase addressed the crowd for two hours and forty-five minutes. "Tall, broad-shouldered, and proudly erect," Schurz wrote of Chase, "his features strong and regular and his forehead broad, high and clear, he was a picture of intelligence, strength, courage, and dignity. He looked as you would wish a statesman to look." Hugh McCulloch described him as "courtly without assumption." Still, although Chase "cared very much for the favorable opinion of other people," as Hart expressed it, he was "habitually grave and reserved in demeanor." Strangers "were not generally at ease in his presence," and Schurz described him as a "majestic figure" plagued by a "bashful shyness" that formed an "icy crust" in public situations. His sense of humor came across as stiff and limited. He could not show much true democratic heartiness. As a public speaker "his utterance was somewhat thick, and his manner lacked in grace." Although "he had few equals in analyzing difficult questions and making abstruse subjects intelligible," McCulloch wrote in 1889, Chase "was not what might be called a fluent, nor according to the American idea (which is rapidly changing) an eloquent speaker."[49] Even with people who knew him, he could be inflexible, overly sensitive to criticism, too blunt in expressing his views, and apt to "break out into reproaches"—rather "dogmatic," McCulloch confessed, although he was "nevertheless genial in social intercourse, and at times fascinating." He did not develop warm personal relationships with many of the men he rubbed shoulders with in his professional and political life. If he lost his temper, Jacob Schuckers said, "it is no exaggeration to say that men *fled* from his presence, as lesser animals take flight before a lion." Needless to say, Chase and the seemingly easygoing Lincoln, known for his country humor and homilies, were never on particularly comfortable terms.[50]

Although Chase was often marked as ambitious by those who wanted to insult him for some particular purpose, some historians have perpetuated the labeling of him as a striver propelled by ambition. David Donald referred to an "unquenchable political ambition." Benjamin Thomas— in a biography of Lincoln, it should be noted—wrote of "the colossal egotism of Salmon P. Chase." Allan Nevins declared that Chase "had a touchy self-importance" and "let political ambition warp his outlook." Hans L. Trefousse referred to his "intense" and "obvious" ambition. In his detailed examination of *The Origins of the Republican Party,* William Gienapp called Chase not only ambitious but "unbearably self-righteous and on occasion decidedly duplicitous."[51] In an effort to explain Chase's ambition as an expression of anxieties about identity and to connect it to the man's personal drive for reform, Stephen Maizlish in a 1998 article accepted the characterizations of Chase's "desperate passion for advancement," his "powerful, legendary," and "unbridled" ambition. Maizlish took careful note of the reform element in Chase's makeup but, reflecting a view shared by some other historians, labeled as "self-delusion" Chase's belief that his striving for achievement was subordinate to a greater cause.[52]

Delusion would only have been necessary, however, if Chase's ambition was coldly self-serving and contrary to his religious and moral principles. But for him, ambition was the striving to do good and to attain that "golden reputation" he had yearned for on his twenty-first birthday. Charlotte Eastman, with whom he had an affectionate relationship, felt neglected because of the attention he gave to his public career. "I wont complain any more of your remarks about my ambition," he responded in August 1863; "but take it for true that I *am* ambitious and forget in ambitious hopes and wishes, some duties of friendship & charity. I will only try to direct my ambition to public ends and in honorable ways," he continued, "and forget friends and claims as little as possible."[53]

According to Schuckers, Chase was cognizant of a direct relationship between his variety of ambition and his morals, and there was no conflict that would have required self-delusion. Stating that Chase "was ambitious. Yes, he was ambitious even of the presidency," Schuckers believed that he "was conscious of the possession of great powers, and he knew he would use them to promote the prosperity and glory of his countrymen. They who censure him for this, would censure every thing that inspires men to great deeds and to noble lives." Roeliff Brinkerhoff, who like Schuckers knew Chase, also stated that while Chase was "a man of high ambition," his aspiration "was entirely subordinate to his sense of duty."[54] As Harold Hyman expressed it in a more recent assessment, "By his own monocular lights Chase was ambitious less for power than for realizing the single antislavery purpose, one paired with patriotism." Noting the "remarkable consistency" of Chase's views, Hyman wrote that during the Civil War "Chase remained confident that substantially decent law-and-order procedures would moderate man's tendency toward anarchy." Chase advocated a "secular solution" to the nation's troubles—a "confidence in equal justice under law as the sovereign prescription for most of the nation's ills"—yet did so with "certainty that he was on the side of the godly." Another historian, Michael Les Benedict, characterized

Chase as "a man of powerful convictions and strong passions. Convinced that he was right in his principles, Chase was determined to make them public policy. He was a master of constitutional politics, utilizing politics and law to achieve change. In this, Chase represents something profoundly, perhaps uniquely, American."[55] A. B. Hart thought that Chase's failing was not cynical ambition but almost its opposite: too little "healthful pessimism" and too much self-examination. "His greatest fault was a life-long habit of self-introspection," Hart wrote, "to assure himself how upright were his purposes; but his belief in himself does not lessen the truth that the roots of his private character were a strong sense of duty and a high standard of conduct."[56]

Unfortunately that dedication to his personal religious precepts could seem self-righteous and smug. His moral self-sufficiency, moreover, isolated him from much of the world around him, contributing to his apparent aloofness and making it more difficult for others to accept him on his own terms. Cynics saw him committed to advancement and action, obsessed with his own performance, yet pious, and branded him not just with ambition but with hypocrisy. It was to his enemies' advantage to put him in that light. The day after Chase's death, James A. Garfield wrote in his diary: "It is hard that a man should be treated with so much wicked abuse as Chase has suffered during many years of his life, and have all credit at last with the confession that they were lying about him when they have spoken evil of him."[57] Unfortunately for Chase's historical reputation, the taint of "ambition" has stayed with him and become a commonplace.

Interestingly, his older daughter has also frequently been called ambitious, a label that has marked her identity as a historical figure. The titles of biographies of Chase have not featured ambition and its consequences, which are the overt theme of some books that center on Kate: *Proud Kate: Portrait of an Ambitious Woman,* by Ishbel Ross (1953); *Kate Chase, Dominant Daughter,* by Mary Merwin Phelps (1935); and *So Fell the Angels,* by Thomas Graham Belden and Marva Robins Belden (1956).[58]

Those characterizations of Kate place emphasis on a presumed connection between her attention to her father's political career and her marriage to William Sprague, which has been interpreted as a crass maneuver to finance her father's presidential aspirations.[59] Kate projected a strong personality that elicited infatuation from some people and distrust or dislike from others. "Wherever she appeared, people dropped back in order to watch her," one observer later recalled.[60] And Kate, like her father, was called cunning by influential people who resented her or considered her a threat. In Washington during the Civil War, Mary Todd Lincoln famously despised the young, attractive, and socially energetic daughter of the secretary of the Treasury.[61] The eventual collapse of Kate's marriage in scandal and divorce after her father's death made her even more susceptible to charges that she had been selfishly and tragically covetous of power. Moreover, some of the onus of ambition could be shifted to her from her father. Roeliff Brinkerhoff, for example, in his memoir published in 1900, asserted that Chase's nods toward presidential aspiration late in his life sprang "more from a desire to gratify the ambition of his daughter rather than his own."[62]

Kate actually fulfilled a version of her father's insistent program of self-attainment, in which achievement and assertiveness were reciprocally coupled with responsibility and obligation. She was seventeen years old when, as illustrated by letters in this volume, her father gave her the responsibility of buying furnishings for their residence in Columbus. At times she assumed the role of the parent or guide in her correspondence to Nettie. Her actions and traits, like her father's, made it easy for detractors to slight her as "ambitious." Her sister avoided the charge, partly because by age and circumstance Nettie did not engage with her father's political world in the same way. He nevertheless made a certain form of striving the dominant theme in all their lives: ambition, as he thought, to accomplish a purposeful life on earth, to prepare oneself and others properly for the life beyond death, to meet demanding expectations and fulfill significant obligations.

PENS TO PAPER

This volume is a testament to the role that written communication played in the relationships among the Chase sisters and their father. If circumstances often kept the three of them apart, even as the girls were growing up, letters were the means by which they stayed in touch. They might have communicated less frequently than they did—not all families, when their members were apart, corresponded as often or as fully as did the Chases. In the development of the correspondence among the three of them, the father's emphasis on letters and on the practices of writing was as important a factor as the necessity of communicating over distance.

Law business or politics took Chase away from home from time to time even when his daughters were quite young. Those absences became prolonged with his election to the U.S. Senate. When he first sat with the Senate for a full session beginning late in 1849, Kate was nine years old and Nettie only two. He was not the only member of the family to make long trips away from home: for example, the letter that opens the first chapter of this volume was written by Kate's mother, Lizzie, at Cumberland, Maryland, in 1844. Nettie's mother, Belle, had prolonged stays at sanatoriums to treat her tuberculosis. During Belle's illness and after her death, Nettie stayed with relatives in Hillsboro, Ohio, and near Cincinnati. And both Kate and Nettie attended boarding schools for several years. During all of those times the family remained connected through correspondence.

Chase began to exchange letters with his children when they were still too young to correspond without assistance. About three months past her sixth birthday, Kate vowed that "she shall not write or send any word" to her father until he sent her a letter as he had promised to do.[1] Apparently he complied, for not long afterward Kate, with an aunt's help, dispatched an epistle to her father and stepmother (see November 18, 1846, in this volume). In March 1852, when Nettie was four, her Aunt Charlotte reported that Nettie was "delighted" with a letter from her father and sister: "She insists on learning the lines written by Katy—but it is rather too long to task her memory with the whole of it at once."[2] A history of the Clopper family, who were related to the Ludlows, prints a little note that Chase wrote to Nettie in July 1852:

> Darling little Nettie
>   Pa wants to see you very much. He hopes you are a very good girl. He will come home after a while. He now sends you a kiss, and some pictures in a book, which he hopes will please you. May God our Father bless you for Christ's sake. Your own Father,
>   S. P. Chase[3]

At the age of three, Nettie attempted to write to her sister herself and found relatives to put her words on paper for her (see below at September 28, 1850, and January 9, 1851; for a letter written in her own hand at the age of six, see April 1, 1854).

Chase knew, and constantly reminded Kate and Nettie, that writing good letters required attention and effort. He believed the skills could be mastered, however, and that it was important to achieve the best results. Several of his letters printed in this volume, addressed not just to his daughters but also to Belle, show how didactic he could be in his insistence on accuracy and the observance of proper forms in their writing. He wrote to a married niece in 1864: "Please don't set me down as a faultfinder if I say I wish you would pay more attention to your composition & spelling. One so intelligent as you are ought to take all possible pains to be correct. Just to show you what I mean I do by you what I sometimes do by Nettie—mark all the places where there are mistakes in grammar or spelling & send your letter back to you. Take a Dictionary, a Grammar & some book on English Composition and determine that you will correct the mistakes & make no more in future letters."[4] As intimidating as that demand for correctness could be, he insisted that people write to him. After the death of his brother Alexander in 1847, for example, Chase asked that relatives in New Hampshire send him a letter at least once a month.[5] His letter to Kate on September 5, 1850, not long past her tenth birthday, was blunt in its insistence that she keep up her side of their correspondence.

Nettie and Kate also learned about writing in school. During the period in which they received their education, most female seminaries taught not just grammar and parsing but composition also, in many cases requiring students to write compositions once a week. Henrietta Haines, not long after Kate was in her school, gave such importance to students' compositions that she began to send out some papers to be graded by the well-known writer Susan Warner (author of *The Wide, Wide World*, 1850). Warner's journal entries regarding the strenuousness of this correcting work suggest either that she received a very large number of compositions or that she put care and time into her responses.[6] In the late eighteenth and early nineteenth centuries, the teaching of writing in female academies emphasized classical oratorical traditions and rhetoric. By the time Kate was in boarding school, the emphasis had shifted to composition, which educators thought would prepare girls to be able conversationalists and letter writers. Christie Anne Farnham, who studied female education in the antebellum South, notes that composition writing was seen as beneficial "training for epistolary writing, which held a central place in women's lives by the late antebellum period."[7]

Composition topics varied greatly, although when Kate and Nettie were in school in the middle of the century, teachers tended to encourage relatively objective discussions of broad issues. Truly "personal" expression only gained precedence in the late nineteenth century. To borrow an example from S. Michael Halloran, in the early and mid-1800s "students might have been asked to develop a broad and general topic like 'patriotism,'" whereas in the century's last decades they may have been "urged to narrow the subject to something like 'How Can a Boy Be Patriotic?'" But while addressing these broad topics, student writers in Kate's and Nettie's era were often encouraged to engage in detailed description and spiritual contemplation. For instance, Farnham quotes a young Southern student who chose "Home" as a composition topic in 1852 and lists a selection of weekly assignments given at Mount Holyoke: "beauties of nature, the uncertainty of earthly things, the virtues of early rising, and the meaning of 'home' and 'mother.'"[8]

In his letter of July 5, 1854, printed in this volume, Chase praised Kate's composition on "the Hand." Although we do not have that composition itself, it could have fit into many of the commonly used assignment categories of the era. Students were sometimes asked to answer philosophical questions or prove propositions—for example, to support a claim such as "The hand of the diligent maketh rich" (one of the topics in *Outlines of a Philosophical Education*, 1825). Since thoughtful responses to lectures and readings were also encouraged, a composition on "the hand" might be a report on an anatomy lesson or lecture, similar to the assignment on glaciers that Henrietta Haines gave students in 1854 after a lecturer spoke on that topic. Such responses might have been descriptive or expository pieces—in the latter, as prescribed by rhetorical guides, "the object should be defined with a class of objects (genus) with the particular properties of the object identified and explained (differentia)." Narration and argumentation were the two other popular compositional modes taught to students. The comments of Kate's fellow student at Haines's school, Catharine Beekman, indicate that the boundaries between the modes were indefinite. "I have written a composition this week on presence of mind," Catharine wrote her mother; "mine is a story I once read, which is true, it is some time ago since I read it, and I have written down all that I could remember, besides I put in some of my own ideas also."[9]

Compositions, as shown by Catharine's description, were not necessarily expected to be entirely original, reflecting the continuing influence of George Campbell's *Philosophy of Rhetoric* (1776). That work did not emphasize invention, but rather "adapting the message, managing it, so as to affect the audience in the desired way." As James A. Berlin notes, Campbell's ideas, along with Hugh Blair's *Lectures on Rhetoric and Belles Lettres* and Richard Whately's *Elements of Rhetoric,* constituted a kind of "blessed trinity" of American instruction in rhetoric through much of the nineteenth century. Much antebellum discussion of writing instruction debated the degree and significance of invention in student compositions, which gives context to Chase's eagerness to know how much of Kate's composition was her own invention. "Coincidences in thought and expression will occur," the South Carolina Female Collegiate Institute observed, in terms reminiscent of Blair. Some commentators, however, suggested that such approaches were occasionally taken to the extreme. Critiquing the compositional technique that left to the student "only the arrangement," a *Ladies' Repository* writer asked, "Why is not the younger composer not required to invent simultaneously, whilst she composes and writes?"[10]

We have not seen Kate's 1854 essay on "the Hand," but another of her compositions, from Columbus a couple of years later, is extant. She very likely wrote it for an assignment at Lewis Heyl's school:

The [folly] of devoting too much time to accomplishments.
Accomplishments, when seen in their perfection, always afford much enjoyment, both to those possessing them; and also to those who may only witness them. Yet they are but a secondary consideration in the early training of a mind—An education, consisting chiefly of accomplishment is [like] a house without a foundation— it must ere long, totter and fall, likewise they will in time be forgotten, and become useless.

The term education is frequently misconstrued. Our education, may be said to extend through the entire life-time—Every day some new idea is presented to our mind. They differ of course in value, some may be of material service in our after life, some again may not be called so prominently into play, but each day adds a little to our store of knowledge, and tends towards the completion of our education.

Our term of instruction, which is generally, but erroneously denominated education, only extends through the period in which[11] our minds are under the direct control and supervision of others. Then it is, that we lay the foundation for the super-structure, which we are to rear hereafter. If then, this time is wasted in the *acquirement* of accomplishments, instead of the fundemental[12] branches of a substantial education, the tone of the mind is weakened, and it is rendered incapable of receiving and retaining that which is elevating and useful.
Columbus—
Nov. 11th. 1856.[13]

The subject matter of the piece (certainly appropriate for a daughter of Salmon P. Chase) and the diction are probably typical of the compositions required in the schools that Kate and Nettie attended.

In her study of Henry Adams's correspondence, Joanne Jacobson aptly observed that scholars have come "to challenge the assumption" that unpublished letters are "rhetorically innocent, and to recognize the strategies of performance and construction which the form makes available to writers." The language of letters in the nineteenth century "is not a direct transcription of daily speech," Marilyn Ferris Motz has noted, "but follows the formal grammatical structure and vocabulary of written discourse, producing a style to a great extent unique to personal correspondence." During that period, writers in periodicals, as well as teachers and parents, "devoted much attention to proper and improper modes of correspondence" as well as to differences in masculine and feminine styles of writing letters. For Adams and his contemporaries, according to Jacobson, "the letter straddled a set of rhetorical boundaries which were crucial to the conditions of transition taking place during this period: between public and private; between literary and nonliterary; between elite and democratic discourse."[14] To this list, we would add—in the case of women's letters in particular—the boundary between visual and verbal, or the surface appearance of the letter and the substance of its rhetoric and content.

Following a pattern employed by many nineteenth-century paternal correspondents, Chase often began letters to Kate with a critical evaluation of her last letter's form and content.[15] His desire for her to produce letters written in an "elegant lady's hand—free, clear & elegant," as well as "full of thought," reflects the equal interest in surface appearance and substantive content that marks much antebellum instructional discourse about letter writing.[16] Good handwriting carried a great deal of significance not only as a marker of class and gender status, but also as a sign of careful thought. Instructional texts, periodical articles, school publications, and family correspondence from this era often present elegant penmanship and clear thinking as interrelated skills, emphasizing that to write and rewrite a letter or essay not only eliminated surface errors but also helped develop ideas.[17] Although she did not do so consistently, by the early 1850s Kate followed standard conventions for organizing her correspondence, endorsing some of the letters she received with the name of the sender, the date of the letter, and the date on which it was received.[18]

Even when Kate and Nettie were old enough to write on their own, their correspondence with their father was not always direct and private. Henrietta Haines had the "supervision" of Kate's correspondence and saw all of the pupil's letters to her father. Mary Macaulay, Nettie's headmistress in New York, may have done the same, and certainly acted as an intermediary in all correspondence, distributing letters that came for her students and likely handling the outgoing missives as well.[19] We find other reminders also of the semipublic nature of family letters in this period, when multiple relatives and friends might read letters, which parents urged children to make presentable and praiseworthy. One scholar has said that family letters "became a kind of expressive tug-of-war between intimate meaning and social act." What to modern readers might seem like unreasonable and mutually exclusive demands— that a schoolgirl's letter be confessional and natural, yet still polished and precise—were oft-repeated ideals of mid-nineteenth-century epistolary discourse that Chase echoed when he insisted that Kate must write both correctly and "unreservedly" (July 5, 1854). His intense concern with how often Kate wrote and when her letters went in the mail, though perhaps scolding in tone, also shows an undisguised eagerness to hear from her. Perhaps aware of other children who wrote their parents more often— such as his Senate colleague Thomas Hart Benton's daughter Jessie, who wrote daily letters to her father even after her marriage—Chase would have been likely to view his insistence upon a weekly letter from Kate as a very reasonable request.[20]

As Kate and Nettie matured, they found that their father valued them as confidantes. Nettie was sixteen when her father, after chiding her for carelessness in her letters, acknowledged that she was "quite a woman in intelligence and judgment" and vowed to overcome his own reserve in order to write to her "more freely." To fulfill the pledge, he went on to tell her about his political circumstances in the approaching presidential election.[21] In a long letter to Kate that is not included in this volume, written in June 1862, he gave details of a bleak Federal military situation—"I write you this morning with a very sad heart"—and groused that his advice on military matters was not heeded by Lincoln. "I write you very freely," he said in a postscript. "Say nothing of what I write unless the news be in the papers. I trust your sense & prudence."[22] Networks of sensible and prudent correspondents were essential to him. As governor of Ohio and secretary of the Treasury, he relied on reports from friends and officials to keep him informed. Throughout his career, correspondence played a critical role in politics, as like-minded people who kept in touch by letter provided the sinews of state and national parties. This was especially true of political affiliations such as the Liberty and Free Soil parties. Kate and Nettie, then, assumed places in the networks of people who corresponded with their father on matters of public interest.[23]

One function of his official and political correspondence was to supply him with information—lots of it, on various subjects. During the Civil War, he wanted the Treasury agents who were in charge of plantations controlled by the Federal government to write monthly reports without fail: "These reports are important and should embrace all the suggestions of the practical experience of the Assistant Agents who make them." Even after he left the Treasury he craved information from locales that were distant but, to him, important. "I wish that in addition to the information you give of civil & military movements you would add impartial sketches of your prominent men, as seen by friends and as seen by enemies," he wrote to a contact in New Orleans. "I desire to be informed & it may become important that I should be informed fully as to persons as well as things."[24] He did not exempt himself from the requirement of recording detailed observations. In the first letter of chapter 7 below, Chase, who had set off with Nettie on a tour encircling the just-defeated Confederate states, asked Kate to retain the often lengthy letters he wrote during the trip: "for I mean they shall serve as my diary." Detailed letters that he wrote to Nettie from a trip to the Hampton Roads vicinity with Lincoln and the secretary of war in 1862 performed a similar function.[25] As shown by the correspondence in this volume, he wanted his daughters, while they were away at boarding school, to keep him up-to-date and allow him to monitor, from a distance, their education and their social and moral development.

"What a pity it is," Chase lamented to Kate on August 18, 1863, "that one cannot establish some sort of electrical communication between mind and paper of which the pen should be the conductor just as a wire leads electricity from its source to its reservoir." Yet he recognized that the craft of writing a good letter required more than capturing a stream of thoughts on paper. "Excuse this long letter, which I have not had time to make shorter," he once apologized at the end of an epistle on politics.[26] When crafting letters, he could skillfully adapt his tone to suit a particular recipient or set of circumstances: some of his letters to Charles Sumner, for example, are positively oratorical in timbre. He knew that his letters on political topics and public issues could end up in the newspapers, and sometimes he deliberately wrote a statement for publication in the form of a letter.[27]

His law mentor, William Wirt, had been able to write in different voices for diverse audiences, penning fiction and biography as well as masterful legal arguments. As a young man, Chase may have contemplated a similar course even before he came under the influence of Wirt's example. The first portion of Chase's earliest extant diary, beginning in Washington just before his twenty-first birthday in January 1829 and almost certainly not the first journal he kept, is almost a writer's notebook. Its entries record his observations, with only incidental details of his own activities. In the margins he penned names or headings to help him locate his impressions of people, events, or topics of interest: for example, "President's Levee," "Dr. Huntt's Wedding," "Mr Calhoun," "Hagerstown," "Beauty," "A Glance at Futurity." In entries marked by such labels as "Sentences for Conversation" and "Yankee Phraseology," he recorded clever retorts, bons mots, phrases that caught his fancy, and regional expressions. He kept journals intermittently throughout his life, but at different stages of his career they served varying purposes. None of the others was so self-consciously writerly in intent and form as that early journal.[28]

That diary also records a half-dozen instances in which an unmarried young Chase wrote verses in young ladies' albums or on calling cards, sometimes composing the lines himself and sometimes recalling poetry that he had committed to memory. He tried to amuse one of Wirt's daughters with a composition "in doggrell" about an imaginary meeting of a temperance society.[29] Later on, even though he could not always fulfill his intent as a diarist, he still adhered to the principle that a journal furnished regular practice in writing, and in sifting and organizing one's thoughts. By the time Kate was nine, he pushed her to keep a daily journal.[30]

As he began to fashion a career in law, he gave attention to nonfiction writing. In 1831 the respected *North American Review* published an essay he wrote on British reformer Henry Brougham, and the next year the same journal printed a version of a talk he had given to the Cincinnati Lyceum on the "Effects of Machinery" on society. In the same period, he wrote for the *Cincinnati American* and was an acknowledged or silent editor of that newspaper, the *Western Quarterly Review,* and the *Western Monthly Magazine.* At one point he attempted to recruit Daniel Webster to write something for the *Western Monthly Magazine.* Undertaking a three-volume compilation of the statutes of Ohio and the Northwest Territory, Chase decided that the work must have a good survey of the region's history to serve as a preface. He wrote that introduction himself, confiding to a friend that the research and writing required "great labour." He also participated in a Cincinnati group called the "Semi-Colon Club," a literary salon that met on Monday evenings for readings of its members' poetry and prose. Among the members were Catharine Beecher and her sister Harriet, who began her career as a writer by composing satirical pieces for the club.[31]

Language and written composition were of course central to his career as lawyer, politician, and jurist. Perhaps because he lacked the facility to stun crowds, and perhaps because of the limited and transient function of political stump speeches meant only to stir a little interest among audiences of strangers interested in their own local concerns, he found it difficult to motivate himself to write speeches. "It is *so* hard for me to *write* a *speech*," he confided to a friend. "The flesh & spirit both rebel against it."[32] He recognized, however, that after the passing oratorical moment in which an address might or might not motivate its hearers, speeches took on new, longer-lasting, and often more crucial lives in print. Early in September 1851, for example, he had on hand printed copies not only of the "Union and Freedom" speech that he had made on the floor of the Senate in March 1850, but also of a speech that he gave in Toledo in May 1851 and a letter addressed to the publisher of an Ohio newspaper, all available for enclosure in his correspondence as statements of his political position.[33]

The appearance and presentation of a letter could be as important as the correctness of grammar and spelling of its contents. In this regard the Chases followed wider cultural norms. For several months after Belle's death, Salmon Chase used letter paper edged with a black border as a sign of his mourning.[34] Sometimes he penned family letters on official letterhead stationery. Although we have his letters to both daughters on August 17, 1863, only in the form of his retained letterpress copies, we know that he used printed Treasury Department letterhead paper for both missives, as the "18" is lacking from the year in both datelines. Those digits were already printed in the heading at the top of the departmental stationery, so the writer needed only to fill in the rest of the date. The letterpress process did not pick up the printed portion of the letterhead (including the heading "Treasury Department"). On that particular August day, the secretary of the Treasury used different styles of the department's letter paper to write his daughters, since the version he used to write Nettie had a printed "186" and required him to fill in only the last digit of the year, whereas he wrote to Kate on paper that needed two digits—"63"—to complete the date. Pressed copies of letters written on official stationery also lack any designation of the place at the top of the page, since that information, too, was already printed on the letter paper.[35] His use of departmental stationery and the making of the letterpress copies suggest that when he was secretary of the Treasury he often wrote to his daughters at the office when he took care of other corre-spondence. Indeed there is some direct evidence of that, as in his letter to Kate on September 9, 1863, in which he refers to leaving home earlier in the day.

Kate and Nettie did not have access to all the appurtenances of corre-spondence that were available to their father as a government official—clerks, departmental letter paper, systems for making letterpress file copies—but as married women of social and economic standing, they did have their own stationery. Kate wrote to her father on July 7, 1868, on paper that bore an ornate multicolor monogram of her initials, *K, C,* and *S,* superimposed on one another. In October of that year she wrote from Rhode Island on paper embossed with an elaborate *S* and the place names "Canonchet" and "Narragansett" printed in a distinctive font. In 1872–73, Nettie used two forms of stationery, one with her and her hus-band's Manhattan address and one without. Both featured a fancy mono-gram in which all of her initials—*J, R, C,* and *H*—intersected in intricate filigree. Nettie may well have designed that pattern herself, and perhaps her sister's stationery also. Their monograms, like their father's official stationery and like the sketches that Nettie sometimes incorporated into her letters, highlight the inextricable link between visual and verbal aes-thetics in correspondence of the day.

Through their education and from their father's example, direc-tion, and encouragement, Nettie and Kate developed habits of writing and a familiarity with different forms of composition. Kate's gift to a bride in 1872 was "a pretty piece of verse." A few years later, Nettie penned anonymously for *Scribner's* an account of a trip into the Maine woods with her husband and children, and in 1891 she wrote articles for the *New York Tribune* to recall life with her father three decades earlier.[36] Although not professional wordsmiths as their father was by necessity, both sisters, in the course of their maturation as members of the family, acquired a com-fortable facility for written expression and a lasting, appreciative interest in writing.

NOTES — KATE AND NETTIE

1. James Ralston Skinner to Salmon P. Chase, Dec. 18, 1848 (Chase Papers, LC).
2. *Chase Papers,* 1:197; 2:201, 204–7.
3. Recollections of Eliza Chase Whipple, [1873] (Chase Papers, HSP).
4. See the appendix for biographical information about members of the immediate and extended families.
5. Eliza Chase Whipple to [Jacob W. Schuckers], June 27 [1873], and memorandum of recollections [ca. 1873] (Chase Papers, HSP).
6. *Chase Papers,* 1:255; 5:105.
7. Emily Jones to Chase, Dec. 13, 1852 (quoted), Mar. 2, 1853, Kate Ludlow to Chase, Jan. 7, 1850, Charlotte Ludlow Jones to Chase, Mar. 9, 1852 (Chase Papers, LC); *Chase Papers,* 1:142; and see the appendix for the Collins family.
8. Janet Chase Hoyt, "A Woman's Memories," *New York Tribune,* Feb. 15, 1891.

9. Chase had given some initial support to the free-state cause in Kansas, but rejected Brown's violence. "How rash—how mad—how criminal," he said of the Harpers Ferry raid. *Chase Papers*, 3:22–23. Kate's involvement in Nettie's *Tribune* anecdotes about Columbus is not clear. Nettie used the words *we* and *us*, but also mentioned a young cousin and was not explicit about which activities involved Kate. Conversely, Nettie does not appear in the accounts of visitors to the household in Columbus such as Trotter and Howells. The seven-year difference in the sisters' age may have had its greatest social effect in the late 1850s, when Kate was in her teens and Nettie was about ten to twelve.

10. Nettie in *New York Tribune*, Feb. 15, Mar. 8, Apr. 5, 1891; *Chase Papers*, 1:260, 267, 271; 2:451, 452; 3:19.

11. Nettie in *New York Tribune*, Mar. 8, 1891. See the letters of June 18, 1866, and Apr. 30, 1871, in this volume, for the Chases' familiarity with Hawthorne's short stories.

12. Eliza Whipple recollections [ca. 1873] (Chase Papers, HSP); *Chase Papers*, 1:79, 82, 84. The book he gave Kitty was a volume of *The Percy Anecdotes*, a series of stories written by two English journalists, Thomas Byerley and Joseph Clinton Robertson, to impart moral instruction in a light, humorous tone. *ODNB*, 9:300; 47:256.

13. Leon Burr Richardson, *History of Dartmouth College*, 2 vols. (Hanover, N.H.: Dartmouth College Publications, 1932), 1:376–77; Hart, *Chase*, 4–5.

14. *Catalogue of a Most Superb Collection*, items 1018, 1036, 1057, 1085, 1116, 1126, 1139, 1140, 1142, 1171, 1233, 1275, 1341, 1421, 1422, 1469; *Chase Papers*, 1:24, 57, 75, 79, 122, 128, 129, 153, 155, 177, 178, 216, 241, 280–92, 306, 307, 309, 362, 501; 2:49, 304–5; *New York Tribune*, Feb. 22, 1891; his letters to Belle of Mar. 16, 1850, and to Kate of Feb. 14, 1851, are printed below in this volume.

15. Schuckers, *Chase*, 627; *Catalogue of a Most Superb Collection*, items 1004, 1180, 1199, 1393, 1432; *Chase Papers*, 1:19, 57, 83–84, 94, 216, 252, 277–80, 309, 504; 2:11.

16. Howells, *Years of My Youth*, 132–34; Nettie in *New York Tribune*, Feb. 15, 1891; Coyle, *Ohio Authors*, 320.

17. *Chase Papers*, 1:174–77. Unfortunately he was an erratic diarist, and it was unusual, rather than the norm, for him to record details of Kate's and Nettie's childhood.

18. Father to Kate, Mar. 23, 1855, in this volume; Emily Jones to Chase, May 26, 1852 (Chase Papers, LC).

19. Garniss to Chase, Jan. 7, 1850 (Chase Papers, HSP).

20. Herr and Spence, eds., *Letters of Jessie Benton Frémont*, 384; Margaret Ayer Barnes and Janet Ayer Fairbank, eds., *Julia Newberry's Diary* (New York: W. W. Norton & Co., 1933), xi, 30, 32; Wheeler, *Ogden Family*, 249, 364, 365. For Sarah Platt Haines Doremus, see also *Notable American Women*, 1:500–501.

21. *Doggett's New York City Directory* (New York: John Doggett Jr., 1848), 180; *Trow's New-York City Directory* (New York: J. F. Trow, 1854), 313; *New York Times*, July 9, 1853; Stephen Garmey, *Gramercy Park: An Illustrated History of a New York Neighborhood* (New York: Balsam Press, 1984), 189.

22. Philip L. White, *The Beekmans of New York in Politics and Commerce, 1647–1877* (New York: New-York Historical Society, 1956), xxix, 618, and chaps. 17–19 for Catharine's father, the philanthropist and politician James William Beekman.

23. See Nettie's letter of Feb. 20, 1864, in this volume. The walks by Miss Haines's schoolgirls played a role in the novel by Rachel Field, *All This, and Heaven Too* (New York: Macmillan Co., 1938), 367–70; see Garmey, *Gramercy Park*, 83.

24. Catharine Beekman's letters to her parents and brother, Feb. 2, 9, 16, Mar. 2, 9, 16, 28, and school bill of June 1, 1854 (New-York Historical Society).

25. In 1847, sparking a scandal that gained international notoriety, the duc de Praslin murdered his wife and committed suicide. Police in France held the governess for three months, then released her with no charges. Victor Hugo wrote about the events, which became the subject of novels and a motion picture in the twentieth century. Henriette Deluzy Desportes left Haines's school upon her marriage to Henry M. Field, a clergyman who had several well-known brothers. Chase later had professional or political relationships with three of them: lawyer David Dudley Field, transatlantic telegraph entrepreneur Cyrus W. Field, and Stephen Johnson Field, who was an associate justice of the Supreme Court when Chase was chief justice. Alison L. McKee, "'L'affaire Praslin' and *All This, and Heaven Too*: Gender, Genre, and History in the 1940s Woman's Film," *Velvet Light Trap* 35 (1995): 33–51; Stanley Loomis, *A Crime of Passion* (Philadelphia: Lippincott, 1967),

276–88; Garmey, *Gramercy Park*, 82–83; *DAB*, 6:364–65; *Chase Papers*, 1:367, 372, 373, 513, 686, 699, 706; 4:73–75, 109–12, 293–96, 364–66, 439, 440n; 5:88–90, 115–17, 369–70.

26. *New York Times*, June 27, Aug. 20, 1863; Burton J. Hendrick and Daniel Henderson, *Louise Whitfield Carnegie: The Life of Mrs. Andrew Carnegie* (New York: Hastings House, 1950), 15–16; copy of Henrietta Haines's will, 1879 (New-York Historical Society). Louise Whitfield, who married Andrew Carnegie, grew up near the school and attended as a day student in the 1860s and 1870s, from the age of six until she turned eighteen. Hendrick and Henderson, *Louise Whitfield Carnegie*, 12–14.

27. Catharine Beekman's letters of Feb. 2, 9, 16, Mar. 9, 28, 1854 (New-York Historical Society); Hendrick and Henderson, *Louise Whitfield Carnegie*, 15; *ANB*, 6:750–51; 9:752–54.

28. Catharine to her mother, Abian Steele Milledoler Beekman, Mar. 16, 25, 1854 (New-York Historical Society); *ANB*, 22:189–90.

29. *Chase Papers*, 1:225, 228, 233, 235; Jane Roland Martin, *Reclaiming a Conversation: The Ideal of the Educated Woman* (New Haven, Conn.: Yale University Press, 1985), 124, 105; Richard D. Brown, *Knowledge Is Power: The Diffusion of Information in Early America, 1700–1865* (New York: Oxford University Press, 1989), 162; Alexander H. Sands, "An Address Delivered before the Hollins Female Institute, at the Commencement, on the 6th April, 1859," published as "Intellectual Culture of Woman," *Southern Literary Messenger* 28, no. 5 (May 1859): 324, 328. For additional examples of the antebellum discourse regarding child obedience and female submission, see Heman Humphrey, *Domestic Education* (Amherst, Mass.: J.S. & C. Adams, 1840), 15; Elias Marks, *Hints on Female Education* (Columbia, S.C.: Printed by Isaac C. Morgan, 1837), 35; Lydia Sigourney, "Address on Female Education," *Southern Literary Messenger* 1, no. 4 (Dec. 1834): 169; "Where Our Daughters Go to School," *Harper's New Monthly Magazine* 15, no. 89 (Oct. 1857): 676.

30. See his letters to Kate of Feb. 6 and Mar. 9, 1853, in this volume. Alice Hunt Sokoloff offered a different interpretation, declaring that Chase was "hiding behind the skirts of Miss Haines." Sokoloff, *Kate Chase*, 33.

31. To Kate, Apr. 13, 1855, in this volume; to the Ohio State Teachers' Association, July 6, 1857, *Chase Papers*, 2:457–59; Hart, *Chase*, 5–6.

32. See his letter to Kate of July 31, 1854, in this volume; Catharine Beekman to her father, Mar. 9, 1854 (New-York Historical Society).

33. 1850 census for Pennsylvania, Delaware County, Aston Township, fol. 56 (the "household" also included a girl of four who had the same last name as a young woman of eighteen, who was either the oldest student or one of the employees); Ashmead, *History of Delaware County*, 299–300; Huntington, *Genealogical Memoir*, 282. Regarding Kate's last academic report from the school in New York, see her father's letter of July 5, 1854, in this volume.

34. Margaret Leech, *In the Days of McKinley* (New York: Harper, 1959), 14; see Chase's letter to Kate of Sept. 15, 1854, in this volume.

35. Mrs. A. K. Pearce, "Esther Institute," *The "Old Northwest" Genealogical Quarterly* 9 (1906): 143–49; Peacock, *Famous American Belles*, 212; *Chase Papers*, 1:256, 263, 264, 278.

36. Pearce, "Esther Institute," 148; for Catharine Collins, see the appendix. Though Catharine's husband, William O. Collins, was a trustee of the Hillsboro Academy (and of the Hillsboro Female College founded in 1855), there is no indication that Nettie attended any academy in Hillsboro. Thompson, *History of the County of Highland*, 57–58, 60.

37. Pearce, "Esther Institute," 143–49; Deborah Jean Warner, "Science Education for Women in Antebellum America," *Isis* 69 (1978): 61–62; *Chase Papers*, 1:256, 258, 259.

38. *Chase Papers*, 1:73n, 243, 247, 250, 254, 282.

39. She and Kate did accompany their father on a trip to Baltimore in July 1857 to attend ceremonies celebrating the completion of a continuous railway connection between that city and St. Louis. *Chase Papers*, 1:281, 294.

40. *New York Tribune*, Mar. 8, 1891; *New York Times*, Apr. 15, 1861.

41. *New York Tribune*, Mar. 8, Apr. 5, 1891.

42. Burlingame and Ettlinger, *Inside Lincoln's White House*, 97. For Kate's role as hostess in Columbus, see Howells, *Years of My Youth*, 133–34, and in Washington, Jacob, *Capital Elites*, 49–50.

43. Ellet, *Court Circles*, 581; Reid quoted in Ernest B. Furgurson, *Freedom Rising: Washington in the Civil War* (New York: Knopf 2004), 270; *Chicago News* quoted in Claude G. Bowers, *The Tragic Era: The Revolution after Lincoln* (Cambridge, Mass.: Houghton Mifflin

Co., 1929), 253; Mrs. John A. Logan, *Reminiscences of a Soldier's Wife: An Autobiography*, foreword by John Y. Simon (1913; repr., Carbondale, Ill.: Southern Illinois University Press, 1997), 300, 301. See *ANB* for John A. Logan. Bowers, *Tragic Era*, 252–55, and Belden and Belden, *So Fell the Angels*, 375, cite several sources of descriptions of Kate.

44. *New York World*, Feb. 20, 1870; Beale, ed., *Diary of Gideon Welles*, 1:306. "Miss Grundy" was M. A. Sneed, according to Alice Kahler Marshall, *Pen Names of Women Writers: From 1600 to the Present* (Camp Hill, Pa.: Alice Marshall Collection, 1985), 57.

45. Ellet, *Court Circles*, 554; Elizabeth Fries Ellet, *The Queens of American Society* (New York: C. Scribner & Co., 1867), 455; *New York World*, Feb. 20, 1870; Hamilton Gay Howard, *Civil-War Echoes: Character Sketches and State Secrets* (Washington, D.C.: Howard Pub. Co., 1907), 130. Virginia Tatnall Peacock, in *Famous American Belles*, 206, 210–11, 216–17, 223, 225, described Kate's appearance and traits. However, Peacock, whose book appeared two years after Kate's death, was born in 1873 and had no personal experience with Kate as a great "belle." Oscar Fay Adams, *A Dictionary of American Authors*, 5th ed. (Boston: Houghton, Mifflin, 1904), 540.

46. [Isabella Strange Trotter], *First Impressions of the New World on Two Travellers from the Old* (London: Longman, Brown, Green, Longmans, & Roberts, 1859), 191. When Kate was born, her father wrote in his diary: "The babe is pronounced pretty. I think it quite otherwise. It is however well formed and I am thankful." *Chase Papers*, 1:142.

47. Howells, *Years of My Youth*, 133–34.

48. Schurz, *Reminiscences*, 2:169.

49. *Chase Papers*, 3:8–10.

50. *New York Herald*, July 8, 1865; Oberholtzer, *Cooke*, 1:154.

51. Trotter, *First Impressions*, 193; Ellet, *Court Circles*, 581; *New York World*, Feb. 20, 1870. Howells later referred to Kate as her father's "brilliant young daughter," although sometimes it is difficult to know if such references are to her intellect or a brilliant social aura. Howells, *Years of My Youth*, 133.

52. Burlingame and Ettlinger, *Inside Lincoln's White House*, 97; Logan, *Reminiscences*, 300–301; *New York World*, Feb. 20, 1870; Lamphier, *Kate Chase and William Sprague*, 96–104, 131–37, 157–79.

53. Beale, ed., *Diary of Gideon Welles*, 1:306; *Daily National Intelligencer*, Nov. 13, 1863; Clemmer, *Ten Years in Washington*, 187.

54. Burlingame and Ettlinger, *Inside Lincoln's White House*, 98, 111; for Hay's use of "statuesque," see also Burlingame, *At Lincoln's Side*, xxiii. In October 1863, Hay wrote to a friend that Kate's impending marriage "disgusts me with life. She is a great woman & with a great future" (Burlingame, *At Lincoln's Side*, 67). Virginia Tatnall Peacock, looking at Kate from the perspective of the next generation, thought that Kate had a combination of masculine traits such as "virility" and feminine characteristics such as "delicacy." Peacock called Kate's personality "singularly enigmatical." Peacock, *Famous American Belles*, 206, 215, 225–26.

55. See the undated letter on page 187 of this volume; Howells, *Years of My Youth*, 132.

56. Burlingame and Ettlinger, *Inside Lincoln's White House*, 110; Ellet, *Court Circles*, 581; Logan, *Reminiscences*, 239, 300; *New York World*, Feb. 20, 1870; Burlingame, *At Lincoln's Side*, 45.

57. Rutherford B. Hayes to Lucy Webb Hayes, Dec. 7, 1865 (Hayes Papers, Library of the Rutherford B. Hayes Presidential Center [microfilm edition]); Worthington Chauncey Ford, ed., *War Letters, 1862–1865, of John Chipman Gray and John Codman Ropes* (Boston: Houghton Mifflin Co., 1927), 488. For both Hayes and Gray, see *ANB;* for the journey that Nettie made with her father in 1865, around the Southern coast and up the Mississippi, see chapter 7 of this volume. Historians and biographers of S. P. Chase often try to account for Kate but generally fail to notice her sister.

58. Father to Nettie, Nov. 28, 1863, in this volume; *New York World*, Feb. 20, 1870.

59. Adolph Schmitz, *Brooke Hall Polka* (Philadelphia: G. André & Co., 1859); *Guide-Book to the West Chester and Philadelphia Railroad* (Philadelphia: Printed by Sherman & Co., 1869), 29; John W. Jordan, *A History of Delaware County, Pennsylvania, and Its People* (New York: Lewis Historical Publishing Co., 1914), 448; Smith, *History of Delaware County*, 388; Ashmead, *History of Delaware County*, 601, 608; Brooke Hall Female Seminary, *Catalogue*, 11; *The American Educational Year-Book: February, 1858* (Boston: James Robinson, 1858), 157; *DAB*, 15: 124–25.

60. Eleanor Wolf Thompson, *Education for Ladies, 1830–1860: Ideas on Education in Magazines for Women* (New York: King's Crown Press, 1947), 46.

61. Brooke Hall Female Seminary, *Catalogue,* 3; 1860 census, Delaware County, Media Borough, 440; *Guide-Book to the West Chester and Philadelphia Railroad,* 29; Saul Sack, "The Higher Education of Women in Pennsylvania," *Pennsylvania Magazine of History and Biography* 83 (1959): 48.

62. *New York Times,* Aug. 1, 1862; *Chase Papers,* 5:125; Nettie to Kate, Feb. 15, 1864; Nettie to Father, Feb. 20, 1864, printed in this volume.

63. *Chase Papers,* 4:156.

64. Maria Eastman's and Mary Macaulay's letters of June 23, 1862, and Sept. 9, 1863, respectively, are printed in this volume.

65. Father to Nettie, Feb. 26, 1864, in this volume.

66. *Chase Papers,* 5:105; *Catalogue of a Most Superb Collection,* items 1240–42, 1310; Father to Kate, Sept. 10, 1866, in this volume.

67. New York *World,* Feb. 20, 1870.

68. *Harper's New Monthly Magazine* 42 (Jan. 1871): 302–3; *Atlantic Monthly* 39 (Jan. 1877): 116; *Appletons' Journal* 2 (Jan. 1877): 96. On the title page of *Janet et ses Amis,* published by D. Appleton and Company of New York, probably in 1876, Nettie is identified as author, and as one of the illustrators, only by a monogram of the initials of her married name: J, R, and C interlocked above an H. That monogram also appears as a signature in some of the pictures in the book. The title page identifies the other illustrator only as "R.E." The Janet of the book, a very young girl, no doubt represented Nettie's daughter of that name. Nettie's *Mother Goose Melodies,* printed by Porter and Coates in Philadelphia in 1870, had the title *Mother Goose in a New Dress* on its cover. It had its origin as a present from Nettie to her father. Jay Cooke arranged for the publication and Charles M. Walker, a journalist and writer who was a clerk and auditor in the Treasury Department under Chase, contributed to the book's verses. *Chase Papers,* 1:529, 668; Oberholtzer, *Cooke,* 2:477; Coyle, *Ohio Authors,* 664; S. P. Chase to Charles M. Walker, Dec. 8, 1870 (Chase Papers, LC).

69. See her letter to Kate of Feb. 15, 1864, in chapter 6.

NOTES — FATHER: SALMON PORTLAND CHASE

1. The arguments appeared under the titles *Speech of Salmon P. Chase, in the Case of the Colored Woman, Matilda* (Cincinnati: Pugh & Dodd, 1837) and *Reclamation of Fugitives from Service* (Cincinnati: R. P. Donogh, 1847). *Chase Papers,* 1:119, 166.

2. Benedict, "Salmon P. Chase," 463, 465–68; *Chase Papers,* 1:162, 172, 180–84; 2:76, 112–13, 116–18; *The Address and Reply, on the Presentation of a Testimonial, to S. P. Chase, by the Colored People of Cincinnati* (Cincinnati: H. W. Derby & Co., 1845).

3. *Chase Papers,* 1:11, 36, 121; 2:70.

4. Ibid., 1:121–23, 125, 129, 133–34, 149; 2:57–58, 73.

5. William Birney, *James G. Birney and His Times: The Genesis of the Republican Party* (1890; repr., New York: Bergman Publishers, 1969), 259–61; *ANB,* 2:816–18.

6. Hart, *Chase,* 58–59; *Chase Papers,* 1:138, 147–48, 166; 2:111, 134.

7. *Chase Papers,* 2:433, 445–46; 4:156–57. Don E. Fehrenbacher, *The Slaveholding Republic: An Account of the United States Government's Relations to Slavery* (Oxford: Oxford University Press, 2001), 224, 241, 408, called Chase's argument in the Van Zandt case an "eloquent effort to blend moral principle with legal argument."

8. Niven, *Chase,* 8–15; *Chase Papers,* 2:9, 11, 14; Schlesinger, "Salmon Portland Chase," 130, 132, 137–38.

9. Another Chase uncle was a senator from Vermont, but Salmon Chase seems to have had limited contact with him in Washington. *Chase Papers,* 1:3, 9–11, 22–23, 29, 36, 49–50; 2:13, 16, 21–22, 43–46; 4:281–82.

10. Hart, *Chase,* 46–47.

11. Ibid., 39–43, 49; *Chase Papers,* 1:68; Joan D. Hedrick, *Harriet Beecher Stowe: A Life* (New York: Oxford University Press, 1994), 82; Blue, *Chase,* 29; Niven, *Chase,* 45.

12. *Chase Papers,* 1:12, 15–16, 28, 113, 115, 121, 150–52, 155–57, 173.

13. Hart, *Chase*, 49–51; Leonard L. Richards, *"Gentlemen of Property and Standing": Anti-Abolition Mobs in Jacksonian America* (New York: Oxford University Press, 1970), 92–100, 134–50; David Grimsted, *American Mobbing, 1828–1861: Toward Civil War* (New York: Oxford University Press, 1998), 59–61; Blue, *Chase*, 28–31; Niven, *Chase*, 46–49.

14. Stowe, *Men of Our Times*, 257–58; *Chase Papers*, 2:77–79; Richards, *"Gentlemen of Property and Standing,"* 34–35, 113, 122–29.

15. Hart, *Chase*, 53, 88; *Chase Papers*, 1:147.

16. Niven, *Chase*, 88–89; Blue, *Chase*, 50, 62, 73, 288; Gienapp, *Origins*, 88–89, 114; Chase to Quintus F. Atkins, July 2, 1845, *Chase Papers*, 2:109–11. For Chase and the Constitution before the Civil War, see Benedict, "Salmon P. Chase," 465–70.

17. Foner, *Free Soil*, 90–92. Morris and Chase joined forces as attorneys in John Van Zandt's first trial in 1842. For the 1844 election, Morris was the vice-presidential candidate on a ticket that was headed by Birney and put forward first by the American and Foreign Anti-Slavery Society and subsequently by the Liberty Party. Hart, *Chase*, 76; *Chase Papers*, 2:82, 83, 86, 103.

18. Stephen E. Maizlish, *The Triumph of Sectionalism: The Transformation of Ohio Politics, 1844–1856* (Kent, Ohio: Kent State University Press, 1983), 121–46.

19. *Chase Papers*, 1:xxvii–xxviii, 227n; 2:xvii, 381–83, 385, 386n; Blue, *Chase*, 80–83, 93–96; Gienapp, *Origins*, 71–73, 75; Foner, *Free Soil*, 94–95. According to Fehrenbacher, *Slaveholding Republic*, 228, 415, Chase was at one key point in 1850 the sole "militant voice" in the Senate.

20. *Chase Papers*, 1:243; 2:389, 401–2, 405, 408–9, 414, 420, 432; Gienapp, *Origins*, 19, 47, 56–58, 88–90, 114–17, 192–203.

21. *Chase Papers*, 5:40. Gen. Benjamin Butler had first used the term *contraband of war* as a legal fiction to authorize protection of runaway slaves who came under the army's protection at Fortress Monroe, Va., in the early part of the war. Rose, *Rehearsal for Reconstruction*, 13–14.

22. *Chase Papers*, 1:206, 216; 2:220–21.

23. Ibid., 1:179, 503; Dorothy S. Provine, comp., *District of Columbia Free Negro Registers, 1821–1861*, 3 vols. (Bowie, Md.: Heritage Books, 1996), 3:613. Vaudry appears in the latter source as "Catherine Vandery." She was set free by New York attorney Joseph B. Varnum, who was the Chases' landlord for a time in Washington. *Chase Papers*, 1:364; 4:106, 205.

24. Dorothy S. Provine, comp., *District of Columbia Indentures of Apprenticeship, 1801–1893* (Lovettsville, Va.: Willow Bend Books, 1998), 219; *Chase Papers*, 1:115–16, 587; Warden, *Chase*, 271–72; Howells, *Years of My Youth*, 133, 135.

25. *Address and Reply on the Presentation of a Testimonial*, 10–11, 20–23, 27.

26. *Chase Papers*, 4:90–92, 129; 5:519, 521; Hyman, *Reconstruction Justice*, 84–85; James P. McClure, Leigh Johnsen, Kathleen Norman, and Michael Vanderlan, eds., "Circumventing the Dred Scott Decision: Edward Bates, Salmon P. Chase, and the Citizenship of African Americans," *Civil War History* 43 (1997): 279–309; Burlingame and Ettlinger, *Inside Lincoln's White House*, 65, 183; Benedict, "Salmon P. Chase," 470.

27. *New York Times*, May 12, 22, 1873, Oct. 15, 1886; Frederick A. McGinnis, *A History and an Interpretation of Wilberforce University* (Wilberforce, Ohio: Brown Pub. Co., 1941), 44, 46; Daniel Alexander Payne, *Recollections of Seventy Years* (Nashville, Tenn.: A.M.E. Sunday School Union, 1888; repr., New York: Arno Press, 1968), 229–30. Chase's benevolence to Wilberforce University extended back at least as far as 1857. *Chase Papers*, 1:268–70. The only other institution to receive a bequest of money from his will was his alma mater, Dartmouth, to which he also gave $10,000.

28. *Chase Papers*, 1:249, 253, 254, 265, 267, 271, 273, 275, 280–84, 292, 294; 2:432–33, 452–57.

29. Ibid., 1:261, 284, 289, 291; 2:446–49; 3:10–12; Fehrenbacher, *Slaveholding Republic*, 239.

30. *Chase Papers*, 4:226, 231, 235, 237–39, 323–29.

31. Gienapp, *Origins*, 235–36, 248–53, 307–9, 338–39; *Chase Papers*, 2:440–43.

32. *Chase Papers*, 1:266, 276, 281; 3:11–12, 25.

33. Ibid., 1:243; 3:14–16, 33–34.

34. Foner, *Free Soil*, 73–79, 84–86, 132, 290; Merrill D. Peterson, *The Jefferson Image in the American Mind* (Charlottesville, Va.: University Press of Virginia, 1998), 190, 192, 197, 205–6.

35. Donald, *Lincoln*, 264, 281; *Congressional Globe*, 37th Cong., spec. sess., 1861, 1433; *Journal of the Executive Proceedings of the Senate*, vol. 11, *Dec. 6, 1858 to Aug. 6, 1861* (Washington, D.C.: U.S. Senate, 1887), 289–90.

36. *Chase Papers*, 3:101–2, 141, 291.

37. Ibid., 3:126–29, 291, 299–300, and illus.; 4:246, 356–58; Melinda Lawson, *Patriot Fires: Forging a New American Nationalism in the Civil War North* (Lawrence, Kans.: University Press of Kansas, 2002), 40–64; McPherson, *Battle Cry of Freedom*, 443–47; *ANB*, 5:398–99; Larson, *Cooke*, 102–3.

38. Historian Michael Les Benedict has asserted that "Chase proved a great secretary of the treasury." Benedict, "Salmon P. Chase," 459, 464, 490; McCulloch, *Men and Measures*, 185; *Chase Papers*, 1:364, 383, 425, 462, 464–65; 3:104–5, 114, 142, 171, 217–18, 292, 358–59, 368; 4:128, 400, 404; McPherson, *Battle Cry of Freedom*, 447–48. Still cited with reference to financial policies during Chase's secretaryship are Bray Hammond, *Sovereignty and an Empty Purse: Banks and Politics in the Civil War* (Princeton, N.J.: Princeton University Press, 1970), and Irwin Unger, *The Greenback Era: A Social and Political History of American Finance, 1865–1879* (Princeton, N.J.: Princeton University Press, 1964).

39. The department's employment of women was at the instigation of Francis E. Spinner, the treasurer, who argued that women could cut notes more adeptly than men—and, of course, for lower pay. Clemmer, *Ten Years in Washington*, 300, 372; Hyman, *Reconstruction Justice*, 78–80; *ANB*, 20:479–80; Slotten, *Patronage*, 166; *Chase Papers*, 5:363–64. See also the fourth illustration following 234 in *Chase Papers*, vol. 4.

40. *Chase Papers*, 1:238, 268–69; 3:133–34, 138–40, 146–48, 159–65. Rose, *Rehearsal for Reconstruction*, is a detailed study of the "Port Royal Experiment" in the Sea Islands.

41. Hyman, *Reconstruction Justice*, 69, 75, 84–90; *Chase Papers*, 3:350–1; 4:32–33, 119, 202, 225; Louis S. Gerteis, "Salmon P. Chase, Radicalism, and the Politics of Emancipation, 1861–1864," *Journal of American History* 60 (1973): 42–62; Donald, *Lincoln*, 479.

42. *Chase Papers*, 1:xxxiv–xxxv, xl–xlii; 5:12; Hyman, *Reconstruction Justice*, 90–91; Donald, *Lincoln*, 507–8, 535–37, 551–52; Burlingame and Ettlinger, *Inside Lincoln's White House*, 93, 133–34, 217, 241, 323.

43. *Chase Papers*, 1:512, 598; 5:12–13, 109–10, 116–17, 189.

44. Ibid., 5:66, 70–71, 94–96, 104–5, 125–28, 133, 224–28, 287, 311.

45. Ibid., 3:126–27; 5:xxi, 328, 344–45.

46. Ibid., 1:xlvii; 5:159, 297–98.

47. Ibid., 5:xx, 186; Hyman, *Reconstruction Justice*, 123–39.

48. *Chase Papers*, 1:xlvii; 5:xxi, 369–70. For the Chase court, see Benedict, "Salmon P. Chase," 470–90.

49. *Chase Papers*, 5:15–19, 47–52; Simpson et al., *Advice after Appomattox*, 3–38.

NOTES — OBLIGATION AND FULFILLMENT

1. *Chase Papers*, 1:142.

2. Ibid., 1:113, 134, 165, 166, 178; Diana Hochstedt Butler, *Standing against the Whirlwind: Evangelical Episcopalians in Nineteenth-Century America* (New York: Oxford University Press, 1995), 150–58, 177.

3. *Chase Papers*, 1:282, 569, 584, 593, 626, 644, 682; 2:11; 5:162–63; letter to Kate, Aug. 4, 1853, below.

4. *Chase Papers*, 1:607; see also 1:39–41, 386, 474, 511, 526, 531, 541, 634, 636, 647, 649, 671, 675, 677, 706; *Catalogue of a Most Superb Collection*, items 1033–35.

5. He was pushed there, again, by the weather, being unable to reach his intended destination, the Episcopal Rock Creek Church. He took communion at Rock Creek at least twice after doing so at the Methodist church. *Chase Papers*, 1:592, 667–68, 679, 686. He abstained from communion when he did not think himself worthy of it. On one occasion in 1862 he wanted to participate "but felt myself too subject to temptation to sin." Ibid., 1:324.

6. *New York Times*, May 12, 22, 1873. His library also contained Benjamin T. Tanner's *An Apology for African Methodism* (Baltimore: privately printed, 1867). *Catalogue of a Most Superb Collection*, item 1075.

7. *Chase Papers,* 1:97, 100, 121, 122, 124–29, 131, 134, 136–38, 140–41, 143, 178, 210–12, 219, 256, 259; and his letter to Belle, Aug. 19, 1849, printed in this volume.

8. *Chase Papers,* 1:121.

9. Ibid., 1:98, 106, 111, 120, 130, 143, 162, 163, 169, 179, 187, 214.

10. Ibid., 1:178.

11. Ibid., 2:278. Chase turned twenty-five in January 1833. For the deaths of his siblings in that period—one of the deaths, and probably another also, occurring in Cincinnati—see ibid., 1:19, 184, 186–87, 229–30.

12. Ibid., 1:92–93, 97–98.

13. Ibid., 1:161; 2:121–22.

14. Ibid., 1:6, 281.

15. Ibid., 1:34–35, 45, 102, 125–43, 146, 178, 204.

16. See in this volume the letter from Lizzie Chase, June 22, 1844, and the one to Belle of Aug. 19, 1849.

17. To Kate, Jan. 8, 1855, and to Nettie, May 5, 1869.

18. See Father to Nettie, Aug. 9, 1866, and to Kate, July 5, 1854; Kate to Father, July 2 and July 10, 1868; Nettie to Kate, Feb. 15, 1864; Nettie to Father, July 21, 1868, in this volume.

19. See in this volume his letter to Belle dated "Sunday night" [Dec. 7, 1851]; to Kate, Nov. 18, 1863, and May 4, 1869; to Kate, Jan. 8, 1855; to Kate, Aug. 9, 1868; and see to Kate, May 10, 1868, where he asserts that William Sprague would be "nearly perfect" if he were "a true Christian."

20. To Helen Chase Walbridge, Feb. 11, 1864 (Chase Papers, HSP).

21. Introduction by David Roberts to Chesterfield's *Letters* (Oxford: Oxford University Press, 1992), ix–xxiii.

22. Harold G. Syrett et al., eds., *The Papers of Alexander Hamilton,* 27 vols. (New York: Columbia University Press, 1961–87), 25:288–89; Julian P. Boyd et al., eds., *The Papers of Thomas Jefferson,* 33 vols. to date (Princeton, N.J.: Princeton University Press 1950–), 29:349, 379; 30:608; 33:570.

23. *Chase Papers,* 1:118; Slotten, *Patronage,* 166–67; Cincinnati *Commercial Gazette,* Dec. 18, 1887.

24. *Chase Papers,* 5:302–3, 363–64, 369–70.

25. June 15, 1866, below.

26. *Chase Papers,* 1:5. For an articulate expression of his sister Abigail's views on education, see ibid., 2:33–36. For Elizabeth Wirt, see also Jabour, *Marriage in the Early Republic.*

27. *Chase Papers,* 1:3, 29, 35–36.

28. Ibid., 1:3, 13, 26, 37.

29. Ibid., 1:39.

30. Schuckers, *Chase,* 602–3.

31. *Chase Papers,* 5:303, 367.

32. See his letter to Kate, Sept. 10, 1866, in this volume.

33. *Chase Papers,* 1:6.

34. Ibid., 27.

35. Warden, *Chase,* 329; Maizlish, "Salmon P. Chase," 50; Niven, *Chase,* 62, 84–85; Burlingame and Ettlinger, *Inside Lincoln's White House,* 77; Hans L. Trefousse, *Benjamin Franklin Wade: Radical Republican from Ohio* (New York: Twayne Publishers, 1963), 140, 189, 192, 235; Benedict, "Salmon P. Chase," 462. Maizlish, "Salmon P. Chase," 49–50, has citations to several of the charges that Chase was ambitious.

36. James Brewer Stewart, *Wendell Phillips: Liberty's Hero* (Baton Rouge, La.: Louisiana State University Press, 1986), 95. Joshua Leavitt, initially scornful of Chase for not being of the pure abolitionist fold, became an ardent supporter of Chase for the presidency from 1856 on. Hugh Davis, *Joshua Leavitt: Evangelical Abolitionist* (Baton Rouge, La.: Louisiana State University Press, 1990), 209, 264, 279, 284.

37. Schurz, *Reminiscences,* 2:171–74.

38. Burlingame and Ettlinger, *Inside Lincoln's White House,* 93, 242; Maizlish, "Salmon P. Chase," 49; Beale, ed., *Diary of Gideon Welles,* 2:121, 192–93; Bates quoted in Benjamin P. Thomas, *Abraham Lincoln: A Biography* (New York: Knopf, 1952), 412; Benedict, "Salmon P. Chase," 461. Hay also noted negative comments by others about Chase; see Burlingame and Ettlinger, *Inside Lincoln's White House,* 99–100, 119, 214, 233, 241, 242.

39. Burlingame and Ettlinger, *Inside Lincoln's White House*, 323; John Bigelow, *Retrospections of an Active Life*, 5 vols. (New York: Knopf, 1909–13), 2:110.

40. Burlingame and Ettlinger, *Inside Lincoln's White House*, 78, 103, 313; Maizlish, "Salmon P. Chase," 49.

41. Donald, *Lincoln*, 480–83. Supposedly Lincoln said that "Chase is about one and a half times bigger than any other man that I ever knew." Hart, *Chase*, 435; Benedict, "Salmon P. Chase," 460.

42. Hyman, *Reconstruction Justice*, 67–68, 72.

43. Maizlish, "Salmon P. Chase," 49.

44. Hart, *Chase*, 428–30; Hyman, *Reconstruction Justice*, 72–73; *Chase Papers*, 5:199. Chase learned to avoid leaving any impression of political ambition. In 1863, when given the opportunity to make corrections to an 1856 letter to Theodore Parker, he wanted to alter the passage "an ambitious man, anxious to get to the top"—meaning, in the context of the letter, getting to the "topmost" or broadest goal in the dismantling of slavery—to say "an earnest man." *Chase Papers*, 2:445–46.

45. Stowe, *Men of Our Times*, 257.

46. Hart, *Chase*, 423.

47. Hyman, *Reconstruction Justice*, 85, 89.

48. Allan Nevins, *The Emergence of Lincoln*, 2 vols. (New York: Scribner, 1950), 1:26.

49. Hart, *Chase*, 415, 421; Harry James Brown and Frederick D. Williams, eds., *The Diary of James A. Garfield*, 2 vols. (East Lansing, Mich.: Michigan State University, 1967), 1:341–42; Schurz, *Reminiscences*, 2:170, 3:99–100; McCulloch, *Men and Measures*, 181; Schuckers, *Chase*, 595, 613; Benedict, "Salmon P. Chase," 462. Chase had a moderate speech difficulty, sometimes characterized as a lisp, and Harold Hyman concluded that his stiffness as an orator was a product of his efforts to control his enunciation; Hyman, *Reconstruction Justice*, 14.

50. Hart, *Chase*, 415, 421–24; McCulloch, *Men and Measures*, 181; Schuckers, *Chase*, 598–99; Donald, *Lincoln*, 478–79.

51. Donald, *Lincoln*, 551; Thomas, *Lincoln*, 411; Nevins, *Emergence of Lincoln*, 1:26; Hans L. Trefousse, *The Radical Republicans: Lincoln's Vanguard for Racial Justice* (New York: Knopf, 1969), 7; Gienapp, *Origins*, 72.

52. Maizlish, "Salmon P. Chase," 47, 50, 53, 62, 67, 69–70. Thomas, *Lincoln*, 411, wrote: "Few men found it so easy to delude themselves as the Secretary of the Treasury." Like Maizlish, Peter Walker was willing to stipulate Chase's "alleged duplicity" and reputedly "rapacious ambition" in order to confront, with mixed success, the apparent conflict between Chase's moral principles and personal ambition. Peter F. Walker, *Moral Choices: Memory, Desire, and Imagination in Nineteenth-Century American Abolition* (Baton Rouge, La.: Louisiana State University Press, 1978), 305–29.

53. *Chase Papers*, 4:113.

54. Schuckers, *Chase*, 594, 610, 614; Roeliff Brinkerhoff, *Recollections of a Lifetime* (Cincinnati, Ohio: Robert Clarke Co., 1900), 108.

55. Hyman, *Reconstruction Justice*, 70, 73; Benedict, "Salmon P. Chase," 490.

56. Hart, *Chase*, 424–25.

57. Brown and Williams, *Diary of James A. Garfield*, 2:176–77.

58. Benjamin Thomas, in his biography of Lincoln, called Kate "restlessly ambitious," while a biographer of New York financier August Belmont deemed her "a social python." Thomas, *Lincoln*, 411; David Black, *The King of Fifth Avenue: The Fortunes of August Belmont* (New York: Dial Press, 1981), 555.

59. The Beldens' book made the most overt and protracted argument in this direction. Aaron Burr's opponents had made a similar accusation when Burr's daughter Theodosia married Joseph Alston of South Carolina. Charles R. King, ed., *The Life and Correspondence of Rufus King*, 6 vols. (New York: G. P. Putnam's Sons, 1894–1900), 3:459; *ANB*, 4:40.

60. Mrs. Daniel Chester French [Mary Adams French], *Memories of a Sculptor's Wife* (Boston: Houghton Mifflin Co., 1928), 148. Mary French's uncle, who as commissioner of public buildings was active in the official life of Washington in the 1860s, deemed Kate "one of the most lovable women I ever saw." He considered the slandering of Chase "wicked & malicious in the extreme" and said that Kate was "deservedly beloved by all who know her." Benjamin Brown French, *Witness to the Young Republic: A Yankee's Journal,*

1828–1870, ed. Donald B. Cole and John J. McDonough (Hanover, N.H.: University Press of New England, 1989), 443, 564.

61. Donald, *Lincoln,* 459, 476. Mary Lincoln appears to have obsessively distrusted both Chase and Seward as "ambitious fanatics" and threats to her husband. Justin G. Turner and Linda Levitt Turner, eds., *Mary Todd Lincoln: Her Life and Letters* (New York: Knopf, 1972), 136, 138; Keckley, *Behind the Scenes,* 111–15; Jennifer Fleischner, *Mrs. Lincoln and Mrs. Keckley* (New York: Broadway Books, 2003), 211, 250, 269–70.

62. Brinkerhoff, *Recollections,* 113.

NOTES — PENS TO PAPER

1. Ithamar Chase Whipple to Chase, Nov. 10, 1846 (Chase Papers, LC).
2. Charlotte Ludlow Jones to Chase, Mar. 9, 1852 (Chase Papers, LC).
3. Clopper, *American Family,* 423.
4. To Virginia Shook, May 6, 1864 (Chase Papers, HSP).
5. E. C. Whipple to Chase, May 1, 1847 (Chase Papers, LC).
6. Olivia E. Phelps Stokes, *Letters and Memories of Susan and Anna Bartlett Warner* (New York: G. P. Putnam's Sons, 1925), 22; Anna Bartlett Warner, *Susan Warner* (New York: G. P. Putnam's Sons, 1909), 393.
7. Farnham, *Education of the Southern Belle,* 76–77; Catherine Hobbs, ed., *Nineteenth-Century Women Learn to Write* (Charlottesville, Va.: University Press of Virginia, 1995), 13; Lynne Templeton Brickley, "Sarah Pierce's Litchfield Female Academy" in *To Ornament Their Minds: Sarah Pierce's Litchfield Academy, 1792–1833,* ed. Catherine Keene Fields and Lisa C. Knightlinger (Litchfield, Conn.: Litchfield Historical Society, 1993), 43.
8. S. Michael Halloran, "From Rhetoric to Composition: The Teaching of Writing in America to 1900," in *A Short History of Writing Instruction: From Ancient Greece to Twentieth Century America,* ed. James J. Murphy (Davis, Calif.: Hermagoras Press, 1990), 164; Farnham, *Education of the Southern Belle,* 77.
9. Catharine Beekman to her mother, Feb. 2, 16, 1854 (New-York Historical Society); Winifred Bryan Homer, "The Roots of Modern Writing Instruction: Eighteenth- and Nineteenth-Century Britain," *Rhetoric Review* 8 (1990): 340; Nan Johnson, *Nineteenth-Century Rhetoric in North America* (Carbondale, Ill.: Southern Illinois University Press, 1991), 177, 179.
10. James A. Berlin, *Writing Instruction in Nineteenth-Century American Colleges* (Carbondale, Ill.: Southern Illinois University Press, 1984), 21, 35, 25; Farnham, *Education of the Southern Belle,* 76; Marks, *Hints on Female Education,* 30; Caroline M. Burrough, "Girls and Their Training," *Ladies' Repository* 1 (1841): 374; Robert J. Connors, "Textbooks and the Evolution of the Discipline," *College Composition and Communications* 37 (1986): 179, 185, 193n.
11. "In which" is an interlineation, substituted for "that."
12. Kate wrote "fudemental," then placed a caret for the insertion of the "n" but neglected to write the letter.
13. Brown University Library, manuscript in Kate's hand, and with her endorsement: "Composition by Kate Chase." The words in brackets are partially obscured by drops of ink.
14. Joanne Jacobson, *Authority and Alliance in the Letters of Henry Adams* (Madison, Wis.: University of Wisconsin Press, 1992), 3; Marilyn Ferris Motz, *True Sisterhood: Michigan Women and Their Kin, 1820–1920* (Albany, N.Y.: State University of New York Press, 1983), 53, 54; George W. Brush, "Woman as a Letter-Writer," *Ladies' Repository* 24 (1864): 598–600.
15. Steven M. Stowe, "The Rhetoric of Authority: The Making of Social Values in Planter Family Correspondence," *Journal of American History* 73 (1987): 923–24. For other examples, see John C. Calhoun to Anna Maria Calhoun, Mar. 10, 1832, or William H. Bradbury to Jane Bradbury, Feb. 17, Apr. 6, 1864, May 24, 1865. Robert L. Meriwether et al., eds., *The Papers of John C. Calhoun,* 28 vols. (Columbia, S.C.: University of South Carolina Press, 1959–2003), 11:561; Jennifer Cain Bohrnstedt, ed., Kassandra R. Chaney, comp., *While Father Is Away: The Civil War Letters of William H. Bradbury* (Lexington, Ky.: University Press of Kentucky, 2003), 128, 150, 278.
16. Feb. 12, 1852, and Aug. 4, 1853, in this volume.

17. The published syllabus of the South Carolina Female Collegiate Institute (c. 1837), for example, describes the advantages the student gains through such revision: "In carefully reviewing what she has written, she is to be sure not to spare herself in correcting errors; recollecting that the art of writing, is that of judiciously blotting out. She is to transcribe again and again; and in thus transcribing, she will find that new views of the subject, and new forms of expression, will present themselves." Historian S. Michael Halloran points out that such strategies of revision could only be employed because of nineteenth-century technological developments: "With pens that do not require constant sharpening, ink that requires little or no blotting, and cheap yet serviceable paper, it becomes possible to write in the free, exploratory manner." Marks, *Hints on Female Education,* 31 (includes "Plan of Instruction Adopted in the South Carolina Female Collegiate Institute" and "Syllabus of A Course of Study, Recommended to the Students of the South Carolina Female Collegiate Institute, During Its Vacation"); Halloran, "From Rhetoric to Composition," 170.

18. Examples are her father's letters of Jan. 22, 1851, Jan. 23, 1853, and Feb. 6, 1853, the originals of which are in the Chase collection at the Historical Society of Pennsylvania.

19. See Chase's letters to Kate, Feb. 1, 1851, Mar. 4, 1852, and July 31, 1854, and his to Mary Macaulay, Oct. 21, 1863, all in this volume.

20. Stowe, "Rhetoric of Authority," 921, 925; Andrew Rolle, *John Charles Frémont: Character as Destiny* (Norman, Okla.: University of Oklahoma Press, 1991), 31.

21. See Mar. 15, 1864, in the letters below.

22. To Kate, June 29, 1862 (Chase Papers, HSP).

23. In April 1869 he wrote Nettie from the Supreme Court chamber, describing dinner parties attended by President Grant, General Sherman, and other notables. He also asked that she and Kate give him "the compliment" of reading his opinion in the *Texas v. White* case. *Chase Papers,* 5:295–98.

24. *Chase Papers,* 4:229, 436.

25. Those letters, not included in this volume, are printed in the *Chase Papers* and are cited in the introduction to chapter 7 below.

26. To August Belmont, May 30, 1868, in *Chase Papers,* 5:224.

27. *Chase Papers,* 1:225, 227, 229; 2:323–33. For his letters to Sumner, see, for instance, that of Dec. 2, 1847, which spins a theme of "Servilism" and poses a series of questions beginning with "But what next?"; the one of Mar. 7, 1850, which laments a speech by Webster and asks, "Will not Faneuil Hall thunder once more? *Will* the tempest of popular indignation blast Jonah's gourd?"; and the letter of Sept. 8, 1850, which begins, "Clouds and darkness are upon us at present," goes on to quote Milton, the "glorious child of Freedom though blind," and uses a biblical allusion to urge Sumner: "Rouse up in Massachusetts, and quit you like men. God's Providence has devolved political duties and responsibilities upon you my friend from which you must not shrink." *Chase Papers,* 2:160–61, 284, 304–5.

28. For the early journal, which runs with many gaps from January 1829 to June 1835, see *Chase Papers,* 1:3–81.

29. *Chase Papers,* 1:5, 12, 13, 42–43, 56, 60–61, 83–84.

30. See the letters of July 22 and Aug. 13, 1850, below.

31. *Chase Papers,* 1:55, 57, 65–68; 2:49–52, 55; Joan D. Hedrick, *Harriet Beecher Stowe: A Life* (New York: Oxford University Press, 1994), 82–85.

32. *Chase Papers,* 3:17.

33. The text of an important speech would also appear in sympathetic newspapers. Ibid., 1:225, 227; 2:286, 289.

34. The black band appears on the first six letters of chapter 2, all written to Kate from February to May 1852.

35. See *Chase Papers,* 3:xxvi and 4:xx, regarding the department's printed letter paper and the press copies of letters written on it.

36. *Chase Papers,* 5:350; *New York Tribune,* Feb. 15, 22, Mar. 8, Apr. 5, June 7, 1891; "Babes in the Woods," *Scribner's Monthly* 14 (1877): 488–501. Some of the illustrations accompanying "Babes in the Woods," although not attributed to her, resemble the style of her drawings in letters and the depictions of children in her *Janet et ses Amis.*

CHRONOLOGY

September 1839   Father and Eliza Ann (Lizzie) Smith marry in Cincinnati, Ohio

February 1840   First daughter Kate (b. Nov. 1835, daughter of Father and Kitty) dies of scarlet fever

August 1840   Kate is born

May 1842   Kate's sister Lizzie is born; she dies in August 1842

June 1843   Second baby Lizzie is born; she dies in July 1844

September 1845   Eliza Chase dies of tuberculosis (twenty-three years old)

November 1846   Father and Belle Ludlow marry in Cincinnati

September 1847   Nettie is born

February 1849   Ohio legislature elects Father to U.S. Senate; special Senate session, 31st Congress, in March

July 1849   Josephine (Zoe, Josey) is born

December 1849   Belle suffers tuberculosis attack, travels to Parkeville, N.J.; first session of 31st Congress opens

by January 1850   Kate enters Miss Haines's school in New York

May 1850   Belle, with Nettie and Zoe, is at Northampton, Mass.; Father in Washington, D.C.; Kate at school

July 1850   Zoe dies

September 1850   First session of 31st Congress ends

December 1850   Belle and Nettie visit relatives in Matagorda County, Tex.; second session of 31st Congress opens (closes March 1851)

Spring 1851   Belle and Nettie return to Ohio

January 1852   Belle (thirty-two years old) dies of tuberculosis (Clifton, Ohio)

CHAPTER 1

"Whom He Loveth He Chasteneth"

JUNE 1844–JANUARY 1852

A FEW WEEKS after Kate's second birthday, Noah Worcester, a physician and her father's friend, examined her mother and found "the upper lobe of each lung infiltrated with tubercles." Even at the age of twenty, Lizzie Chase surely understood the gravity of the diagnosis. Two of her older sisters had already died, aged twenty-one and twenty-four, and another, her last surviving older sibling, would expire at twenty-three, within months of Worcester's assessment of Lizzie's condition. In his prescription for Lizzie's treatment—"plain nutritious diet, daily exercise in the open air," routine sponging of the chest with water, and "attention to the state of the digestive organs"—the doctor acknowledged that the medical science of his day could concoct no potion, apply no medicine or course of treatment, that would avert the fatal outcome of an aggressive case of tuberculosis. Lizzie died in September 1845, three years after Worcester's diagnosis. As her younger brother Edmund succumbed to consumption a year and a half later, Father lamented in his journal: "He is following all the elder members of his family to the grave." Ironically, Edmund's death came less than three weeks after Lyman Beecher addressed a throng of grieving Cincinnatians at the funeral of the much-admired Dr. Worcester, dead of consumption at thirty-four.[1]

Belle Chase, twenty-six years old when Father wed her in November 1846, also contracted tuberculosis. Three years after they married she suffered an attack of "most threatening symptoms of rapid consumption" that caused her husband to despair of her recovery. "Neither she nor I had confidence in the efficacy of ordinary treatment," he noted. "Both of us had some in the Water cure, especially in the hands of a judicious physician."[2] Accordingly, in the year following her acute attack, Belle made a cycle of visits to far-flung hydropathic institutions: the Round Hill Water Cure at Northampton, Massachusetts; a facility in Morris County, New Jersey; and the Parkeville Hydropathic Institute in New Jersey not far from Philadelphia. Those establishments had in common an affiliation with Dr. George T. Dexter, who also practiced in Boston and New York City and incidentally cultivated, in addition to his hydropathic treatments, an interest in spiritualism and communication with departed souls. His work at the Parkeville Institute, in which patients or others could invest financially, was promoted by Gamaliel Bailey, who, trained as a physician himself, was the ardent proprietor of the prominent antislavery newspaper, *The National Era,* and Father's very close friend. If George Dexter was bolder than some hydropathic physicians in promoting his water cure as efficacious against rapidly progressing consumption, Father appreciated the attention that the doctor and his wife gave to Belle as she began her treatments with Dexter.[3]

In the middle reaches of the nineteenth century, the water cure, like homeopathy and other forms of treatment, offered an alternative to the harsh methods and heavy dosing that characterized allopathic medicine, at least according to its contemporary critics. It is not known if Belle Chase partook of the full range of hydropathic techniques, which utilized cold water in an effort to stimulate the body to return to a presumed natural state of health and could include tightly wrapping the patient in cold wet sheets for hours at a stretch, plunge baths, sitz baths, and standing or sitting under a jet of frigid water. Yet in a more general context, practitioners of the water cure stressed a good diet, fresh air, exercise, and the avoidance of heavy medication—a program similar to what Noah Worcester had advised for Lizzie. "The great principle which should never be lost sight of in the treatment of such cases," Worcester had written, "is to improve the general state of the system, and elevate the general health to the highest possible standard."[4] Father seized upon those factors of environment, diet, and dress that might forestall the progress of the disease. With concern that would be echoed in later admonishments to his daughters, he asked Belle to regulate the temperature of her room and avoid "risks of any kind," to attach "shoulder straps on your petticoats so as to keep them off your hips," and to "be careful of your diet" by eating "simple things, well cooked."[5]

He was more than casually interested in finding alternatives to the overbearing methods of aggressive doctors. In 1835, when his first wife, Kitty, fell seriously ill after childbirth, she was dosed with morphine, quinine, and calomel, and her prescribed diet featured porter and oysters. During what proved to be the final two days of her life, doctors led by Daniel Drake, Cincinnati's preeminent physician, drained fifty fluid ounces of blood from the veins of the pitifully failing young woman. Father, away on business during Kitty's last illness and death, carefully reconstructed the details of her treatment on his return. He also studied medical texts, especially some relating to obstetrics and diseases of women, and questioned the approach to medicine that, for all its infliction of misery, had failed to save Kitty. Later, when Dr. Worcester enjoined that the consumptive Lizzie should avoid "all fat and grease of every description, all narcotics as articles of diet or Medicine, every thing in short of a debilitating tendency; especially, the loss of Blood," Father, believing that doctors had in effect bled his first wife to death, was receptive to approaches that shunned the heavy-handed methods of allopathic medicine.[6]

Kitty's demise confirmed spiritual as well as medical precedents in her grieving husband's mind. In his world, if one could not withstand the ravages of terrible disease, one must at least approach death spiritually prepared. Kitty's last moments were spent under interrogation by her father, John Garniss, who roused her to ask, "My daughter, have you thought of God?" and "Are you willing to die, my daughter?" "What grieves me most," Father wrote in his journal in the aftermath of her death, "is that I was not, while my dear wife lived so faithful with her on the subject of religion as I should have been, and I have now no certain assurance that she died in the faith."[7] Again, during Lizzie's final illness it was her husband's "chief employment to care for her. I prayed with her: I read the Bible to her: But oh how defective and insufficient was my performance of this part of my duties." Nevertheless, he noted, "The cloud is fringed with light. She died trusting in Jesus, as I trust, though for eighteen hours before she expired she was able to articulate but three words."[8] If death could not be evaded, then both the expiring patient and those around her had responsibilities to fulfill. In Belle's case, as shown by letters in the pages that follow, her husband hoped that she would maintain a state of spiritual preparation in anticipation of what both of them understood would be the fatal outcome of her disease.

In addition to their similar experience battling tuberculosis, both Lizzie and Belle lost children who died in infancy. Between Kate's birth in 1840 and Lizzie's death five years later, Lizzie bore and lost two daughters, each of whom had her name. And in addition to Nettie, Belle had little Zoe, who was also called Josey and who died shortly after her first birthday while with her mother at Morristown, New Jersey.

Whatever solace Belle had hoped to find under Dr. Dexter's care, after making the rounds of his hydropathic establishments in 1850, she and Nettie traveled to New Orleans with Belle's brother Ben, her sister Charlotte, and Charlotte's husband.[9] Belle, Nettie, and Ben then continued on to Texas to spend the winter with some of their kin along the Gulf Coast. Returning north with the advent of warm weather in 1851, Belle evidently spent the final months of her life in Ohio. Kate already attended Henrietta Haines's school in New York and was by necessity accustomed at an early age to learn of important family events, and to maintain contact with loved ones, by means of written correspondence. A combination of circumstances—Lizzie's and Belle's illnesses, Father's law work and his election to the Senate in 1849, and Kate's attendance at distant boarding schools—contrived to keep members of the family apart much of the time during Kate's and Nettie's formative years. And being apart, they wrote letters.

Belle Chase died on January 13, 1852, her husband's forty-fourth birth-day. Nettie was four years old, Kate eleven. Their father did not marry again.[10]

1. Noah Worcester to Father, Sept. 5, 1842 (Chase Papers, LC); "Family Memoranda" (Chase Papers, LC); *Chase Papers*, 1:170, 188, 189–90; Kelly and Burrage, *Dictionary of American Medical Biography*, 1334.

2. *Chase Papers*, 2:271, 278; "Family Memoranda" (Chase Papers, LC).

3. *Chase Papers*, 1:224; 2:272, 286, 297, 302; Harry B. Weiss and Howard R. Kemble, *The Great American Water-Cure Craze: A History of Hydropathy in the United States* (Trenton, N.J.: Past Times Press, 1967), 128–29, 138–39, 146–50; Susan E. Cayleff, *Wash and Be Healed: The Water-Cure Movement and Women's Health* (Philadelphia: Temple University Press, 1987), 78–79, 98–99. Another prominent water-cure doctor admitted that "consumption, true developed consumption, can seldom, very seldom be cured by any means earthly." Joel Shew, *The Water-Cure Manual: A Popular Work* . . . (New York: Fowlers and Wells, 1849), 224.

4. Worcester to Father, Sept. 5, 1842 (Chase Papers, LC). For hydropathy in a larger medical and historical context, and particularly its appeal to women of families prominent in social and political reform, see Cayleff, *Wash and Be Healed*, 3–9, 17–39, 52–53, 148, and Weiss and Kemble, *Great American Water-Cure Craze*, chap. 5.

5. Father to Belle, Jan. 2, 1850, in *Chase Papers*, 2:272–73.

6. Worcester to Father, Sept. 5, 1842 (Chase Papers, LC); *Chase Papers*, 1:87–93, 96, 99–100, 103, 104.

7. Father later noted the details of a similar conversation that the dying Noah Worcester had with those keeping vigil at his bedside. *Chase Papers*, 1:92–93, 97, 191–92.

8. *Chase Papers*, 2:121.

9. Ibid., 2:309.

10. "Family Memoranda" (Chase Papers, LC).

ELIZA TO FATHER

Cumberland, June 22nd. 1844.

My Dear Husband

I have postponed writing for half a day considering, whether I should tell you the real state of my health or not. I believe on the whole it is best always to be candid and speak the truth. You must not be alarmed at what I say for there is no occasion for it. I have taken cold I think and do not feel near as well as I did when I left home. I cough incessantly and am taking something all the time, nights I rest but very little on account of my cough. I expectorate a great deal of thick heavy phlegm. My appetite is very poor, and I am afraid to eat scarcely any thing at all on account of a very severe pain I have in my chest. I seem to be relieved of this pain when riding. The day we were on the Brownsville boat was my sickest. I had a high fever all day, and night, but the moment I got into the stage I felt better and were it not for the bad nights I have, I think I would be as well if not better than when I started. I am confident when this additional cold goes off I shall improve.

I feel rather uncomfortable travelling in this state, but I do not feel any uneasiness about myself at all.

I do not want you to think from this that I wish you to come to me, or that I wish to go home. I am sure I shall be better than I am now, and may improve very much. You must not think that I have been imprudent. I have been as careful as possible, and every one has been careful for me. Mrs Wiggins even neglects herself I think to attend to me.[1] She is exceedingly attentive and kind. We took two days for our ride, the morning of yesterday it rained, we waited for the afternoon and had a very pleasant ride. We arrived here last night and intend taking the cars in the morning.[2] We shall stay one day in Baltimore I suppose. You do not know how quiet and contented and submissive I am, one would think me almost a saint. You would hardly know me. No one would ever believe that I was ever tyranicul, ever scolded, or ever fretted. So far I have been benefitted by travelling. Tell Alice I miss her very much.[3] How anxious I do feel to hear from you all. I trust all will be right when I do hear. My dear dear little children I am almost crazy to hear from them. I talk about them so long sometimes that I find no one listening to me, but that is no matter it does me good. I suppose Jane has entirely recovered.[4] You must not expect to hear any thing very interesting in my letters untill I get stronger and can write about something else besides myself. We get along very pleasantly indeed. The house we are staying at is called the United States Hotel. It is a delightful house.

I believe I will not write often it makes me want to see you so much. I miss you more than I can begin to tell. Nothing is half so pleasant to me as it would be if you were along. But I am anticipating your going with me next winter. How I do wish your business was such that we would never be separated. Remember me to Mr Ball and his wife.[5] Give my compliments to Dr Worcester, tell him I am sorry I am not as well as he anticipated.[6] Remember me to Mr Melen.[7]

Kiss the children for me, and give my best love to Alice and Jane. How does little Maria[8] and Kate get along. Do not let my letters go out of your hands to any one, for I do not wish any one to read them but yourself. My hand trembles so I can scarcely guide my pen. Read them or parts of them if any wish to hear.[9]

Your affectionate wife
Lizzie Chase

Library of Congress.

1. Cornelia Wiggins, the wife of Cincinnati businessman Samuel Wiggins. She died in 1845. *Chase Papers*, 1:171.

2. Cornelia Wiggins and Eliza had evidently traveled by boat up the Ohio and Monongahela rivers from Cincinnati to Brownsville, Pa., and then along the National Road to Cumberland, Md. In 1842, construction of the Baltimore and Ohio Railroad had reached Cumberland, making it possible to travel by rail from there to Baltimore. James D. Dilts, *The Great Road: The Building of the Baltimore and Ohio, the Nation's First Railroad, 1828–1853* (Stanford, Calif.: Stanford University Press, 1993), 19, 21–22, 277–78; J. G. Pangborn, *Picturesque B. and O.: Historical and Descriptive* (Chicago: Knight and Leonard, 1882), 30–31.

3. Father's sister, Alice Jones Chase.

4. Evidently Father's (and Alice's) sister Janette Logan Chase Skinner, on a visit from her home in Lockport, N.Y. Eliza's and Father's children at the time were Kate, three years old, and their second daughter named Lizzie, who was just a year old and died a little more than a month after her mother wrote this letter. Their first daughter Lizzie had died in infancy in 1842.

5. A native of New York City, Flamen Ball (b. 1809) moved to Cincinnati in 1832 with his wife, Evelina Candler Ball (d. 1864). He studied law at Cincinnati College and in 1838 joined Father in a general law partnership that existed for more than twenty years. Benefiting from Father's rise in public office, Ball was U.S. attorney for the Southern District of Ohio during the Civil War. In 1867, when a new law allowed Father, as chief justice, to recommend registers in bankruptcy, Ball received one of the appointments. A founder of the Young Men's Bible Society, for many years he was a trustee of local common schools and of the Ohio Medical College. Joblin, *Cincinnati Past and Present*, 150–54.

6. In 1838, Noah Worcester (1812–47), a native of New Hampshire who had attended Harvard College and received medical training at Dartmouth, followed his mentor, Dr. Reuben Dimond Mussey, to the Medical College of Ohio in Cincinnati. There Worcester, who had taught anatomy at Dartmouth, occupied the chair of physical diagnosis. He continued his medical study in London and Paris in 1841–42 and on returning to the United States married an old acquaintance, Jane Shedd of Vermont, who suffered from an advanced case of tuberculosis. She died in 1843. Her husband, who accepted the professorship of general pathology at the new Western Reserve College in Cleveland, where he lectured and wrote on dermatology, succumbed to tuberculosis four years later. Kelly and Burrage, *Dictionary of American Medical Biography*, 1334–35.

7. Father and William P. Mellen were considering the possibility of joining in a law partnership, both of them wanting to cultivate clients in eastern cities who needed legal assistance in Cincinnati. Although the merger did not come about, the men remained friends. After the start of the Civil War, Father had his old acquaintance, who then lived in Kentucky, appointed a special treasury agent. Mellen became a supervising special agent in the Ohio and upper Mississippi valleys and, by the end of the Civil War, chief agent of all the Treasury's special agencies. He also supplied Father with political intelligence and advice. Simpson et al., *Advice after Appomattox*, 32; Father to Mellen, July 2, 1844 (Clara H. Mellen Papers, Bowdoin College); Mellen to Father, Oct. 28, 1844 (Chase Papers, LC); Mellen to Father, Dec. 24, 1844, Sept. 24, Dec. 10, 1859 (Chase Papers, HSP); *Chase Papers*, 1:316, 430; 3:66, 83–85, 374–75; 4:65–66, 285–91, 421–22.

8. Maria J. Southgate, Kate's cousin.

9. This letter was postmarked at Cumberland on June 23. Father endorsed it "Mrs Chase" and "Went East day after recg it—Recd. Thursday June 27, 44 / Left Home June 28 " ." He reached New York City on July 2. Lizzie was then in Connecticut, evidently the final destination of her journey. Father to William P. Mellen, July 2, 1844 (Clara H. Mellen Papers, Bowdoin College).

KATE TO FATHER AND BELLE

Cin: Nov 18. 1846

Dear Father—

I am very sorry that poor man got killed by the engine

Aunt Alice is well—How soon will you be back. I hope that Mother is well and you are too

The little Curly lap dog is dead; but I am goin to have a straight haired one with red eyes.

They are all well here.

Your Affec daughter
C. J. Chase

Dear Mother.
> I will write you a few words. I wish to see you very much & father too.[1]
>> Your Affec Daughter.
>> C. J. Chase

Probably in the hand of Alice Jones Chase. Library of Congress.

1. Father and Belle Ludlow had married twelve days earlier, on Nov. 6, 1846. Lizzie Chase had died on Sept. 29, 1845, at the age of twenty-three. "Family Memoranda" (Chase Papers, LC). Although we do not have his reply, Father endorsed this letter as "Ansd.," recording its author as "C. J. Chase."

FATHER TO BELLE

Delevan House,[1] Albany, Aug. 19. 1849

Well, my dearest Belle, I do think that people get through the world—at least over its superficies—about as fast as can be reasonably desired. Here I am at Albany—and here I have been ever since three oclock this morning: having left Cincinnati at 3 oclock Thursday afternoon, making the whole distance in sixty hours—a distance of nearly 800 miles. If we had arrived in Buffalo half an hour earlier, we should have been in time for the first train from that place east, and might have reached New York at the same time that we reached Albany. However I was not anxious to be so whisked through—but, on the contrary well pleased to have a chance to wash myself, according to my manner, and eat a quiet breakfast in Buffalo, before starting, for which the delay till the 9 oclock train gave us opportunity.

On the road here I saw of course very little of the country. The glimpses I caught of it were enough to shew me a constant series of villages; from one to the other of which we were hurled along, so rapidly, that we scarce seemed out of one before semianimate monster of a locomotive screamed out that we were just entering another. All countries almost and almost all ages find their representatives along the route. Attica and Batavia, Syracuse and Rochester, Rome & Utica, Albion & Schenectady—remind the traveller of Greece & Holland—Sicily and England—Italy & Africa—the Seagirt isle & the Indian forest home. If some old gentleman—an educated Rip Van Winkle of 1749—after a century sleep could be placed behind a locomotive and whisked through these towns, and told their names, would he not think that Satan himself had got him, and was taking him zig zag round the world?

What a country it is! and what a development does it exhibit! How anxious may we well be for its future! And yet what is there for us to do, but asking wisdom and guidance from on high, fulfil the duties which the *present* imposes and leave the events of the future, in faith & hope, to the Allwise and All Merciful Disposer.

This morning I went to church—and to the Presbyterian hoping to hear my old friend Dr. Campbell.[2] But a stranger preached. After the services I learned that Dr. Campbell was at Lake George, and would not return before the first week in September. I feel I have not spent this Sunday as I ought. I have allowed myself to look over some news papers which Mr. OReilly brought in,[3] and their contents diverted my mind much from the appropriate topics of the day. I see no warrant in the New Testament for rigid Sabbatarianism; but I do think that, while the New Testament requires us to hallow all time, and maintain constant communion with God by the offering of the Christian sacrifices of prayer & thanksgiving, the merciful provision of the day of rest ought to be used exclusively for the preparation of the heart for this Christian communion during the days of toil & care; and that all reading, which does not belong to such a purpose & action should be laid aside. I pray that I may be enabled henceforward to conform my conduct more closely to my own convictions.

You know that sometime since I commenced committing portions of the Scripture. I have since then committed about twelve chapters—the first six of Proverbs and the six which constitute the Epistle to the Ephesians. I think this Exercise very valuable—though my memory is neither ready enough nor retentive enough to enable me to profit so much from it as many would. I mean, however, to persevere, and would earnestly recommend it to you.

I intended before I left home to speak to you on the subject of maintaining family prayer in my absence; but neglected to do so. I do wish you keep up this service. As you would probably be embarrassed in extempore prayer I would recommend the form of Family Prayer you will find in the prayer book as one of the best I know of.[4] It is of great importance that religious services should not be intermitted because one of the heads of the family is absent: and you, especially, able as you are to conduct it, have no excuse for the omission. Do think of this, and, if you agree with me, take the first opportunity of saying that you will continue family prayer as usual notwithstanding my absence, and commence, at once, on the next morning. You will derive great benefit from it every way, and when once you have begun, will find the duty easy & pleasant.

Give my best love to all and believe me,

Your affectionate husband,
S: P: Chase

P.S. You will wonder that I say nothing as to our destination & route; but the reason is that it is undetermined. I have heard that the gentleman— Professor Henry,—whose testimony I wished to take first was, day before yesterday, in Boston,—instead of Washington where he resides—and we may, if we learn in the morning that he is still there proceed at once to that point.[5]

P.S. Monday. We go this evening by River to New York.

Library of Congress.

1. E. C. Delevan opened his Albany hotel in 1845. Originally operated as a temperance establishment, it came to be known not only as a fine hotel but as a favorite meeting site of New York state politicians. George Rogers Howell and Jonathan Tenney, *Bi-Centennial History of Albany: History of the County of Albany, N.Y., from 1609 to 1886* (New York: W. W. Munsell & Co., 1886), 651.

2. As early as 1829 Father attended—and critically assessed—sermons by John Nicholson Campbell, who was then the popular minister of the New York Avenue Presbyterian Church in Washington. Also that year Father made note of Campbell's role in bringing out the Peggy Eaton scandal that agitated Washington society during Andrew Jackson's first term. For Father to call Campbell his "old friend" would seem to indicate that the two became personally acquainted sometime before Father left Washington for Cincinnati in March 1830. The following year, the clergyman accepted the pulpit of the First Presbyterian Church of Albany. *Appletons'*, 1:514; *Chase Papers*, 1:4, 22–23; 2:43–44.

3. In 1845, Rochester, N.Y., newspaper editor Henry O'Reilly contracted to develop telegraph lines for Samuel F. B. Morse and his agent, Amos Kendall. O'Reilly's formation of his own company spawned litigation by Morse and his associates over franchise rights and a claim that O'Reilly's telegraph equipment infringed on Morse's patent. Father acted as one of O'Reilly's attorneys in the protracted legal contest, and Edwin M. Stanton, later Father's colleague on the Cabinet, worked on a financial reorganization of O'Reilly's venture. O'Reilly won the initial court action over the contract but in 1848 lost in federal district court on the patent issue. The matter finally reached the U.S. Supreme Court on appeal. In 1854 the high court ruled in Morse's favor on most points but did not allow him to claim exclusive rights to the principles of electromagnetic telegraphy. Marc Rothenberg et al., eds., *The Papers of Joseph Henry*, vol. 7 (Washington, D.C.: Smithsonian Institution Press, 1996), 174–75, 601–2; *Chase Papers*, 1:214–15, 216, 222, 235; *DAB*, 14:52–53.

4. American Episcopalians used a Book of Common Prayer adapted from the 1662 standard of the Church of England. The American book included morning and evening prayers for use in private family worship. An 1845 version of the prayer book was the American church's standard until 1871. William McGarvey, *Liturgiae Americanae; or the Book of Common Prayer as Used in the United States of America Compared with the Proposed Book of 1786 and with the Prayer Book of the Church of England, and an Historical Account and Documents* (Philadelphia: Sunshine Pub. Co., 1895), lv, lxix–lxxi, 404–11.

5. For a deposition to be used in the O'Reilly case, Father sought Joseph Henry, who directed the recently founded Smithsonian Institution and had performed seminal research on both the principles of electromagnetism and their application to the telegraph. Father finally located Henry in September at a base camp outside Portland, Maine, collecting data with Alexander Dallas Bache of the Coast Survey. Henry, who thought Morse's claims too broad but regretted being pulled into the dispute, lamented the two days he had to spend "with Mr chase in the Library" of the American Academy of Arts and Sciences in Boston to answer Father's painstaking inquiries. For his part, Father considered Henry "a fine specimen of humanity," and later, when as chief justice he served as a regent and the chancellor of the Smithsonian, the two enjoyed a cordial relationship. *ANB*, 10:613–15; Rothenberg et al., *Papers of Henry*, 599–602; *Chase Papers*, 2:254–55; 5:144, 300; Memorandum Book, 1864–69 (Chase Papers, HSP).

FATHER TO BELLE

Washington, January 6, 1850.

My dearest Belle,

I have no report from you yet today, for no morning mail has reached Washington from any place east of Baltimore.[1] The reason is that the

Philadelphia & Washington Trains failed to connect at Baltimore. I hope a very good account of you is on its way and will reach me by the evening mail.

I opened the New Testament this morning at these words: "If ye endure chastening, God *dealeth with you as with sons;* for what son is he whom his father chasteneth not? But if ye be without chastisement, whereof *all* are partakers, then are ye bastards, and not sons. Furthermore, we have had *fathers of our flesh* which *corrected* us and we gave <u>*them*</u> *reverence:* shall we not <u>*much rather*</u> be in subjection unto the *Father of Spirits* and live? For *they,* verily, for a few days chastened us *after their own pleasure;* but *He,* <u>*for our profit,*</u> that we might be <u>*partakers of His Holiness.*</u> Now *no chastening,* for the present, seemeth to be *joyous,* but *grievous;* nevertheless, *afterward,* it yieldeth the <u>*peaceable fruit of righteousness*</u> unto them which are exercised thereby."[2]

How full of comfort is this passage! Read it my dear wife, and the chapter (12th Hebrews) from which it is taken, & join me in prayer that it may be blessed to us. How it rebukes our lack of faith in dwelling so much on the grievousness of the present chastisement and in looking so little to the fruit of righteousness, which requires this torrid heat for its ripening. May you, my precious wife, find your trial drawing you nearer and nearer to your Savior, so that you may even desire to depart and be with Christ, though willing, if such be His holy will, to abide in the flesh for usefulness in His Service and for the joy of those dear to you. I trust God's purpose concerning you is the restoration of your health. That will, indeed, be a rich—a transcendant blessing:—but, it will be a richer & more transcendant blessing, if, with renovated health He shall please to give you renovated faith & penitence which will lead you to a more entire consecration of yourself to His service than you ever before attained. To this end let the season of sickness be with you a season of much selfexamination, searching of the scriptures, and prayer; and may the peace of God be shed abroad in your heart, so that when you shall have regained your health, as I trust you will, you will feel, indeed, that "it is good to have been afflicted."

I am still at the National.[3] Yesterday I had my things brought down from Dr. Bailey's, and spent some little time in putting them into some kind of order.[4] I shall not remain, here, long however. I do not like the place; though, in many respects, I am quite comfortable. Dr. Bailey was here a few moments ago. He is quite out of patience with the servility of Northern Men, and wants the Freesoilers to speak out more strongly than ever in condemnation of slavery. He is for abandoning defensive operations, and carrying the war into Africa.[5] It is probable that he may be gratified, in some degree, tomorrow; for Hale intends to speak on Cass' Resolution in relation to suspension of diplomatic relations with Austria on which its author was speaking, when I wrote you on Friday.[6]

How I wish I could look into your little room and see what you are about at this moment. I suppose you are eating your dinner. I hope you have a good appetite—though it is hardly to be expected that you have a good one. That you may have some more than you had, I hope, it is not unreasonable to expect. Dr. Dexter writes me that he has consented to your taking the Cod Liver Oil, once, for an experiment, in wine. I hope you have not found the experiment injurious. Taking it in capsules will be best, I believe; and, I suppose, the Doctor has got these for you by this time; as Mr. Garniss writes me that Rushton & Co of New York wrote the Doctor on Thursday informing him where he could get them in Philadelphia.[7] Mr. Garniss writes me that Delia Austen is in very delicate health and is, also, taking the cod liver oil. So you have company you see in this misery.

I hope I find your little carriage just the thing. Have you got the new front curtain? It was to have been ready, Thursday Evening: and was to be made to fit accurately to the carriage, which the one you had at first did not, and to be well lined so as to make it perfectly comfortable.

Yesterday was a very beautiful day here. I hope you enjoyed it. Today the sky is clouded, but the temperature is not disagreeable. I suppose you ride every day. You should ride just as much as you possibly can, without fatiguing yourself—morning & afternoon, if possible.

I send you a letter from Dun[8] which I took the liberty of opening. Love and kisses for the children.[9]

Ever your affectionate husband,
S: P: Chase

Library of Congress.

1. Father was writing Belle on a daily basis. He had spent Christmas with her and escorted her to the Parkeville Hydropathic Institute in New Jersey. Extremely anxious about the state of her health, he hoped that she might improve there under the care of Dr. George Dexter. Leaving Parkeville on January 2, after a brief stopover in Philadelphia he proceeded to Washington and resumed his place in the Senate on the third. Elected to the Senate by the Ohio legislature in February 1849, he took the oath of office the next month during a special session. He was back in Washington after the first full session of the 31st Congress convened in December 1849 before he joined Belle for the holidays. Father to Belle, Jan. 2, 3, 4, 5, 7, 1850 (Chase Papers, LC); *Chase Papers*, 1:xxvii; 2:229–36, 265–76.

2. Hebrews 12:7–11. In his letter to Belle of Dec. 14, 1851 (below), Father quoted an adjacent verse to reiterate the same theme.

3. The National Hotel in Washington. *Chase Papers*, 1:403.

4. Gamaliel Bailey, Father's close contemporary in age and his fraternal ally in the antislavery cause, was educated as a physician and practiced medicine early in his career, but made his name as a newspaper editor and political activist. Originally from New Jersey and Philadelphia, he moved to Cincinnati in 1832. There he became committed to the opposition to slavery and, drawing on previous experience as an editor, in 1836 became James G. Birney's assistant on the *Philanthropist*, succeeding to the editorship of that paper the next year. He played a very active role in organizing and mobilizing the Liberty, and subsequently the Free Soil, political movement and relocated to Washington in 1847 to edit the new *National Era*. In that capacity he encouraged such writers as Harriet Beecher Stowe, whose *Uncle Tom's Cabin* first appeared in the *Era* as a serial in 1851. Until his death in 1859,

Bailey's home served as the regular gathering place of antislavery politicians as well as authors who contributed to the *Era.* Early in 1851 he and his large family took up residence on C Street, in a large house that some critics decried as opulent. *ANB,* 1:881–82; Harrold, *Bailey,* 133–34, 141, 142–43, 195–96.

5. Roman generals finally countered Hannibal's invasion of Italy during the Second Punic War by abandoning a defensive strategy based on delay and mounting an offensive strike against the Carthaginians' own homeland. The allusion so appealed to Father that he used it at least twice again with reference to political strategy in August 1852. *Chase Papers,* 2:348–49.

6. The resolution, introduced by Lewis Cass of Michigan, protested Austria's crushing of the Hungarian independence movement led by Louis (Lajos) Kossuth. Cass, a Democrat who advocated granting the Western territories "popular sovereignty" on the slavery question, spoke at length on the resolution on Friday, January 4. Father wrote to Belle while sitting in the Senate chamber that day, abruptly ending his letter as Cass spoke because "I must listen to him." Three days later Free Soiler John Parker Hale of New Hampshire, who like Father had been elected to the Senate by a combination of Whigs and "Independent" Democrats in his state's legislature, offered an amendment to condemn Russia along with Austria. *Congressional Globe,* 31st Cong., 1st sess., 1850, 103–6, 113–15, app., 54–58; Donald S. Spencer, *Louis Kossuth and Young America: A Study of Sectionalism and Foreign Policy, 1848–1852* (Columbia, Mo.: University of Missouri Press, 1977), 31–34; *ANB,* 4:546–47; *DAB,* 8:105–7; Father to Belle, Jan. 4, 1850 (Chase Papers, LC).

7. Rushton, Clare & Co., the Manhattan firm of druggist William L. Rushton, had two locations on Broadway and one in the Astor House. *Doggett's New York City Directory, for 1850–1851* (New York: John Doggett Jr., 1850), 435.

8. James Dunlop Ludlow.

9. Nine-year-old Kate; Nettie, who had turned two the previous September; and Josephine ("Zoe"), born the previous July.

FATHER TO BELLE

Washington, Feb. 28, 1850

My Dearest Belle,

I saw your Aunt McLean this morning.[1] She said she had just recd. a letter from you, & that you wished her to take Catharine home with her.[2] I thought it had been determined when I left you that Catharine should remain, at least, until some time in April; and I told Mrs McLean so. She said that in that case she would not visit you at Parkeville but proceed directly to New York. I want you to write her immediately, or rather have Dun write, for you *must not* exert yourself much—you *should not* at all—in writing; and let me know whether there is any change in your wish as regards Catharine. *It seems to me* very important that she should remain. You may think yourself capable of the additional fatigue which the care of the children would impose on you. But remember that you are apt to *presume* a little on your strength, and have had some severe warnings against *presuming too much.* You are far from well, and, though decidedly improving, you might by what would *seem,* to you, a slight matter arrest the progress of improvement, and reinstate all the unfavorable symptoms.

If you let Catharine go you must have another nurse, and whom can you get at present. Find one first. Keep Catharine Egan where she is if you can. Get a good nurse whom you can confide in & then Catharine can return home if she wishes. But this movement is too sudden. You cannot transfer Catharine Egan to the children, and run the risk of any attendant you may pick up for yourself. It will never do.

Your own,

S. P. C.

Library of Congress.

1. Sarah Bella Ludlow McLean.
2. We know practically nothing about Catharine McDonald, the children's nurse discussed in this letter. If she had a connection to the McLeans through kinship, employment, or otherwise, it could account for the fact that she did not accompany the Chases on their departure from Washington in May 1850, when she "grieved to part with her little Nettie whom she had nursed so long." At that time the family's entourage included an unidentified "nurse," perhaps the Catharine Egan mentioned later in this letter as Belle's own "attendant." If so, and if her responsibilities shifted during 1850 from Belle to the children, then Egan was probably the Catharine referred to in Father's letter to Kate of Sept. 10, 1851 (below). The spelling of both women's names as "Catharine" was likely Father's doing and may not reflect how either of them would have rendered the name. *Chase Papers,* 1:223.

FATHER TO BELLE

Washington Mar. 8, 1850.

My dearest Belle,

I feel extremely concerned about little Zoe.[1] I wish I could be with you, and unless the intelligence is more satisfactory tomorrow I mean to come tomorrow night. It is, indeed, very desirable to me to remain here *now*, but I cannot bear to be absent from you, if she is dangerously ill.

Let me beg of you dearest, not to expose yourself. Such exposure will do Zoe no good, and yourself much harm. I entreat you not to do so. Remember how precious your health is to me and all of us. Remember that in your present state a little over fatigue, broken rest, or exposure may bring on your disease in an aggravated and most dangerous form. Be careful—exceedingly careful.

As to your baths, as long as you suffer no immediate ill effects from them, which are perceptible, but gain 2½ lbs per week, I think you had better follow orders. Keep the Doctor[2] constantly advised of your symptoms, and the effects of the baths. Is there not some mistake about 2½ lbs;—surely you can hardly have gained so much as that.

I am very glad the horse pleases you so much. I wonder if a good match could not be found for him, and then when you are able to come to Washington again you could have your own horses.

Your own affectionate

S: P: Chase

Library of Congress.

1. Their youngest child, Josephine Ludlow Chase.
2. George T. Dexter.

FATHER TO BELLE

Washington, Mar. 16, 1850.

My dearest Belle,

Your good resolutions and your improving health almost equally gratify me. May God bless you in both.

You will, indeed, have much time at Parkeville for reading and I shall be very glad to have you improve it by making yourself acquainted with as many useful works as you can. I wish especially you would read American History, and the English Classics both in prose and poetry. You need the knowledge of our History daily & an acquaintance with the classics—I mean the Spectator, the Rambler, the Essays of Elia & the like in prose[1]—& Milton, Cowper, Pope & the like in poetry[2]—will be a great help to you in the art of composition.

These greater things being attended to you must not neglect the less—I mean penmanship and spelling & punctuation. I wish you would imitate Dun's resolution of perseverance in forming a good hand. A few years ago his was bad as yours. Now it could hardly be improved. Formerly he made frequent mistakes in spelling—now he rarely makes one. I was sorry to notice in your last letter such errors as "*tewsday*" for Tuesday. Attention while writing—keeping your mind engaged on what you are about—will enable you to detect & and correct these inaccuracies.

My cold is much better. It has neither disturbed my rest, nor impaired my appetite nor detained me from any duty. Of course, it has not been serious. I am still ignorant when I shall speak. I have in fact very little time to get ready in. But I must speaky,[3] ready or unready.[4]

You must not walk to fatigue—but dont forego the exercise of walking. You need it, and will find yourself gradually able to extend your excursions.

Ever your own
S. P. C.

Library of Congress.

1. Joseph Addison and Richard Steele first published the *Spectator,* a compendium of essays on literature and criticism, as a daily paper in 1711–12. Among the other English writers influenced by their work was Samuel Johnson, who composed his own series of periodical essays, the *Rambler,* in 1750–52. Beginning in 1820 Charles Lamb assumed the pen name "Elia" to contribute a renowned run of essays to the new *London Magazine.* They were published in book form in 1823 and 1833. Pat Rogers, *The Samuel Johnson Encyclopedia* (Westport, Conn.: Greenwood Press, 1996), 321–22, 376; *ODNB,* 32:262.
2. John Milton, William Cowper, and Alexander Pope.
3. So written.
4. Without seniority and as part of the small Free Soil contingent in the Senate, Father had little control over when he might contribute to the debate over the measures that became the Compromise of 1850. He opposed the proposed legislative package, which had been the subject of Senate debate since early February, as an establishment of slavery in the Western territories. He finally got his chance on March 26–27, when he delivered his major speech, "Union and Freedom, without Compromise," which looked to the Northwest Ordi-

nance of 1787 as an embodiment of the notion that the territories should remain free of slavery. *Congressional Globe*, 31st Cong., 1st sess., 1850, app., 468–80.

FATHER TO KATE

Senate Chamber, July 22, 1850

My dearest little daughter,

I have received your Journal of two days.[1] It is quite as good as I could expect from you as a first effort. I look, however, for great improvement, and shall expect you to copy and send me your journal every week.

I hope you enjoy yourself very much. Miss Haines is very kind to you and your companions will be very kind if you are kind to them.[2] It is a beautiful principle which God, in his goodness, has implanted in the human heart, that she who thinks least of her own and most of others' convenience, will always be happiest. A selfish girl can never be a happy girl. I hope if you feel, as no doubt you often do, for we are all naturally selfish, risings of selfishness in your own heart you strive to suppress and ask God to help your endeavors.

I want you to be as active, and as much in the open air as possible. You must get all the strength you can in the country to carry with you to the city.

I had a very interesting letter the other day from Ruhamah. She seems to be learning very fast and improving greatly. She and Josey are both at Mr. Burnets near Cincinnati and both are very well. Mr. Burnet [calls] his place Hygeia, for the meaning of which word you must ask Miss Haines.[3]

I had a letter this morning from your dear mother. Her health is improving. Kate Ludlow is still with her.[4] Nettie has had a bowel-complaint, caused by eating green fruit. Josey is improving.[5]

Give my best regards to Mrs Haines and Miss Sallie McGrew.[6]

Your affectionate father,
S: P: Chase

Historical Society of Pennsylvania.

1. We have not located Kate's journal from this period.
2. The head of Kate's school, Henrietta Brown Haines (1816–78) was the youngest of seven children of a New York City family. Her siblings included reformer and philanthropist Sarah Platt Haines Doremus and their older brother, Daniel Haines, a former governor of New Jersey who became a justice of the state's supreme court. In 1872 Henrietta Haines brought European educator Maria Boelté (later Kraus-Boelté) to the United States and sponsored Boelté's first efforts to promote Friedrich Froebel's kindergarten system in America. Wheeler, *Ogden Family*, 249, 364, 365; *Nat. Cyc.*, 13:467.
3. In 1850, Belle Chase's sisters Ruhamah and Josephine turned seventeen and twelve years of age, respectively. Their sister Kate had been a student at the same school in 1846–47. David Staats Burnet was the son of Isaac Burnet, Nicholas Longworth's law partner and the mayor of Cincinnati for twelve years, and a nephew of Ohio politician Jacob Burnet, who in 1830 had advised a young Salmon P. Chase on the prospects of beginning a career as an attorney in Cincinnati. D. S. Burnet left the Presbyterian church while still in his teens and became a Disciples of Christ preacher, educator, and periodicals editor. Although lacking in

formal education, he learned Latin, Greek, and natural science, and by the early 1840s he established the Hygeia Female Atheneum about seven miles from Cincinnati. His wife, Mary Gano Burnet, was also involved in the school, which offered, in addition to its regular curriculum, instruction in music, French, and art. Burnet evidently gave up full-time supervision of the school after 1844, when he became the pastor of a church in Cincinnati, but for some years thereafter he continued to be in residence at the institution he called "Mt. Healthy" as well as "Hygeia." W. T. Moore, ed., *The Living Pulpit of the Christian Church: A Series of Discourses, Doctrinal and Practical, from Representative Men among the Disciples of Christ* (Cincinnati: R. W. Carroll, 1869), 33–46; Alanson Wilcox, *A History of the Disciples of Christ in Ohio* (Cincinnati: Standard Publishing Co., 1918), 343; Noel L. Keith, *The Story of D. S. Burnet: Undeserved Obscurity* (St. Louis, Mo.: Bethany Press, 1954), 17–21, 62, 103, 133, 135; *Chase Papers*, 1:42; statement of account with Catherine Ludlow Baker, Feb. 10, 1852, or after (Chase Papers, LC).

4. In the spring of 1850 Belle's sister Catherine traveled to Washington escorted by their uncle by marriage, John McLean. In May she went to Northampton, Mass., and stayed there with Belle until the first week of July, when they relocated to Morristown, N.J. Statement of account with Catherine Ludlow Baker, Feb. 10, 1852, or after (Chase Papers, LC).

5. Nettie's and Kate's baby sister, Josephine.

6. As is clear from this and other references in the correspondence, Sallie McGrew was one of Kate's schoolmates in New York. Sixteen years old in 1850, Sallie was the daughter of Cincinnati silversmith and jeweler Wilson McGrew. Her mother, Sarah McGrew, had died when Sallie was very young, and Sallie treated Evelina Ball, the wife of Father's law partner, as a surrogate mother. Henrietta Haines's mother, Mary Ogden Haines (1778–1852), was the widow of merchant Elias Haines, who had died in 1824. John Garniss described her as "lively" and "elegant." Beckman, *In-depth Study of Cincinnati Silversmiths*, 93–94; interment record for Sallie B. Williams, Spring Grove Cemetery, Cincinnati; *Chase Papers*, 1:87; 2:309; Wheeler, *Ogden Family*, 249.

FATHER TO BELLE

Washington July 28, 1850.

My dearest Belle,

I know your heart must bleed under the sad affliction which Mr. Baker's despatch has just informed me of. But be consoled my own sweet wife. Our dear little Zoe suffers no longer.[1] Her portion of pain is over forever. Few & evil have the days of her pilgrimage been, and yet while I write the words with tearful eyes and a sad-sad heart, the spirit speaks to itself and says How know you that her few days were evil. The Lord loveth whom he chasteneth—and who shall say that the sufferings of that patient little one were not intended to prepare her for the fullness of joy on which she is now entered.

Surely I do not weep for her. She is happier now than either of us could be were all the blessings which we covet ours; and she is spared a life of sickness and suffering which might have and very probably would have been hers had she lived. When I think of such instances as your Aunt Clarkson's poor Margaret, and remember the fear that would sometimes intrude in spite of me that little Zoe would never be well, and, though I did not anticipate any *such* destiny for her, might always be a sufferer from disease of the heart and never able to develope her mental powers, I cannot but feel almost glad that she is safe in the bosom of her God and Savior.

I fear the effect of her death on you: but, dearest, do not look on the dark side only. Think of the bright side also. Remember our little one as suffering and sick; think of her as rejoicing and bright, where disease comes not. Bless God for this exceeding consolation which brightens with celestial glories the clouds of sorrow. I would hasten to you immediately; if my presence were really required. But I must not at this moment allow private grief to withdraw me from my public duties. The great questions which we have been discussing all winter approach their decision. A single vote may be of vast consequence. It may be required tomorrow. Almost certainly it will be wanted on Tuesday or Wednesday. These questions once decided I shall come to you.[2] Meantime, dearest, remember how unspeakably precious your own health is to me, and that indulged grief may be hurtful to you. Be cheerful, therefore, in your submission to God's will. Continue your exercise. Take all possible care of yourself. Today I thought I could look *with faith* to God for your recovery. May God give me more faith, even that faith which will assure a favora[*torn*] answer to my prayers for you.

Mr. Bakers despatch says that little Zoe was to be buried this evening at 6 oclock. It is now past eight. Would that I could have been with you! Should it be yet possible I shall wish to take some measures when I come for her removal to Cincinnati where my other little ones lie.

Goodnight, dearest. May God Almighty, our Father, bless, comfort and restore you.

Your own affectionate
S. P. C.

Library of Congress.

1. Josephine Ludlow Chase died on this day. Father apparently received the news from the otherwise unidentified Mr. Baker who late in 1850 married Belle's sister Catherine Ludlow (see appendix).

2. During the next few days the Senate debated and voted on amendments to the "Omnibus" bill that incorporated the various compromise measures—governments for California and New Mexico territories, resolution of the Texas boundary, the status of slavery in the District of Columbia, and a fugitive slave law. As the bill neared a final vote on Wednesday, July 31, Father attempted in vain to have it postponed indefinitely. The Omnibus crumbled anyway on that day when its managers could not successfully reinsert one of its measures. The compromise passed Congress in the subsequent weeks as a series of bills rather than a single piece of legislation. *Congressional Globe*, 31st Cong., 1st sess., 1850, 1474, 1481–82, 1490–91; app., 1470–85; David M. Potter, *The Impending Crisis: 1848–1861*, completed and ed. by Don E. Fehrenbacher (New York: Harper & Row, 1976), 99–100, 107–11.

FATHER TO BELLE

Washington City,
Senate Chamber, July 29, 1850: Monday

My dearest Belle,

I received only this morning the notes of Kate[1] and yourself written on Friday. I have come to the Senate Chamber today hoping that the question upon the Omnibus Bill may be taken today. It may be, but the prospect is not very favorable. Gen Houston, however, has suggested to me that he may wish to pair off for a few days; and I have told him that I will if he desires it.[2] I shall know this afternoon whether I can come in virtue of either event. If I do, there is hardly any use in this letter, for I shall probably be with you before you get this; if I do not, I fear you will consider this letter as an aggravation of my absence as it will let you know how near I have been to coming, while I have not come.

I hope, dearest Belle, you do not indulge unprofitable grief. Indeed apart from the hope I entertained of the entire recovery of our little Zoe—a hope with which a great deal of fear was mingled—and of her growing up with little Nettie, I cannot feel that there is cause of grief. Happy little angel, how would she now commiserate our mistake, could she know that we grieve for her.[3]

May God bless and recover you, dearest.

Your own
S. P. C.

Library of Congress.

1. Catherine Ludlow.
2. In the complex politics of voting on seemingly innumerable amendments and motions relating to the compromise measures, Father and Sam Houston did not always split their votes. Nevertheless Houston, hero of the Texas war for independence from Mexico and former president of the Republic of Texas, voted staunchly for all components of the compromise, and so he and Father were in opposition on the fundamental questions before the Senate. Both were present for the crucial voting on the compromise during the final days of July. *Congressional Globe*, 31st Cong., 1st sess., 1850, 1481–82; app., 1455–57, 1473, 1479–85; *ANB*, 11:279–81.
3. Father's filing note on this letter includes the notation, "Zoes death."

FATHER TO KATE

Senate Chamber, Aug. 13, 1850[1]

My dearest little Kate,

I am very sorry that you delayed your answer to my letter so long. You should remember that I have very many engagements to attend to and very little time to devote to writing to anyone and very many to write to. You are a little girl and can easily command time to write a journal every day, and can copy that journal once a week and send it to me with a short letter. That is all I have *asked* of you, and this you certainly might have done. I have not *required* even that, for I did not wish to owe to your obedience what I desired to receive from your affection. You have said a good deal in your letters in excuse of your delays and bad writing. I do not like excuses. They are not often strictly true, and they are almost invariably in bad taste.

My dearest child, you do not know how much I grieve whenever you deviate at all from the straight line of duty. I am sure you have an affectionate heart and that you love me sincerely and earnestly. But you are young—very young, and you have not cultivated those habits of self denial which are necessary to enable you to devote regularly some portion of your time to such work as writing a journal daily. I know that such regular employment is sometimes quite irksome, and I make every allowance for you. But I want you to try.

There is another thing which I want to speak to you about. You do not always speak the exact truth. This is a *very-very* bad *habit.* If you do not overcome it, it will grow upon you and will ruin you forever. You must strive against it continually and earnestly, with constant prayer to God for his blessing on your endeavors. You have some peculiar difficulties to contend with. You are naturally somewhat nervous and timid. You fear censure and displeasure. When, therefore, you feel that you have done something for which you may be blamed, you are peculiarly tempted to swerve from the truth in order to conceal or excuse it. Am I not right? If your conscience tells you I am, do, my dear child, strive by all means, to overcome that fear which leads you to do wrong rather than to suffer.

I am very anxious about you. Your dear mother,[2] was extremely solicitous that you should become a sincere, devoted christian; more than anything else do I desire this for you. I want to see you true, gentle, forbearing towards your companions, loving towards all around you—loving your fellows and loving God. Shall not this, my hope be realized? It depends on you, my dear child—for if you earnestly strive, in dependance on God's grace to be what you should be, His assistance will not be wanting.

I went to see your dear mother[3] last week. She was quite weak, though otherwise comfortable and able to ride and walk a good deal. You have not heard yet perhaps of the death of your sweet little sister Josey. She died quite suddenly and unexpectedly, a fortnight ago last Saturday night. She had only been sick a day or two, and seemed not so much to die as to fall asleep. There seemed to be nothing to weep for in her departure, but our loss. That loss however was so deeply felt by your dear mother as to check materially her improvement, and make it necessary for her to change her residence. Accordingly I took her to Schooley's Mountain last Wednesday.[4] Miss Haines is, I believe, well acquainted with this place and can tell you all about it. I left your mother there on Thursday and was here in Washington the next morning. I have heard from her twice since my return and both letters were encouraging. Yesterday Evening I sent her your letter; and, saying this reminds me to say to you that I am well pleased by the improvement in your handwriting which your last letter manifests. Go on to improve and you will soon write an excellent hand. Having found some fault with you in this letter I am glad that I can conclude it with this commendation.

Give my best regards to Miss Haines, and thank Mr. Doremus in my name for his kindness to you.[5]

Your own affectionate father,
S: P: Chase

Historical Society of Pennsylvania.

1. Kate's tenth birthday.
2. Presumably Eliza Chase.
3. Belle.
4. Belle, Kate Ludlow, and Nettie had been in Morristown for about a month before moving to another location in Morris County, Schooley's Mountain, where a mineral spring was located. While there, Belle Chase continued to give her letters the heading "Morristown." *History of Morris County, New Jersey* (New York: W. W. Munsell & Co., 1882), 379–80; statement of account with Catherine Ludlow Baker, Feb. 10, 1852, or after (Chase Papers, LC).
5. Merchant and importer Thomas Cornelius Doremus was married to Henrietta Haines's sister Sarah Platt Haines Doremus, who was several years older than Henrietta. A founder of New York University, he collected a large personal library and helped subsidize the influential role his wife played in progressive social causes, including prison reform and improved medical care for women. William Nelson, *Genealogy of the Doremus Family in America* (Paterson, N.J.: Press Printing, 1897), 92–93; *DAB*, 5:377–78; *ANB*, 6:750.

FATHER TO BELLE

Washington, Aug. 26, 1850.

My dearest wife,

I sent you a letter this morning by the six oclock cars, and about half past nine I received your long letter. It had really, a very formidable appearance, but, apart from the reflection that the effort of writing it must have been rather too much for you, it gave me great pleasure. I thank [our] Heavenly Father that, though he deprives you of health and strength, he gives you a cheerful heart. Trust Him entirely, dearest. He who withheld not His Son but gave Him to die for us shall he not, also, with Him freely give us all things? What though He turns us aside from the path in which we would walk[1] and separates us from the companions we would choose, hereafter when we look back upon the line by which His Providence has led us we shall see that all is right & all was right. Would we *could* trust Him entirely. But want of faith,—which is sin—prevents. Let us strive against that. And meditating upon his goodness, endeavoring to realize his presence & protection, let us humbly cry Lord increase over faith! Help, Lord, our unbelief.

I am half expecting you at Washington. If you do not arrive before day after tomorrow—Thursday—Evening I think I shall be with you on Friday.[2] I am going today to look at some rooms on Capitol Hill, which may suit you. My impression is very strong in favor of your going to Cincinnati or to Texas.[3] But all shall be, if it please God, as you will.

I am very thankful for dear little Netties restora[*torn*] She is a dear sweet little creature. She is too much set on having her own way and has rather too much temper[.] But I think she is disposed to be ingenuous and that [is] a great thing.

I feel anxious about little Kate. She is situated in most respects as well as I could wish—better, I think, than if she were with me. Still I cannot help fearing for her. Her want of truthfulness distresses me greatly. I attribute much of this defect in her character to her nervousness and timidity. She startles at every thing[,] and to avoid danger however slight is apt to make any kind of excuse. May God strengthen her!

Goodbye, dearest.

Your affectionate husband,
S. P. C.

Library of Congress.

1. "Get you out of the way, turn aside out of the path, cause the Holy One of Israel to cease from before us" (Isaiah 30:11).

2. Three days later Father still considered himself bound to attend the Senate's proceedings, apprehensive that key legislation could require votes when several Free Soil senators were absent. He declared, "It is very important that every friend of freedom should be at his post." However, as he indicated on Sept. 5 to Kate (below), he did manage a trip to New York, bringing Belle and Nettie back to Washington on his return. Father to Belle, Aug. 28, 29, 1850 (Chase Papers, LC).

3. He first wrote "Cuba," then crossed it out and substituted "Texas" above the line.

BELLE TO KATE

Morristown Aug 29th 1850

My darling little daughter

Nettié says I must not call you little, because you are a great tall girl, and you are her big sister. There is a good deal in what she says, you are growing so fast. Nettié talks a great deal about you, & if any strangers say they are going to New York, she immediately tells them. her sister Katey is in New York, and they will see her. & sometimes, she wants to go with them to see you. she writes in her own style, a nomber of letters to you, and thinks you will be delighted to get them. The play things you sent her, gives her great amusement and employment. she has a table in the corner, where she has a dinner party two or three times a day. she always invites Charlotte to dine with her.[1] and she will spend a long time arrangeing them. and her dolls also must come, and stands them against the wall.

I have not been well, and have felt so little like writing, that since the death of dear little Zoe I have trusted all my corrispondence to your Father, & aunt Kate.[2] but I imagine they did not tell you any thing particularly about it, As you would like to know, I will tell you. After we left Northampton, she grew so well and strong, that I was sure she would soon sit alone. she was so strong that Charlotte could hardly hold her, whilst I poured watter on her from a pitcher; which the Dr[3] said would strengthen her limbs. she was growing so wise and was good as possable. and on Friday, wakened up in the morning, with high fever. I sent for a Dr who gave her some medicines which seemed to have a good effect. your aunt Kate set up all night. and the next day, she seemed well. went down stairs into the garden, & was glad to see the flowers, when she came up she slept until I went to bed. she was sleeping by my side but in a few moments awoke, and looked at me so intensely, that I took her in my lap while I set in the bed. and in quarter of an hour she had gon to him, who says, suffer little children to come unto me. and forbid them not. for of such, is the kingdom of heaven. I could hardly give her up. but the Lord gave her to me, and she was his to take again. She died with out pain, [*illeg.*] in my lap. she had inflamation of the brain. She is at rest now, and we must not grieve.

Nettié is well, and so fat, that her face looks as broad as it is long; she is as funny as she ever was, and a grand chatterbox. she is now in bed, she goes to bed at seven oclock, but it takes her about twenty minuits, before she can quiet her self enough to go to sleep. she is kicking up her heels, turning summersets, & singing at the top of her voice. I do wish you could see her in her night drawers. she is so droll.

You have not spoken of Sallié McGrew, in any of your last letters, if she is still with Miss Hain's give my love to her.

Good night my dear Katey. I pray constantly that our heavenly Father may watch over you.

Your affectionate Mother
Belle Chase

When you write, tell me Miss Hains address. as I have forgotten it.

Historical Society of Pennsylvania.

1. Charlotte Ludlow Jones. Years later Father would refer to her as Nettie's former "Nurse" (see his letter of Oct. 15, 1866, in chapter 8).
2. Belle's sister, Catherine Ludlow.
3. Perhaps George Dexter, Belle's hydropathic physician.

FATHER TO KATE

Washington City, Sep. 5, 1850.

My dearest little Kate,

You have not in any letter, taken any notice of what I wrote some weeks since on the subject of your negligence in not writing punctually and some other matters. What is the meaning of this? The least it *can* mean is that you are very thoughtless. This thoughtlessness gives me pain and I shall be very glad when you shall have overcome it. You must be aware that your letters are far from giving me the pleasure they would if they were written punctually and with a manifest wish on your part to gratify me by your careful compliance with my advice and recommendations.

I was in New York last Monday, and expected to see you, and was much disappointed when I found you had not returned. I met your mother on my return from New York at Newark and she and Nettie came with me to Washington. Your Aunt Kate went to Weverton.[1]

When you write me better letters, I will try to improve the quality of mine.

Your affectionate father,
S: P: Chase

Historical Society of Pennsylvania.

1. Weverton, Md., a manufacturing town a few miles downriver from Harpers Ferry. Belle's and Kate Ludlow's uncle by marriage, Caspar W. Wever, seeing potential in a site that had abundant water power and was located on both the Baltimore and Ohio Railroad and the Chesapeake and Ohio Canal, had established the town in 1834. Thomas J. C. Williams, *A History of Washington County Maryland,* 2 vols. (Chambersburg, Pa.: J. M. Runk & L. R. Titsworth, 1906; repr., Baltimore, Md.: Regional Publishing Co., 1968), 229, 248.

NETTIE TO KATE

Aunt Wever's
Sep 28th.[1]

Dear Sister Kate.

Our Sweet Mother left here this afternoon, on horseback, for the West—. She hopes to be able to ride all the way to Cincinnati—; She has a very easy going horse—. Uncle Dunlop arrived here on last tuesday for the purpose of accompanying dear Mama home.[2] Uncle Dun's horse is so big, & strong that I might have gone on behind him if they would have let me.

Aunt Kate, & I start with our Cousin[3] On Monday—We will stay at Aunt Charlotte's in the country—until Mother comes. I will be so happy to see Lilly & Aunt Josse—& Luddy, & Josse Jones will be so glad to see me, you must write to me as soon as you receive this direct to Aunt Kate's care[4]— Cummingsville. Hamilton Co. Ohio; We can send to that office every day, as it is so near Uncle Charles'[5]—Aunt Kate is so kind to me, she sends her love to you—I sleep with her—29th[6] this morning when I woke—I got close up to her, & said dear mama—& when I found out it was not her, I cried so hard—but she told me a story, & I soon become pleasant—I have been good all day, but I would not permit Aunt Kate to go to church

Do not fail dear Katy to write soon

to your own Sister *Nettie.*

In Kate Ludlow's hand. Brown University Library.

1. This letter is from September 1850, as confirmed by one from Kate Ludlow to Father of September 29, 1850 (Chase Papers, LC). Nettie was at the Weverton residence of her great aunt, Jane Catherine Dunlop Wever.

2. Belle's escort was her brother, James Dunlop Ludlow. Kate Ludlow learned that when Belle and Dun passed through Harpers Ferry on the twenty-eighth, Belle attracted attention by getting down from her horse to give aid to a little boy who had been injured. A traveler reported that although Belle stopped "but a few moments," she won the acclaim of Harpers Ferry: "She has been talked about all over town—as 'a lady with a most benevolent heart'—'got off to lend all assistance necessary to a boy.'" Ibid.

3. Evidently Catharine Wever Collins, whose husband, William O. Collins, was expected to return through Weverton from a trip to Washington, D.C. Ibid.

4. We have been unable to identify a "Lilly" associated with the Ludlows. The other relatives named here were Charlotte Chambers Ludlow Jones, Josephine Ludlow, Ludlow Jones (later Ap-Jones), and Josephine Jones.

5. Charles A. Jones. Cumminsville or Cummingsville, a name associated with a local post office established in 1844, originated as Ludlow Station, a military outpost built north of Cincinnati in 1790 on a tract of land owned by Belle Chase's grandfather, Israel Ludlow. The city of Cincinnati annexed the town in 1873. Maxwell, *Suburbs*, 170–71; Goss, ed., *Cincinnati*, 2:530; John Hayward, *A Gazetteer of the United States of America* (Philadelphia: James L. Gihon, 1854), 811.

6. Kate Ludlow inserted the date above the line.

BELLE TO KATE

Dec 11th 1850

My dear daughter.

I am a great way off from you, and Pa, and it makes me very sad to think it will be so long befor I can see you.[1] it takes very nearly a month, before I can get a letter from either your father or your self. If you both were with me, I should enjoy myself vastly. The weather is as warm and soft as summer, and flowers are blooming all around; one rose bush, has at least twenty roses on it, and more buds than you can count. If you were here, you could fish in the river close to the house and catch fish and crabs in abundance. Ben shoots geese, and ducks, every day, that swim in the river, within a yard of the door. they are wild, and as soon as any one makes thier appearance away they go. Ben has to creep with out noise near enough to kill them, & even then, they often dive, and the shot glances on the water over them. There are plenty of deer, one morning as I was riding I saw six or eight and got quite near them. they were lieing in the tall grass, & when they heard us, they sprang up and were soon out of sight.

Ben went out on Matagoda bay, in a vessel called a lighter, having two sails. A terrable storm came up, and blew the boat up-on a sand bar where it stuck fast five days, before they could get off. At last, a boat passing, saw thier distress & came to the assistance of the poor mariners. The weather was so cold, that Ben and two of the men had thier feet frozen, and Ben cannot get his boots on yet, although it is a week since; they had no beds, or fire and nothing to eat; but fortunately, I had a couple of barrells of apples, and Ben broke one of them open, and that was all they had to eat or drink for five days. Ben says he will not be a sailor.

Nettié grows very fast. and we often have long talks about you, and think how pleasant it will be, when I am well, and you home from school.

Nett gets quite beyond her self when I talk to her of you, & she jumps about, clapping her little hands, saying oh Katey oh Katey coming home! She was very sea sick as we crossed the Gulf: we had a storm, and were 38 hours longer than we should have been which affected the stoutest stomach. I often laugh now, at the specticle we made. Nett & I on the same berth. both as sick as possable and a wash bason at my side, for Nett or I were vomiting all the time. if she began first, I had to hold her up, and that would start me, & both at once in the same bason, was quite too familiar for Nett's ideas, and she would fight as long as her strenght held out, & then fall back exhausted. Ann, her nurse, was no more use to her or I, than a post, as she was too sick to move. but we got safely to Galveston. & some days after arrived here. found all delighted to see us, & the weather so warm that the windows all open, and summer dresses on Emily & aunt[2] but the cold storm, which they call "*a Norther*" coming, froze us up for a week. but it is again too warm for comfort.

I should like to see you so much. You must have grown greatly since you were with me at Northampton. and I hear, you are getting very fat. I hope you will not loose any of it. until I see you next summer. I hope to leave here in May or the last of April. Which will soon roll around.

Tell Belle & Jose Kenner—that Lottie & Mary are at school. and Buttler also.[3] the name of thier teacher, is Miss Duval. Send my love to them both, and keep a great bundle of my

affectionate love for Your Self

Your Mother
Belle Chase

When you write tell me Miss Hain's address. Emily & I do not agree about it. and I will direct this to the care of Mr Garniss.

Direct to me, to Matagoda. Texas. care of Mr G R Kenner.

Historical Society of Pennsylvania.

1. Belle; her brother Benjamin Chambers Ludlow; their sister Charlotte; Charlotte's husband, Charles Jones; and three-year-old Nettie had traveled down the Ohio and Mississippi rivers to New Orleans. From there Belle, Nettie, and Ben had continued by boat on the Gulf of Mexico to Matagorda County, Tex., where Charlotte Riske Kenner, Belle's half-aunt, and her husband, George, lived on a sugar plantation. Appendix; *Chase Papers,* 2:309.

2. Charlotte Riske Kenner and her daughter by her first marriage, Emily Jones.

3. As later correspondence reiterates, Belle's young cousins Belle and Josephine Kenner attended Henrietta Haines's school in New York, where Kate was. They and their siblings Charlotte ("Lottie"), Mary, and Frederic Butler Kenner were children of Ruhamah Riske Kenner, Charlotte Riske Kenner's sister, who had married a brother of George Kenner.

NETTIE TO KATE

Jan 9th 1851

My dear Sister Kate.

Almost every day I write two or three letters to you, and beg, uncle Ben to take them to the post office and then he, and uncle George both laugh as hard as they can.[1] I was so much distrist to day about it, that our dear Mother said, she, would write one for me. that uncle Ben would take to the office. I am now sitting on my chair beside her, and she says I talk so fast, that the letter will not hold quarter of what I tell her to write. so, that is an other trouble. I wish you were here, and then I could talk, and tell you every thing with out the trouble of a letter.

If you were here, I would show you so many things. you would like to see. I would show you the playthings uncle George has given me, & he gave me, a real live calf, white, with black spots on it, and I would show you the trees covered with long moss, it is an ugly grey colour, but when it is dry, it turns black; it is the kind that is put in mattresses. Henry the gardner, pulled a quantity down, and made me a beautiful little play house of it, against an old oak tree, and the tree is close to the river. Uncle Ben caught some fish in the river. which were longer than I am.

This morning, uncle George went out on his horse. to see how his sugar cane was growing. and the dogs started a[2] deer, it ran in to a corner of the fence. & uncle George went up and killed it. dont you think it was bad to Kill a poor little deer.

To day, Aunt Charlotte sent Henry in the cart to get some trees to plant in the yard, I went along and as I was stooping about among the grass, a lizzard got down my back, but I did not know it. until I got home, and cousin judge, was dressing me for dinner.[3] it jumped out on to her. we screamed. and Aunt Charlotte caught it in the bason and threw it out the window.

good night dear Katey

your affectionate sister
Nettié

In Belle Chase's hand. Historical Society of Pennsylvania.

1. Ben Ludlow and George R. Kenner.
2. Belle repeated "a" in the manuscript, at the turn of a page.
3. Georgine Jones, one of Charlotte Riske Kenner's daughters. Another observer, writing a decade earlier when Georgine was a girl, gave the nickname as "Jud." Clopper, *American Family*, 386.

FATHER TO KATE

Washington City, Jany 15, 1851.

My dearest little Kate,

I have very little time to write in and a great many letters to write. I should like to write you as long letters as you would wish to receive, but I am obliged generally to be quite short. Now I have only time to thank you for your last letter. It was quite well written. I should be glad, however, to have you describe more of what you see and do every day. Can't you tell me all about your school mates one by one.

Hannah Whipple[1] enjoys herself very much here. Last night she went with me to a party at the house of Mr. Graham, the Secretary of the Navy.[2] It was dreadfully crowded. Grace Greenwood is staying at Dr. Bailey's, and keeps them all very cheerful. She is you know the author of those stories of her pets which you liked so much.[3] When do you think you will be able to write such stories / Take pains, use your eyes, reflect, and you will do well enough.

Your affectionate father
S. P. Chase

Historical Society of Pennsylvania.

1. Kate's and Nettie's cousin, Hannah Ralston Whipple of New Hampshire.
2. North Carolina Whig politician William Alexander Graham was secretary of the navy, 1850–52. *ANB*, 9:392–93.
3. Author Sara Jane Clarke was known socially by her pen name, Grace Greenwood. She was twenty-seven years old at this time. Dismissed from a position with *Godey's Lady's Book* because of an antislavery piece she contributed to the *National Era*, during the early 1850s she lived in the household of Gamaliel Bailey, acted as governess to the family's children, contributed regularly to the *Era*, and was a lively participant in the Baileys' social and intellectual circle. She published *History of My Pets*, aimed at young readers, in 1851. In 1853 she married Leander K. Lippincott, ceased her contributions to the *National Era*, and with her husband began publication of a children's magazine while continuing her own writing. *ANB*, 13:723–24; Harrold, *Bailey*, 89, 133–34, 142, 189.

FATHER TO KATE

Washington City, Jany 22, 1851.

My dearest child,

I ought to have written to you several days ago, though I have nothing to tell you of any particular interest. The days come and go very much like each other, though every one brings new blessings with it. If I had more of what the phrenologists call marvellousness I should take more notice of passing events and find in them more ample materials for letter writing. I suppose your cousin Janette Skinner must have this bump very large, for she writes the most entertaining letters of any person I know. You, I think, are like me. You set down only naked facts without any embellishment whatever. I wish you could put a little more life into your letters, but I cannot blame you much seeing there is so little life in mine.

Do you read the Bible regularly and carefully? I have begun to read it with the New Year and make it a practice to read so much of the Old Testament each morning and so much of the New each evening, that I shall finish the whole during the year if I keep on which I intend to do.

Give my best regards to Miss Haines and all the young ladies whom I know and to Mrs Haines mother. Give my love also to Mrs Garniss and all the rest when you see them

Your affectionate father
S. P Chase

Historical Society of Pennsylvania.

FATHER TO KATE

Washington Feb. 1, 1851.

My dearest little daughter,

I am quite to blame for not having written you immediately after receiving your letter of last week. I was so much pleased with it, that I wished to answer it at once; but I put it off, and I dare say you know by experience that what is put off once will be very apt to be put off twice. Your letter was indeed very well written. I quite agree with Miss Haines in thinking it your best. It was even better than your last which I received yesterday, though that also was very good. I am much gratified by your improvement, and hope you will do your best to improve still further.

I am quite well; but the death of Mr. Kauffman of Texas yesterday admonishes us that no one is secure of life for an hour. At two oclock he was in his place perfectly well to all appearance—at four oclock he was dead.[1]

I had a long letter from your mother a day or two ago. She appears to be enjoying herself and to be improving in health. I send you another little halfsheet letter that came with it because I think it will amuse.

Your affectionate father
S: P: Chase

Historical Society of Pennsylvania.

1. Texas attorney David Spangler Kaufman served in the U.S. House of Representatives from 1846 until his sudden death on Jan. 13, 1851, at the age of thirty-seven. *Appletons'*, 3:494; *Bio. Dir. U.S. Cong.*, 1288.

FATHER TO KATE

Washington, Feb. 14, 1851.

My dearest little daughter,

I was so much pleased with your last letter that I must answer it at once. It is indeed written very well and would do credit to a young lady. It shows what you can do if you take pains: but you must not be content with doing so well. You must try to improve more and more until you write a really elegant hand and express your ideas with ease and fluency.

I do not wish you to send me the daguerreotype of your dear mother. It was taken for you. I have one taken for myself.

Ask Miss Haines if it is not time for you to read some history. When I was of your age I had read Rollin through. The Abbot Histories of Charles the 2nd &c are very interesting, and, if you read them with maps, so as to improve in geography at the same time, will do you a great deal of good.[1]

May our Heavenly Father bless my child.

Your affectionate father
S P Chase

Historical Society of Pennsylvania.

1. Charles Rollin's massive work on *The Ancient History of the Egyptians, Carthaginians, Assyrians, Babylonians, Medes and Persians, Macedonians and Grecians* was first published in French in 1730–38 and subsequently appeared in various editions in English. Rollin also wrote a history of Rome and on other aspects of the ancient world. Beginning in the 1830s, teacher and school principal Jacob Abbott wrote numerous books for young readers, most notably a series of morally instructive volumes centered on the fictional character "Rollo" but including as well a *History of King Charles the Second of England*, biographies of other English monarchs, and a *History of Hannibal the Carthaginian*. *ANB*, 1:27–28.

FATHER TO KATE

Washington City, Mar. 2, 1851.

My dearest little Kate,

I was not quite so well pleased with your last letter as with the one before it. You did not take quite so much pains in forming your letters. They were too small and pinched looking as if they were cold and shrunken. You must acquire a good, large, neat, bold hand.

This is a beautiful day. The sun shines bright and warm and all out doors seems quiet and cheerful. The grounds about the capitol are already clothed with green, tender grass, and the trees are budding. The other morning we had a thunder shower. But this is very little compared to what your mother writes from Texas. Her last letter was dated on the 2nd of January and she said they had had young potatoes for some time, and had just received an invitation to dinner at a *neighbor's* (only fifteen miles off) on green peas.

I expect to leave here for Cincinnati on Tuesday—day after to morrow: but may be detained a day or two if the President should think fit, as he may, to notify an Executive Session of the Senate. Perhaps you don't know what an Executive Session of the Senate is; but you can ask Miss Haines.[1]

Give my kindest regards to Miss & Mrs Haines; to Belle and Josephine Kenner and our other friends.

Direct your letters hereafter to Cincinnati. I will try to send your Pilgrims Progress to you.[2]

Your affectionate father,
S P Chase

Historical Society of Pennsylvania.

1. Father did not realize that the Senate itself would soon wrestle with the question of just what constituted an "executive session." He also misjudged how long the extra session would take. On March 3–4, the Senate spent long hours trying to complete the last business of the second session of the 31st Congress—Father drawing the ire of some of his colleagues when he tried to make major changes to a large river and harbors bill, his amendment being drubbed by a vote of 38 nays to only 3 yeas. At midday on March 4, the regular session ended and the Senate reconvened for a special session called by President Millard Fillmore to consider a number of unresolved nominations and military appointments. The question soon arose whether the special session was entirely an "executive" meeting of the Senate, during which the galleries would be emptied of spectators, the doors closed, and the body's proceedings recorded in a special journal. After vigorous discussion the Senate determined to hold closed executive meetings on the nominations, but also to meet in its more everyday posture to consider other issues as well. The Senate did not adjourn the special session until March 13. Fillmore, prominent in a faction of New York Whigs who took a conservative stance on the slavery issue, had been inaugurated as vice president in 1849 and succeeded to the presidency on Zachary Taylor's death in July 1850. *Congressional Globe*, 31st Cong., 2d sess., 1851, 823–24; app., 398–425; *Journal of the Executive Proceedings of the Senate of the United States* (Washington, D.C.: U.S. Senate, 1823–), 8:299–336; *ANB*, 7:910–12.
    2. John Bunyan's *Pilgrim's Progress*, first published in 1678.

FATHER TO KATE

Cincinnati, April 19, 1851.

My dearest little Kate,

I received day before yesterday two letters from you one dated on the 4th and the other on the 11th of April. The time of the mail between New York and Cincinnati is not more than four days. Now I suppose you know Arithmetic enough to be able to tell how many days more than enough to bring them to Cincinnati elapsed between the date of each of these letters and their receipt here; and I want you to find out and tell me in your next letter, and, also, the reason why they did not come directly through.

You are mistaken about your not writing as well in a large hand as in a small one. The two letters I have received from you in a large hand were the best you have ever written me. Your small hand looks cramped and awkward. You can never write it with boldness and freedom. I hope your writing master teaches you so to hold your pen as to have the freest use of all the motions of the hand.

In your letters I want you to tell me more about what you see and hear—about your studies—your rooms—your little daily employments and enjoyments. I suppose Gramercy Park begins to look quite pretty by this time. The trees have been in foliage here for two weeks—especially the maples—and the peach, apple & pear trees have been in full bloom. But for several days the weather has been quite cold and vegetation has been much retarded. The peaches are said to have been generally killed by the frost.

Jenny Lind has been here more than a week. Her concerts have been very fully attended, many persons having come from the Northern part of the State and from Kentucky and Indiana to hear her.[1] Cassius M. Clay and his wife have been here all the week. Mrs Clay is a very superior woman.[2]

I expect your mother up about the middle of April. I believe however I have told you this before. I think of meeting her at Louisville, or, perhaps, if I can get the time at Cannellton. Possibly we may make a visit of a few days at Mr. Hamilton Smith's near Louisville.[3]

Your Aunt Charlotte Jones came up the River from New Orleans yesterday and has gone to her place in the country. Ruhamah is with her.[4]

You ask me what is the relation between yourself and Bishop Chase of Vermont.[5]—Not very near, I believe, nor do I know precisely how near or distant. My impression is that a second or third cousinship might be established between him and me upon investigation; but I have never attempted to trace it. One Bishop in the immediate connection is enough.[6]

Your affectionate father,
S: P: Chase

Historical Society of Pennsylvania.

1. Soprano Jenny Lind, on a popular tour of the United States arranged by impresario P. T. Barnum, had arrived in Cincinnati on April 12. She and her entourage gave four concerts, at the first of which police dispersed the crowd that clamored outside the windows of the concert hall. Gladys Denny Shultz, *Jenny Lind: The Swedish Nightingale* (Philadelphia: J. B. Lippincott Co., 1962), 272–73; C. G. Rosenberg, *Jenny Lind in America* (New York: Stringer & Townsend, 1851), 205–11.

2. Kentucky newspaper publisher, antislavery reformer, and politician Cassius Marcellus Clay had married Mary Jane Warfield in 1833. His chronic infidelity eventually led to their divorce forty-five years later. *ANB*, 5:18–20.

3. Father knew Hamilton Smith (1804–75), a New Hampshire native, from his student days at Dartmouth College. Like Father, Smith migrated to the Ohio Valley after teaching school in Washington, D.C. He practiced law in Louisville, Ky., then beginning in 1851 was president of the American Cannel Coal Company in Cannelton, Ind. George T. Chapman, *Sketches of the Alumni of Dartmouth College* (Cambridge, Mass.: Riverside Press, 1867), 250; *Chase Papers*, 1:26.

4. Ruhamah Ludlow.

5. Between December 1849 and September 1852, Carlton Chase, the Episcopal bishop of New Hampshire since 1844, made three visitations to New York City, which was without a functioning bishop. Prior to his consecration as bishop, Chase, a native of Hopkinton, N.H., had been the minister at Bellows Falls, Vt., for more than twenty years. *Appletons'*, 1:584.

6. Father's uncle Philander Chase (1775–1852), who as a student at Dartmouth College joined the Protestant Episcopal church, had converted his parents and siblings to Episcopalianism from their accustomed Congregational practice. He became a priest in 1799 and ten years later was consecrated as the first Protestant Episcopal bishop of Ohio, where he also promoted and directed various educational institutions. In 1831 he gave up his episcopate and the presidency of Kenyon College, which he had founded, when the Ohio convention would not allow him to keep both positions. In 1835 he became the first bishop

of Illinois. Energetic, strong-willed, self-assured, he vigorously raised funds in England for his projects. Father's first residence in Ohio was during his early teens when his widowed mother sent him to live in his uncle's household. According to Father's later recollection, the stern bishop "liked to Govern." *Chase Papers,* 1:xiii–xiv; 4:263–66; *ANB,* 4:736–37; Niven, *Chase,* 7, 10–15.

FATHER TO KATE

Cincinnati, Aug 30, 1851.

My dear child,

Your excuses for writing are not very good and I am sorry that you have to make them so often. There is an old saying that a person, who is good at making excuses, is seldom good for anything else. I hope you will take care that this saying do not prove true as to you. A great many things happen every day which you might relate in a letter. It would be a good plan to keep a little journal, not putting down every thing that happens, but describing fully every day or two, the most striking incidents: or relating the most interesting conversations. You do not seem to me to notice enough. There are many young girls not older than you who make their letters very interesting by telling all about what happens to them.

Your handwriting I am glad to see continues to improve. You must take pains not to let it grow worse, but, on the contrary, to make it better. It will help you a good deal if you get a good gold pen with a silver penholder and always use it. The pen I am now writing with is one which I have had some time and it is now better than when I first began to use it. Miss Haines will get you one when you return to New York, if you ask her and will be careful of it.

Your dear mother's health is about the same as usual. She will probably start for Florida, about the middle of October taking little Nettie with her.[1] We are at present boarding on Mt. Auburn at Mrs Hamilton's,[2] which is a very pleasant place, I have bought a nice carriage and a fine large grey horse and hired her a good driver, so that she is quite independent.

Little Nettie remembers with a great deal of pleasure the little letter in the little envelope which you sent her when she was in Texas, and wants another. You must send her one.

Your Aunt Ruhamah is going to Madame Chegaray's school in Union Place: so she will be quite near you.[3] She will leave home next week and will be in New York about as soon & perhaps a little sooner than you will.

Write me one of your very best letters, immediately after receiving this. I am afraid you will think I had better take some of my lessons about handwriting to myself.

Your affectionate father,
S: P: Chase

Historical Society of Pennsylvania.

1. Belle and Nettie did not make the anticipated trip to Florida.
2. Father boarded with Eliza Hamilton again in 1853. *Chase Papers*, 1:242.
3. Heloise (or Eloise) Desabaye Chegaray (1792–1889), a native of Paris who had emigrated to the United States at a young age, established her school in New York City in 1814. The institution was later called "one of the best known in the country, and numbered many well-known people among its pupils." Around 1851 she relocated the school from Union Place and East 15th Street to Madison Avenue and East 28th. Later it was in Philadelphia, as the Chegaray Institute. *Appletons'*, 7:57; James Pyle Wickersham, *A History of Education in Pennsylvania* (Lancaster, Pa.: Inquirer Publishing Co., 1886), 485; *Doggett's New York City Directory, for 1850–1851* (New York: John Doggett Jr., 1850), 99; *The New York City Directory, for 1851–1852* (New York: Doggett & Rode, 1851), 105; Inglis Stuart to Morrison Weyent, Dec. 4, 1939 (Haines's School Papers, New-York Historical Society).

FATHER TO KATE

Cincinnati, Sep. 10, 1851.

My dear little daughter,

I expected to have had a very nice letter from you, before now, giving an account of all your goings on at Appoquogue.[1] I have been disappointed. I hope the other little girls, under Miss Haines' care, are more punctual and better correspondents that you are. If not their parents will not be very well satisfied with them.

I suppose that by this time you are in New York and that your school will commence next Monday. You must remember that you are now eleven years old and that you ought to commence trying to improve yourself in earnest. When I was younger than you I had read almost all Rollin's History and had made pretty good progress in my Latin.

Your Aunt Ruhamah is in New York now I presume. She left us last Monday morning with the intention of spending a year at Madame Chegaray's school in Union Square. I hope Miss Haines will let you see her occasionally.

Your dear mother has been much better for several days past. To-morrow she goes into the country for a few days, leaving me at Mrs Hamilton's and Nettie and Catharine[2] at Aunt McLeans's. She will be gone I suppose about a week. Her brother Dunlop goes with her. She intended to go today, and went down to the River with that intention; but the Boat was so crowded with people, returning from the great Fireman's Parade yesterday, that we all concluded the trip would be too uncomfortable and it was given up.[3] I think now she will probably take the carriage and go by land. The place she is going to is about forty miles from the City on the bank of the Ohio. The name is Rural & it is in Clermont County, but I don't think you can find it on the map.

Last week Tuesday, little Nettie went with her mother out to your aunt Charlotte's[4] where she spent the day. When I came home in the Evening they had not returned. Pretty soon however they came. Nettie was lying in her mother's lap apparently asleep but her mother said she was ill.

Her nurse Catharine carried her into the house, and undressed her. She seemed to have some fever, but not to be very sick. Her mother did not think it necessary to send for a doctor. Not long after she was put in bed, however, her mother heard her making a strange noise, apparently in distress. Immediately she took her up; but she was quite insensible. Her eyes were open & staring and glazed. Her teeth were closed and set fast. Her mother spoke to her; but she made no answer. She heard nothing saw nothing. We were very greatly alarmed. Without stopping to put on my vest or my boots I ran as fast as I could to the stable, some five or six hundred feet from the house, and told Thomas to put the horse in the carriage as quickly as possible.[5] While he did this I ran back to the house, and was somewhat relieved to hear that Nettie had revived a little & showed some little consciousness. I hurried again to the stable; Thomas was ready; I jumped in and told him to drive as quick as possible to Dr. Ehrman's on 7th Street. We were soon there but Dr. Ehrman was not at home. "Where does Dr. Pulté live?" I enquired of the boy who came to the door. "Round the corner, Sir, Said he. Telling Thomas to follow with the carriage I ran round the corner & rang the bell. Dr. Pulté came to the door himself. "I want you to come immediately and see my little daughter" said I. "What? Is she quite sick" said he, going back towards the parlor where Mrs Pulté was sitting.[6] "Yes" said I, "very sick. Don't wait a minute. Put on your hat and get into the carriage with me and go." Seeing that I was pretty thoroughly alarmed, he did not hesitate; but without even saying goodbye to his wife, got into the carriage and we were off instantly. I was hardly fifteen minutes—certainly not over twenty—in going from Mrs Hamiltons on Mt. Auburn to the Doctor's and back again. Your mother was much astonished when she saw me and the Doctor come in; and I was as much delighted to find little Nettie pretty decidedly better. The doctor said that her illness was attributable to green corn she had been eating at her aunt Charlottes; and left some medicines for her to take, directing them to be given at intervals through the night. I took upon myself the duties of nurse and was as punctual in my administration as possible. In the morning she was much better and is now quite as well as usual. I was very glad to have a homœopathic physician for her. If she had been treated after the fashions of the old school she would have suffered much more than she did, and might have been sick much longer and more seriously. I was so frightened however that I wanted to send for Dr. Mussey, an excellent man and a skilful allopathic physician who lives on Mt. Auburn very near Mrs Hamilton's: but her mother would not consent.[7]

We are just about starting for Aunt McLean's and Charlottes intending to leave Nettie and Catharine at the first place and to make arrangements with your uncle Dunlop about your mother's going into the country at the other. Little Net is in the front yard playing with a little child near her own age and amusing the boarders. Your mother is just finishing her preparations for a start. We are expecting the carriage every minute; and I am almost at the bottom of my page. Goodbye my dear child. May God ever bless you is the constant prayer of

Your affectionate father

S P Chase

Historical Society of Pennsylvania.

1. Apaquogue, a hamlet at East Hampton, toward the eastern end of Long Island, was a resort site with easy access to the ocean. Jason Epstein and Elizabeth Barlow, *East Hampton: A History and Guide,* 3d ed. (New York: Random House, 1985), 138; Karl H. Proehl and Barbara A. Shupe, *Long Island Gazetteer: A Guide to Current and Historical Place Names* (Bayside, N.Y.: LDA Publishers, 1984), 5.

2. Probably Catharine Egan or, less likely, Catharine McDonald (see Father to Belle, Feb. 28, 1850, above).

3. That year the Cincinnati parade, which the Chases did not attend, included fire companies from Louisville and Nashville and stretched for three miles. *Chase Papers,* 1:228.

4. Charlotte Chambers Ludlow Jones.

5. If this Thomas was the person of the same name who also appears in this volume in letters of Apr. 30, 1859, Aug. 18–19, 1863, and June 15, 1866, driving or performing other functions in Columbus and Washington, he was in the family's employ for many years. It is uncertain if he was the Thomas Handy who was later Kate's personal driver and helped her flee from her husband in 1879. Lamphier, *Kate Chase and William Sprague,* 179–80; *New York Sun,* Sept. 5, 1879.

6. Joseph Hippolyt Pulte and his medical partner Benjamin Ehrmann were prominent homeopathic physicians. Ehrmann had written a pamphlet, *What Is Homeopathy?* (Chillicothe, Ohio: Eli & Allen, 1848), and Pulte, one of the founders of the American Institute of Homeopathy in 1844, was the author of a substantial guide, *Homeopathic Domestic Physician* (Cincinnati: H. W. Derby & Co., 1850), which appeared in numerous editions. Both doctors were natives of Germany, where Samuel Hahnemann first articulated the principles of homeopathic treatment, but Ehrmann and Pulte learned homeopathy in the United States. Pulte, who prospered as a physician and wrote about world history as well as homeopathic medicine, advocated linking the earth's hemispheres by way of a telegraph connection across the Bering Strait. Father had presented Pulte's memorial on the subject to the Senate in March 1850. Pulte's wife was Mary Jane Rollins Pulte, originally of Pittsburgh. In June 1852 Nettie fell ill at Cumminsville with a suspected case of measles, and Ehrmann was the physician summoned by Charlotte Jones. *DAB,* 15:264; Otto Juettner, *Daniel Drake and His Followers: Historical and Biographical Sketches* (Cincinnati: Harvey Publishing Co., 1909), 384–88; *Congressional Globe,* 31st Cong., 1st sess., 1850, 538; C. C. Clopper to Father, June 30, 1852 (Chase Papers, LC).

7. Reuben Dimond Mussey's decision in 1837 to accept the professorship in surgery at the Medical College of Ohio had changed the topography of Cincinnati's medical community. Daniel Drake, long a dominant feature in the city, was affiliated with the rival medical department of Cincinnati College. He wrote Mussey a letter that called attention to factional rifts among local physicians. After that letter appeared in newspapers, the embarrassing episode prompted Drake—the domineering physician who had insisted on a relentless and copious bleeding of Kitty Garniss Chase during her tragic final illness in 1835—to relocate to Louisville. Mussey, who had taught anatomy and surgery at Dartmouth College and other institutions before moving to Cincinnati, built a reputation for his surgical accomplishments, often achieved after prayer sessions with his patients. In 1850 the American Medical Association elected him president of its annual meeting, which was held in Cincinnati that year. Juettner, *Drake and his Followers,* 162–70; *ANB,* 16:190–91; *Chase Papers,* 1:91–93.

FATHER TO KATE

Washington City, Dec 5, 1851.

My dearest child,

Since arriving here I have received your letter dated Nov. 17, and sent to Cincinnati. I am glad that I can say with truth that it is the best written letter I have yet received from you, I refer to the handwriting, not to the composition, though I have no fault to find with that. I should be pleased, however, if instead of repeating the stories told by Dr. Tyng, you would tell me all about your studies, your schoolfellows and your daily doings and enjoyments.[1]

I need not tell you that I was greatly delighted to hear Miss Haines speak so well of you. I am sure that she is conscientious and speaks only the truth, which makes my satisfaction the greater. I earnestly hope you will strive to improve in every respect, and carefully observe all the school regulations, and especially avoid all harshness and abruptness towards your schoolmates, and all wrong doing of every kind. Remember, my dear child, that the eye of a Holy God is upon you all the time, and that not an act or word or thought is unnoticed by Him. Remember, too, that you may die soon, and cannot, in any event, live very many years, and make your peace with God, by loving and trusting in Christ. Already eleven years of your life are passed. You may not live another eleven years; perhaps only a very small part of that time; certainly or almost certainly not many times eleven years. How short then is this life! And how earnest ought to be our preparation for another! None of us lay this enough to heart.

I went to see the President today.[2] I found him very well, and very pleasant, and we had quite a long talk. It may be of some interest to you to know how visits at the Presidents are made; and so I will give you a pretty full account of ours. Two members of the House of Representatives went with me. The front door was opened by the porter, who knew me well as I have often been at the House.[3] After entering we went up stairs to the Anteroom. This is an apartment in which gentlemen who come see the President sit or walk while other persons who have come before them have had their interviews. At the door of this room a person waits to receive visitors and take their names into the President and inform them when he is ready to receive them. I gave him my name and the names of my two companions on a card and he took it in, & immediately came back saying that the President was engaged and asking us to wait a while. There were several other gentlemen in the Antechamber who wished to see him, but it is a rule that Senators and Representatives must be admitted before others. So we spent several minutes in the Anteroom, looking at the busts, pictures and newspapers there, until the usher came and invited us to walk into the President's Room which we did leaving several who came before us to wait until we came out. This is the way all morning visits are made to the President. The rule I have mentioned often operates hardly upon persons who do not happen to be Senators or Representatives; for sometimes they are compelled to wait a whole morning and after all go away without accomplishing their object.

After seeing the President I went to the Patent Office, where I saw numerous curiosities. If you will remind me of it in your next letter I will tell you about a cake of lava which a gentleman scooped up in a pan from the crater of the great Volcano of Hawaii, and came near losing his own life in doing so.[4] But it is now late at night and I cannot write anymore.

Your affectionate father,
S: P: Chase

Historical Society of Pennsylvania.

1. Episcopal clergyman Stephen Higginson Tyng, whose evangelical style focused on the individual conversion experience, was a popular orator who drew immense audiences both in churches and in nonreligious settings. Since 1845 he had been pastor of St. George's Church in New York. *ANB*, 22:86–87.
2. Millard Fillmore was president; see note from Father to Kate, Mar. 2, 1851, above.
3. Edward McManus was doorkeeper of the White House. Elbert B. Smith, *The Presidencies of Zachary Taylor and Millard Fillmore* (Lawrence, Kans.: University Press of Kansas, 1988), 198.
4. Under the command of Lt. Charles Wilkes of the U.S. Navy, from 1838 to 1842 the United States Exploring Expedition made detailed investigations of the Antarctic coast, islands of the Pacific, and the Northwest Coast of North America. During the squadron's visit to the island of Hawai'i in 1841, Gerrit Parmele Judd, a missionary physician at Honolulu, volunteered to descend into the crater of Kilauea to obtain samples of gases and lava. Assisted by some native Hawai'ians, Judd barely escaped a sudden eruption in the crater but used a frying pan lashed to a pole to retrieve a specimen of molten lava. According to Wilkes, the lava, after it hardened, "resembled precisely a charred pound-cake." For a time the Patent Office in Washington housed the specimens gathered by Wilkes's expedition. Charles Wilkes, *Narrative of the United States Exploring Expedition. During the Years 1838, 1839, 1840, 1841, 1842*, 5 vols. and atlas (Philadelphia: Lea and Blanchard, 1845), 4:169, 171–74; Gerrit P. Judd IV, *Hawaii's Friend: A Biography of Gerrit Parmele Judd (1803–1873)* (Honolulu, Hawai'i: University of Hawaii Press, 1960), 99–102; *ANB*, 23:394–95; Kenneth W. Dobyns, *The Patent Office Pony: A History of the Early Patent Office* (Fredericksburg, Va.: Sergeant Kirkland's Museum and Historical Society, 1994), 134.

FATHER TO BELLE

Sunday Night.[1]

My own dearest wife,

Before I bow myself in supplication to our Heavenly Father for blessings on us and ours this night, I wish to commune a few moments with my beloved, afflicted, precious wife. My heart goes up to God in invocations of blessing upon you. Oh May He be very near you in this time of trial, and may the consolations of His Spirit abound towards you. May your faith be perfected and your hope established in Christ. Jesus died that we might live. He has risen and ascended into Heaven to prepare mansions for them who love Him and trust in Him. He has sent to us the Holy Spirit, the Comforter. Every holy desire, every feeling of affection towards God comes from the Spirit. Let us take care not to grieve the Spirit; but by continual acts of thanksgiving, faith, penitence and love endeavor to invite His residence in our breasts. My darling, I cannot tell you how I long for the restoration of your health. I know of no earthly blessing so great. It may please God to grant my earnest prayer for it. If not, I desire above all things your cheerful, loving submission to the Divine Will here and your eternal happiness. Oh, could we but be sure of the Divine Favor and Acceptance through Christ, parting would not be so grievous. I hope you do feel a true penitence and faith, and then there can be no doubt of acceptance, for the promise is clear and express. None who repent and believe in Christ can be lost—none who come to Him shall be cast out. For myself, I hope I repent & believe but the workings of sinful thoughts and inclinations are so strong in me, and my love,—if indeed what I feel be love—towards God is so feeble and cold, that I dare not be confident. Pray for me, dearest. Let us pray for each other. Goodnight— May God bless you and be very near you and give you a blessed sense of His Presence and loving kindness towards you. It is just past twelve oclock and Monday has commenced. Goodnight, dearest.

Monday Evening. My first moments after tea are given to you / Every evening between 7 & 8 I make it a point to write a few lines. Today I received your notes of the 4th & 5th. I am sorry that Miss Clopper has left you even for a short time; but I suppose she has already returned or will return tomorrow. I hope, also, to hear of the restoration of your voice.

I received your letter postmarked Cumminsville; but as it had no place-date inside I do not know which it was, certainly. I believe however it was the one in which you propose that I should bring Eliza Whipple. You say you should like to know its fate, when I got it and what I think of its contents. Its fate was to be received & placed among the other letters I get from home; I received it, if it is the one I think on Saturday or Sunday; and I thought its contents as I do almost every thing that come from you—quite right, and complied at once with your wish. I do hope Eliza may come, and that you will find her an acquisition. The only thing that troubled me in the letter—except that it gave no account of improvement—was the erasure of a line which had been written. This makes me fear that something is concealed from me which I ought to know, but which you withhold lest it may pain me. This, dearest, you ought not to do. Let me know every thing just as it is. Tell me all you want and all you feel. You are sure of my most affectionate sympathy, and that I will do all I can to satisfy all your desires.

My Ohio Bill was referred to the Committee today, and I have the promise of the chairman of immediate attention to it. I hope to get it reported on Wednesday and through the Senate early next week.[2] If I succeed I mean to leave for home, unless obliged to go for Eliza Whipple, on Thursday and may possibly reach you on Monday, a fortnight from today.

I was greatly disappointed by learning from Dun that he did not succeed in getting Louisa's carriage for you. I have written to Ralston to buy another Dun spoke of and if it is the one I think, it will answer better than Louisa's & in the end prove nearly as cheap.[3]

I wish I could think of something to do for you or get for you. If I was at home I could; but I hope you are as comfortable as your state of health permits. I wish you would have curtains for the dining room and have the parlor thoroughly warmed occasionally for a change, & to keep out the cold feel from the house.

I saw Judge & Mrs Peters the other day. Ann & her little boy are with them, and an old black woman who, I believe, belonged to Judge Peters father & nursed the Judge in his infancy. Ann's little boy has improved a good deal and Ann seems much recovered from her cough.

You write too much, I fear. A line is all I expect from you—and not even that do I ask for, if writing it gives the slightest inconvenience. Let Ralston write the rest.

Your own affectionate
S: P: Chase

Library of Congress.

1. According to the endorsement that Father later added to this letter, he wrote it on Dec. 7, 1851.

2. Father had first introduced his bill "to grant to the state of Ohio the unsold and unappropriated public lands remaining in that State" in December 1850, during the second session of the 31st Congress, but it languished after referral to the Committee on Public Lands in February 1851. He reintroduced it on Dec. 2, 1851, but the 32d Congress had just convened and the Senate did not have committees established until December 8 (Father, as a Free Soiler and an opponent of the Compromise of 1850, was banished to the committee concerned with lingering Revolutionary War claims). Since the bill had been referred to a committee once and the amount of land was less than 300,000 acres of what Father depicted to the Senate as "chiefly worthless" land, he hoped for expeditious treatment of the measure. The Senate finally passed it on Apr. 15, 1852, but in July the House of Representatives tabled it after a committee report objected to "separate legislation in giving away the public lands." He persisted, introducing the measure again in the second session of the 32d Congress, when it died in committee, and again in the 33d Congress. To his disgust the House finally replaced the entire bill by an amendment, substituting language by which Ohio would receive rights only to certain canal lands. Doomed to accept that mite or nothing, he allowed the measure to proceed in that form, and it became law in March 1855. *Congressional Globe*, 31st Cong., 2d sess., 19, 541; 32d Cong., 1st sess., 1851–52, 4, 11, 21, 30, 34, 112, 1065–68, 1083, 1235, 1653; 2d sess., 24, 69; 33d Cong., 1st sess., 5; 2d sess., 991, 1009, 1038, 1084.

3. Belle's brother, James Dunlop Ludlow, their cousin, Louisa Ludlow, and Father's nephew James Ralston Skinner.

FATHER TO BELLE

Washington City Dec 14, 1851.

My dearest wife,

I am gratified to hear that you still continue comparatively comfortable, though your inability to speak remains. Ralston writes me that on the evening before you spoke loud but that the next day your trouble returned. The swelling of your feet and the loss of your voice indicate, I fear, that the disease is making progress. May God, in his mercy, prepare us for all his will. It is hard to yield hope, and we need not yield it; for all is in God's power; but when you tell me that you do not feel that you shall ever get any better, my heart sinks within me. How wonderful and mysterious are the ways of God! What consolation would remain if we had not the consoling assurance that "whom He loveth he chasteneth."[1] I rejoice, in my distress, to think that you do not conceal from yourself your danger or the possibility of its nearness; but, while you find it hard to part with earthly blessings, trust yourself in the Hands of a Merciful God, through faith in Christ. My darling wife, think continually of your Father in Heaven and of the Mansions prepared for the Redeemed in Heaven.[2] Try to exercise constant faith in Christ and penitence for sin. Trust wholly in Him, and open you heart wide to the influences of the Holy Spirit. I have been reading today some of the Hymns in the Prayer Book.[3] They seem to have acquired additional meaning for me. I hope my heart is more in sympathy with their expressions than it formerly was.

I still mean to come to you at Christmas. Perhaps I may be with you sooner by a day or two. I shall know positively by Wednesday.

Yours most devotedly,
S: P: Chase

Library of Congress.

1. "For whom the Lord loveth he chasteneth, and scourgeth every son whom he receiveth" (Hebrews 12:6). See Father to Belle, Jan. 6, 1850, above.
2. A reference to the well-known passage from the New Testament: "In my Father's house are many mansions: if it were not so, I would have told you. I go to prepare a place for you" (John 14:2).
3. The American Book of Common Prayer, like its English counterpart, included a Psalter that contained the text of all the Psalms in meter. McGarvey, *Liturgiae Americanae,* lxix–lxx, app. 1.

FATHER TO KATE

Cincinnati, Jany 7, 1852.

My dear Child,

I have been at home some days, and am glad to be able to say that your dear mother is better than when I came home. The Doctor[1] thinks I may now return to Washington and, if she continues to improve, I shall probably start in a few days. Little Nettie is kneeling in a chair close by me ready to tell me something to write to Sister Katie. She says "Ma's housekeeping at Cousin Louisa's house. Aunt Charlotte is here and the baby.[2] Miss Clopper was staying here, and is going to come here again when Ma sends for her. Lud was here one day, I don't know when.[3] Cousin Ralston is staying here. I've got a garden. Ann has got a little dog. It licks me on my hand and on my face. Ann lives over by Cousin Louisa's house. Mrs Ball has got a baby.[4] I made a snow man. Mary made a snow man—little Mary lives with mother and takes care of me. That's enough."

So her letter is finished. Your aunt Charlotte Jones with her little baby, and Josey, a year older than Nettie has been staying here for near a week past. She came with Aunt Clarkson, who is going to remain with your mother two or three weeks, if she can. Your Aunt Charlotte expects to go to housekeeping again, in her house, near Cumminsville, as soon as Dunlop Ludlow gets home from St Louis. She has been spending the early part of the winter at Dr. Clarkson's in Kentucky.

There has been a great deal of snow here this winter, and the ground is now covered. This makes it quite difficult to visit much in this neighborhood. Mr. & Mrs Bowler, who live nearest, are gone to the City. Bishop McIlvaine, our next nearest neighbor, comes over oftener than anybody else.[5]

Your Cousin Ralston comes out every evening, and goes in every morning in the Omnibus, which runs between Clifton and Cincinnati. It happens that it comes out no further than just to our gate.

[I feel quite sorry that I was so situated this year as not to be able to attend to your Christmas & New Year presents. I hope, however, that you will be satisfied this time with the assurance that I love you dearly—as dearly as if I gave you ever so many presents. Next year I trust, circumstances will be more favorable. But who can tell. God only, and we must trust all to Him.)

You may direct your next letter to Washington. I find that you do not succeed well in writing one letter a week. Try a while to write one good letter a fortnight and remember that it is important to be punctual in whatever you undertake.

I am anxious to hear from you, and shall be delighted to learn that you have got rid of your cold and are quite well.

Your affectionate father
S P Chase

Historical Society of Pennsylvania.

1. Apparently George Dexter.
2. Charlotte Ludlow Jones, at Louisa Ludlow's. We do not know the name of Charlotte's baby (see appendix).
3. Charlotte's son Ludlow, later called Ludlow Ap-Jones.
4. Evelina Ball, who bore twelve children during her marriage to Flamen Ball, gave birth to a little girl, Alice, on Nov. 12, 1851. The baby died of whooping cough in August 1852. Interment record, Spring Grove Cemetery, Cincinnati; Joblin, *Cincinnati Past and Present*, 151.
5. In November, Father had rented and furnished a house in Clifton, a residential suburb of Cincinnati, in hopes of providing Belle with "a pleasant home in the country" for the winter. Clifton originated in the Lafayette Bank's division of a five-hundred-acre tract into plots of ten to forty acres in size. In 1849, Father, who had become solicitor and a director of the bank in 1834, and R. B. Bowler, a dry goods wholesaler, had been among the signers of a petition drawn up by Flamen Ball to ask the state assembly to incorporate the town. Ball, who established his residence on twenty acres in 1843, became mayor upon the assembly's granting of incorporation. Father had heard Charles Pettit McIlvaine (1799–1873) preach as early as 1833, soon after McIlvaine succeeded Philander Chase as Episcopal bishop of Ohio. McIlvaine, whose theology stressed evangelism rather than high-church ritual, and Father developed a long, cordial relationship. Since 1846 the bishop and his family had resided in a "comfortable mansion" on fourteen acres in Clifton. Cincinnati annexed the community, which was "noted for its numerous magnificent residences and the exceeding beauty of its situation," early in the twentieth century. *ANB*, 15:84; *Chase Papers*, 1:77, 80–81, 229; Maxwell, *Suburbs*, 27–28, 35, 44; Goss, *Cincinnati*, 2:529; Joblin, *Cincinnati Past and Present*, 153; Clopper, *American Family*, 220–21.

CHRONOLOGY

February 1852	Father in Washington, D.C.; Kate at Haines's school in New York; Nettie with relatives in the Cincinnati area
July 1852	Kate in Lockport, N.Y.
August 1852	Kate at Haines's, turns twelve; first session of 32d Congress closes
September 1852	Nettie turns five
December 1852	Second session of 32d Congress opens
January 1853	Father's forty-fifth birthday
March 1853	32d Congress closes; special Senate session, 33d Congress, March 4 to April 11
by August 1853	Nettie with Collins family in Hillsboro, Ohio
August–October 1853	Father on speaking circuit in Ohio
December 1853	Father to Washington; first session of 33d Congress opens
June–July 1854	Kate finishes term at Haines's school, goes to Concord, N.H., with Eliza Whipple
August 1854	First session of 33d Congress closes

CHAPTER 2

"The Respect and Affection of the Excellent"

FEBRUARY 1852–JULY 1854

I N THE years following Belle's death in January 1852, the surviving family members lived apart much of the time. While Father served his U.S. Senate term in Washington, D.C., Kate remained at Miss Haines's school in New York except for summer visits with family, and Nettie stayed primarily in Hillsboro, Ohio, under the care of Belle's cousin Catharine Collins. Father's duties—which necessitated trips to his home state— allowed him to visit his younger daughter more often than he could see Kate, though he did travel to New York in March 1853.[1] In the letters from these years we glimpse daily life in the Senate chamber, Washington social circles, and a New York boarding school and see Nettie enter the dialogue as a full-fledged writer. Father's letters to Kate at school—which constitute the majority of the extant correspondence from these years— give us further insight into the language of letter-writing instruction, precepts and practices of women's education, anxieties about health, re- sponses to death, and the difficulties a single father faced in attending to his daughters and his career.

Father wished for Kate, under Haines's guidance, to be "respected and beloved." He was "very anxious" that she "be worthy of the respect and affection of the excellent."[2] Winning such respect, his comments make clear, required substantial intellectual development. He certainly wanted Kate to learn much more than social graces. In an era when the definition of an "accomplished" woman was much debated—the term often used derisively to describe the shallow and fashionable—he chose to apply the term to a scholarly woman, who translated and published books (see his letter of Aug. 4, 1853, below).

These letters also mention a number of specific topics—Latin, geog- raphy, French, composition—that Father wanted Kate to study. His desire for her to read Latin, while hardly radical, reflects a liberal assessment of women's intellectual capacity and an acceptance of a fairly advanced curriculum in an era when some commentators still questioned wom- en's ability to learn classical languages.[3] His advice to Kate on February 6, 1853, that she "pay particular attention" to geography reflected his hope that she would visit foreign countries herself. Geography, "the first science for girls," had widespread cultural approval as a manageable and beneficial topic for female students. Commonly used nineteenth-century geography texts "contained physical, demographical, racial, political, historical, and economic data," suggesting that learning the subject involved a good deal more than merely memorizing names and locations.[4] Most of Father's contemporaries would have seconded his opinion that "French is a most important language," but increasingly at midcentury, commentators argued that girls' schools should prioritize English composition over foreign languages.[5] We know from Father's letter of July 5, 1854, which is included in this chapter, that Kate wrote a composition on "the Hand" while at Haines's school, and Catharine Beekman, who was also at the school that year, mentioned composition writing in her letters to her family.[6]

Catharine's copy books contain pages with the same phrase or sentence copied eighteen times, suggesting that penmanship exercises were a regular part of the curriculum at Haines's school—for example, "Birds borne along on the joyous wing" and "Luxemburg Manchester Martinique my." Letter writing time seems to have been limited even for students who liked the task. Catharine wrote to her mother from Haines's school that "my happiest hour in the week is spent in writing to you," but it was difficult "to write more than one letter a week." Catharine also confirmed that the headmistress read all the outgoing mail: "I cannot seal my letters as Miss Haines reads them, before they are sent, and also seals them."[7]

Kate knew some of the students at Haines's school, including the daughter of Clifton resident William Resor, Kate's cousin Maria Southgate, and Josie and Belle Kenner. The sudden and untimely demise of young Belle (Father to Kate, Apr. 3, 1852) is only one of several deaths mentioned in this chapter. Father often used such passings as opportunities to offer Kate moral guidance and religious instruction, reminding us that it was not unusual at that time to ask young people to think about issues such as dying in faith or God's will, or to move easily from comments about death to discussion of quotidian events. The constant reminders of the fragility of life, as well as the ongoing public dialogue regarding the physical frailty of American women, certainly would have fueled Father's apprehensiveness regarding his daughters' health. His belief in the value of exercise and concern for Kate's "naturally very delicate" constitution (July 23, 1854, below) echo the epistolary writings of other parents. Commentaries on women's education argued for more attention to students' physical well-being, often in terms likely to fan anxieties regarding current school conditions even as they suggested remedies.[8]

These expressions of concern for their health provide evidence of Father's attentiveness to both daughters, as does his clear interest in

Kate's education and pleasure in Nettie's developing personality. Yet other passages—such as one recounting how he first forgot to get Nettie a birthday gift and then had the belated present inscribed with Kate's name by mistake—reflect a high degree of distraction.[9] Though he did not discuss politics in his letters to the girls when they were still children, he certainly had much to preoccupy him in these years. Indeed, awareness of his outsider status helps one to understand his comments to Kate regarding ways to cope with her loneliness and his descriptions of events in the Senate chamber. In Ohio, hard feelings remained in some quarters about the arrangement that got him the Senate seat, and his status as one of the few Free Soilers isolated him in Washington. His active campaigning for Free Democratic candidate John P. Hale in 1853 earned him back the goodwill of some abolitionists, yet his views on the slavery issue were too advanced for most Ohio Democrats, and the legislature did not give him a second term in the Senate. Yet some of his most noted Senate activities took place during the latter part of his term. Though he did not delve into politics in his letters to Kate in that period, she could have known about newspaper accounts of her father's much-discussed "Letter to Hon. A. P. Edgerton" in November 1853, his resistance to Stephen Douglas's Kansas-Nebraska bill, and the "Appeal of the Independent Democrats."[10]

Father's letters did give Kate glimpses of the Washington social world she would one day join. He mentioned diplomatic dinners and well-known figures such as Russian Minister Count Bodisco and Senator Thomas Hart Benton. Although his antislavery politics may have limited his social options, he regularly attended the salon hosted by *National Era* editor Gamaliel Bailey. These gatherings included other Washington residents and visitors mentioned in this volume, such as Eva Ball, Elizabeth Ellicott, and Judge McLean. Journalist Grace Greenwood (Sara Jane Lippincott), a member of the Bailey household, later affectionately described the "little militant band of Free-Soilers" ostracized by many in Washington: "We knew we had been 'sent to Coventry,' and set about making 'Coventry' a jolly sort of place." Father eventually moved into a house on C Street, not far from the Baileys' home, "where the gathering of the faithful was made a regular Saturday-night event." As Greenwood recalled, "though still democratically informal, and quite simple in matters of dress and refreshment, these receptions were evidently found very enjoyable by men and women of the highest culture; even by certain 'society people,' eager for a new diversion." She wrote of the senator from Ohio specifically: "Mr. Chase, at that time a superb specimen of vigorous manhood and senatorial dignity, was most faithful to the reunions." Apparently he was not too dignified to take part in parlor games, contributing to a game of epigrams a rhyme about Mrs. Bailey that Greenwood recorded:

When Margaret Shands was young and fair,
She sung "Love in cottage" gaily;
But later years brought graver cares,
She now is prisoner of "Old Bailey."[11]

1. *Chase Papers*, 1:237.

2. See, below, his letters to her of Aug. 10, 1852, Mar. 9, 1853, and the undated one from the spring of 1854.

3. See his letter of Dec. 10, 1853. In the nineteenth century, as Eleanor Wolf Thompson points out, "generally a discussion of whether girls should be taught Latin involved their mental ability, not the value of Latin." Thomas Woody's study of American female seminaries between 1742 and 1871 indicates that a minority of the schools offered Latin. Similarly, Carl F. Kaestle observes that one noticeable distinction between schooling for males and females was that "girls less often studied Latin and Greek." Mabel Newcomer also found that private girls' schools tended not to teach Greek and often offered not more than a year or two of Latin: typically, "Latin and mathematics were taken seriously only in the seminaries concerned primarily with teacher training." Eleanor Wolf Thompson, *Education for Ladies, 1830–1860: Ideas on Education in Magazines for Women* (New York: King's Crown Press, 1947), 54; Thomas Woody, *A History of Women's Education in the United States*, 2 vols. (New York, 1929; repr., New York: Octagon Books, 1966), 1:563; Carl F. Kaestle, *Pillars of the Republic: Common Schools and American Society, 1780–1860* (New York: Hill & Wang, 1983), 54; Mabel Newcomer, *A Century of Higher Education for American Women* (New York: Harper, 1959), 10, 73.

4. Woody, *History of Women's Education*, 1:415; Caroline M. Burrough, "Girls and Their Training," *Ladies' Repository* 1 (1841): 374; Barbara Finkelstein, *Governing the Young: Teacher Behavior in Popular Primary Schools in Nineteenth-Century United States* (New York: Falmer Press, 1989), 81.

5. Father to Kate, July 5, 1854, below. The American Woman's Educational Association stated emphatically in 1853, "It is regarded as much more important for a woman to understand the History of our race, to be familiar with our own literature, and to be able to speak and write our own language with elegance, than to take a larger course of Mathematics and Foreign Languages." An earlier magazine commentator stated that an "American girl should be complete mistress of the English language. If she incline to the Latin, French, Italian, Spanish, German, let her study them after her sixteenth year has, by usage, rendered her *too old* for school—that is for school of all-work." Sarah Josepha Hale, in a January 1859 *Godey's* magazine piece, decried the presence of "dead languages" on the curriculum of the Baltimore Young Ladies' College, noting that current languages were more important, and she especially praised the placing of English composition "in the first rank" of subjects. Of the 162 female seminaries Woody studied, 139 offered English grammar, and 96 offered composition. *First Annual Report of the American Woman's Educational Association* (New York: Kneeland, 1853), 32; Burrough, "Girls and Their Training," 373; Hale quoted in Thompson, *Education for Ladies*, 54; Woody, *History of Women's Education*, 1:563.

6. Catharine Beekman to her mother, Feb. 2, 16, 1854 (New-York Historical Society).

7. To her mother, Feb. 16, Mar. 2, 1854; to her father, Mar. 9, 1854; copy book, Jan. 1854 (New-York Historical Society).

8. John C. Calhoun to Anna Maria Calhoun, Mar. 10, 1832, in Robert L. Meriwether et al., eds., *The Papers of John C. Calhoun*, 28 vols. (Columbia, S.C.: University of South Carolina Press, 1959–2003), 11:562; "Our Daughters," *Harper's New Monthly Magazine* 16 (1857): 73; Jane Roland Martin, *Reclaiming a Conversation: The Ideal of the Educated Woman* (New Haven, Conn.: Yale University Press, 1985), 112; Archibald Maclaren, "Girls' Schools," *Macmillan's Magazine* 10 (1864): 409–16; Linda J. Borish, "The Robust Woman and the Muscular Christian: Catharine Beecher, Thomas Higginson, and Their Vision of American Society, Health and Physical Activities," *International Journal of the History of Sport* 4 (1987): 142.

9. Father to Kate, Oct. 8, 1853, in this volume.

10. Blue, *Chase*, 76–77, 90–91; *Chase Papers*, 2:xvii; Niven, *Chase*, 145–46, 148, 152.

11. Grace Greenwood, "An American Salon," *Cosmopolitan* 8 (1890): 442, 444–46; Niven, *Chase*, 147; *Chase Papers*, 1:231.

FATHER TO KATE

Washington, Feb. 12, 1852.

My beloved child,

I have not written to you for several days. I believe I have had two letters from you since I wrote. I have been very busy. Night before last I was at work till near two oclock in the morning, and last night until near one. I feel quite exhausted and it is now a quarter past eleven; but I am not willing to go to bed before writing you a few lines.

I was very much comforted by your letter written about ten or twelve days ago. It is delightful to me to know of your affectionate love towards me and to see your improvement. You and I have lost one who was to me a devoted comforter & supporter, and to you a kind and affectionate guide.[1] Now, my dear child, we must think of her as in Heaven whither a purer & gentler spirit has seldom gone. You, I hope, will manifest your sincere devotion to her memory, by constant endeavors to do what you know she would wish in every respect—by cultivating your intellect and your manners; by doing all the good you can; above all by devoting your heart to God, and seeking reconciliation with Him through Christ.

I notice, with gratification your constant improvement in penmanship and composition. Your last two letters do you great credit in these respects. Continue to improve. Make each letter such as you would not be ashamed to have me shew to any body. You will if you take pains write after a while with great ease an elegant lady's hand—free, clear & elegant.

Today I attended the funeral of a little child—a young boy, only two months old—the son of my friend Dr. Bailey. He was born a few days after I came here this winter, and now he is in the grave. His it seems to me is a happy lot. He just entered into life and straightway became immortal. He suffered but he did not sin. His mother's heart was very much set upon him; but surely she would not recall him from the deeper love with which the Savior welcomes to Heaven the little ones of whom is His Kingdom there.[2]

I heard from home today, Mr. Garniss had been ill but was much better. Dear little Nettie was well and as happy as possible. She is a sweet child and every one seems to love her. Ralston Skinner writes that Mr. Jones went out to Clifton the other day carrying with him some cakes for the children. Josey[3] took hers & commenced eating: but Nettie carried hers to the table and laid them on it saying "papa would not let her eat them."

Mrs Kate Baker wrote me that Mrs Garniss was going to Cincinnati immediately on account of Mr. G's illness. Has she gone?

I want you to send me the daguerreotype of your mother and little Net which I gave you, by Express. Miss Haines will be kind enough to have it properly put up and directed & placed in Adams & Co's Express Office.[4] I want it for the use of a painter.

Goodbye, my darling child. May our Heavenly Father watch over you with the eyes of love.

Your affectionate father,

S: P: Chase

Miss Kate Chase

On paper edged with a black border. Historical Society of Pennsylvania.

1. Belle had died on Jan. 13, 1852.
2. Margaret Lucy Shands Bailey (1812–88), the wife of *National Era* editor Gamaliel Bailey, was herself an abolitionist and journalist. The Baileys' infant son, Charles G. Bailey, had died on February 11. Mrs. Bailey's grief was perhaps heightened by the fact that this was the sixth child she had lost. The Baileys' first baby was stillborn in 1834; their next two children died soon after birth; a healthy girl born in 1838 died of "brain fever" before she was two. Their next two children, Marcellus, born in 1840, and Frederick, born the following year, survived, but the parents had another scare in September 1842 when Marcellus was seriously ill. Between 1841 and 1845, the Baileys had two healthy daughters, but they lost another infant son in 1846. Their daughter Frances and son Frank were born healthy before the death of infant Charles, Margaret's last child, in 1852. Harrold, *Bailey*, 13, 16, 27, 55, 71, 150.
3. Nettie's cousin, Josephine Jones.
4. Alvin Adams established Adams & Co. in 1840 as an express mail route between New York and Boston with limited service to New London, Norwich, and Worcester. The company expanded its routes and in 1854 would join with Thompson and Co. and Kinsley and Co. to form the Adams Express Company. *Appletons'*, 1:11; A. L. Stimson, *History of the Express Business* (New York: Baker & Godwin, 1881), 53–57.

FATHER TO KATE

Washington City, Feb. 21, 1852.

My dearest child,

I received this morning your letter of the 19th. If a letter is written in New York one day and put in the Post Office in season for the five oclock mail of the afternoon I receive it the next morning. I always, for example, get the New York Evening Post the morning after it is published in New York. I wish you to notice this, and have your letters mailed so that I can get them on the morning of the day after they are written.

It gave me very great pleasure to receive a letter—or rather a short note from Miss Haines,—by the same mail which brought yours. Little children cannot imagine the anxiety of their parents about them. You cannot understand how deeply solicitous I am for your improvement in all respects, particularly in moral respects. I am delighted to learn from Miss Haines that you do improve—that you try to avoid untruth, try to be just and conscientious in your intercourse with your schoolmates—try to cultivate habits of self control & self denial and an obliging disposition; and that you, in consequence, gain more and more the love and good will of your associates and instructors. Dear Kate, this is very pleasant news to me. I would rather hear it, than be made President. Persevere, my own dear child, and may God help you. Pray to Him for his grace. Ask for the assistance of the Holy Spirit for the sake of Christ.

We have had a beautiful day here. The snow and sleet which fell & froze yesterday has melted away, and it seems as if Spring were coming. How much this is like what we often feel. Passion and Evil inclination interrupt our pleasant paths, and make them slippery, miry and dreary. The Sun of Divine Grace—rays from pleasant circumstances—shine upon them again; and all that was troublous & disagreeable seems to disappear. But alas, the winter is not over yet. Other storms will come. The snow and ice will fall again & again encrust our paths. And so life is again disturbed, after a season of exemption, by temptations without and temptations within. The eternal Spring is beyond the Grave. God grant we may enjoy it.

Mrs McLean, with Emily Jones and Miss Avery[1] who have been been spending the winter with her, will leave for Cincinnati about the first of March. I suppose you don't remember[2] Emily Jones. She has not been much in Cincinnati. She is a lovely girl. I hardly ever knew one of a more amiable and sweet disposition.

I received a letter from Aunt Charlotte Kenner a day or two ago. She was spending a little time in Matagorda. Her enquiries after you were very kind.

You must still pay a little more attention to your handwriting / Can't you *join* all your letters? Give me more particular accounts. Describe to me—your school room—your sleeping apartment—you companions. Make me *see* what you describe.

I must give you an example I believe in my next by describing my own quarters.

Give my very best respects and thanks to Miss Haines; and give my love to Sallie McGrew, Fanny Breese,[3] & Josephine & Belle Kenner—not forgetting your aunt Kate & Ham, when you see them, or Cousin Delia.[4]

Your own affectionate father,
S P Chase

Miss C. J. Chase.

On paper edged with a black border. Historical Society of Pennsylvania.

1. Likely a relative of the Mr. Avery who sold land in the Clifton area in 1843. Maxwell, *Suburbs*, 27.

2. In the manuscript Father repeated "remember."

3. Cornelia Fanny Breese (c. 1842–80), the only child of Adeline Wiggins and William Gregg Breese, later married John Gerard Coster of New York. The 1850 census lists Fanny and her parents as members of her maternal grandfather Samuel Wiggins's household in Cincinnati. William Breese took over the Front Street grocery store of S. S. Smith in 1841.

Edward Elbridge Salisbury, *Family-Memorials: A Series of Genealogical and Biographical Monographs on the Families of Salisbury, Aldworth-Elbridge, Sewall, Pyldren-Drummer, Walley, Quincy, Gookin, Wendell, Breese, Chevalier-Anderson and Phillips* (New Haven, Conn.: Tuttle, Morehouse & Taylor, 1885), 519; 1850 census, Hamilton Co., Ohio, Cincinnati, Ward 2, 151; *Cincinnati Daily Gazette,* July 3, 1840, June 8, 1841; *DeBow's Review* 4 (1847): 18; Charles Cist, *Sketches and Statistics of Cincinnati in 1851* (Cincinnati: W. H. Moore & Co., 1851), 88, 93.

    4. Cordelia Picket Austen. "Ham" was Ruhamah Ludlow.

FATHER TO KATE

Washington, Mar 4, 1852.

My dear child,

I only received your letter dated 25th February yesterday. There must be some delay in sending to the Post Office. Ask Miss Haines about it. I have not received the daguerreotype of your dear mother and Nettie at all yet. I want it very much: and am at a loss to know what can have become of it.

It gratifies me very much to have such good accounts of your health and progress. I pray God to preserve your health and enable you to persevere in your endeavors at self improvement. Remember, my darling, that you have a naturally evil heart and that it is through God's grace alone, that you can overcome sinful inclinations. Be watchful over yourself and look constantly to God through Christ for his blessing.

Miss Haines, in a note on the back of your letter, says that you did not copy it. I am not sorry for it, but rather pleased that you sent the first draft. It shews better what your handwriting is and whether you really improve or not. I think your hand will be a very good one, if you pay attention to it. It is now as good as I could expect a child of your years to write, and I am not ashamed to shew it to any body. It is the basis of an excellent hand, if you do not become careless: which, I hope, you will not allow.

Several years ago I was at Quincy, the residence of two Presidents of the United States, John Adams and John Quincy Adams. It was after the death of John Quincy Adams and his son Charles Francis Adams was living in the House.[1] His wife took me and another gentleman into the Library. It was a very extensive collection of many thousand volumes of the works of the best authors of Ancient or modern times. But what interested me most were several quartos containing the manuscript diary of John Quincy Adams. The whole was written in a clear, round, legible hand even to the very last. Paralysis and age affected the characters of the Manuscript with tremor, but the last was as legible as the first. The concluding pages were not written by Mr. Adams. His paralysis at last affected his hand so much that he could not write. So for the last days of his life he was accustomed to dictate his diary to one or other of the ladies of his family, who would write from his mouth.[2] I wish you could see the elegant, lady like penmanship of these pages. I am sure that after seeing them you would never be willing to write a scrawl, or any other than an elegant hand.

Perhaps you are thinking, Father had better write a good hand himself and set me an example: but, my dear child, don't imitate my illegible writing, but follow my precept rather than my practice.

Can't you send me some of your drawings? That was a very pretty little poem you enclosed with your last letter. I sent it to Nettie with the Valentine, and a letter I wrote her myself.

I think I shall come to New York in the beginning or about the middle of next month, and perhaps I shall go out to Cincinnati. In that case, if Miss Haines does not disapprove of it, I shall want to take you with me on a short visit.

I had a letter from Ralston Skinner today and another from Miss Clopper. Nettie was very well & happy. Every body loves her for her winning ways and sweet disposition. Mr. Garniss was not quite so well & Mrs Garniss was persuading him to go south. Mr. Wiggins had bought his interest in the Ferry.[3]

Present to Miss Haines my kindest remembrances and sincerest thanks for her care of you: and give my love to Sallie McGrew, Fanny Breeze & Belle & Jose Kenner.

Your affectionate father
S: P: Chase

Miss Kate Chase.

On paper edged with a black border. Historical Society of Pennsylvania.

1. As a young man in Washington, Father had attended "levees" or receptions at the White House during the presidential administration of John Quincy Adams. At one such event in 1827, he met Charles Francis Adams (1807–86), the fifth child of six born to John Quincy and Louisa Catherine Johnson Adams. At that first meeting Father found "nothing remarkable either in person or in mind" about Charles Francis, and he later considered Adams's nomination for vice president the least satisfactory result of the 1848 Free Soil convention. Charles Francis Adams was a lawyer and Massachusetts politician, serving in the U.S. House of Representatives, 1858–61, and as minister to Great Britain, 1861–68. In December 1852 he attended a meeting of "free democrats" at Father's house in Washington, where according to Father's journal there was "a good deal of talk and little done." Adams edited his grandfather's *Works* and the diaries of his father, who died in 1848. The Adams home visited by Father was in Quincy, Mass. *Chase Papers*, 1:3, 231; 2:16, 17, 185; *DAB*, 1:40–48.

2. Abigail ("Abby") Brown Brooks (1808–89) married Charles Francis Adams in September 1829. The women of the Adams household in John Quincy Adams's final days included wife Louisa Catherine Johnson Adams; daughter-in-law Mary Hellen Adams, widow of his son John; and his granddaughter Mary Louisa Adams (Johnson). The elder Mary and Louisa worked with the ex-president, who had been disabled by a stroke in 1846. Paul Nagel, *The Adams Women* (New York: Oxford University Press, 1987), 237, 243, 257; Lynn Hudson Parsons, "Louisa (Catherine Johnson) Adams," in *American First Ladies*, ed. Louis L. Gould (New York: Garland Publishing, 1996), 93, 95.

3. Cincinnati ferry owner and bank director Samuel Wiggins also had ferries at St. Louis, owning a fleet of four ferries crossing the Mississippi by 1832. He owned a million

dollars' worth of vessels and real estate when he incorporated the Wiggins Ferry Company in the early 1850s. John Garniss long harbored dissatisfaction over his business relationship with Wiggins, who died in 1852 (see the appendix). *Chase Papers,* 1:94; Federal Writers' Project, unpublished guide to East Saint Louis, Illinois (1936), available through East St. Louis Action Research Project, University of Illinois at Urbana-Champaign; U.S. Supreme Court, *Wiggins Ferry Co. v. City of East St. Louis* (1883), 107 U.S. 365; Thomas Ford, *History of Illinois* (Chicago: S. C. Griggs & Co., 1854), 175.

FATHER TO KATE

Washington, March 25, 1852.

My darling child,

I have had two letters from you since I have written you one, and on looking at the date of your last I see that it is a week since it was written.

I am glad to see that you pay a good deal of attention to your handwriting, and that you are improving in it. Let me, however, recommend to you a little more care in *joining* all the letters of each word. For example, in your last letter there is the word "pleasure." You write it "pleas ure."

I wish, also, that you would tell me more about your school and schoolmates and your studies. Describe your school companions and give me an account of what you learn—not merely the names of the books, but the subjects you have been engaged upon during the week and what new ideas have occurred to you.

The weather has been very disagreeable here / After a few pleasant days of sunshine and soft air winter suddenly came back and fires were again necessary. For more than a week now we have had a succession of raw, chilly days almost without exception.

Last week, Thursday, I was at the President's at dinner. He gives a dinner every week. The different Senators and members are invited from time to time together with such distinguished or undistinguished folks as happen to be in the city and to attract enough of the Presidential notice. Each guest is assigned to a particular place at the table. The two extremes are appropriated to gentlemen without ladies. The central portions of the table—which is quite long and extends from the east to the west—are occupied by gentlemen and ladies. The President occupies the exact centre on the north side—his wife, generally, but on this occasion his daughter, Miss Fillmore, occupied the opposite centre on the South side.[1] Those gentlemen, selected for the purpose, are expected to take charge of the ladies assigned to them respectively, and the ladies are expected to be content with their allotted gentlemen whether agreeable or disagreeable. It happened that Mrs Morton of Florida wife of Senator Morton of Florida was assigned to me and our seats were next to the President on his left—Mrs Morton between me and him.[2] This arrangement placed me in an agreeable association, and made the dinner pass off pleasantly enough to me. The table is ornamented with mirrors laid flat upon it & extending nearly its entire length upon which mirrors a[3] placed flower vases—gilt & supported by figures of women also gilt. Mrs Morton remarked that a gentleman, who was with her on another occasion, asked her: "Don't you think those women must be tired holding up those vases. They have been doing it ever since Gen Jackson's time." From this you may infer that all the furniture is pretty old—I mean the table furniture. No meats or pastry or any other food is placed on the table. The several courses are brought round by waiters: and there is nothing particularly nice. A simple dinner at home would be quite as good: but social forms make such dinners necessary perhaps.

I should like to see my darling Katie very much, and still expect to visit you next month and to go west. Though the going west is not positively certain.

Love to Sallie McGrew, Fannie Breese & the Kenners if they care enough about me to value it: and kindest regards to Mrs & Miss Haines

Your own father

S P Chase

On paper edged with a black border. Historical Society of Pennsylvania.

1. Millard Fillmore was in the final year of his presidency. He and Abigail Powers had married in 1826. According to one contemporary observer, Abigail was "the envy of the wives in their circle of friends as her husband continued to bestow on her the attentions and courtesies other men reserved for guests." After her death in 1853, Fillmore married a second time, in 1858, to Mrs. Caroline C. McIntosh. Due to Abigail Powers Fillmore's poor health toward the end of her husband's presidency, their daughter Mary Abigail "Abby" Fillmore (1832–54) often took over her mother's social duties. A graduate of a Massachusetts finishing school, fluent in French and Spanish as well as being a talented musician, the teenaged Abby excelled as a hostess and earned praise from White House visitors. She was considered an asset to her father, much as Kate Chase was later on. Abby Fillmore died unexpectedly in July 1854. *DAB*, 6:380–82; Frank H. Severance, ed., *Millard Fillmore Papers*, vols. 10–11 of *Publications of the Buffalo Historical Society* (Buffalo, N.Y.: Bigelow Brothers, 1907), 10:15, 25; 11:489; Benson Lee Grayson, *The Unknown President: The Administration of President Millard Fillmore* (Washington, D.C.: University Press of America, 1981), 55; Robert J. Rayback, *Millard Fillmore: Biography of a President* (Buffalo, N.Y.: Buffalo Historical Society, 1959), 47, 254, 395.

2. Elizabeth F. Archer, daughter of Col. William Archer of Powhatan County, Va., married Jackson Morton in 1838. A former member of the Florida territorial legislature and navy agent, Jackson Morton served one term in the U.S. Senate, 1849–55. Brian R. Rucker, *Jackson Morton: West Florida's Soldier, Senator, and Secessionist* (Milton, Fla.: Patagonia Press, 1990), 6, 40; *Nat. Cyc.*, 5:259.

3. So in the original.

FATHER TO KATE

Washington City, Apl. 3, 1852.

My darling Child.

I received yesterday two letters from you. They were very well written so far as penmanship goes, but I wish you were not quite so stiff in your style. You must try to write exactly as you would talk. and tell me, just as you would in conversation, of all I wish to know.

I was very sorry to hear of Belle Kenner's death. It shocked me, it was so entirely unexpected. You say that Miss Haines is confident that she died in the confidence of the Christian Faith. It is consolatory to know this. The Christian death is not terrible. It is triumph rather than loss. Oh, if we could but lean humbly on the cross of Christ, repenting truly of sin and endeavoring to walk by faith in newness of life, how little should we dread death. It would then be but the ivory gate opening from gloom to glory.

This is a beautiful morning. The Sun shines clear and bright. Some Canary birds, at the next house are singing cheerily. The trees begin to shew signs of outcoming foliage. And the grass about the Capitol is green and luxuriant. I should like to have you with me and we would take a ramble together. But as I have no such companion for a walk, I content myself with remaining in my room, writing and reading.

I received a letter from Ralston Skinner a day or two since. Your aunt Charlotte was still at Clifton.[1] Nettie—little precious darling—was quite well. I still hope to go out in about two weeks and in that case mean to take you with me, if Miss Haines approves of it.

Eva Ball is here.[2] She was at the Capitol yesterday in the Gallery of the Senate Chamber. I never see any body being so nearsighted: so, to attract my attention just as the Senate adjourned she dropt her handkerchief over my head. Looking up I saw a lady beckoning to me, and knew at once who it was.

Your affectionate father,
S P Chase

On paper edged with a black border. Historical Society of Pennsylvania.

1. Probably Charlotte Kenner.
2. Eva Candler Ball (b. 1831), one of the five surviving children of Father's law partner Flamen Ball and his wife, Evelina Candler Ball. Eva later married Charles H. Glover of Brooklyn, N.Y. Joblin, *Cincinnati Past and Present,* 151.

FATHER TO KATE

Washington City, May 21, 1852

My darling child,

I have no reasonable excuse for not writing to you before. I can't tell you how often I have thought of you, but my intention to write has always given way to something which seemed to require more immediate attention.

I learn from Miss Haines through Miss Soley[1] that she will not make her accustomed arrangements for retaining a number of her pupils with her during this vacation. I should regret this the more had I not determined to gratify your grandmother with a visit from you this Summer. I have written to your Aunt Carrie offering her my house at Clifton for a Summer residence, and I suppose she will accept it. If she does so, it will be a pleasant home for you while in the west. I mean to ask Mr. Resor to take charge of you to Cincinnati when he takes his daughter home, unless some other opportunity presents itself.[2] I hardly think I shall be able to accompany you myself.

I wish you could be here now for a few days. The Capitol grounds are looking beautifully and the country is lovely. If you were here we would have some nice morning and evening walks. The grounds are filled with people every evening and once a week at the Presidents and at the Capitol, on different days, the Marine Band plays for the gratification of the promenaders.

Dr. Baileys family is well. Little Fan[3] enquires for you very often and wants to know when you are coming to see her.

Give my best regards to Miss Haines and to Sallie McGrew and Fanny Breese and any others who remember me

Your affectionate father
S: P: Chase

On paper edged with a black border. Historical Society of Pennsylvania.

1. A Miss Soley worked for Henrietta Haines and was signing receipts for tuition payments in the 1850s. "E. C. Soley for H. B. Haines," Papers of James W. Beekman, box 1 (New-York Historical Society).

2. William P. Resor was a resident of Clifton, having been one of the first to move to the Cincinnati suburb in 1844. A prominent Cincinnati businessman, Resor was president of both the American Patent Company and William Resor and Company, a stove manufacturing firm. He received numerous patents for stove designs. He and his wife, Mary, had three daughters of school age in 1852: Sallie Resor (1837–64), Mollie Resor (1841–93), and Kate Gordon Resor (1842–1928). Clara Longworth de Chambrun, *Cincinnati: Story of the Queen City* (New York: R. Long & R. R. Smith, Inc., 1939), 183; Charles Cist, *Sketches and Statistics of Cincinnati in 1851* (Cincinnati: W. H. Moore & Co., 1851), 123; George W. Hawes, *Geo. W. Hawes' Ohio State Gazetteer and Business Directory for 1860–'61* (Indianapolis: G. W. Hawes, 1860), 88, 901; *DAB, Suppl.*, 7:641–42; *ANB*, 18:353–54; *Nat. Cyc.*, 53:86; Interment Records, Spring Grove Cemetery, Cincinnati.

3. Gamaliel and Margaret Bailey's daughter Frances (Fanny). She was probably about Nettie's age, or a bit younger. Harrold, *Bailey*, 71, 239n.

FATHER TO KATE

Washington, July 6, 1852.

My dear child,

I have just received your letter dated last Friday. It ought to have been here sooner. I want you to write me every week, and to write just as you would talk, a full account of all your doings, and be sure to have it put in the mail so that it will leave Lockport on the day it is written.[1] Your letter is not written quite so well as usual. Your hand appears to have been un-steady, as if your nervous system was excited, like that of a person who is in the habit of drinking coffee. You must not drink coffee or tea, or allow yourself in anything which will derange the nerves.[2] You are natu-rally delicate, and what would not greatly harm another might be fatal to you.

I shall expect quite a treat in the cake you are to make for me. I de-light in you making yourself useful and in your acquainting yourself with the ways of being useful.

Above all things, however, I am anxious, with unspeakable anxi-ety, that you may dedicate yourself soul and body to the service of God. The highest usefulness is to promote the glory of God by sincere and continued obedience. God will help if we sincerely try, and look to Him through Christ. My dear, dear child do try and try faithfully and perse-veringly. You may feel discouraged by finding that you are not able to or rather do not overcome all sinful dispositions immediately. But you must not be discouraged. Persevere and you will conquer. To give up is to per-ish. Did you ever read the story of the young man who tried to carve his name higher than every other on the almost perpendicular wall of the great chasm at the Natural Bridge of Virginia. He climbed highest and carved his name: but then he found it impossible to descend.[3] Above him towered the precipice; below him yawned the gulf. He must ascend or perish. So he commenced the painful and perilous ascent. His hands were cut—his feet were torn—his clothes rent—his body bruised. He felt as if he should never gain the summit: but he must hold on, for behind and below was death. At length he succeeded for God was merciful. Something like this is our escape from Sin. But there is this difference. If we trust thoroughly in Christ, He will help: and we shall find victories, impossible to nature, become comparatively easy to faith.

A letter from Miss Clopper tells me that dear little Nettie is unwell. I am exceedingly anxious about her.

Your affectionate father,
S. P. Chase.

Historical Society of Pennsylvania.

1. Lockport, N.Y., was the home of Father's brother Edward and his wife, Mary Eliza, and of Father's sister Jane—Janette Logan Chase Skinner—and her family (see the appendix). Situated on the Erie Canal sixty-five miles west of Rochester and eight-een miles from Niagara Falls, Lockport was the county seat of Niagara County. In 1850 the city had a population of 10,327. Frederick A. P. Barnard and Arnold Guyot, eds., *Johnson's New Universal Cyclopædia*, 4 vols. (New York: A. J. Johnson & Son, 1876–78), 3:84; *First Cen-tury of National Existence; the United States as They Were and Are* (San Francisco, Calif.: F. Dew-ing & Co., 1875), 686.

2. Such concerns about coffee's impact on the nerves were not uncommon in this era. Many Americans associated the beverage with substances such as alcohol and tobacco—and with immoral and unhealthful desires. For example, an 1852 *Southern Literary Messen-ger* article lamented that "the poor waste much of their earnings on tobacco, whiskey, coffee and—dogs;—much more do the rich consume upon their lusts what might be put to far

better use." H. R., "Essay on the Slow Progress of Mankind," *Southern Literary Messenger* 18 (1852): 405; "Coffee, Its History and Uses, All the Year Round," *Ladies' Repository* 6 (1870): 252, 253.

3. The Natural Bridge is a 215-foot rock formation over Stock Creek in Scott County, Va. The young man Father referred to may be Colonel Piper, an "adventurous youth" described by his friend, the Reverend C. Collins, in an 1855 periodical article. "Journal of a Trip to the Mountains, Caves, and Springs of Virginia, Chapter VII–VIII," *Southern Literary Messenger* 4 (1838): 517–18; C. Collins, "Virginia's Two Bridges," *Ladies' Repository* 15 (Oct. 1855): 579; "An Excursion to the Natural Bridge," *Southern Literary Messenger* 20 (1854): 163.

FATHER TO KATE

Washington City, August 10, 1852.

My dear child,

I have received your letter and journal. That of July 26–31 was extremely well written—the last was marked by a good deal of carelessness. I am sorry that you feel so lonely and wish very much that Hannah had remained with you. But the best remedy against loneliness is busying yourself with duties and, so far as circumstances admit, with amusements. I wish I could feel it safe to allow you to visit more freely: but your conversations with Miss Haines have made known to you the reasons why I think it safest for you not to do so at present. You cannot tell how much it pains me, not to be able to gratify you in every respect. I do hope that your action during your next year with Miss Haines will be such as to satisfy her and all your friends that hereafter full confidence may be reposed in your own self control and discretion. Most earnestly do I pray and long for your improvement in every respect. I long to have you beloved and honored by all: but, my dear child, you cannot expect it unless your conduct shows that you love others and are willing to make some sacrifices of your own will & pleasure for their sake.

Since my return to Washington two of my friends have died—Mr. Rantoul a member from Massachusetts and Mrs Ellzey, an old lady with whom I used to board when I lived here about twenty five years ago.

Mr. Rantoul was a very eminent man, and a very highly valued friend. His disease was very little thought of at first: but soon became very serious. Mrs Rantoul was telegraphed for on Wednesday to Boston from whence a messenger was sent to Beverly. She left by the first train the next morning and reached Washington, Friday morning, and the same evening he died. It was a terrible grief. I was in his room almost at the moment he breathed his last.[1]

Yesterday afternoon a black girl came into my room and said Mrs Ellzey wanted to know if I had received her note. I said "No." "She says she would like to see you once more—she's very sick." I told the little girl I would come up, and, after attending to another engagement I went. When I entered the room I saw she was very ill indeed. She turned towards me as well as she could and said "Oh! Mr. Chase, I am almost gone." She had been sleeping very quietly, a lady told me, but on awaking had immediately had been attacked by a bad turn. After speaking to me she said almost nothing intelligibly, but grew worse rapidly and in a few moments was no more.[2]

So the gifted and strong and the old & decrepid pass away. My dear child, remember how worthless life is, if not consecrated to God.

You ask in your last letter about riding. I have no objection to your riding two or three times a week, if any one can go with you without inconvenience. I want you to take as much exercise as you can conveniently— and your aunt won't do you any harm, I am sure, with the gymnastics, or twitches as you call them.[3]

Congress will adjourn on the 31st of August and I expect to be with you by the 5th or 6th September and to take you to Cincinnati for a short visit.

Your affectionate father
S: P: Chase

Historical Society of Pennsylvania.

1. Robert Rantoul (1805–52), an antislavery Democrat in the U.S. House of Representatives, died on August 7 of a sudden illness described as erysipelas (rash and inflammation), which affected his face and then his brain. Jane Elizabeth Woodbury Rantoul (1807–70) took her husband's remains back to Beverly, Mass., along with four congressmen chosen as escorts. *National Intelligencer,* Aug. 9, 1852; *Chase Papers,* 1:273; 2:344; *DAB,* 15:381–82.

2. Henrietta Elzey (c. 1767–1852), the widow of President James Madison's physician Dr. Arnold Elzey, died on August 9. A friend of the Wirt family, she had been reduced from affluence to living in a single room in a boardinghouse in her later years. A later memoir mentioned "a colored woman, Peggy," who was Henrietta Elzey's only servant. Sarah E. Vedder, *Reminiscences of the District of Columbia, or, Washington City Seventy-Nine Years Ago, 1830–1909* (St. Louis, Mo.: A.R. Fleming Printing Co., 1909), 53–54; *History of the Medical Society of the District of Columbia, 1811–1909* (Washington, D.C.: Medical Society of the District of Columbia, 1909), 219; *Chase Papers,* 2:42.

3. The aunt was perhaps Jane Chase Skinner. Neither her interest in gymnastics nor Father's approval of such exercise would have been unusual in this era. Respected female educators such as Mary Lyon and Catherine Beecher promoted calisthenics for girls, as did *Godey's* magazine editor Sarah Josepha Hale, who approved of this type of structured physical exercise as appropriately decorous and restrained for women. Jan Todd, *Physical Culture and the Body Beautiful: Purposive Exercise in the Lives of American Women, 1800–1870* (Macon, Ga.: Mercer University Press, 1998), 33, 57, 88, 120, 129.

FATHER TO KATE

Washington City, August 27, 1852

My dearest child,

I have received your journal of last week and was pleased with most of it—with some of it very much. One thing, however, you must remember—not to grow weary in well doing. You must not begin well and then towards the end grow careless in any thing you do.

I am writing in the Senate Chamber. It is growing dark, and Senators are growing uneasy. They have not had their dinners—at least most of them have not. Some of them I am sorry to say have visited the refectory a little too often, and are not as sober as they should be. The gallery is full: and the scene is quite animated. A Senator offers an amendment— the President says it must be reduced to writing—the Senator replies there are but two words—the President puts the question.[1] The Ayes evidently have it, but the President declares it lost. A division is required. A Senator demands that the amendment be reduced to writing, and when that is done offers an amendment to the amendment. A tipsy Senator gets up & opposes it. Wine makes him merry and he makes Senators merry / So we go. It is sad and wrong; but almost unavoidable when so many men get together under circumstances of so much excitement, and of such different characters.[2]

I must stop for the present. I expect to be in Lockport on Thursday Evening or Friday morning, and to leave on Friday. Give my love to all.

Yours affectionately

S: P: Chase

Historical Society of Pennsylvania.

1. On the evening of August 27, the Senate was debating an appropriations bill. There was no vice president of the United States since Millard Fillmore had become president on the death of Zachary Taylor in July 1850, and the presiding officer of the Senate was Alabama Democrat William Rufus de Vane King, the president pro tempore. Senators proposed a series of amendments having to do with printing expenses for Supreme Court decisions and Taylor's obituary notices. Father probably referred to James A. Pearce, a Whig (later a Democrat) from Maryland, whose proposal was to add the two words "Provided, however" to one sentence in an amendment. *Congressional Globe*, 32d Cong., 1st sess., 1852, 2399; *Bio. Dir. U.S. Cong.*, 147, 151, 1314–15, 1624.

2. According to the *Congressional Globe*, Isaac P. Walker, a Democratic senator from Wisconsin, offered the amendment to the amendment. Then Senator Willie Person Mangum of North Carolina, a Whig, opposed Walker's proposal—thus Mangum may be the "tipsy" senator. The record suggests that many senators were growing impatient with the debate, and Father's reference to his colleagues being "merry" might be ironic. After complaints that they could be there all night, Father rose to say that "those who introduced the amendment, originally, are responsible for the consumption of the time of the Senate at this late hour of the session, and not those who oppose it." Then, after Virginian Robert Mercer Taliaferro Hunter noted that he "was not charging any one with the loss of time," Alabama Democrat Jeremiah Clemens made what sounds like a sniping comment that the "Senator will allow me to suggest that the country will never hold the Senator from Ohio responsible for anything." *Congressional Globe*, 32d Cong., 1st sess., 1852, 2400; *Bio. Dir. U.S. Cong.*, 791, 1236, 1418, 1995.

FATHER TO KATE

Washington, Decr. 21, 1852.

My dear Child,

I am very-very sorry that Miss Haines thinks you had better not come to Washington at this time. In a note received from her today she says "in my judgment it will be much better for Kate not to go to Washington, both on account of her health and other considerations, indeed I do not feel that she deserves this pleasure at present and would much prefer that she should remain in New York."

As long as you are under the charge of Miss Haines I think it my duty to acquiesce in her views respecting what is best for you. She may be mistaken, sometimes, as I or any other person, however devoted to you, might be; but she has shown too deep and too earnest a solicitude for your welfare to permit any doubt that she seeks, in all her decisions and requirements, your truest happiness, and her knowledge of all the facts and circumstances necessary to a decision make it more probable that she will decide right in any particular instance, than that I would. I feel it my duty, therefore, to leave you in New York during the coming holidays.

This is a great disappointment to me, and no doubt will be to you. I reckoned confidently on the pleasure of having you and Maria[1] with me, and my grief that *you* cannot come is all the greater because I am sure you must have done something wrong or neglected some duty, or Miss Haines would have been willing that you should come. You can hardly think, dear Kate, how much of a father's happiness is in the power of his child. Reports of your good conduct and improvement give me the greatest pleasure; but when any thing occurs which makes me think you have incurred the censure or displeasure of your teachers by misconduct I am pained exceedingly / It seems to me that the knowledge of this should be a strong stimulus to the performance of your duty: but how much stronger should be the thought "Thou God! seest me."[2]

You must not be angry on account of your disappointment. Take it with a gentle and loving spirit. Make Miss Haines see that you acquiesce in her views, though not without regret, yet with the fullest confidence in her goodness and discretion and with the sincerest desire to please her and regain whatever you may have lost in her good opinion. Be sure, my darling, that this is the wisest course and the one most pleasing to God. *Improve* your disappointment and, like an unsightly bush, it will bear beautiful flowers for you yet.

You have not written me your regular letters. Why is this? I expect you to write once a week, and though I do not wish you to take that time which should be given to exercise or recreation, yet, I trust, Miss Haines will give you some proper & sufficient time for it

Your affectionate father,
S: P: Chase

Historical Society of Pennsylvania.

1. Kate's cousin, Maria Southgate.
2. Genesis 16:13: "And she called the name of the Lord that spake unto her, Thou God seest me: for she said, Have I also here looked after him that seeth me?"

FATHER TO KATE

Washington, Jany 23, 1853.
My dear child,

I received your last letter day before yesterday: and it was welcome although it had been so long in coming. It was my wish that you should write me regularly once a week, and that your letters, instead of being mere dry bones should expressly freely your thoughts in the confidence of a beloved child to a beloved father, and should also, contain natural & easy accounts of what you see, do, and experience from day to day, just such as you would give if talking to a schoolfellow. For several weeks past however I have received no letters at all; and now the one which comes commences with saying that you have a great deal to write about; proceeds with a very "dry bones" account of your visit to Keller, the Magician, & closes with an apology for a short letter.[1] I do not like this: if I did not believe you could do better, I should not, however, say a word about it. But you can.

You are allowing yourself in habitual disregard of your father's wishes, and are permitting the growth of a habit, which will cost you a great deal of misery. It makes me very sad to think of it.

I did not mean to write you any more this winter, for I thought it hardly worth while to write to a child who took so little pains to obey, and so little pleasure in complying with my wishes. I expected to see you and speak to you in March.

But the receipt of your letter has inclined me to write you once more, and once more repeat my wishes. Perhaps you will try to comply with them.

I will do you the justice to say that your last letter is quite well written so far as the penmanship goes. There are a few errors in spelling, evidently the results not of ignorance, but of carelessness.

I wish you, my dear Kate, to think seriously what you do when you neglect complying with your fathers wishes. You are old enough now to reflect, and judge your own conduct. I wish you to consider what happiness your prompt and cheerful endeavors to do what I require will give me: and how much pain I must receive from careless & indifferent conduct. Remember also that the welfare and happiness of yourself and little Nettie are now my greatest cares, and that you have it in your power greatly to promote my happiness by your good conduct, and greatly to destroy my comfort and peace by ill conduct.

I mean now to leave you to your thoughts, praying earnestly that God may make you a dutiful, affectionate, studious and happy child.

Perhaps you will after receiving this try to write regularly. If so I will endeavor to write you oftener and give you an account of what goes on here, as far as I see it.

Remember that there is no reason for so long a delay between the dates of your letters & their arrival here. The Mail leaves New York twice a day and comes through in 12 hours. I ought always to receive your letters the day after they are written.[2] Your last was dated the 18th and did not get here till the 21st or 22nd.

Give my love to Maria & Fanny Breese & Sallie McGrew.

Your affectionate father[3]
S: P: Chase

Historical Society of Pennsylvania.

1. Although Father clearly wrote "Keller," it seems likely that Kate actually wrote to him about "Heller" the magician. The famous magician Harry Kellar did begin performing as a ten-year-old, but if his autobiography and other contemporary accounts of his life record his birth year correctly, he was still only four years old in 1853. Robert Heller, born William Henry Palmer in England in 1828, came to New York City and began performing in a leased hall on Broadway in December 1852. Billing himself as "The Prince of Wizards," Heller had a run of more than two hundred shows in his "Saloon of Wonders," which featured regular performances that Kate might have attended in December 1852 or January 1853. Heller was best known for his "second sight" routine, wherein he went into the audience and held articles and an assistant on stage who could not see those articles was able to describe them in detail. *New York Times*, Dec. 1, 14, 1852, Jan. 3, 20, 1853; Milbourne Christopher, *The Illustrated History of Magic* (New York: Crowell, 1973), 211–12; Harry Kellar, *A Magician's Tour Up and Down and Round About the Earth* (Chicago: R. R. Donnelley, 1886); *Nat. Cyc.*, 14:221; *Appletons'*, 4:641.

2. According to Kate's filing endorsement, she received this letter on January 24 and answered it on the twenty-fifth.

3. Father apparently first wrote "daughter," then partially blotted the word away and wrote "father" in its place.

FATHER TO KATE

Washington, Feb. 6, 1853.

My dear child,

It is Sunday Evening, and before going to church I will give a few moments to conversation with you. Your letter dated 2nd Feb. was only received here today, when it should have come the morning, or, at latest, the evening after it was written. You speak of a letter written very carefully before. I do not think I received that at all; for the one received today is the first which I have received since my last to you. Can't you tell me exactly what day is allowed you for writing, & when your letters are sent to the Post Office?

I was very sorry to learn that you were prevented from going to Mrs Garniss' by being unwell. I feel very much troubled when I hear of your being in the slightest degree indisposed: for you can hardly realize my anxiety about your health. I will believe, however, that on this occasion nothing serious could have been the matter as you were able to dance & play till bedtime. You must be very careful of your health. Your constitution is not strong naturally; but by eating only wholesome food, and taking sufficient exercise, and avoiding every thing which weakens, you may become a vigorous & healthy woman, when you grow up. Miss Haines will give you excellent advice, and you must pray continually to God for strength to enable you to follow it

I was pleased with your account of your visit to the Panorama of the Holy Sepulchre. It must have been a very interesting sight to you.[1] You must learn all about such places that you can, and pay particular attention to your Geography that you may know where they are and which way to go to them. If you live and improve, as I hope you will, it is very probable that in a few years you may see many of these places with your own eyes.

The Church bell is now ringing and I must close. I mean to write to you another letter in a day or two as this is a short one. May God bless you my dear child, and make you all your affectionate father longs to have you. Give my best respects to Miss Haines & kindest regards to Fannie Breese & Sallie McGrew.

Your devoted father
S: P: Chase

Historical Society of Pennsylvania.

1. Panoramas, or massive paintings in circular rooms that provided 360-degree views for spectators, gained popularity in both Europe and America during this period. Depictions of the Holy Land were particularly prevalent subjects. Painter John Banvard exhibited his "Panorama of the Holy Land" in New York City for sixteen months in 1852–53. Banvard's exhibit provided not only rolling painted images, estimated to be between twenty-five and forty-eight feet tall, but also dramatic explanatory lectures accompanied by music. A major section of the panorama was devoted to a visual tour through the many rooms of the Church of the Holy Sepulchre, the Jerusalem Church believed to be the site of Jesus's tomb. Ralph Hyde, *Panoramania!: The Art and Entertainment of the "All-Embracing" View* (London: Trefoil in association with Barbican Art Gallery, 1988), 7, 11, 13, 37; John Davis, *The Landscape of Belief: Encountering the Holy Land in Nineteenth-Century American Art and Culture* (Princeton, N.J.: Princeton University Press, 1996), 3, 53–55, 65–68, 70; George Horatio Derby, *Phoenixiana; or, Sketches and Burlesques* (New York: D. Appleton & Co., 1856), 252.

FATHER TO KATE

Washington City, March 9, 1853.

My dear Kate,

Your last letter came this morning. It is dated March 2nd, but this I suppose is a mistake, as, if that be the true date the letter must have been *written* a week ago, whereas it is postmarked Mar. 8, which was yesterday. You must learn to be careful about dates, as well as every thing else.

The time is very near when I shall have the pleasure of again embracing my darling child. I am very happy in the thought that I shall find you improved, and enjoying the approval of your kind guardian as well as instructress, Miss Haines. You can never be too grateful to her for the tender solicitude with which she has watched over you, supplying the place of your sainted mother. God give you wisdom and strength, my dear child, to act as she counsels, that you may be respected and beloved here, & happy hereafter.

A great many of the friends, whom I have been accustomed to meet during the winter have left Washington, and the place is, comparatively, quite dull. A crowd of officeseekers, however, remain from whom I receive more visits than I wish.

I suppose you will see Mr. Ball & Miss Eva in New York, as Mr. B——— told me he intended to remain there some days. Miss Eva has been very much liked here this winter, and leaves many friends behind her, won by her in Washington. My friend Mrs McLanahan, also, told me that she should call on you: and I shall be glad if Miss Haines will let you go and see her,—should she invite you to do so,—while she remains in New York. Mr. McLanahan was a member of the last and the next preceding Congress from Pennsylvania, and has been a much valued friend of mine. Mrs. McLanahan is a daughter of Mr. McBride, who lives on 5th Avenue, I believe, not very far from Mr. Austen's. She is an excellent, intelligent, christian lady, full of kindness, abounding in good sense, and without the least particle of affectation.[1]

It will be very pleasant, indeed, for Josey Kenner to see her family in May after so long a separation. I am glad that she is to have such a pleasure so soon. I suppose that Aunt Charlotte & Cousin Emily will come up to Cincinnati about the same time.[2] Would it not be pleasant if we could all be together at Clifton this Summer?

Tell Sallie McGrew that I am much obliged to her for her kindnesses to you and give her my love;—and give my love, also, to Maria and Fanny Breese. Tell Maria I wish she would write me a very nice letter. I should prize it much.

I had a letter from Ralston today. He says that Ben. Ludlow has gone to New York to be with Kate in her great sorrow. Terrible indeed has been her visitation.[3] My heart aches for her.

I meant to give you a description of a dinner I was at yesterday at the British Minister's where I met a number of people you would like to hear about; such as the Russian Minister, his wife & sister in law, secretaries, Senators, Ministers, attaché's &c but I am at the bottom of my sheet and it is time to go to the Senate Chamber especially as I wish to call on Judge McLean and Mrs McLean on my way.[4]

Your own affectionate father
S: P: Chase

Miss C. J. Chase

P.S. As I shall not be in New York till week after next you will have time to write me at least two more letters.

Historical Society of Pennsylvania.

1. Anne McBride, daughter of New York merchant and diplomat James McBride, married lawyer and politician James Xavier McLanahan in 1843. A Democrat and a former

member of the Pennsylvania state senate, James McLanahan had just concluded his second term in the U.S. House of Representatives, 1849–53, the same week Father wrote this letter. David Austen lived on 12th Street in New York City. *The New York City Directory for 1853–1854. Twelfth Publication* (New York: Charles R. Rode, [1853]), 48; *Nat. Cyc.*, 13:470; *Bio. Dir. U.S. Cong.*, 1476.

    2. Charlotte Kenner and her daughter, Emily Jones.

    3. Possibly the death of Kate Ludlow's husband, Mr. Baker, about whom we know very little.

    4. Sir John Fiennes Twistleton Crampton served as British minister to the United States from 1852 to 1856, when President Franklin Pierce severed diplomatic relations because of Crampton's attempts to enlist American soldiers in the Crimean War. The Russian minister, Count Waldemar de Bodisco, and Harriet Beall Williams, the daughter of a U.S. government clerk, married in 1840, when he was fifty-six and she was still in her teens. *ODNB*, 13:983; *Appletons'*, 1:299; Green, *Washington*, 149–50.

FATHER TO KATE

Cincinnati, Aug. 4, 1853.

My darling child,

    I have received your two letters one written before I saw you and the other last Friday. I think your plan of writing every Friday a very good one. Now keep your eyes open and see every thing worth seeing and your thoughts active that you may apprehend what you see, and describe it in a lively manner. I want your letters to be as full of thought and affection as it is possible for a young girl to make them. Somehow or other I dont think your handwriting improves. Exercise your taste on this.

    I wish to see you as accomplished as a lady whom I saw in Philadelphia—a Miss Furness who understands French, Italian & German, converses in all three languages, writes beautifully and talks as well as she writes.[1] I hope you will not merely equal but excel her before you are twenty. But don't think because twenty to you is seven years off you have plenty of time to spare. No, indeed. Every minute is precious. You must not lose any of them. Not that you must study all the time: but that the disposition of *all your time*, whether in study, or society, or amusement, may have reference to the great end of the highest self improvement for the happiness of yourself & others and the glory of God.

    On my way to Washington I spent a couple of days at Mr. Ellicotts—the house of the father of the lady to whom *that* letter was addressed. It is a very old mansion, situated upon the slope of a hill, which runs off into a valley through which a little stream finds its way. The house fronts the rise, and upon its walls, worked someway in the brick are the dates at which its several parts have been built. One of these dates is 1731 and the other a number of years later, but what year I dont remember. So you see the house stood there before the declaration of independence and a part of it more than forty years before. How interesting it would be if the old walls could tell the story of all they have witnessed! Was it the home of liberal or tory? Were schemes debated there for the security of American liberties or for the perpetuation of colonial dependence? Who can tell.

Long since, though the walls stand yet the actors in those scenes have all disappeared forever. Old Mr. Ellicott is himself a good deal older than this century: a white haired, but erect and vigorous old gentleman of about seventy five. His wife is more infirm than he is. There are several children of whom my friend Miss Lizzie is the youngest, I think, though there is another sister who is smaller and may be junior. My visit was a very pleasant one.[2] Miss Mary and I climbed up the hill I have mentioned and looked at the pretty prospects: we all together took a stroll to the spring, gushing out boldly in a quarry where the piles of rocks almost deny access, over the knolls, through the woods & back again; then on Sunday I went with Miss Lizzie to the Quaker meeting: where we had a "waiting opportunity" of an hour or so, and then a *hearing opportunity* of half an hour or thereabouts when two old women delivered exhortations.[3] Mr. Ellicotts family are quakers and most of them adhere to the forms and formulas of the sect. Some of them, however, do not and this is the case with Miss Lizzie and her sister Mary. Miss Lizzie is the best looking of them all, and is really a very superior woman, with a great deal of sense and a great deal of heart. You need not however be alarmed for me, for a gentleman in New York is said to be her accepted lover, and I look only for *friends* among ladies as I do also among gentleman.

But I have said so much about the Ellicotts, who by the way, expressed great regret that you did not come with me, that I have no time to tell you of my stay in Washington or my homeward journey. I can only say that I came and here I am.

Your Aunt Mary and your cousins Missouri & Virginia have gone to Lockport, where they will reside with your Uncle Edward.[4]

Yesterday Ralston received a despatch from Mrs Adela Ludlow at Buffalo, saying that George could live but a little—very little while—and imploring him to come immediately to her. He started by the next train and will be in Buffalo this afternoon. I hope he may be able to comfort Mrs Ludlow, if not to be of any other service.[5]

Clifton is looking very pretty. I rode out there yesterday with George Sumner the brother of the Senator, who has been a great traveller in Europe.[6] He was delighted with Eva Ball. At Aunt McLean's they were too much in a litter to receive him. We rode also to East Walnut Hills and visited the beautiful places of Mr. Wheeler and Mr. Joseph Longworth, taking our tea with the latter.[7]

I have not yet seen Nettie: but mean to go up to Hillsborough on Saturday.[8]

Give my kindest remembrances to all the party at Mr. Carpenter's,[9] and my special love to Mrs Garniss and Maria—and also to Delia if she has returned. I am sorry I could not get to Sharon.[10]

Your affectionate father,
S. P. Chase

Historical Society of Pennsylvania.

1. Annis Lee Furness (1830–1908) was educated at home by her mother, Annis Pulling Jenks Furness, and father, William Henry Furness, a Unitarian minister, biblical scholar, and translator of German literature. Daughter Annis, known as Annie to her family, began translating at a young age and published more than thirty volumes of adapted German novels and fairy tales, in addition to coauthoring *Metrical Translations and Poems* (1880) and *Worthy Women of Our First Century* (1877). In 1854, soon after Father met her, Annis married Dr. Casper Wister. She later corresponded about writing with her husband's nephew Owen Wister, author of the best-selling novel *The Virginian* (1902). *DAB*, 7:80; *Appletons'*, 2:565–67; 6:583; *New York Times*, Nov. 16, 1908; Darwin Payne, *Owen Wister: Chronicler of the West, Gentleman of the East* (Dallas, Tex.: Southern Methodist University Press, 1985), 206.

2. Thomas Ellicott was a businessman involved in mills and the Baltimore and Ohio Railroad, who also served as president of the Union Bank of Maryland. He married Mary Miller in 1806. They had nine children: William, Sarah Ann, Hannah, Lydia, Mary, Esther, Rebecca, Catharine, and Elizabeth, who was born in 1822. At the time of Father's visit the Ellicotts lived on the Miller family estate in Avondale, Chester County, Pa. In 1855, Elizabeth Ellicott married James Shepherd Pike (b. 1817), who during his career was Washington correspondent for the *New York Tribune*, U.S. ambassador to the Netherlands, and author of *Chief Justice Chase* (1873). C. W. Evans, *American Family History: Fox, Ellicott, Evans* (Cockeysville, Md.: Fox, Ellicott, Evans Fund, 1976), 84–85; *DAB*, 14:595–96; *Chase Papers*, 1:236, 587.

3. In the "waiting opportunity," congregants worshipped silently. A "hearing opportunity" allowed ministers and anyone else to speak. Thus Quaker meetings were relatively silent and not programmed. William Wistar Comfort, *Just among Friends: The Quaker Way of Life* (New York: Macmillan Co., 1942), 30–31; Thomas D. Hamm, *The Transformation of American Quakerism: Orthodox Friends, 1800–1907* (Bloomington, Ind.: Indiana University Press, 1988), 7, 8, 59.

4. Mary Gillespie Chase was the widow of Father's brother William, who had died in St. Louis late in November 1852. *Chase Papers*, 1:229–30.

5. George Ludlow's relationship to Adela Ludlow is unknown. This episode marked an early symptom of Ralston Skinner's mental illness. As he later revealed to Father, Skinner had delusions that caused him to feel "implicated" in George's death. Appendix; *Chase Papers*, 1:511–12.

6. Charles Sumner was born in Boston in 1811. He and Father corresponded in the 1840s, when Sumner, originally a "Conscience" Whig, joined the Free Soil ranks, and they became firm political allies. In 1849, Gamaliel Bailey published one of Father's letters to Sumner in the *National Era* as a statement of "Political Affairs in Ohio." The Massachusetts legislature elected Sumner to the U.S. Senate in 1851. Five years later, he became a symbol of the antislavery cause when Congressman Preston Brooks of South Carolina attacked him on the floor of the Senate. After a prolonged recovery from the effects of Brooks's caning, Sumner returned to the Senate and remained a senator until his death in 1874. His younger brother George (b. 1817), a political economist and reformer, had studied in Europe. *ANB*, 21:137–39; *Appletons'*, 5:750; *Chase Papers*, 2:144–45, 147–50, 160–63, 195–99, 236–41, 359.

7. The Cincinnati suburb of Walnut Hills was known as the home of the Reverend Dr. Lyman Beecher and his two famous daughters, Catharine Beecher and Harriet Beecher Stowe, as well as the site of Lane Seminary. Mr. Wheeler may have been I. D. Wheeler, who owned a large section of East Walnut Hills in the 1870s. Joseph Longworth was the only son of wealthy Cincinnati real estate magnate Nicholas Longworth. Joseph married Annie Rives in 1841 and brought her to live in his father's Walnut Hills home on Pike Street. Works Projects Administration Writers' Program, *Cincinnati*, 283, 289–91, 303–4, 306; *Chase Papers*, 1:65; Chambrun, *Making of Nicholas Longworth*, 40, 47.

8. Hillsboro, Ohio, between Columbus and Cincinnati, had about 1,400 people in 1853, including Nettie's relatives, the Collins family. Fisher, *Gazetteer*, 290.

9. Possibly Latting Carpenter (1771–1858) and his wife, Martha. They had a 223-acre farm near Glen Cove, N.Y., on Long Island (see the next letter). Daniel H. Carpenter, *History and Genealogy of the Carpenter Family in America from the Settlement at Providence, Rhode Island, 1637–1901* (Jamaica, N.Y.: Marion Press, 1901), 174–76.

10. Probably Sharon in Schoharie County, N.Y., a mineral springs resort, or perhaps Sharon, N.H. Smith, *Harper's Statistical Gazetteer*, 1600.

FATHER TO KATE

Ravenna,[1] Sep. 6, 1853.

My dear child,

I have no time to write you a long letter. I have packed my valise and am waiting for the cars which are to take me to Cleveland this morning. But I must give these few moments to you. I have had but one letter from you for a long time, and that was the one written on your birthday. It was, I must say, rather a poor beginning for your new year. You should have put your best hand to it, and written the best letter you were capable of and in your best handwriting. I dont wonder you were "ashamed to send this miserable scrawl" especially as the first letter of a young lady of thirteen. But I will say no more on this subject. I will accept your excuse of a miserable pen and hope that when you get your new one you will write better letters and in a less sprawling hand.

I suppose that by this time you are returned to New York and, I hope, in invigorated health. I am anxious to hear how your summer residence at Glencove has affected you.[2] I am afraid you have not so seriously[3] of your religious duties as you should have done: and I am afraid, also, that your health may not have improved so much as it has hitherto done in the summer season. You cannot know a fathers anxiety for a child without a mother. I have endeavored to place you in such circumstances as I believed your angel mother, could she express her wishes, would approve, and wish. My heart's desire and prayer is that you may be all she would desire. Next to the motive of duty to God and honoring that Savior who died for us I know none which seems to me so powerful in its promptings to right action as love to a dear mother now no more. I remember well her anxieties about you and our conversations about you. It was her most earnest wish that you should be a child of God as well as a useful and well qualified member of society. Many prayers for you ascended from her heart and lips to the throne of Her Heavenly Father. Dear Katie, see to it that, with Divine Grace aiding you, your part be done towards fulfilling your mothers hopes.

I have told you that I go to Cleveland this morning. I have been speaking in different Counties of the State on the subject of the duties of American citizens in respect to slavery.[4] I expect to return to Cincinnati in a few days. I was at Syracuse last week Wednesday.

If I had time I should like to tell you about some places, persons and things I have seen: but I must hurry to a close.

Give my best love to Mrs Garniss & Cousin Delia & the children & Uncle John & Mr. Austen; and my truest regards to Miss Haines.

Your affectionate father
S P Chase

Historical Society of Pennsylvania.

1. Ravenna, the county seat of Portage County, is east of Akron in the northeastern quadrant of Ohio. It was a stop on the Cleveland and Pennsylvania Railroad. The town grew from a population of 2,240 in 1850 to 3,500 in 1854. Smith, *Harper's Statistical Gazetteer,* 1454.

2. Glen Cove was a Long Island resort community of about two hundred inhabitants on the east side of Hempstead Harbor, connected to Manhattan by steamboat service. Smith, *Harper's Statistical Gazetteer,* 695; Benjamin F. Thompson, *History of Long Island From Its Discovery and Settlement to the Present Time,* 3d ed., 3 vols. (New York: R. H. Dodd, 1918), 2:452.

3. So in the original.

4. By August 1853, Father was giving speeches in a number of Ohio towns supporting Norton S. Townshend for the Ohio Senate and speaking outside the state in support of the Free Democratic cause. Sometimes his travel schedule allowed him to speak only in towns close to railroads. "I do not want to hold any meetings at all unless they can be rousers," he instructed Townshend. "Get up your songs, and your banners & get out your music and your people, and we will have good times." Townshend won the election. *Chase Papers,* 1:241–42; 2:359–40; Niven, *Chase,* 146.

FATHER TO KATE

Cincinnati, Oct. 8, 1853

My darling child,

Your little letter of last Tuesday came this morning Saturday—only four days time, while the same mail brings me a newspaper printed in New York on the evening of the next day!

It was short and not *very* funny, though you say you were full of fun. It reminded me of my own ideas of my own speeches sometimes, when I have thought myself quite eloquent, while others held, as it turned out, quite another opinion. However your letter was very interesting to me for it came from my precious daughter, and breathed the warm affection, which I doubt not she feels, for a father who loves her dearly. It always gives me pleasure to hear of your improvement, of your increased interest in your studies and of your happiness. It will give me increased pleasure to know that you derive your motives for exertion and your grounds of happiness from religious obligation and love to your Savior.

I have been absent from the City several weeks and only returned day before yesterday. My letters have been sent to Cleveland and among them I suppose one or two from you. I expect them here today.

Last evening I was out at Clifton at Mr. Balls and Judge McLean's. Aunt Charlotte Kenner and Cousin Emily, and Ammie Ludlow were at the Judge's. Little Nettie was there also having come down from Hillsboro where she will probably pass the winter with Mrs Collins.

Aunt Charlotte was quite sad. The thought of her own loss of husband and daughter and of her sister's widow hood, so recent and under circumstances so distressing was evidently pressing upon her heavily.[1] Still she endeavored to be cheerful. Emmie was as lovely as she always is—and it would be hard to find any one sweeter and lovelier. Ammie was sweet too, but not as winning, though I think more richly endowed in mind &

person. Little Nettie was herself—pleasant, gentle, pretty, dear little one. Every body loves her; and nobody can help loving her. The 19th of last month was her birthday, and I had neglected to provide her a present at the proper time. So yesterday I went to Mr. McGrews,[2] and bought a beautiful silver goblet, and gave them the name to put on it with this inscription

"from her father

19 September 1853."

At the appointed time I called for it, and it was ready—so I had it wrapped up and took it along. But I had hardly got seated in the buggy, before it occured to me, all at once, that instead of giving Netties name to Mr. McGrew, I had given yours and that I should find the goblet marked for you and not for her / And so it turned out: and so dear little Nettie missed her present last evening: and so you will get one for her birthday as well as your own—and so I must provide another for her. I dare say you wont be very sorry for the goblet is a very pretty one &, though small, quite large enough for your use.

I have not half finished what I had to say to you: but I have not time for another sheet, and so will bid you goodbye with love to Maria & Fanny & best regards to Miss H——.

Your very affectionate father

S P Chase

Historical Society of Pennsylvania.

1. Charlotte Kenner's husband, George, and her daughter Georgine Jones had both died in 1852 (see appendix). We have not identified her recently widowed sister.

2. Sallie McGrew's father, Wilson McGrew, was a prominent silversmith in Cincinnati, working from 1825 to 1859. Until 1836 he was an employee of Alexander McGrew (d. 1843), probably his older brother, who passed on his stock to Wilson when he retired. When Wilson died in 1859, he left the business to his son William Wilson McGrew, who was born in 1832. Beckman, *In-depth Study of Cincinnati Silversmiths*, 93–94.

FATHER TO KATE

Cincinnati Oct. 19, 1853.

My darling Kate,

I dont know why I have received no letter lately. Perhaps there was one in the Mail which were burnt in the Mail Car last Monday Evening.[1]

But I will write just to let you know that I am well and that Nettie is well & we all are well.

Little Nettie was in my rooms today with Ammie Ludlow, Emmie Jones & Israel Ludlow and Luddy Jones. She is the most winsome little creature you can imagine. I wish very much I could bring her with me and let you all see her. But I have pretty much made up my mind to have her stay with Mrs Collins, her mothers cousin, in Hillsborough this winter. Aunt

Charlotte Kenner wants to take her to Texas, and Aunt Clarkson urged me strongly to let her go to St. Louis but I said no. It was too far away.

Write soon and often to your

affectionate father
S P Chase

Historical Society of Pennsylvania.

1. Mail due to arrive in Cincinnati from the east, including New York City, on the morning of Tuesday, October 18, burned when sparks from the locomotive of a night express train ignited a fire in the train's baggage car between Cleveland and Columbus. *Ohio Statesman*, Oct. 18, 22, 1853; *Daily Missouri Republican*, Oct. 19, 26, 1853.

FATHER TO KATE

Washington, Dec. 10, 1853.

My darling child,

It is just a week today since I left you at New York. I have received one little letter from you since: and a very little letter it was. I am glad Maria is going to write me. You must tell her not to neglect to do so. I wish you had her talent at letter-writing; but you can cultivate what you have and by and by you will write as well. I know, however, from experience, that it is not very easy for those whom nature has not gifted with the talent to write good letters.

I found here several letters from you which had been to Cincinnati. In two of them you gave me some account of your studies. I was pleased by this, and shall be glad to have you give me me an account of each book you have in hand. From the specimen I had of your translating french, I am afraid you do not think enough. You should not be content either in French or English to pass over any word or sentence which you do not fully understand. It may answer, sometimes, to run over a page or two in order to get a general idea of the whole. This will often help greatly to the understanding of particular words: but this, by itself, will generate a careless, superficial habit, which, in the end, will give great inconvenience as well as impair the general tone of character. Avoid it, my child. What you do at all, do well.

What books have you read in Latin? You say you have just commenced Cæsar. I wish you would translate a few sentences, and send them to me writing the Latin in one column & the English in a parallell column: Say, dividing a page of letter paper into two equal parts by a line from top to bottom through the centre, and writing the Latin on one side & the English on the other.

The day here is very beautiful. The sky is clear and the sun shines bright. It was cold when I went to breakfast but I suppose it is mild enough now.

I have taken the second story of a house occupied by a private family in a very convenient & pleasant situation not far from the Hotels. I take my meals at Brown's where Judge McLean & family are.[1] I like this better than boarding with the family or having my meals sent from a restaurant: I have three rooms—a sitting room; bed room; & the small room over the hall.

Give my best regards to Miss Haines, & love to Maria & Fanny.

> Your loving father,
> S P Chase

Historical Society of Pennsylvania.

1. Brown's Indian Queen Hotel, located at Pennsylvania Avenue and 6th Street, opened in 1820 and became a prominent Washington meeting place. Kermit L. Hall, ed., *The Oxford Companion to the Supreme Court of the United States* (New York: Oxford University Press, 1992), 93.

FATHER TO KATE

Washington, Dec. 20, 1853.

My dear child,

I shall refer the matter of your coming to Washington during the holidays entirely to Miss Haines. I do not think, inasmuch as Christmas & New Year come on Sunday that Washington will offer much attraction this year; but it would be very pleasant for me to have you with me for a little while provided it would not interfere with your progress in your studies. Of that Miss Haines can judge best. Her past watchful care of you—as vigilant & kind almost as that of a mother could be,—makes me entirely willing to confide the decision of all such matters entirely to her. You do not know how much you owe. You cannot yet feel the grateful sense of her attention to you which you will some day hereafter. But you do feel enough I hope to be entirely willing to be guided by her judgment, and to be thankful to her for her counsel.

I am exceedingly anxious for your improvement now. In a few years you will necessarily go into Society. I desire that your life may be a useful one, and not only useful, but refined & tasteful. I desire that you may be qualified to ornament any society in our own country or elsewhere into which I may have occasion to take you. It is for this reason that I care more for your improvement in your studies, the cultivation of your manners, and the establishment of your moral & religious principles, than for any thing else in respect to you. To secure this improvement I know no way so certain as to pay the utmost regard to the advice and wishes of Miss Haines.

So my dear Kate just ask Miss H. about coming to Washington. If she says she thinks you had better come, you shall come. But if not, be sure that it is best for you not to come.

I had a letter from Mrs Collins today. Little Nettie was very well. I enclose you the letter as you will no doubt like to read it. Send it back to me.

> Your affe. father
> S P Chase

NETTIE TO KATE

Hillsborough—O. April 1st. 1854.[1]

Dear sister Katie

I love you very much. When will you return to Cincinnati. again? I would like you to write to me again.[2] Josie is my play mate and she is a year younger than me.[3] We have a little garden. we have violets, daffodils Hyacinths, starflowers flags, tulips, belldaffodils and a good many more. Josie sends hur love to you. Pa was to see me a week ago and showed me the slippers you worked for him. They ware beautiful[4] he buowght me an ivory thimble and a box to keep it shaped like an acone. goodby your affection sister.

> Nettie Chase

In Nettie's hand, with intervention by an adult. Brown University Library.

1. This line is in the hand of an adult, very likely Catharine Wever Collins. She also made several corrections to Nettie's text, the most apparent of which have been noted.
2. The adult wrote the final two words of the sentence above the line to replace an attempt by Nettie to write them. The "again" in the preceding sentence and the question mark after it are probably the adult's reworking of "agane" by Nettie.
3. Josephine Collins.
4. This word was written by the adult above Nettie's attempt, which may have been reworked from "beatulful" to "beautlful." A false start by Nettie, "it was but" (or "bul"), appears at the beginning of this sentence.

FATHER TO KATE

Dear Katie,[1]

I enclose to you a little letter from dear little Nettie. You must write her (so plain that she can read it herself) the sweetest answer you can. It delights me to see that she loves you so dearly, though she has seen so little of you. I want you to be very affectionate sisters and to make each other very happy.

The weather is delightful here. The Jays are on a visit to Washington. Ella speaks very kindly of you and Mrs Jay wishes you to make them a visit. I hope Miss Haines will allow you to go. It is an excellent family, of the highest tone and most elevated sentiment, and just such a one as I should like to have you know.[2] I am very anxious that you should be worthy of the respect and affection of the excellent.

Your affe. father

S P Chase

Historical Society of Pennsylvania.

1. This undated letter may be from the spring of 1854.
2. Attorney John Jay, grandson of Chief Justice John Jay and son of Father's friend and antislavery ally Judge William Jay, resided in New York with his wife, Eleanor Kingsland Field Jay. *DAB*, 10:10; *Chase Papers*, 1:237; 2:102, 104, 338–39.

FATHER TO KATE

Washington July 5, 1854

My dear Child,

Yesterday I had a note from "Uncle John"[1] informing me that you had gone to Mr. Jay's. I half regret this as Miss Haines seemed so clearly of opinion that it was not best for you; And my wish has always been that her judgment in all things should be observed by you. I hope, however, that your visit has been a pleasant one, and that Mr. & Mrs Jay were gratified by your visit. It gives me always the greatest pleasure to know that by kind, obliging, cheerful conduct you have endeared yourself to any of the friends I love. It would give me the greatest pain to think that you had failed through heedlessness or want of right judgment, to do so.

Miss Haines sent me your Report.[2] It is not so creditable to you as I hoped & expected. To rank eighth in your class ought not to satisfy you & does not satisfy me. You know I have never desired to have you apply yourself so as to injure your health; but the time has come when you must put on your thinking cap & use your brains, & qualify yourself for a part in society. The report of your French Teacher is not favorable to you. This is bad. The French is a most important language, and gives great advantages to one who can speak and write it. I regret few things more than my neglect of early opportunities to acquire it, and even now devote some time nearly every day to its acquisition. You must take some French Book with you to Concord, & try to improve, instead of losing ground during the Vacation.[3]

I suppose that, at this moment, Wednesday Morng. 8 3/4 o'clock you have just finished breakfast & that tomorrow you will return to New York. I am glad that Mr. Garniss is there to meet Cousin Eliza & take the best care of her. Your journey to Concord will, I hope, be a pleasant one. I have no fears for you safety under Eliza's care.

Dr. Bailey tells me that he & Mrs Bailey and the family are going to spend six weeks on the Sea Shore not far from Portland towards Portsmouth,[4] and that Fanny Bailey and Frank are to spend some time at Mr.

Whipple's. Fanny is a pleasant, lively girl, and Frank is a fine little boy. You will like them I have no doubt, and will I hope be useful to them by setting them an example of perfect propriety of behavior.

I cannot help feeling a good deal of anxiety about this summer's experience for you. You have always had some very kind & judicious person to watch over you, & will now have one in our dear Cousin Eliza. But you are now just at that age when girls are apt to feel that they ought to be allowed to think & act for themselves a good deal more than they are capable of, and I fear lest you may not, in every thing, act, so as to secure the regard of your friends, the approbation of your own conscience and the favor of God. Remember, my dear, dear child that no one—not the youngest child—liveth to herself. All that you do becomes a part of your future and of the future of others. By acts and words of pleasant kindness; by careful abstinence from the appearance of evil; by constant memory of the presence of a Holy God; by continual thought of the sacrifice made for you by your Savior; may you My dear Child be made a blessing to yourself, your friends & your loving, anxious father.

You must write me very often—at least twice a week—and tell me unreservedly all that happens. If you feel any repugnance to letter writing you must overcome and think to yourself "How much pleasanter I shall feel if I gratify My dear father than I shall if I indulge my laziness."

It is very warm here. Yesterday was the hottest day that has been known here for seven years as I was told. In the morning however I called at Col Benton's & Col. Fremonts. I should like to tell you about Mrs Benton, who sat in the Hall near the Colonel, absolutely helpless, without reason, with only perhaps a half consciousness of his kindness & love towards her, which made it pleasant for her to[5] be there; and about Col. & Mrs Fremont & the daguerreotype pictures he took of many features of landscape in his late journey across the continent to the Pacific—some of them are of great interest.[6]

But I must stop I have already written you a very long letter for one who has so little time for writing.

Yet I must add a word or two to tell you that I was much pleased with your Composition on the Hand. Were you not helped in it. Were the thoughts & the expression of them your own? If not absolutely your own, how much was? You must tell me all about this when you write.

Your affectionate father,
S: P: Chase

Show this letter to Cousin Eliza.

Historical Society of Pennsylvania.

1. John P. Garniss.
2. Though we have not found any of Kate's school reports, the report for another Haines student from a slightly later era gives us some idea of how these records were formatted. The collections of the New-York Historical Society include the "Yearly Report of

Miss Margaret E. Parmly" from Haines's school, dated June 16, 1870. The printed form includes three columns labeled "Standard," "Marks," and "Rank." Written in by hand on Parmly's report are the numbers 7,000 under "Standard," 7,038 under "Marks," 1 under "Rank," and under all the numbers the phrase "not absent once during the year." The report is signed by Henrietta Haines and Camille de Janon. Margaret Parmly was possibly a child or relation of Eleazar Parmly, a noted dentist in New York City. Herr and Spence, eds., *Letters of Jessie Benton Frémont*, 185.

3. The family of Father's sister Hannah Ralston Chase Whipple, who had died in 1850, lived in Concord, N.H. A railroad hub and the capital of New Hampshire, Concord had a population of more than eight thousand in 1850. Smith, *Harper's Statistical Gazetteer*, 448.

4. Gamaliel and Margaret Bailey arranged for their children to remain in New Hampshire while they traveled to Europe in the summer of 1854. Located about fifty miles from Portland, Maine, Portsmouth was the largest town in New Hampshire in 1853. Harrold, *Bailey*, 154; Fisher, *Gazetteer*, 694.

5. Father repeated "to" in the manuscript, at the turn of a page.

6. Missourian Thomas Hart Benton served in the U.S. Senate, 1821–51, and the House of Representatives, 1853–55. In 1854 the Bentons lived on C Street in Washington. After their house burned down in the next year, Benton moved in with his daughter Jessie Frémont, who maintained a home nearby. Mrs. Benton, Elizabeth (Betsy) Preston McDowell Benton, first fell ill in 1842, suffering from mysterious attacks that slowed her speech and left her weak and depressed. In January 1846, she was diagnosed, possibly misdiagnosed, with epilepsy. By the summer of Father's visit, Mrs. Benton had lost the ability to speak. She died two months later. Jessie Ann, the second of Thomas and Elizabeth Benton's five children, was born in 1824. She married John Charles Frémont, who was eleven years her senior, in 1841. John Frémont returned in May 1854 from his fifth western expedition, this one searching for the best railroad route to the Pacific. *DAB*, 2:210–13; 7:19–23; *Washington Evening Star*, Sept. 13, 1854; Andrew Rolle, *John Charles Frémont: Character as Destiny* (Norman, Okla.: University of Oklahoma Press, 1991), 23–24, 30; William Nisbet Chambers, *Old Bullion Benton: Senator from the New West* (Boston: Little, Brown, 1956), 303–4, 393, 413; Elbert B. Smith, *Magnificent Missourian: Thomas Hart Benton* (Philadelphia: Lippincott, 1957), 139, 184, 230, 301–3; Pamela Herr, *Jessie Benton Fremont* (Norman, Okla.: University of Oklahoma Press, 1988) 63, 236–37.

FATHER TO KATE

Washington July 23, 1854

My darling child,

Your letter so abruptly terminated & Cousin Eliza's note saying that you had been suddenly taken ill alarm me a good deal; and her second note saying that you were well enough to be up & dressed & would, with proper care, escape any serious illness was very welcome indeed

I hope you will be very careful. You are disposed to be otherwise; even more so than young persons generally of your age I fear. But you *must* reform this. Your constitution is naturally very delicate: as was your dear mothers. By proper care & proper exercise you can strengthen it, and ensure to yourself comparative exemption from disease. It will cost some little effort, and a considerable perseverance but the benefits will be worth more than they cost.

Your indisposition makes me very reluctant to blame you for any thing and yet I must say that I *do not* hold you quite excusable for not writing for so long a time. Where there is a will there is a way. As a set off to this blame I must tell you how much gratified I was by Eliza's account of your behavior at Middletown[1]—she says that you conducted yourself with the greatest propriety and won the regard & goodwill of all who became acquainted with you. You may depend upon it this pleased me very much. I hope you will never give me the pain of hearing different accounts of you. There is a very simple rule for getting along well which is Always *think* as kindly as possible of all you associate with and *try* always to make them happy. Thinking kind thoughts & doing kind acts is a certain fountain of happiness for the thinker and doer as well as for the objects of the kindness.

The day of adjournment is rapidly approaching. The session will terminate next week Friday. The probability is that I shall be able to leave that night, & shall soon after be at Concord. I want to be at Quebec on the 9th of August at the opening of the Provincial Parliament & for two or three days after: but it is possible that I may be at Portland on the 12th. I want Eliza to write me about the best and quickest way of getting to Quebec. I suppose it is through New York, Albany & Montreal but I dont know. If you were "a little older" I should like to take you with me.[2]

The weather has been extremely hot here. Today we have a pleasant breeze, & the air feels fresher than it has felt of late, as if there had been a thunder-shower some where in the neighborhood.

This morning I saw Mr. Hale in Church: and he went home with me to Dr. Baileys & took part of my little dinner. He is in good spirits about the election in New Hampshire.[3]

I have been at Church twice today, & heard two excellent sermons: one on the duty of parents to children & the other on the duty of earnest endeavor to secure an interest in Christ, and to meet faithfully the various responsibilities of life. Dr. Butler, the preacher, is an excellent man.[4]

You must write me, if well enough, a nice, sprightly letter when you receive this: and thus prove your love for me. Give my love to Mr. Whipple & Eliza & Hannah, & be sure that you get a great deal for yourself from

Your affectionate father
S: P: Chase

Historical Society of Pennsylvania.

1. Eliza Whipple and Kate apparently stopped at Middletown, Conn., on their way from New York City to New Hampshire. Middletown was a commercial center of more than eight thousand people and the home of Wesleyan University. Fisher, *Gazetteer,* 474.

2. Father was still in Washington on August 8 and in New Hampshire by August 11, suggesting that he did not make his proposed trip to Quebec. The Canadian Parliament was to meet in the Music Hall in Quebec City due to problems with other sites. Canadian politics were riven that summer by controversies stemming from transcontinental railroad contracts. Following the collapse of the government and new elections, Parliament did not

meet until September, by which time Father was in Ohio. J. M. S. Careless, *The Union of the Canadas: The Growth of Canadian Institutions, 1841–1857* (Toronto: McClelland & Stewart, 1967), 143, 189, 191–92; Margaret Conrad, *A History of the Canadian Peoples* (Toronto: Copp Clark Pitman, 1993), 426–29; Donald Creighton, *A History of Canada* (Boston: Houghton Mifflin, 1958), 277–78; Stanley B. Ryerson, *Unequal Union: Confederation and the Roots of Conflict in the Canadas, 1815–1873* (New York: International Publishers, 1968), 248; Father to John Jay, Aug. 8, 1854 (Jay Family Papers, Columbia University); to John P. Hale, Aug. 11, 1854 (John Parker Hale Papers, New Hampshire Historical Society); to Charles Sumner, Sept. 13, 1854 (Houghton Library, Harvard University).

3. As an antislavery Democrat, John Parker Hale was sympathetic to the American or Know Nothing Party in New Hampshire. Know Nothings, while anti-Catholic and anti-immigrant, were also strongly antislavery, and in New Hampshire they favored school reform and temperance as well. The state had an 82 percent voter turnout in 1854 and elected a slate of Know Nothing candidates, including Ralph Metcalf for governor. A contemporary of Hale's saw the election as a stern rebuke to the "panderers of slavery." Lex Renda, *Running on the Record: Civil War-Era Politics in New Hampshire* (Charlottesville, Va.: University Press of Virginia, 1997), 48–55.

4. Dr. Clement Moore Butler had been the chaplain for the U.S. Senate from 1849 to 1853 and would be the minister of Christ Church in Cincinnati from 1854 to 1857 before returning to Washington. *Appletons'*, 1:478; *Nat. Cyc.*, 10:34.

FATHER TO KATE

Senate Chamber, July 31, 1854

My darling Kate,

Mr. Dawson, of Georgia, is making a very *loud* speech, but it does not interest me enough to make me listen to him.[1] I prefer to spend the time in the more agreeable occupation of writing to you.

Your last letter gave me a great deal of pleasure, first, because it assured me that you were nearly well again, and secondly because it was so well written. By "well" I do not mean merely that it is is well composed, but that it breathes a freer and more affectionate spirit than your letters have usually exhibited. I dare say one reason for the dryness of your letters is that to which you refer—namely that they were to pass under the supervision of Miss Haines. Now that no body is to read them but your father I am glad that your pen runs with more facility.

I wish I had something pleasant to say to you: but, in truth, my own pen does not run very freely at this time. My thoughts are any thing but clear. The weather is very hot: we have been sitting here a great while— the night is coming on and I feel dull. I do wish I felt more in tune; for I should like to write a very clear letter to you. But it is quite out of the question.

In a few days I hope to see you, but you must answer this note to this place; and give me something to make me laugh.

I have just been called out of the Senate Chamber to subscribe for a Kansas Paper to be devoted to the establishment of Freedom in that Territory.[2]

And now the chandelier has been lighted up and the gaslight fills the chamber. Senators look dull & cross and as if they wanted their dinners.

Some of them look more pleasantly and as if they had been off & got something to eat. I am one of these last, for I paired off with Gen. Houston and went home & got my dinner quietly.[3]

It is past seven o'clock & I say good night.

> Your affectionate father
> S P Chase

Historical Society of Pennsylvania.

1. William Crosby Dawson, a senator from Georgia, 1849–55, took part in a debate on appropriations for river and harbor improvements that the Senate held late on July 31. *Congressional Globe,* 33d Cong., 1st sess., 1854, 2024; app., 1189–90, 1196–97, 1204; *Bio. Dir. U.S. Cong.,* 885.

2. Two Kansas abolitionist newspapers began publication in October 1854: John and J. L. Speer's *Kansas Pioneer,* which was renamed the *Kansas Tribune* in 1855, and G. W. Brown's *Herald of Freedom,* first printed in Wakarusa, Kans. The *Herald* was moved to Lawrence, where it was destroyed in the May 1856 sack of the city but began publishing again in November of that year. In May 1857, framed copies of the *Herald of Freedom* hung on the wall of Kate's bedroom. William G. Cutler, *History of the State of Kansas* (Chicago: A. T. Andreas, 1883), 190–91; *Chase Papers,* 2:451.

3. That is, he and Houston were on opposite sides of the issues before the Senate and agreed to be absent from the chamber at the same time in case any votes should be called. The two of them had cooperated before in this fashion; see Father's letter to Belle, July 29, 1850, above. Earlier in 1854, Houston, who had strong unionist views, had surprised and angered many of his colleagues by voting with Father and other antislavery politicians against the Kansas-Nebraska Act, which he considered to be a violation of the sacred compact of the Missouri Compromise. The senator from Texas presciently argued that the slaveholding South would "reap the whirlwind." Niven, *Chase,* 124, 148–53; M. K. Wisehart, *Sam Houston: American Giant* (Washington, D.C.: R. B. Luce, 1962), 542–44.

CHRONOLOGY

September 1854	Father in Cincinnati; Kate, age fourteen, at school in Pennsylvania; Nettie, staying with relatives in Hillsboro, Ohio, turns seven
January 1855	Father in Washington, D.C.; has his forty-seventh birthday
March 1855	33d Congress and Father's Senate term end; in Ohio, he campaigns for governor
January 1856	Father is inaugurated governor of Ohio; the Chases board in Columbus with the Snowden family
February 1857	Kate and Nettie are in the Clifton-Cincinnati area
May–July 1857	All make visits to Cincinnati
July 1857	Father, Kate, and Nettie go to Baltimore for railway celebration
August–October 1857	Nettie and Kate stay with Collins family in Hillsboro; Father campaigns throughout Ohio and is reelected governor
December 1857	They buy and furnish a house in Columbus
October 1858	Father campaigns for Lincoln in Illinois
February 1859	Aunt Alice, Father's sister, dies in Columbus
September 1859	Father in Columbus, then speaking elsewhere in Ohio; Kate in Philadelphia; Nettie in Hillsboro
February 1860	Ohio legislature elects Father to U.S. Senate (to begin with 37th Congress, March 1861)
May 1860	Republican convention in Chicago chooses Lincoln as presidential candidate
Summer 1860	Father and Kate in Columbus, Nettie in Hillsboro; Kate turns twenty in August

CHAPTER 3

"Be Patient Under Reproof"

SEPTEMBER 1854–AUGUST 1860

W HEN KATE arrived at Maria Eastman's school in Aston Ridge, Pennsylvania, for the fall term in September 1854, she traveled there from Concord, New Hampshire, and was accompanied by her older cousin, Eliza Whipple. Maria Eastman was originally from Concord, and though we do not know when the decision was made for Kate to attend the boarding school in Pennsylvania, the letter of September 15 printed in this chapter indicates that Kate and her father were both in Concord toward the end of the summer and saw Eastman there. Father had gone to New Hampshire after the Senate's adjournment in August. Apparently he then traveled from New England to Cincinnati, sending Kate to her new school under Eliza's care.[1] At school, Kate grew restive (see her father's letter of April 13, 1855) and perhaps not just from the regimen of the institution. She was fourteen when she went to Aston Ridge, and her father's letters reflect his anxious desire to shape her character before she attained full adulthood.

Control was a theme of his correspondence with her in this period. He conceded that it might require "hard doctrine" for her to believe that her school's discipline was based in love, harder still for her to respond to that discipline with love.[2] The starkest example of the authority that he, and others by proxy, maintained over her was his short letter of July 25, 1856, in which he commanded her to "*Go nowhere*" and "*do nothing*" except with her aunt's permission. Early in 1857, when Kate and her father were together in Columbus, he left brief indications in his diary of "trouble" with her (arguments over what she could and could not do, apparently) and of "false conduct" on her part that he did not elaborate on in his journal.[3]

There was hope, though, for the recognition of wrongdoing could bring remorse and lead to better conduct. "We are all sinners," he vouched, ranking himself among the most unworthy.[4] External discipline could foster self-control, self-discipline—and self-reliance. By late in 1857 he gave Kate, who was then seventeen, responsibility for buying furnishings in Cincinnati for their house in Columbus. Not surprisingly, he involved himself in the purchasing decisions and cautioned her to follow his instructions. Still, he took pains to declare his confidence in her: "you have capacity & will do very well," he assured her. A few months earlier he exulted in his diary that Kate was "sprightly & intelligent & right minded" when she conversed with Charles Sumner's political protégé Edward L. Pierce.[5]

We continue to see but one side of the discourse in this period, his letters to her, with only partial reflections of her responses. One of the matters he instructed her in, by letter, was letter writing. He coached her to develop "a *noticing habit*" and to develop "a conversational, & even dramatic style." He outlined the components of a good letter, praised her when she approached that standard, and attempted to follow his own strictures, briefly describing funeral services for a Latin American diplomat and conjuring sights and sounds of Cincinnati.[6] It was in regard to letter writing that he cited the aphorism from the earl of Chesterfield (although misattributing it to Samuel Johnson): "What is worth doing at all is worth doing well." Ironically, while placing that stress on perfection, he tried to encourage creativity and a lack of inhibition. "Let your pen *run* freely," he urged in 1859—quite a challenge when the writer must concentrate on "doing well" by her father's high standards.[7]

His political future was uncertain in 1854–55 as the various groups that finally took shape as the Republican Party sorted themselves out. But he attained the nomination for governor of Ohio in 1855 and set out through the state to speak in numerous towns and counties, contending with impassable roads and swollen watercourses. During one two-day period he traveled by open wagon, canoe, carriage, horseback, and railroad handcar. He won the election—one of the significant early victories for the national Republican effort—and was inaugurated in Columbus on January 14, 1856.[8]

For his family, his election as governor meant that the three of them could rejoin as a single household. Nettie had been spending much of her time with the family of her mother's cousin, Catharine Collins, in Hillsboro, while Kate was in school in Pennsylvania and their father was in Washington, D.C., or campaigning around Ohio. Their coming together in Columbus meant fewer occasions for them to exchange letters. Nettie's recollections for the *New York Tribune* decades later recorded some aspects of their home life, however, especially from the latter part of their time in Columbus.[9] And her father left some tidbits in his journal from 1857.

Many mornings in January and February of that year, the three of them set out from home together, either by sleigh or on foot. Father went to his office in the State House, and Kate and Nettie continued on to school at Lewis Heyl's Esther Institute a couple of blocks away on Broad Street. At that time there was no official governor's mansion, and in 1856–57, Governor Chase and his daughters boarded with the family of Philip T. Snowden, a dealer in silks and embroideries and a Republican supporter. The Snowden home was on Town Street, a few blocks east of the capitol. On at least one occasion, Kate met her father at his office in the afternoon and they went home together.[10]

There was church together on Sundays, of course—often at Trinity Protestant Episcopal Church. On one occasion the three of them all went to a shoe store to get overshoes for Nettie.[11] There were frequent evening parties, some of which Kate attended with her father, and in February 1857 he hosted a big reception for members of the state government and other guests. Both girls went to official ceremonies, including an event dedicating the new state capitol, and in July 1857 they went to Baltimore with him for celebrations marking the completion of railways to connect the eastern seaboard and St. Louis.[12]

Father took Kate to a lecture on "Success," and Ralph Waldo Emerson spoke at the Columbus Atheneum.[13] In addition to Nettie's and Kate's studies at Heyl's school, their father initiated a program to improve their French. He hired Adolphus Mot, a native of France, to come to their home for regular evening lessons in written and spoken French. Father threw himself into the enterprise, studying grammar books, adding a French devotional guide to his religious reading, and undertaking Victor Hugo's *Notre-Dame de Paris* and other works in French.[14] He was also reading, during the same period, Edmund Spenser's *The Faerie Queene*, Gibbon's *Decline and Fall of the Roman Empire*, the *Aeneid*, Longfellow's *Hyperion* and *Song of Hiawatha*, a work on Egyptian antiquities, and the Septuagint, the Greek Old Testament. In February he traveled to Cleveland to deliver a talk on Galileo.[15]

Only late in 1857, after his election to a second term as governor, did they give up their rented lodgings and move into a house of their own in Columbus. Occupying that residence on the corner of 6th and State streets represented a second reunion of the three of them in Columbus. Knowing at the outset that the 1857 political campaign would be difficult and that he would have limited help mobilizing the vote, Father had left both Nettie and Kate with the Collins family in Hillsboro for two months, from mid-August until the election was over in October, while he completed a grueling itinerary of speaking engagements in counties throughout the state.[16] It was the house in Columbus, where they came together again after the separation of the campaign, that Nettie recalled decades later for readers of the *Tribune;* there that Kate made an impression on the visitor from England, Isabella Strange Trotter; and there that a young William Dean Howells first dined "in society." The occasion was a Thanksgiving dinner, unusual in Ohio in that day, when the holiday was generally observed only in New England and by "families of New England origin" elsewhere. At that house in Columbus, too, the girls'

Aunt Alice died in February 1859. She was staying with them and died after suffering "an apoplectic fit" on the doorstep after returning from church one evening.[17]

Father once again traveled around the state giving speeches during the 1859 campaign, but not as a candidate, and his second term as governor ended in January 1860. The following month the legislature once again elected him a U.S. senator, for a term to begin in 1861, and in March the state's Republican convention endorsed him for the presidency. During the latter part of April and early part of May 1860, Kate accompanied him on a visit to Washington, where he conferred about politics, but in May the Republican national convention in Chicago gave its nomination to Abraham Lincoln.[18]

Nettie, meanwhile, was well into her own apprenticeship in letter writing. In September 1857, while both daughters were in Hillsboro, Father wrote to Nettie from Columbus to report on his political campaigning. Referring to a letter he had received from her, he deemed it "a pretty good letter for such a little girl, but not nearly as good as some little girls write who are no older than you are."[19] About six weeks before her thirteenth birthday, he unlimbered the slogan from Chesterfield, this time, however, without any attribution of its source. He called it simply an "old saying." Nettie could not easily have forgotten the principle, for she now had not one, but two, instructors. "Your last letter was a great improvement upon the others," Kate wrote her in July 1860, sounding very much like their father—"still the spelling is not perfect."[20]

1. Maria Eastman's bill, Feb. 17, 1855 (Chase Papers, LC); Father to James Mackenzie, Aug. 7, 1854 (Huntington Library); to John P. Hale, Aug. 11, 1854 (John Parker Hale Papers, New Hampshire Historical Society); to Charles Sumner, Sept. 13, 1854 (Houghton Library, Harvard University).

2. Apr. 13, 1855, below.

3. *Chase Papers*, 1:260, 263–64.

4. Apr. 13, 22, 1855, below.

5. Letters of Dec. 4, 5, 1857, below; *Chase Papers*, 1:277–78.

6. See his letters of Sept. 15, 1854, Feb. 8, Apr. 13, 22, 1855, below.

7. Apr. 13, 1855, Sept. 4, 1859, below.

8. *Chase Papers*, 1:243; 2:421–25, 434.

9. "A Woman's Memories," *New York Tribune*, Feb. 15, 1891.

10. *Chase Papers*, 1:247, 251–52, 255, 257, 263, 271, 279, 305; *Williams' Columbus Directory . . . 1856–'57*, 43, 109, 186; *Williams' Columbus Directory . . . 1858–'59*, 86, 191.

11. *Chase Papers*, 1:252, 253, 267, 269, 277.

12. Ibid., 1:249, 258, 263, 265, 266, 269, 271, 273, 274, 281, 292, 294.

13. Ibid., 1:257, 262, 273.

14. Ibid., 1:257, 258, 259, 263, 265–72, 277–81, 287, 290–93.

15. Ibid., 1:248, 253, 256–59, 264–65, 268–69, 277–80, 290, 293, 306–7, 309.

16. *Williams' Columbus Directory . . . 1858–'59*, 67; *Chase Papers*, 1:296–306, 309–10; 3:16–17.

17. Howells, *Years of My Youth*, 133; *Chase Papers*, 1:310.

18. *Chase Papers*, 1:312, 3:25–28; Blue, *Chase*, 122–23.

19. *Chase Papers*, 2:459.

20. Father to Nettie, Aug. 10, 1860; Kate to Nettie, July 25, 1860, below.

FATHER TO KATE

Cincinnati Sep. 15, 1854.

My dear Kate,

I found your first letter from Aston Ridge on my table last night when I came back from Hillsborough.[1] It was very acceptable as it informed me of your safe arrival and of your satisfaction with your new home. But I must add that it would have been much more acceptable, if it had been not quite so meager & dry. I once knew a gentleman who had visited Europe. He was fond of telling of his travels, and would give his friends an account of them some what after this fashion. "On such a day of such a month I left New York & crossed over to Liverpool. From Liverpool I went up to London. Then I went to Dover & crossed over to Calais. Then I went to Paris. From Paris I crossed over into Switzerland, & then I crossed over to Rome. From Rome I went back to Liverpool & crossed over to New York again." This gentleman got the name of Crossover Lane. He was a very worthy man, but dont you think his account of his travels was rather dry?

You must keep your eyes open, my dear child. They were given you expressly to see with: and your mind was given you expressly to observe with. It is a curious fact that some blind people see more, than many who have good eyes.

In your next letter give me some proof that you have seen & observed. I want especially to hear all about your school and your teachers: how you employ your time: what you do on Sundays. I must say, candidly, that I was disappointed the evening we visited at Mr. Eastman's to see Miss Eastman setting all her guests to playing games of chance.[2] I do not say that all such games are wrong: but still I think that they might as well be let alone and I would not on any account have you learn cards, and would rather that you should abstain altogether from all such games. I know that some good people think differently about this; but if I err I err on the safe side. The most that can be said of such games is that they relax & divert the mind: but there is danger that they may absorb and excite it: and, as there are many modes of diversion and relaxation which are not dangerous, it is best to avoid those which are.[3]

I am quite willing and indeed would prefer that you should show this to Miss Eastman; though I do not require you to do so. It is my wish to be perfectly frank and sincere, & that you should be so also.

Your cousin Belle Skinner (now Mrs Walbridge) came here the same night that I returned. The next day she was taken sick & for a week was confined to her bed. For a time we were much alarmed about her; but she recovered so much by Wednesday that I thought I might properly go to see Nettie, & now she is so nearly well again that she will leave tomorrow for Toledo, but will make, as she expects, two days journey, of what if she were well would only require about ten hours. Her husband is with her. He is a good looking, pleasant gentleman of excellent business capacities and makes her an excellent husband.

I have seen nobody here whom you know except Mrs Adela Ludlow, who enquires for you always very kindly. She is living on Broadway, & Ralston Skinner lives with her. Her daughter, Mrs Louisa Goodloe, is to be married next December, to a gentleman from Virginia of whom Ralston speaks very well.

I found Nettie very well and very happy. She was highly delighted to see me, & had a great deal to tell me. You are a great deal in her thoughts and talk. She thinks it very strange that sister Katie never answered her letter. A very lovely child, every body thinks her. Artless, guileless, truthful, affectionate, & winning she gains all hearts. It is by loving others that she makes others love her. There is a lesson in this, dear Katie. Can't you tell what it is. May our Heavenly Father bless you my child.

Your affectionate father
S P Chase

Historical Society of Pennsylvania.

1. Aston Ridge was an area on the Concord Pike, above the community of Village Green in the township of Aston, in Delaware County, Pa. In 1850, Aston Township had a population of 1,558. Smith, *History of Delaware County,* 400.

2. Maria L. Eastman was the principal of the seminary for young ladies in Aston Ridge that Kate attended in the 1854–55 school year. Not long afterward, Miss Eastman became the principal of the Brooke Hall Female Seminary in Media, Pa., which was also in Delaware County. She was the principal there for the remainder of her career and died in Media in 1895. She also taught science at Brooke Hall. Nettie, like Kate, had one year of her schooling under Miss Eastman, at Brooke Hall in 1861–62. Born about 1821, Eastman was from Concord, N.H., and had a school for young ladies there by about 1842. The poet Edna Dean Proctor was a boarding student at that school. By the early 1850s, Eastman moved to Pennsylvania and took the position at the Aston Ridge seminary. Her connection to Concord accounts for Kate's enrollment at Aston Ridge, as the Chases had relatives in Concord, including Eliza Whipple, who had been a teacher there for one term in the town's public schools in 1845. The call at "Mr. Eastman's" mentioned in the letter above almost certainly took place in Concord late in the summer of 1854, before Kate started at Aston Ridge and when she and her father were both in New Hampshire. Maria Eastman was one of thirteen children of Robert Eastman of East Concord village, and the social evening may have been at his house or the home of another male relative. Lyford, *History of Concord,* 2:1250, 1286; Rix, *Eastman Family,* 1:301–2; *Philadelphia Inquirer,* Feb. 19, 20, 1895; 1860 census, Delaware County, Pa., Media Borough, 440; Brooke Hall Female Seminary, *Catalogue,* 3.

3. Although many of Father's contemporaries shared his disapproval of games of chance, and a good deal of reform fiction was published in the 1840s and 1850s warning of the dangers of wagering, antigambling crusades never achieved the same prominence and influence as other midcentury reform movements. Negative depictions of deceptive gamblers and their victims were common, however, and games of chance had many negative connotations. The 1854 edition of one *Home Cyclopedia,* for instance, included in the definition of "vagrant" all "idle or disorderly" people, such as "persons playing at games of chance in public places." Young women were considered especially vulnerable to the temptations of gambling. Ann Fabian, "Unseemly Sentiments: The Cultural Problem of Gambling," in *The Culture of Sentiment,* ed. Shirley Samuels (New York: Oxford University Press, 1992), 144, 148, 153; George Ripley, *The Home Cyclopedia or Library of Reference* (New York: A. S. Barnes,

1854), 620–21; David C. Izkovitz, "The (Other) Great Evil: Gambling, Scandal and the National Anti-Gambling League," in *Victorian Scandals: Representations of Gender and Class,* ed. Kristine Garrigan (Athens, Ohio: Ohio University Press, 1992), 235–38.

FATHER TO KATE

Cincinnati Sep. 23, 1854.
My dear Kate,

Your letter which came this morning gave me a great deal of pleasure. I shall certainly if it is at all in my power visit you before the commencement of the next session.

I am glad that you are so contented and happy, and especially that you are so well pleased with your room & roommate. You must give my best regards to her and make me acquainted with her by telling me all about her.

Mrs Collins wrote me a letter which I received yesterday, enclosing one from our darling little Nettie. You know Netties Birthday was last Tuesday the 19th. I sent up a box for the occasion containing some gifts for the whole family; for Mrs Collins a set of Silver forks & Castors; for Nettie a Panopticon; for Josie, a crying doll, & for Caspar a drawing book "Studies of Animals."[1] They were all much delighted. To add to their pleasure Mrs Trimble gave Nettie a little party on the occasion.[2] Mrs Collins says that after they got to Mrs Trimbles she asked Nettie how she liked her visit. "I liked my ride very much" she replied, "but my visit is not over yet." Pretty discreet, was it not for a seven year old. She is the most guileless & perfectly truthful little one I ever saw. You must write her as often as you can and as nice letters as possible.

One word about your studies. Don't try to do too much but *be sure you understand everything as you go along.*

Give my best regards to Miss Eastman.

Your affectionate father,
S P Chase

Historical Society of Pennsylvania.

1. Possibly *Studies of Animals: With Instructions for the Lead Pencil and Crayon* by Otis N. Fessenden (New York: D. Appleton, 1852). The panopticon for Nettie may have been an optical device combining features of a microscope and a telescope. Philip Babcock Gove et al., *Webster's Third New International Dictionary of the English Language Unabridged* (Springfield, Mass.: G. & C. Merriam Co., 1963), 1631.

2. In 1811, Rachel Woodrow Trimble became the second wife of politician Allen Trimble, who was Ohio's acting governor in 1822 and governor, 1826–30. They maintained the family home in Hillsboro, Ohio, even during his years in public office. They were neighbors of the Chase family's Collins relatives. Once when Catharine Beecher visited the Trimbles, Rachel asked her about her writing. Beecher told her she was writing about housekeeping. "How would you like some practical experience?" Rachel asked her. Beecher replied, "Oh, it is so much easier to write about than to put into practice." Allen Trimble, *Autobiography and Correspondence of Allen Trimble, Governor of Ohio* (Columbus, Ohio: "Old Northwest" Genealogical Society, 1909), 237; Eliza Jane Trimble Thompson et al., *Hillsboro*

Crusade Sketches and Family Records (Cincinnati: Cranston & Curts, 1896), 25–28; *Notable American Women*, 3:451–52.

FATHER TO KATE

Washington, Jany 8, 1855

You cannot think, my precious child, how much pleasure it gives me to hear you praised, and to find that you left so agreeable an impression on those whom you met. Mr. Sumner commends you in a measured, discriminating way, which gives value to his appreciation, while all others who saw you, Mr. Wood, Dr. Bailey, Ada Smith, of Cincinnati, Addie Smith, of Washington, Mrs Bailey Miss Tenney,[1] and the rest all speak of you with the greatest kindness and with real apparent esteem. Of course I make much allowance for the natural wish of people to give pleasure to a father; but I feel sure that much of what is said is sincere, and I feel the more sure, because I have some confidence in my own judgment even when exercised upon you, where affection would be so apt to bias it, and your conduct, manners & conversation all met my approval while you were here

You, my darling, are you not in some danger of becoming vain? I hope not. Rather let me hope that comparing these opinions of you with your own sense of your own deficiencies you will be stimulated to make constant & earnest endeavors to realize in yourself these favorable regards.

Especially and most anxiously do I desire that you may become a follower of Christ, and that you may adorn the profession of Christianity by a life of faith & obedience. I want you to read the Bible daily, and through each year: and I trust you will not read it without earnest prayer for the influence of the Holy Spirit to make its teachings effectual to the regulation of your life and the perfecting of your faith. Our life is very short at the longest; and after this life, there is a long life to come. Let us secure that whatever becomes of this

Mrs Smith (Cincinnati) & Ada expressed great regret that they did not see you at their house. I called there today. They are living very pleasantly indeed, & my morning visit was a very agreeable one

Col. Taylor was here today. He said that Mrs Taylor & Belle were disappointed that you did not spend a little time in Baltimore.[2] I am sorry myself that you did not: but I hope you will have an opportunity of becoming better acquainted with them at some future day.

I send you a Washn. paper today & will send one frequently.

Your affectionate father
S P Chase

P.S. I wrote you a note from Philadelphia which I suppose you received yesterday. I am looking for an answer tomorrow.

Historical Society of Pennsylvania.

1. Likely a relative of Dr. Lyman Tenney of Oberlin, Ohio. His daughters, Minerva Emeline Tenney (later Nettleton) and Melissa Roxena Tenney (later Daniels), both of whom graduated from Oberlin College later on, would have been teenagers in 1855. The seventeen-year-old Minerva might have been called "Miss Tenney." Another candidate would be a cousin of theirs, Luna Maria Tenney, who was born in 1831 and may have been the Miss Tenney who participated in the Literary Club at Oberlin in 1849. Jonathan Tenney, *The Tenney Family; or, the Descendants of Thomas Tenney of Rowley, Massachusetts* (Concord, N.H.: Rumford Press, 1904), 238; *General Catalogue of Oberlin College, 1833–1908* (Oberlin, Ohio: Oberlin College, 1909), 966; Robert Samuel Fletcher, *A History of Oberlin College from Its Foundation through the Civil War* (Oberlin, Ohio: Oberlin College, 1943), 763.

2. Joseph Pannell Taylor, an army officer born in 1796, was Zachary Taylor's brother. His wife, Eveline Aurilla McLean, was a daughter of John McLean. "Belle" was Eveline and Joseph's daughter, Arabella Taylor. Holman Hamilton, *Zachary Taylor: Soldier of the Republic* (New York: Bobbs-Merrill Co., 1941), 1:76; Holman Hamilton, *Zachary Taylor: Soldier in the White House* (New York: Bobbs-Merrill, 1951), 260, 492; *Appletons'*, 6:55; *Chase Papers*, 1:209.

FATHER TO KATE

Washington, Jany 15, 1854.[1]

My darling Katie,

I must take a few moments though I am much pressed for time to write a little letter to you.

It *was* hard for you to be left at the Station by yourself. I felt it keenly after I had left you, which I should not have done had you not suggested and rather urged it. It was a blunder, as a good many of my acts are, and teaches the necessity of forecast even in small matters.

Let me explain this to you. A "Railway Guide" was lying on my table in my bedroom.[2] I meant to consult it in respect to the precise times of the arrival & departure of the Philadelphia & Baltimore trains. I thought of it two or three times, but put it off and finally went away with you without doing it / Now if I had done this little thing at the right time, the doing of which would not have taken three minutes, I should have learned that the train on which we went would arrive at Chester at 58 minutes after two, and that the Express Train from Philadelphia for Baltimore & Washington would arrive at Chester at 31 minutes after three. Thus I should have learned that I could leave the cars with you, have thirty three minutes to look after your baggage and see you safe in the Stage & well cared for, & then take the Express Train & be back in Washington at half past nine. Thus you would have saved from all inconvenience and annoyance; I should have had the pleasure of staying with you half an hour longer & attending to all your wants; should have spared myself the journey to Philadelphia & back and the night ride; & should have had time in Washington which I much needed.

I have been thus particular about this matter because I want you to learn a lesson from it: Which is "Don't procrastinate; keep your wits about you; and avoid harumscarumitiveness."

The Baileys are all well. They talk of you with the greatest kindness. Miss Eva Ball is staying with them just now. I delighted Fanny by a bon-bon yesterday morning, which I brought the day before, as the custom is here, from a dinner party at Col. Benton's, where by the way I had a very pleasant time. The dinner was given mainly to an old fellow student of Mr. Bentons, three years older than himself, & of course seventy six years old now. It was pleasant to hear these old people talk of their young days.

Affectionately your father
S P Chase

Historical Society of Pennsylvania.

1. Misdated in original; later corrected in pencil to 1855 by an unidentified hand.
2. Possibly the *American Railway Guide* of Dinsmore & Co. or *Disturnell's American and European Railway and Steamship Guide.* Both included railroad timetables and were updated regularly.

FATHER TO KATE

Washington, Feb. 8, 1855.

I am writing, dear Kate, in the Senate Chamber. A confused hum of conversation fills the hall, and a Senator is on the floor, speaking earnestly to a very inattentive audience, and now and then a sentence reaches my ears and rather disturbs the current of my thoughts.[1] So you see I write under disadvantages.

Since I wrote last I have received I believe, two letters from you, each of which gave me a great deal of pleasure. I observe a gradual improvement in your style of composition, and your handwriting is becoming not only neat but elegant. All the rest necessary to make you a charming letter writer will come with more extensive knowledge and more practice in the use of it. It will be a great advantage to you to cultivate a *noticing habit.* See all you can whereever you are, and see everything all over. It is a source of great inconvenience to me that I did not cultivate this habit more in my youth. Then accustom yourself to talk of what you see and to write details, and in a conversational, & even dramatic style. There is the greatest possible difference in charm between the same narrative told by one person and by another, as doubtless you have often felt. No doubt a large part of this difference is to be ascribed to constitutional differences of temperament: but any intelligent person can greatly increase facility of apprehension & expression by careful self culture.

I know you do not like writing. I am sorry for it, for I know a natural repugnance to any pursuit is a great hindrance to excellence; and I am very desirous to have you excel in this respect. But I trust you have aspiration enough to enable you to make the effort necessary to overcome this feeling. You can overcome if you will: just as one can by an effort of will convert what would otherwise be disagreeable into tolerable if not pleasant. I dislike for example to bathe myself all over with cold water in the morning especially when the thermometer is so low as at present: but I find I can when I determine to do so overcome my feeling of dislike and even substitute a certain pleasurable sensation. So you must determine to write and enjoy writing.

Did you receive Mr. Sumner's Lecture? He told me he would send you one.[2]

I was at a great party at Willard's last night.[3] Mrs Bailey and the Doctor, with Miss Eva Ball were there and a great crowd. To me it was dull, simply because I knew so few except politicians / Washington you know is always full of strangers: and a party brings together hundreds who never saw each other before and will never see each other again.

The most interesting spectacle I have witnessed lately was the celebration of High Mass at the funeral of Mr. Molina, the Minister from Guatemala.[4] The Diplomatic Corps attending in full dress—the Archbishop with his clergy in full robes[5]—the coffin upon a lofty catafalque draped in black surrounded by a large number of lighted candles—the wail of the organ—and the chanting of the priests all formed a scene of great solemnity and interest. But I must stop.

As ever your affectionate father
S P Chase

Historical Society of Pennsylvania.

1. The speaker might have been Senator James Chamberlain Jones of Tennessee, who gave a long speech that day on a bill to grant railroad companies three years to pay duties on imported iron. *Congressional Globe*, 33d Cong., 2d sess., 1855, 623.

2. Very likely an address by Charles Sumner before the Mercantile Library Association of Boston in November 1854 praising British emancipation activist Granville Sharp. The lecture was published as *The Position and Duties of the Merchant* (Boston: Ticknor & Fields, 1855). *Chase Papers*, 2:401.

3. Willard's Hotel, located on the northwest corner of Pennsylvania Avenue and 14th Street, was one of the significant social and political meeting places of nineteenth-century Washington. Lincoln's secretary William O. Stoddard described it in 1861 as filled with "great men from all over the country and more of a strangely mingled society than you can find anywhere else in Washington." Goode, *Capital Losses*, 204–5; William O. Stoddard, *Inside the White House in War Times: Memoirs and Reports of Lincoln's Secretary*, ed. Michael Burlingame (Lincoln, Neb.: University of Nebraska Press, 2000), 30.

4. Felipe Molina was born in Guatemala in 1812, but at the time of his death he represented Costa Rica in commercial negotiations with the United States. *Appletons'*, 4:353.

5. The archbishop of Baltimore, Francis Patrick Kenrick. *Daily National Intelligencer*, Feb. 5, 1855.

FATHER TO KATE

Cincinnati, March 23, 1855.

My darling child,

A short letter from father to daughter and a still shorter one from daughter to father! This will never do. I accept your excuse for brevity however, only hoping that you will remember that it is an old saying a person good at making excuses is seldom good at any thing else. As you are certainly good for something else I shall hope to hear no excuses from you for the future unless under really extraordinary circumstances.

Yesterday I went up to Hillsborough to see Nettie. She saw me far off and came running to meet me. Never was a child so delighted to see a father. She clung round my neck, and kissed me with a real transport of affection. Her little cousin Josie Collins seemed to share her joy almost like a sister.

After a while the porter brought my valise in which I had stowed away a drum of figs, a box of prunes and a dozen oranges. The children were highly gratified to find I had remembered them in this way, though Nettie said she would rather have had something that would last long. Books, I found, were her passion.

She reads very well and with very good emphasis for one so young. She has also begun to take drawing lessons which Mrs Collins is kind enough to give her.

I hear the cry of Fire! Fire!! I must look out and see where it is.

All seems quiet enough out of doors. A false alarm I suppose.

Nettie draws very prettily and evidently has a decided taste for it. She shewed me her drawing book which, of course was rather rough, being her very first attempts; but there was manifest progressive improvement. Today before I came down she shewed me a tree she had been copying and really it was very well done.[1]

Night before last I called to see your grandmother & Maria.[2] They are both quite well. Maria has been out a good deal this winter, but has so far escaped bad colds. Her grandmother thinks she is careless & so do I. I fear very much that she will someday suffer from her self exposure. You and she both should remember that your constitutions require especial care at least till you are twenty five. You must *always* avoid exposure to sudden changes by going *uniformly* warmly clad, and you must take care *never* to wear tight dresses / I meant to speak to you about this: but it escaped me. Remember particularly this point. Loose dresses & warm clothing will save you from much suffering & probably prolong your life many years. Don't neglect this.

Maria spoke very affectionately of you, and praised your letters. Your grandmother, too wanted to know when I would bring you out to see her and was pleased to hear of your improvement.

I have been very busy since I came home. The very day after my arrival I was called upon to argue the cause of two persons claimed as slaves;[3] and when that was over I had a very important cause to attend to which however was settled by a compromise. I find I have no more leisure here than I had in Washington.[4]

You will find some trouble in reading this letter I am afraid: but it is nearly twelve oclock at night and I am writing as fast as I can so as to be sure of getting it off to you by tomorrows mail.

Please remember me very kindly to your roommate, and to Mr & Mrs Huntington[5] & Miss Eastman, & believe me

Most affectionately your father
S. P. Chase

Historical Society of Pennsylvania.

1. He noted in his journal, "talk with Nettie—her tree prettily drawn." According to his diary, he returned from Hillsboro to Cincinnati on Saturday, March 24. He clearly dated this letter March 23. *Chase Papers*, 1:244.

2. Mary Colton Smith and Maria Southgate.

3. Immediately on Father's return to Cincinnati from Hillsboro, Cincinnati attorney William M. Dickson informed him that a marshal had brought Rosetta Armstead, a sixteen-year-old slave, before John L. Pendery, a commissioner under the federal Fugitive Slave Act. Armstead, who was traveling through Ohio with her owner's agent, had already been liberated once by antislavery advocates using a writ of habeas corpus in Columbus. Father and Dickson were particularly incensed because Pendery, who would get a fee of ten dollars if he ruled that the young woman was a fugitive slave but only five dollars if he released her, had borrowed ten dollars from Dickson and then bragged that he would soon be good for the money. Father worked with Timothy Walker and Rutherford B. Hayes to win Armstead's release, again by means of a writ of habeas corpus in a state court, although ultimately that would not free her from the reach of the Fugitive Slave Act. Father later described Pendery as "notoriously venal." Another slavery-related case apparently also came to Father's attention the day he returned to Cincinnati. *Chase Papers*, 1:244, 246; Stephen Middleton, *The Black Laws: Race and the Legal Process in Early Ohio* (Athens, Ohio: Ohio University Press, 2005), 226–27.

4. In addition to the court cases, including the one resolved by compromise, he was involved in political discussions. Dickson, who was affiliated with the Know Nothings, confided to him that the party might nominate an acceptable candidate for governor to win antislavery votes but pack the remainder of the state ticket with proslavery people. Father advised Dickson to stall any Know Nothing nomination for governor. Preventing an early Know Nothing nomination helped Father consolidate Free Soil and Know Nothing interests to win the Republican nomination for governor. *Chase Papers*, 1:245.

5. Benjamin Snow Huntington married Frances Seal Huntington in 1838. About five years after his 1840 ordination as an Episcopal minister, B. S. Huntington established the "seminary for young ladies" at Aston Ridge. An 1884 history records that the school was popular, "the scholars being drawn largely from the Southern States." Huntington, however, "was constantly enlarging the building until he finally became bankrupt" and sold the estate in 1859. Huntington, *Genealogical Memoir*, 282; Ashmead, *History of Delaware County*, 299–300; 1850 census, Delaware County, Pa., Aston Township, 56.

FATHER TO KATE

Cincinnati April 13, 1855.

My dear child,

Your last letter was a very successful one. You say you meant to make it as good as you could, and it is another proof that what one really has the will to do she generally finds herself able to accomplish. It was the best written letter I ever received from you and satisfied me that you have only to *persevere in doing your best* to become an excellent letter writer.

It was Dr. Johnson I think who said that "What is worth doing at all is worth doing well."[1] And certain it is that what is not well done had better generally be left undone.

To write a good letter three things only are necessary: first, observation of what passes under one's eye or within one's circle; secondly Narration or the disposition, which with some is acquired & with others natural, to tell easily & naturally, just as one would talk, what has been observed; & thirdly correctness and ease of style which can only be gained by practice and cultivation. I hope you will profit by this short essay on letterwriting.

I suppose Maria has written you about the death of your Uncle Henry Southgate. It was quite unexpected until within a few days of its occurrence. He had been sick during the winter but was supposed to be recovering. In fact not long after I got home Richard Southgate[2] told me that he was quite well again. After this however he was attacked by Erysipelas, and, after an illness of ten days, expired. I was not in town when the event occured and did not know of it till all was over. Poor Henry! His life was not such as he must have wished it had been when he came to die. But who dare judge him? We are all sinners and I, with the restraining influences which have been continually cast about me, have yet so transgressed that I fret that in the sight of God I must be regarded the greater sinner. I therefore judge not: but, dear Katie, let us take warning from each instance of mortality to make our peace with God through Christ by true repentance and earnest faith.

It gives me some pain to find you growing discontented. You complain of Miss Eastman. You must remember that she began by loving you; that she was kind in providing you with a pleasant little room; and that you were, in some sort, specially confided to her care. You must make a great deal of allowance for one who has so many cares upon her. I remember that when I was a teacher I used to go to my school every morning resolved to control my temper and be very kind and pleasant all day.[3] But I should be ashamed to tell you how the petty vexations and cares of the schoolroom swept away the defences of good resolutions with which I had surrounded myself. You must think of your teachers cares: of her trials: and vexations. She is responsible for you all, and is anxious about you all. She wants you all to love her. Every human heart yearns for love even from the youngest. Make then, my dear child, as much sunshine for Miss Eastman as you can. Be patient under reproof. Sometimes you may not deserve it. Comfort yourself then with the apostle's reflection, "It is better to suffer for well doing than for evil doing.["][4] Sometimes, you may deserve it. Be thankful then for it, and strive to amend by it. In all circumstances be patient and make Miss Eastman and all others love you by loving them. I know what the heart whispers. It says this is hard doctrine. An evil nature would rather have a fit of grumbling, or an angry countenance, or rude words: but these are evil and the fruit of them is sorrow. Dear Katie, resist the evil one, and persist in loving and being kind. Think of Christ and his grand patience and ineffable sweetness.

I saw your grandma & Maria two days ago. They were both well only Maria had a headache. They both spoke affectionately of you; and Maria said you had not quite lived up to your arrangement about writing.

A letter from Mrs Collins came today telling that Nettie is very well and very happy.

Gov. Fish & Mrs Fish with their eldest daughter Sarah were here two or three days ago on their return from Cuba.[5] They had enjoyed their visit very much. I took the ladies out riding and shewed them some of the beautiful views around Cincinnati. They were much pleased. Mrs Fish enquired very kindly for you.

Your cousin Jane Auld is here from St Louis. She has gone out to Clifton where she occupies a cottage near Mr. Ball's. She is to be principal of the Female Department of the Clifton School. She has three sweet little girls.

But I must stop writing. Goodbye. Give my best regards to Mr. & Mrs Huntington, Miss Eastman and your sweet roommate. When you next write tell me more particularly about your studies.

Your affectionate father,
S P Chase

Historical Society of Pennsylvania.

1. Actually it was one of Samuel Johnson's rivals, the earl of Chesterfield, who gave currency to the maxim; see the introduction to this volume. Chesterfield's *Letters,* ed. David Roberts (Oxford: Oxford University Press, 1992), 29; *Chase Papers,* 2:404.

2. Richard Southgate lived in Covington, Kentucky, across the Ohio River from Cincinnati. Other members of the Southgate family who were related to Maria Southgate (and Kate) were from Covington, but we do not know Richard's connection to them. *Chase Papers,* 2:404.

3. In Washington, after his graduation from Dartmouth College and before he qualified as a lawyer, Father was master of a school attended by the sons of several members of John Quincy Adams's cabinet. He confessed to a friend in 1829: "I always feel when I have been absent from the city a little while and pass by the Capitol on my return, a sort of involuntary sinking of the heart for which I cannot account unless it be that I detest the drudgery and thanklessness of school-keeping." He had taught for short stints earlier, in New England when he was a student at Dartmouth. "I counted the hours, minutes and even seconds with the utmost impatience," he reported after one of those teaching jobs. Schlesinger, "Salmon Portland Chase," 123–25, 127, 143–44, 154–55; *Chase Papers,* 1:xv–xvi; 2:43.

4. "For it is better, if the will of God be so, that ye suffer for well doing, than for evil doing." 1 Peter 3:17.

5. Hamilton Fish and his wife, Julia Kean Fish, were prominent in American political society during this period. A former governor of New York, Fish entered the U.S. Senate in 1851, one of only six antislavery Whigs. He and Julia had eight children, including their daughter Sarah, who was born in 1838. A member of the Committee on Foreign Relations who opposed expansionism, Fish was particularly interested in Cuba because of the Ostend Manifesto, an 1854 document produced by the American ministers to Spain, France,

and Great Britain that advocated the seizure of the island by force if Spain refused to sell it. *Nat. Cyc.*, 4:15; Alan Nevins, *Hamilton Fish: The Inner History of the Grant Administration* (New York: Dodd, Mead & Co., 1937), 17–19, 22, 45, 48.

FATHER TO KATE

Cincinnati, April 22, 1855.

My darling Katie,

Just fancy a bright beautiful Spring morning—as bright and beautiful as if made expressly for the consolation of hearts wearied of the long cold winter—then conceive of me as having just come from my breakfast at the Burnet House, and seated before a tall Secretary, drop leaf let down for desk, pen in hand & thoughts of you in my head & love for you in my heart, and you will get a pretty good notion of my present position and surroundings.[1]

The roar of multitudinous sounds comes up from the city: for the most part resembling the roar of the ocean / You might think it such in fact, but for the particular noises which every now and then make themselves heard in the general volume. There just at this moment I heard footfalls distinctly on the pavement;—now voices of conversing men; now a tinkling I know not what; a moment since and now again the rattle of wheels & the hoof strokes of horses; then the clangor of the Sunday bells, summoning so many people of so may creeds to prepare for the worship of the same God—the Merciful Father of all, Who doth prefer,

Before all temples, the upright heart and pure.[2]

But who, alas! possesses "this upright heart and pure"? "There is none that doeth good, no, not one."[3] "All we, like sheep, have gone astray."[4] Even St Paul was forced to exclaim, when he had announced that Christ came to save sinners "Of whom I am chief."[5]

It is very sad to think that we are all sinners—that none can hope for eternal life as the reward of well doing—that none can escape the consciousness of desert of punishment as a just recompense for ill doing. Sadder still is it to think that living as we do in God's world; sustained evermore by his Providence; adorned with immortality; blessed actually exceedingly and with blessings offered to us passing all comprehension, we should still sin against the Author of our being and the kind Provider for all our wants.

When I think of my own short comings and sin I feel humbled and ashamed. All I desire is to feel more & more so—more and more deeply and truly penitent—until it shall be impossible for me to offend Him to whom my whole heart is due.

And my darling child I pray that you may think much of these things. Life is short. We know not the hour of death. Make life long by devoting yourself to the service of God—for then though the body may perish *you* will never die. Make death impossible by giving up yourself to that Savior who has conquered death. What do I mean? That you should become dull, melancholy, recluse? Oh no! If you see your sins as they are you will feel sorrow and contrition: if you feel sorrow and contrition you will guard against offences in future. Especially will you be more apt to find fault with yourself than with others. But you will be cheerful, for you will have the assurance of God's goodness, and you will have the love of those to whom out of a Christian affection you render offices of kindness. With these sources of happiness you will be happier than is possible for any one who seeks happiness only in the world.

I have been too remiss in writing of late. I must endeavor to amend in this respect: but you will easily comprehend that my engagements make it difficult for me to do all I could wish as a correspondent

When is that French letter coming? It seems to me about time that you should be able to write one: and I shall be well pleased to have all your letters written in French. If I had more time I would endeavor to reply in the same language. When you write always tell me what you have been studying during the preceding week. *Dont neglect this*.

Jane Auld has arrived. I believe I mentioned this before. She has got established in her little cottage at Clifton and has commenced her school. I hope she will be happy there & I think she will.

I was at Toledo last Sunday, Monday & Tuesday; staying at Geo Walbridges. Your Aunts Jane & Alice were there.[6] Aunt Janes health was bad, & Aunt Alice's, though she seemed healthy, is precarious. Your cousin Mary,[7] your aunt Helen's daughter, a very sweet girl of seventeen has been thought to be past hope in consumption. This spring, however, hear health seems to improve and there is a possibility that she may get well. A few weeks ago her little brother, the baby, died to the great grief of all the household.

I have not heard from Nettie since I wrote you, nor have I seen your Grand mother or Maria. Write regularly.

Your own father,
S P Chase

Historical Society of Pennsylvania.

1. Opened in 1850 on the site once occupied by Judge Jacob Burnet's home, the Burnet House was a prominent Cincinnati hotel. Works Projects Administration Writers' Program, *Cincinnati*, 156.
2. John Milton, *Paradise Lost*, 1:17–18.
3. This expression appears identically at Psalms 14:3 and Romans 3:12.
4. Isaiah 53:6.
5. In 1 Timothy 1:15, St. Paul notes, "This is a faithful saying, and worthy of all acceptation, that Christ Jesus came into the world to save sinners; of whom I am chief."

6. Janette Logan Chase Skinner and Alice Jones Chase.
7. Mary Walbridge.

FATHER TO KATE

Cincinnati, May 27, 1855.

My darling child,

You can hardly imagine how much pleasure my brief visit to Aston gave me. To an affectionate father nothing is more delightful than the fond greeting of a beloved child, improving in intelligence, in manners, in physical development, and giving promise of a rich & delightful future. It was a great comfort to me to look at you, and feel that I could trust you, and, under Gods blessing, expect for you years of health & usefulness. Darling Katie, be careful not to disappoint your father. Take care of your health. Be as much in the air as possible. Avoid stooping. Take such exercise as will expand the chest & give freest Motion to the lungs. Avoid tight dresses and every thing which, in the least, compresses the lungs. Don't foolishly imagine that you can trifle with yourself and neglect precaution and yet escape.

I need not repeat my anxious wishes for your spiritual improvement. I want to see you a consistent Christian above all things. And to be a Christian is nothing but to follow Christ. Consider his Character, his goodness, his Death for us and you must love him. Remember that you are always to depend for help on the Holy Spirit, always freely afforded those who sincerely desire it. And remember also that it is not in some great thing you are to commence the life of a Christian. You are to commence, perhaps in some very little thing, & that right away. You [feel] you *ought* to do something you don't want to do or not to do something you want to do. Follow, at this moment, the dictate of your conscience, and you will take one step in the right way. This, I think, is the main thing, to do the present, immediate duty of the moment. Do you feel inclined to say something bitter or unkind of some one or to some one? And does conscience tell you you ought not to say it. Suppress it then at once. Remember, "Charity thinketh no evil." Do you suffer from some unkindness & feel a rising spirit of revenge? Suppress it. "Charity suffereth long and is kind."[1] I know it is not easy to suppress the natural evil workings of the heart, but I know it can be done and by many is done. And I know that every such victory over Wrong within is a source of peace and sweet delight. Let me hope that, my dear girl, will attend to what I say.

I reached Washington the Evening of the day I left you, where I went at once to Dr. Bailey's & found my room all ready for me and all, especially the children, delighted to see me. The Baileys enquired very kindly after you, and, in every way, possible for them endeavored to make my stay agreeable.

On Saturday I dined at Major Smith's, where I found Miss Addie as pretty and charming as ever Miss Virginia as sensible & kind, and their mother and Miss Ellen & the Major just as I had left them.

After dinner I called at Mrs Geo (Cincinnati) Smith's, and finding that Miss Ada had walked over to the Presidents grounds to enjoy the stroll and hear the music, I, with her brother, Tom, went there also. We were rather late but I found a number of persons whom I knew, and interchanged pleasant greetings. Then I called at Judge Blairs & at Mr. Marcys &, so wound up the Evening.[2] The rest of my time at Washington, except a few hours devoted to business was spent pretty much in the same way. On Thursday Morning I left for Cincinnati & the afternoon of the next day found myself once more in my own rooms.

Mr. Ball was absent at Columbus & I have had but a glimpse of him since his return: but he is well as is also his family. I have not yet seen your grandmother or Maria. Ralston is well & is returned from Lockport

It is very uncertain whether I shall be Governor or even a Candidate: but some of the papers begin to abuse me a little which is a good sign.

Your very affectionate father
S P Chase

Historical Society of Pennsylvania.

1. "Charity suffereth long, and is kind; charity envieth not; charity vaunteth not itself, is not puffed up, Doth not behave itself unseemly, seeketh not her own, is not easily provoked, thinketh no evil." 1 Corinthians 13:4–5.

2. Lawyer and former New York governor William Learned Marcy was serving as Franklin Pierce's secretary of state in the spring of 1855. Montgomery Blair, who turned forty-two years old that May, lived at the time in a three-story home called "Montgomery Castle" on Pennsylvania Avenue with his second wife, Mary (Minna) Elizabeth Woodbury. Blair was a son of Jacksonian political operative and journalist Francis Preston Blair. A former mayor of St. Louis, Montgomery Blair was a judge of the common court of pleas before returning to Washington in 1852 to work as a practicing attorney regularly arguing before the Supreme Court. He was later postmaster general in Abraham Lincoln's cabinet when Father was secretary of the Treasury. Father did not then have the smoothest relationship with the Blair family, particularly Montgomery's brother, Francis (Frank) Preston Blair Jr. *DAB*, 2:339; 12:274–77; Niven, *Chase*, 335, 344, 346–48; *Nat. Cyc.*, 44:190.

FATHER TO KATE

Cincinnati, June 21, 1855.

Your nice letter, my darling child, came yesterday or day before. I have not time to answer it as I would wish: but must say a few words.

I call your letter a nice one and so it was: but I must say that it had rather a sleepy air. The words seemed occasionally chosen and arranged under the influence of the drowsy god. Not quite life enough.

Do you know they have been getting up a picture of me at Boston: a copy was sent me and I liked it well enough to order quite a number that I might have some to give my friends. It is a lithograph and presents me with my head turned to one side and in rather a speaking position. Some like it very much. Others of course condemn.[1]

The picture which Walker painted has been sent here & I rather think I shall take it for you. It is not quite what I would like for you; but perhaps as good as anything I shall get.[2]

The prospect now is that I shall be nominated for Governor. If I am and accept I shall not be able to spend much time in New Hampshire this summer.

But I must stop.

Your ever affectionate father,
S P Chase

P.S. I was at Hillsborough Saturday & Sunday. Nettie grows more & more charming. She continually talks of Katie & loves you dearly.

Historical Society of Pennsylvania.

1. Probably a lithograph of Father published in 1855 by Charles H. W. Brainard and the S. W. Chandler and Brothers Lithography Company of Boston. The likeness was by French-born artist Leopold Grozelier, who worked in Boston beginning in 1854. Groce and Wallace, *Dictionary of Artists*, 119, 278.

2. Portrait not identified. The artist may have been James Walker, a historical painter who worked in New York and Washington and became known for his depictions of Civil War battles. Father may also have received a work that Cincinnati portraitist Samuel Swan Walker produced before his death in 1848. Groce and Wallace, *Dictionary of Artists*, 655, 656.

FATHER TO KATE

Cincinnati July 25, 1856[1]

Dear Katie,

I have time today only to write you one word. *Go nowhere & with nobody & do nothing* of the least consequence with consulting freely your aunt Charlotte.[2] You are at a time of life when all your acts will be observed. Think above all that God *Sees* your most secret thoughts. May He bless you & keep you from all harm.

I saw Aunt Adela today. She is well. I go to Clifton this Evening & to Eaton, Preble Co, tomorrow morning / Love to darling Nettie

Yours affy.
S P Chase

Historical Society of Pennsylvania.

1. Father had been inaugurated governor of Ohio in January 1856, and the family resided in Columbus.

2. Charlotte Ludlow Jones, apparently. Father evidently intended to write "without consulting." A story has Kate taking unchaperoned buggy rides with a married man around this time period. Phelps, *Kate Chase*, 89.

FATHER TO KATE

Read this carefully & note all directions on your Memorandum—

Columbus, Decr. 4, 1857

My dearest child,

Enclosed you will find a list of the Articles taken from Mr Crane, copied from the one I sent you yesterday. It is for him. Two small chairs are marked for Room No. 10. They are not yet ordered. Please select them not exceeding $6 for both & give the list to him and let him send up the articles as soon as possible.[1]

I shall not object to your taking the furniture from John according to the list sent yesterday: except that the Sideboard *must* be left out, and I think a cheaper table would do as well. There are tables—not extension—with two leaves hanging down & not more than a foot & a half wide when the leaves are down. I saw some at John's on the first floor. They occupy little room when not in use. Why would not two or three of these answer, & be cheaper? I still think that before deciding you had best visit some other establishments. As soon as you decide all except the parlor can be sent up next week.

I forgot to tell you that Mrs John C. Huntington our White Mountain acquaintance[2] called to see you & with her Miss Augusta Mitchell whom you remember. Mrs. H. is at 121 8th St & Miss Mitchell was with her. You had best call.

I enclose Shillito's bill or list of Carpeting priced there. In a few instances it differs from my memorandum a copy of which I sent you yesterday. It seems to me you had better look at the stocks of Falls & Ringwalt before buying.[3] The bill is large and it is desirable to make it smaller if possible. Perhaps it will be best to take 3 Ply for the middle Room. If you do you will want 12 yds more of the same for the hall next it. If you retain the Brussels you will want 15 yds more. If you find it best to take all from Shillitos have it understood that it is to be delivered in Columbus free of charge—and if you buy of any body else have the same understanding. Remember this: The carpet for the parlor is to be cut but not sewed. Notice this & have it done.[4] Henry Fraas will sew it here & put it down. Nobody can do better work.[5]

I enclose also, a list of Pieces in a plain gold band set from Mr. Huntington. He says they have imported too many fine goods for the hard times.[6] He wishes it regarded as confidential; but I apprehend that he would make the same list for any purchaser. Still you must observe his request. The price of the set he states to be $88.—He wishes you to look at his furnishing goods on 4th St. & says he will sell at auction prices. You will want tin sets of foot tubs & water urns for several rooms. But I suppose you have made out a list of room by room. Mr. H—— will give you a little book shewing what goods he has.

I brought up with me the Trunk containing the silver. The key I handed you, which was handed back to me by Mr. Brown, fits it.[7] There are one or two blankets &c in which the Silver is packed and all appears safe except one of the bottles of the castor is broken.

I do not think of any thing more to say about furniture. Dr. Carter has moved out except from Library & small Sitting Room. They have taken their plants out of the Green House: and will leave for good next week Monday or Wednesday.[8]

Aunt Alice has not come nor have I heard from her which is Strange.

Enclosed I send you two letters which have come for you. One, I see is from Concord & I presume from Eliza Whipple.

Mr. Snowden went to Baltimore today.[9] Nettie's cold still clings to her. She wants you back. I hope earnestly that you are getting better of your cold. You Cant be too careful. I expect to hear from you today.

Affectionately your father
S P Chase

Keep my letters & lists so that I can see how you have managed. It is too much to put on you, I feel, to have you make these purchases & attend to these matters. But if you are young you have capacity & will do very well.

Historical Society of Pennsylvania.

1. Kate was in Cincinnati looking for furnishings for the family's house in Columbus. The Cincinnati furniture dealers mentioned in this letter were likely Lemuel M. Crane, whose "Cabinet Furniture Manufactory" was located at 81 Sycamore; S. J. John, who sold "Fashionable Furniture" at 23 East 4th Street; and the firm of John C., William C., and Albert W. Huntington, who sold china, glass, imported fancy goods, and home furnishings ranging from bathtubs to feather dusters. The Huntingtons' emporium was near the intersection of 4th and Main, not far from John's. C. S. Williams, *Williams' Cincinnati Directory, City Guide, and Business Mirror; for 1857* (Cincinnati: C. S. Williams, 1856), 75, 166, 168; F. W. Hurtt, *Cincinnati Guide and Business Directory, for 1857–1858* (Cincinnati: F. W. Hurtt, 1857), 68, 91, and unpaged advertisement for Huntington Brothers & Co.

2. The White Mountains of northern New Hampshire and western Maine were a popular resort area. The area's scenery made it a center for artists and the well-to-do sightseer. Frank A. Burt, *Among the White Mountains* (Mount Washington, N.H.: Among the Clouds, 1886), 4–7.

3. John Shillito and Company, a wholesale and retail dealer in dry goods and carpeting, occupied a large building on 4th Street in Cincinnati. Both Henry Falls and J. C. Ringwalt and Company, both located also on 4th Street, advertised themselves as carpet and oilcloth dealers. *Williams' Cincinnati Directory . . . for 1857*, 105, 225, 238; *Picturesque Cincinnati* (Cincinnati: John Shillito Co., 1883), 198.

4. Father inserted this sentence above the line.

5. In 1856, Henry Fraas was sexton of the First Presbyterian Church in Columbus. *Williams' Columbus Directory . . . 1856–'57*, 83.

6. Father inserted this sentence above the line. The financial panic of 1857, which began with financial institutions, widened into a nationwide depression marked by business closings and unemployment. The trouble started in Ohio toward the latter part of August, when the Ohio Life Insurance and Trust Company suspended payments. Kenneth M. Stampp, *America in 1857: A Nation on the Brink* (New York: Oxford University Press, 1990), 221–30.

7. Probably Thomas Brown. He and Father had been acquainted since at least 1848, when Brown was heavily involved in Free Soil politics. Initially a Cleveland lawyer, Brown in

1850 cofounded a newspaper, the *True Democrat*, and in 1853 he left that paper to establish the *Ohio Farmer*. When Father was secretary of the Treasury, Brown became a special agent of the department. He traveled to California in that capacity and involved himself in various business ventures, including mercury mining and petroleum production. After the war he was a special agent for the Treasury Department in New York City. *Appletons'*, 1:411; *Chase Papers*, 1:197, 238, 495, 517, 586; 2:201; 4:53–54; Father to Nettie, Aug. 9, 1866, below in this volume.

8. Father had purchased the large residence of Francis Carter, a physician who was on the faculty of the Starling Medical College, for twelve thousand dollars. The house stood at the corner of 6th and State streets in Columbus. Carter was moving into a newly built house nearby. *Chase Papers*, 1:309.

9. P. T. Snowden, with whom the Chases boarded until they moved into the home purchased from Carter, later moved to Baltimore. *Chase Papers*, 1:247.

FATHER TO KATE

December 5, Saty. 1857

My darling daughter,

There must be, I think, a mistake in John's list in respect to the two arm chairs coasters for the parlor. They are set down at $30 each—it must be for both / The two Carved chairs in the same list are $13 each or $26 for the two. The other two chairs cannot be more than $2 a peice dearer. At $30 each they come to nearly as much as the Sociable & had better be left out.[1] Since writing the above I have summed up the total asked for the parlor furniture & am satisfied that the chairs should be set down at $30 for both.

I find I have a surplus Dressing Bureau on looking over the list. We will put it into the North Room & so dispense with a Mirror for that room.

Have I mentioned that the Stair case has 22 Steps & of course needs 22 rods instead of 20?

I am much disappointed not having heard from you. You promised me full reports of your doings. I *presume* you have found very little time for writing, and am *distressed* by the fear you have been Sick. I mean to come for you as soon as I hear you have got through.

Nothing has been heard from Aunt Alice but Dun[2] writes again earnestly for a visit from you and Nettie

Let me again remind you *not* to buy any thing in Cincinnati which you can as well buy in Columbus. The expense & risk of transportation is to be considered & there are other reasons. I fear that I am trusting a good deal to the judgment of a girl of 17; but I am confident I may safely trust yours.

Let Crane send up the furniture ordered from him as soon as he can: and let the other furniture also come up without delay except that for the parlor, which must remain where purchased for a week or two.

The painting &c is going on well. You must not buy curtains for the parlor windows.

Nettie had Maggie Andrews with her last night, & has been with her in turn all today[3]

Affy. your father
S P Chase

Mr. Snowden went to Balt yesterday—but I told you this before

1. A sociable, also called a conversation sofa or "tête-à-tête," was an S-shaped couch that allowed two people to sit facing each other. They were popular from the 1840s into the mid-1850s. *OED*, 15:904.
2. Nettie's uncle, James Dunlop Ludlow.
3. Probably Margaret Andrews, a daughter of Columbus banker John Andrews and his wife, Phebe. Maggie was the same age as Nettie. 1860 Census, Franklin County, Ohio, Columbus Ward 2, 83–84.

CATHERINE LUDLOW BAKER AND NETTIE TO KATE

Dear Kate.

As Josie Ludlow has ill, and is not quite well—('tho' almost) we cannot leave as we had though't of doing tomorrow—(Monday 26th.) but must defer it until Thursday—and if then not able to go to St Louis (Uncle Clarkson's) with Brother,[1] we will wait until Monday, to-morrow week.

Nettie, the darling, is much disappointed, yet exclaims "oh well it will give me more time to gather, the remainder of the seeds for sister"; you dear Kate, must be an affectionate sister, as she speaks of you in glowing, and loving terms—

She is a dear child, and needs, & deserves all the devotion, and tenderness you can bestow—

I hope to spend a few days with you, before going to Aunt Adela's, in Covington; I quite long to see you, so many years have elapsed since, I had that pleasure

Sep 2[7]'th Sunday—

love for your Father and much, from your Aunt Kate for your self; in haste[2]

PS

My Dear Sister.

Have you all seen the comet, is it not splendid? how fast it go's.[3] I have quite a large assortment of seed's, for my sister. I sapose Aunt Kate said that we thought of coming Wednesday or Thursday tell Alice I want to see her so bad[4] and all of you and tell Mrs Decker that she will not long be without a cat. for there is a nice little cat here that I am going to take home if you have no objecktions give my love to dear Father and Alice and Aunt Alice frome your loving little sister

Nettie

1. Probably James Dunlop Ludlow.

2. The letter to this point is in the handwriting of Catherine Ludlow Baker, who altered the second digit of the date at least once, her final intention evidently being "6" or "7." If she was accurate about "Sunday," she wrote this letter on Sept. 26, 1858 (the year confirmed by Nettie's reference to the comet). The remainder of the letter is in Nettie's hand.

3. At the height of the comet's visibility during September and October 1858, "multitudes of star-gazers" in the U.S. viewed Donati's Comet, which Italian astronomer Giovanni Battista Donati had discovered the previous June. Much of the information the American public received about the comet came from Ormsby M. Mitchel, then a professor at Cincinnati College, who tracked the celestial body from his observatory in Cincinnati. Donati's Comet, easily seen with the unaided eye, was the most noticeable comet since the 1830s, when Halley's Comet had last appeared. *New York Times*, Sept. 23, Oct. 2, 11, 1858; *Cincinnati Daily Gazette*, Sept. 28, 1858; Goss, *Cincinnati*, 1:186–87: *Nat. Cyc.*, 3:440.

4. Probably Alice Skinner, who had visited the family in Columbus a year before and was likely the "Allie" mentioned at Apr. 30, 1859, below. Mrs. Decker may have been a housekeeper. A city directory listed a Mrs. Roseanna Decker, who was probably a widow, or perhaps Mrs. Decker was a relative of one of several men named Decker in the directory. *Chase Papers*, 1:302; *Williams' Columbus Directory . . . 1858–'59*, 77.

FATHER TO KATE

Warren, near Galena,[1] Oct. 28, 1858

My darling Katie,

How often I have thought of you! Mr Barney indeed would have made me think of you if I had been disposed to forget. It was delightful to me to see what a favorable influence you had made on him. He is a man of very sober judgment and his praise is worth having.[2] Study my dear child to deserve such good opinions & be the joy of your father's heart

My reception in Illinois has been cordial & I have been so much urged to remain & speak on Monday that I have felt obliged to consent; and so shall not reach home before Wednesday or Thursday. There is to be a meeting here today & tonight I go to Galena not to speak but to spend the night with my friend Washburne[3] / The best opinion here seems to be that Douglas will be defeated. It is not so certain that Lincoln will be elected: as it is possible that the Senate may be held by the Dems & the House by the Republicans & So have no joint Convention to Elect a Senator.[4] Love to all especially to Nettie

Most Affectionately

S P Chase

Say to Mr. Breese that I shall be detained beyond Monday

Historical Society of Pennsylvania.

1. He started to write "Colum," struck through it, and began the dateline anew with "Warren." The small community of Warren and the city of Galena, which had a population of 9,000 in 1854, were in Jo Daviess County, the most northwestern county of Illinois. Smith, *Harper's Statistical Gazetteer*, 663, 1851.

2. Father's old friend and fellow antislavery advocate Hiram Barney (b. 1811) had been Ohio's commissioner of education before moving to New York, where he opened a law practice and later served as customs agent. Niven, *Chase*, 180; *Chase Papers*, 1:237.

3. Illinois politician Elihu Benjamin Washburne served in the U.S. House of Representatives, 1853–69, initially as a Whig, then as a Republican. He had two brothers who were in Congress from other states during the same time period. *DAB*, 19:505–6.

4. In the original, there are three vertical strokes in the margin next to the passage from "The best opinion" to "will be elected." Abraham Lincoln and Stephen A. Douglas were engaged in their famous contention for Douglas's seat in the U.S. Senate. Although Lincoln received the majority of popular votes, his Republican Party was outnumbered in the state legislature, which voted 54 to 46 in favor of sending Douglas back to the U.S. Senate. *DAB*, 5:402.

FATHER TO KATE

Columbus, Apl. 30, 1859

My darling Katie,

We must not when absent from each other be so uncommunicative. My conscience reproaches me with having allowed three whole days to elapse without writing; and, if I, who have so much to do & so much to think of, ought to have written sooner & more than once, what ought your conscience to say to you?

Yesterday I received Aunt McLean's note written some six or eight days sooner. It was very welcome because it assured me that you did not find yourself unexpected on going to Clifton as I suppose you did, on Thursday. I hope you had there a very pleasant visit & did all in your power to make yourself agreeable & beloved.

Of course you saw Mrs Eastman Monday &, I trust, were so cordial in your invitation as to obtain her promise to return with you, on Wednesday or Thursday.[1] I shall be very much disappointed if she does not come. You were so suddenly roused from sleep the night I came away that I feared you did not understand exactly what I said and what I stopped at Mr. F——'s expressly to say for fear of some misunderstanding.[2] But I hope you remembered enough of it to call the next morning at Mrs Mussey's & that you found Mrs Eastman returned from Clifton, & that you said all that could be said to induce both Mrs E—— & Mrs L—— to pay us a visit—and that you said it so well & so cordially as to prevail at least with Mrs E——. I had less hope in regard to Mrs L—— because of her natural wish to be with her daughter.[3]

I enclose you a couple of letters for yourself and one for Aunt Charlotte.[4] You must not let her off from coming up with you. Let us have a pleasant housefull & a pleasant time

Tell Nettie she must join you in writing. Say to her that James has taken very good care of *Nichts*, but that he is nearer *nothing* than ever. His sister Nelly, poor thing, is dead. Nichts has a pretty good chance to live. In fact there is too little of him almost for Death to get a fair hold.[5]

Mr Jones came back last evening. He was here a little while ago, and told me that he had given you an account of his adventures in the letter which I enclose. He looks extremely well and seems much pleased with his prospects.[6]

Thursday Evening I spent at Col Swaynes & had a long talk with Mrs King.[7] She spoke very highly of you. Last evening I spent at Dr. Smith's.

Miss Anthony was as handsome & agreeable as usual[8] / Mrs Smith and I played five games of chess & I beat her in four out of the five: and ought to have beat her in all. I tried to persuade some of them to come and breakfast with me this morning; but in vain. Not a soul has sat down with me since you left home.

The grass begins to shew itself plainly in the new lot and about a dozen right pretty evergreens have been planted. It makes quite a change in the appearance of things. The lilacs are coming out & will be in full bloom by the time you return and so will some of the peonies. Mr. Coggeshall brought in some wild flowers for you which Thomas has planted under the washroom window, west side[9] / Anne and Co[10] have been very busy cleaning house up stairs: and I hope you will find every thing as you would wish.

Love to all—especially Nettie and Allie[11]

> Your affectionate father
> S P Chase

Historical Society of Pennsylvania.

1. Charlotte Sewall Eastman was the widow of Ben C. Eastman of Wisconsin, an attorney and member of Congress, 1851–55, who died in 1856. Charlotte—"Lottie"—was a close friend of Jane Rantoul of Beverly, Mass., whose husband's death Father reported to Kate in his letter of Aug. 10, 1852, above. Father and Lottie Eastman corresponded beginning in 1857. They also saw one another in Washington, where she sometimes spent the winter, and in Massachusetts. In 1866, fending off a rumor that he and Mrs. Eastman intended to marry, Father characterized her as only a "very dear friend," and his letters addressed her in that fashion. However, his journal from that time contains evidence of at least a burst of amorous feeling. To Jacob Schuckers, with regard to the matrimonial rumor, Father described Lottie as "a sweet & lovely woman, unaffected & unpretending, good looking enough, though no longer Young, to be pleasant to the eyes, and intelligent enough though not learned, to be an agreeable talker." Charlotte and Ben Eastman had married in 1841. Ben Eastman, who was born in Maine, and Maria L. Eastman were seventh-generation descendants of a common ancestor, but we do not know if they or the Chases were aware of that distant connection. *Chase Papers,* 1:273, 309, 353, 483–84, 491–92, 494–95, 601, 607, 624–25, 639, 683; 4:112–13; 5:29–31, 125; Rix, *Eastman Family,* 1:463.

2. Kate may have been staying in Cincinnati at the home of George L. Febiger, whose wife, Caroline Smith Febiger, a sister of Kate's mother, died in 1852.

3. Emeline Colby Webster Lindsly and her husband, Dr. Harvey Lindsly, were acquaintances from Father's early days in Washington, D.C. Their daughter Caroline was the wife of Dr. William H. Mussey of Cincinnati. Before Emeline's marriage, Father had "vindicated her character" against accusations of a relationship with a married man. Even after he learned that there might be substance to the "base slanders," he was forgiving of Emeline's part in the affair. "Man is always the seducer, woman the seduced and which is the more guilty," he wondered to a friend about the matter in 1828. *Chase Papers,* 1:65, 236; 2:20–21, 23, 26; Kelly and Burrage, *Dictionary of American Medical Biography,* 896; *DAB,* 13:372.

4. Charlotte Chambers Ludlow Jones.

5. Apparently James was a household servant and Nichts and Nelly were pets. For a later Nellie, see Father's letters to Nettie of August 1863, in chapter 5.

6. Possibly Thomas Dow Jones, a Cincinnati sculptor. He had made a death mask of Alice Chase in February 1859, and the year before, a group of Cincinnatians had commissioned him to make a bust of Father. Jones long endured a tenuous financial situation. His best-known work was a bust of Abraham Lincoln modeled in 1860, which was commissioned, but not paid for, by a group of Ohioans. *Chase Papers,* 1:311, 354; Coyle, *Ohio Authors,* 345.

7. Probably Elizabeth Jane Neil King, a Columbus resident and the widow of Thomas Worthington King. Columbus attorney Noah Haynes Swayne was later on the U.S. Supreme Court throughout Father's tenure as chief justice. *DAB,* 18:239; *Chase Papers,* 1:291.

8. Dr. Samuel M. Smith of Columbus was a professor at Starling Medical College and the surgeon general of Ohio. Miss Anthony was likely Anna J. (Annie) Anthony, whose sister, Susan H. Anthony, had married Smith's son in 1843. *The Alpha Delta Phi, 1832–1882* (Boston: privately printed, 1882), 34, 45; *Chase Papers,* 1:257, 279.

9. Author and journalist William T. Coggeshall served as state librarian, 1856–62. In 1860 he compiled *Poets and Poetry of the West,* which included three poems by Father, called "The Sisters," "To a Star," and "Themes," introduced by a biographical sketch by William D. Gallagher drawing on biographical information drafted by Edward L. Pierce. "The Sisters" dated from when Father was a young man in Washington and was inscribed to two of William Wirt's daughters. "Themes" began, "Lightly that feather floats upon the wind! / yet in the eternal balance mightiest deeds / Of mightiest men are lighter!" and ended, "How shifts the varying scene! The great, to-day, / Are by the turn of fickle Fortune's wheel / To-morrow mingled with the general mass." William T. Coggeshall, *The Poets and Poetry of the West: With Biographical and Critical Notices* (Columbus, Ohio: Follett, Foster, 1860), 167–71; *Chase Papers,* 1:247; 3:17.

10. Presumably the household staff.

11. Probably Alice Skinner.

FATHER TO KATE

Columbus, September 4, 1859.

My dear Katie,

Your letter of August 31 came Saturday—yesterday. I should have been very much disappointed indeed if I had come home the week before as I intended and had found no letter from you. But I was saved the disappointment by yielding to the pressing invitation of my friends in Medina to remain there, after finishing my speech Saturday afternoon, over Sunday instead of riding sixteen miles to the cars & then a hundred & ten to Columbus.[1] When I came home in fact on Friday night I *was* disappointed that I found no letter from you—but the disappointment did not last very long, for the morning mail of Saturday bro't one—and a very nice one. I just mention the disappointment however that you may see and realize that it is always better to adhere to your first plan—especially when you make a promise—than to change it, *however probable* it may be that it *will be just as well.*

But having given you this little bit of censure let me making amends by telling how much I like your letters from Philadelphia. They are very good indeed—and—what pleases me greatly—the last, so far, is the best. Keep on improving / Let your pen *run* freely. Talk of every thing that interests you—the beaux you see—the acquaintances you make—the places you visit—and the whole string of "so forths."

I doubt not that your visit to Miss Haines was very pleasant to both of you. Few things are so pleasant to a conscientious teacher as the manifested remembrance and gratitude of a pupil who has won a good place in Society. And to a good pupil I can easily imagine that the affectionate remembrance of a valued teacher must be very pleasant.

If you desire it I have no objections to your remaining through the month especially if you are well and are growing fat. Act your own pleasure about coming home with Mr. Cooke.[2] It will be a good opportunity if you are ready and wish to come; and your coming as you know will be hailed with joy by the whole household: but if you think it best all things considered and especially your own health and happiness to remain a little longer do so. Col. Parsons told me that he should go to New York day after tomorrow and stay there about a week.[3] He may come back by way of Philadelphia, and if so he will be coming home about the same time with the Cookes[4] / I don't want you to come unless with some elderly staid gentleman except some other lady is of the party to matronize you. But if Parsons is of the party when you come it will be agreeable to you I am sure / By the way I am glad to be able to say to you that he is nominated for reelection. There was some—and a good deal of unfair & ungenerous opposition to him but he overcame it all to the great gratification of all of us who admire & love him.

Your cousin Jane Auld came last night with her two children Jennie & Alice, who are nice little girls. She brings sad news from Missouri. She is in a rapid consumption and no hope of recovery remains. She is at Lockport with your uncle Edward. Poor girl, how sad! She took cold & neglected it. Other disorder supervened—She did not make her real condition known, until too late to check the progress of the malady. How Short her life has been & how full of trouble—almost all of which could have been so easily Shunned. Sad—sad—very-very sad.

Nettie is now at Hillsborough. I intend to go for her on Thursday and return with her on Friday. She writes me that Mr Collins has met with an accident, hurting his back badly: but gives no particulars. I hope it is not serious. Do you know that he is nominated for the Senate?

I have neglected to send you the Journal, but will send you a package tomorrow & tell Mr. Simkins to send them regularly.[5]

Do you want more money & how much will answer?

I go to the north part of the state next Saturday but hope to get your next letter before I start. I expect to be absent about six days. Mr Dennison's prospect of election is very good—almost a certainty; and it is highly probable also that we shall elect a considerable majority in both branches of the Legislature among whom *probably* will be Mr. Collins.[6]

With best regards to all & special thanks to Lottie[7] for making your visit so pleasant I remain,

Your loving father
S P Chase

Miss Katie Chase[8]

Historical Society of Pennsylvania.

1. Father had written to a friend a few days earlier that he was in Medina, Ohio, "fulfilling a series of appointments to speak for the State Ticket." *Chase Papers*, 3:16–17.

2. Born in Sandusky, Ohio, in 1821, Jay Cooke was a clerk in different businesses before he worked himself into a full partnership in a Philadelphia banking firm by the age of twenty-one. That establishment failed in the 1850s, and after managing some of the reorganized firm's assets, Cooke was on his own from 1858 to 1861. He then opened his own banking firm, Jay Cooke and Company. He had experience marketing bonds during the war with Mexico, and during the Civil War he was highly successful as the agent for several government bond issues. During the war and after, Father called on Cooke for personal loans and investment advice. After the war Cooke's firm moved into the financing of railroads; the company's inability to meet its obligations in September 1873 precipitated one of the great financial panics of the nineteenth century. The connection between Father and Cooke before the Civil War was primarily through Cooke's younger brother, Henry David Cooke, who from 1856 to 1861 was the politically engaged editor of the *Ohio State Journal*, a Columbus newspaper. *ANB*, 5:398–99; *Chase Papers*, 1:532; 3:249; Blue, *Chase*, 153, 208, 311.

3. A longtime friend, Richard C. Parsons was a lawyer and Republican politician from Cleveland, and later marshal of the Supreme Court, 1867–72. *Chase Papers*, 1:268.

4. Jay Cooke had married Dorothea Elizabeth Allen in 1844. *ANB*, 5:398.

5. The night following Alice Chase's death in February 1859, Mr. Simkins and Allen Gangewer, an Ohio newspaperman who became Father's secretary that year, sat up in the library of the Chases' home while two women watched over Alice's body. Simkins may have been F. A. B. Simkins, who, like Gangewer, had been the editor of an Ohio newspaper. By 1860 he advertised his services in Columbus as an attorney and notary public. *Chase Papers*, 1:233, 311; *Ohio Statesman*, Apr. 4, 1860.

6. The 1859 election did result in a Republican majority in the state legislature, and William O. Collins had a seat in the Ohio Senate, 1860–61. Lawyer, banker, and Republican politician William Dennison won the election to succeed Father as governor. Dennison was later U.S. postmaster general, 1864–66. Thompson, *History of the County of Highland*, 33; *DAB*, 5:241–42; Niven, *Chase*, 211.

7. Charlotte Eastman.

8. Kate endorsed this letter to indicate that she received it on September 7 and answered it on the eighth.

KATE TO NETTIE

Columbus. July 25. 1860.

My dear Nettie,

Your last letter was a great improvement upon the others, still the spelling is not perfect. When you are not perfectly sure about a word, you should look at it in the dictionary, or ask someone how it is spelt.

Henry, I think, is learning a little. He reads to me every morning for two hours. I make him use the Dictionary freely—he is very slow about finding the words, & will call d, t & v. f, still, I have great hopes of him.[1]

I have commenced taking singing lessons of a Miss Gibbs, a young lady, who has come here from Newark.[2] You would have laughed, if you could have seen me on Monday, when I took my first lesson. Miss Gibbs made me stand with arms folded *behind* my back, & a quarter between my teeth to keep my mouth open.

Poor little Bob, has hurt his foot, & walks quite lame, but I hope he will soon get over it. He seems very lonesome, & goes wandering about the house as if he was lost. In the evening he strays into the sitting-room,

& last evening, with-out any invitation jumped into Father's lap, & laid down & went to sleep. I think, Nettie, he misses you.

If you feel that you need a sack to protect your arms & neck from the sun, you had buy enough of some material that will wash, & *make it yourself,* Your Aunt[3] will, cut it out for you I have no doubt. How about the handkercheifs—have you hemed any of them yet.

To-day we have quite a little dinner-party, & a very nice dinner. Father invited a number of gentlemen to meet President Hitchcock, among them Dr. McMillen.[4] He inquired very kindly about you, as all your friends do. This is quite as long as one of your letters, & I am very tired, so good night dear Nettie, & pleasant dreams.

Your Affectionate Sister

Historical Society of Pennsylvania.

1. According to the 1860 census, Henry Kepler, age thirteen and a native of Germany, was a servant in the Chase household in Columbus. The other servants listed on the census return were Anna McElvoy, age twenty-six, a native of Ireland; Ann Jones, twenty-five years old, born in Wales; and Mary Richards, who was also from Wales and twenty-five years old at the time of the census. For Mary, see the letter written by Nettie and Will Hoyt, Apr. 30, 1871, in chapter 11. 1860 census, Franklin County, Ohio, Columbus Ward 2, 86.

2. Newark, Ohio, with more than 3,000 inhabitants, was about thirty miles east of Columbus in Licking County. Smith, *Harper's Statistical Gazetteer,* 1215.

3. Catharine Collins.

4. The Reverend Henry Lawrence Hitchcock became president of Western Reserve College in 1855. William Linn McMillen, M.D., practiced in Columbus and socialized with Dr. Samuel M. Smith. Alfred E. Lee, *History of the City of Columbus, Capital of Ohio,* 2 vols. (New York: Munsell & Co., 1892), 2:609; Frederick Clayton Waite, *Western Reserve University: The Hudson Era* (Cleveland, Ohio: Western Reserve University Press, 1943), 325; *Chase Papers,* 1:293.

FATHER TO NETTIE

Columbus, Aug 10, 1860.

My darling Nettie,

Your letters, though not quite long enough or quite full enough, give us a great deal of pleasure. It is a happiness to know that you are well and that you are enjoying yourself so much: and I am very grateful to your kind Uncle & Aunt Collins for all the interest they take in making your visit so pleasant; and I am particularly gratified that you get along so happily with Caspar, & Josie & Fanny.[1] One of the most agreeable sights to me in the world is to see children enjoying themselves together, and that not selfishly as too many do, but finding their highest enjoyment in promoting the happiness of each other.

The Republican State Committee has appointed a meeting for me at Greenfield on the 23d of August: but as Mr. Clay has also been invited it is very possible that I may not be there.[2] If Mr. Clay promises positively to be present or if some other Speaker with whom the people will be satisfied will make such a promise, it is thought best that I should go to Indiana at that time. If however no one is found to take my place I shall not allow any disappointment, but shall give up the idea of going to Indiana and shall be at Greenfield, if alive & able to get there. I take it for granted that Mr. Collins will be there and, if I go, I hope to see you and Josie there too with Mrs Collins. Perhaps Mr. Collins will conclude also to go to Batavia where I am also to speak if I speak at Greenfield.[3]

Next week I expect to go to Michigan and to make two speeches there: but I hope to be at home again on Saturday.

Katie has been writing to you and has told you I suppose all about her preserves. She has been very busy; and you never saw prettier jelly or prettier preserves than she has made out of our crabapples. But she will tell you all about these things herself.

Every thing is looking beautifully here. The [rain] has kept the grass & the foliage bright and green: and thanks to Mr. Bannisters advice our roses, kept cut down, continue to bloom profusely.[4] The only thing likely to fail seems to be the figs. They dont seem to grow much, and, I am afraid, will not be worth eating. Our new strawberry beds however are doing nicely and promise next year great things.

You must take a great deal of pains with your spelling my darling. Your hand writing will be very good if you do not become careless. Remember the old saying that whatever is worth doing at all is worth doing well.

Goodbye—dear—for the present. I expect to write you again before I go to Michigan & to have you keep writing to me as usual. I shall get your letters.

Your affectionate father
S P Chase

Miss Nettie Chase

Library of Congress.

1. We have not identified this Fanny.

2. Cassius M. Clay's place in the movement against slavery was assured in 1845, when inhabitants of Lexington, Ky., closed down his newspaper, *The True American*. In 1860, Clay hoped that he might receive the favor of the Republican national convention, but after the party nominated Lincoln, Clay worked earnestly for the Republican cause, particularly in the states bordering Kentucky north of the Ohio River. Party stalwarts expended considerable energy in Indiana, which had not gone for the Republicans in 1856. David L. Smiley, *Lion of White Hall: The Life of Cassius M. Clay* (Madison, Wis.: University of Wisconsin Press, 1962), 90–99, 159, 169–70; *Chase Papers*, 3:24, 25.

3. Batavia and Greenfield were both in southern Ohio. Batavia was between Cincinnati and Hillsboro, where the Collins family lived, and a railroad connected the two places. Greenfield was west of Chillicothe in Highland County, the same county as Hillsboro. Smith, *Harper's Statistical Gazetteer*, 149, 720, 796.

4. Dwight Bannister was a law student and a bookkeeper in a state office. Later he managed property for Father in Columbus. *Williams' Columbus Directory . . . 1858–'59*, 45; *Lathrop's Columbus Directory* (Columbus, Ohio: Richard Nevins, [1860]), 4; *Chase Papers*, 1:379.

NETTIE TO KATE

I do want to see you and Father so bad dear Sister. Every little while I wonder what you and Father are doing.[1]

Sister Aunt Collins said that cold water just out of the pump hurts the flower's so she lets a tub of water stand all day in the sun to water the flowers with / She say's the water ought to be of the same temperature as the air I wish you would tell Thomas to make some liquid manure and water the roses around the roots it would do them so much good water them twice a week. I put some around the verbena's and it did them good.

It has been very hot—the last few day's hardly any air it makes a person feel very lasy

Josie had a little party on her birthday no boy's only a few girls we had a very nice time we played charades we had Phantom for one word[2] the ghost was Mary Waite she held a broom in her hand covered with a sheet which made her seem very tall[3]

The recipe for sweet pickles is "Take half of the weight of the peaches in sugar and what vinegar will be sufficient to make a syrupe boil up the vinegar and sugar—and pour it boiling hot over the peaches let them stand till the next day then pour of the syrupe boil it up again and let it stand till the next day the third day put peaches syrupe and spices and boil all about fivteen minutes put the peaches carefully in the jar and pour the syrupe over them when cold tie it up tight the spices should be cloves broken nutmeg green peper stripes of lemon or Orange peel Horse radish, mace and a little ginger" Please give my love to Father

Your loving
Nettie

PS
The peaches should be clings

Brown University Library.

1. Nettie wrote this letter at Hillsboro and may have done so, judging from the contents, in the summer of 1860.

2. She originally wrote, and then struck through, "name."

3. Nettie wrote "with with a sheet." Mary was perhaps the daughter of Morrison R. Waite, who joined the Supreme Court in 1874, after Father's death, and succeeded him as chief justice. A native of Connecticut, Morrison Waite attended Yale, then moved to Ohio as a young attorney in the 1830s. He lived in Toledo beginning in 1848. His connection to Hillsboro is not evident, but he had a daughter named Mary Frances. *ANB*, 22:457–58; C. Peter Magrath, *Morrison R. Waite: The Triumph of Character* (New York: Macmillan, 1963), 79, 93, 137.

CHRONOLOGY

February 1861	Chases move to Washington, D.C.
March 1861	President Abraham Lincoln appoints Father secretary of the Treasury
April 1861	Kate and Nettie in New York City; Civil War begins at Fort Sumter, S.C.
July 1861	Nettie and Kate visit Fortress Monroe; first battle of Bull Run
September 1861	Nettie, at Maria Eastman's school in Pennsylvania, has her fourteenth birthday; Kate (twenty-one years old) traveling
December 1861	All are in Washington for Christmas
January 1862	Nettie falls ill returning to school, convalesces in Philadelphia
May 1862	Father visits Fortress Monroe and Norfolk in Virginia with Lincoln and Secretary of War Edwin M. Stanton
June 1862	Kate travels to Ohio
July 1862	Father in Washington, Kate in Ohio, and Nettie completes her term at Eastman's school in Pennsylvania

CHAPTER 4

"Please Write Soon"

September 1861 – July 1862

THE FALL of 1861 found the Chase family in entirely new circumstances. In March of that year Abraham Lincoln was inaugurated
as the sixteenth president of the United States, and he named Father as
his secretary of the Treasury. Although Ohio had returned Father to the
U.S. Senate, he resigned that post and joined Lincoln's cabinet as the secession crisis brought the nation to the brink of war. When he and his
daughters moved to Washington, D.C., they made their home first at the
Rugby, a well-known residential hotel. Father took Kate to the inaugural
ball, where her trim figure and white silk gown made quite an impression. At the age of twenty, her life as a society lady had officially begun.
She and Nettie, who was thirteen, were visiting friends in New York in
April when the war began at Fort Sumter, South Carolina, and their trip
back to Washington was quite an adventure. Maj. Robert Anderson, who
had been in command at Fort Sumter and had been forced to surrender
the garrison to the Confederates, arrived in New York by sea and was intent on getting to Washington. He offered to take Kate and Nettie with
him. Baltimore, on the direct route from New York to Washington, appeared to be in the control of Rebel sympathizers, and Kate's and Nettie's
friends urged them to stay put in New York. Nettie later recalled, though,
that she and her sister were "too anxious to be at home" to heed those
cautions. With Anderson, they went by train through Philadelphia to
Perryville, Maryland, at the mouth of the Susquehanna River. There they
boarded a steamer that took them down Chesapeake Bay to Annapolis,
outrunning a suspicious vessel on the way. Massachusetts troops at Annapolis had the railroad operating from there to Washington, and in the
"chill dawn" of an April day, Major Anderson safely returned his charges
to the capital city they now regarded as their home.[1]

Kate and Nettie made another excursion without their father in
the first week of July. Secretary of War Simon Cameron and Lorenzo
Thomas, the adjutant general of the army, made a one-day visit to Fortress Monroe at Hampton Roads, where the James and York rivers joined
Chesapeake Bay. Although Norfolk, across the water, had fallen to Confederates at the start of the war, the Federals kept control of Fortress

Monroe, and the ostensible reason for the visit by Cameron and Thomas was to assess the place's readiness as a base for an offensive campaign. They also used the fact-finding mission as an opportunity for a pleasure trip, for they took along their wives, their daughters, and the Chase sisters. The group reviewed the troops at Fortress Monroe and two other locations and called on the navy's commanding officer before returning to Washington, by water along Chesapeake Bay as they had come, their heads undoubtedly filled with the ominous sights of war.[2]

By midsummer the Chases had set up housekeeping at a rented but imposing brick house at the corner of Sixth and E streets, only blocks from the White House and Capitol.[3] Nettie later reported that she found the "combination of grandioseness and actual squalor" of Washington "very disappointing." Like other newcomers to the nation's capital, young Nettie noticed that cows and pigs seemed to freely roam the muddy streets, creating a sharp contrast to grand halls of government and dashing men in uniform.[4] In late July the Chase house was used as a temporary hospital in the wake of the first battle of Bull Run. As men flooded into Washington, fleeing the nearby battlefield, local hospitals were quickly filled. Wounded soldiers were brought into the Chases' home and ar-ranged on sofas and the floor. When one wounded young man used profane language, the Chases' friend Charles P. McIlvaine, the Episcopal bishop of Ohio, warned him, "God can help you much more than the devil can."[5]

The heart of this chapter is a series of letters from Nettie to Kate, in part because after the move to Washington Kate stepped into the breach created by the overwhelming nature of Father's work and became, in some ways, a de facto parent. Though we do not have Kate's replies, her sister's letters create a vivid picture of a teenage girl's interests and anxieties as she entered a new phase of her life. Apparently pleased with the education that Kate had received in Pennsylvania under the tutelage of Maria Eastman, Father sent his younger daughter to the Brooke Hall Female Seminary. Eastman had become the director of Brooke Hall, which was located outside Philadelphia in Media, after she left the Aston Ridge school. Although we do not know the details of the curriculum offered by Miss Eastman in 1861–62, Nettie faced a rigorous course of study in literature, history, mathematics, logic and rhetoric, sciences, and foreign languages. Girls at Brooke Hall were also encouraged to exercise outdoors and take gymnastics. Father apparently did not object to the "bloomer costumes" the girls were required to wear for gymnastics, despite the fact that critics of dress reform charged that the split skirt, or bloomer, caused female promiscuity and other unladylike behaviors.[6]

Nettie's entry into boarding school coincided with her father's increasing responsibilities as Lincoln's secretary of the Treasury. Early in the war, Congress, the president, and his cabinet were still debating whether the seceded states remained part of the United States of America, and thus entitled to treatment as such, or were a hostile and independent nation whose citizens and combatants deserved no U.S. civil rights. The permutations of these questions affected issues as diverse as prisoner of war treatment to the question of whether western Virginia could legally become a new state. Father was also deeply mired in the problem of how to pay for the war, which appeared by this time to be settling in as a long-term conflict. In the midst of his concerns, the needs of a fourteen-year-old girl could play only a small part.

Thus it was to Kate that Nettie made requests for warm clothing, permission to join gymnastics, pictures of the family, books, and other essentials. Nettie also wrote Kate about her new friends and teachers, and it was Kate who brought her sister home for Christmas break. At home it was Kate who took charge of Christmas when Father spent the day writing remarks for a cabinet meeting about the *Trent* affair, and Kate who acted as hostess of their New Year's celebrations. The Chases received a crowd of Washington luminaries, including a number of politicians, diplomats, and military officers. Helen McDowell, who was married to Gen. Irvin McDowell; Charlotte Bridge, a friend from when the Chases first moved to Washington; and Susan Walker, an antislavery activist and one of Father's closest female friends, acted as Kate's helpers at that reception. The next day the family had a more intimate gathering, sitting down to a "big Turkey" with Charles Sumner and the McDowells.[7] It must have been terribly exciting for the girls to have a father in the wartime cabinet, though one wonders if the thrill wore off as official demands on his time took his attention away from his family.

When Nettie's break was over, she set out for Media escorted by her cousin Ralston Skinner but fell ill with scarlet fever along the way. Kate hurried to see her, but then had to leave her sister in Philadelphia under a doctor's care until she fully recovered. Nettie's boredom as she recuperated was eased by the attentions of Jay and Dorothea Cooke, who lived nearby in Chelten Hills. The Cookes were the Chases' best friends in the Philadelphia area, and as the war developed and required financing far beyond what could be met by short-term loans, Jay Cooke would play an ever-increasing role as he and Father began the program of selling war bonds directly to the public. By the end of the war Cooke was selling bonds faster than the government could spend the money, and one of every four Northern families had purchased war bonds.[8] In January 1862, Cooke took care to send Nettie a canary to keep her company.[9]

The Chases' home became one of Washington's social and political centers, and Kate developed her skills as a political hostess—a job that entailed far more than serving tea and managing the help. A good Washington hostess had to know her politics as well as she did social niceties. Kate was very much the belle of Washington in the early years of the war, so successful in combining the social and political worlds that the president's wife, Mary Todd Lincoln, detested her and forbade her husband to dance or talk with the young woman. Indeed, though belles are often thought of as empty-headed young ladies, with no more on their minds than fashion and gossip, young society women like Kate often experienced this period of their lives as empowering. Through her popularity and social position a belle could "bend men to her will," while controlling her own.[10] Kate excelled at this game, for she had both a pretty face and an astute grasp of politics learned at her father's knee.

The chapter ends in the summer of 1862 with a series of letters from Father to Kate, who was visiting family and friends in Ohio and West Virginia in June and much of July. Nettie had to stay in school through June, in part to make up time she lost earlier in the year when she was ill, but was back in Washington by early July. Father's July letters to Kate suggest how much he missed his daughter and how immersed he was in Civil War politics. The war was going badly for the Union that summer, with defeats in the Shenandoah Valley and the Peninsula campaign. Father's and Nettie's irritation with General McClellan's unwillingness to meaningfully engage the Confederates mirrored many Northerners' frustrations.[11] A little more than a year into the war, any heady optimism and romanticism of war had worn off for noncombatants and soldiers alike. This set of family letters only hints at how destructive and deadly the war had become, but they also suggest that despite the parade of disheartening battles, many Americans, like the Chases, carried on with their day-to-day lives.

1. Janet Chase Hoyt, "A Woman's Memories," *New York Tribune*, Mar. 8, Apr. 5, 1891; Niven, *Chase*, 234; McPherson, *Battle Cry of Freedom*, 264–74, 285.

2. *New York Times*, July 7, 1861. Simon Cameron and his wife, Margaretta Brua Cameron, married in 1822 and had ten children. Their unmarried daughters at the time of the excursion to Fortress Monroe were Virginia (Jennie) and Margaretta. There was also a widowed daughter, Rachel Cameron Burnside. Lorenzo Thomas, whose wife's name we do not know, had a daughter named Mary. Erwin Stanley Bradley, *Simon Cameron, Lincoln's Secretary of War: A Political Biography* (Philadelphia: University of Pennsylvania Press, 1966), 23, 51; *Chase Papers*, 1:637; undated letter from Nettie to Kate, following Nettie's letter of Nov. 27, 1861, below.

3. Niven, *Chase*, 234, 255.

4. *New York Tribune*, Mar. 8, 1891.

5. Ibid., June 7, 1891.

6. Nancy Isenberg, *Sex and Citizenship in Antebellum America* (Chapel Hill, N.C.: University of North Carolina Press, 1998), 45–55; Sylvia D. Hoffert, *When Hens Crow: The Women's Rights Movement in Antebellum America* (Bloomington, Ind.: Indiana University Press, 1995), 23. For the courses offered at Brooke Hall a decade later, see Brooke Hall Female Seminary, *Catalogue*.

7. On November 8, a U.S. naval ship stopped the British ship *Trent* and removed two Confederate commissioners who were charged with trying to make diplomatic alliances with Britain and France. The incident caused a diplomatic crisis between the United States and Great Britain, which claimed its neutrality had been violated. On New Year's Day the girls first accompanied their father to a White House reception, then received callers at the 6th and E street house afterward. Though Father's diary does not mention Helen Mc-

Dowell at the dinner on January 2, it seems likely that she was there with her husband. *Chase Papers,* 1:318–21.

8. McPherson, *Ordeal by Fire,* 202–4; *Chase Papers,* 1:323.

9. Nettie to Father, Jan. 26, 1862, below.

10. Farnham, *Education of the Southern Belle,* 180; Keckley, *Behind the Scenes,* 106–9.

11. McPherson, *Ordeal by Fire,* 235–48; Nettie to Father, June 25, and Father to Kate, July 4, 1862, below.

FATHER TO KATE

My dear Katie,

I forgot to say to you last evening that I called on Mrs Eastman, just before dinner, and *en causant*[1] asked why she had not called on you". She replied that she really thought you ought to call first on her, being younger and no stranger: adding that Mrs Blair had called immediately to see her on learning her arrival.[2] I answered that I thought that the first call was due *de rigueur* from her to you: and she said that if I thought so she would make.[3] She will doubtless call this morning; and I hope you will make it just as agreeable as possible to her, and wipe out all past disagreeable remembrances on both sides.[4]

Affy your father
S.P.C

Historical Society of Pennsylvania.

1. In the course of conversation.

2. Probably Mary Elizabeth ("Minnie") Woodbury Blair, who married Montgomery Blair after his first wife died in 1844. It seems less likely that this Mrs. Blair was Appoline ("Apo") Alexander Blair, the wife of Francis P. Blair Jr. Virginia Jean Laas, *Wartime Washington: The Civil War Letters of Elizabeth Blair Lee* (Urbana, Ill.: University of Illinois Press, 1991), 50, 125; William Earnest Smith, *The Francis Preston Blair Family in Politics,* 2 vols. (New York: Macmillan Co., 1933), 1:206, 212–13.

3. So in the original.

4. Too little is known of the chronology of Charlotte Eastman's visits to Washington to assist in dating this note, which Father perhaps wrote before departing for his office one morning. The note may date from early in the Chases' residence in Washington, before Kate's position in the capital city's social and political hierarchies was clear.

FATHER TO KATE

Washington, Sep. 2, 1861

My dear Katie

I write at a venture not knowing where you may be, as you have not thought it worth while to keep me advised of your movements.

The last I heard of you was that you went some time last week to Orange, where I doubt not you had a pleasant visit.

Mr. Hamilton writes me that he had heard nothing of you since you were at Newport.[1] I supposed you intended making a brief visit there & hoped that Gertrude Stevens wd. accompany you.[2]

I always feel anxious about you when I do not hear. It would hardly be too great a tax on your time to send me a few lines every day

Your affe. father

S P Chase

Miss Kate Chase

1. New York lawyer and politician James Alexander Hamilton, born in 1788, was a son of Alexander Hamilton. He advised the Lincoln administration about financial policy beginning in April 1861. The next year he drafted an emancipation proclamation that he hoped would be used by the president and, representing the "War Committee of New York," criticized William Seward's influence over policy. Hamilton and an unmarried daughter sometimes saw Kate in New York City and invited her to their residence near Dobbs Ferry, in Westchester County up the Hudson River from Manhattan. On at least one occasion Hamilton stayed with the Chases when he was in Washington. *DAB,* 8:188–89; *Chase Papers,* 1:378–79, 393, 398; 3:63, 269, 333.

2. Gertrude Stevens was a year younger than Kate. She was a daughter of John Austin Stevens Sr., the president of the Bank of Commerce in New York, and Abby Weld Stevens. During the Civil War, Gertrude Stevens worked with Louisa Lee Schuyler in the New York branch of the United States Sanitary Commission, performing services similar to those later fulfilled by the Red Cross, and in the 1870s and 1880s the two were associated again in the New York State Charities Aid Association. Stevens, who married William B. Rice in 1869, continued her social service work as a trustee and vice president of the Russell Sage Foundation and vice president of the National Committee for the Prevention of Blindness. She died in 1926 at the age of eighty-four. Early in the Civil War, John A. Stevens was one of the representatives of the "Associated Banks" of New York advising the secretary of the Treasury and negotiating loans to the government. He and Father established a cordial relationship that continued after Father left the Treasury. Gertrude's brother, John A. Stevens Jr., a New York merchant, was also on good social terms with the Chases, a political ally, and in 1863 the founder of the Loyal National League, a pro-Union organization in New York. *New York Times,* Mar. 25, 29, 1926; Eugene R. Stevens, *Erasmus Stevens, Boston, Mass., 1674–1690, and His Descendants,* ed. William Plumb Bacon (New York: Tobias A. Wright, 1914), 41; John M. Glenn, Lilian Brandt, and F. Emerson Andrews, *Russell Sage Foundation: 1907–1946,* 2 vols. (New York: Russell Sage Foundation, 1947), 1:9, 11, 18, 232, 270; 2:423, 669, 670; *Chase Papers,* 1:312, 328, 412, 413, 482, 502, 595; 3:69–70, 115, 119–20; 4:135; *DAB,* 17:616.

NETTIE TO KATE

September 29 1861[1]

Dear Sister

To day is my birthday, I ought to have some proper thought for the *great?* occasion, and I fully intended to have them, but I can not for the life of me think what they were. except that I want to see you and Father ever so much but I think of that often or rather always.

Is Gov Sprague back yet? I wish (if you do not think me impertinent) that you would marry him. I like him very much wont you? but of course not until I grow up I shant give my consent before that. prehaps though he may get tired of waiting.[2]

I study English History, Philosophy, Spelling, Arithmetic, French, & Parsing. today is composition day I do not succeed very well in that. I like Carrie Gwin well enough.[3] I do not beleive she cares for either North or

South only for beaux & cadets I get tired of lisening to her I like Lula Bowman the best of the girls[4]

I just received a letter from Father I was *so* glad to get it but I could not read it all. Gen McDowel's "Phiz" (as Father called it)[5] was in the letter the first picture in my Album I wish you would send me some. Please write soon to your

loving
Nettie

Miss Kate Chase
Washington D.C.

Historical Society of Pennsylvania.

1. Nettie probably wrote the date originally as "19," which would accord with her statement in the opening sentence that she was writing on her birthday. For unknown reasons, perhaps teasing her sister over the faulty recollection of family birthdays, Nettie or someone else altered the first digit to a "2" and underlined the date with two strokes. Kate, according to her filing endorsement, received this letter on September 21 and answered it on the twenty-third.

2. In the spring of 1861, thirty-year-old William Sprague came to Washington at the head of the First Rhode Island Regiment, which established a cantonment on the outskirts of the city. William and Kate soon entered into a courtship that was apparent to Washington society. In the summer of 1861, William, who was first elected governor of Rhode Island in 1859, returned to his home state and his family's very large cotton textile milling business, which prospered during the war. There he raised more military units for the Union. Lamphier, *Kate Chase and William Sprague*, 43–44; *DAB*, 17:475; Thomas Aldrich, *The History of Battery A, First Rhode Island Light Artillery* (Providence, R.I.: Snow & Farnham, 1904).

3. Carrie was the youngest daughter of Senator William McKendree Gwin of California and Mary Bell Gwin. Lately Thomas, *Between Two Empires: The Life Story of California's First Senator* (Boston: Houghton Mifflin, 1969), 161–62.

4. Lula Bowman and Lalie Bowman (who appears in letters below) may have been related to Alexander Hamilton Bowman, an army engineering officer who beginning in March 1861 was the superintendent of the United States Military Academy. That supposition gains reinforcement from the Bowman girls' friendship with Mary Thomas (see Nettie's undated letter following the one of November 27, below). Mary was the daughter of Lorenzo Thomas, who beginning in March was the army's adjutant general. *Appletons'*, 1:339; *DAB*, 18:441–42.

5. Writing to a friend in 1870, Father again used "phiz"—derived from "physiognomy," meaning facial features—to indicate a photograph. Irvin McDowell, born in Columbus, Ohio, in 1818, was a graduate of West Point and a veteran of the war with Mexico. Most of his experience, however, was as a staff officer. Early in the Civil War he became a protégé of Father, who was eager to promote the career of an Ohioan and liked McDowell's plans for an offensive campaign. In the spring of 1861, at Father's urging, Abraham Lincoln and Secretary of War Simon Cameron put McDowell at the head of Federal forces charged with making the first Union advance in northern Virginia. That project ended with the rout of the army at Bull Run in July. In the period after that disaster, McDowell commanded a division in the forces protecting Washington. Niven, *Chase*, 254; *ANB*, 15:21–22; *Chase Papers*, 5:333.

NETTIE TO KATE

Media September[1] 18 1861.

Dear Sister

I received your letter a few days ago, I was so sorry you, and Father, were troubled about me; I was perfectly well. I have dated my letter September, instead of October, but I cannot take another sheet, so please excuse it.

I am so delighted that you are coming here I shall be so glad that I will not know what to do; be sure and come. I shall be dreadfully disappointed if you do not. I have almost finished one stocking for the soldiers I guess that is more than you have done is it not. I will be so much obliged you send me those things you spoke of Fathers picture particularly. the books also I shall be delighted to have, I am much obliged to you for thinking of me. We have a new teacher, Miss Ellsworth, she is very cross. I do not like her much. Please come to Cousin Robert's wedding.[2] I cannot think what to say every day here passes like the one before. In eight weeks school is out

Your own loving
Nettie

Historical Society of Pennsylvania.

1. Actually October, as Nettie corrected herself in the first paragraph. According to Kate's filing endorsement, she received this letter on October 21 and answered it the same day.
2. We do not know whom Nettie meant by "Cousin Robert."

NETTIE TO KATE

Media Nov 7th. 1861.

Dear Sister

I am afraid you will not be here Saturday. I want you so much. Miss Emma Loeser will be here to see Sarah, are you in Washington now? I cannot tell where you are, half the time. Have you forgotten my "card de visits"?[1] I want to put them in my Album. Please send with them another of those vignettes of you for you know that other old Photograph of you Well! when I got the new one Lalie Bowman took it and it is not a bit pretty of you and I want her if she has any to have a pretty one. for I do not want that old one to be shown as you. My drawing teacher picked up that new one and she said if I did not put it away she would carry off for it was so pretty. How can I get my pictures which are being framed in the city? I cannot tell. Gov Sprague has gone back to Rhode Island hasent he I am afraid I can not get my autograph.[2] I can not write long letters on Wednesday

Your own
Nettie

Historical Society of Pennsylvania.

1. Cartes de visite, small portrait photographs.
2. In the fall of 1861, William Sprague returned to Washington and with his troops was engaged in a brief skirmish in Virginia. He then went back to Rhode Island and did not re-

visit the capital until May 1862. Thomas Belden, "William Sprague: The Story of an American Tragedy" (M.A. thesis, George Washington University, 1948), 13–14; *OR*, ser. 1, 2:397; vol. 11, part 3, 301–2, 311.

NETTIE TO KATE

Dear Sister[1]

I received your long letter and was so glad to get it. I begin to get along very well but I cannot keep the rules. Will you please ask Father if I can take gymnastics I want to so much if I can shall Miss Eastman get me my bloomer dress? she is going to get those of several of the girls. I wish you would please[2] send me my trunk I get so cold I have no warm dress but that red one, and will you send me a bureau I have not even my trunk to keep my things in I have to put all in the bottom of the wardrobe. My roomate is Sallie Potter from *N. Carolina* she is a rebel we discuss the subject very warmly somtimes. but Miss Eastman says as our opinions would not have much weight we had better be silent and tend to our studies. something litk your old gentleman.

I received a letter from Josie Jones saying she had read of you in one of the Chicago papers as an "angel of mercy tening to the sick soldiers" quite romantic. I heard a lady say the other day it was such a pity for a young & charming girl like you to throw herself away on a widower with six children it would be such a change for you. how glad I was to contradict her. I am[3] told so often I look like Father. I do hope I shall grow like him in character he is so noble.

In your next letter please tell me if I may join the gymnasts I hope I have im-[4] in my letters. I like Lula & Lalie best of all the girls

Please write very soon to your

loving
Nettie

Brown University Library.

1. We have placed this undated letter at a likely place in the sequence of correspondence, based on its contents.
2. After this word Nettie wrote, then struck through, "let me."
3. She originally wrote "was," then altered it to "am."
4. She probably meant to write "improved" but hyphenated at the turn of a page and neglected to complete the word.

NETTIE TO KATE

Media November 16th. 1861.

Darling Sister

Miss Eastman says Father is in New York and for all I know you may be also. It is awful cold I shiver & freeze all the time when I go to my bath it is horrid I have no dressing gown or slippers please send them *when* you send my trunk. I do not know whether you will receive this. or not. I have nothing in the world to say but I am very well

Your own loving
Nettie.

Historical Society of Pennsylvania.

NETTIE TO FATHER

Brooke Hall.
November 20th. 1861.

Dear Father.

I received your long, and very welcome letter, on the 19th. I was delighted to have your photograph. I think it is very good, but not yet as hansome as you; I suppose you have heard me say, that Senator Gwin's daughter was here. She received a letter from her Father, a little while ago telling her to go to N. York, meet her Mother, and Sister, and then for them all to come to Cuba, to meet him & spend the winter. the day after, when she was packing up, the news of his arrest came. but she was not told of it here, the first she hears of it will be from he[1] mother, Poor thing, I pity her sincerely. I could not tell what I should do if you were in his place. is there any danger of his estates being confiscated? I hope not for his family's sake. for I am afraid they could not do much with him in prison.[2]

Sallie Potter, one of the southern girls, said while looking at your picture "It is impossible, for such a noble looking man, to be an abolitionist he looks so good, and if he would never do a mean act, I do not believe it"

I received a letter from Alice Skinner, saying she could not come Christmas. I am so very sorry. You know you said I might invite the Bowmans if she did not accept our invitation, I have done so, but I am afraid they cannot come

The girls are going to give Miss East man a Christmass present, will you please send me some money to give? Very soon I will be with you I will be delighted. to see you again and in our own house and the prospect of staying two whole weeks I will not what to do I am so glad. It will be very interesting for the girls now if they come. I am so afraid Lizzie can not come, I shall be so disapointed if she does not.[3] All the girls around me and I can hardly write, there is so much noise.

I received another letter from you, a little while ago. I was so glad to get it Lieutenant Ammon's letter was very interesting it is splendid to think that our "off scourings of the populace" "Mudsils" &c have established them on their "sacred soil" I should not think it would be very palatable to them to have "hirelings" "invading" their land.[4]

Your own loving
Nettie

P.C.
I have not seen Sister I am afraid she will not come
N.C.

Historical Society of Pennsylvania.

1. So in the original.

2. Arrested for sedition while on board a vessel near Panama, William McKendree Gwin was taken to New York, held prisoner in Fort Lafayette from November 18 to December 2, 1861, and then released for lack of evidence. Though it was rumored that Gwin, who owned a plantation in Mississippi, was on his way to Havana to meet John Slidell and James Mason at the time of his arrest, the family never went to Cuba. In March 1862, Carrie and her mother sailed for France. Later, Gwin joined them in Paris with Carrie's older sister Lucy, who had marked Confederate sympathies and had spent much of 1861 in Richmond, Va. Thomas, *Between Two Empires*, 91, 161, 265–79; *DAB*, 8:65.

3. Lizzie was the daughter of Ohioans George M. and Jane Swan Parsons (see Father's letter of July 2, 1862, in this chapter). A year later Lizzie did visit the Chases in Washington over the holidays, accompanying them to a reception at the White House on New Year's Day, 1863. Later that year Kate and Father accompanied Lizzie home to Columbus. *Chase Papers*, 1:424; George M. Parsons to Father, June 8, 1863 (Chase Papers, LC); Father to Parsons, June 12, 1863 (Chase Papers, HSP).

4. Nettie quoted some of the language that Southerners had used to characterize their opponents. On November 7, the Union's South Atlantic blockading squadron attacked Port Royal, S.C. That assault resulted in the capture of Port Royal and the occupation of the coastal islands from Savannah to Charleston by Federal forces. A great many Southern whites fled the area, leaving behind thousands of slaves and hundreds of plantations and setting the stage for the "Port Royal Experiment." Treasury Department agents who reported to Father played an influential role in that venture, whereby freed slaves worked to produce their own cotton in the Sea Islands. Daniel Ammen, one of the fleet's officers, had Ohio connections and wrote to Father regularly in 1861, before and after the Port Royal attack. Rose, *Rehearsal for Reconstruction*, 6, 18–22; Niven, *Chase*, 323–29; McPherson, *Ordeal by Fire*, 177; *DAB*, 1:258–59; Ammen to Father, Aug. 20, [Sept.], Dec. 21, 1861 (Chase Papers, LC).

NETTIE TO KATE

Media November *27th.* 1861

Dear dear Sister.

In the excitement of seeing you &c I forgot to tell you that Father said if Alice Skinner did not come I could invite the Bowmans I have done so but I am very much afraid they cannot come / Please write very soon my Sister and say you approve

Miss Eastman has gone to New York, so I have not seen her yet. I had my card de-visit taken[1] I think they will be very good I will send you some as soon as they come. I saw the new one of you I think it is very pretty but not *near* as much so, as you I saw Mrs Jay Cook she wanted me to stay over Thanksgiving with her, I wanted to very much but I thought you would not like it, so I came back to school / It seems quite dull I have put my Photographs in my album they look so nice we had quite a heavy fall of snow Sunday. did you have any thing of it in Washington? I have not time to write long letters on Wednesday so I must stop you will write to me soon wont you? Please give my love to Father I remain

Your

Nettie.

PS
I enclose this letter in an envelope to Father

N.C.

Historical Society of Pennsylvania.

1. Carte de visite.

NETTIE TO KATE

Darling Sister

I received your letter yesterday, it was very welcome, as yours always are. It is growing very cold, when our walking hour comes, it is very hard to keep warm. I am trying, very hard, to improve in my handwriting, composition, &c. I write in my copy book every day.

Miss Eastman's little neice is here her name sake she is a dear little thing and so pretty. Miss Eastman says she means to educate her and then take her to Europe. she has laid plans rather far in the future I think dont you / You said you sent two photograph I guess you forgot them for I have not received any I send you some of mine I think they are very good but I wish they would flatter me more.

Mrs Morehead told me to ask you if you would send her one of your vignetts every one says it is so much prettier than your full length.[1] Beau is getting more sedate and does not get whipped any more. I have not received a letter from Lizzie for a good while I wish she would write to me.

We had some experiments with electricity last night I dont like the shock at all it feels to say the least of it *very* piculier / Have the Miss Stevens left yet? if they have not please remember me to them[2] Do you see much of Fannie Bailey? I received a letter from her a little she is not quite as patronising as she was. when you see her Please give her my love and say I am going to take her example and bill my time in answering her letter. she informed me in her last letter that "I was very fluent in talking and there she could not come up to me but she could beat me in writing any day and there fore she could say what she pleased.

This letter is quite long for me. isent it? so I must stop for I am "run out." Our subject for composition "the use of slang" Phrases I do not like it much

Your own

Nettie

Miss Kate Chase.
Washington, D.C.

Dear Sister[3] I put this in because I have nothing to do and am in the parlour. Lalie & Luila "are much obliged for the invitation and will be very happy to come the last week" the first week they have a visitor themselves

Mary Thomas you remember her she went to Fort Monroe with us, Gen Thomase's daughter[4]

I send you a peice of poetry I found and copied tell me in your next letter what you think of it I think it very pretty.

Your own
Nettie

Historical Society of Pennsylvania.

1. Jay Cooke's and H. D. Cooke's sister, Sarah E. Cooke, had married William G. Moorhead in 1833. Moorhead, from western Pennsylvania, was involved in building railroads and canals and became a business partner of Jay Cooke. Oberholtzer, *Cooke,* 1:3, 40–41; 2:16, 146.

2. At the time, Gertrude Stevens, who was born in September 1841, had three unmarried sisters: Laura Gibbs Stevens (b. 1832), Abby Austin Stevens (b. 1836), and Julia Curtis Stevens (b. 1843). Stevens, *Erasmus Stevens,* 41–44.

3. Nettie added this long postscript in pencil.

4. Their trip down Chesapeake Bay to Fortress Monroe with Secretary of War Cameron and Adjutant General Thomas and their families was on July 5. See the chapter introduction and *New York Times,* July 7, 1861.

NETTIE TO KATE

Media December 14th. 1861.

Dear dear Sister

One week yesterday we go home please do not let me stay after the girls leave if you want me to come as much as I want to go I will be sure of not staying / Please write imediately and tell me who will come for me, Please come your self, I would like it so much. I can go in town[1] Friday evening and start for *home* Saturday if it is not too much trouble please write as soon as you receive this.[2]

Almost all of Miss Eastmans boxes[3] &c come marked. M. L. Eastman. no Miss about it it looks so queer. Like a man. Please excuse all mistakes I am so glad at the idea of going home that I hardly know what I do, say, or write

Please answer to oblige

Your loving sister
Nettie

Historical Society of Pennsylvania.

1. Philadelphia.

2. Following this sentence Nettie wrote "A," probably a false start for the next sentence.

3. She first attempted to write "packages," but apparently got tangled in spelling or forming the word, canceled it, and wrote "boxes" instead.

FATHER TO KATE

Washington, Jan'y 10, 1862

My darling Katie

Mr. Cooke's dispatch today comforted me somewhat concerning Nettie. But I am still very-very uneasy. "A light case" may so easily turn into a serious case. But I earnestly pray that God will watch over her and bring her safely through. It seems—nay, why speak such a language?—it was providential that Ralston discovered her illness & that Mrs Cooke determined to keep her in town & that Dr. Kitchen was sent for.[1] I remember how Dr. Colby thought that scarlet fever was peculiarly manageable under homoepathic treatment; and I shall never forget how futile was allopathic practice in the case of my own dear child, whose name you bear.[2]

Mr. Garrett tells me he placed a private car at your disposal at Baltimore; for which I am much obliged to him. I hope you have not suffered.[3]

I send you a parcel [*illeg.*] & letter under cover to Mr. Jay Cooke, which you will receive I suppose at the same time with this.

Kindest regards to Mr. & Mrs C. & children[4] & a multitude of love to dear Nettie. Write every day or have some one write.[5]

Your affe. father
S P Chase

Historical Society of Pennsylvania.

1. Father was poring over a map with General McDowell at the Treasury Department on Thursday, January 9, when Kate and Jay Cooke came in with the news that "Nettie was ill, but doing well, at Philadelphia." Ralston Skinner was apparently escorting Nettie back to school after the holidays when she fell ill. Kate and Cooke left Washington by an evening train. Jay and Dorothea Cooke's main residence at the time was "The Cedars," in Chelten Hills, outside Philadelphia. Dr. James Kitchen, of 715 Spruce Street in Philadelphia, had an affiliation with the Southern Homœopathic Dispensary at 519 South Third Street. *Chase Papers*, 1:324; Oberholtzer, *Cooke*, 1:154; *McElroy's Philadelphia City Directory for 1860* (Philadelphia: E. C. and J. Biddle & Co., 1860), 529, 1408.

2. Father's first child, also named Catharine Jane and called Kate, died of scarlet fever in February 1840 at the age of four, about six months before Kate was born. In medical practice, homeopathy espoused the use of small quantities of remedies that, in larger doses, produced effects similar to the disease being treated, whereas allopathy utilized remedies that produced effects differing from those of the disease being treated. *Chase Papers*, 1:85, 120; Martin Kaufman, *Homeopathy in America: The Rise and Fall of Medical Heresy* (Baltimore, Md.: Johns Hopkins Press, 1971), 27, 23–25; George Vithoulkas, *The Science of Homeopathy* (New York: Grove Press, 1980), 136–38.

3. The Chases had known John Work Garrett at least since the ceremonies in 1857 celebrating the completion of railroads between the Mississippi Valley and the seaboard. Long involved with the Baltimore and Ohio Railroad, Garrett became the company's president in 1858. He and Father kept up a good relationship, and in the autumn of 1863 the B. & O. was one of the railroads called into service to transport 20,000 soldiers rapidly from the Army of the Potomac to Tennessee to bolster Union forces around Chattanooga. *Chase Papers,* 1:294, 392, 448, 454–56; *DAB,* 7:163.

4. Dorothea and Jay Cooke had eight children from 1845 to 1857, three of whom died in infancy. Larson, *Cooke,* 56.

5. According to her filing notation, Kate received this letter on January 11 and answered it the next day.

FATHER TO KATE

My dearest Katie,

The welcome letter came today—I read enough to assure me that Nettie was doing well—confirmed happily by Mr. Cookes despatch of today—& then was obliged to lay it aside because of the influx of callers of all sorts & sizes & errands and could only resume & finish its reading after I got home this evening.[1]

And now I have only a moment to write as I must go to the Presidents to a consultation on military matters. Every body growls dreadfully—worse I think than ever—and the President is trying to put life and motion into the inert army. The truth is McClellans sickness has cost the country more than can be estimated, & the loss is aggravated by the fact that he has had no man "of his counsel"—thoroughly conversant with his plans able to comprehend & able in event of disease or disaster to himself to execute them. Here has been his great error.[2]

I had learned all about Lander (except the Parrott Gun & Lieutenant) before I received your letter. Large reinforcements have been ordered to him but he has not been treated well, or well supported. If his wishes had been heeded I think Jackson would have been discomfited if not captured. But instead of that he was snubbed and almost insulted by Gen McClellan. Nothing but the weakness & irritability of disease could excuse it.[3]

Your suggestion that Miss Walker should make her other visits and then return to you is very well; but I cannot make it to her. You can write her yourself—say how long you will be absent, & with your own delicate tact suggest that as she must find it lonely, you would not urge her to stay longer than is absolutely agreeable to herself, but beg her to return to you when you come home[4]

Ulke succeeded very well with his picture of me—unless he spoils it by finishing too much.[5]

Oh how I long to see you and Nettie. Give my warmest-warmest love to the darling—May God bless & keep you both. How kind Mrs Cooke has been & Mr. Cooke. I feel their kindness most deeply & shall never forget it. Give my love to them & the children.

You are right in getting a nurse for Nettie / Relieve Mrs C—— & yourself too as much as possible.

Goodbye—Gen McDowell is sitting by me waiting for the consultation tonight. The Gen. says "tell Miss Katie to get Nettie well & come back before we vanish" And give my love to Nettie

Your Affectionate father
S P Chase

Historical Society of Pennsylvania.

1. Kate endorsed this letter as received on Jan. 13, 1862, which, according to the usual exchanges between her and her father, would imply that he wrote it on the previous day. In this case, however, January 12 was a Sunday. He may have written this letter on Saturday the eleventh, a day on which he had numerous callers at the Treasury Department and Abraham Lincoln held a late meeting of generals and cabinet officers, one of a series of conferences the president had with his military advisers over several days. Lincoln accepted the resignation of Simon Cameron as secretary of war on January 11. Four days later the Senate confirmed Edwin M. Stanton as Cameron's replacement. *Chase Papers,* 1:324–26; Miers, *Lincoln Day by Day,* 3:89; Long, *Civil War Day by Day,* 159–60.

2. Lincoln placed George B. McClellan in charge of the Army of the Potomac in July 1861. In mid-December, McClellan contracted typhoid fever, effectively depriving the army of a commander. Three homeopathic physicians treated McClellan, who did not return to work until Jan. 6, 1862. Stephen W. Sears, *George B. McClellan: The Young Napoleon* (New York: Ticknor & Fields, 1988), 136–37; McPherson, *Battle Cry of Freedom,* 348–50, 367–68; *DAB,* 11:582–83.

3. On January 5–6, Frederick West Lander, a brigadier general of volunteers since May 1861, prevented Stonewall Jackson from crossing the Potomac River at Hancock, Maryland—not in a pitched battle but by deploying his outnumbered forces as best he could to resist Jackson's advances and refusing Jackson's demand to evacuate. Lander repeatedly implored his superiors, including George McClellan, to cross the river and cut Jackson off from behind, but his pleas were not heeded. Lander had only two artillery pieces, a smoothbore cannon and a Parrott gun, under the command of Lt. Edward D. Muhlenburg. The smoothbore cannon was virtually useless firing across the river at the Confederates, but Muhlenburg carefully managed a scant supply of ammunition to harass Jackson's army with the Parrott gun, which had a rifled bore and much greater accuracy at long range. Ill health, compounded by war wounds, caused Lander's death early in March 1862. McClellan did not care for Lander, who had participated in five transcontinental surveys from 1853 to 1858. In October 1853, while on an expedition to find passes for railroad routes in the Pacific Northwest, McClellan refused to go through two of the passes during winter to test them. Lander, who was stationed at nearby Fort Walla Walla, volunteered to cover one of the routes, which infuriated McClellan. Gary L. Ecelbarger, *Frederick W. Lander: The Great Natural American Soldier* (Baton Rouge, La.: Louisiana State University Press, 2000), 166–84; Sears, *McClellan,* 37–39; *DAB,* 10:569–70.

4. Father had known Susan Walker (b. 1811) since the 1830s. She was the sister of Cincinnati attorney Timothy Walker, who early in Father's career had been his law partner. Timothy died in 1856. Susan worked as a "computer" for the U.S. Coast Survey before the Civil War. In March 1862, she accompanied a group of Northern women to Port Royal to serve as teachers to freed slaves in the Sea Islands. After the war she opened an industrial school at Washington, D.C., to teach freedwomen, and a few men and boys, sewing skills to help them find employment. She and Father were good friends and frequent correspondents. At times he seemed uncertain about the relationship. In his journal late in 1852 he recorded a call he made on her in Washington as "indiscreet & wrong." *Chase Papers,* 1:64, 118, 232, 247–48, 320, 636, 710; 3:138, 144, 147–48, 160, 184; Carol Faulkner, *Women's Radical Reconstruction: The Freedmen's Aid Movement* (Philadelphia: University of Pennsylvania Press, 2004), 12, 133, 136–39, 188; Father to Oliver O. Howard, Apr. 3, 14, 20, 1869 (O. O. Howard Papers, Bowdoin College).

5. Prussian Henry Ulke (1821–1910) emigrated to the U.S. in 1851, after several years studying painting in Berlin. He painted the portraits of a number of notable politicians, among them Charles Sumner, Ulysses S. Grant, and James G. Blaine. An oil portrait he made of Father is in the possession of the U.S. Treasury Department. Ulke was also a photographer, and earlier in January he had taken "a number of Photographs" of Father at the request of Tracy Robinson Edson, president of the American Bank Note Company. *Chase Papers*, 1:321, 323; *Who Was Who*, 1:1263.

NETTIE TO KATE

Philadelphia Jan 24th. 1862

Dear Sister

I have not received any letter from home since you left and when *you* were here Father wrote every day. Please do write to me. I have nothing to tell you except that I was going out to [Mr] Jay Cooke's tomorrow but I got worse alittle and the doctor said I must stay at home. give my love to dear Father

Your own
Nettie.

I wrote this yesterday I am very well to day Dear Sister write soon to N.C.

Historical Society of Pennsylvania.

NETTIE TO FATHER

Philadelphia Jan 26th. '62

Dear Father

I received your welcome letter yesterday, with one of dear sister's, by the way when *is* she coming back and take me home the doctor says I can go next week this is Sunday & I feel very well to day, Mr. Jay Cooke sent me a canary bird it sings all the time, they all are so kind to me.

I have been reading Dickens a great deal lately I think his writings are the strangest mixture of the grotesque & delicacy of feeling joined up and scattered around in the queerest manner. I think some times I like him and then again I dont, he is so strange[1]

I am so glad we have really commenced fighting[2] I do hope will will[3] soon be victorious so we can "go at" England I would so like to see her arrogance humbled.[4] Please give my love to Sister and remember me to my friends

Your loving
Nettie.

Historical Society of Pennsylvania.

1. Nettie may not have read *Great Expectations*, Charles Dickens's most recently published novel, by January 1862, but most of his best-known works were available before then,

including the *Pickwick Papers, Oliver Twist, Nicholas Nickleby, Martin Chuzzlewit, A Christmas Carol, David Copperfield, Bleak House, Hard Times,* and *A Tale of Two Cities.* Dickens, born in 1812, died in 1870. *ODNB,* 16:59–73.

2. In January 1862, Union operations up the Cumberland and Tennessee rivers probed Confederate strength in the west, while the Army of the Potomac prepared to attack Roanoke Island, near Hatteras, N.C. Denney, *Civil War Years,* 116–19.

3. So in the original.

4. On May 13, 1861, Great Britain declared neutrality with regard to the American Civil War, an act that gave the Confederacy the right under international law to contract loans and buy arms from England. In November, the captain of a U.S. gunship boarded the British steamer *Trent* and arrested two Confederate diplomats, James Mason and John Slidell. British outrage forced the United States to release the Southerners in December. The Union never gave serious thought to going to war with England, and in fact took considerable measures to avoid war. McPherson, *Battle Cry of Freedom,* 388–91; Denney, *Civil War Years,* 44, 96, 98.

NETTIE TO KATE

Philadelphia Jan 28th '62

Darling Sister,

I received your letter the other day, I was so glad to have it, but I thought it very long coming. Dear Sister I am going to ask you a question, which you may think I have no right; but I do love you so dearly, that all that concerns you, *seems* to concern me also, Are you really ingaged to Gov Sprague? if you think it is not my business and I have no right to ask you Please say so and I will never ask you again.[1]

I received a letter from Gen Butterfeild this morning he wrote to me as if I were a four year old baby.[2] telling me to take my medicines, if they are bitter & "such like" I did not know if he was in fun or otherwise. I hope the former for I should be sorry to have any one think so poorly of my understanding. He told me to "cultivate those charm & graces which render your so charming." as if I did not. When are you coming back, the doctor says he thinks I can go home the last day of this week & Mr Cooke is going on Friday. If you do not come before that time can you not send on the car & I go with Mr Cooke? Doctor says if I go in the public car I will have to wait two weeks or more Please write or telagraph imediately to

Your own loving
Nettie

Miss *Katherine* Chase

Historical Society of Pennsylvania.

1. Kate and William did not become engaged until late in May or early in June 1863. Nineteenth-century engagements were not publicly announced but communicated privately to friends and family. Rothman, *Hands and Hearts,* 161–62; William to Kate, June 3, 1863 (Brown University Library).

2. Daniel Butterfield probably became acquainted with the Chases in the spring of 1861. While Kate and Nettie were in New York in April, Butterfield's Twelfth New York Regiment set up camp in a park in front of the Chases' residential hotel. The sisters returned

to Washington to find the square filled with rows of military tents "arranged with symmetrical exactness." Butterfield was then a colonel, and his headquarters stood in the center of the park. His regiment drilled every day and put on a dress parade every afternoon. After a few weeks they left Washington to move into northern Virginia. Butterfield, who was born in 1831, became a brigadier general of volunteers in September 1861. Father visited him when he was sick in September 1862. *New York Tribune*, Apr. 5, 1891; *ANB*, 4:114–16; *Chase Papers*, 1:379.

NETTIE TO KATE

Media June 7th. 1862

Dearest Sister.

I have just received your letter, long expected, and eagerly welcomed. for it is two weeks to day since I have heard from home. I think that your cart de visite with Mr Robinson[1] is charming you I mean his is an excellent likeness do not have the negative destroyed it will be such a pity. Please. do not

About the dresses I do not need any except one for the flag raising, any thing will do. I think both the samples of the silk and organdy are beautiful. is Auntie with you now? The girls are looking at you picture I like to hear their comments apon it

School closes the eleventh of July 1862 I might almost have written 63 / Miss E——. keeps us all because a few did not come back on the appointed day. need I stay? I was here the first day / you said when you were in Philadelphia that if you had any influence with Father I could come home. Please write to me very soon and tell me. The young ladies are chattering all around me so please excuse my many mistakes.

I have to write two more letters so I must stop.

> Your own loving
> Nettie.

I send you a photograph of a *dog* which is exactly like Scamp dont you think so? N.C.

Historical Society of Pennsylvania.

1. Possibly John P. Robison, whose name Father wrote as "Robinson." Robison served in the Ohio Senate from Cuyahoga County, 1862–63. Late in October 1862, Father reported to a political associate that Robison had been in Washington "some months since," professing political support for Father. *Chase Papers*, 3:311, 312.

NETTIE TO FATHER

Media June 21st.

Dear Father.

As Sister has gone West I write to you instead[1] / When will you come on? very soon I hope, I am so very anxious to see you. Eulalie Bowman cannot come home with me, I am very sorry I think you would like them.

Miss E——. is making out my report / I hope it will be what I wish. I have tried in my lessons, but I fear my many misdemeanors, will out weigh the other, in the balance.

We all are in the excitement, of a near vacation. Do you remember the feeling? In your next letter will you send me one of your carts de visites for Lalie Bowman? with your autograph. please

The Misses Cummings have just come, so I am obiged to stop. this is hardly worth reading. Wednesday I will write a longer letter

Your own
Nettie.

Historical Society of Pennsylvania.

1. Kate had left Washington on June 19 and was in Zanesville, Ohio, on the twentieth on her way to Cincinnati, where she visited her grandmother, Mary Colton Smith, and saw family friends. Father to Kate, June 24, 1862, *Chase Papers*, 3:220–22.

MARIA EASTMAN TO FATHER

Brooke hall
June 23d 1862

Mr. Chase

Dear Sir—Nettie is so anxious to reach home before the 4th. that I think it best to allow her to go, though it would be possible for her to learn something if she remained another week—She lost a great deal during the period of her absence & I have felt anxious to keep her on that account—She is gifted with a quick & comprehensive intellect, but she is deficient in mental discipline—She never likes to complete anything, but is always ready to commence anything that is new—She lacks perseverance—She has been very good & has tried to get on well in her studies & I think she has made some considerable improvement in her habits of regularity & in promptness—She is still inclined to keep confusion on the throne over her own personal effects, but I hope in a reform there after a while. I hope she will return to school in the Fall—School opens on the 2d. wednesday in Sept. which comes I think, on the 10th.—As I have to keep 2 rooms for Nettie I would like to be advised of your intentions in regard to her return as early as possible

Nettie would like to go from here on the 2d. of July & I will have her ready to leave at that time if you will attend to her escort

I shall send her Report next week

With highest respect[1]

Yours truly
M. L. Eastman

Library of Congress.

1. The filing endorsement on this letter is in the handwriting of Homer G. Plantz, a Treasury clerk who served as one of Father's secretaries and assisted him with correspondence. *Chase Papers,* 3:xxv, 197; Father to Kate, Aug. 18, 1863, in chapter 5.

NETTIE TO FATHER

Media. June 25th.

Dear Father

Your letter was received with great pleasure as they always are. The one you enclosed, was a note from Major Brown, enclosing his photograph. it was very good / poor fellow I wonder how he is, do you ever hear from the general? Why dont he *move.*[1]

Miss Eastman says I can go home Wednesday, one week from to day. I will be so happy to be home. I have finished, all that can be completed this week. You said Sister would stay some time West. when will she be home? it will seem lonely to you, I am afraid.[2]

After we finish a book, review and advance, Miss Eastman has what she calls "contests" / two nights in a week we have them, we take on an average six chapters a lesson, on the last night if we have recited the entire book, without a mistake, she gives each one of those a diploma as a certificate of the fact / I am in two "contests" one of History of England, and the other of Philosophy / I received my diploma for not failing in Philosophy, last night, and will receive that for History, to night.

We have a hospital near here, or at least will have, for the wounded soldiers, they are those who are not dangerously wounded or the convelesing. who need good food, and fresh air. The girls take a great deal of interest in it, being so near / they want to raise a sum of a hundred dollars, I beleive, among ourselves. What can I give? Miss E. is going to take me there Saturday. Poor fellows. You told me to keep an account of my expenses / I have done so, and I send you my list. I do not think I have been extravagant do you? I will write only one more letter to you, and then— I shall be with you.

Your own loving
Nettie.

Who will you send for me? do not forget next Wednesday.

N.R.C.

Hon S. P. Chase.

Historical Society of Pennsylvania.

1. Nettie probably referred to George McClellan. During April, May, and June, McClellan hesitated to attack, erroneously convinced that the Confederates greatly outnumbered his army. The day after Nettie wrote this letter, Robert E. Lee attacked McClellan's army. By July 1, more than twice as many Confederates had been killed as Union soldiers, and still McClellan retreated. McPherson, *Battle Cry of Freedom,* 425–27, 464–71; Denney, *Civil War Years,* 184–87.

2. Kate went from Cincinnati to Columbus and then on to White Sulphur Springs, Virginia (later West Virginia), in mid-July. By July 20, both Kate and Nettie were home in Washington with Father. *Chase Papers*, 3:226–27, 231.

FATHER TO KATE

Washington, June 25, 1862.[1]

My dear Katie,

I know of no better way of using up this Presidential paper than by writing to you.[2]

Day before yesterday I wrote last. In the afternoon I went with the McIlvaines to dine at Mr Seward.[3] The company was very pleasant. Mr. & Mrs Stanton, Mr. & Miss Welles, &c.[4] Only two foreigners, Mr. Stewart— who told me that Lord Lyons mentioned to him that I had called to say goodbye & was gratified by it—& Mr. Treilhard, who talks English very well and wears huge black whiskers.[5]

The McIlvaines went away the next morning, leaving a very pleasant memory of their visit. I hope you will see them.

You telegraphed Wilson about some express goods.[6] Please dont do so any more. When you want any thing done let me know it. A bag was sent you by express which came from New Orleans—a mystery to me. Some articles were sent by express from New York from Stewarts—a dress I believe.[7] And I send today also by express your veil returned cleaned from New York.

A letter also came from New York in a peculiar hand addressed to Mrs Chase. I supposed it some application for office & opened it. It was a note from a Frenchwoman, whom another Frenchwoman had advised to apply for a situation as seamstress. Madame Grafauche the recommender—cant recall the name of the applicant / If you know Madame G—— you had best write a line saying you will probably be absent during the summer & wish to make no Engagement, at any rate before fall.

It is very agreeable to me to have you fulfil so kindly and affectionately all your duties to your grandmother, & if she will accept your invitation her home here will be made as pleasant as possible.

The President astonished every body by his rapid trip to West Point & return / What he got from Gen Scott I dont know not having yet seen him.[8]

After breakfast this morning I was astonished by a visit from Gen & Mrs McDowell. The General is recovering rapidly. Mrs McD—— is as delightful as ever[9]

Miss Eastman writes that Nettie may leave on the 2d. July which will be next Wednesday. Should Congress adjourn soon I hope to bring her out. Miss E—— wants her to return & wishes an early decision on this point. What do you think

Your affectionate father

S P Chase

Historical Society of Pennsylvania.

1. Internal evidence, including the references to the dinner party at Seward's and Abraham Lincoln's movements, suggests that Father misdated this letter and actually wrote it on Thursday, June 26. According to Kate's filing note, she received the letter on the twenty-ninth.

2. He wrote this letter on presidential letterhead stationery, marking through the printed "Executive Mansion" heading.

3. Charles P. McIlvaine and his daughters, Margaret ("Nain") and Anna, stayed with Father June 23–25. A son, Joseph Heathcote McIlvaine, was already in Washington and accompanied the young ladies on a sightseeing tour during their visit. William H. Seward was secretary of state in Lincoln's cabinet. *Chase Papers*, 3:221–22; *DAB*, 12:64; *Nat. Cyc.*, 7:2.

4. Ohio native Edwin M. Stanton (b. 1814), a former U.S. attorney general from the latter part of James Buchanan's presidency, had succeeded Simon Cameron as secretary of war. Stanton and Father were old friends and had corresponded on politics and other subjects since the 1840s. In 1856, Stanton married Ellen Hutchison, daughter of a Pittsburgh merchant. They had four children together. Lincoln's secretary of the navy, Gideon Welles (b. 1802), and Pennsylvanian Mary Jane Hale married in 1835. They had nine children together, but by 1862 six of their children, including both of their daughters, had died. Father may have meant to write "Mrs." Welles, or referred to a niece, since Gideon Welles had three brothers but no sisters. *ANB*, 20:558–62; *Chase Papers*, 2:134–36, 138–40, 163–65; Richard West Jr., *Gideon Welles: Lincoln's Navy Department* (New York: Bobbs-Merrill, 1943), 55, 68–69, 192.

5. Alexander Turney Stewart, a native of Northern Ireland, was a prosperous New York merchant and noted philanthropist. During the war he supplied clothing to the U.S. military. Before Kate's marriage, Richard Bickerton Lyons, the British minister to Washington, was often spoken of as a leading contender for her hand. He never married. Viscount Jules Treilhard was secretary of the French legation in Washington and acted as chargé d'affaires whenever the ambassador was absent. *ANB*, 20:740–42; *DNB*, 12:358–59; Sokoloff, *Kate Chase*, 57; Phelps, *Kate Chase*, 113–14; Daniel B. Carroll, *Henri Mercier and the American Civil War* (Princeton, N.J.: Princeton University Press, 1971), 4, 188, 353–54; Lynn M. Case and Warren F. Spencer, *The United States and France: Civil War Diplomacy* (Philadelphia: University of Pennsylvania Press, 1970), 16.

6. Charles Wilson was employed as a servant in the Chase household from 1861 to 1863, when he was dismissed for episodes of drunkenness. *Chase Papers*, 3:126.

7. In 1846, Alexander T. Stewart had opened a large store on Broadway that was the innovative model for the large American department store. That Italianate edifice came to be known as the "Marble Palace." In November 1862, Stewart opened his "New Store" farther up Broadway at Astor Place. When it opened, the new emporium was the largest retail store in the world. Stewart's store included its own highly regarded dressmaking department. Burrows and Wallace, *Gotham*, 639, 666–68, 716, 878–79, 945, 990.

8. On June 25, while the Army of the Potomac fought off Lee's forces, Lincoln went to West Point to consult with retired general Winfield Scott. The president wanted Scott's opinion as to whether he should reinforce McClellan's army with troops under McDowell's command. Scott later sent Lincoln a telegram urging McClellan's reinforcement. Donald, *Lincoln*, 357.

9. In 1849, Helen Burden married Irvin McDowell, with whom she had four children. Father was surprised to see Irvin McDowell in Washington because the general had been injured in Virginia only the week before, when his horse, named Ohio, reared and fell backward on top of him. Stanton and Lincoln had made a hurried visit to Manassas, Va., to check on the injured officer before Father heard of the accident on Friday, June 20, and the next day Father went to McDowell's headquarters himself, taking A. T. Stewart and a few

others with him in a single-car train. McDowell was up and around by then but suffered from "dreadful contusions." He had been knocked unconscious by the accident and had no memory of the day on which it occurred. *Chase Papers*, 3:220–21; *DAB*, 12:30; *Nat. Cyc.*, 4:50.

FATHER TO KATE

Washn. June 30, 1862

My dear Katie,

Your two letters, one a real nice letter & the other covering one from Dr. Stone[1] have just reached me in time to change the direction of the long one which you will find enclosed with this—which had been already sealed & directed to Cincinnati & handed to Clark for the Post.[2]

Your explanations about the diamonds relieved me much. I will pay your proportion myself and send the bill with your explanation extracted from your letter to Miss Stanley. I hope not always to be obliged to restrict myself in regard to you in the matter of diamonds though in truth I attach no great value to their possession.

I enclose the note to your grandmother which you suggested: and shall be glad to join you in making her as contented here, if she comes as possible

One of the things in you which I love best is your thoughtfulness of her.

May God bless and keep you my dear child.

Affy
S P Chase

Historical Society of Pennsylvania.

1. In 1862, Father nominated James W. Stone, a friend from Massachusetts, to an internal revenue collectorship. *Chase Papers*, 4:113.

2. Henry Clarke was the Treasury Department messenger. In 1871, he got a similar position with the Supreme Court, functioning as Father's personal attendant as well as his messenger. John Disturnell, comp., *Blue Book; or, Register of Officers and Agents, Civil, Military and Naval, in the Service of the United States; Corrected to November, 1862* (New York: J. H. Colton, 1863), 32; *Chase Papers*, 1:665; 5:342–43.

FATHER TO KATE

Washington July 2, 1862

Your letter from Loveland has just reached me, my dear child, and was much welcome.[1] How little you thought when writing it of the terrible anxiety we were enduring here! I fear from what you say that you have not received your summer clothes. Three packages have been sent—the bag—which contained the secession flag—; the box,—containing your lace veil—& the dress which went direct from New York—

"Wilson"! enter Wilson—"Has any thing gone for Miss Katie besides the little bag & the box"? "Yes, Sir a trunk" "Did it come from New York" "Yes, Sir; I thought it contained the curtains but found it did not & sent it right on." Did you open it? "Yes, Sir; it was only strapped and I thought it contained the curtains: but it did not & I nailed it right down & sent it on." "When?" "Last Thursday." Exit Wilson noise of forks, knives & plates in the pantry.[2]

Now is not that dramatic? At any rate it relieves my apprehensions for you, and makes me hope that if the trunk dont reach you today you will get it very soon.

I wish I *could* tell you when I shall come on: Congress will probably adjourn in three weeks—perhaps sooner. I mean to come within the first eight days after. If I cannot accomplish this I cannot expect to come at all.

I think very well of your French woman plan; but wish you had put its execution off till reestablished here in the fall. The poor woman, getting no answer has been disappointed I fear. I could not make out her name: and don't know the address of Madame Graf &c / Would it not be well for you to write her.[3]

I have not visited the War Dept today and have not heard a word of military news. Every body is full of speculation concerning the Causes of our late disasters. *I know them*[4]

Mr. Washburne, of Illinois, was here a few moments ago. He tells me Hunters answer to Mr. Stanton's letter enclosing the House resolution of Enquiry about arming the contrabands &c was read in the House today & that it was admirable. A gleam of light![5]

Yours affy
S P Chase

Best regards to Mr. and Mrs. P—— & Lizzie[6]

Historical Society of Pennsylvania.

1. Father owned property in Loveland, Ohio, northeast of Cincinnati. *Chase Papers*, 5:333.
2. He added this sentence as an insertion.
3. It seems likely that Kate planned on hiring a French seamstress. Father to Kate, June 25, 1862, above.
4. McClellen's Peninsula campaign, culminating in the Seven Days battles of June 25–July 1, was a military and strategic failure. Also, in May and June, Stonewall Jackson defeated the Federal army in five successful battles in his Shenandoah Valley campaign. McPherson, *Battle Cry of Freedom*, 454–71.
5. In the House of Representatives on July 2, a letter was read from Gen. David Hunter, the commander of the Department of the South based at Port Royal, S.C. Addressing Edwin Stanton in the letter of June 23, Hunter responded to a House resolution of June 9 that asked for information about a reported "regiment of volunteers composed of black men, fugitive slaves," in Hunter's department. Hunter claimed to be ignorant of any "regiment of 'fugitive slaves'" but said there was a good regiment composed of "persons whose late masters are 'fugitive rebels.'" Noting that his orders authorized him to employ "all loyal persons," the general wrote: "The experiment of arming the blacks, so far as I have made it, has been a complete and even marvelous success." On May 9, Hunter had issued

a declaration abolishing slavery in South Carolina, Georgia, and Florida by martial law. He did so without consulting Lincoln. Father advised the president to support the general, but Lincoln revoked Hunter's May order on the grounds that policy on abolition and emancipation must come from the administration, not commanders in the field. Father did not conceal his disappointment—"I do not believe in fighting rebellion & upholding its main cause, prop & element"—but thought the president might take some action on emancipation if the right circumstances should develop. *Congressional Globe,* 37th Cong., 2d sess., 1862, 3087; *Chase Papers,* 3:202–3, 205, 219; McPherson, *Battle Cry of Freedom,* 499, 503.

6. Father squeezed this sentence in at the foot of the page after signing the letter. From their time in Columbus, the Chases were good friends with George M. Parsons and Jane Swan Parsons. Mrs. Parsons was the daughter of Judge Gustavus Swan, an Ohio jurist. Her husband, a prominent Columbus lawyer, had been a member of the state legislature when Father was governor. *History of Franklin and Pickaway Counties, Ohio* (Cleveland, Ohio: Williams Bros., 1880), 44, 65, 528; *Chase Papers,* 1:73, 247, 281, 290, 582–85.

FATHER TO KATE

Washington July 4, 1862

My dearest child,

You have done admirably. All your letters have come and all have been good—some very good.

I was half amused—though very sad—sadder than on the day of Bull-run[1]—by your want of news thinking, how soon your wishes would be gratified, though the news would be none of the best.

Nettie has not yet returned. Hoping to be able to go for her, I requested Mr. Jay Cooke to take charge of her till I should come, which he has most kindly done. Now I have made up my mind not to go; but Nettie will return Monday with Mr. Henry D Cooke & his family.[2] I urge them all to take up their residence with me till their house in Georgetown is quite ready. I enclose your letter to Nettie to her today

The news from McClellan's Army seems to be little better; though as I have had neither time nor Opportunity to analyze the despatches & other intelligence of the last few days I can say nothing certainly.[3]

McClellan's army—or rather what is left after the heavy losses of the last eight days estimated at not less than 25.000 men,[4]—was when I last heard from them at Harrison's bar, hoping some respite.

I must close—being called away.

Your aff. father
S P Chase

Historical Society of Pennsylvania.

1. The first Battle of Bull Run, or Manassas, took place a morning's carriage ride away from Washington, July 21, 1861. The Confederate Army routed Union troops, filling the capital with wounded and disconsolate soldiers. Denney, *Civil War Years,* 59–60; McPherson, *Battle Cry of Freedom,* 339–45.

2. Journalist and banker Henry David Cooke, originally of Ohio and the brother of Jay Cooke, was married to Laura ("Lollie") Humphreys Cooke, who was originally of Utica, N.Y. *DAB,* 4:382–83; Oberholtzer, *Cooke,* 1:93.

3. On July 2, 1862, McClellan's army retreated from Malvern Hill, at the end of the Seven Days battles, to Harrison's Landing on the James River outside Richmond, the Confederate capital. Denney, *Civil War Years*, 189–90; McPherson, *Battle Cry of Freedom*, 465.

4. Confederate casualties for the Seven Days battles numbered around 20,000, while the Union suffered about 16,000. Denney, *Civil War Years*, 186–88.

FATHER TO KATE

Washington, July 6. 1862.

My dear Katie

Your last letter, received last evening, bears date 2d July—last Tuesday—and in it you acknowledge the receipt of mine of 28th, 29th & 30th, the last of which only it appears went direct to Columbus.[1] It seems that it takes three days for letters to go either way—a little too slow.

Your appreciation of my long letter as a mark of love and confidence and the gratification it gave you are more than ample reward for the time & trouble of writing it. It is quite as agreeable to bestow love and confidence as it can be to receive it. You have my love always and I confide greatly in you on many points. My confidence will be entire when you entirely give me yours and when I feel—that is am made by your acts & words to feel that nothing is held back from me which a father should know of the thoughts, sentiments & acts of a daughter. Cannot this entire confidence be given me? You will, I am sure be happier and so shall I. One other thing now that I am upon this subject. A daughter ought in all things to respect a father's feelings and if wishes conflict and no moral principle is compromised by yielding she ought to yield gracefully, kindly, cordially. You will easily remember instances in which you have tried me pretty severely by not doing so.

But enough of this. I will trust your good sense and what I believe is your real affection for me to correct what your own conscience & judgment tell you ought to be corrected.

Nettie has not yet returned. I expect her tomorrow evening with the Cookes, as I told you, I believe, in my letter of yesterday. I am glad to have an opportunity of returning a little of the kindness of that charming connexion. I know no family which includes more worth & more mutual affection. The more of such Cookes there are the better the broth.

I am sorry that I must tell you some bad things of John Austen.[2] You know I thought him remarkably frank and honest: and you may judge then that I was not less surprised than grieved to find him deliberately attempting to deceive me, and also guilty of acts which he would not do before either of us & which he knew neither his father nor I could approve.

Last Sunday morning a little after nine say half past he asked me if I had any objections to his going to the Capitol to hear Mr. Channing; to which I answered no.[3] "Then" said he "I will go early because I want to get young Johnston." He went & I thought no more of it. In the afternoon I asked him something about the attendance or the sermon. He then told me that he did not go to Church; but met a boy who wanted to go to ride with him & he went. "Was the boy, Johnston?" "No, another boy,—the boy I told you I did not like much." The next morning he told me more. He did not go home with his father on Friday for what reason told his father I do not know. He told me it was because he was waiting for money from Mr. Garniss. On Monday morning I was speaking to him about going home, and he then told me he had spent a couple of dollars of the money he had of that I handed him on account of a payment made by his father for you in New York, and had been waiting till Mr. Garniss shd send him some, as he had not enough to pay his expences otherwise. That now however his father had given him some money & he could go. I asked him whether the two dollars had been paid for the horse the day before; to which he replied "no—that was paid by himself & the other boy, divided between them.[4]

I then told him that as he had money enough he had best go home & that I would send him Mr. Garniss letter if it came. He proposed to go the next day (Tuesday) but I told him I thought it useless to delay & that he might as well go by the eleven AM. train.

I then left him to go to the Dept, & the horse happening to move off rather briskly I remarked to Clark that he seemed to have benefitted by the rest of yesterday. As Clark said nothing, I enquired if the horse did not rest yesterday? Clark answered "Yes, except while Mr. Austen had him." This surprised me very much. "Mr. Austen had him! What do you mean." "Mr Austen, came to me & said he wanted the horse & carriage to take a ride & as he lived with you I supposed it all right & went with him to the Stable & let him have them."

When I reached the Dept I wrote a note to John telling him what I had heard & saying that he had any explanation to make he might stay & make it. He sent me a note in answer saying he wd. write from Phila. And he did so but his letter only showed that he had done all I heard he had, and that he had no proper sense of the wrong of the deception he had practiced.

A day or two afterwards on enquiry of Wilson about the wine I learned that it was Johns practice to make himself a sherry cobbler every day at his lunch, which he took regularly; that he also was in the habit of taking the key to the sideboard & helping himself to wine there; that he drank nearly two bottles of that best Catawba (Grape Juice) from Yeatman;[5] and that he told the servants—Wilson especially when he asked if this was right—that you told him he could take any thing he wanted. One day he took two bottles with some wine in each and a Champagne glass and went up into the hall near your room where Cassy was cleaning it out. Cassy mentioned this to Richd. I think & he told me.[6] Cassy confirmed. Where he was going to take these bottles I dont know.

These things are discouraging. What to do I don't know. I don't want to have him come back and I don't like to let him go altogether. I cannot think that a boy who seems so frank and ingenuous and to desire improvement in all ways can be really very bad. What do you think.

I had one letter from Hunt after you saw him & have written to him. After his three months are out I want him to come & stay with us a few months at least.[7]

Our war news is not important today so far as events go. Gov Seward has returned from his visit to the Governors / I have not seen him, but do not hear that he has accomplished a great deal. Gen. Mitchell came today. He impresses me more favorably than any man I have seen. I do hope he will be *allowed* to be of some use. Unfortunately the do somethings are generally neutralized by being put under do nothings.[8]

It is not settled what will become of McClellan's army. In my judgment it ought to have been already embarked and on its way here or somebody should have been put in command who has resources & energy to retrieve its disasters.[9]

Goodbye, for the present darling and may God in his mercy keep you from all harm.

> Your own father
> S P Chase

Dont forget always to remember me most cordially to Mr & Mrs Parsons Lizzie & the children who I suppose have all forgotten me.

Tell me if you have been in our old house? I got Mr. Aston to send me [6][10] sets of the views. Tell me of all the people you see.

Historical Society of Pennsylvania.

1. See above for his letter of June 30. That of the twenty-eighth discussed news of friends and gave advice to Kate regarding her grandmother, Mary Colton Smith. The next day he wrote of war news, specifically criticizing McClellan and Lincoln for their prosecution of the war (both in Chase Papers, HSP).

2. The son of Cordelia Picket Austen, who was the adopted daughter of John and Amelia Garniss.

3. When the Civil War began, Unitarian minister William Henry Channing left his position with a church in Liverpool, England, to return to the United States, where he became the chaplain of the U.S. House of Representatives. Channing, who was a native of Boston and a nephew of William Ellery Channing, was very interested in intellectual, spiritual, and social reform movements, including Transcendentalism and Fourierism. He had been a minister in Cincinnati from 1838 to 1841. *ANB*, 4:683–85.

4. Initially Father began a new paragraph with this sentence, which he subsequently struck through: "This conversation may have been & probably was on Sunday Evening instead of Monday Morning." Before canceling the sentence he struck out "probably" and substituted "possibly."

5. Promoted by Nicholas Longworth beginning in the late 1820s, the Catawba grape, a variety native to America, played an important role in the production of wine in the Cincinnati region. At the great Crystal Palace exposition in London in 1851, Thomas H. Yeatman's Catawba wine won a gold medal, but the Catawba vineyards of the Ohio Valley were

devastated by rot and mildew beginning at the end of that decade. Father was long ac-quainted with Yeatman, a Cincinnati banker and industrialist, and his wife, Elizabeth Hart-zell Yeatman. During the Civil War, Thomas Yeatman received appointments to U.S. govern-ment positions in Memphis and Vicksburg. Linda Walker Stevens, "Old Nick: Cincinnati Winemaker," *Timeline* 13 (April 1996), 24–35; *Chase Papers*, 1:190–91.

 6. Catherine ("Cassy") Vaudry, a former slave, was Father's Washington housekeeper. In July 1862 he also characterized her as Kate's "chambermaid." Cassy Vaudry worked for Father until his death, nursing him through illnesses and attending family prayers. Richard was also a member of the household. Father once described him as "a colored American Citizen." *Chase Papers*, 1:503, 520, 667; 3:237; 4:193.

 7. See the appendix for the sad military history of Kate's and Nettie's cousin W. Hunt Walbridge.

 8. Ormsby MacKnight Mitchel had been a professor of mathematics at Cincinnati College and, during the war, brigadier and major general of volunteers. In July 1862, Father urged Stanton and Gen. Henry W. Halleck to send Mitchel to help secure the Mis-sissippi River. Soon after, Mitchel was placed in command of the Department of the South at Hilton Head, S.C., where he was fatally stricken with yellow fever and died on October 30. *Nat. Cyc.*, 3:440; Long, *Civil War Day by Day*, 282; *Chase Papers*, 1:352–54, 358, 404.

 9. Many of the soldiers were wounded or sick, and the administration decided to with-draw the Army of the Potomac from the Peninsula. Brooks D. Simpson, *America's Civil War* (Wheeling, Ill.: Harlan Davidson Inc., 1996), 62–65; McPherson, *Battle Cry of Freedom*, 488.

 10. Father evidently wrote "5" and altered it to "6," or possibly vice versa. Mr. Aston may have been Isaac C. Aston of Randall & Aston, a Columbus firm that sold "Books, Sta-tionery, Paper Hangings, etc." *Williams' Columbus Directory . . . 1858–'59*, 41, 169.

FATHER TO KATE

             July 7, 1862

My darling Katie,

 I believe I did send you the letter to your grandmother a day or two ago? did I not.

 I hope she will go and stay with Jane.[1] What she could easily allow for board for herself and servant would help Jane a good deal, & it would I hope be pleasant to both of them.

 The President has gone down to Fortress Monroe. I hope he will ac-complish as much as when Stanton & I went with him.[2]

 Dont think of coming back to Washington. It is hot, hotter, hot-test. Get to Lockport & I will try & join you there, if I find I cannot go to Ohio.

           In haste yours affy
           S P Chase

I expect Nettie this afternoon

Historical Society of Pennsylvania.

 1. Apparently Jane Auld.

 2. On the day of this letter Lincoln boarded the USS *Ariel* to travel down Chesapeake Bay to Fortress Monroe. Up the James River at Harrison's Landing, he visited the Army of the Potomac and met with McClellan. He returned to Washington on July 10. In May, Father, Lincoln, and Secretary of War Stanton had taken a revenue steamer to the Hamp-ton Roads area, where they watched the navy block off the *Merrimack*. Lincoln, Stanton, and

Father also involved themselves in preparations for an attempt to capture Norfolk. The campaign was successful, and when the officials left to return to Washington, Norfolk was in Federal control and the Confederates had scuttled the *Merrimack.* Father described the momentous events in three detailed letters addressed to Nettie and meant for Kate also. *Chase Papers,* 1:336–45; 3:185–88, 189–91, 193–98; Miers, *Lincoln Day by Day,* 3:126–27.

FATHER TO KATE

July 11, 1862

My darling Katie,

No news—at least no good news. Mr. Stanton's little child which has suffered so much and so long is released at last—The poor mother grieves, but the little one doubtless rejoices.[1]

I am anxious to know your programme. It is more & more doubtful whether I can remain here. The war is at a stand still. Halleck is, I am told, invited here. I *fear* we are to have a repetition of McClellanism in him.[2] I *hope* better.[3] Heaven save our poor country!

Your affectionate father
S P Chase

Miss Kate Chase

Historical Society of Pennsylvania.

1. Edwin M. Stanton had two children with his first wife, Mary A. Lamson Stanton: Lucy Lamson Stanton (1840–41) and Edwin Lamson Stanton (1842–77). After Mary Stanton's death, her husband married Ellen Hutchison, with whom he had Eleanor Adams Stanton (b. 1857), Lewis Hutchison Stanton (b. ca. 1860), and the baby mentioned here, James Hutchison Stanton (b. 1861). James was a healthy baby until vaccinated, after which he became sick and died at nine months old. Lincoln and most of the cabinet attended his funeral. In 1863, Edwin and Ellen Stanton had another child, Bessie, for whom Father acted as godfather. Benjamin Platt Thomas, *Stanton: The Life and Times of Lincoln's Secretary of War* (New York: Knopf, 1962), 21, 37, 29, 75, 175, 211, 368.
2. Maj. Gen. Henry W. Halleck officially replaced George McClellan as general in chief of the army in July 1862, in part because McClellan was not forceful enough in his engagement of the enemy. Encouraged by Halleck's successes in the Department of the Missouri and in Tennessee, Abraham Lincoln hoped he would redress the problems of "McClellanism." Unfortunately Halleck also proved less than aggressive in field campaigns, tended to blame others for his failures, and had a poor reputation by the time U. S. Grant replaced him as general in chief early in 1864. At that time Halleck assumed the role of chief of staff. *ANB,* 9:875–77.
3. Father originally ended the paragraph with "in him" and began a new paragraph with "Heaven save." He subsequently inserted the sentence "I *hope* better" in the space at the end of the line after "him" and in the indentation before "Heaven."

CHRONOLOGY

December 1862	Nettie at Mary Macaulay's boarding school in New York City, where Kate surprises her with a visit; Father in Washington, D.C.
January 1863	Emancipation Proclamation takes effect
March 1863	Special session of the U.S. Senate; William Sprague takes his seat as a senator from Rhode Island
May–June 1863	Kate accepts William's proposal of marriage
July 1863	Union victories at Gettysburg and Vicksburg; Father takes Kate and Nettie to Rhode Island to see William's family; Father returns to Washington
August–September 1863	Kate turns twenty-three (August 13); Kate, Nettie, and Cousin Eliza Whipple travel in New England; Aunt Charlotte Jones visits Washington, where renovations are under way at the family's residence
September 1863	Term begins at Mrs. Macaulay's school; Nettie turns sixteen (September 19); Battle of Chickamauga
September–October 1863	Kate shops for trousseau in New York, staying with Helen McDowell
October 1863	Father makes speaking trip to Ohio and Indiana; Cousin Alice Skinner comes to Washington in anticipation of Kate's wedding
November 4–5, 1863	William writes to his future father-in-law; Nettie prepares to leave school for the wedding

CHAPTER 5

"I Heartily Wish I Was Home"

DECEMBER 1862 – NOVEMBER 1863

T HE CHASES could hardly count their family as representative of
the new companionate model of the nineteenth century, in which
familial happiness focused on a mother-centered household. By midcentury, middle-class wives dominated child rearing, while their husbands'
main job was to make money. That transformation of fatherhood from
patriarch to breadwinner provided Father no paradigm for raising his
motherless children. This problem was exacerbated by the fact that his
children were daughters, in a time when society particularly valorized the
mother–daughter bond.[1]

By 1862, moreover, Kate was an adult who made trips away from Washington, D.C., without him. Nettie was old enough to go with her sister
on some of those travels. During school terms from September 1862 to
the spring of 1864, Nettie was at the Madison Avenue boarding school
of Mary Macaulay, under a firm headmistress's authority in the familiar
pattern that Father found comfortable. New York City was an appealing
destination for Kate, though, and her visits reduced Nettie's cloistered
isolation at school, as shown by the tandem letter written by the two
of them that opens this chapter. Father's letters to Kate exhibit his anxiety and frustration when she rambled beyond his ability to control what
were, to him, important details. Away from Washington, she could take
power over her movements, and she did not always give her father prior
notice of changes in her itinerary. He was anxious, too, about her spending, cautioning her in letter after letter that their expenses seemed likely
to exceed his income.

Some expenditure was necessary, however. In late May or early June
1863, Kate and William Sprague became engaged. Father traveled to
Providence to meet William's mother, and in August Kate and Nettie
had a long stay with the Sprague family in Rhode Island. In Providence
and at the family "cottage" at Narragansett Pier, the sisters enjoyed William's hospitality and the cool ocean air. The sisters then traveled to New
Hampshire and the White Mountains. Returning with their cousin Eliza
Whipple, they stayed with the Spragues again in September. The visits to

Rhode Island effectively announced the couple's intention to marry: Americans in the nineteenth century did not generally make public announcements of engagements. Engaged couples regarded the event as intensely private and generally spread the word of upcoming nuptials in person or by letter.[2] As the November wedding date approached, Kate began to assemble a trousseau, and her Father—the secretary of the Treasury—confessed, "I know nothing of such matters, so far as ladies expences go."[3]

Money and the prospective marriage were closely related topics. The Civil War created cotton shortages for the Sprague mills, and Father had the authority to issue cotton permits so that manufacturers could purchase cotton from Southern areas that came under Federal control, including the Sea Islands, parts of Louisiana, and in the Mississippi Valley. One of the richest men in the country, William Sprague had parlayed his family's cotton milling business into a multimillion dollar conglomerate of lumber, iron, cotton, and other businesses. When Rhode Island elected him, at the age of thirty, the country's youngest governor, many said that the wealthy "boy governor" had bought the election for $50 per vote.[4] Some thought that the young magnate's wealth was meant to fund the presidential aspirations of his future father-in-law. Of more immediate practical importance, William renovated and purchased the mansion the Chases occupied at 6th and E streets, N.W., in Washington, so that he and Kate, after their marriage, could occupy the house along with Father and Nettie. Although Father conceded that Kate must have dresses that were "*just* right," he knew that he, and Kate, before her marriage, must not appear to be too beholden to William. "You were quite right in not allowing the Gov. to pay your bills," he wrote to Kate after chastising her for borrowing spending money from a relative.[5]

For all the monetary aspects of the betrothal, William and Kate's courtship letters strongly suggest that the two fell in love. Indeed, the ethos of romantic love played a central part in their courtship. By midcentury, romance, a sentiment Americans of the previous century had considered of dubious value, became the primary emotion on which women and men could base a lifelong commitment. In effect, William and Kate had to fall in love to marry. "True love" became a normative cultural value, one so strongly held that it became compulsory rather than merely desirable. Karen Lystra, in her study of Victorian courtship, suggests that Americans of the Civil War era created a "new theology of love," a religion in which one's lover replaced God as the central figure in the individual's life.[6] Kate exemplifies the generational nature of the new theology, for her father found his primary personal identification with a stern God, while Kate, and later Nettie, saved their emotional energy for their husband and children, leaving God at the periphery of their lives. Kate's and Nettie's notions of duty lay rooted in a more personal, less religious ideology than their father's.

As his elder daughter's independence grew, Father's attention was heavily absorbed in public affairs. His involvement in politics and in public office had always taken time and attention that he could have given to his family. The demands on him as secretary of the Treasury overmatched anything he had encountered before. In January, March, April, and August 1863, he traveled to New York to talk to bankers and solicit loan subscriptions, and in the spring he went to Philadelphia and Boston on similar errands.[7] Financing the enormous expenses of the war was difficult, even with a cooperative Congress, which authorized paper greenback currency, a national banking system to help manage the currency supply, bond issues, and other measures. Despite victories at Gettysburg and Vicksburg in July 1863, the Lincoln administration had not found the formula to overall success in the war. The establishment of a military draft sparked rioting in New York City in July that left more than a hundred people dead.[8] If McClellan's lack of progress in Virginia was the theme in 1862, Gen. William S. Rosecrans's inability to break through in Tennessee was the focus of the cabinet's worried attention for much of 1863. Lincoln's Emancipation Proclamation took effect on January 1, but the limitations on its scope frustrated Father and others who thought that it was past time for a more aggressive policy to eliminate slavery. Some of those progressives, including Horace Greeley of the *New York Tribune*, believed that Father might be the candidate who could win the presidency in 1864 and bring a new focus to Federal policy. Father was, Greeley had assured him earlier, the "only man who could successfully prosecute the war and free the slaves." Although that movement to dump Lincoln and elect Father president collapsed early in 1864, during 1863 it seemed to have momentum.[9]

When Kate made her surprise visit to New York to see Nettie in December 1862, and Father stayed in Washington, Nettie wrote him: "I think a little relaxation would have done you so much good."[10] Nettie, who turned sixteen in September 1863, continued to have a more ebullient letter-writing style than her sister. Her father's letters to her continued to emphasize his desire that she write elegant and intelligent letters. Time and again he urged her to pay more attention to her efforts, use a better pen, and write more often. He emphasized the seriousness of these requests when he wrote her, "Count nothing trifling which involves the idea of duty."[11] We have only the one letter from Nettie to him in the period of this chapter, the one written with Kate, but the sheer repetition of his admonitions suggests that Nettie's nature made it hard for her to please him in these matters. Though he urged the same standards on both his daughters, Kate's letters demonstrated more discipline and less humor than her sister's. Nettie sometimes fell short of the family's standards of spelling and punctuation, although her sense of fun and her ability to delight her father in spite of her epistolary failings is clear in his letters to her. Mary Macaulay's letters further elucidate Nettie's personality, for the teacher found the girl to be "of strong nature," yet with great academic potential.

Kate, for all her growing independence, still cherished home life. "I heartily wish I was home," she wrote her father after she came down with a bad cold during her unannounced visit to Nettie in New York late in 1862.[12] In Washington, Kate had more than familiar surroundings and the comforts of home. Her father's intense involvement in public affairs, while it competed with the intimate domestic circle for his attention, gave his older daughter an identity as his hostess and as a perceptive individual near the core of decision making about policy and politics. She had a certain independence when traveling and making many of her own choices, but at 6th and E she was near the fonts of power. She was yet to sort out how her roles in the family and in the larger social and political world would change upon her marriage.

1. Robert Griswold, *Fatherhood in America: A History* (New York: BasicBooks, 1993), 13–17. See also Steven Mintz, *A Prison of Expectations: The Family in Victorian Culture* (New York: New York University Press, 1983), chap. 5; Nancy M. Theriot, *The Biosocial Construction of Femininity: Mothers and Daughters in Nineteenth-Century America* (New York: Greenwood Press, 1988), chap. 2; Linda W. Rosenzweig, *The Anchor of My Life: Middle-Class American Mothers and Daughters, 1880–1920* (New York: New York University Press, 1993), 23–25.

2. William's letters to Kate suggest that he took both approaches, though he followed up letters to some family friends with a visit. The actual moment of Kate's and William's engagement is difficult to determine for a number of reasons. There was, of course, no newspaper announcement of the event, and letters can only suggest a window of opportunity. In a letter of May 1, William suggested that Kate might someday marry a politician, apparently without assuming that it would be him. His June letters took on a new tone of intimacy. He began to sign letters "your own Wm.," and a June 3 letter to Kate suggests he was spreading the news to family friends. William to Kate, May 1, June 1, 3, 1863 (Brown University Library); Rothman, *Hands and Hearts*, 161–62; Lamphier, *Kate Chase and William Sprague*, 52.

3. Sept. 17, 1863, in this chapter.

4. A Providence paper claimed that the Democrats, whom William Sprague represented, led voters to the polls and paid them after they cast their ballots. William admitted that he spent more than $100,000 on the election. See *Providence Daily Post*, Apr. 2, 4, 1860; John J. Turner, "The Rhode Island State and National Elections of 1860" (M.A. thesis, University of Rhode Island, 1955), 55.

5. See Aug. 19 and Sept. 30, 1863, below.

6. Lystra, *Searching the Heart*, 8–13; Lamphier, *Kate Chase and William Sprague*, 50–52. See also Rothman, *Hands and Hearts;* Ellen Plante, *Women at Home in Victorian America: A Social History* (New York: Facts on File, 1997); Ward, *Courtship, Love, and Marriage*.

7. *Chase Papers*, 3:xiii; 4:xi, 15.

8. McPherson, *Battle Cry of Freedom*, 600–601, 609–10.

9. Greeley to Father, Nov. 3, 1862 (Chase Papers, LC); Niven, *Chase*, 343–45, 360–62.

10. Dec. 10, 1862, below, the only letter from Nettie to her father in this chapter.

11. Aug. 19, 1863, below.

12. Dec. 10, 1862, below.

KATE AND NETTIE TO FATHER

Fifth Avenue Hotel[1]
Dec. 10th. 1862.

My dear Father,

I have just received your short note, & have wondered why you did not say more. I did not know that Aunt Helen was here, but will try & see her the first thing in the morning. I have been quite sick ever since I arrived here & most of the time have been forced to lie in bed / To-day Dr. Macay came to see me, & gave me some medicine[2] / It is a severe cold I have taken arising from the change of weather & climate, & not being sufficiently warmly dressed / To-day I am more free from the pain in my chest, & the annoying swelling in my face has gone down, but I heartily wish I was home. Nettie dear child is looking very well, & is anticipating the Christmas Holidays with much pleasure. She however will speak for herself.

Very affectionately your daughter
Kate Chase

Dearest Father.

I was so much surprised to see Sister, I had not an idea she thought of coming to New York. I was so delighted. I am so sorry you can not come on also. I think a little relaxation would have done you so much good. But I will see you one week from next [Tues]day. I shall be at home for two weeks. Minnie Vail, and Lizzie Parsons, are coming with me.[3] we will have quite a house full.

We saw Mr Russel in the hall a few minutes ago. it looked quite like Columbus.[4] I am limited to this page so I must say good night your own
Nettie

Library of Congress.

1. Father and Kate sometimes stayed at the Fifth Avenue Hotel when they visited New York in the 1860s. When it opened at 190 Fifth Avenue in 1859, the immense hotel was the city's grandest, boasting private bathrooms, an elevator, and a staff of four hundred servants. It was an important social and political center for decades. It stood at the intersection of Broadway, Fifth Avenue, and 23d Street, a few blocks from where Kate had attended school a decade earlier at Miss Haines's on Gramercy Park. For several years Mary Macaulay's school had been nearby, on 21st Street, a little east of Broadway, but by the time Nettie entered Macaulay's school in September 1862, it had moved several blocks to the north as fashionable society moved uptown. *Chase Papers*, 1:594–95, 612, 630; 4:67; Burrows and Wallace, *Gotham*, 672, 902, 903, 958, 1021, 1103, 1154; Mary Macaulay to Father, Sept. 9, 1863, below.

2. Perhaps Dr. James G. McKee, who resided at 319 Broadway. Hiram Barney saw Kate and Nettie on December 9, "looking very well—except Miss Kate had a cold." Wilson, *Trow's New York City Directory, For . . . 1862*, 546; *Chase Papers*, 3:330.

3. Minnie Vail was the daughter of Henry F. Vail, a New York banker who was one of Father's acquaintances. See Nettie to Father, Feb. 20, 1864, in the next chapter.

4. Nettie and Kate probably ran into Addison Peale Russell, a former Republican newspaper editor who had been a member of the Ohio legislature, 1855–57, and the state's secretary of state, 1847–61. From 1862 until 1868, Russell was Ohio's financial agent in New York City. He then retired to his home town of Wilmington, Ohio, where he wrote several

books that earned him comparisons to Emerson and Washington Irving. Coyle, *Ohio Authors*, 544–45.

FATHER TO KATE

Washington, Aug. 12, 1863.

My dear Katie,

Enclosed I forward a letter for you.

Two letters have come from Nettie—none from you. I hope your not writing is not occasioned by indisposition. You must not expose yourself at all but take the best possible care of your health. I sent from New York two waterproof cloaks, one for you & one for Nettie which looked to me like very comfortable garments. Take care of changes in the weather[1]

Please let me know, exactly, or as exactly as possible what bills you are making that I may provide for them. Expence now largely overruns salary and my resources are not great enough to admit of carelessness.

Best love to dear Nettie & to the Governor.[2] Be careful to do nothing which will in the slightest degree diminish his respect for you; for love cannot be perfect where respect is impaired. Make him read Betrothal, Espousals & Faithful Forever, & have them by heart yourself.[3]

Your affe. father

S P Chase

It is still very warm here—Ever since I came home it has been excessively hot: but last night it rained & was somewhat less oppressive and I think the weather will change soon.

Letterpress copy. Historical Society of Pennsylvania.

1. As amplified by the letters that follow, Kate and Nettie were in New England visiting, in particular, William Sprague's family in Rhode Island.

2. Like Father (see Nov. 4, 1863, in this chapter), William Sprague could claim the courtesy title "Governor" for the rest of his life. The Rhode Island legislature had elected William a U.S. senator beginning with the 38th Congress. During that Congress, the Senate first met in a special session in March 1863. The first regular session of the Congress convened in December of that year. *Bio. Dir. U.S. Cong.*, 1856.

3. English writer Coventry Kersey Dighton Patmore wrote a connected series of poems, *The Espousals* (1854), *The Betrothal* (1856), and *Faithful for Ever* (1860). With a fourth poem, *The Victories of Love* (1862–63), they were known by the collective title *The Angel in the House*. The verses were an exposition of traditional values of married love that later came under attack from Virginia Woolf and feminists for the constrained role Patmore's poems gave the married woman. On a snowy Sunday in Columbus in January 1857, Father read *The Espousals* through and noted in his journal: "calm gentle pure." *Chase Papers*, 1:252; *ODNB*, 43:40–44.

FATHER TO NETTIE

Aug 17,   3[1]

My darling Nettie

I had a pleasant little note from you yesterday; not very well written nor with very good ink; and of course not very easily read. You may say that my letters are not very easily read either: And I am willing to confess it. But please remember that my time is a little more important than yours.

I am glad that Katie did not undertake to ride that pony. She must run no risks.

Last night Mr. Stanton called for me in his carriage, and we took a long starlighted ride, out round Soldiers Home, through its grounds not stopping however to call on the President (who probably was abed and asleep)[2] & back by 14th Street; around the circle, and so back to our House where he stopped and we took tea together.[3] Of course we talked of many things—armies—generals—negro soldiers—reconstructions &c &c &c. I wish you could have heard his account of some of the transactions towards the close of the Buchanan Administration.[4] But I have no time for details.

Charlotte is still on the mend.[5] All the rest (including Nellie who called on me dogfashion this morning) quite well. Wilson seems straight.[6]

Your Affe. father

S P Chase

Your letter was dated on the 8th and mailed on the 13th—a mistake somewhere or too great negligence.

I enclose a letter for Sister.

How is the weather "at Tucker's"[7]

Letterpress copy. Historical Society of Pennsylvania.

1. Father no doubt wrote the original of this letter on Treasury Department stationery that included, in the printed letterhead, the "18" of the year. The letterpress process that he or his clerks used to create this copy for his files did not pick up the printed text of the letterhead, which explains the gap in his date here, and similar spaces in the datelines of other letterpress copies from this period printed in this volume. Some versions of the letterhead included three digits of the year, "186" (see editorial method and volume introduction, pp. xiii and 52).

2. The Soldiers' Home opened in 1853 as a residence for invalid veterans of the war with Mexico. In the summers of 1862–64, Lincoln and his family followed James Buchanan's example and escaped some of the heat and stress of the capital by staying in a stone cottage at the facility, which occupied a 240-acre farm in the District of Columbia a couple of miles north of the city. Lincoln rode in to the White House each morning. Edgewood, the estate that Father made his residence in 1871, was not far from the Soldiers' Home. Matthew Pinsker, *Lincoln's Sanctuary: Abraham Lincoln and the Soldiers' Home* (Oxford: Oxford University Press, 2003), 2–5, 13; Green, *Washington*, 200, 201; Burlingame, *At Lincoln's Side,* 109, 133, 137, 261; *Chase Papers,* 1:650.

3. Father had leased a spacious house at the northwest corner of 6th and E streets, N.W., in Washington. The house, in Greek Revival style with Italianate elements, was built in 1851 (and torn down in 1936 to make way for a department store parking garage). Goode, *Capital Losses,* 60–61; *Chase Papers,* 3:342.

4. Edwin Stanton was practicing law in Washington in December 1860 when Buchanan asked him to be attorney general. In the closing months of Buchanan's administration, Stanton urged the president to resist the secession of Southern states. Stanton also passed information about the administration's deliberations to William Seward and others. *ANB,* 20:559.

5. Apparently Nettie's aunt, Charlotte Chambers Ludlow Jones, was visiting.

6. Charles Wilson, the family butler, had a drinking problem. Wilson to Father, July 22, and Father to Wilson, July 29, 1863 (Chase Papers, HSP); *Chase Papers*, 3:126.

7. Joshua C. Tucker and his son J. A. Tucker ran a resort hotel at Narragansett Pier, Rhode Island, a small town near the Spragues' summer retreat. *Chase Papers*, 1:661.

FATHER TO KATE

August 17, 63

My dear Child,

Your letter from Providence came this morning. Certainly I cannot disapprove of your going with Mrs Sprague, to her home; though I would a little have preferred that she had refrained from asking. After all however it may be for the best, and I am not sorry to have her have an opportunity of knowing you or to have you have an opportunity to see her as I saw her in her own house, without company. She is a lady of such true sense and genuine dignity that you cannot fail to gain by being with her.[1]

You must not think of coming home. I do not at all need you. Though Charlotte is not yet able to cook she is getting better & will soon be at the head of the kitchen again. Wilson is doing very well—at all events, so far as I can see. As for me, my health seems to be excellent & I want for nothing.

Your visit to the White Mountains is quite unexpected by me.[2] You must want money for it, & must not receive any from any body but me. Let me know precisely what you want a reasonable time before you will actually need it & I will try to supply you. Let me know too exactly what debts you have made that I may provide for them.

Mr. Ball writes me that the Bowen place, near him in Clifton, is soon to be sold. I have thought of buying it in order to try and save the debt secured? to me by mortgage in it. But I am too much pressed to do so. So I must lose there some $2000 dollars [certainly] & probably a good deal more.[3]

I should not mention these things to you, if I did not fear you think matters go easier with me than they really do. Not that I am pinched or what I *call* poor—though New Yorkers would so *call* me—but that I cannot afford to be extravagant, since I am determined to be honest.

> Yours most affectionately
> S P Chase

Best love to dear darling Nettie and to the Governor & all. In great haste this morning

Letterpress copy. Historical Society of Pennsylvania.

1. Fanny Morgan Sprague, Kate's future mother-in-law, lived in Providence, R.I. Father had gone with Kate and Nettie to Rhode Island in the latter part of July. After leaving them

there he returned to Washington by way of New York, where he negotiated with bankers about Treasury-note subscriptions. *Chase Papers,* 4:98, 206–7.

2. Father originally wrote "a little unexpected," then replaced "a little" with "quite." After visiting William's family, Kate and Nettie traveled through the Boston area and stopped in Portsmouth, N.H., to see Charlotte M. Bridge. Mrs. Bridge and her husband, Horatio, a civilian employee of the Navy Department, had lived in the same hotel as the Chases in 1861. After Portsmouth, Nettie and Kate embarked on their trip to the White Mountains. *Chase Papers,* 4:112–13; Father to Nettie, Dec. 15, 1872, in chapter 11.

3. A prior mortgager had foreclosed and forced a sale of the property. Father's mortgage on the Bowen property secured three notes of indebtedness from 1856, totaling more than $4,400 that was only partially paid off by 1863. Flamen Ball, who was himself a security for the three notes, feared that the property might not fetch a sufficient price at sale to pay both the prior claim and any part of Father's. Ball obtained an advance of funds to bid in Father's behalf and by his bidding at the sale on August 28 advanced the price so that Father could expect to receive approximately $2,300 against the debt. "I am extremely pleased with your conduct of the Bowen business," Father wrote to Ball on August 31. Ball to Father, Aug. 14, 28, 1863 (Chase Papers, LC); Father to Ball, Aug. 18, 31, 1863 (Chase Papers, HSP).

FATHER TO KATE

Washington, Aug. 18. 1863.

My darling Katie,

I have thought of a great many things to say to you this morning; but now that I have taken my pen in hand, they seem obstinately resolved not to come off its point. What a pity it is that one cannot establish some sort of electrical communication between mind and paper of which the pen should be the conductor just as a wire leads electricity from its source to its reservoir. Then let the brain work chemically and send thought of unconsciously![1] Perhaps some genius will discover some such conductor one day. Now this was *not* one of the things which I thought of saying to you.

But this was:—to congratulate you on your twenty third birthday, which I omitted doing yesterday and to express my most anxious wishes that the next may find you happier, better, and stronger than this.

Just as I was finishing the last sentence Wilson called me to breakfast—a call which I obeyed with an article on the Pacific Railroad as my breakfast company. I wish you could have some of the good peaches & nice melon which Wilson's care had provided: but I dare say you fare better wheresoever you may be. As for me I had good appetite and was quite content—thinking now of my dear children & wondering if Katie would be careful to guard herself against these sudden changes of the weather by dress and by exercise perhaps even more necessary to stir the blood, air the lungs and send out the perspiration; and thinking now of the great work which is to link the east to the west and carried back by association to the old days in the Senate when I ventured almost if not quite alone to stand up for the line which has been finally adopted. And then I thought of Gwin, of Davis, of Benton and the contests and—so on.[2]

But I must stop this letter—yet before I stop I will just step up stairs and see how Aunt Charlotte is. And lo & behold, no Charlotte is there. Down I come & finding Richard at the foot of the stairs ask "Is Charlotte down stairs?" "No, Sir, she went over to Georgetown yesterday." "To Georgetown?" "Yes Sir for a few days; she is much better" "How did she go" In a hack."

And now I must stop. Here is Mr. Plants come in to look for some papers;[3] and here is Mr. Hutchins, come in to enquire after his New Orleans report;[4] and here is Thomas with the carriage (which reminds me to say that our carriage is not yet finished) to take me to the Department;[5] & there is somebody ringing the bell & Richard going to the door. And here's the end of this letter except love to Nettie, the Governor, Eliza[6] and anybody else whom I love & who may be near you.

Your Affe. father
S P Chase

I enclose two letters—one of Judge Turner of Nevada. The silver bar is here.[7]

Letterpress copy. Historical Society of Pennsylvania.

1. So in the original. Perhaps he meant "send thought off unconsciously."
2. Father felt he had initiated "the first practical measure looking to the construction of a Pacific Railroad" in 1853, when as a U.S. senator he successfully proposed an amendment for funds to survey routes for a transcontinental railway. At that time Jefferson Davis, who in 1861 became president of the Confederate states, was secretary of war, and his department had responsibility for surveying the routes. Some months later, when Father moved that a standing committee should report on the construction of a railroad across the west, William McKendree Gwin—the same senator who in 1861, when his daughter was one of Nettie's schoolmates, came under suspicion for Confederate sympathies—successfully diverted the matter to a special committee that Gwin chaired. Thomas Hart Benton, who had previously served thirty years in the Senate, was then in the U.S. House of Representatives, where he supported the idea of a Pacific railroad but insisted that St. Louis rather than Memphis or another Southern city should be the eastern terminus. Benton also fought against giving government subsidies to railroad companies. *Chase Papers*, 2:355, 356; 4:199–202; Robert L. Frey, ed., *Railroads in the Nineteenth Century* (New York: Facts On File, 1988), 437; *ANB*, 2:619–20; 9:755–57; Nettie to Father, Nov. 20, 1861, in the previous chapter.
3. Ohioan Homer G. Plantz was a Treasury clerk whose responsibilities included assisting with the secretary of the Treasury's correspondence. Later in 1863 Plantz became the U.S. district attorney at Key West, Fla. *Chase Papers*, 1:308.
4. Father had made John Hutchins, an Ohio attorney who earlier in 1863 had concluded two terms in Congress, a special agent of the Treasury and assigned him to report on accusations of bribery against the deputy collector of customs at New Orleans. Later in the year, Hutchins returned to New Orleans as one of the Treasury's agents and one of Father's sources of information about the region's politics. *Chase Papers*, 1:252; 3:224; 4:77–78, 211–14, 332; *Bio. Dir. U.S. Cong.*, 1239.
5. It is likely that Thomas was the employee of that name mentioned by Father in his letters to Kate of Sept. 10, 1851, and Apr. 30, 1859, printed in this volume. Father sought a light, enclosed, two-person carriage in the latter part of 1861 and enlisted Jay Cooke in the

search. Cooke and his brother-in-law and business partner, William G. Moorhead, bought a coupé and offered it to Father as a gift. Father felt strapped for private funds and pronounced himself "strongly tempted" to accept. He decided that Kate might take the gift, if he could not, but he then reconsidered and returned the vehicle, saying that it was not heavy enough for his family's needs. *Chase Papers*, 3:102–3; Oberholtzer, *Cooke*, 1:180–84.

6. Kate's and Nettie's cousin Eliza Chase Whipple.

7. George Turner of Ohio had supported Father for the presidential nomination in 1860 and subsequently became chief justice of Nevada Territory. Obliged for what he perceived to be Father's support during an attempt to oust him from his judicial position, Turner sent a "Silver Paper Weight, made of the ore of Nevada," along with other items— "as proofs," Father acknowledged, "of your interest in me and mine." Turner to Father, July 20, 1863 (Chase Papers, LC); Father to Turner, Dec. 26, 1863 (Chase Papers, HSP); *Chase Papers*, 4:54.

FATHER TO NETTIE

August 19, 3

My darling Nettie,

Your somewhat ragged looking letter came yesterday. I am afraid you do not take with you a very good supply of paper, pens, and ink. If you used the writing case I gave you you would do better. And don't you think yourself that, knowing as you do how it pains me to have you careless in any thing, that you owe me enough to make it your duty to be more attentive to my wishes—saying nothing of your duty to yourself. Think of these things now, and you will save yourself much pain in thinking about them hereafter. Count nothing trifling which involves the idea of duty.

I wrote your Sister yesterday and very little has happened since. To be sure Nellie comes to see me every evening after dinner and puts her nose up in my face in a sort of sympathetic way—whether offering or asking sympathy it is hard to say. But Nellie is almost the only individual whom I have seen & cared to see.

Mr. Cooke (H. D.) was seized by a violent attack of Cholera Morbus last Sunday night and for a time seemed to be in great danger. He is much better now however, and will I hope soon be well again. I am going to see him this morning as soon as I finish this and a little note to Katie.

The workmen are still busy about the house.[1] What *they* are doing I do not know; for I was not consulted in their employment and have not thought it best *to* enquire. They have painted the blinds white which makes no very agreeable contrast with the oak coloring of all the other woodwork. They have really improved the looks of the bath room however; and I suppose when they get through we shall see a general bettering. Very few however would think it worth while to put so much expence on a house which at most can be occupied under the existing lease only some eighteen months.

But Thomas is waiting and I must write a line to Katie and go. I hope your trip to the White mountains is pleasant and beneficial. Love to Katie, Eliza, the Governor & all

Your Affe. father

S P Chase

Letterpress copy. Historical Society of Pennsylvania.

1. William Sprague planned to purchase the 6th and E streets house after his marriage to Kate. He was having some renovations done so that the new couple could co-inhabit the house with Father and Nettie. Father to William, June 6 and July 14, 1863 (Chase Papers, LC).

FATHER TO KATE

Aug. 19

My dear Child,

Your note added to Netties informs me that you borrowed $200 of Prentice for the expences of your trip.[1] Had you informed me of your intention to make it, when I was at South Pier and of the sum you wanted it would have been furnished, and the borrowing would have been unnecessary. It would also have been much more agreeable to me to be called on in the first instance, than to have you resort to borrowing— which cannot but seem somewhat strange to lenders. However I prefer that you should *borrow,* rather than omit anything which the proper care of your health may seem to require. To protect *that* is the first object: all I ask is that you avoid *unnecessary* expence, for as I have told you the present scale of our expenditure cannot be met from income; but must be supplied, as to the the excess over income, by loans: or, in other words, from the principal.

The money you borrowed will be sent Prentice today.

Your affe. father

S P Chase

You were quite right in not allowing the Gov. to pay your bills—including Netties and Eliza's.

Letterpress copy. Historical Society of Pennsylvania.

1. Josiah Prentice Tucker, Hannah Whipple Tucker's husband (and Eliza Whipple's brother-in-law). He had a position in the Boston Custom House. Appendix; *Chase Papers,* 4:107.

FATHER TO NETTIE

Wash. Aug. 22, 186.[1]

My darling Nettie,

Don't you think I must have a great deal of leisure & that certain young ladies must bear the load of the national finances on them when

I can find time to write every day or almost every day & they can find time to write only once a week or so? Of Course, you do.

Mr. Swann has past the night with me & we have just finished breakfast and are going out immediately: so I can write little this morning.[2]

Last night the sad news came by telegram that Dr. Stone, of Boston, was very ill and not expected to live more than a few hours. This is very distressing. He has been so faithful a friend—so kind a man—& so good an officer.[3]

But I must stop. Enclosed with this are two letters

Your affectionate (idle) father
S P Chase

Library of Congress.

1. He apparently wrote, or started to write, a digit after the "8," then perhaps canceled that digit, wrote the "6" legibly, and neglected to write the "3." The appearance of the date led the editors of the *Chase Papers* microfilm edition to misdate this letter as Aug. 22, 1856. The reference to James W. Stone's impending death confirms that the year of this letter was 1863.

2. In a messy political contest between factions of the Union Party in Maryland, Thomas Swann Jr., former president of the Baltimore and Ohio Railroad and former mayor of Baltimore, had lost the nomination for a congressional seat to Henry Winter Davis. Swann, who led a movement for emancipation in Maryland, later became governor of the state, 1865–69, and congressman, 1869–79. Father had been friends with him since at least 1829, and Nettie and Kate knew Swann from their visit to Baltimore with Father for the railroad celebration in 1857. *Chase Papers,* 1:8, 30, 38–39, 292, 294–95; 4:115–16, 127, 222; *DAB,* 18:237–38.

3. Father considered James W. Stone to be a good friend and had nominated him for an internal revenue collectorship in August 1862. Father called Stone "an excellent public officer," but apparently some criticism had arisen. On Stone's death Father wrote to Charlotte Eastman: "No office was more ably or honestly conducted than his: and neither to me nor to the country can his loss be easily made good: Those who censured him will now let censure sleep." *Chase Papers,* 4:113.

FATHER TO KATE

August. 27   3.

My dear Katie,

The Governor's telegram, giving the pleasing information that you are all "returned safely and in health," has just come.

If it is as cool in Providence as in Boston I am glad that you are out of the Mountains.

What is your purpose now? When you left "Tuckers" was it to return again or did you give up your rooms? If you go back how long do you propose to stay. The arrangement with him was $39 per week while the little room was not occupied—that is while there were but three persons—and $44 per week when it was occupied. I paid him $50 on account. Have his bill made out & let me pay till now if you return & if not whatever is due. Let me know exactly also how your money affairs stand.

I asked Mr. Clark today if the repairs at the house were proceeding under his direction & he said they were and that he was corresponding with you on the subject.[1] Would it not have been *much* better to let me know just what you proposed doing?

When will Nettie's vacation end? I suppose she will hardly return to Washington before going to school again. I was unable to meet Mrs Macaulay's bill when it was presented: but will make all right with her before school begins.

I presume this will reach you at Providence. I make no suggestions as to your future movements, not supposing that they will be of any benefit to you. I only desire that you will be specially careful to avoid exposure; to let me know what you are going to do, and how I can promote your comfort & happiness. I will come for you at almost any time or any where. It is not very inviting here just now.

With dear love to dear Nettie and kindest remembrances for the Governor, Mrs Sprague, and all the ladies[2] including Eliza, I am still

Your Affectionate father
S P Chase

Letterpress copy. Historical Society of Pennsylvania.

1. This was probably Edward Clark, an architect born in Philadelphia in 1822. In the early 1870s, he designed and oversaw construction and renovation work at Edgewood, Father's home in the District of Columbia. Clark's father was an architect and his uncle an engineer. He began to study and work under Thomas U. Walter in Philadelphia and then went to Washington with Walter in 1851 when Walter became the architect for the dome of the U.S. Capitol and the expansion of the building. In 1865, Clark succeeded his mentor as architect of the Capitol. During his career in Washington, Clark designed or supervised the expansion of the Patent Office and the General Post Office, in addition to the marble terraces of the Capitol. *Who Was Who,* 1:222; *Chase Papers,* 1:665, 666, 682, 705; Henry F. Withey and Elsie Rathburn Withey, *Biographical Dictionary of American Architects (Deceased)* (Los Angeles: Hennessey and Ingalls, 1970; repr., Detroit: Omnigraphics, 1996), 121; Sandra L. Tatman and Roger H. Moss, *Biographical Dictionary of Philadelphia Architects: 1700–1930* (Boston: G. K. Hall, 1985), 147.

2. William's mother, Fanny Sprague, and Almira Sprague, his sister.

FATHER TO NETTIE

Washington, Septr. 7, 1863.

My darling Nettie,

I fear this letter will not find you in Rhode Island: and as it is uncertain when it will reach you I will make it short. Your note of the 4th only came today. I am sorry that your last days at Tucker's were made so unpleasant by the cold rains: but if you take back with you to school renovated strength and a cheerful resolution to make next year the best year yet I shall be satisfied. I want you to be a lady in every sense of the word and above all a Christian lady. May God bless and keep you.

> Your Affectionate father,
> S P Chase

Letterpress copy. Historical Society of Pennsylvania.

FATHER TO KATE

Washington, Septr. 9, 1863.

My dear Katie,

Your letter of the 4th has only just come. It comforts me much. Pardon me, darling, if I have caused you any trouble; but please remember how terribly annoyed I must be by having your name being brought into any public charges against employees in the Department. Your explanation relieves me greatly and will enable me, I hope, to get your name out of the paper altogether. At any rate, out or in no harm can come—only not a little annoyance.

As to the house I do not pride myself on my memory; and perhaps the fault is mine that I did not go a little more into details, when you talked of repairs & improvements. I received the impression that they were to be confined to the rooms to be occupied by yourself and the Governor; and when I found them going on to an indefinite extent and really never knew or had quite forgotten that I knew any thing of their being made, I felt uneasy about the pocket. You know that what I have goes pretty easy, but that I dread debt; and *expences this fall are heavy.*[1]

Now we will dismiss these topics: and say no more of money except that I sent to Gov. Sprague $250 to pay bills at Tuckers.

Wilson has been quite sick for a few days—that is since [Sun]day. Dr. Lindsly has been to see him.[2] Richard is doing very well & so is Cassy. James Schureman lends a helping hand as wanted.[3] Yesterday I thought Charlotte was in the house & at work a little: today I am not sure whether she is or not. I had a notion she is not, when I left the house this morning, but did not enquire.

Some delicious grapes came today from Mr. Browne with the largest banana branch crowded with fruit I ever saw—larger than I supposed to exist. I wish you could have them: and Nettie.[4]

I quite approve your plan of taking rooms at the Brevoort House:[5] and if I can get a parlor & bed room to suit shall feel inclined to join you there.

There is reason to fear that I shall lose Mr. Plants. Mr. Lawrence (a Judge in Ohio whom you may possibly remember) will probably be appointed U.S. District Judge for the Western District of Florida & Plants wants to be Clerk & may be.[6] I shall find it difficult if not impossible to make his place good.

There is nothing new of a public character. Mr. Lincoln comes nearer & nearer to the true ground on the slavery question; but won't urge the War as I wish him.[7] Mr. Stickney tells me that the Florida sales are advertised for the 26th October. How would you like to go down in a Cutter as a Wedding trip? The Governor talked of buying a farm![8]

Most affectionately
S P Chase

Letterpress copy. Historical Society of Pennsylvania.

1. William Sprague purchased the house at 6th and E from Joseph B. Varnum for $30,000 and assumed the costs for remodeling. Each family member had private rooms, the Spragues paid for food, and Father paid the servants. Lamphier, *Kate Chase and William Sprague*, 73.

2. Father's old acquaintance from his early days in Washington, physician Harvey Lindsly, was president of the American Medical Association, 1858–59, as well as a professor of obstetrics at the National Medical College. *Nat. Cyc.*, 12:205–6.

3. Father apparently employed James H. A. Schureman to perform various tasks. In June 1863, Father offered to have Schureman accompany Kate on a trip to Ohio to handle baggage, and according to a letter of Feb. 26, 1864, to Nettie (in the next chapter), Schureman acted as Father's barber. Schureman was not a Treasury Department employee, and a city directory listed his occupation as messenger. *Chase Papers*, 4:73, 309.

4. Albert Gallatin Browne Sr. was the supervising special agent of the Treasury Department at Beaufort, S.C. *Chase Papers*, 1:492; Father to Browne, June 9, Aug. 24, Sept. 23, 1863 (Chase Papers, LC).

5. Built in 1854, the Hotel Brevoort stood at the corner of Fifth Avenue and Eighth Street. Federal Writers' Project, *New York City Guide* (New York: Random House, 1939), 135.

6. William Lawrence, previously a judge in Logan County, Ohio, later became a Republican congressman. On Father's recommendation, Abraham Lincoln offered Lawrence the federal judgeship at Key West, but the Ohioan declined the post. *DAB*, 11:52–53; *Chase Papers*, 1:431.

7. The president's Emancipation Proclamation carried many exceptions, including parts of Louisiana and Virginia and all of West Virginia. Through 1863, Father pressed Lincoln to remove the exemptions. In August, Father prepared a draft of an executive order to revoke all exceptions except West Virginia, but Lincoln was concerned about the political consequences of a broader challenge to slavery. Father was also very supportive of the organization of African American regiments, asserting in a public letter to the Loyal National League in April that "American blacks must be called into this conflict, not as cattle, not now even as contrabands, but as men." He was sometimes disappointed in military decisions and wished "the war could be more efficiently & more economically conducted." To Horace Greeley, however, in October 1863, Father stated that "Mr. Lincoln, with sentiments which divide him between the border state and the progressive policy, advances slowly but yet advances." *Chase Papers*, 1:428–29, 447, 527; 4:8, 103, 119–20, 133, 142, 150–51, 262.

8. Lyman D. Stickney was the U.S. direct tax commissioner in Florida and had called on Father three days previous to this letter to tell him that he believed that 5,000 men could easily take Florida from the Confederacy. In May 1865, Stickney was indicted for fraud a short time before he was to buy a Florida estate for Father. Lyman Stickney to Father, Apr. 16, 17, 1863 (Chase Papers, LC); *Chase Papers*, 1:553; Jerrell H. Shofner, *Nor Is It Over Yet: Florida in the Era of Reconstruction, 1863–1871* (Gainesville, Fla.: University Presses of Florida, 1974), 15.

MARY MACAULAY TO FATHER

Wednesday
Sept 9th.

My dear Sir

I return the bills of Nettie's expenses receipted, and thank you for your renewed expression of confidence in returning her to my care[1]—

I must ask your aid in helping me to enforce a rather more rigid discipline than that I [pursued] last year, tho' I am satisfied the first thing to be done with a child of her nature is to secure her affection—She is full of talent—but erratic—and must be *compell'd* to apply herself systematically—I will do all that I can to secure her improvement

It is no easy task to enforce application when a child has wrapp'd herself around one's heart as closely as she has around mine—I have thought of the subject a great deal this summer, and I shall be grateful for any suggestions you can make that will ensure the goal which I am confident both you and I desire the dear child to reach—to be a good, and happy woman—

I hope Miss Kate is well—that she is happy I cannot doubt—

Believe me with much respect—Truly &c &c[2]
Mary Macaulay

To Hon S P Chase

I hope Nettie will return punctually—My school will open next Wednesday—the 16th.

Library of Congress.

1. A bill dated June 20, 1863, indicates that Father owed Macaulay $232.42, expenses that included extra German lessons, washing, books, trips to the museum and theater, pencils, dress material, and cash advances. Nettie's school bills for February, June, and September 1864 totaled $1,143.80. Macaulay to Father, June 20, 1863, Feb. 9, June 28, Sept. 24, 1864 (Chase Papers, LC).

2. Of the three women who directed boarding schools attended by Kate and Nettie—Henrietta Haines, Maria Eastman, and Mary E. Macaulay—we know the least about Macaulay. New York City directories identified her as a widow, as did Father in a letter to Jacob Schuckers in 1866. She had a school in Manhattan as early as 1853, apparently teaching at the same location as her residence, 43 East 21st Street. She was at that location through the 1850s and by the end of that decade called her establishment a "French and English Boarding and Day School." By the time Nettie entered the school in 1862, Macaulay had moved it uptown to 253 Madison Avenue. There, at the southeast corner of Madison Avenue and 40th Street, Macaulay continued the school through the 1860s, also acquiring the building at 251 Madison Avenue by 1864. In the 1860s, her late-summer newspaper advertisements announcing the September opening of school noted the date when she would be back "in town," usually early in September, implying that she went away for a portion of the summer. *New York Times*, July 15, 1853, Oct. 10, 1859, Aug. 1, 1862, July 25, 1865, Aug. 11, 1866, Aug. 7, 1867, Nov. 1, 1868, Aug. 7, 1869; Wilson, *Trow's New York City Directory, For . . . 1862*, 557; Wilson, *Trow's New York City Directory, For . . . 1863*, 568; Wilson, *Trow's New York City Directory, For . . . 1864*, 564; Wilson, *Trow's New York City Directory, For . . . 1865*, 576; *Chase Papers*, 5:125.

FATHER TO KATE

Washington Septr. 17, 1863.
My dear Katie,

I received your first letter from South Pier: none since.

You say nothing as to the amount of the bill at Tuckers or of what you have left, and leave the whole question of money very much at loose ends.

You only say that you will probably want $1000 for what is to come from abroad: and intimate that you will want something more to pay for what you wish to buy in New York and want me to give the sum. How can I? I know nothing of such matters, so far as ladies expences go. I want you to ascertain what you would need for a becoming outfit (not what you could spend) and let me know the amount. As you have not done this I suppose I must guess, and so will guess $500 in addition to the $1000 & what you have already had. Will it answer?[1]

I have no idea what the repairs of the house are to come to, but in connection with what Wilson had done they must cost a large sum. I was not consulted at all about them; and let every thing go just as carpenters and painters please.

> Yours affectionately
> S P Chase

Charlotte is much better and at work moderately. Wilson has got over again; but is now right except sick. Every body else comme il faut.[2]

Letterpress copy. Historical Society of Pennsylvania.

1. Kate had arranged for a considerable trousseau, including some clothing from New York and Paris dressmakers. The surviving wedding trousseau bills total just over $1,900. Another $1,500 was spent on catering, carriages, flowers, invitations, and other wedding-related items. C. W. Cambell et al. to Father, Nov.–Dec. 1863 (Chase Papers, LC).
2. "As it should be."

FATHER TO NETTIE

Washington Septr. 19, 1863.
My darling Nettie,

You and Sister or one of you try my patience a good deal. Some time ago you wrote me that you were going to return promptly to your school &, try, this year, to make improvement which would fully satisfy my wishes. Instead of that, I learn that on the evening of the very day before your school was to open in New York you all went off from Providence to Boston, and Gov. Sprague, who tells me this, adds "I don't know their further movements."[1] This pains me very much. If your sister wanted to go to Boston & could not possibly manage to go in time to take you to New York before your school was to open, you ought to have insisted on going yourself, and should have asked Gov Sprague to have the goodness to send an escort with you to New York. Had I supposed that you would be prevented from returning by want of somebody to go with you I would have sent some one from Washington, for Mrs Macaulay had written me, particularly desiring that you should be present at the opening of the school.

I am not at all certain that this letter will find you in New York but I hope it will: and I hope also most earnestly that you will now give your mind to the duties of the school & set every thing else aside.

If you and Katie could only realize how much distress it occasions me to have you treat so lightly the plain every day duties—such as that of being present when your school opens—you would, *I hope*, be more careful. I say, "I hope"—I wish I could say, "I am sure."

I have had no letter from your sister for a long time: and your last dated the 13th did not state where you were or what you intended to do

Your affe. father

S P Chase

Letterpress copy. Historical Society of Pennsylvania.

1. William was in Providence tending to business matters related to A. and W. Sprague and Co. William to Kate, Sept. 19, 20, 1863 (Brown University Library).

FATHER TO KATE

Washn. Septr. 24, 1863.

My dear Katie,

I have just received your letter from Brookline, dated the 16th! Had it come earlier I should have understood matters more clearly; though I should have still regretted that you did not see that Nettie reached her school a day *before* instead of a day *after* the opening. Mrs Lander told me you crossed the bay to Newport which consumed some time.[1]

I wrote yesterday to Mr. Barney giving him directions to have your Paris Case sent to you.[2] I enclosed the letter of the importer not being able to make out his name with certainty.

We are all very busy here. No battle at Chattanooga up to last night. Strong reinforcements on their way.[3] I enclose a telegram from Garfield which read & return.[4]

Yours most affy

S P Chase

Letterpress copy. Historical Society of Pennsylvania.

1. Jean Davenport Lander was the widow of Gen. Frederick W. Lander, whose spirited resistance to Stonewall Jackson on the Potomac River came up in correspondence between

Kate and Father in January 1862. Jean Lander, born in England in 1829, had made her stage debut as a child actor in Scotland in 1837 and had her American debut—as Shakespeare's Richard III—in New York not long after her ninth birthday. She retired from the theater when she married Frederick Lander in 1860. After his death in March 1862, she and her mother became nurses for the Union troops at Port Royal, S.C. Early in 1865, Jean Lander resumed her theatrical career and acted until she retired for good in 1877. She split her time between Washington, D.C., and New England and was a friend of the Chases. *ANB*, 13:103–4; *Chase Papers*, 1:483; 3:382.

2. Hiram Barney had been collector of customs at New York since the spring of 1861. *Chase Papers*, 3:60–61.

3. In the indecisive Battle of Chickamauga, Tenn., Sept. 19 and 20, 1863, Union major general William S. Rosecrans dropped back and held Chattanooga from Confederate forces. In a conference held in the middle of the night of September 23–24, Secretary of War Stanton argued that the U.S. could, and must, rapidly move troops from the Army of the Potomac to reinforce Rosecrans in the west. When Lincoln doubted that enough troops could be moved fast enough and far enough by rail, Stanton countered: "It is certain that 30.000 bales of cotton could be sent in that time . . . and I do not see why 30.000 men cannot be sent as well." Father and William Seward supported Stanton, and after Lincoln and General Halleck assured themselves that the troops could be spared from the Army of the Potomac, they ordered two corps under Joseph Hooker to go to Rosecrans's relief. The reinforcements arrived October 2 and occupied Chattanooga. This not only cut Confederate supply lines to Georgia and South Carolina but also caused, as Southern diarist Mary Chesnut wrote, "gloom and unspoken despondency" in the South. *Chase Papers*, 1:450–54; 4:222–23; McPherson, *Battle Cry of Freedom*, 672–81; Denney, *Civil War Years*, 325–28, 331, 341–42.

4. Before the war, James Abram Garfield of Ohio earned a degree from Williams College in Massachusetts, returned to his native state to teach ancient languages at Hiram College, and then became the president of the college in 1857, the year he turned twenty-six. He went to the Ohio legislature as a Republican in 1859. When the war broke out he led a regiment from Ohio. With support from Father, he was promoted to brigadier general in 1862. He was also elected to the U.S. House of Representatives from Ohio. The 38th Congress did not convene until late in 1863, and Garfield remained in the army until the congressional session began. During the fighting around Chickamauga and Chattanooga he was Rosecrans's chief of staff. Father telegraphed Garfield on Sept. 22, 1863, and received a reply "confirming the report of great losses at Chickamauga, and urging reinforcements." Garfield served in the House of Representatives until 1880, the year he was elected the twentieth president of the United States. Garfield to Father, Sept. 23, 1863 (Chase Papers, LC); *ANB*, 8:715–17; *Chase Papers*, 3:142–43.

FATHER TO KATE

Washn. Sep. 30. 1863.

My dear Katie,

Your letter of the 28th came yesterday—the first time that I have received a letter from you in the regular course of the mail.

I am glad that your dresses suit you so well. To meet the demands of your taste they must be *just* right.

The great expedition to reinforce Rosecrans is going on admirably. If no luck occurs the advance from the army of the Potomac will begin to arrive at Chattanooga or within supporting distance within the next two days.

How much would have been gained had Rosecrans attacked when Bragg was weak![1]

I am expecting a letter from you which will determine whether I go to New York. Cant you come under Mr. Barney's escort? On Saturday? The Governor will be a most welcome member of the party; if he thinks best to come at this time.[2] I love him now for his love to you as much as I have always honored him for his courage & patriotism. I expect to be very proud of him, but shall hope to have more occasion to be grateful for him. Best regards to him & Mrs McDowell

Your affectionate father
S P Chase

The trunk was delayed by Cassy's failing to get it packed till yesterday— Then by Wilson's carelessness till today. Today it goes directed to the care of Mr. Barney at the Custom House. He will send it to you. I do not remember the No of Mrs McDowell and so cannot direct to it.

Letterpress copy. Historical Society of Pennsylvania.

1. "Rosecrans is moving—not rapidly enough I fear," Father had worried in his diary some months earlier. William Starke Rosecrans was a native of Ohio, but his performance as a commander had tended to alienate Secretary of War Stanton and others in Washington. President Lincoln characterized Rosecrans's state of mind after the Battle of Chickamauga as "confused and stunned like a duck hit on the head." A West Point graduate, Rosecrans in the fall of 1863 was a major general of volunteers and a brevet major general in the regular army. For months his Army of the Cumberland had opposed the troops of Confederate major general Braxton Bragg, who later suspended three generals for slowness or refusal to obey orders during the crucial days of Chickamauga. It was not so much Rosecrans's failure to attack that hurt him in that battle, but in pushing forward he inadvertently created a gap through which Bragg's forces could attack the Federal position. *Chase Papers*, 1:427, 432; Burlingame and Ettlinger, *Inside Lincoln's White House*, 99; McPherson, *Battle Cry of Freedom*, 672–76; Denney, *Civil War Years*, 327; *ANB*, 18:868–70; *DAB*, 2:585–87; 16:163–64.
2. William did visit Kate over the weekend, though whether they went to New York or stayed at Buttermilk Falls with Helen and Irvin McDowell is unknown. William to Kate, Sept. 26, Oct. 1, 1863 (Brown University Library).

FATHER TO NETTIE

Washington, Sept 30, 1863

My darling Nettie,

You want just one word: there is only one which comes near expressing my feeling for you & that is *love*. Take it, darling.

I bought a beautiful writing table for you the other day, which is your birthday present from me. How old *we* grow![1]

Those little girls you write about are not *much* smarter or more political than you were at the same age: but it is so far back that you have forgotten. You were "precocious" too. Mind, I spell precocious, preco*c*ious—

not precosious. Overhaul your dictionary, and "when found make a note of it."

Your affe. father
S P Chase

Letterpress copy. Historical Society of Pennsylvania.

1. Nettie turned sixteen on September 19.

FATHER TO KATE

Washington, Oct. 3, 1863

My dear child,

Your pencilled letter of the 1st is just received—Had it come yesterday I should have been tempted to start for New York this morning. Now my engagements will prevent. I expect Mr. Barney today.

Enclosed you will find a check for $700, $500 for your own expences and $100 each for Nettie and Alice.[1] I fear you will never learn to be definite in money matters—But you ought to say for such object I want so much & for such so much & for such so much, making the whole matter clear.

I regret that *the day* is to be so late on your account chiefly. It will make any excursion hazardous to your health, and I should be glad to have you make one so as to be recovered for the winter. But I hope all will turn for the best.[2]

Your charge concerning the two trunks and the saddle shall be attended to.

I expect to *love* the Governor. Why should I not? Will he not be my only son? And shall I not be very proud of him? I trust he will never have cause to feel otherwise than happy and honored in the alliance he is about to form. My aim always has been and I trust yours will be to exceed—not disappoint—expectation.

You show your usual good sense in the matter of escort. By all means take that of Col. Howe. Can't you persuade his charming wife to come with him & stay with us a few days. We can make them all with baby and nurse very comfortable.[3]

It is rather late to have my memory refreshed as to Mrs McDowells No. But this letter shall be addressed accordingly: and I hope you will get it a few hours earlier than you otherwise would. The Penny Post is more reliable for you than the Brevoort House. Though your last mailed yesterday came regularly.

I am much gratified by Mrs Macaulay's account of Nettie. I expect she will be a great woman—great in all excellencies as well as as in cultivated intelligence. Love to her and Lizzie. Mrs M—— must let Lizzie come if she can get her father & mother's consent.

Kindest remembrances to dear Mrs McDowell

Your affectionate father
S P Chase

Miss Kate Chase
at Mrs McDowells,
No 58 West 9th Street
New York

Letterpress copy. Historical Society of Pennsylvania.

1. Kate's and Nettie's cousin Alice Skinner.
2. Father's unfulfilled wish that Kate's wedding be earlier than November illustrates two important points about nineteenth-century weddings. First, parents had less power over their children's decisions regarding whom and when they wed, compared with the previous century. Also women tended to draw out the courtship phase of their lives as long as possible, both enjoying the relative freedom and power of premarital life and putting off the responsibility that would become theirs upon marriage. "Men tended to see engagement as the time before they *could* marry," Ellen Rothman explains, "while women viewed it as the time before they *would* marry." Rothman, *Hands and Hearts,* 119–22, 146–57; Lystra, *Searching the Heart,* 164–66.
3. During the course of the war, Frank E. Howe was Massachusetts state agent at New York City, an assistant quartermaster with the rank of colonel, the director of the New England Soldiers' Relief Association in New York, and a temporary agent of the U.S. Treasury reporting on affairs in Louisiana. Howe, originally from Boston, was a friend and, on occasion, a political helper to Father, as in September 1865, when Father let Howe deal with a *New York Herald* writer looking for information. *Chase Papers,* 1:482, 483, 594; 4:35, 67, 298–300, 361–64.

FATHER TO MARY MACAULAY

Oct 21, 3

My dear Mrs Macaulay,

I enclose a check for Nettie which is intended for her quarterly allowance 1st Sepr. to 1st Decr., and which I will thank you to hand her if you do not disapprove of it, together with the letter herewith also enclosed.

Katie thinks $300 a year will suffice for Netties clothing; and I add $60 for incidentals of all sorts. We both agree that if you see no objection it will be best to allow her to make her own purchases under your advice. Under no circumstances should she contract any debts whatever outside of your regular bills for board, tuition & books.

The Enclosed check is for the first quarter on this plan—$75 for clothing & $15 for other incidental expences.

Yours very truly
S P Chase

We are expecting the pleasure of seeing you soon with Nettie & Lizzie.
Mrs M. E. Macaulay.

Letterpress copy. Historical Society of Pennsylvania.

FATHER TO NETTIE

Washington, Oct. 23, 1863.
My darling Nettie,
Your nice little note came just now: and gave me an appetite for the
nice long one you promise.
You must not be elated by the praises just now showered upon your
father.[1] Nobody can tell how soon the tide may turn. There is only one
judgment by which any man should supremely wish to stand approved—
I mean the judgment of God. Young folks & some old folks attach far too
great importance to human breath and [praise].
Alice is here and well. She went down the river with a party yesterday
& was delighted.
Enclosed is something. I know not what
Your affectionate father
S P Chase

Letterpress copy. Historical Society of Pennsylvania.

1. Father had made a trip to Ohio and Indiana, October 10–16, speaking on behalf of
Republican tickets in those states and using the opportunity to publicize his views on the
war and policy matters. His speeches were published as a pamphlet, *"Going Home to Vote."*
He was the favorite candidate of several influential Republican radicals and some moderates, who felt that Lincoln should be replaced in the next presidential election by someone
who might prosecute the war more vigorously and could be relied on, in particular, to
work harder to eradicate slavery. "I know no man in our country who is in my view better
qualified for President than yourself," Horace Greeley of the *New York Tribune* wrote to
Father in September 1863, "nor one whom I should more cordially support." "If in 1864 I
could *make* a President (not merely a candidate)," Greeley wrote, "you would be my first
choice." Father replied: "I am proud of your approval and your preference." *Chase Papers,*
1:xxxvii–xxxviii; 4:xiii, xvi, xvii, 145–46, 150, 154–55; Niven, *Chase,* 343–45; Blue, *Chase,*
216–22.

WILLIAM SPRAGUE TO FATHER

Providence[1] Novr 4th. 1863
My dear Governor,[2]
Your letter has filled me with a great deal of pleasure. When you
was writing to me, probably the same hour, I wrote Katie that her fathers
care was attributable far more to his anxiety for her future, than to other
causes. This could not well be otherwise. I think I realize the delicate link

which has so long united father & daughter. I think I realize something of that high & holy relation, and that I know something of the great soul of the one, and its counterpart in the other, hightened & electrified by the extreme delicacies of female character. My dear Sir you will not think less of me, for being in love with both these characters—I shall strive to so conduct myself to be worthy of the connection, and shall never be happier than when contributing to continue the same relation between father & daughter—that has heretofore existed, excepting if possible to share something of it, myself. If resolves are anything, If a single mind & heart absorbed in the happiness of another, can be my guarantee of a bright and happy future for Katie, I think I can faithfully and truly promise it to her.

I have taken little or no care for myself during my past life. It has been my luck to have others interests in my keeping; from my earliest youth, I have neglected both mind & body—I have for some time given more attention to the latter, & think I have worked out a remedy for physical ills so that with good health and a proper exercise of the talent God has been pleased to give me, I hope to to do something usefull for my day and generation

I am not satisfied with having done well

Past honors or acts have no attraction to me,—the very much over estimated ability given me, whatever of real talent I may have of business or family, they all have no charms for me unless they are contributing to something more usefull for the future than has been done in the past. My creed was (tho somewhat blurred by my hurried advent into public life) was to prove a worthy son of my father & mother & of the superior advantages of this day over those of the past.

Infirmities of nature, increased by improper remedies to asuage the disease, has made my life an excited & excentric one.

I feel I have found a remedy against all this, & with good health & disposition I have more hopes for a successfull accomplishment of the work God has for me to do in the future than I ever have had in the past. I need not say here I rely much upon your guardianship, expecting to receive a fathers council & the benefits of a fathers experience, and a faithfull reliance upon Him who always smiles upon the efforts of those who in relying upon Him make every effort to help themselves, and having another and better half I think I have a right to feel I commence my new life in great hopefullness for myself & for those who are dependent upon me. Dont think me weaker my dear Sir for thus uncovering so much of my real nature I believe they are true ones, & I am far happier to be weak if such must be weakness. I have not had a fathers care for 20 years,[3] Katie has missed a mother's, while my mother with her whole heart has gone out to her; I shall, repeating again, try to desire from you a fathers guidance, council & affection. I note your remark as to the Govt, and am gratefull at the Baltimore meeting appreciation / I have been so many times interupted while writing my letter that I hope you will overlook its hurried style, & get Katie to read it if you cannot

Faithfully & affectionatly

Yours

Wm Sprague

Library of Congress.

1. William made his home at his mother's Providence house, "Young Orchard." Lamphier, *Kate Chase and William Sprague*, 54.

2. Here William reciprocated his future father-in-law's address of him as "Governor"; see Father to Kate, August 12.

3. William's father, Amasa, cofounder of A. and W. Sprague and Co., was murdered in 1843, when William was thirteen years old. Ironically, given William's penchant for strong drink, Amasa was said to have been killed over his opposition to the sale of "intoxicating liquors" in one of his mill towns. Knight, *History of the Sprague Families*, 19–21; Belden and Belden, *So Fell the Angels*, 52–53; William to Kate, Dec. 31, 1863 (Brown University Library).

MARY MACAULAY TO FATHER

New York

Thursday

Nov 5th.

My dear Sir

I beg you to excuse my neglect in not acknowledging the receipt of your letter enclosing a check for dear Nettie—

Incessant recuperation must be my apology; I shall be most happy to aid Nettie by my advice, or in any other way in reference to her wardrobe, I think your allowance ample, and that the systematic expenditure which it involves will be a great advantage to Nettie—

She is greatly excited at the prospect of going home tomorrow[1]—but proposes to return without loss of time for her school—I wish to say that she has applied herself much more earnestly to her studies than she did last year, and I hope very *very much* that her improvement will be recognised by you—

You were a little disappointed last year, at least in her discipline, but you can hardly understand how difficult it is to influence a child of her strong nature—

She really merits praise for her good beginning at least, [and] I think (perhaps it is self-flattery) she gives evidence that the influence of last year's training, imperfect as it may have been, has produced good results—

I regret exceedingly that I cannot be present at Miss Kate's wedding— but my duties at home are too numerous for me to leave at this moment—

Hoping that you will gain a son who will be an additional blessing to you, and yours,

I remain very truly &c &c
Mary Macaulay

Library of Congress.

1. Kate's wedding, in which Nettie was to act as bridesmaid, was a week away.

CHRONOLOGY

November 12, 1863	Kate and William are married in Washington, D.C.
November 13, 1863	Kate, William, Nettie, and William's relatives leave Washington for New York City and Providence, R.I.; Father is in Washington (niece Eliza Whipple visits)
November 23, 1863	Nettie resumes school at Mrs. Macaulay's; after leaving her in New York, Kate and William travel to Ohio
December 7, 1863	38th Congress convenes (William is a senator from Rhode Island)
late December 1863	Kate and William return to Washington; William goes to Providence for Christmas without Kate
March 1864	Kate, ill with a cold, spends time with Helen McDowell at Buttermilk Falls, N.Y.
June 1864	Kate is in Washington, then to Rhode Island; President Lincoln accepts Father's resignation (June 30)
July 4, 1864	William makes speech in Senate; congressional session ends
July 16, 1864	Father meets Kate and Nettie (who has finished at Macaulay's school) in New York; the three leave for Rhode Island
July–September 1864	Father travels in New England
August 13, 1864	Kate's twenty-fourth birthday
September 19, 1864	Nettie's seventeenth birthday
December 6, 1864	Lincoln names Father to the Supreme Court
December 15, 1864	Father is sworn in as chief justice; he turns fifty-seven on January 13
March 1865	Kate and Nettie make a visit to Rhode Island
April 1865	Robert E. Lee surrenders at Appomattox Court House, Va., and the Civil War ends; John Wilkes Booth assassinates Lincoln in Washington

CHAPTER 6

"Rejoice with Trembling"

NOVEMBER 1863 – MARCH 1865

T HE NOVEMBER 12 wedding of Kate Chase and William Sprague was one of the highlights of Washington's winter social season. Kate wore white velvet and lace, though white was not yet the de rigueur bridal color, and a Tiffany diamond and pearl tiara, earrings, and bracelet set worth $6,500.[1] The groom cut a dashing figure in a new black suit and a silk shirt with diamond studs. Nettie, Cousin Alice Skinner, and William's niece Ida Nichols were bridesmaids, while William's attendants were resplendent in military uniforms. Fifty guests, including President Lincoln, most of the cabinet, and several senators, attended the wedding ceremony, which was held in the front parlor of the Chases' house. Hundreds more guests were invited to the reception, which began immediately after the wedding ceremony. There was dancing music, including Frederick Kroell's newly composed "Kate Chase Wedding March," which the U.S. Marine Band played three times that evening.[2] A caterer provided food, including oysters, truffle terrines, roast partridges, veal, and other delicacies. For the gentlemen there were "segars" to smoke, while the wine, brandy, and champagne flowed until after midnight. For the Chases the wedding was an astounding social and political success. Lincoln's secretary John Hay saw Kate in her rooms at the end of the evening and wrote, "She had lost all her old severity and formal stiffness of manner, & seemed to think that she had *arrived*."[3]

After the wedding Kate and William took a wedding trip to Rhode Island. Not to be confused with a honeymoon, a wedding trip represented an older public ritual wherein the newly married couple, accompanied by friends and family, journeyed to relatives' houses. The Spragues' bridal company consisted of William's sisters, mother, brother, and sister-in-law, as well as Nettie, Alice, and William's three groomsmen.[4] The happy group stopped over at New York. The hotel erupted in fire twice in the same night, driving Kate, Nettie, and the others on to Providence. Though Nettie greatly enjoyed herself, Kate found the reception at William's mother's house less than pleasing. Cousin Alice wrote Father that the bunting and flags that festooned the Sprague house made it look ready for "a horse fair" and found the whole scene "very funny." Professing fatigue, Kate retired to her room.[5] Gardeners soon after removed the offending decorations.

Kate also may have noticed that none of Rhode Island's elites, people who had been so happy to receive her and her sister the previous summer, attended the reception. Kate quickly came to realize that Rhode Island society did not receive the Spragues. As one arbiter of taste put it, "Governor Sprague never had the manners of a gentleman, only the veneer of refinement, and in a mental lapse might put his feet upon a rose satin chair, That was a Sprague trick—they all did it."[6] This attitude was perhaps more than a matter of simple snobbery. Providence elites had not forgotten the scandalous affair Kate's new husband had had with one of their own—a girl named Mary Viall who became pregnant by William in early 1860, right before he left on a trip to Europe. According to local gossip, William abandoned the young woman, who eventually gave the baby to relatives to raise. Mary would eventually write a thinly veiled novel defending her lover, much to the considerable consternation and scandal of those who knew of the story.[7]

It is difficult to discern just what Father knew of this scandal, if anything, but he did know that his daughter's new husband was intimately acquainted with other vices, chief among them a weakness for intoxicating beverages. By William's own admission to Father he had "neglected both mind & body" and "applied improper remedies" to "infirmities of nature." He had led an "excentric" life.[8] Thus Father's first letters to Kate during this period contain considerable trepidation regarding her future. "I rejoice greatly in all your happiness, & fervently pray that it may be continued to you," he wrote Kate within a week of the wedding. "But I rejoice with trembling. Few lives are so unclouded as yours has been hitherto; and I fear the dark days." Father continued to remind Kate of her duty to act as a Christian, believing she could find happiness in faith.[9]

After the wedding trip Nettie returned to Mrs. Macaulay's school in New York, while Kate and William made their home with Father in Washington, D.C. William purchased the house at 6th and E streets, N.W., that Father had been renting, paid to have it remodeled so as to provide private quarters for the two branches of the family, and arranged to share some expenses with Father. William had originally resisted the idea of living with his august parent-in-law, writing Kate that "I could never consent to occupy any house with dimmed authority."[10] Whether because Kate desired to live with her father, or because William saw the advantage of so closely associating himself with a cabinet member, William soon after professed himself "delighted" to share a roof with Father.[11] Kate spent that winter and spring assisting her father and husband with their political careers, hosting breakfasts, and taking a lively part in political

Nettie (left) and Kate in an undated photograph. *Courtesy of Cincinnati Museum Center—Cincinnati Historical Society Library.*

Salmon P. Chase as secretary of the Treasury during the Civil War. *Courtesy of the Library of Congress.*

Facing page: The first page of his letter to Nettie, January 17, 1867. At the bottom of the page he attempted to imitate Nettie's handwriting. *Courtesy of the Library of Congress.*

Washington, Jany 17. 1859. 6215

My darling Nettie

I have received two of your always welcome letters within the last week. The first was without a date except December - the second was the 26th: the day after Christmas.

You say in your last that I have only to tell you what to do or omit and your greatest pleasure will be to comply with my wishes. Now I am going to put you at once to the test. I do want to have you write a plain good hand, with the letters joined and no long lines drawn through your ts. and shorter legs to your gs, and shorter horizontals at the end of many of your letters. And then I want your spelling right - it is pretty nearly so - and your points and capitals rightly made & placed. Just let me give you some specimens of what I mean

Your Long looked for letter came Last night. the h

14738

Kate as a young woman. *Courtesy of the Library of Congress.*

Facing page: The first page of her July 2, 1868, letter to her father. The monogram, embossed in gold, blue, red, and green, spells Kate's first name in rings
suspended below the upper half of a rearing lion (a "demi-lion rampant" in the
terminology of coats of arms). *Courtesy of the Historical Society of Pennsylvania.*

94. Fifth Avenue
New York. 2 July
/66

Dearest Father.

Your dear loving
letter came this morning. Don't
pray worry your-self about me. I
feel perfectly well. & dont cough at
all. The perfect quiet & rest.
I find here. is perfectly delightful
to me. Mr. Hoyt's family are all
at Astoria but one or the other of
its members come in to see me
every day — Amasa is here &
writing

Nettie, notebook on her lap, is both participant and observer in an illustration from her article describing a trip to Maine. John Tinkey made this wood engraving from an image that may have been drawn by William L. Sheppard. "Babes in the Wood," *Scribner's Monthly* 14 (1877): 495.

Facing page: The first page of her letter to her father, July 21, 1868. Other pages of the letter include sketches of sights in Minnesota. The monogram, in blue, consists of the superimposed initials JRC (for Janet Ralston Chase) with a lion similar to the one on Kate's letter of July 2. *Courtesy of the Library of Congress.*

Frontenac
July 21st 1868

My own dear Father

I am on fire with
Minnesota — We have just returned from a
most perfect trip to St Paul and vicinity,
I say perfect because my enjoyment of it was
without a drawback. Do you know I think
that I have inherited a soupçon of the old
pioneer spirit, for when I feel myself beyond
civilization, a kind of wild delight comes over
me, my Indian wakes and gives a war whoop.
Do you remember Burnet McLean? a son of the
Generals, he went with us on our expedition
and was a great comfort to me, for he is even
more venturesome than I am, and Jep is rather
lazy — Lazy, but so good natured and thoughtful.
Flo hef and Minnie stayed in the inn, and
Burnet and I tramped and explored to my
hearts content — St Paul is an exceedingly

My own dearest Perceval

I have not written for the few last days, but think you should be satisfied with the twelve pages I send. I will also send you a sketch of my yesterdays employment. I rode eight miles from home to see them catching beeves. Uncle George has two killed a week. I rode about eighteen miles yesterday which is doing pretty well.

No 1. is the striker, with his lasso around the horns of a large ox which has fallen down.

No 2. is Ben equiped for a hunt, as we expect to kill a deer on this on our way home.

No 3. represents George making desperate, but vain attempts to lasso an ox.

No 4. You may descrive as my prudent self getting out of harms way. Do not be alarmed at my proximity to a furious cow; it is intent on joining No 6 which you are to

On this page of an undated letter to her husband (not printed in this volume), Belle illustrated an episode of "catching beeves" while she and Nettie were visiting relatives in Texas during the winter of 1850–51. As Nettie did later in letters of her own (see that of April 30, 1871), Belle drew herself in the picture as one of the actors in the scene (in a bonnet, on horseback, in the upper left of the sketch). Belle here playfully addressed her husband as "Perceval." *Courtesy of the Historical Society of Pennsylvania.*

Henrietta Haines's school, where Kate was a boarding student from 1849 to 1854, was in New York City at No. 10 Gramercy Park South. The brownstone townhouse, three window bays wide, appears in the center of this tax assessment photo taken about 1940. Originally the building's roof line would not have had the slanted notch in the center—the cornice and top story reflect modifications by the artist Robert Henri, who had a studio and apartment here, 1909–29. *Courtesy New York City Municipal Archives.*

ESTHER INSTITUTE.

Kate and Nettie took classes at the Esther Institute, Lewis Heyl's school, during the Chases' residence in Columbus, Ohio, 1856–60. This picture is from William T. Martin's *History of Franklin County* (Columbus, 1858), facing p. 401.

FIFTH AVENUE.

As Nettie related in her letter of February 20, 1864, Mary Macaulay's students took regular walks along Fifth Avenue in Manhattan. This undated view looks south down the avenue from its intersection with 31st Street, which is where Nettie and a friend, with permission, diverted from the school's usual route one morning to call on the Vail family. *Courtesy of the Museum of the City of New York, Print Archives.*

Two sketches by Francis H. Schell, an artist affiliated with *Frank Leslie's Illustrated Newspaper*, depict a July 1861 visit to Fortress Monroe by an official party that included Kate and Nettie. Here, the figures at the far left, heading the procession, are Maj. Gen. Benjamin F. Butler and Secretary of War Simon Cameron. The Chase sisters are probably the woman in a dark dress and the girl in a light dress walking side-by-side in the second rank behind the carriage. *Courtesy of the Casemate Museum, Fort Monroe, Virginia.*

In this sketch of an artillery demonstration, Schell identified the woman in the right foreground, in a feathered hat and standing with her back to the viewer, as Kate. The girl to her left, turned to face her, is Nettie. *Courtesy of the Casemate Museum, Fort Monroe, Virginia.*

William Sprague, who married Kate in November 1863. *Courtesy of the Library of Congress.*

In this photo by Matthew Brady or an assistant, Kate visits Brig. Gen. John J. Abercrombie and his staff. In 1862–63, Abercrombie commanded a division of the Federal troops protecting Washington. *Courtesy of the National Archives.*

The community of former slaves at Hampton, Va., was photographed about six months before Nettie and her father visited the town in the spring of 1865. The ruins of the town's colonial-era church, mentioned by Chase in a letter to Kate, are in the tall trees visible in the right background of this picture. *Courtesy of the Library of Congress.*

discussions. Father's letters to Nettie during this period suggest that she too desired to be involved in his political life. He described one letter in which he wrote about his position vis-à-vis the upcoming presidential election as "a dish of politics" and declared that he would be "satisfied & pleased" if it fulfilled her desire for news.[12] Indeed both the girls acquired good understandings of the political machinations of the day, belying the historiographical rubric of nineteenth-century "true womanhood" that places women in the private sphere, primarily concerned with domestic matters. Too, these letters suggest that even traditional political history may be found within the so-called private sphere.

Kate and Nettie had good reason to be concerned with politics during the first half of 1864. Not only did the first six months of the year see a military stalemate in the war. Father's position in the cabinet became increasingly untenable. In January, Frank Blair made a speech charging Father with "profligate administration of the treasury Department," calling it "rank and fetid with fraud and corruption."[13] This combined with fallout from the "Pomeroy Circular," a pamphlet Father's unofficial presidential election committee had used to attack Lincoln, caused Father to offer his resignation in February. Lincoln refused to accept. In the coming months matters continued to deteriorate. Late in June, over a bitterly contested patronage appointment, Father again offered his resignation. The president surprised Father by writing him that they had "reached a point of mutual embarrassment in our official relation" and accepting the resignation on June 30.[14] Father became, with one stroke of Lincoln's pen, a private citizen.

In the meantime Father's worries for Kate's marital prospects quickly came to fruition. William and Kate had stretched the wedding trip into a honeymoon, traveling alone to Ohio to visit friends and family. A cousin wrote Father that Kate looked "so well and happy."[15] Days later the honeymoon ended. The couple returned to Washington, but soon after William returned to Rhode Island without his new wife. Kate stayed with Father through Christmas and New Year's, receiving only the most cursory letters from her husband. When Kate wrote him that her holidays were "a bitter disappointment," William admonished her for proving "an additional burden" to his already busy schedule.[16] The couple's early married years suggest that they had considerable difficulty sustaining the romance of courtship and living up to the ideals of companionate marriage.[17] Kate placed so much importance on her relationship with William that even Nettie's presence during the holidays did little to mitigate her deep unhappiness. William would prove unable to sustain the weight of Kate's expectations.

Nettie appears to be the bright spot in an otherwise troubled family milieu. She worked "faithfully" to make up the time she lost at school due to Kate's wedding and certainly pleased her father with her "sweet grace" and engaging writing style. "You are certainly the genius of the family for this sort of composition," he exalted of her letters. Nettie finished up at Macaulay's school with the spring term and spent the summer of 1864 with Kate in Rhode Island, where by all accounts they had a delightful time. That summer found Father traveling about New England visiting friends and fishing.[18] In September he and both daughters spent time in Providence and Narragansett with the Sprague family. William had purchased a large parcel of land with a farm house on it on the west side of Narragansett Bay, and that summer Kate initiated work on the residence that would eventually transform the modest dwelling into a four-story, sixty-eight-room mansard-style mansion called Canonchet.[19]

Not long after his reelection, Abraham Lincoln nominated Father to succeed the recently deceased Roger B. Taney as chief justice. The Senate promptly and unanimously confirmed the nomination, and Father joined the Supreme Court in mid-December 1864. The court was well into its term, and as he had never had a judicial position, he had to immerse himself in the cases coming up for argument and step into the role of presiding judge. He also had to adopt the court's calendar cycle, hearing cases in Washington through the winter months and preparing to go on circuit in the spring. Pregnancy took Kate out of the busy whirl of Washington's late-winter social season, but perhaps her father did not mind. In mid-March 1865, when William left Washington to take one of his sisters back to Rhode Island, Father wrote to his old friend Susan Walker, "Kate, Nettie & I compose the present family: quite the old triangle." Kate and Nettie went to Rhode Island themselves the latter part of that month, but they were back in Washington by mid-April. When there was a grand "illumination" of buildings in the capital one evening to celebrate the Confederate surrender at Appomattox, their father was too tired to go. Appropriately, the two sisters, who had been together in New York when the war began four years before, went out together to commemorate its end.[20]

1. Rothman, *Hands and Hearts,* 168–70; Ward, *Courtship, Love, and Marriage,* 110–11; Lamphier, *Kate Chase and William Sprague,* 62. Although historians have reported that Kate's "parure," the jewelry set, cost upward of $50,000, Irvin McDowell, who handled the transaction with Tiffany, reported to William that Kate's changes in the set, which allowed for the tiara to be worn also as a necklace and brooch, increased the cost of the set from $5,500 to $6,500. McDowell to William, Sept. 18, 1863 (Brown University Library); *Harper's Weekly,* Nov. 28, 1863; Niven, *Chase,* 343.

2. *New York Times,* Nov. 15, 1863; *Washington Evening Star,* Nov. 13, 1863; Lamphier, *Kate Chase and William Sprague,* 58–60.

3. C. W. Cambell to Father, Nov. 10, 11, 1863 (Chase Papers, LC); Burlingame and Ettlinger, *Inside Lincoln's White House,* 111.

4. *Washington Evening Star,* Nov. 14, 1863; Ward, *Courtship, Love, and Marriage,* 115–17.

5. Alice Skinner to Father, Nov. 22, 1863, and William to Father, Nov. 21, 1863 (Chase Papers, LC).

6. Phelps, *Kate Chase,* 142–43.

7. Mary gave birth to a boy, whom her sister refused to adopt. Mary and William's affair would reignite in later years. Lamphier, *Kate Chase and William Sprague,* 34–35; Phelps, *Kate Chase,* 300–304; Mary Viall Anderson, *The Merchant's Wife, or He Blundered: A Political Romance of Our Own Day* (Boston: privately printed, 1876), 21, 29.

8. William to Father, Nov. 4, 1863, in the previous chapter.

9. Father to Kate, Nov. 18, 1863, below.

10. William to Kate, June 15, 1863 (Brown University Library).

11. William to Kate, July 22, 1863 (Brown University Library).

12. Father to Nettie, Mar. 15, 1864, below.

13. *Congressional Globe,* 38th Cong., 1st sess., 1864, app., 50–51.

14. *Chase Papers,* 4:409–11; Niven, *Chase,* 346–66.

15. Jane Auld to Father, Dec. 7, 1863 (Chase Papers, HSP.).

16. Kate to William, Dec. 29, and William to Kate, Dec. 31, 1863 (Brown University Library).

17. Lamphier, *Kate Chase and William Sprague,* chap. 3. For more on companionate marriage, see Carl Degler, *At Odds: Women and the Family in America from the Revolution to the Present* (New York: Oxford University Press, 1980); Steven Mintz and Susan Kellog, *Domestic Revolution: A Social History of American Family Life* (New York: Free Press, 1988); Jabour, *Marriage in the Early Republic.*

18. Father to Nettie, Nov. 28, 1863, and May 5, 1864, both printed in this chapter; *Chase Papers,* 1:479–86.

19. *Narragansett Times,* Oct. 15, 1909; *Providence Daily Journal,* Oct. 12, 1901; *Chase Papers,* 1:587; Lamphier, *Kate Chase and William Sprague,* 79–80.

20. *Chase Papers,* 1:xli–xliii, 522, 528; 4:445–46; 5:14; Father to Kate, Mar. 28, 1865, below.

FATHER TO KATE

Washington, Nov. 18, 1863.

My darling child,

Your letter—so full of sweet words and good thoughts—came yesterday and I need not tell you how welcome it was.

I rejoice greatly in all your happiness, & fervently pray that it may be continued to you. But I rejoice with trembling. Few lives are so unclouded as yours has been hitherto; and I fear the dark days. But you are beginning right; and there is one infallible security against unhappiness. I thank God that He puts it into your heart to take shelter under this security. "The fear of the Lord is a strong tower; the righteous man runneth into it & is safe." I don't know that I quote the precise words; but I preserve the idea.[1] It is this that trust in God, proved by conformity to His will, is a sure defence against all the ills of life. The same idea was expressed by the great Roman Orator when he said that "no ill can befall a good man."[2] He meant that the man who conforms his life to the principles of rectitude is in harmony with the everlasting laws and therefore cannot miscarry. But who can conform his life to the unvarying rule of rectitude? Who does? Here the Christian faith comes in to save us from despair. For perfect conformity it substitutes repentance and faith—repentance which is unfeigned sorrow for transgression, proved by steadfast endeavors to keep the law & faith, which is trust in God &

His appointed Salvation through Christ, proved by constant endeavors towards conformity & tranquil reliance on His merits instead of our own.

Dear Katie, I desire nothing so much for you and your beloved husband as that you may be Christians in heart & life. Then though sickness & misfortune may come, and death must come, you will indeed be safe: and many will be blessed through you. No duty will be neglected belonging to your station nor any work appropriate to it omitted. But duty will be made easy by the spirit of its performance and the work lifted out of its grosser material character, by the nobleness of the motives which prompt the doing of it.

Things are going on very nicely at the house. Marshall[3] & Richard seem to be doing their best and Eliza is beginning to take on housekeeping ways: while Claire is pleasant and ornamental.[4] Wilson has not yet gone; but I shall send him off tomorrow. I hate to do so: but see no alternative.

The President, with all the "Heads" except Mr. Stanton & myself go to Gettysburgh today. I should like to go; but cannot leave my work. The Report is hardly begun, and I must finish, if possible, before Congress comes together.[5]

I shall send with this a short letter to the Governor, and so send no special Messages to him: but warm love for him, & for dear Nettie and Allie.

Please remember that Dudley Walbridge is at the Custom House & get Mr. Barney to have him come to see you. Try also to see John Wallace & the Bakers.[6]

Your very Affectionate father
S P Chase

Mrs Kate Sprague

P.S. I enclose a bill and a check for $50. Please pay all little bills made prior to your marriage; and have the large ones made out & sent to me at once or as early as practicable. The Governor as a good business man will approve of this I am sure.

Private collection, 1987 (*Chase Papers*, 4:191–92).

1. In Proverbs 18:10, the passage reads: "The name of the Lord is a strong tower: the righteous runneth into it, and is safe."
2. Cicero, who got the sentiment from Socrates and Plato, said in his *Tuscalan Disputations* that "no evil can befall any good man either in life or in death nor will his welfare ever be neglected by the immortal gods." *Chase Papers*, 4:192; A. E. Douglas, ed. and trans., *Cicero: Tuscalan Disputations* (Chicago: Warminster, Wiltshire, Aris & Phillips, 1985), 75; B. Jowett, ed. and trans., *The Dialogues of Plato*, 4th ed., 4 vols. (London: Clarendon Press, 1953), 366.
3. Marshall's full name remains unknown, but he was a member of the Chase-Sprague household staff for several years. *Chase Papers*, 1:503; Father to Nettie, Nov. 27, 1866, and Father to Kate, Sept. 29, 1868, both in this volume.
4. Eliza Whipple and Claire Albrecht, a Chase family friend. Albrecht, who was born in Switzerland, worked in the Treasury counting U.S. notes and postal currency. She later

married Charles Manning Walker, an Ohio native who was a Treasury clerk in 1861–62, then one of the Treasury auditors until 1869, as well as a historian and journalist. *Chase Papers*, 1:499–501; 4:68–69; *Appletons'*, 6:325–36; Coyle, *Ohio Authors*, 664.

5. Father was busy with the *Report of the Secretary of Treasury on the State of Finances for the Year ending June 30, 1863*. Lincoln's train arrived in Gettysburg the evening Father wrote this letter. The next day at the battlefield dedication ceremony the president delivered his now-famous Gettysburg Address. Garry Wills, *Lincoln at Gettysburg: The Words That Remade America* (New York: Simon & Schuster, 1992), 24–26; *Congressional Globe*, 38th Cong., 1st sess., 1863, House Exec. Doc. 3.

6. Dudley was Kate's cousin, a son of Helen Chase Walbridge of Toledo. Wallace may have been John William Wallace, the reporter of Supreme Court cases, 1863–75, but there were several people named John Wallace in New York City at the time. The Bakers were the family of Jacob S. Baker, the deceased husband of John Garniss's sister. *Chase Papers*, 4:193; Wilson, *Trow's New York City Directory, For . . . 1864*, 895.

FATHER TO WILLIAM SPRAGUE

Washington, November 18, 1863.

My dear Governor,

I was delighted by your subscribing yourself "son" and said in my heart "God bless him for this sign of Affection." It makes me feel stronger to have you to lean upon & confide in; and, though somehow it seems too familiar to call myself "father," believe me I cherish all affection of one from you. If I live to grow much older I am afraid I may somehow become foolish in my fondness for you and yours.

My whole time now must be devoted to my report and I shall write briefly therefore.

Nothing here is specially important. The President goes to Gettysburgh today and I should like to go with him; but yield inclination to the obligation to remain & work.

From Tennessee I hear that Burnside has had a smart fight with Longstreet & has fallen back to Knoxville. He reports his men in good spirits and expects to hold the place. The enemy is between him & Grant which Gives Grant an opportunity of putting himself between Longstreet & Bragg, an opportunity he will not be apt to miss.[1] Foster has gone to take command in Burnsides place; which I hope will prove a good change; though I cannot say that my *impressions,*—I have no opinions—of Foster are exactly such as I would like to have.[2]

In our immediate front there is no change—nor elsewhere—save that Butler is infusing some administrative activity into his department. I do not know that he will have force enough to accomplish any thing in a military way.

There is, I see, to be a War democratic Convention at Chicago. If my name is to be brought forward in connexion with the next canvass it will be useful to look to the character of this Convention. If you could send for Dickinson to meet you in New York—or get him to join you at

Binghamton & travel with you to or towards Cleveland, you can easily ascertain his drift. I shall write him arguing some ideas about a platform[3]—See any others you conveniently can.

Faithfully & Most Affectionately
S P Chase

Hon Wm Sprague.

Letterpress copy. Historical Society of Pennsylvania.

1. In November, Confederate general Braxton Bragg sent a corps under James Longstreet to take on Maj. Gen. Ambrose Burnside, who had taken Knoxville, Tenn., in September. Burnside, like William Sprague, was a Rhode Islander. Longstreet besieged Knoxville throughout November, only to be repulsed by early December. Longstreet's absence cost Bragg one quarter of the strength of his Army of Tennessee, and Ulysses S. Grant, who had replaced Rosecrans in command of the Army of the Cumberland, took advantage of that weakness to launch a successful campaign against Chattanooga. McPherson, *Battle Cry of Freedom,* 670–81; Denney, *Civil War Years,* 322, 338, 341, 343–46, 350.

2. On November 11, Benjamin F. Butler succeeded Maj. Gen. John G. Foster in command of the Department of Virginia and North Carolina. Foster in turn succeeded Burnside as commander of the Department of the Ohio at Knoxville. Foster was soon relieved of those duties because of injuries. Denney, *Civil War Years,* 340, 351; *DAB,* 6: 549–50.

3. "War Democrats" supported the prosecution of the war against the seceding states and on that subject allied themselves with Republicans. "Peace Democrats" were willing to negotiate a settlement with the Confederacy. Although he thought it was "not exactly proper" for a leading Republican to offer suggestions to the other party, Father did write to Daniel Stevens Dickinson, a Democrat from Binghamton, N.Y., about the November 25 convention. Father thought the platform should include a pledge of support for Southerners loyal to the Union and a renunciation of slavery. Dickinson and Father had been in the Senate together, and during the Civil War Father considered Dickinson to be a reliable Democrat. Dickinson was one of the people who thought that Father should be preferred over Lincoln in the 1864 presidential election, and Dickinson hoped to attain the vice-presidential nomination himself. Father to Dickinson, Nov. 18, 1863 (Daniel S. Dickinson Papers, Newberry Library, Chicago); McPherson, *Battle Cry of Freedom,* 506; *ANB,* 6:560–61; *Chase Papers,* 2:241, 356; 4:255, 256, 284–85, 414, 416.

FATHER TO NETTIE

Washington, Nov. 18, 1863.

My darling Nettie,

You will be at school on Monday and I shall be really glad of it. Not that I am not glad, also, that you have had so much enjoyment; but because I am so sensible of the importance of all your time to you.

Your letters have come and I am much pleased with your writing them. I do not know what time, "before breakfast" was exactly; but take it for granted that writing at that time implies some degree of early work.

But do take more care of your handwriting, your punctuation & your spelling. Unless you now acquire good habits in these respects you never will: and the mortification you will suffer and will occasion to your friends will be very great. I wish you would constantly discipline yourself in these particulars.

Your Affectionate father
S P Chase

Miss Nettie Chase

Letterpress copy. Historical Society of Pennsylvania.

FATHER TO NETTIE

Washington, Nov. 23, 1863

My darling Nettie,

I send back your letter with some corrections. I hope you will find time to copy it and return it to me, together with the corrected letter, that I may see whether you understand the corrections I make.

You ought always to have a book about composition, including punctuation, together with a dictionary at your side, until by practice you become perfect in spelling and writing. You may think, I lay too much stress on these matters: but I do not: and some time hereafter you will be convinced of it, by painful mortifications, if you do not now correct your faults.

Your great defect is in heedlessness and it pains me more than I can well tell you. It will cost you an effort and a continued effort to amend. Have you the courage and the conscience to make it? Let your letters show.

I am very glad you have enjoyed yourself so much. It would have suited me better, had you, yourself, showed your sense of the value of your time & insisted on going back to school. Today I think you would have been happier had you done so. But I was not willing even to seem harsh to you: especially when all united in desires that you should go. Of course I did not doubt what was *pleasantest* for *the week to come;* though I preferred for you the more self denying & beneficial course.

It is over now and I rejoice in your rejoicing for all the pleasure you can have, if innocent, is pleasure to me.

It pleases me also to read your resolutions of improvement. May God help you to keep them.

If you determine to come home for the holidays instead of making up lost time by remaining in New York—(if indeed Mrs Macaulay thinks you can thus make up lost time—) I will very gladly invite Minnie Vail to accompany you. It seems to me however that you are so breaking up the first half of your year that it will be of little benefit to you.

Your affectionate father
S P Chase

Miss Nettie Chase

Letterpress copy. Historical Society of Pennsylvania.

FATHER TO NETTIE

Washington, Nov. 28, 1863.

My darling Nettie,

You wish I would write you one letter of praise. Well, I will try. There are plenty of things to admire and love in you: and it is not because I am insensible to them that my letters have so much criticism in them. There is no one who feels so deep an interest in your welfare as I do and I am naturally prone to think most of those things which most endanger it. This is the reason, why I generally leave the more pleasing office of commendation to others, and take the less agreeable part of pointing out errors & faults to be corrected. What I write however I hope is not *always* in censure, though it is oftener doubtless than you like. Still if you would only make up *your mind to like it,* you would find it most useful.

However I have promised this time to write in praise.

So I will begin by commending your last letter. The sweet grace with which you took my correction of your last letter and the patience with which you wrote it over again is admirable. The letter you sent with your rewritten copy is also marked by a decided improvement. The handwriting is very good and the spelling quite faultless. The style too is very agreeable. Indeed all your letters lately have been so pleasing in this respect that I have only regretted they were so short. We all laughed heartily over your account of James' sentimental speeches.

Your letter has quite convinced me that you should come home at the holidays. I could not think of your staying at New York with almost all the girls and Mrs Macaulay too away and especially after labouring so faithfully to make up lost time. So we shall expect you and Minnie Vail with you, or, if she will not come, any other of your young friends you may select.

It is really very praiseworthy in you to go to work so much in earnest to make up what you have lost. I hope,—indeed I feel quite sure— you will succeed perfectly; and what a satisfaction that will be to Mrs Macaulay, to me, to sister, to all who love you.

Everybody here is rejoicing over the great victory at Chattanooga.[1] I have just been reading a telegram from Gen Meigs—sent to me from the War Department—giving a full account of the three days fighting, and its grand results.[2] I suppose you will see it all in the papers; but I meant to send you the telegram itself; but Aunt Eliza[3] wanted it to send home to Hannah & I could not deny her.

Aunt Eliza received a letter today from Mrs Lander who said she was at Mrs Sprague's reception in Providence and that you filled your new part of Miss Chase, charmingly. And we hear nothing but good of you from every one.

There, darling, have I not kept my promise. May our Heavenly Father bless you and make you understand that there is a grace, which adds charm to all other graces,—that comes down from Heaven & lifts those to whom God gives it—and He gives to all freely & withholds from none who sincerely ask—to Heaven. May that Christian grace be yours.

Your affectionate father

S P Chase

Letterpress copy. Historical Society of Pennsylvania.

1. On November 25, the Army of the Cumberland, with the corps sent in its support from the Army of the Potomac earlier in the fall, broke the siege at Chattanooga by defeating the Confederacy's Army of Tennessee. McPherson, *Ordeal by Fire,* 338–42; Denney, *Civil War Years,* 344–45.

2. Quartermaster General Montgomery C. Meigs had gone to Tennessee to supervise the establishment of supply lines for the army. He kept a journal of his experiences, as well as sending dispatches to Washington. He sent a report to the secretary of war dated November 26 about the Chattanooga victory that the *New York Times* published on the twenty-ninth. Russell F. Weigley, *Quartermaster General of the Union Army: A Biography of M. C. Meigs* (New York: Columbia University Press, 1959), 289–91; *Chase Papers,* 4:171, 174, 207.

3. Eliza C. Whipple, who like her sister Hannah Whipple Tucker was actually Nettie's cousin.

WILLIAM SPRAGUE TO FATHER

Cincinnati Dec 2. 1863

My dear Governor.

Your letter to me of the 26th. has been the only one which has reached us since we left New York.[1] Katie became anxious for intelligence from her father & I turned over to her the ever welcome hand, and waited my turn for the share which fell to me. I am delighted that you see brighter future for us, as I have known that you trembled a little, for that which was yet a solution of that which was to come. We are happy. We feel we have it upon a foundation which will not give way. With God on our side, and the ever watchful eye & council of one so dearly loved we share with you, in feeling that misfortune can never come, tho trials may. I am glad you speak so of Katies anxirity for your future, & I am doubly glad to have you speak of your connections with Mr Lincoln. could that paragraph find its way into print as from you, it would destroy the effect of the whole bitter work, of Seward, Blair[2] Lincoln & Co attack upon you. We have both taken colds. I am quite over mine. Katie holds to hers, but will relinquish it later. You know she is very tenacious of every thing

Faithfully & affectionately your son.

W Sprague

Gov Chase

Library of Congress.

1. The hotel at which the wedding party was staying caught fire twice in one night, causing the group to cut short their visit to New York. They went on to Providence, where they stayed for one week. Then, finally alone, Kate and William left for Ohio. On November 26,

Father wrote William about his happiness for the marriage, though he worried that the new couple might have "some inequalities of temper." He also discussed the coming election, his relationship with the president, and William's imminent purchase of the house at 6th and E. Belden and Belden, *So Fell the Angels*, 97–99; *New York Times*, Nov. 19, 1863; *Chase Papers*, 4:204–5.

2. The eldest son of Francis Preston Blair Sr., Montgomery Blair functioned as the U.S. postmaster general in Lincoln's cabinet. In an October 3 speech he attacked radical Republicans, most notably Father. Montgomery and his brother Frank (Francis P. Blair Jr.), a congressman, vociferously opposed Father's candidacy for the upcoming presidential election. Montgomery Blair was the only cabinet member who did not attend Kate's and William's wedding. Niven, *Chase*, 335, 347; William E. Smith, *The Francis Preston Blair Family in Politics* (New York: Macmillan Co., 1933), 2:237–40; *DAB*, 2:339–40.

FATHER TO NETTIE

Washington Jany 29, 1864

My darling Nettie,

I have been quite unfatherly in neglecting to write you so long. I will try to do better.

Enclosed with this is a check for ninety dollars your quarterly allowance for the winter.

You will remember that you are to have that sum every spring, summer, fall & winter & make it pay all your expences excepting Mrs Macaulays bills, which are to include nothing but board, tuition & books.[1]

I hope you will make it go as far as possible & save a good deal for the poor.

Your affectionate father
S P Chase

As to skates & skating Mrs Macaulay knows best. You can do whatever she approves.

Letterpress copy. Historical Society of Pennsylvania.

1. Under Father's agreement with Mary Macaulay, he sent $90 per quarter for Nettie's expenses. Macaulay charged $250 per quarter for tuition. Books, which cost $1 to $3 apiece, totaled less than $20 each quarter. Mary Macaulay to Father, Feb. 9, Sept. 24, 1864 (Chase Papers, LC).

NETTIE TO KATE

New York
Feb 15th. 1864

My own darling.[1]

There is an old scotch woman here, who comes every other Saturday to mend my clothes, which pleasant duty she fills to perfection.

She has a great admiration for you; and every time she sees me, it is. "Weel Mees Chase hows yes bonnie Sister." She read of your marriage in the papers, and found it very interesting, and wanted to know if you were much in *love,* "as to the husband," she said, "I need na ask" She is a funny old soul, as she speaks of you I mentally exclaim in that time honored quotation, "thems my sentiments.

I was at Minnie's for lunch to day, after which Minnie Mary and myself went to church,[2] as it is lent, It always seems so strange, to go into church on a week day, all is so quiet, so different from the noisy bustle, without. I think one always realizes so much more the solemnity of the church, when taking a moment from the week day's pleasures.

In returning, we met Pauline Hecksher she looked as pretty, and fresh, as possible / Georgie you know is to be married in the Spring.[3]

It seems it is the fashion nowadays. Alas! Alas! why does not some one ask *me*—, Looking into the future I see old maidism and forty cats before me—

I must turn from such subjects as I can not control my sensitive feelings.

The world is all hollow to me,

And my doll's stuffed with sawdust I see,

If your dress does become me,

I will enter among ye,

Oh nuns, quit the world & its cruelty

That terrible bell is ringing, and I must seek my downy couch (spoken *"sar caustically"* you know, as it is any thing but downy.) Really my bed is quite a study. there are hills and valleys, rolling slopes and steep declivities.

Mademoiselle threatens to bring my letter to a sudden tirmination. by turning the gas. So good bye dearest

Nettie.

Brown University Library.

1. A filing endorsement by Kate confirms that she was the receiver of this letter.

2. Mary Vail was Minnie Vail's sister and the daughter of Henry F. Vail. *Chase Papers,* 1:312; Nettie to Father, Feb. 20, 1864, below.

3. Pauline and Georgie were probably New York merchant Charles A. Heckscher's daughters. Heckscher occasionally handled Father's private investments. Father to Heckscher, June 28, July 5, Oct. 18, 1866 (Chase Papers, HSP); Wilson, *Trow's New York City Directory, For . . . 1864,* 386.

NETTIE TO FATHER

New York Feb 20th. 1864

Dearest Father.

The other day Lizzie Phipps, and I, made a raid on the residence of Mr Henry F Vail, at eight oclock in the morning;[1] thereby verifying the ancient saying, that "the early bird catches the worm" for we obtained a splendid breakfast. His house is near the corner of Fith Avenue, on which is our morning walk. On this particular morning, we had obtained permission to give a note, from Minnie, to her Sister, as the school passed the house, and to rejoin it on its return. It was bitter cold, and we found them at a hot breakfast. We did not require much urging, to share it for we had had our's an hour before, and they say a school girl's appetite is never satisfied, at all events I never enjoyed a breakfast more. Mr Vail piled up our plates, and as Miss Mary would speak, he would say, "Dont talk, dont talk, let the children eat," which we *did* We accomplished it all in seven minutes by the clock, and then went on our way rejoicing; but forgot the *note.*

I will tell you now of another visit I made lately, though it was not as agreable as the last, indeed I may say it was decidedly disagreable, for it was to the dentist's; and he halfed killed me. Mrs Macaulay places great trust in him, indeed he is one of her particular "hobbies"; and she rides him at every new scholar. Having had a severe toothache I resolved to try this wonder of the nineteenth century, and accordingly I presented myself before him last Tuesday. He invited me to remain two or three hours, which kind invitation I accepted. But how he did torture me! and when I suffered the most he would assure me with the softest voice, that "it did not hurt" I disagreed with him in that particular. I must say however that he filled my tooth beautifully—I have not been to the dentist's now for about eight months, and my teeth are in quite a bad condition. Would it not be better for me to go to Dr Gunning,[2] rather than take the time from my studies, to go to Philadelphia?

We had quite calamnity the other night, owing to the intense cold the gas was frozen in the pipes; and we were left in the dark. As the gas goes to every part of the house, there were no candles; however after much searching some were produced; and we converted cologne bottles into candlesticks. We told ghost stories until my hair almost stood on end like "quills of the fretful porcupine"[3] And at last I realized the horrow of going to bed in the dark.

Please tell Sister that I never enjoyed a letter more than her last; and give her much love,

Good night dear Father
Nettie

1. New Yorker Henry F. Vail was the cashier of New York's Bank of Commerce. The Vails lived at 7 West 31st Street. Henry Vail and John A. Stevens Sr., also of the Bank of Commerce, worked with Father on bond sales and the legalization of U.S. notes that assisted in underwriting the Union's war effort. *Chase Papers,* 1:312, 502; *New York Times,* June 3, 1865; Niven, *Chase,* 266–67.

2. Englishman Thomas Brian Gunning settled in New York in 1840. There he practiced dentistry and was an inventor, creating devices such as his 1861 hard rubber splints for fractured jaws. Rossiter Johnson, ed., *The Twentieth Century Biographical Dictionary of Notable Americans,* 10 vols. (Boston: Boston Biographical Society, 1904), vol. 4.

3. In Act 1, Scene 5, of *Hamlet,* the ghost of Hamlet's father says that he could tell a tale that would cause "each particular hair to stand on end / Like quills upon the fretful porcupine."

FATHER TO NETTIE

Washington Feb 2[6], 1864

My darling Nettie,

Your letters have wonderfully improved. The handwriting is good, the spelling almost perfect, and the style extremely agreeable. We are all delighted with them and each that comes has quite a run, as the book people say.

Katie will no doubt give you soon if she has not done so already a full account of the grand review and ball; the latter given by the officers of the 2d. Corps and the former of I know not what divisions of the Army of the Potomac. Miss Sprague & Josie Ludlow had never seen anything of the sort before; and they came back delighted.[1] For my part, when I thought of the suffering which exists throughout the land; of the dangerous condition of our finances; of the urgent necessity for the prosecution of the war, & the speediest possible suppression of the rebellion, I did not feel inclined to participate in such scenes. And yet why should I blame those who did? It is not worth while, under almost any circumstances, to refrain from all amusements; perhaps listlessness & discouragement would creep in and paralyze all action. There are a few earnest souls who seem willing to work without much other pleasure than that of their work and its results. But almost all men and almost all women must have a good deal of relaxation and recreation to keep them in condition to accomplish any thing. In this matter as in many things else the middle is best—Not too much work & not too much amusement and in all innocence & love to God and man.

Claire says she has written you two long letters in French and that you have not replied. Can't you make your exercises [contribute] [*illeg.*] [beautifi]cation by writing your french in the form of a letter. I hope you will and that you will keep up the practice. She will be delighted to receive such letters and Katie & I will be glad to read them. And you will find the exercise very improving. Indeed I suppose it is impossible to acquire any real mastery of french without writing it a good deal—Most talking by Americans in French is simply translating quite literally thoughts first conceived in English. The idioms cant be acquired in this way and without a pretty good knowledge and pretty familiar use of them one cant talk well in French. As soon as I can honorably leave the Treasury Department I want to do so; & then I may visit Europe & I shall want you for my interpreter & Secretary.[2] So qualify yourself thoroughly.

Have you ever read the French Translation from the Italian of Silvio Pellicos Treatise on Duties—*des devoirs*. If not I wish you would. The style is beautiful & the sentiments full of piety and devotion; and these things I desire to see in you above all things else.[3]

But here comes Schureman to barberize me and then breakfast—So I must close. Goodbye, darling, and never forget

Your affectionate father

S P Chase

Miss Nettie Chase.

Letterpress copy. Historical Society of Pennsylvania.

1. On February 22, Kate, William's sister Almira, and Josephine Ludlow, who was Nettie's aunt but only a couple of years older than Kate, attended the ball in Virginia. *Chase Papers*, 4:309.

2. Father never traveled to Europe.

3. Italian playwright and writer Silvio Pellico was jailed in the 1820s for nationalistic activities. His memoir of his imprisonment, *Le Mie Prigioni*, documented the reinvigoration of his faith and his reflections on duties to God. The book was very popular. Translated into French, it appeared in several editions as *Mes Prisons*, often with the subtitle *Des Devoirs des Hommes* ("of the duties of men"). Peter Hainsworth and David Robey, eds., *The Oxford Companion to Italian Literature* (Oxford: Oxford University Press, 2002), 108, 450, 483.

FATHER TO NETTIE

Washington, March 15, 1864

My darling Nettie,

You must never be ashamed of any thing you do when you do your best.

If you don't begin to write French you will never learn; and you can write to no one with more assurance of being set right kindly than to Claire. So don't fail to write if only a page & send your letter every week.

Your last letter to me is not quite so correct as your other letters have been of late. "Babarous" is not, and yet is—barbarous; & "conscious stricken" is not conscience stricken.

I am not in the habit of writing or expressing my opinions very freely: for on some points I am not certain they are correct and on others they differ so much from those most current, that I fear the expression of them may be ascribed to a wrong motive & to do harm rather than good.

But to you, my dear child, who, though in some respects a little too thoughtless & careless, are, in others, quite a woman in intelligence and judgment, I believe I will hereafter write more freely.

And, perhaps, I cannot interest you more than by telling you what I have just done about the Presidency and why I did it.

I have declined to be considered as a candidate for that office. A good many of the best and most earnest men of the country desired to make me a candidate; but I always felt that being so considered would greatly impair my usefulness as Secretary of the Treasury and subject me to attacks from the mere partizans of the President as a candidate for re-election against which I could not defend myself without neglect of duties more important to the country. There was so much dissent from this view and I was so unwilling to seem even to shrink from responsibilities which many insisted I ought to assume, that I allowed myself to be named. It was not long before my apprehensions were realized. The two Blairs assailed me indirectly & directly; the most ungenerous influences were used to injure me; my relations with the President were in danger of becoming unfriendly; and it was becoming daily more & more clear that the continuance of my name before the people would produce serious discords in the Union Organization and might endanger the success of the measures & the establishment of the principles I thought most indispensable to the welfare of the country.[1]

While things were in this condition a majority of the Union Members of our Legislature declared Mr. Lincoln to be the first choice of Ohio and her soldiers. I had already said that the wishes of our friends in Ohio would be controlling with me, and I gladly accepted this action of the Union Members as an indication of their wishes, & redeemed my promise by asking that no further consideration might be given to my name.[2]

I expect Mr. Lincoln will be nominated for relection and I expect to support him as I did in 1860 & for the same reason that he is presented by the majority of those with whom I act as the representative of the views and principles which I believe sound & important.

There, darling, is a dish of politics. I have almost hated to write it; but shall be satisfied & pleased if I have gratified you.

Your affectionate father
S P Chase

Miss Nettie Chase

Letterpress copy. Historical Society of Pennsylvania.

1. A group of Republican congressmen authorized an anti-Lincoln, pro-Chase manifesto called "The Next Presidential Election." One of the group, Senator Samuel C. Pomeroy, issued a public letter denouncing Lincoln and promoting Father for the Republican nomination. This "Pomeroy Circular" put Father in an awkward position with Lincoln, and their relationship became extremely strained. Late in September 1863, Frank Blair directly attacked Father in a speech in St. Louis. A week later his brother Montgomery followed suit, though his diatribe did not mention Father by name. In January, Frank attacked again, this time in a two-hour speech from the floor of the House of Representatives

accusing Father and the Treasury of corruption. Niven, *Chase,* 335, 347, 360–62; *Chase Papers,* 1:xxxviii–xxxix; Roy P. Basler, ed., *The Collected Works of Abraham Lincoln,* 9 vols. (New Brunswick, N.J.: Rutgers University Press, 1953–55), 7:212–13; *DAB,* 2:332–34; *Congressional Globe,* 38th Cong., 1st sess., 1863, app., 47–51.

2. In 1864, in an effort to attract War Democrats and Southern Unionists, the Republican Party began calling itself the National Union Party. Nonetheless, the party adopted a straight Republican platform. In the post–"Pomeroy Circular" negotiations, Lincoln deferred his acceptance or rejection of Father's offer to resign until he saw the returns from the Ohio Republican-Union convention. When the Ohio delegates overwhelmingly supported the president's renomination, Lincoln refused the resignation. McPherson, *Battle Cry of Freedom,* 716; Niven, *Chase,* 361–62.

FATHER TO NETTIE

Washington, May 5, 1864

My darling Nettie,

It is a shame that I should be so poor correspondent; but then remember how many more words I put on a paper than you do, and how little time I have for any thing but hard office work.

All your letters give great pleasure. You are certainly the genius of the family for this sort of composition. Every one of your letters is quoted and commented in a way that *must not* excite your Vanity. But really it is quite delightful to read your free & easy talk—just what letters should contain to be interesting.

Katie is almost herself again after her illness, which frightened me not a little. Her husband was all devotion & to be so petted it was almost worth while to be sick.[1] We have just been riding out under the hills which skirt the city on the north, across Rock Creek into Georgetown & back through that old town[2]

When I had written thus far the gentlemen I was waiting for, at my room in the Department came in & I went to work with them, and have had two hours or so of pretty busy writing & reading. It is now ten oclock and I am pretty tired—So I shall not write much more tonight.

I wish I were out of official harness. It constantly grows more irksome. I have toiled hard & patiently and it is painful to find my labors made the occasion of calumny & reviling. I am thankful, however, that no calumny or reviling can destroy any good I have accomplished. So, dear child, do good for the sake of doing it; not for reward or applause. Your Heavenly Father will see & bless you.

Your affectionate father
S P Chase

Miss Nettie Chase

Letterpress copy. Historical Society of Pennsylvania.

1. Kate and William were currently in Washington at 6th and E streets. The spring of 1864 was particularly cool and wet, and Kate had been troubled by colds and upper respi-

ratory ailments. In March, she spent some time at the McDowells' home in Buttermilk Falls, N.Y., attempting to recuperate under Helen McDowell's care. Father probably feared Kate's illness was a recurrence of her mother's tuberculosis. Belden and Belden, *So Fell the Angels*, 116–17, 122; Lamphier, *Kate Chase and William Sprague*, 73; *Daily Congressional Union*, Mar. 19, 1864.

2. When the city of Washington was first laid out as the national capital, Rock Creek was the boundary between it and the existing community of Georgetown. Green, *Washington*, 4.

FATHER TO NETTIE

Washington May 25, 1864

My darling Nettie,

Your description of your night alarm is capital and gives me a good laugh in the midst of my perplexities and troubles. But I must tell you that you are allowing your handwriting to degenerate, and that you are too careless about your "myselfs" and "howevers" putting them in, as it were, to fill up; and that though paper is dear I prefer on the whole to have you write on untorn sheets.

Sister received some days ago your pictorial-poetical success which ought to have been entitled "The neglected young Lady." It was very funny—

And now about what else shall I tell? In the first place we are all pretty well—very well for us—In the next place we take our meals—but nonsense.

Dear Bishop McIlvaine has been with us, and at the Army. He gives most interesting accounts of the wonderful work the Christian Commission is doing—There was never any thing like the self denial—the activity—the usefulness of these men. They seem to have the very spirit of Christ—a sort of Divinity in Manhood.[1] He left us day before yesterday & thinks of [*illeg.*] to Europe in July. Sister would like to go too, [*illeg.?*] [her][2] if the Governor *would* or *I could* go.

Have you seen the Ferry Boy yet? There is a good deal of truth in it, but some embellishment.[3]

And here I must stop—for I have ever so much work to do before I can go home to dinner.

Your affectionate father
S P Chase

I enclose a picture. I don't know whether you ever had one of these.

Letterpress copy. Historical Society of Pennsylvania.

1. Founded in 1861, the Christian Commission provided medical services similar to those of the Sanitary Commission, but with a more evangelical bent. Both organizations attracted thousands of female volunteers. McPherson, *Ordeal by Fire*, 386–87.

2. Father inserted this word or fragment above the line, probably with an unknown number of words preceding it that cannot be seen on the letterpress copy and are represented here by [*illeg.?*].

3. In early 1864, Father began a series of autobiographical letters to light fiction writer John Townsend Trowbridge, who was to write a biography of the prospective candidate. Trowbridge produced *The Ferry-Boy and the Financier,* which on its surface was aimed at a juvenile audience. It first appeared in the *Atlantic Monthly* in April and was published as a book by Walker, Wise and Co. of Boston. If the author intended to make further use of the biographical information he collected, that notion apparently collapsed with the failure of the movement to nominate Father for the presidency. Niven, *Chase,* 358–59; *DAB,* 18:655–56; *Chase Papers,* 1:xii, xxxviii, 611; 4:xvi, 263–66, 274, 277–78, and title page of *Ferry-Boy* illustrated between 234 and 235.

FATHER TO NETTIE

Washington July 5, 1864

My darling Nettie,

Your broadspaced, large lettered, scantworded, but after all really welcome letter arrived here today after what must have been a very fatiguing journey of seven days from Newport. After such hardships it was *as well as could be expected.* I am glad that you are enjoying yourself at Newport.[1] Remember in all your enjoyments, only, the duties of a young lady and a Christian.

Today my successor Mr. Fessenden took his seat.[2] I am heartily glad to be disconnected from the administration; though a little sorry to miss the opportunity of doing the great work I felt confident I could with God's blessing accomplish. I took Mr. F—— to the Department, explained to him as well as I could the situation of things; introduced him to all the Head of Bureaus &c: and, in short, did what I could to [show] not merely my personal regard for him, but that my interest in the public service and in the welfare of the country is as earnest as it would have been had I remained myself in office.

Give my best love to Sister. I do not know whether I shall go to Ohio before coming north or not. I shall determine in a week or two.[3]

Senator Sprague went to the front today. His little Speech of yesterday morning is much commended.[4]

I enclose one of the bills which I omitted from Katie's letter.

Miss Ransom's picture of me is quite a success.[5]

Your affectionate father
S P Chase

Miss Nettie Chase

Library of Congress.

1. Nettie was with Kate, who summered in Rhode Island. William had purchased several hundred acres near Narragansett Pier (or Narragansett Beach), on the west side of Narragansett Bay across from Newport. A ferry daily traversed the bay, and Kate occasionally took rooms at one of the resort hotels on the side of the bay near the new property.

Narragansett Times, Oct. 15, 1909; Sokoloff, *Kate Chase,* 105; Lamphier, *Kate Chase and William Sprague,* 79–80.

2. After battling with Lincoln about New York Custom House appointments, Father tendered his resignation on June 29, 1864. The next day the president accepted the resignation and offered the position to David Tod, former Union Party governor of Ohio. Tod declined, and Lincoln asked William Pitt Fessenden of Maine, Republican chairman of the Senate finance committee, 1861–64, who became secretary of the Treasury on July 1. *Chase Papers,* 1:295, 468–72; 4:409–11; *DAB,* 6:348–50.

3. After his resignation, Father spent two weeks familiarizing Fessenden with Treasury matters. He then spent the rest of the summer traveling in the Northeast, fishing with friends and visiting his daughters in Rhode Island. Niven, *Chase,* 369–70; *Chase Papers,* 1:479–502.

4. On July 4, the last day of the Senate session, William made a speech rebutting Francis P. Blair Jr.'s attack on Father of two and a half months earlier. Blair's charges had included an accusation that William stood to gain a huge profit from cotton he purchased under a permit granted by his father-in-law. Father had reviewed a draft of William's speech, which denied that the Rhode Islander had received any "special privileges." Buried in the bustle of the last day of business and coming five days after Father's resignation, the speech made little impression, although Charles Sumner assured Father that senators had listened "with breathless attention." *Congressional Globe,* 38th Cong., 1st sess., 1864, 34, pt. 4:3543; *Chase Papers,* 1:465, 475.

5. Artist Caroline L. Ormes Ransom was a native of Newark, Ohio. She graduated from Oberlin College; studied art in New York and Munich; painted in Sandusky, Ohio, from 1858 to 1860; and then had her studio in Washington, D.C. Born in 1838, she was a couple of years older than Kate and nine years older than Nettie. Ransom worked on Father's portrait in the summer of 1864. A year later he reported that she had made little progress on the picture and that it "don't impress me so favorably as then." The portrait, which depicts him standing in the south portico of the Treasury Building, with a white summer hat in his hand and with the Potomac River and the unfinished Washington Monument in the background, is illustrated in vol. 4 of the *Chase Papers* edition. Groce and Wallace, *Dictionary of Artists,* 524; *Chase Papers,* 1:583, and illustration facing 4:234.

FATHER TO KATE

Washington July 11, 1864.

My darling Katie,

Your good husband, I think, in his indignation against those who contrive evil against me, has magnified the trial of my resignation to me. I really have not felt it as such. I resigned because I thought I ought to resign and have seen no cause to change my opinion. Had I chosen I might have held on to the office and if I had valued it for its own sake I should have done so. But I valued it only as an opportunity for useful work & when that opportunity seemed gone because of the Presidents disposition toward me duty & honor alike required me to lay it down, unless he should be willing to make my position useful by giving me his entire confidence and the entire control, subject only to him, and not subject to any outside control, of the administration of my department. He was not willing, and that was the end. I do not know to what the

Governor refers; but he [doubtless] has heard something said or of something being said [which has] disturbed him more than it would me.

Let us all possess our souls in patience and remem[ber only] our duty to our country and the cause of our country.

I am very glad that you did not put your idea of coming here into execution. It would [done] no good at all, & exposed you very unnecessarily.

I am getting ready to leave for New York.[1] As I have already told you it is barely possible I may go to Europe. If I go it must be before long: within eight or ten days.

I propose to give up all connexion with the house: only leaving my books in the rooms they now occupy & retaining a right to come and see you when I please and occupy my old chamber. Perhaps I may want a little more definite arrangement than this: but, of course, I shall not wish to have things continue on the same footing as if I had remained in the Department. I shall leave every thing in the house except my books as yours—and except also a few small articles such as the little bust & such like; and I shall leave you to settle with Mr. Varnum concerning that portion of furniture which is hired.[2] If the Governor inclines to keep my horses & carriage I shall ask to have them set off against the rest accruing from his purchase of the house. So every thing will be settled without trouble: and when I come again & you take me in it will be as visitor or boarder at home.

I hope to see your husband today; but am not at all sanguine about it. If he does not come today I may go to New York tonight. If Mr. Fessenden telegraphs for me I shall certainly do so. At any rate I expect to be there before the end of the week and may possibly even see you before Sunday.[3] Love to darling Nettie[4]

Your affectionate father
S P Chase

Mrs Kate C. Sprague

If you think me wronged or not appreciated, let nobody *think* you *think* so. People never sympathize with such feelings.

Letterpress copy. Historical Society of Pennsylvania.

1. He left Washington "a private citizen" on July 13 and arrived in New York City two days later. *Chase Papers*, 1:479–81.

2. Joseph Bradley Varnum Jr., a New York attorney and politician, owned the house at 6th and E streets, N.W., in Washington until William bought it in late 1863. Varnum was also the former owner of the Chases' housekeeper, Cassie Vaudry. *Chase Papers*, 1:364; 4:106, 205; Dorothy S. Provine, *District of Columbia Free Negro Registers, 1821–1861*, 3 vols. (Bowie, Md.: Heritage Books, 1996), 3:613.

3. In New York City on Saturday, July 16, after seeing Jay Cooke, Henry F. Vail, and John A. Stevens Sr. and discussing political problems of Treasury appointments with William P. Fessenden, who was also in the city, Father had dinner with Kate and Nettie at the Astor House hotel on Broadway. That evening the three of them left for Newport. *Chase Papers*, 481–82.

4. Father apparently inserted this sentence after he wrote the complimentary closing.

KATE TO FATHER

Newport. July 26. 1864—

My dearest Father,

Your letter to me received yesterday, & the one to Nettie that came to-day, were very welcome, because they brought the assurance that you were well, & really enjoying your-self.[1] The very afternoon you left Mr. Larz Anderson, & his son the Colonel came to see you, & were quite disappointed to find you gone. They with Mrs. A, & several others are staying at the Ocean House.[2] Nettie & I think of going up this evening to call, & to see if the Ocean rivals the Fillmore in gaiety.[3]

The poor Governor spent most of the time he remained here in bed, & was not well enough to go to work when he left here yesterday morning, but he was very impatient to complete & arrive at a perfect understanding with Amasa about the Pier arrangements.[4] He really seems to look forward with a great deal of pleasure to establishing him-self there, & says he hopes you will consider it your summer home, where you will come & go just as it suits you. My husband, now that he is so unwell, seems to dread the idea of my leaving him & hopes on every account that the trip to Europe is abandoned for this summer. Indeed that feeling seems to be very strong among your friends that you will not leave the country at this time.[5] They seem to depend upon your aid for the coming Presidential Campaign. The Governor attended to your Bill, which was very large, but no more than all Hotels charge at present, & I made the calls. You left me no cards, but Nettie wrote some a very fair facimile of your autograph. I enclose one that you may see.[6] I must write to the Governor by this mail, & have but a few minutes. Nettie sends much love. She has achieved a few inches of me.

Affectionately your daughter
Kate C. S.

Library of Congress.

1. Father left Newport for Boston on July 22. Kate and Nettie remained in Rhode Island, joining others who gathered in Newport each summer for a season of yachting and dancing. *Chase Papers,* 1:482–83; Belden and Belden, *So Fell the Angels,* 130.

2. Larz Anderson of Cincinnati was the brother of Robert Anderson, who had escorted Kate and Nettie from New York to Washington after the fall of Fort Sumter. Larz Anderson's wife was the former Catherine Longworth. In the early 1830s, before she married Anderson and Father married Kitty Garniss, Father had socialized with Catherine, calling on her and her sister and writing poetry for her. *Chase Papers,* 1:56–57, 60–61, 72–73, 578, 581.

3. The Ocean House, the second Newport hotel by that name, opened its doors in 1845. Antoinette F. Downing and Vincent J. Scully, *The Architectural Heritage of Newport, Rhode Island, 1640–1915,* 2d ed. (New York: C. N. Potter, 1967), 118, 131–32, pl. 157.

4. That is, the property that William had purchased at Narragansett Pier.

5. As Father wrote to Nettie on February 26 (above), he had hoped to travel to Europe as soon as he could "honorably leave the Treasury Department." During July, following his

departure from the cabinet, he considered making a European trip with Kate and Nettie but gave up the plan. *Chase Papers*, 4:422.

6. Politics was by no means confined to the formal halls of government, and social calls could obviously serve an important political function. Calling cards were about three inches by two inches and either engraved or handwritten with the caller's name. Cards could be offered by visitors to household staff, who then determined if the resident was "at home" to the visitor. Cards could also be left when only servants were home as a way of signifying that a visit had been attempted. It was not improper for Kate to make calls and leave cards on her father's behalf, since it was presumed that a man might be too busy to make calls and it was common for a woman to leave her husband's card even if he did not accompany her on the visit. Allgor, *Parlor Politics*, 120–24; Kenneth L. Ames, *Death in the Dining Room and Other Tales of Victorian Culture* (Philadelphia: Temple University Press, 1992), 35–43, 247; C. Dallett Hemphill, *Bowing to Necessities: A History of Manners in America, 1620–1860* (New York: Oxford University Press, 1999), 152.

FATHER TO KATE

Cherry Hill,[1] Aug. 26, 1864

My darling Katie,

Your letter fills me with great concern for your health.[2] Is it not possible that you can join me at Concord next Monday & go with me to the White Mountains? I have consented to the excursion more in deference to the wishes of some friends than from inclination but must make it very short. I mean to return so as to be in Narragansett next Saturday at 1.24 P.M. according to Appleton's Guide. So whether you join me at Concord or not I hope to see you very soon.[3]

Meantime let me counsel you to take all the interest possible in the place. Imitate Aunt McLean's example. Go out among the workmen: see what is being done & why. Occasionally take a row: but do not exercise too violently. Open air; interest in common objects; cheerfulness; and an active life are the best medicines. Perhaps we may arrange the more extensive journey when I see you.

May God bless you & keep you, my precious one.

Your affectionate father
S P Chase

Mrs K. C. Sprague

Historical Society of Pennsylvania.

1. Cherry Hill was not far from Salem, Mass. Merchant and politician Richard Palmer Waters lived there. Father visited him July 28–29 and again August 19–27. *Chase Papers*, 1:484, 491–95.

2. Kate's cold or respiratory infection from the spring lingered on through the summer. She was still ill in September. Belden and Belden, *So Fell the Angels*, 135; Sokoloff, *Kate Chase*, 108; Father to Kate, Sept. 23, 1864 (Chase Papers, LC).

3. Traveling by train, Father left the Boston area for Concord, N.H., on Saturday, August 27. On the thirtieth he went to the White Mountains. Kate did not go with him but stayed in Rhode Island. On Friday, September 2, Father traveled to Boston and the next day took a train to Providence, where William met him. Together they took another train to Kingston, R.I., and then had a "dusty ride to Narragansett," which Father found to be

"delightful." *Appleton's Guide to the United States and Canada,* printed in New York by the William Reese Company, which revised and updated it each year, contained railway maps, plans of cities, and tables of railway and steamboat fares. *Chase Papers,* 1:497–99.

FATHER TO KATE

Washington, March 28, 1865.

My dearest Katie,

Mrs Goldsborough[1] came in just after you left to tell you that the person whom she recommended to you for housekeeper is in Baltimore but in such infirm health that she fears she will not be able to come to you: though possibly she would be competent to the duties at Chez Nous—or Merlac—or Melluna, or Sea-Pond, or "the Peir" & might find herself renovated completely.[2] She will doubtless come over to see you if you wish when you come back.

Mrs G—— went up to see the suit & commended it warmly. Mr. Phillip was delighted. She was his only visitor today.

She says that the Admiral will be much gratified by my company across the ocean: & that she and Lizzy are talking about going out to be near him as soon as he finds a suitable place.[3] I told her that if I should go I should expect her to take Nettie with her, to meet me in Europe. And she said that would be delightful. So much for so much.

Mrs Goldsboroughs call was the event of today, but not the only event.

The mirror came and was got into the parlor safely: it is splendid; but how extravagant! You must contract your ideas. It is not yet set up in its place: but leans gravely against the wall where it is to be.

Mr. Reid came in & eat shad with me, & told me of his well doing, & of his cane just sent him by a New Orleans friend, and made himself generally agreeable according to his wont. I took him round the Capitol & set him down at his office near Willards.[4]

Then I called at Mr Sherman's—but saw nobody. Mr. S—— was "out"; Mrs S—— indisposed; and the young ladies begged to be excused.[5] I got here and found to my disappointment that Mr. R. J. Walker had called & left his card. I should have so liked to see him.[6]

I forgot to mention that I went up to Judge Wayne's this morning: and had quite a pleasant call. I saw Mrs W—— and a couple of ladies who like myself were callers & the Judge: who was as kind & courteous as he always is.[7] He mentioned one very sad incident. A neice of his has just died at Savannah. She was a lady of large fortune; most respectably connected; who unfortunately took the secession fever. In the result she lost all she had & was absolutely reduced to set up a little shop,—or perhaps without a shop—to make & sell cakes & other small things for the bare means of sustenance. She could not endure the terrible reverse & died of a broken heart, as the Judge said. What a terrible sample of terrible afflictions & humiliations. "Let him that thinketh he standeth *take heed*—lest he fall."[8]

Love to Nettie—be *very* kind to her & very considerate for her. Let your *thought* supply her thoughtlessness.[9]

Goodbye darling. May God keep you & make you wholly his.

Your affectionate father
S P Chase

Mrs Kate C. Sprague[10]

Historical Society of Pennsylvania.

1. Elizabeth Gamble Wirt, one of William Wirt's four "uncommonly intelligent" daughters, had married naval officer Louis Malesherbes Goldsborough in 1831. In the late 1820s, Father taught Elizabeth's brothers, studied law under her father, and lived on the same block as the Wirt family in Washington. Of the Wirt daughters, Father liked Elizabeth the best. He admired her "richly cultivated mind" and "most amiable disposition," but also noticed her "bright raven locks" and "fine frank open brunette countenance." "She moves like a wind-borne thing over the earth," he confided to his journal in 1829. *Chase Papers,* 1:4–5, 337; 2:21, 23.

2. Kate and William had yet to pick a name for the property at Narragansett Pier. "Melluna" was still one of the possibilities in July 1865, at which time Father also referred to the property as "Sprague Farm." Another prospective name at that time was "Canonchet," the name that Kate and William decided to give the estate. Canonchet was the leader of the Narragansett Indians in King Philip's War in the 1670s. *Chase Papers,* 1:587; James D. Drake, *King Philip's War: Civil War in New England, 1675–1676* (Amherst, Mass.: University of Massachusetts Press, 1999), 131–32.

3. Louis M. Goldsborough was a rear admiral of the U.S. Navy. Earlier in the war he had commanded the North Atlantic Blockading Squadron along the Virginia-North Carolina coast. In 1865, he received command of the European Squadron, which was meant to deal with Confederate ships raiding on U.S. commerce. He and his wife had three children, including a daughter, Elizabeth Wirt Goldsborough—"Lizzie." *ANB,* 9:202–3; George A. Hanson, *Old Kent: The Eastern Shore of Maryland* (Baltimore: John P. Des Forges, 1876; repr., Baltimore: Regional Publishing Co., 1967), 291.

4. Willard's Hotel on Pennsylvania Avenue was a great political center during the Civil War, and many political leaders and military officers stayed there when they visited Washington. When Henry D. Cooke formed a horse-drawn streetcar corporation in the city in 1862, the first line the company opened was between Willard's Hotel and the Capitol building. Whitelaw Reid, who was born in Ohio in 1837, was a correspondent for Ohio newspapers and for the Western Associated Press during the war. He had strong Republican connections and received an appointment as librarian of the U.S. House of Representatives, 1863–66. He supported the failed movement to replace Lincoln with Father in the 1864 election. Reid became editor of the *New York Tribune* in 1872. *ANB,* 18:315–16; Goode, *Capital Losses,* 204–5; *Chase Papers,* 1:209, 325, 352, 365, 385, 402, 403, 531, 532; 3:68, 227, 228.

5. John Sherman of Ohio, the brother of Union general William Tecumseh Sherman, had been in the U.S. Senate since 1861. Sherman, a Republican and a political supporter of Father before the war, served as Father's crucial connection to the Senate Committee on Finance. He also participated in the effort to elect Father president in 1864. Sherman and Margaret Stewart married in 1848 and adopted one daughter. The "young ladies" at the Sherman house when Father called may have included one or more of General Sherman's four daughters. *ANB,* 19:813–15; *Chase Papers,* 1:xxxvi, xxxviii–xxxix, 257, 322, 680; 3:240–41, 376–77; 4:321–23; Theodore E. Burton, *John Sherman* (Boston: Houghton, Mifflin Co., 1906), 18–19.

6. In 1863–64, Robert J. Walker, former Democratic senator from Mississippi, secretary of the Treasury, and antislavery governor of Kansas Territory, traveled to Britain and Europe at Father's request to bolster the government's credit standing and promote bond sales. *ANB,* 22:511–13.

7. Andrew Jackson had appointed James Moore Wayne of Georgia to the Supreme Court in 1835. Wayne, who had a relatively undistinguished career as an associate justice, remained on the Supreme Court until his death in 1867. He and Mary Campbell had married in 1813. *ANB*, 22:828–29.

8. 1 Corinthians 10:12.

9. On March 15, when the Chases were all in Washington, Father wrote in his journal: "Nettie came in, greatly distressed by trouble with her sister—talked with her quietly & affectionately—hoped good from it—she is a dear but thoughtless child & as sensitive as she is thoughtless." *Chase Papers*, 1:522.

10. On the back of the last page of the letter Kate wrote: "*Please keep this for me.*"

CHRONOLOGY

May 1, 1865   By revenue steamer from Washington, D.C., Father and Nettie depart on a journey around the Southern coast; Kate, pregnant with her first child, is in Rhode Island

May 4–24, 1865   Father and Nettie visit the North Carolina coast (May 4–9), Charleston (May 11–13), Savannah (May 16–17), and Key West (May 23–24)

May 25–28, 1865   Father and Nettie see Havana, Matanzas, and other places in Cuba

June 2–12, 1865   Traveling through Key West again, they visit Mobile (June 2–3) and New Orleans (June 5–12)

June 13–22, 1865   They travel by river steamer up the Mississippi and Ohio rivers to Cincinnati

c. June 20, 1865   Kate's son Willie is born at Canonchet, Narragansett Beach, R.I.

June 30–July 3, 1865   Father and Nettie are in Cleveland

July 5–6, 1865   They travel by night steamer from New York City to Providence, R.I., and by train and carriage to join Kate at Canonchet

July 15–August 6, 1865   Father is in New Hampshire and Boston

mid-August 1865   Kate turns twenty-five; Father returns to Washington; Nettie remains with Kate in Rhode Island

September 19, 1865   Nettie's eighteenth birthday; Father goes to New York City

September 21, 1865   Father leaves for Buffalo, Cleveland, and Jay Cooke's retreat "Gibraltar" in the Lake Erie islands

October 11–12, 1865   Father returns to Washington

November 4, 1865   He leaves Washington for circuit court in Wilmington, Del.; Kate and Nettie are in the house at 6th and E streets, N.W., in Washington

CHAPTER 7

"So On We Went"

MAY – NOVEMBER 1865

As a child Nettie had often stayed with relatives while members of her immediate family traveled for one reason or another, but at the age of seventeen she accompanied her father on the most notable journey of his public life. While the two would travel together on other occasions, their loop around the defeated Confederacy in the spring of 1865 was a public event with an intended significance beyond that of any electioneering trip Father had made in earlier days.

Kate, pregnant with her first child, remained behind. Father had already anticipated that Nettie might go with him as an assistant should he travel to Europe (see his letter to her of February 26, 1864). She got some taste of that role on the Southern trip: as she later recalled, an agitated Gen. William Tecumseh Sherman drew her father into the cabin of the *Russia* for a private conversation at Morehead City, North Carolina, and "I followed, simply because I did not know where else to go."[1]

As the stay-at-home, Kate received descriptive letters from the travelers. In the spring of 1862, Father had written Nettie long, detailed narratives of his visit to Hampton and Norfolk with President Lincoln and Secretary of War Edwin Stanton, and his letters to Kate during his Southern tour performed the same dual purpose, capturing the scene for an absent daughter as well as documenting the journey for his own purposes.[2] He wrote Kate on May 2 that his letters to her would "serve as my diary" of the trip. In fact two of his surviving journals contain memoranda from the journey, but those entries are compressed notations made for his own information.[3] He likely thought of the "diary" provided by his letters to Kate as a different kind of record.

We have not found any of Nettie's correspondence from the trip or any of her sketches. She made candid drawings of members of the traveling party, including a sleeping Capt. James Merryman and "gentlemen struggling up a sandy hill" on the windy North Carolina coast, "eyes and ears and mouth full, hands clapped on hat to secure its tenure, and coat tails manifesting strong tendencies to secede bodily, while in the distance, small and indistinct, could be perceived the ambulance that could n't be made to go."[4] She retained the habit of sketching during her travels. Her letters of July 21, 1868, March 28, 1871, and April 30, 1871, later in this volume, contain examples of her drawings. In 1877 she wrote for *Scribner's* an account of a camping trip in the Maine woods with her husband and children, and apparently drew at least some of the pictures for it. One illustration in that article depicts her seated quietly in a canoe amidst a tangle of dead trees in an overflowed forest, pencil in hand and small sketchbook open on her lap.[5]

As Nettie later recalled, the ostensible reason for her father's journey south in 1865 was to visit parts of his Supreme Court circuit that had been cut off from federal judicial process. More important, as made plain by his comments to public figures both before and during the trip, was his desire to influence the president's Reconstruction policy, which Father urged should be founded on the extension of voting rights in the Southern states to African Americans. While cynical observers attributed his motivation to personal political ambition, he advocated his "thorough conviction that *universal suffrage* is essential to *thorough pacification*," expecting the combined elective franchise of loyal Southerners irrespective of race to counter any resurgence of prewar political tendencies.[6] He developed the idea of traveling to the defeated South before Lincoln's assassination in mid-April, which delayed his departure on the trip until the beginning of May. In the course of the journey he wrote seven letters to the new president, Andrew Johnson, as an on-the-scene report from the former Confederacy.[7]

William P. Mellen, an old friend whom Father had appointed as a special agent of the Treasury early in the war, was supervising special agent, at the top rank of the system developed to regulate trade in those portions of the South that fell under Federal control during the conflict. Secretary of the Treasury Hugh McCulloch authorized Mellen to visit the ports of the lately rebellious states, and Stanton ordered Federal commanders to assist the chief justice in his journey.[8] Under those official auspices, Father and Nettie traveled with Mellen on U.S. Revenue Service steamers as far as New Orleans, where military and civilian officials arranged for transportation up the Mississippi.

"A day or two" before the departure was all the notice Nettie had that she might go along. Although Father warned her that she could not bring a maid and would have "limited accommodations," she eagerly accepted, dismissing such inconveniences as, "under the circumstances, mere bagatelles."[9] In fact she was miserable much of the time from the terrible seasickness that had plagued her, as a child of three, on the Gulf of Mexico with her mother in 1850. Some other members of the party also suffered from the pitching of the revenue steamer, but not Nettie's father, who cheerfully cracked Latin-English puns about his fellow travelers' fate: "O *si sic omnes!*"[10]

They were attended on the journey by one "Marshall," evidently a male servant, known in their correspondence and in Father's journals by just the one name, and by William Joice, a Supreme Court messenger who was Father's personal attendant.[11] Four men, each with a different purpose on the trip, made up the rest of the traveling party. Mellen's son, William S. Mellen, acted as his father's assistant. Russell R. Lowell was a detective who had worked for the government. His function on the trip is mysterious—perhaps investigative, to assist Mellen, or protective, in the backwash of the conspiracy that had assassinated Lincoln, gravely wounded William Seward, and intended harm to others. Richard Fuller, a Baptist divine, born in South Carolina and transplanted to Baltimore, was in the process of undergoing a new kind of conversion, from pragmatic slave owner to pragmatic, if reluctant, apostle of a transformed political and social order. Whitelaw Reid, a clever Ohio journalist, had made a name for himself during the war writing under the pen name "Agate." Reid publicized the chief justice's visit along the margins of the recently vanquished Confederacy. Like Father, he kept a journal of the trip, and the following year he published his observations as a book, called *After the War.* Reid later became editor in chief of the *New York Tribune.*[12]

The first stop on the itinerary was Fortress Monroe at the end of the Virginia Peninsula, which had remained in Federal control through the course of the long conflict. Nettie and Kate had seen the fort in July 1861, and their father was in the area the following spring. From Fortress Monroe, Nettie, Father, and their party traveled by water south along the coast, stopping at Beaufort, North Carolina; Charleston, South Carolina; and Savannah, Georgia. They saw Fernandina, Florida, and the Sea Islands of South Carolina, Federal outposts during the war and sites of early attempts to transform plantation economy and society following the emancipation of the labor force. From Key West, the travelers steamed to Cuba, a side trip given some official purpose by a wish to see the Confederate raider *Stonewall* at Havana. Returning to Key West, they continued around the Gulf coast, stopping briefly at Mobile and for a week at New Orleans. They traveled up the Mississippi on a river steamer, and after a visit in Ohio, Father and Nettie returned east by rail, through New York to Rhode Island to see Kate and her new baby boy.

John Chipman Gray, the army's judge advocate in the Department of the South at Hilton Head, offered a disillusioned realist's assessment of the local effects of the chief justice's Southern journey. "It was sickening to see the packs of thieving villainous traders and officials come fawning round Judge Chase and talk about negro suffrage, when I knew they were lying," Gray wrote to a friend. "I believe in negro political equality myself, but I believe that I am one of a minority and that when the present pressure is relaxed, the majority will express itself and with some violence." Gray, who held a low opinion of carpetbaggers who owed their official positions to Father's former patronage as secretary of the Treasury, noted with regard to the African Americans of the Sea Islands: "The more I think of Judge Chase's visit here the more unbecoming and probably pernicious in its results it seems, for though moderate in his tone, particularly when compared with the men who generally talk to the negroes, he must have raised hopes that are doomed to disappointment." Father, who by the end of his Southern tour was disillusioned with Johnson's policies, still believed that suffrage for the formerly enslaved was essential to Reconstruction.[13]

In August, Nettie remained with Kate and her family in New England while Father, less than a year into his tenure as chief justice, returned to Washington, D.C. There, as indicated by the final letters in this chapter, he sorted out the routines of temporary solitude in the house at the corner of 6th and E streets, N.W., which also continued to serve as the residence of Kate, her husband William, and Nettie when they were in Washington.

Despite an intention to travel to Europe in the succeeding years, Father never crossed the Atlantic. Many of the people he spoke with on his Southern journey were federal officials or local politicians anxious about the future of the defeated Southern states and their own futures, but the trip in 1865 was his venture into an exotic world—his real introduction to a region and culture with which he had been engaged in a relationship of tension for most of his public career.

1. Janet Chase Hoyt, "Sherman and Chase: An Interview at Beaufort," *New York Tribune,* Feb. 22, 1891; *Chase Papers,* 1:538–39.

2. *Chase Papers,* 1:336–44; 3:185–88, 189–91, 193–98.

3. Ibid., 1:536–78.

4. Reid, *After the War,* 35–36; *Chase Papers,* 1:562.

5. Janet Chase Hoyt, "Babes in the Wood. Through Maine to Canada in a Birch-bark Canoe," *Scribner's Monthly* 14 (1877): 488–501, illus. 495.

6. *Chase Papers,* 1:531–34; 5:15–20, 52–56 (quotation 5:52); Simpson et al., *Advice after Appomattox,* 3–16; *New York Tribune,* Feb. 22, 1891.

7. Simpson et al., *Advice after Appomattox,* 17–38; Reid, *After the War,* 11.

8. *Chase Papers,* 1:533, 535.

9. *New York Tribune,* Feb. 22, 1891.

10. As he used the phrase in his journal on a day in 1862 when he felt himself fortunate not to have been pestered by callers at his office, it was "O si sic omnes dies!"—that is, "Oh, if all days were this way!" In his bilingual play on words it became, "Oh, everyone's seasick!" *Chase Papers,* 1:354, 537.

11. *Chase Papers,* 1:503, 535, 557, 558.

12. His manuscript journal of the trip is in the Reid Family Papers, LC.

13. Worthington Chauncey Ford, ed., *War Letters, 1862–1865, of John Chipman Gray and John Codman Ropes* (Boston: Houghton Mifflin Co., 1927), 490, 495, 502; see Father's comments to Charles Sumner, June 25, 1865, in *Chase Papers,* 5:55–56.

FATHER TO KATE

Northerner, May 2, 1865

My darling Katie

The jar of the boat dont allow a full display of the beauties of my penmanship; but you will probably think it nearly as good as common.

It was a beautiful night last night. After we left the Navy Yard we all went on deck. The air was a little chill but the stars were very bright; and we were all in good spirits. Capt. Henriques told us how narrow the channel was—how difficult the pilotage—as if I did not know all that. I had been aground just there in the Tiger, and so I let him know.[1] He seemed to think that if his pilot had been on her that accident would not have happened. "It takes a very careful pilot to get through safe"—he said "its a mere ditch." Then he left us—"us" meaning Nettie, Mr. Reid & myself. Just then a tow boat came along close to us, & I thought I noticed that our boat did not move. "We are aground" said I. "Oh no; said Mr. Reid we are moving;" but it was the tow boat "Seth Low" that was moving not we.[2] Then somebody rushed by us & went back with a fender one of those bags which are put down at the side of a vessel to prevent injury from another coming along side. Then came the hay boats,—lashed in pairs—a long string—grinding along one side as they followed their tow. At last they were all by & our boat was safe, but *fast* without *moving*. Only a little while however & she had worked herself off & we were on our way again. Then we went to the cabin & I beat Will Mellen three games at chequers,[3] & we tried to read & tried to talk without much success; and then we turned in. Nettie & I have a little cabin answering very much to that of the Wayanda: her part being curtained off very much I suppose as that is to be. Our berths were very comfortable & we both slept quite well. I was up this morng earlier than any body else except Mr. Lowell.[4] Nettie followed my example as soon as I left the cabin. When she made her appearance on deck she looked a little wrong & I asked her if she was well. "No:" she said "I felt quite sick when I got up, but I am better now." And to be sure she was brisk enough. When breakfast came, however, she had no appetite; but after we left the table Dr. Fuller took her some hard tack which she dispensed of with great relish:[5] and is now quite well. We had a very pleasant breakfast. Dr. Fuller asked a blessing; and then we all talked of great men & great things & little men & little things Nettie silent for a wonder! Poor child, she was thinking of seasickness & feeling a little of it.

The officers of the boat are gentlemen—two of them at least appointments of mine—and all our party disposed to make themselves as aggreeable as possible to each other.

We are now about two hours from Fortress Monroe. I will keep this open till we get there & perhaps add a postscript before mailing. Possibly you may get it before you leave Washington. You must keep it and all my letters for I mean they shall serve as my diary. Love warm & earnest to your dear husband; and may God bless you both.

Your affectionate father
S: P: Chase

We are approaching the Fort, and there is nothing more to add; so good bye.

Historical Society of Pennsylvania.

1. When Father left Washington for Philadelphia after resigning from the cabinet in July 1864, he traveled down the Potomac River and around to the head of Chesapeake Bay aboard the *Tiger,* a steamer of the Treasury's Revenue Cutter Service. *Chase Papers,* 1:480–81; Lytle and Holdcamper, *Merchant Steam Vessels,* 212.

2. The prosaic *Seth Low,* displacing 236 tons and driven by propeller, drew less water than the revenue cutter *Northerner,* a 319-ton sidewheeler built in 1864. Lytle and Hold-camper, *Merchant Steam Vessels,* 160, 197.

3. William S. Mellen, the son of Supervising Special Agent William P. Mellen. *Chase Papers,* 1:535.

4. A former deputy U.S. marshal and later a private detective in Rochester, N.Y., Russell R. Lowell had carried out investigative and other tasks for the Treasury Department during the Civil War. Father subsequently consulted him about a suspected theft, and in 1867 he helped manage the affairs of Father's aged maternal aunt. The following year he provided intelligence regarding Father's strength as a Democratic candidate. *Chase Papers,* 1:535, 637; Father to Lowell, Mar. 2, 4, 15, Apr. 20, Oct. 21, 1867, Father to Mary Eliza Chase, Mar. 16, 1867, Lowell to Father, June 15, 1868 (Chase Papers, LC).

5. Harvard-educated Richard Fuller, since 1847 the pastor of Baltimore's Seventh Baptist Church, had been born into a Beaufort, S.C., plantation family in 1804. Long a proponent of theological justifications for slaveholding, he continued to own slaves until the Civil War. Seemingly baffled to learn from Father in March 1862 that the Federal seizure of the Sea Islands had effectively emancipated his slaves, Fuller by April 1865 welcomed his own freedom from the responsibilities of slave owning and yielded a "qualified assent" to Father's advocacy of universal suffrage. Accompanying Father along the Southern coast that spring gave him an opportunity to see his former slaves in their new status. *Chase Papers,* 1:331, 526; *DAB,* 7:62–63.

FATHER TO KATE

Beaufort N.C. May 5, 1865.

My dear Katie,

I finished my last letter as we were approaching Fortress Monroe. It was about noon and a lovely day. The Perit,[1] a large steamer from up the James had just arrived, and was discharging her passengers—some hundreds of rebel prisoners from Lees Army. Some of our party talked with individuals among them. They [showed] the usual variety of tempers. Most of them, however, were thoroughly glad the war was over & that they were free from military duty. As usual they were ragged & dirty. A set of plantation negroes would not appear badly in comparison.

Among the gentlemen who came on board of our cutter was Major James the Quarter Master in charge of the Department, who was extremely civil.[2] On learning that we wished to visit the Freedmens Village at Hampton he sent for carriages—his own & another—and volunteered to accompany us. Nettie and I got into his double seated, one horse buggy, while the other gentlemen, Dr. Fuller, Mr. Reid, & the two Mr. Mellens followed in a two horse barouche. The Major knew every thing & proved a very pleasant as well as very intelligent companion. He had married a Miss Janney of Columbus whom you may remember. She is a daughter of John Janney a good friend of mine & a most worthy gentleman.[3] The Major is himself a Pennsylvanian but his connexion with Ohio & my Ohio friends made him ready to serve me.

We went out over the old road, passing the houses of John Tyler, Mallory and other residences of rebels now inhabited by better men or women.[4] The Mission School, under the auspices of the American Missionary Society is, I believe, established in the Tyler House & Dr. McClellan, the able & efficient Surgeon in charge of all the hospitals in the vicinity, occupies the Mallory House.[5] A drive of about an hour brought us to the principal school. It was built, after a plan suggested by Gen. Butler in the form of a cross, each of the four arms being of equal length with a large space at their intersection, somewhat thus ⚕ . The square in the centre or intersection was occupied by a raised platform on which was the table of the Superintendent & chairs for visitors or others. Standing on this platform we could keep a pretty good observation of the scholars dispersed in the four arms. Three of these were pretty fully occupied. One was not yet completed & the carpenters at work in it somewhat disturbed the school, or rather us the visitors.[6] The seats, the desks, the slides for slates & the other conveniences for the scholars were if not so elegant quite as complete as in any school I ever visit. In each arm rows of seats extended back to the farthest side leaving on each side a space to move up & down; occupied also by a series of moveable arrangements which could be shut up as it were against the wall or expanded in a series of little recitation squares with a monitor for each mounted on his stool, and as conscious of his importance as a corporal. Every thing was done in military order. For example when we went in the children were engaged in some lesson under the charge of the monitors. Mr. Raymond for that was the name of the Superintendent took his place with us on the platform. "Attention Monitors"! Every little darkey was on his feet in an instant. "Take!"—all hands extended, "Stools!" All hands grasped stools "Place!" Stools elevated "Stools!" Stools all put one side in their places. Then came "Attention! School!" & all the children are on their feet: "March!" and they all, under the lead of their respective monitors, marched in perfect order to their rows of seats & stood expectant; the rank & file behind their several seats & the monitors at the end of each row. Then came the orders in obedience to which they were all seated & took their slates preparatory to writing. The drill had in it something ludicrous; but it was plain that it secured great promptitude, without confusion, & was calculated to make the children themselves orderly & methodical. We heard one class read and they read very well. Dr. Fuller made them a short address. Some specimens of hand writing were shown & they were very good. Mr. Day the principal of the Mission School & several ladies connected with it were present & manifested much interest[7]

From this school we went to Hampton where Freedmens cottages have taken the place of the old aristocratic mansions—& in place of the old brick church where the first families worshipped of old there is a plain little chapel for Freedmens prayers & praise[8]

Returning we took leave of the kind Major & went up to Norfolk. General Gordon met us at the wharf & took us to his house and to the old entrenched camp through which we passed as we went to Norfolk three years ago—right glad to find it abandoned & undefended. I had a long talk with General Gordon about civil & military government & reorganization; taking good care to let him understand what part I thought the new made citizens must take in the latter.[9]

It was dark when we returned from Norfolk & got on board the Wayanda, which was lying in the Roads to receive us. Mr. Henriques, the commander & Mr Allen & Mr. OBrien the lieutenants had been very attentive & we were more than have[10] sorry to exchange the Northerner for the Wayanda: which we found in by no means so perfect condition as Mr. Harrington thought it. The after cabin however was very well arranged for myself & Nettie, and except the fear of seasickness we thought ourselves very well off.[11]

Capt Merryman did not think it best to go out that night; but, at daylight Tuesday Morning, the 2d. we were under way. The day was beautiful; but before breakfast time Nettie, (who by the way had lost her cloak & taken Ben Ludlow's military cape instead—we happened to meet him at Norfolk) was too sick to eat. Mr. Reid was in the same condition & young Mr. Mellen also.[12] The rest of us thus far remained very well. After breakfast however I felt some qualms which evidently had more connexion with the stomach than the conscience. But I did not get sick and could eat lunch & dinner with appetite which I felt it prudent to restrain. Poor Nettie however had a hard time. She got up very early & went on deck hoping to avoid the tiger: but she soon came down & took up her quarters on the floor & there remained all day, suffering greatly all the time & sometimes very much. At night she was better & came on deck for a while but when she came down would not take her berth. A nice mattress was arranged on the floor & she was made very comfortable & slept well. She was still sick in the morning & eat nothing till after we arrived here yesterday Morning. Then however she recovered at once. We had very pleasant weather around Cape Hatteras / The sky & air were all that could be desired: & but for the slight nausea I was as well as could be desired.

Early yesterday morning we arrived here. Poor Nettie could not be persuaded to get up until just before we came into the harbor: but we had hardly come to anchor before she was as bright as possible. Mr. Mellen & Dr. Fuller went over to Beaufort to take observations.[13] They had not been gone long before Capt West of the Navy, Who is stationed here came along side in his cutter & coming on board asked us to visit his vessel the Orletta. We complied nothing loth: and found her very nice though with rather contracted quarters. She is moored close along shore, so that a plank gangway reaches the beach. A few feet, two or three hundred perhaps from the water he has built a little frame of two rooms about ten by twelve each, in which he has established Mrs West, a handsome, sprightly, agreeable lady who received us with great kindness.[14] After a little talk with her we visited Fort Macon, one of our old fortifications seized by the order of the Gov. of N. Carolina before the state seceeded as the operation of inaugurating rebellion is facetiously called. A young Massachusetts officer, Lt. Hinckley, was in command: and as attentive as possible.[15] We saw where Burnsides' shells shattered the wall, & came so near exploding the magazine that the rebels thought it best to surrender.[16]

Returning to the boat we found our party who had been in Beaufort. They had seen some of the natives & had talked with them about the situation. One of them a Senator in the rebel Legislature, just returned, to his home which he left when our troops took possession, afterwards came to see me with the Clerk of the County Court[17] / They did not seem exactly to relish my suggestions about admitting the negroes to the ballot, & thought it wd. be better to let the Legislature (rebel [late] supposed Union now) assemble & call a Convention & bring the State back into the Union. They did not seem much surprised however when I told them that the Natl. Govt. could not consistently recognize any official body or individual who owed his position to rebel election or appt.; but must look directly to the people for reorganization. Our interview was pleasant. They [stayed] & lunched with us & then we started for Newberne.[18] *Love to Wm.*

Your affectionate father
S P Chase

Historical Society of Pennsylvania.

1. The *Thomas Perrit* was an infantry transport. *Chase Papers,* 5:35.

2. Col. William L. James, chief quartermaster of the Department of Virginia. *Chase Papers,* 1:536; *OR,* ser. 3, vol. 5:346.

3. From 1851 to 1865, John Jay Janney was secretary of the board of control of the Ohio State Bank. Before holding that office he had been assistant clerk of the state House of Representatives for four legislative terms and chief clerk in the office of the Ohio secretary of state. Raised as a Quaker and unhappy with the effects of slavery in his native Virginia, he had moved to Ohio as a young man during the 1830s. Having a limited education himself, he was a strong advocate of public education, libraries, antislavery, and temperance. Robson, *Biographical Encyclopædia,* 469–70; *Chase Papers,* 1:536.

4. John Tyler called his summer home near Hampton "Villa Margaret," after a vivacious sister-in-law. A strong supporter of Virginia's secession from the Union, the former president sat in the Provisional Congress of the Confederacy and then won election to the Confederate House of Representatives, but died in January 1862 before he could take his seat. Jefferson Davis had only accepted the resignation of Stephen Russell Mallory, the Confederate secretary of the navy, two days before Father wrote this letter. Following his confinement at Fort Lafayette in New York City from June 1865 to March 1866, Mallory returned to his home state of Florida to practice law. A U.S. senator from 1851 to 1861, his tenure in that body had overlapped with Father's term. Oliver Perry Chitwood, *John Tyler: Champion of the Old South* (New York: Russell & Russell, 1939), 387, 405, 419, 421, 457–65; *ANB,* 14:380; Long, *Civil War Day by Day,* 685.

5. A large Federal hospital had been established on the site of the former Chesapeake Female Institute (or College), which had been founded by a Baptist minister in 1854. After the war it became a government home for disabled soldiers. Ely McClellan, who had received his medical training at Jefferson Medical College, stayed in the army, gave particular study to cholera and problems of sanitation, and eventually achieved the rank of deputy surgeon general. Kelly and Burrage, *Dictionary of American Medical Biography,* 772; Lyon G. Tyler, comp., *History of Hampton and Elizabeth City County Virginia* (Hampton, Va.: Board of Supervisors of Elizabeth City County, 1922), 50, 52, 54; Reid, *After the War,* 14; *Chase Papers,* 5:35.

6. Whitelaw Reid described the school for the formerly enslaved children at Hampton as a "barn-like" building of "rough board" construction. Three wings of the cruciform structure were occupied by the approximately two hundred pupils in attendance that day. "The fourth," wrote Reid, "completing the cross, was designed for girls, and was yet unfinished. Down these three long halls were ranged row after row of cleanly-clad negro boys, from the ages of six and seven up to sixteen or seventeen." The students were taught by "convalescent soldiers from the hospitals, moving noiselessly about among the benches in their hospital slippers and cheap calico wrappers." Charles A. Raymond, the superintendent, was a military chaplain. Reid, *After the War,* 15, 16; *Chase Papers,* 1:536.

7. Reid also noted "the general adherence to military forms" at the school. For three and a half years Charles P. Day had taught African Americans at Hampton under the auspices of the American Missionary Association. Reid, *After the War,* 17; Ira Berlin, Steven F. Miller, Joseph P. Reidy, and Leslie S. Rowland, eds., *The Wartime Genesis of Free Labor: The Upper South,* ser. 1, vol. 2 of *Freedom: A Documentary History of Emancipation, 1861–1867* (Cambridge: Cambridge University Press, 1993), 217; Robert Francis Engs, *Freedom's First Generation: Black Hampton, Virginia, 1861–1890* (Philadelphia: University of Pennsylvania Press, 1979), 29, 33, 54.

8. After the Confederates torched Hampton and withdrew early in the Civil War, African American refugees built residences, some of which utilized the still-standing chimneys of substantial houses destroyed by the fire. St. John's Episcopal Church, the brick walls of which had survived the fire, had been one of the town's notable buildings. Engs, *Freedom's First Generation,* 10–11, 27–28, 34, 83.

9. Brevet Maj. Gen. of Volunteers George Henry Gordon, a West Point graduate and Harvard-trained lawyer, commanded the Eastern District of Virginia from March to June 1865. *DAB,* 7:421–22.

10. He apparently meant to write "half."

11. Of the revenue steamer *Wayanda,* at anchor in Hampton Roads off Fortress Monroe, Father jotted gruffly in his journal: "first impressions not agreeable." Reid described the craft, which would be the party's home and primary conveyance as far as New Orleans, as "a trim, beautifully-modeled, ocean-going propeller, carrying six guns, and manned with a capital crew." He detected, however, "not a little dismay at the straitened proportions of the cabin." George Harrington, who first obtained a position as a Treasury clerk during the administration of James K. Polk, had ascended the department's clerical ranks to become chief clerk and finally, from 1861 to 1865, assistant secretary. Later he was U.S. minister to Switzerland. Second Lt. S. Allen O'Brien was one of the officers of the *Northerner. Chase Papers,* 1:537, 5:35; Reid, *After the War,* 13, 21; *Nat. Cyc.,* 12:337.

12. The weather may have been fair, but Reid described "plunges fore and aft, and lurches from port to starboard" through heavy seas. James H. Merryman of the Revenue Cutter Service commanded the *Wayanda.* Reid, *After the War,* 21; *Chase Papers,* 1:427, 540.

13. During the war the U.S. Treasury's special agencies had taken on responsibility for captured and abandoned property and the leasing of plantations, as well as commerce, in areas wrested from Confederate control. *Chase Papers,* 3:xxiv; 4:75–76, 221, 227–29.

14. William C. West's vessel, a wooden mortar schooner, was actually called the *Arletta.* Mrs. West was a former Miss Jamison of Maryland. *Chase Papers,* 1:538.

15. First Lt. Wallace Hinckley of the 2d Massachusetts Heavy Artillery. Returns from U.S. Military Posts, 1800–1916, Records of the Office of the Adjutant General, Record Group 94, National Archives; Adjutant General's Office, *Official Army Register of the Volunteer Force of the United States Army for the Years 1861, '62, '63, '64, '65,* 8 vols. (Washington, D.C.: War Department, 1865–67), 1:132.

16. Fort Macon, a masonry fort on the Outer Banks that controlled access to Beaufort and Morehead City, was unoccupied by Federal troops when North Carolina soldiers

seized it on Apr. 15, 1861. John W. Ellis, who died in July of that year, was governor at the time. On Mar. 23, 1862, a Federal expeditionary force under Ambrose Burnside laid siege to the fort. After a personal appeal from Burnside to the commander failed to evoke a surrender, a punishing bombardment forced the capitulation of the post on April 25. William Marvel, *Burnside* (Chapel Hill, N.C.: University of North Carolina Press, 1991), 78–79, 86–87; Long, *Civil War Day by Day*, 60, 188, 204; *DAB*, 6:106–8.

17. The callers were Michael F. Arendell, who represented Carteret County in the state senate in the early 1850s and again from 1860 to the session of 1865–66, and James Rumley, longtime county clerk. Whitelaw Reid, who if less the politician than Father was more vivid in characterizing individuals, had little patience for Arendell: "A large, heavily and coarsely-built man, of unmistakable North Carolina origin, with the inevitable bilious look, ragged clothes and dirty shirt." Reid, *After the War*, 23; John L. Cheney Jr., *North Carolina Government, 1585–1979: A Narrative and Statistical History* (Raleigh, N.C.: North Carolina Department of the Secretary of State, 1981), 318, 319, 327, 329, 330, 332; *Chase Papers*, 1:538.

18. In a second letter dated Beaufort, May 5, Father described New Bern, N.C., and a conversation with Gen. William Tecumseh Sherman at Morehead City. Father to Kate, May 5, 1865 (Chase Papers, HSP); *Chase Papers*, 5:36–40.

FATHER TO KATE

Fernandina, May 20. 1865.

My dear Katie,

I wrote you from Savannah.[1] Since then we came here from Hilton Head, & have visited day before yesterday Jacksonville & yesterday St. Augustine.

Here I found a store of Hoyt, Sprague & Co in full operation: and it seemed to me as if I was near home again. Tell the Governor that the agents of the firm here seem to be active; and as they have the advantage of being among the very first to whom the new regulations, (which virtually make trade free once more, except the high tax on cotton,) are communicated will I hope be able to do something very profitable.

Jacksonville—though much smaller & poorer than Savannah—represents it in some fashion—the same trees—the same squares. Mr. Yulee called on me full of reconstruction on a basis satisfactory to the south—meaning the Southern Aristocracy—he left me I fear not altogether satisfied with the prospects.[2] It is very hard for these southern gentlemen to believe that we owe any duty to the loyal blacks. They dislike the idea of free labor—And, though having minds made up emancipation from personal slavery, want some plan of coercing labor by law. They most dislike the idea of the blacks being citizens & voters. I hope President Johnson will not fail to insist on absolute freedom & on the only practical guaranty of freedom universal suffrage.

Whom do you think I found here elected by the suffrages of blacks & whites as Mayor of the City of Fernandina? Why no other than our friend Professor Mot, who came here with Judge Stickney & is as zealous as ever for all sorts of industrial improvement. He has been manufacturing olive oil—better than any other in the world—arrowroot, do.,[3] has planted a vineyard; has planted a grove of olives; but, alas, has failed again on beets. His beet seed was lost coming from France, in sight of land.[4]

But the Mayoralty compensates for the loss. He is full of zeal for good government [*torn*] doubt not make an excellent offic[*torn*] desired that I should administer the [oath] [*torn*] office & I was not at all unwilling— So it w[as] done: & I had the honor of swearing in the first Mayor, chosen by universal suffrage south of Mason & Dixon's Line; an event to be remembered.[5]

I have not time to say much of St Augustine / It is an old Spanish town, with an old Spanish Fortress metamorphosed into an American fort; an old Spanish Palace, in ruins; a profusion of orange trees, fig trees, myrtle trees, magnolias, oleandars, cactuses, palmettos &c—Minorcan girls & boys, &c &c almost a new world.[6]

Nettie has been very well, except a little seasickness for change, & is greatly delighted. I shall be disappointed if she does not give you a pretty vivid sketch of St Augustine.

Gen. Gillmore goes visiting these places & took us with him.[7] He has been very kind, & has impressed me with a high opinion of his sense, capacity & tact in Administration. We leave today for Key West. Love to Governor

Your affectionate father
S P Chase

Historical Society of Pennsylvania.

1. A long, descriptive letter of May 17, Father's only one to Kate since May 5, was actually written at Hilton Head just following the group's departure from Savannah (Chase Papers, HSP). Before Savannah the travelers had seen Charleston and the Sea Islands of South Carolina. *Chase Papers,* 1:539–51.

2. Florida railroad promoter and plantation owner David Levy Yulee had not held any official commission from the Confederacy but in June 1865 was temporarily imprisoned at Fort Pulaski, Ga. His service as a United States senator, 1845–51 and 1855–61, had overlapped with Father's term in that chamber. *DAB,* 20:638; *Chase Papers,* 1:552.

3. That is, "ditto."

4. In Columbus in January 1857, the aptly named Adolphus Mot—*mot* is French for "word"—contracted to tutor Father, Kate, and Nettie in the French language for $24 per quarter. The lessons, which involved both conversation and reading and were held in the evening at the Chases' home in Columbus, often more than once a week, continued at least until June 1857. After the beginning of the Civil War, Mot, a native of France, experimented with the production of beet sugar. In 1863 he went to Florida as clerk to the U.S. direct tax commissioners. In Fernandina he continued his agricultural innovation, cultivating olives and, in 1867, seeking aid for a plan for former slaves to homestead land and grow sesame. Mot was in Washington, D.C., in January 1870, when Father hired him to give Nettie twenty lessons in French for $20. *Chase Papers,* 1:257, 272, 273, 287, 647; Father to Mot, Feb. 17, 1867, Mot to Father, Sept. 25, 1861, Apr. 7, 1863, Jan. 8, July 10, 1867 (Chase Papers, LC); Simpson et al., *Advice after Appomattox,* 36.

5. The new city government for Fernandina had been organized under the authority and protection of U.S. military authorities, and the Federal direct tax commissioners and tax collector saw to it that African American men would have the franchise in local elections. Those local whites who objected to the arrangement boycotted the election on May 1, when Mot was unanimously elected mayor. *Boston Daily Advertiser,* May 29, 1865.

6. In 1768, when East Florida was a British colony, the Scottish proprietor of the New Smyrna indigo plantation seventy miles south of St. Augustine recruited 1,400 people from the island of Minorca, with some Italians and Greeks, as an alternative to slaves for a labor

supply. After several difficult years on the plantation, during the American Revolution most of the survivors left in a body for St. Augustine, where they formed a long-lasting component of the city's culture. Patricia C. Griffin, *Mullet on the Beach: The Minorcans of Florida, 1768–1788* (Jacksonville, Fla.: University of North Florida Press, 1991), 28, 98–99, 106, and preface.

7. An 1849 graduate of West Point noted for his skills as a military engineer, Quincy Adams Gillmore, a major general of volunteers since 1863, commanded the army's Department of the South. He accompanied the Chase entourage to Jacksonville, St. Augustine, and Fernandina, as he had their earlier excursion to Savannah, aboard the steamer *W. W. Coit,* a military dispatch boat. *Chase Papers,* 1:550–53; *DAB,* 7:295.

FATHER TO KATE

Key West, May 24, 1865.

My darling Katie,

Here we are in Key West. Since we left Fernandina now four days ago poor Nettie had hardly any comfort until yesterday when the weather was so fair & the sea so smooth that she was able to sit up with something like enjoyment. How I have wished for you! How sorry I should be you are not with us if I could only be sure of your ability to endure the seasickness and the discomforts. We were talking of you today, Nettie & I, & speculating whether you could have stood the voyage. Nettie was pretty sure you could not. I think you could if the close air of the ship and the heat were a little more tolerable, for one constituted as you are. I have borne both splendidly & indeed rather congratulate myself on the goodness of quarters and the pleasantness of the air than complain of any deficiency in the one or oppressiveness of the other.

But I do wish you could have seen the sea & the sky & the porpoises the first night after we came out from Fernandina. So blue a sea except when disturbed by the plank of cutter or fish; so bright a sky so crowded with stars I—but I shall have to revise this. The sky was *not* bright that night nor was a star visible. That part of the description belongs to the second & the third nights not to the first. But the sea was blue, and as the waves dashed against the sides & were thrown back in foam there was a brilliant phosphorescence such as I had never seen. It was most brilliant in the track of the ship. The cutter left a long path of glory behind her; & I observed both at the sides and in the wake what I had never seen before sparks of light which actually resembled fire sparks such are thrown off, on a sudden blow, from a burning brand. And then the porpoises I wish you could have seen them. Three of them ran along by the ship for several miles—darting hither & thither, in all sorts of angles, showing much like preposterous squibs, making flashes & leaving behind them trails of light wherever they darted. I wish I could make you see their gambols.

And here at Key West, how I wish you could have been with us today: and seen the cocoanut trees the date trees, the banana trees, the tamarind trees, the palms, the pomegranates & I know not what else of strange & beautiful. Still more do I wish that you could have visited old Sandy with us—an old negro, seventy two years old, active, energetic, with his plantation of every tree & flower that grows here, of nineteen acres, & heard his talk. He isn't Uncle Tom by any means, but he beats Uncle Tom all hollow. Oh how I wish you could have heard him talk! It was wonderful. I can't even attempt a description. Perhaps I will when I see you.

I am writing at Mr. Plantz table. We are to dine with him; and dinner must be on the table in a minute & a caller has just come in, who must be got rid of before dinner.

But I must tell you how glad we are to hear that the Stonewall has been surrendered to the Spanish Government & how we hope that our Government will make the Spaniards give her up as Confederate property which they have no right to.[1]

We are going to Havana tonight & expect to see the Stonewall tomorrow. We hope to be back here Saturday night; and, after I have seen the General Commanding now absent at Tallahassee, to leave for Mobile & New Orleans on Monday.[2]

I begin to be very anxious to get north. Love to the Governor.

Your affectionate father
S P Chase

Historical Society of Pennsylvania.

1. The Confederacy purchased the *Stonewall,* a French-built ironclad ram, in Copenhagen in January 1865, but due to a series of delays the ship only reached the Bahamas on May 6. Learning there of Lee's surrender at Appomattox, the captain, Thomas Jefferson Page, took the *Stonewall* to Cuba, where, hemmed in by the U.S. Navy, he turned the vessel over to the Spanish authorities in exchange for $16,000 to pay off his crew. Father inspected the ship in Havana harbor on May 26. Raimondo Luraghi, *A History of the Confederate Navy,* trans. Paolo E. Coletta (Annapolis, Md.: University of North Carolina Press, 1996), 287–88, 341, 343–44; *Chase Papers,* 1:557.

2. John Newton, the West Point graduate and military engineer who commanded the District of West Florida, was expected back in Key West on Sunday, May 28, but was still absent when the Chase party passed through again on the twenty-ninth. *DAB,* 13:473–74; *Chase Papers,* 1:555, 560.

FATHER TO KATE

Key West, May 29, 1865.

My darling Katie,

I sent you my last from Havana though it was written here. There is no regular mail from this place except that way: so I took my own letter there[1]

We steamed into the famous Cuban harbor last Thursday Morning, passing between the Mora Castle on our left & Fort Cabañas on the right & coming to anchor about ten o'clock, near the Spanish flagship

Carmen. Mr. Reid & young Mr. Mellen & Mr. Lowell were soon engaged in active negotiations for bananas, & pine apples & cigars, with the boat-men who had pulled along side our ship. Soon after the Consul & Vice Consul, Mr. Minor & Mr. Savage came aboard, & we consulted them as to the best use to be made of our time.[2]

The first thing was to go ashore & establish ourselves in lodgings at the Hotel de Almy, which, being interpreted, Means Mrs Almy's board-ing house. And quite a comfortable house we found it; though quite peculiar to our thinking. It was a large square building,—in the centre an open court surrounded by pillars, which formed with curtains sus-pended between them, the inner sides of a sort of verandah, from which all or nearly all the rooms opened. On one of these sides was the dining hall entirely open to the court, except the curtains were let down which is never the case in Summer, unless in case of storm. The parlor was also on this side—On the other sides lodging rooms. Netties & Mine ad-joined each other & were as pleasant as the climate allows.

In the Evening—that is about five—Mr. Savage the Vice Consul called to take us out for a drive. Nettie was arrayed as I thought quite becom-ingly; with her great black spencer & little cap, & we took the way to the *paséo* or whatever is the name for the fashionable *promenade en Voiture*.[3] Just imagine my *phelinks*[4] when after we had passed the old city wall Mr. Savage proposed to turn off from the drive frequented by the fashion of the city, suggesting that as Miss Nettie was not *in costume*—in dress, I mean,—that she would not wish to be seen on the—what d'ye call it. I laughed & told Nettie, who was, I dare say, as much surprised as I; but she took it very coolly & declined to have our course changed. So on we went; fortunately or unfortunately we were early. We passed a numerous band of musicians on their way to the Capitan Génerals country palace, where the drive ends;[5] and we passed also a few sumptuously got up volantes, each with one horse in the thills & another harnessed at his left or nigh side in traces—the driver in a laced jacket & high spurred boots mounted on the nigh side horse & in sole control of the motive power, with two handsomely dressed ladies reclining on the one seat, their skirts expanded so as to fall largely outside the large[6] & really making a very picturesque effect. No lady wore hat or veil, but every one was handsomely & picturesquely, though not expensively dressed, and they really looked very well. Nettie, I must confess, did not *show* to great advantage,—but she saw every thing & every body whom her glasses brot within range, & as her purpose was to see rather than be seen she en-joyed this part of the drive very well. Afterwards we took our way into the country—through the fashionable Cerro—a street of residences some two miles from the old city—through Puentes Grandes—where are the paper mills—to Marianáo—where is a church & some houses & when we turned—I wish you could have been with us on this drive; you would have been delighted.

But I am near the bottom of my fourth page & at the end of my time. So I must reserve the account of my visit to the Captain General—& to Matanzas & Guines, & the wonderful Cave of Bellamar & the enchanting valley of the Yumari. We leave very soon for Mobile & New Orleans & before we go I must return the Admirals visit.[7]

Oh, my darling; it is hard to be so far away from you & not even have a letter. My heart goes towards you more affectionately than you will ever know, perhaps, in love & blessing. May Heaven keep you & your dear husband. Remember both of you that there is no happiness for either on earth as in that mutual love which always prompts to kindliest offices & never grows weary of them. Hoping soon to see you both,

Your most affe. father

S P Chase

Historical Society of Pennsylvania.

1. Father's last letter to Kate was that of May 24, immediately above. He also recorded the sojourn to Cuba, May 25–28, in his journal, where some of the sights not annotated here are identified (see *Chase Papers,* 1:556–60). Much of what Father and Nettie saw in Cuba was described also by other visitors to the island: Maturin M. Ballou, *History of Cuba; or, Notes of a Traveller in the Tropics* (Boston: Phillips, Sampson & Co., 1854); Samuel Hazard, *Cuba with Pen and Pencil* (Hartford, Conn.: Hartford Publishing Co., 1871); Richard Henry Dana, *To Cuba and Back. A Vacation Voyage* (Boston: Ticknor & Fields, 1859); Henry Ashworth, *A Tour in the United States, Cuba, and Canada* (London: A. W. Bennett, 1861); Eliza McHatton-Ripley, *From Flag to Flag: A Woman's Adventures and Experiences in the South during the War, in Mexico, and in Cuba* (New York: D. Appleton & Co., 1889); and the anonymous *Rambles in Cuba* (New York: Carleton, 1870).

2. Consul General William Thomas Minor, a former governor of Connecticut, and Vice Consul Thomas Savage, an American born in Cuba. *Chase Papers,* 1:556.

3. Father used both Spanish and French terms to refer to the avenue where Havana society showed itself each afternoon. It seems likely that Nettie's "great black spencer" was the military cape she had borrowed from her uncle, Ben Ludlow (see Father to Kate, May 5, above).

4. Southern humorist Joseph Glover Baldwin evidently coined the spelling "phelinks" for "feelings." The first use of the comical twist appears to have been in one of the satirical "sketches" of backwoods Alabama and Mississippi that Baldwin first published in the *Southern Literary Messenger* in the early 1850s. Those pieces appeared in book form in 1853. "*Phansy* his *phelinks,*" Baldwin wrote, to mean "fancy his feelings"—as in, "imagine what he felt in that situation." The expression gained wide currency: as early as March 1853, Emily Dickinson referred jocularly in a private letter to "a young woman's 'phelinks.'" "Phansy his phelinks" and variations—"phancy her phelinks," "phansy my phelinks"—appeared in newspapers in the later 1850s and 1860s. Joseph Glover Baldwin, *The Flush Times of Alabama and Mississippi: A Series of Sketches,* 2d ed. (New York: D. Appleton & Co., 1853), 316; *ANB,* 2:57; Thomas H. Johnson and Theodora Ward, eds., *The Letters of Emily Dickinson,* 3 vols. (Cambridge, Mass.: Harvard University Press, 1958), 1:235; *Daily Confederation* (Alabama), Dec. 20, 1858; *Philadelphia Inquirer,* June 20, 1861; *Constitution* (Middletown, Conn.), Feb. 19, 1862.

5. In Spain's administration of the island colony, the governorship was vested in a captain general, at this time Domingo Dulce y Garay. On May 26, Father called on him, and they discussed prospects for the emancipation of Cuba's slaves. *Chase Papers,* 1:557.

6. So in the original; Father obviously omitted a word. The *volante,* a distinctive open carriage used in Havana, had only two wheels, each about six feet in diameter. The driver (*calisero*), as Father describes here, rode one of the horses, leaving the vehicle's single seat free for the passengers, often a pair or a trio of women. A description published in the 1850s noted that the city's genteel women rode in their *volantes,* which in some cases bore

elaborate gold or silver ornamentation, "to the Tacon Paseo, to meet the fashion of the town at the close of the day." Ballou, *History of Cuba,* 131–32, illus. facing 131; *Chase Papers,* 1:556, 560.

7. Acting Rear Adm. Cornelius Kinchiloe Stribling, commander of the East Gulf Blockading Squadron, had called on Father on the morning of May 29. The travelers left Key West later that day. *Chase Papers,* 1:560.

FATHER TO KATE

Steamer W. R. Carter
Monday Morng June 19 '65

My darling Katie,

We are half an hour from Cairo and I will not omit an opportunity of sending you a line by the first mail.[1]

I received your telegram on the river. The Steamer Fashion bro't it from Vicksburgh & hailed our boat & delivered it. It was a great relief for I was very anxious about you. This was just below Natchez. Of course I was impatient to get to Memphis & find your letter.[2] We got there Saturday Eveng about 8, & young Mr. Mellen & an officer of the Treasury went up into the town, hunted up the Postmaster who was at the Theatre & brought me your letter. It did me a deal of good. I was delighted to hear that you were well & engaged in improvement of the place. It gives you a healthful employment & will be useful every way. Still more delighted was I to read what you say of your excellent husband. You *ought* to be proud of him. I *am* quite as much as you are. He is independent, & manly as well as intelligent: and real manliness & independence are rare qualities in these days. I wish he were not so deeply immersed in business & could give more time to the reading & study necessary to qualify him for the part I hope to see him take in public affairs. Give my warmest love to him. Tell him I saw his agent Mr. Collins at Vicksburgh, who says the plantation will do well this year.

At Memphis we got the papers containing Prest. Johnsons Mississippi Proclamation. It disappointed me greatly. I shall be very glad if it does not do a great deal of harm. I shall stick to my own principles.[3]

We shall keep on up the river on this boat rather than take the cars which will be crowded by returning soldiers. We expect to reach Louisville Wednesday Eveng & Cincinnati Thursday Eveng: and then to determine future course by the letters we get & the circumstances we find.

If Mrs Lander is still with you give her the assurance of my best remembrances & tell dear Eliza that I love her affectionately.[4]

Goodbye, darling. May God watch over you. He will—such is my faith. Nettie is quite well & sends a great deal of love.

Your affectionate father
S P Chase

Mrs Kate C. Sprague

Historical Society of Pennsylvania.

1. Since the previous letter, Father and Nettie had traveled on the *Wayanda* from Key West to New Orleans, stopping at Mobile on June 2–3, and were at New Orleans, June 5–12. No correspondence from the travelers to Kate in the interval has been found. Maj. Gen. Edward R. S. Canby, in command at New Orleans, had arranged for them to travel up the Mississippi on the *W. R. Carter*, a passenger steamboat of the Atlantic and Mississippi Steamship Company. *Chase Papers*, 1:560–71.

2. Father and Nettie reached Memphis on June 17. Kate's telegram and letter have not been found. Father had been chagrined in New Orleans when zealous officials attempted to divert the *Fashion*—advertised as a "new and splendid" steamboat—from its regular weekly schedule in order to accommodate the chief justice's trip upriver. Ibid., 1:569, 574.

3. Instead of guaranteeing the elective franchise to African Americans as Father had advocated, Andrew Johnson's proclamation of June 13, which authorized a convention for the reorganization of the Mississippi government, sanctioned the state's prewar restrictions on voting. Johnson had already revealed the direction of his policy on May 29, when he issued a proclamation for North Carolina that contained the same terms to govern election of that state's convention. James D. Richardson, ed., *A Compilation of the Messages and Papers of the Presidents, 1789–1907*, vol. 6 (New York: Bureau of National Literature and Art, 1908), 312–16; Simpson et al., *Advice after Appomattox*, 16.

4. Eliza Whipple.

FATHER TO KATE

Cincinnati, June 24, 1865.

My darling Katie

The Governor's telegram announcing that "Kate & *her boy* are doing well" did not reach me; but day before yesterday I received his letter saying that it had been sent and confirming its good news. And yesterday I received also his answer to my telegram of the day before saying that you were both still doing very well. And today I have your letter—your own letter—which still more fully assures me; for I reason that if you could write *that* on the 20th & were doing very well on the 22d you must be almost *quite* well today.[1] I am very glad & thankful. I long to see the dear boy whom you must name William. It is natural enough that you should want to name him after me in some way: but my only tolerable name is my surname; and William is not only a better one; but is the name of one to whom *your first duties* belong, and it was the name of his father, was it not? and it *should* be borne by his first boy. So please consider that "case" "adjudged."

We came here on Thursday Morning—day before yesterday: and I have been surrounded ever since; so that it has been impossible to write a decent letter. I am writing this at intervals between calls. If it is not decent lay it to that.

My journey has been one of extreme interest; but as I have lost the thread of my narrative I shall reserve what I have further to say about it as topics of conversation when we meet. Mr. Reid—who went with me through the whole, proposes to write a book about it; and to make a sort of running comparison between the condition as he saw it & the condition as seen by Russell when he traversed substantially the same ground at the outbreak of the war in 1861.[2] I think if he carries out his purpose the book will be interesting.

Mr. Flagg called to see me yesterday. He says that Mrs Longworth is suffering under a disease resembling cancer, but which the doctors call by another name. It has attacked her upper cheek bone on the right side & is gradually eating towards the brain, which it must certainly reach. The termination must be fatal, & she endures great pain. The family are in much distress, and Mrs Flagg is all the time with her mother. I am profoundly sorry. I felt a very great regard for Mrs Longworth: she was so kind to me when I was a young man.[3]

I have seen a good many of your old friends—Bishop McIlvaine, Mr. Ball, Gen Hooker,[4] Young Colonel Anderson, who has been occasionally at our house at Washington, and others. Every body manifests great— three callers, amongst them Mr. LHommedieu, since that last word[5]— regard for you, & I have plenty of congratulations on my promotion to the office of grandfather.

Last night I spent in Clifton at Bishop McIlvaines. It was a charming little visit. You seldom meet girls so sensible, so highly cultivated, and so refined as his: and the Bishop I need not praise to you, nor Mrs McI——[6]

My present plan of journey is to leave Cincinnati Thursday next— spend two or three days at Cleveland & Columbus—leave Cleveland on Monday the 3d. & reach New York Wednesday Morning—& get to Narragansett by the shortest route thereafter. I think we[7] will take the Providence boat Wednesday afternoon and come down Thursday Morning to Kingston Station.[8]

Nettie has gone to Hillsborough. Col. Collins came in yesterday afternoon & insisted on taking her up with him & she wanted to see Mrs Collins. She is to come back on Monday.

We were at Abingdon on Wednesday.[9] Josie Ludlow has had a severe attack of hemorrhage from the lungs, and looks very badly. Kate Whiteman is the same pleasant creature as ever. Ammie Hunt is there having arrived from New Orleans by way of St Louis & the railroad, the same day that we came by Cairo and the River. Charlotte has gone to Cambridge on the earnest appeal of Lud to be present at the Class Speaking.[10] Perhaps she may stay there & thereabout till after commencement. I wish you could ask her to *Melluna*: but it is I suppose out of the question.

Give my best love to dear Eliza. Tell her I saw a good deal of Prentice in New Orleans. He was well; but not so stout & hearty as I should like to see him. I am afraid the climate does not agree with him. I have written Mr. McCulloch asking him to telegraph his permission to come north.[11] I am so glad Eliza was with you at the critical moment. Her presence must have been a great comfort to you. Goodbye. Ask the Governor to show you a Gazette I send to him.[12]

> Your most affectionate father
> S P Chase

Mrs Kate C. Sprague

Library of Congress.

1. We have not located the letters and telegrams that passed among Father, Kate, and William Sprague. In his journal, Father recorded the essence of William's telegram received on June 23 as "We are all well," and noted: "Brief pencil letter from Katie dated 20th—baby bright, black haired & handsome." *Chase Papers*, 1:579.

2. As he and Nettie visited such places as Charleston and Mobile, Father consulted British correspondent William Howard Russell's observations of the region in *Pictures of Southern Life: Social, Political, and Military* (New York: J. G. Gregory, 1861), which included letters written for the *Times* of London in the spring of 1861. *Chase Papers*, 1:544, 562.

3. The failing Susan Howell Longworth was the widow of Nicholas Longworth, a prominent Cincinnati attorney, philanthropist, and horticulturalist who acquired a fortune in real estate during the city's early development. Father had associated with the Longworths and their family of four children from the time of his relocation to Cincinnati in 1830 and maintained the connection, calling on the couple in July 1857, six months before they celebrated their fiftieth wedding anniversary. William Joseph Flagg, a New York attorney and author who continued his late father-in-law's interest in cultivating native grapes, was married to the Longworths' daughter Eliza. Chambrun, *Making of Nicholas Longworth*, 18, 22, 40, 46, 98, 101, 103; Coyle, *Ohio Authors*, 214, 393–94; *Chase Papers*, 1:50, 53, 57, 292.

4. Maj. Gen. Joseph Hooker, who since September 1864 had commanded the Northern Department, with headquarters at Cincinnati, moved to New York City early in July 1865 to command the Department of the East. *DAB*, 9:198.

5. Father's longtime Cincinnati acquaintance Stephen S. L'Hommedieu was president of the Cincinnati, Hamilton, and Dayton Railroad. He had earlier furnished the travelers with railroad passes for use on their trip, and on July 3–4 he escorted Father and Nettie in a private rail car from Meadville, Pa., to New York City. *Chase Papers*, 1:153, 535, 579, 585–86.

6. Charles McIlvaine and Emily Coxe of Burlington, N.J., had married in 1822. *Chase Papers*, 1:578.

7. Father originally wrote "I," then struck through it and wrote "we" above the line.

8. Six days a week, steamers of the Neptune Steamship Company with cabins for overnight travel left New York at five in the afternoon for arrival in Providence, R.I., early the next morning. In accord with Father's intentions, he and Nettie left Cincinnati for Columbus early on Thursday morning, June 29, and continued on to Cleveland the middle of the following day. In both cities Father met with associates and also attended public gatherings that welcomed returning soldiers. He and Nettie left Cleveland by rail on July 3, arrived in New York on Independence Day, boarded the Providence boat after dinner on July 5, and arrived at the station in Kingston, near Kate's and William Sprague's estate, on Thursday the sixth. *Chase Papers*, 1:582–87; *New York Daily Tribune*, June 24, 1865.

9. Abingdon was the Ludlow family home in Cumminsville, Ohio. *Chase Papers*, 1:578.

10. Aunt Charlotte Ludlow Jones and her son Ludlow Ap-Jones, who received an A.M. degree from Harvard that year. Ibid.

11. J. Prentice Tucker, previously assistant surveyor of customs at Boston, was surveyor of customs at New Orleans. In March 1865, Abraham Lincoln had appointed Hugh McCulloch secretary of the Treasury to succeed William Pitt Fessenden. McCulloch, formerly an Indiana banker, had been comptroller of the currency during Father's tenure at the Treasury. *Chase Papers*, 1:495; *DAB*, 12:6–7.

12. The *Cincinnati Daily Gazette* of June 24 printed a front-page article by "Agate"— Whitelaw Reid—titled "President Lincoln on Negro Suffrage," which argued that by the end of the war Abraham Lincoln was more inclined to favor suffrage for African Americans in the Southern states than had been represented. The piece included much of the text of two letters that Father had written to Lincoln about the suffrage issue on April 11

and 12. Father also sent copies of the newspaper to senators Charles Sumner, who had encouraged him to publish the letters to Lincoln, and John Sherman. *Chase Papers,* 5:55–56; Father to Sherman, June 25, 1865 (Sherman Papers, LC).

NETTIE TO FATHER

South Pier
August 26th. 1865

Dearest Father.

Cousin Jennie, Mr Jewett, Alice, and I made a grand expedition yesterday, to the mills at, and around Providence. We had intended to go to the Baltic, but when we arrived at the depôt, we found we were too late for our train by a half hour, and as the Providence train was nearly due, we concluded to change our programme, and visit the mills, and founderys in that vicinity.[1] Reaching Providence we first went out to a large wool delaine factory, belonging to a Mr Chapin, and Mr Hoyt.[2] I seems as if one would never weary of watching the machines. How odd it is that this vast extent of power, almost titanic in its might and strenght, is owned and controlled by so puny a creature as man yes and even generated. It seems rather to be some great giant working out a penance for sins comitted; the great power Steam controlled and put under subjection by the mightier power Intellect. After having *"done"* the delaine factory we went out to Cranston, where the Govenor made glad the hearts of Alice, and myself by giving each of us a couple of calico dresses, with the proviso that one of them was to be made by ourselves.[3] We picked up his gauntlet of defiance on that score, however, and the dresses are to be made. After my former sucess I feel equal to any thing in the dressmaking line. After the mills Mr Amasa Sprague's stables, and horses came in for their share of the admiration which cousin Jennie and Jack bestowed on every thing. The Govenor at last became mischievous and took us to every small manufactory he could think of, until at last we cried for mercy for we began to feel very sensibly that man could not live by sight seeing alone[4] and that as we had had breakfast at seven and it was then four, dinner was not to be despised. The Govenor at last relented and we went to Mrs Sprague's where dinner had been waiting for us since two, and I can assure you we did full justice to it. After dinner more factories, and then at last home, and if I may judge the others by myself we were all very glad to get there. The twins are as funny as usual.[5] Bell one day was opening a drawer, and Alice told her rather sharply, to come away and let it alone. "Wait 'till I go to heaven" said the mite "and God will let me make open his drawers" / Daisy came running towards us the other day, crying "Come, klein Curly hat ein gross fit".[6] This morning we all went down to the bowling alley, it requires great skill in playing here, for the alley instead of being straight, meanders about in the most perplexing way. as in order to be sucessful it is necessary to adapt one's ball to the alley, it is no easy matter. We procured some green peaches and wretched watermelon with which one beguiled the time ad interim. Surf proves himself fully worthy of the name, and dashes into the water with all the boldness one could desire, speaking of the water I must tell you of my own sucess in that element, I can swim a little, float with the most perfect ease, and dive like a duck. the two latter accomplishments I have learned within the last few days only. Mr Jewett says I learn quicker than any one he ever saw, and pleasantly suggests that prehaps it is because I am so light headed agreable is it not? Mr Jewett Cousin Jennie and the babies leave [Tuesday] of next week and Alice is to remain longer / the arrangement is so pleasant for me as I should miss her greatly.

How is Willie getting on? I need hardly ask if he is good, and efficient.[7] We talk and think of you so often it seems so desolate for you to be there all alone. Take more love than my pen can express our my paper contain.

From your own loving
Nettie.

Library of Congress.

1. Nettie's companions were her cousins Alice Skinner and Jenny Skinner Jewett, along with Jenny's husband, Jack. They perhaps had set out to see the sidewheel steamer *Baltic,* which at one time was among the largest ships in the world. The *Baltic* and three sister ships first went into service for the New York and Liverpool United States Mail Steam Ship Company, known as the Collins line, in 1850, to compete with Britain's Cunard line for fast, luxurious passenger and mail service across the Atlantic. In its heyday the *Baltic* once set the record for the swiftest transatlantic crossing. Taken out of that service in 1858, the steamship became a transport during the Civil War. In January 1862, when Father made Charles Sumner's associate Edward L. Pierce the Treasury agent in charge of reform efforts in the Sea Islands, Pierce and an entourage of Northern teachers traveled to Port Royal on the *Baltic.* In 1865 the ship belonged to the Pacific Mail Steamship Company. Gibbs, *Passenger Liners,* 80–82; *New York Times,* Dec. 14, 29, 1865; *Chase Papers,* 3:121.

2. The word "delaine" came from the French term *mousseline-de-laine* ("wool muslin"), meaning a wool cloth that was dyed or printed similarly to cotton muslin. A cotton warp introduced by English manufacturers made the cloth more comfortable, and as its general quality improved it played a significant role in the market as a moderately priced, durable fabric for women's dresses. Manufactured in the U.S. by Providence firms beginning in the 1840s, delaines by the 1860s were printed by mechanized processes. George W. Chapin was the treasurer of two firms that dealt in printed fabrics, the Atlantic DeLaine Company and the Oneco Company. His father, prominent Rhode Island banker and merchant Josiah Chapin, had first sold general merchandise and groceries but moved into the textile trade before turning his business interests over to his sons in 1844. "Mr. Hoyt" may have been Edwin Hoyt. Arthur Harrison Cole, *The American Wool Manufacture,* 2 vols. (Cambridge, Mass.: Harvard University Press, 1926), 1:326–31; *The Providence Directory, for the Year 1864* (Providence, R.I.: n.p., 1864), 34, 39, 204, 205; *The Biographical Cyclopedia of Representative Men of Rhode Island* (Providence, R.I.: National Biographical Publishing Co., 1881), 222.

3. The Sprague firm, which had long engaged in calico printing and devoted special attention to dyes, was the world's largest producer of cotton calico. Thomas Williams Bicknell, *The History of the State of Rhode Island and Providence Plantations,* 3 vols. (New York: American Historical Society, 1920), 3:834–35; Peter Coleman, *The Transformation of Rhode Island, 1790–1860* (Providence, R.I.: Brown University Press, 1963), 131–33.

4. Nettie originally wrote "bread," then struck through the word and wrote "sight seeing" above.

5. The Jewetts' daughters, Belle and Daisy.

6. In a mixture of German and English, the child said, "Come, little Curly is having a big fit." Nettie and her father had both studied German: Nettie took lessons in the language at Mary Macaulay's school in New York, and perhaps at other times in her education, and

Father set out "very zealously" to learn German on his own, and with James A. Garfield as his study partner, in Columbus before the Chases moved to Washington. According to Nettie's later report, her father's studies enabled him to read German with some facility. *New York Tribune*, Feb. 15, 1891; note from Mary Macaulay to Father, Sept. 9, 1863, printed above in this volume.

7. It is likely that W. Albert Wells (b. ca. 1849) was a recent addition to the household staff, and he probably remained at least until Father's death. His first name was surely William, for he seems to have been called "Will" or "Willie" early in his employ. Very soon, however—judging from Father's letter to Kate printed below at the inferred date of Nov. 4, 1865—he was to be known as "Albert." *Chase Papers*, 1:678, 692, 700.

FATHER TO KATE

Washington, September 4, 1865.

My darling Katie,

I have been looking anxiously for a letter from you. The Governor's last letter said that you were somewhat indisposed, and that he feared you had overexerted yourself or had been intemperate in bathing. The former I thought very likely. You have had such a houseful that relaxation was impossible. Three of one's own children create less anxiety, because they can be better controlled, than one of any other body.[1] I felt sorry for you when I was with you; and if I could be of any use would either have staid or returned immediately. All I do here is to read, and attend to some little matters of no great consequence.

It has been awfully hot here for a week—hot & hotter from day to day. Yesterday Morning I was really frightened. Willie came in reporting Mrs Hutchins was very ill with something like Cholera Morbus.[2] I sent him at once for Susan Walker, whose hospital work is pretty much over & who is now staying with Mrs Peter Force.[3] She very kindly came at once & nursed Mrs Hutchins, staying with her all last night, or rather occupying the next room so as to be on hand if needed, as if she had been one of her patients. This Morning Mrs H—— was over the worst of her attack & insisted on getting up & going downstairs though very feeble. Miss W—— has gone back to Mrs Force's. She wrote you a day or two ago about Mrs Hutchins' intention to leave, not because she is unwilling but because she feels herself unable to stay & offering her services to look after the house. She asked me to read her letter and to tell her whether I thought you would take her offer in good part: and I did read it & told her I did not know whether you would avail yourself of her offer but was sure you would appreciate it. I do not think I ever felt so much real respect & esteem for her as I do now—her work all the summer among those who needed consolation & help has been so truly excellent—But even if Mrs Hutchins leaves there will, I think, be no difficulty about the house. I expect Bronaugh here tonight & if he proves what I expect I shall be able to do without any Chamber help & can take care of the house nicely.[4] You need not give yourself the slightest uneasiness about it; but rely on it that you will find every thing when you return in tip top order. Before I leave this subject I must say that I think Mrs H—— has been all that you could expect; nor wd. she think of leaving if her health was tolerable. She is an honest, reasonably intelligent & sincerely religious woman.

Since I began this letter I have received one from Col. Collins enclosing one which I enclose to you as it gives a fuller account than any I have seen of poor Caspar's death. Col. Collins thinks it was little better than Murder, & is full of indignation that all his work in that region was so thrown away, because of the indifference or passivity of the War Dept. I hope his grief makes him mistake. No man can do every thing & I am sure that no ill will has actuated Mr. Stanton.[5]

I enclose also a letter to your grandmother from Maria.[6] It was sent me by, I suppose, the *Rev.* Saml. Cox. He dates, "St Paul's Ch. Cinn——. Sep 1."[7] Poor Maria has had, I fear, a hard time; but I suppose she is just like all the other rebels half consoled for defeat by thinking of their "noble cause & the heroic devotion to it of the brave men overpowered by the Northern hordes."[8]

But I have written a great deal longer letter than I intended, and am afraid you will have trouble in decyphering it. My conscience smites me when I think of my criticisms on poor, dear, Netties chirography. But then she's *young* & *can* improve!

I mean to write the Governor very soon—

Most affectionately, your father
S P Chase

Have you done any thing about a watch for Nettie's birthday? Return the letter about Caspar

Historical Society of Pennsylvania.

1. Kate had recently dealt with three young children in her household, the visiting Jewett twins and her own baby.

2. Willie was W. Albert Wells, and Mrs. Hutchins was apparently the housekeeper.

3. Hannah Evans Force was the wife of Peter Force, the indefatigable gatherer of historical documents best known for the *American Archives* compilation. *DAB,* 6:511, 512–13.

4. Like Albert Wells, Frank Bronaugh was a new employee in the household and still in his teens. Frank, who for a time assisted Father with his correspondence and papers, was perhaps related to Emily Bronaugh, a good friend of Dorothea Elizabeth Allen Cooke. *Chase Papers,* 1:604, 611, 654; 5:153.

5. Caspar W. Collins, who was between Kate and Nettie in age, was a member of the Collins family of Hillsboro, Ohio, that was related to Nettie and well known to Father and Kate as well. Caspar, a lieutenant in the 11th Ohio Volunteer Cavalry on the western frontier, died in July 1865 leading a sortie outside the army's station at Platte Bridge (present Casper, Wyo.), which was under attack by several thousand Cheyennes, Arapahos, and Dakotas. Collins was passing through the area and was not part of the regular complement of officers at Platte Bridge, but the officers assigned to the post all found excuses to decline the assignment when the commandant decided to take belated and ill-conceived action to protect a group of supply wagons. The young Ohioan complied with the order to lead the detachment even though he considered the mission to be suicidal. His father, William O. Collins, had recruited the 11th Ohio Cavalry and oversaw its deployment along the Overland Trail from northern Colorado to South Pass before returning to Ohio in the spring of 1865. In the aftermath of the incident in Wyoming, Colonel Collins made plain to Maj. Gen. Grenville M. Dodge that he considered the commander at Platte Bridge responsible for his son's death. Members of the 11th Ohio recovered Caspar's mutilated

body and escorted it home to Ohio in 1866. Years later Eugene Ware, who as a young officer on the frontier had been acquainted with Caspar, remembered him as "a wild, heed-
less young man." Ware, who perhaps knew Caspar through gossip as much as by personal
acquaintance, portrayed him as "exceedingly brave" but "almost without ballast," an officer
whose recklessness and ambition may have played a role in his death. Spring, *Caspar
Collins*, 50, 72, 82–88, 93–94, 97–99; Alfred James Mokler, *Fort Caspar (Platte Bridge Station)*
(Casper, Wyo.: Prairie Publishing Co., 1939), 22–35, 46–52; Eugene F. Ware, *The Indian War
of 1864* (Topeka, Kans.: Crane & Co., 1911; repr., Lincoln, Neb.: University of Nebraska
Press, 1994), 120, 216–17, 310.

    6. Maria Southgate Hawes, who had evidently written Mary Colton Smith.

    7. Father had attended St. Paul's Episcopal Church in Cincinnati during the 1830s
and 1840s and served on the vestry. He may have emphasized the clergyman's title to distinguish the Reverend Samuel Cox of Cincinnati from the politician Samuel Sullivan Cox
(originally of Ohio, later of New York). *Williams' Cincinnati Directory . . . June, 1865* (Cincinnati, Ohio: C. S. Williams, [1865]), 104; *Chase Papers*, 1:98, 155, 165, 203, 210, 686.

    8. The phrases "noble cause" and "heroic devotion" appeared in Jefferson Davis's in-
augural address as president of the Confederate states in February 1862. Dunbar Rowland,
ed., *Jefferson Davis, Constitutionalist: His Letters, Papers and Speeches*, vol. 5 (Jackson, Miss.: Mississippi Department of Archives and History, 1923), 201–2.

FATHER TO KATE

Washington, Sep. 8, 1865.

My dearest Katie,

    Your letter dated the 5th is just received. Your decision in regard to
Miss Walker is probably best, though she has so much faculty that I think
the House would better satisfy you under some supervision from her
than it is likely to in any other hands than those of Mrs Hutchings.[1] I am
very sorry that her ill health makes her wish to leave—sorry for the cause
and sorry for the effect.

    Miss Walker is at Mrs Force's and I have not seen her since she went
there. I sent your letter to her this Morning.

    Frank's brother in law—I call Bronaugh, Frank—Bowman,—whom
I call Henry—was here just after your letter came. He is not a second
Wilson; but seems to be a fair improvement on Welch; whose awkward-
ness, I must say, in passing, probably arises partly from ill health and
partly from diffidence. He, Henry, says he has had some experience and
thinks he could satisfy you. Frank who pleases me and is I am sure very
honest says *he* thinks so. Your letter leaves it in doubt whether you wish
to have him sent to the Farm. So I tell you all I learn and await your con-
clusions. Please telegraph if you wish him sent.

    You must not be in the least uneasy about me. I am getting along very
nicely. Mrs. G——[2] cooks quite well enough for me and every thing is
very comfortable. I am a great reader these hot days; often not going out
at all and never except to take a walk about Sunset. I have read Judge
Story's Life by his son, some 1100 or 1200 pages; some four hundred
pages of Wallaces Reports of our last winters decisions; Racines Athalie,
a good deal of Coneybeares Life & Writings of St Paul, a few pages here
& there of the Vie de Cæsar, & the newspapers. Is not this pretty well? I
have not for many years read so much consecutively or so thoroughly.[3]

Senator Fessenden and General Fessenden his son came in to see me last night and made me a very pleasant visit. Fessenden is meditating a long western journey to the Lakes, the Mississippi and the Ohio. I dont know what would tempt me to such an expedition. His son is on the Wirtz Military commission.[4]

I don't think that I will bring any silver from the Bank. I find I can get on very well with what we have.

You puzzle me when you ask my advice as a birth day present for your Governor.[5] You know that in such matters I always prefer to be guided by you. My range does not go beyond books and such like. How would it do to begin a collection of American History for him, starting with all the good books that have been written about Rhode Island?

When do you expect to be in New York & where? Perhaps I will join you.

My love to all—not forgetting Nurse Morgan to whom we all owe so much.

Your affectionate father
S P Chase

Historical Society of Pennsylvania.

1. He first wrote "Hutchins," then changed it to "Hutchings."
2. Mrs. Golden (see the next letter).
3. William W. Story, ed., *Life and Letters of Joseph Story,* 2 vols. (Boston: Little and Brown, 1851); the reports that John William Wallace would publish as *Cases Argued and Adjudged in the Supreme Court of the United States, December Term, 1864* (Washington, D.C.: W. H. & O. H. Morrison, 1870); Jean Racine's religious tragedy, *Athalie,* which first appeared in 1691; William John Conybeare, *The Life and Epistles of St. Paul* (London: Longman, Brown, Green, & Longmans, 1852), some editions of which also credited the Reverend J. S. Howson on the title page; and Alphonse de Lamartine, *Vie de César* (Paris: Michel Lévy frères, 1865).
4. As an officer commanding Maine troops during the war, Francis Fessenden, third son of William Pitt Fessenden and Ellen Deering Fessenden, suffered severe wounds, including the loss of a leg. Trained as a lawyer, the twenty-six-year-old brigadier general of volunteers was performing administrative duties in August 1865 when he was appointed to the military commission formed to try Henry Wirz, commander of the notorious Confederate prison stockade at Andersonville, Ga. The commission, presided over by Maj. Gen. Lew Wallace, convicted Wirz, who was executed in November 1865. *DAB,* 6:345; *Trial of Henry Wirz,* 40th Cong., 2d sess., 1867–68, House Exec. doc. 23, 2, 814–15.
5. William's birthday was September 12. He turned thirty-five in 1865. *DAB,* 17:475.

FATHER TO KATE

Washington, [Oct]. 14, 1865.

My darling child

Your letter *did* come "just about in time" to give me "a welcome home". It came last night and I came the night before.[1]

Do not trouble yourself at all about me. I am very well & doing very well. Mrs. Golden is a good enough cook; indeed, quite as good, I think, as Charlotte.[2] I am in no danger of starvation. Nor shall I want any silver from the Bank. I could get along *well enough* with the little I have: but what you have sent, will, when it comes be *very well.* Mrs Golden needs no money. I will supply whatever she wants. I shall have the muslin taken, perhaps, from one or two articles; but I prefer to have it remain on the rest. As to rooms, I propose putting most of the Library in the little room I slept in last winter; using the larger room as an office; and taking the room directly above that for a bedroom; or, if it will be more convenient to you I will go into the third story altogether, taking the three front rooms, putting the Library in the little room there, using the room above the present Library & office for office & the South East corner room for a bed room. The only inconvenience of this arrangement to me will be the necessity of seeing those who call on me down stairs in the sitting room or parlor.

Mrs Golden says she can make the red & green ingrain answer for a carpet for the servants sitting & dining room. She says she can make more out of it than the yellow carpet on the 2d. floor hall, which is too small.

It will be very difficult to get a second hand stove for the room such as you wish; but a good cooking stove can be had for $20, and a parlor cooking stove which would be better for a somewhat higher price say $30.

Mr. Walker has been here today with Mr. Woodward, about the back building, & while here measured the fire places on the parlor floor.[3] I enclose his measurements which you will easily understand; but I will, to make sure, give you those of the Dining room fireplace. The height of that fire place from it's floor to the top of the arch is 2 feet 6½ inches & the width from wall to wall 2 feet 9 inches. The width of the hearth in front of the fireplace is 17 inches & its length four feet ten inches. Mr. Walker says that he has already sent you measurements for the carpets carefully noting the space to left out[4] for the fireplaces.

Nothing has yet been done about the woodshed. Mr. Woodward has been very sick and narrowly escaped with life. He is not yet fully well. This accounts for some delay. Mr. Walker says the old woodshed in t[he cor]ner of the lot can be moved without any considerable expence; or he can build a new & better one either of one or two stories. He says he could build one of two stories, say 30 feet long by [18] wide, making a pair of stairs, leading to two plastered rooms in the 2d. story suitable for servants, with doors & windows for $[9]00. Such a building put up close to the house on the north side of your lot would shut of its 1st & 2d story windows looking into your yard. What shall be done?

Mrs Golden will have the Servants Hall put to rights by white washing, putting down the carpets &c &c & will have every thing arranged rightly, cleaning up the old laundry for Stewards room as you desire. I don't think she will need Cassie but will send for her if she does.

Little Will is at home at his mothers, unwell. Frank is factotum now. Mrs Golden will have a colored woman come to cook on Monday as she will have her hands full otherwise.

There I believe I have attended to all your charges. Write me what you wish done in the undecided matters or any thing else

Give abundant kisses to little Willie & love to the Governor & to the girls.[5]

Your affectionate father
S P Chase

Mrs. K. C. Sprague

Letterpress copy. Historical Society of Pennsylvania.

1. Father had left Washington the night of September 18 to meet Kate in New York City. He then visited Buffalo, N.Y., on the invitation of the builder of a new Revenue Service steamer, the *Commodore Perry*, construction of which had begun during his tenure as secretary of the Treasury. The vessel's trial run on Lake Erie took him to Cleveland, where he attended a "Christian Convention" and subsequently passed a few days at "Gibraltar," the Cookes' retreat at Put-in-Bay. He arrived back in Washington on October 12. Father to Richard C. Parsons, Sept. 18, 1865 (Chase Papers, HSP); to Hiram Barney, Oct. 2, 1865 (Barney Papers, Huntington Library); *Chase Papers,* 1:593–96; 5:70–72.
2. Charlotte Chambers Ludlow Jones.
3. Father apparently wrote "the the fire places." Several people named Walker were carpenters in Washington. Woodward was perhaps C. Woodward, a stove and hardware dealer. *Chase Papers,* 5:74.
4. So in the original.
5. Alice Skinner and Nettie (see the next letter).

FATHER TO KATE

Continental, Phila.
4 P.M. Saturday.[1]

My darling Katie,

I have just arrived & find myself very comfortably situated. It so happened that Mr. Wm E. Dodge, who is one of the best as well as one of the wealthiest of the New York Merchants, was in the cars, and, having discovered me came and took the same seat.[2] We talked and talked and were so much interested that the time seemed shorter than the time tables by a great deal. Of course I have seen nobody here yet.

Willie—I mean Albert[3]—forgot to give me my keys, but it will be easier to get a smith to fit a new key, than to have them sent over. So let him keep them & bring them over when you come.

I hope you have made yourself very comfortable; with new bedrooms, keeping the parlor. That idea seems to me the best. How nice it would be if you & your husband could celebrate the anniversary of your marriage in your own house at Washington? Can't it be so.

Write immediately that I may know when to expect you. You had best direct to the care of Mr. Cooke.

Love to Nettie & Alice & kisses in quantity to the paragon.[4]

I cant send you a check for Nettie till Monday. Meantime if she wants the money Monday please advance it and then take it out of the check. Advance, also, her hotel bill to be paid when we meet.

Affectionately your father
S P Chase

Mrs Kate C. Sprague.

Historical Society of Pennsylvania.

1. Philadelphia's Continental Hotel, which opened in 1860, was the city's finest accommodation. Based on the contents of this letter and the one that follows, Father wrote this one on Nov. 4, 1865. He had been in Washington earlier in the day and was on his way to Wilmington, Del., to hold circuit court. Supreme Court justices sat with U.S. district judges to make circuit courts, and Father's circuit included Maryland, Delaware, West Virginia, Virginia, and North Carolina. Later his circuit included South Carolina but omitted Delaware. Herman LeRoy Collins and Wilfred Jordan, *Philadelphia: A Story of Progress*, 4 vols. (New York: Lewis Historical Publishing Co., 1941), 1:283; Father to Anna Ella Carroll, Nov. 4, 1865 (Anna Ella Carroll Papers, Maryland Historical Society); *Chase Papers*, 1: 596–97; 5:133, 311.

2. William Earl Dodge was wealthy from the wholesale dry goods trade, through his involvement in the copper- and iron-producing corporation of Phelps, Dodge and Company, and by additional investment in timber and railroads. Father probably considered him "one of the best" New York merchants because of his philanthropic activities, including opposition to slavery, support of the Union war effort, an early and prominent involvement in the Young Men's Christian Association, and a lifelong commitment to temperance reform. *DAB*, 5:352–53.

3. W. Albert Wells.

4. Willie Sprague.

FATHER TO KATE

Phil. Tues. Nov. 7. 65

Dearest Katie,

No letter from you yet saying when I may certainly expect you. Please write or telegraph immediately.

I directed $200 to be sent Nettie yesterday by Jay Cooke & Co, which I hope came safe. I have now supplied Nettie with 300 cash & the price of the dress is to be added making over $400, of the $500 which you thought would be enough in September; but which I infer from what you said you do not think enough now. I want her to have enough, and don't restrict her to the $500 but only desire that she will use all the discretion & economy she can under the circumstances.

I passed last night in the country, at Mr. Cooke's.[1] Mr. C—— was in New York but Mrs C—— was very glad to see me & all are very anxious to see you & the baby & Nettie, to whom love. Most affect'y

Your father
S P Chase

Historical Society of Pennsylvania.

1. In the spring of 1865, construction began on what would rise as Jay Cooke's great mansion, "Ogontz." The house was on a two-hundred-acre tract about eight miles north of Philadelphia in the vicinity of "The Cedars," the Cookes' home in the Chelten Hills since 1858. Oberholtzer, *Cooke*, 1:153–54; 2:447–49.

CHRONOLOGY

April 1866	Kate, Nettie, baby Willie, and nursemaid Maggie embark for England on the *Australasian;* Father goes to Baltimore for circuit court
May 1866	Father and William in Washington, D.C.; Kate's grandmother, Mary Colton Smith, is there for an extended stay; Jefferson Davis is indicted for treason by federal court in Virginia
June 1866	Nettie writes from the Isle of Wight
July 1866	Kate and Nettie touring Scotland; Father travels to New Hampshire, Vermont, and Massachusetts; Tennessee ratifies Fourteenth Amendment and is readmitted to the Union
August 1866	Kate and Nettie in London and Paris
September 1866	They travel to the Black Forest region and Swiss Alps
October 1866	Father presides over meeting of American Freedmen's Union Commission in Baltimore; William arrives at Liverpool to join Kate, Nettie, and Willie
November 1866	Nettie and Kate in Dresden
December 1866	Kate, William, Willie, and Maggie return to U.S. from Liverpool; Nettie remains in Dresden

CHAPTER 8

"It Was Hard to Part with You"

APRIL–NOVEMBER 1866

I N THE spring of 1866, Kate, Nettie, baby Willie, and his nurse Maggie made a European tour. They debarked their oceangoing steamship in Liverpool but went straight on to London from there. For the next few months the little group traveled in the British Isles and visited Paris. In October they met William at the fashionable spa resort area of Baden-Baden in the Black Forest region, before the company moved on to Switzerland and back to Germany.[1] To Father's great delight, the Spragues were back in Washington, D.C., in December. Nettie, on the other hand, elected to stay abroad, spending the winter in Dresden studying art and developing her language skills. Father accepted her plans with fairly good cheer but clearly would have preferred she come home with her sister. He was especially concerned about her health, since she had been quite ill in the winter of 1866 and he feared that if she did not stay warm and dry enough in the German winter—Dresden was "a very damp place," he learned with some alarm—she might succumb again.[2] Although we have not located Kate's and Nettie's correspondence from this period, their father's letters illustrate a combination of stern admonition familiar in the girls' school-age letters and a newsy charm. Portions of these letters highlight his gently self-deprecating humor and are at times surprisingly humorous. The letters also convey how much Father loved his adult daughters and missed them.

Kate's and Nettie's travels place them squarely in a larger tradition of "Grand Touring." Popularized in the 1700s, primarily by young Englishmen, the Grand Tour had a fairly standard pattern. Upper-class sons with the leisure time and money to travel journeyed to France, Italy, Germany, and the Netherlands. Such cities as Paris, Geneva, Rome, and Venice were considered standard Grand Tour destinations. Travelers were supposed to educate themselves about foreign countries and view "great art," while enjoying a break from the rigid class conventions of their native land and the warmer climates of southern Europe.[3] Travel was also a kind of work for upper-middle-class and elite women, in that it demonstrated their husbands' financial success. Female travelers thus allowed well-to-do men like William Sprague to display their manly prowess in the economic realm of business life, while at the same time fueling America's burgeoning consumer culture.[4] William clearly understood this when he wrote to his wife and urged her to "go where you like to go, and live as you desire to live so far as the expenditure of money is concerned. Buy all you desire . . . and see your sister is not in any way less in that respect to yourself."[5]

By the mid-nineteenth-century improvements in both ocean and land travel made touring both physically and economically more accessible. The Chases' European tour differed from the usual Grand Tour in that they did not go to Italy, but otherwise Kate and Nettie took a fairly standard approach to traveling.[6] Unlike modern tourists, who often visit great numbers of destinations for short amounts of time, nineteenth-century travelers had the leisure time and money to spend weeks or even months in a single place.

Nineteenth-century travelers also differed from earlier generations of Grand Tour goers in that they placed less emphasis on architecture and art and more on nature and scenery. Thus the sisters' travels in the summer of 1866 to Scotland and Ireland fit neatly into what one historian calls "the search for the picturesque."[7] More remote British destinations became popular during the years when the Napoleonic wars made European travel particularly hazardous, and they remained fashionable throughout the 1800s. While the Lake District in southwest Scotland was overwhelmingly the most popular travel destination within the British Isles, the Scottish Highlands ran a close second. Scotland's road system was considered quite good by the standards of the time, as were the railroads. For example, in 1750 the trip from London to Edinburgh took ten to twelve days, but by 1830 travel time had been cut to just two days.[8] Kate and Nettie were in both Inverness, in the northern Highlands, and on the eastern coast at Berwick, both places sufficiently remote to be considered exotic and romantic.

Nettie, like so many before and after her, did a fair bit of sketching, though unfortunately we do not have her letters and drawings from the trip. She seems, from Father's descriptions of her drawings, to have favored landscapes and ruins as subjects. For more famous landscape artists of the era, natural beauty was found in carefully composed views of valleys or mountains, framed with smaller scale villages, buildings, or people in the foreground. Nature was seen as both beautiful and frightening, so artists often domesticated nature into more manageable and picturesque representations.[9]

The sisters spent time in Paris, the Black Forest, and the Swiss Alps. On the Continent the Alps served much the same purpose the Scottish Highlands did in Great Britain—they provided travelers with domesticated views of exotic mountainous regions. Travelers in the eighteenth and nineteenth centuries viewed the French capital as a necessary stop on the tour, though the English, and sometimes Americans, often found the French people and food repugnant.[10] Kate may have used her sojourn in Paris to visit the fashion designer Charles Frederick Worth, who was said to keep a dressmaker's dummy in Kate's exact proportions so that she might order dresses without the exhausting fitting sessions. Certainly journalists and social columnists commented often enough on Mrs. Sprague's fabulous French outfits in the coming Washington social seasons.[11]

Kate, William, Willie, and Maggie left Nettie in Dresden sometime in late November, made their way back to Liverpool, and from there took a steamship back to New York. Transatlantic travel had vastly improved in the first half of the 1800s, as companies like Cunard, White Star, and Collins introduced steam-powered ships that increased speed so much that crossing the Atlantic in the 1860s took only seven to ten days. Though ship travel improved in the early 1800s, the era of ocean-going opulence, made famous by the *Titanic* and the *Lusitania*, was still in the future when the Chase sisters were making their crossings. Ships tended to be noisy and cramped. Dining was basic, electricity and central heating rare before the 1870s, and until the invention of stabilizers in the 1940s, ships rolled quite a bit in heavy seas.[12] Nettie had suffered from seasickness on the trip she took with Father in 1865, and earlier as a small child with her mother on the Gulf of Mexico, so we can only imagine how ill the transatlantic crossing made her. Perhaps she stayed in Dresden just to postpone the return trip in a pitching, cold, crowded ship!

Nonetheless, the pleasures Nettie, Kate, and company took from travel must have far outweighed the inconveniences. Though their travels to the Scottish Highlands, Black Forest, Swiss Alps, and popular spa resorts such as Baden-Baden were formulaic for the nineteenth-century traveler, it must have been liberating to be out from under the watchful eye of Father, away from the stifling politics of Reconstruction-era Washington, and in the grip of new sensations. However much upper-class women's travel was a "cultural performance," meant to illustrate respectability, economics, and consumerism, the young women's European sojourn must have also been quite an adventure.

1. The modern unified nation of Germany did not exist until 1871, although the name "Germany" was often used to refer to the loose confederation of states before unification. Kate and Nettie were in Bavaria, Wurtemberg, Saxony, and Prussia.

2. See his letter to Nettie of Nov. 27, 1866, below.

3. William Edward Mead, *The Grand Tour in the Eighteenth Century* (Boston: Houghton Mifflin Co., 1914), 29–31.

4. Travel abroad, for example, required purchasing special trunks, new clothing, stationery, travel guides, and farewell gifts before the traveler ever spent any money overseas. Mary Suzanne Schriber, *Writing Home: American Women Abroad, 1830–1920* (Charlottesville, Va.: University of Virginia Press, 1997), 22–35; Thorstein Veblen, *The Theory of the Leisure Class* (New York: George Allen & Unwin, 1945), 40–45; Michael S. Kimmel, *Manhood in America: A Cultural History* (New York: Oxford University Press, 1996), 16–42.

5. William to Kate, Apr. 14, 1866 (Brown University Library).

6. Mary Merwin Phelps claims that the sisters did go to Italy, but evidence for that assertion is lacking. It is impossible to ascertain why Kate and Nettie did not go to Italy. Father's letters suggest he expected that they would go to Florence. Italy was politically unstable in the 1860s, but no more so than the Germanic states, and political instability had not kept away American tourists, like William Sprague, before the Civil War. Phelps, *Kate Chase*, 183; Lynne Withey, *Grand Tours and Cook's Tours* (New York: Aurum Press, 1997), 81–86.

7. Withey, *Grand Tours*, 45–57.

8. Ibid., 52–55, 64; Wolfgang Schivelbusch, *The Railway Journey: The Industrialization of Time and Space in the Nineteenth Century* (Berkeley, Calif.: University of California Press, 1968), 6–7.

9. Anne Bermingham, *Landscape and Ideology: The English Rustic Tradition, 1740–1860* (Berkeley, Calif.: University of California Press, 1986), 33–53; Malcolm Andrews, *The Search for the Picturesque: Landscape Aesthetics and Tourism in Britain, 1760–1800* (Palo Alto, Calif.: Stanford University Press, 1989), 200–201.

10. Withey, *Grand Tours*, 80–81.

11. Phelps, *Kate Chase*, 183–84; Lamphier, *Kate Chase and William Sprague*, 92–93.

12. Foster Rhea Dulles, *Americans Abroad* (Ann Arbor, Mich.: University of Michigan Press, 1964), 40–46; John Maxtone-Graham, *The Only Way to Cross* (New York: Collier Press, 1978), 3–7; Schriber, *Writing Home*, 2, 14.

FATHER TO NETTIE

Baltimore, Apl. 16, 1866.
My darling Nettie,

Your little note by the pilot came safely. I found it in Washington, when I returned from New York: for you must know that I did not return immediately after you went off. I was under engagement to preside at a Meeting under the auspices of the Ladies Centenary Association in New York and of course was expected to make a little speech[1]—so after bidding you goodbye and attending to some little matters in New York I went over to Philadelphia and passed the three intervening days with Jay Cooke, at Chelten Hills.

It was hard to part with you. There was the Australasian lying in the stream when we went back across the Jersey City Ferry: and it was sad to think that she was about to carry away across the ocean all the most precious ones in the world to me.[2] I dare say you and Katie[3] felt badly enough too when the crisis came; while master Willie, no doubt, took every thing very philosophically. Every day since I have thought, now they are so far, & now so far; now half way over; now nearing the English Coast. And today I think of you as probably rattled up towards London by rail. Every day my aspirations for your health & safety & happiness have ascended toward Heaven. If good wishes & sincere prayers can avail you will have nothing but gratification & improvement all the while. I have no fear that we shall be forgotten on your part: and I hope you will find yourself daily drawing nearer & nearer to God in Christ.

The day you left New York the Governor & I went to see Baron Eggloffstein & his new process of photographing on steel. It is really wonderful. He will take your photograph, & then by a chemico-photographic process produce a steel engraving of it in a couple of hours without touching a graving tool of any kind. It really seems magical. Several of us have been talking of setting up an Engraving Company by the new method, & expect it will prove quite a mine. I will divide my profits if I take any shares with you. The Baron—he is a real live baron—had my photograph taken & it has been transferred to steel. If I were writing at Washington I would send you a copy of the engraving. It is awfully ugly— black enough even for my taste: but he will compensate me for this by a better looking one by and by.[4]

My stay at Chelten Hills was pleasant. I did not go into town once: but rode and played billiards at which even little Harry beat me badly[5] & Jay Cooke *Senior* beat me unmercifully—played billiards also with the same reverend gentleman at which I beat him unmercifully. The great palace is well under way & they expect to take a Christmas dinner in it.[6] Wonder if you will be here to take a piece of mince pie. The house will be magnificent. I cant tell how many or what variety of rooms—I could not keep the count but heard of nothing for which there was not a room. Young Jay[7] was sorry that he could not go over with you. He said he would have so liked to go with you for two or three months & then come back to his work. His grandmother insists that he must be allowed to come over with me, if I come—what an *IF!*[8] If there were more room I would make it taller.

I went back to Washington Tuesday, taking the day instead of the night for the ride, and went to work immediately on my Baltimore cases: having three opinions to prepare before I could come over here / Of course I have since been very hard at work, was obliged to take part of yesterday though it was Sund[ay.][9]

But it did not prevent me from going to the Metho[dist] Church & taking the Governor with me yesterday morning. And I must tell you of something that happ[ened.] After the sermon the stewards came forward & told how much their finances had gone behind last year & that they were fifteen hundred dollars in debt & wanted the money badly. Mr. Woodward, the Governor's lawyer, is one of them & this made the matter a little personal you see.[10] Well somebody offered to be one of so many— I forget how many—to take shares of the indebtedness at $25 apiece. Then it was announced that General Grant for himself and family would take four shares.[11] And by & by as one of the stewards went by where I sat I plucked his coat sleeve & told him that I would give $50 but he must not name my name. So he obeyed literally, but had hardly advanced a step before he said "A Friend gives 50" which of course—drew looks towards the friend. At length the subscription dragged & the stewards who had begun with a declaration that they would raise the whole were obliged to say that they were obliged to the people present for their liberality & would not go any further having already $1334. It so happened that just at this moment the same steward who had taken my subscription passed by the step where were & the Governor plucked him & said "Cash will take the balance," telling him to say nothing of the matter; but the good man could not contain himself & sang out "Cash takes the balance!" & then all eyes were turned towards us who blushed to find our good intended to be so quiet all at once so conspicuous

I came here this morning. But I must not omit to tell you that Mr. Leary came last night to enquire for you—when I say you understand the *trio*.[12] Mr. Robert Dale Owen full of reconstruction & spiritualism also came in last evening[13] & so did Mr. Mellen. I must say too that we saw Mr. Wood as we went to church on the other side of the street & flattered ourselves that he *looked sorry* that he did not go with you.[14]

But I must stop. I am at Barnum's very comfortably fixed.[15] Today I have been disposing of cases & hearing an argument. The business will probably keep me here till Saturday night; when I mean to go back to Washington: and go to work again on something. I have not yet determined whether to go to Richmond or not. There are plenty of treason cases here, if the Government wants to have one tried for the purpose of settling the law.

Goodbye darling Nettie, & darling Katie & darling Willie. Remember me kindly to Maggie[16] & believe me most affectionately

Your father
S P Chase

Miss Nettie Chase.

I came near forgetting to say that you did not return your bills to me & Mrs Crawford cant find them.[17] Don't fail to send me a complete list of your creditors & the amounts due that they may be paid. Did you take my ring with you?

Library of Congress.

1. Father used the occasion of the first public meeting of the Ladies' Central Centenary Association of the Methodist Episcopal Church, held at St. Paul's Church in New York City on April 9, to give an address in which he expressed support for the Civil Rights Act and urged the granting of voting rights to former slaves. Judge William Lawrence, who at the time was an Ohio congressman, and two Methodist bishops also addressed the gathering. *Chase Papers*, 1:431; 5:87–88, 103; *New York Times*, Apr. 7, 1866.

2. The passenger liner *Australasian* was a screw steamer operated by the Cunard line and capable of speeds up to 14.5 knots. Father arrived in New York early in the morning of April 4 and made it to the dock in Jersey City just in time to say goodbye to Kate, Nettie, baby Willie, the baby's nurse, and some acquaintances who were also traveling on the *Australasian*. In his journal Father recorded that it was "sad enough to let all my children go; but it seems best on the whole & I commit them to God's gracious keeping." *Chase Papers*, 1:608–9; Gibbs, *Passenger Liners*, 52.

3. He appears to have written "Nettie," then reformed the name into "Katie."

4. Frederick von Egloffstein was showing his "Helographic" or "Heliographic" process, which could transfer photographic images to steel by acid etching, to potential investors, including William Sprague and Joshua Hanna. Father had asked Spencer M. Clark, who had been in charge of the currency printing bureau when Father was secretary of the Treasury, to evaluate the process. *Chase Papers*, 1:384, 609–11.

5. Henry David Cooke Jr., son of Henry D. and Laura Cooke. *Chase Papers*, 1:604, 635; Oberholtzer, *Cooke*, 1:93.

6. Jay and Dorothea Cooke did host Christmas dinner at Ogontz in 1866, for forty-two people, including Jay's business partners and their families. Construction of the house began in April 1865, took about eighteen months, and cost more than a million dollars. The Cookes had a housewarming party for more than five hundred guests on Valentine's Day, 1867. The mansion had a staff of about seventy people. Like Kate's Canonchet, the Cookes' estate bore the name of a Native American chief. Oberholtzer, *Cooke*, 2:447–51; Larson, *Cooke*, 195–96.

7. Jay Cooke Jr., born in 1845, became a financier and banker like his father. Young Jay's grandmother was Martha C. Cooke. *Nat. Cyc.*, 1:123; Oberholtzer, *Cooke*, 1:10; *Chase Papers*, 1:657.

8. Father wrote the *"IF"* in large block letters and underlined the word with four strokes.

9. He was holding circuit court in Baltimore.

10. Possibly Georgetown attorney William R. Woodward. Hunter, *Washington and Georgetown Directory*, 111; *Chase Papers*, 1:647.

11. In the aftermath of the Civil War, Ulysses S. Grant was enormously popular. He and his wife, Julia Dent Grant, had four children. They moved to Washington in 1866 and lived in a Georgetown house presented to them by admirers. That year President Andrew Johnson made Grant a four-star general, but the soldier (and presidential aspirant) began to distance himself from Johnson's soft approach to Reconstruction. *ANB*, 9:410, 419.

12. Arthur Leary of New York City owned a line of merchant ships. When he died in 1893, his funeral in St. Patrick's Cathedral was attended by many prominent New Yorkers, and the *New York Times* noted that his estate was "valued at several millions of dollars." His father, an associate of the Astor family, had made a fortune as a hat manufacturer. Arthur Leary and Father had official connections during the Civil War relating to Leary's shipping line, and the Chases and Leary became social acquaintances. For a long time Leary was a fixture of the fashionable social scene in New York. *New York Times*, Feb. 24, 26, 28, Mar. 9, 1893; *Chase Papers*, 1:595, 639, 699, 708.

13. A newspaper editor and social reformer who had been involved in the experimental communities founded by his father, Robert Dale Owen (b. 1801) was a former member of the Indiana legislature and the U.S. House of Representatives. He wrote several influential books and pamphlets regarding emancipation and assisted in drafting the Fourteenth Amendment. *DAB*, 14:118–22; George B. Lockwood, *The New Harmony Movement* (New York: A. M. Kelley, 1970), 375–76.

14. George Wood took his first position with the government, a clerkship in the War Department, in 1819. He was a Treasury Department employee for many years and had become the chief of the department's navigation division. He was also the author of several books and articles in periodicals. *Appletons'*, 6:593; *Chase Papers*, 1:633, 634; 5:103.

15. Barnum's City Hotel, located at the corner of Fayette and Calvert streets, had been providing accommodations in Baltimore for many years. Father first became familiar with the hotel, and was impressed by its quality, in 1829. *Chase Papers*, 1:18; 5:245.

16. Willie's nurse Maggie may have been the "Maggie English" whom Kate later named in her divorce petition. The petition accused William Sprague of committing adultery with Maggie English, an employee in the Sprague household. *New York Times*, Dec. 20, 1880; Lamphier, *Kate Chase and William Sprague*, 108, 253.

17. We know little about Mrs. Crawford, who was apparently the family's housekeeper in Washington by December 1865. *Chase Papers*, 1:599; 5:104, 121.

FATHER TO NETTIE

Washington, May 14, 1866.

My darling Nettie.

Your last letter, the last date in which is the 2[8]th April, came this morning, and I read most of it at the breakfast table to the Governor & Grandma, who join me in thinking it capital.[1] The illustration of the church-napping is excellent; and I think you would do well to give us more pen or pencil sketches in your letters. Really, dear Nettie, I think you bid fair to prove the best letter writer in the whole family; though you will find it hard to beat Katie. Her letters to the Governor are charming: and I am expecting a great treat in the one which is to contain the account of your visit to the House of Lords.

On Saturday I performed a sad duty in attending the funeral of dear Lizzie Goldsborough. She died Wednesday night. John Ryan, Catherines brother came down the next morning & told me the sad news.[2] I went up & found Mrs Goldsborough in great distress. It is very little that any friend can do in such moments except to sympathize and I did sympathize with her most profoundly, and it seemed to be a little relief. The Secretary of the Navy, whom I went to see, kindly consented to send a boat down for her Uncle William to Westmoreland County Virginia on the Potomac; and thus the whole family was gathered at the funeral. The services were performed in St. John's Church by Mr Lewis & Dr. Pinkney: the latter delivering a short address in which he described dear Lizzie's Christian faith & spirit very touchingly. He had been it seems her constant attendant for some time as a religious advisor & she was one of his communicants.[3] Her death came very suddenly at last. She had been very comfortable Wednesday. The day was beautiful. She sat up part of the time, &, with the help of her nurse, walked to the window & looked out on the bright sky & the green trees & the distant hills: and thought every thing lovely. In the evening her mother read the Bible & prayers to her as usual, & left her to repose with a kiss. About midnight the angel came for her & she went.

This death has made me very sad. It is as if one of my own dear relatives had been taken: and it makes me think anxiously about my treasures beyond the ocean.

Yesterday we attended church at St Johns & Mr. Lewis preached. The Sermon was, like all his sermons, simple, but very able & good. As a preacher he is very much to my taste: but the singing has become very theatrical & my old objections to the formalism of the service remain / It occurred to me that I might do good by trying to get the Methodists to adopt the ritual of our church simplified, & so make a sort of ground for the Union of the earnest portion of our church with theirs.

By the way the Methodists are engaged in an effort to build a great Metropolitan Church[4]—and who, think you, are to be two of the Trustees / Why no less persons than the Chief Justice & the Lieutenant General.[5] They asked and I at first declined as not belonging to their church: but they said it was common to have two or three of the Trustees from other denominations & I consented.

We had a very nice dinner on Thursday. The principal guests were Sir Fredk. Bruce, Baron Gerolt, Mr. McCulloch, Messrs Washburne, Hayes (the General) Patterson of the House, Mr. Garrett, & Mr. Albert from Baltimore & Generals Gillmore & Brice & Professor Henry.[6] Baron Eggloffstein who was also with us ought not to be forgotten nor Col Viall of Providence.[7] So you see all the guests were principal. It was a very plain dinner & got up admirably. Mrs Crawford is distinguishing herself, with the help of Gray & a French Cook. Col Viall who knows what is what says he never sat down to a better dinner at home or abroad.[8]

The next day the Rev. Dr. Brock, Sir Morton Peto's pastor, who brought me a letter from the Baronet, & his traveling friend Mr. Marten dined with us, together with Mr. H. D. Cooke & Judge Lawrence of the House, and I am not sure that the dinner, though not so well got up, was not even pleasanter than that of the day before. Dr. Brock proved himself very agreeable.[9]

Yesterday he was to have preached in the Hall of the House; but the annual refitting for Summer prevented. He preached in the Evening at Mr. Gray's opposite us.[10] I went to hear him, and was rewarded by a very solid, sensible, christian, & in parts eloquent Sermon on the Mediation.

Do you or Katie remember Mr. Biddle, who was at Rio & has been in the East Indies & I don't know where besides? He rode with me Saturday & desired to be remembered to one or both of you, I forget which; and, I promised, &—you see—fulfil.

I am very glad you have seen Mr. Bright & hope you may see more of him. I think him among the foremost of modern men. His course on the Reform bill has proved him a sagacious as well as earnest friend of progress. I wish some of *our* "liberals" had his sterling good sense, as well as his zeal. We are all disappointed that the Reform bill did not command a larger majority, but glad that the Ministry does not give up. Sir Fredk thought they would. I don't think *he* "takes much," to Reform or to Mr. Bright either.[11]

Col. Collins was here yesterday. He says that everything at Hillsborough is pretty much as it was in old times. Caspar's death makes a sad break in their circle. He spoke affectionately as he always does of you & desired to be remembered to both.[12] Wm Neff from Cincinnati was with him.[13] He is an old admirer of Katie's & sends his best regards.

George Wood came in with me from Church last night. The old gentleman comes occasionally to play chess—not last night though! He *half* regrets that he did not go with you; & *quite* that he could not.

Mr. Leary too was here last night evening with Mr Smythe the newly appointed Collector, for New York who was to leave on the Evening train,[14] & called to enquire about [*illeg.*] Thomas Brown (Katie remembers him if you don't) whom he thinks of making his Private Secretary. Mr. Leary was radiant as usual, and sent messages of kind regard.

Mr. Pierce was here last week, going to Richmond for some purpose. The same old six-pence.[15]

And last but not least Mr. Whitelaw Reid has again turned up in Washington: but he is no longer a fixed star in this sky. He remains only a few days, & returns south to his Cotton. In company with General Heron, who since he has doffed his uniform has become a Commission Merchant in New Orleans,[16] he has engaged in planting, & expects if the worms spare his crop to make a profit of $25.000 or $30.000 this year. In which I hope he may succeed & that success may not turn his head.

Speaking of Cotton I will give you an item which may be interesting to some of those you meet. Mr. Brackenridge of Texas has been with me today & says, that the Cotton crop of Texas this year will be 500.000 bales, which at 400 pounds to the bale, is 200.000.000 pounds.[17] I begin to think that the crop this year will reach 3.500.000 bales of ginned cotton, which at 400 pounds (the number of pounds to the bale according to our last census) will give 1.400.000.000 pounds as the product of this year. This is about 600.000.000 pounds less than the product of 1860; but nearly twice as much as was expected at the beginning of the year. Indeed more than twice as much as was expected by many of our most intelligent & best informed men.

The dead lock between the President & Congress still continues: but the world moves on notwithstanding. As far as I can see the People are on the side of Congress: that is to say against letting the lately rebel states be represented in the Senate & House until some further settlement of the basis of representation in the House & some decisive security against the rebel debt & payment for slaves. The Constitutional Amendment which has passed the House will probably be altered somewhat in the Senate; but in these respects at least it will remain unchanged & these are most important. I still hope that the differences between the Executive & Legislative Departments will be reconciled. I see no reason why they may not be with good dispositions on both sides.[18]

The President has not yet issued any proclamation abrogating martial law & restoring the writ of Habeas Corpus & it is still uncertain whether I shall hold the Courts in Virginia & North Carolina. An indictment has been found against Davis for treason, but it is under a statute which does not make death the penalty.[19] Love to Katie.

Your very affe. father
S P Chase

Library of Congress.

1. Technically, Mary Colton Smith was Kate's "Grandma" and not Nettie's, but she was the only surviving grandparent either of them had. She was making a prolonged stay in Washington, as shown by references in Father's letters. Father said of her in a letter to Nettie on June 5: "Grandma Smith is about as usual—pretty well, but rather feeble. I do not see that she changes at all. Mrs Crawford is very attentive to her & we all try to promote her comfort." *Chase Papers,* 5:104, 121.

2. Elizabeth Gamble Wirt Goldsborough's daughter, also named Elizabeth and known as "Lizzie," died after an unknown but long illness. Her Uncle William was her mother's brother, William C. Wirt. George A. Hanson, *Old Kent: The Eastern Shore of Mary-*

land (Baltimore: John P. Des Forges, 1876; repr., Baltimore: Regional Publishing Co., 1967), 291; *Chase Papers*, 1:4.

3. St. John's Church, known as the "Church of the Presidents," was built in 1816. The Episcopal sanctuary stood on Lafayette Square across from the White House at 16th and H streets, N.W. The Reverend John Vaughan Lewis was the church's rector from 1865 to 1880. The Reverend William Pinkney of Maryland was rector of Washington's Church of the Ascension. He later became the Protestant Episcopal bishop of Maryland. *Appletons'*, 5:27; Green, *Washington*, 72; George Morgan Hills, *History of the Church in Burlington, New Jersey* (Trenton, N.J.: W. S. Sharp, 1876), 726; Carolyn Gilbert Benjamin, *Historical Sketches of the Parishes and Missions in the Diocese of Washington* (Washington, D.C.: Episcopal Church, Diocese of Washington, 1928), 65.

4. After a delay during the war years, construction was resumed on the Metropolitan Church on C Street in Washington in 1866. Francis S. De Hass ran a successful fund-raising campaign to cover the building costs. The completed church was dedicated in 1869. Lillian Brooks Brown, *A Living Centennial: Commemorating the One Hundredth Anniversary of Metropolitan Memorial United Methodist Church* (Washington, D.C.: Judd & Detweiler, 1969), 4–10.

5. That is, Father and U. S. Grant.

6. Sir Frederick William Adolphus Bruce, Great Britain's representative in Washington since 1865; the Prussian minister to the United States, Friedrich Karl Joseph von Gerolt; Hugh McCulloch; Elihu Benjamin Washburne; Rutherford B. Hayes, who as a Cincinnati lawyer had assisted Father on the Rosetta Armstead case, then became a major general during the war and a congressman from Ohio, 1865–67; James Willis Patterson, a Dartmouth College professor who represented New Hampshire in the House, 1863–67, and the Senate, 1867–73; John Work Garrett of the Baltimore and Ohio Railroad; Baltimore banker William Julian Albert; Quincy Adams Gillmore; Gen. Benjamin W. Brice, former Ohio militia officer, judge of common pleas, and state adjutant general, who in 1866 was paymaster general in Washington; and Joseph Henry of the Smithsonian Institution. *ODNB*, 8:295–96; *ANB*, 10:400–403; *DAB*, 14:303; *Who Was Who*, hist. vol., 17; *Appletons'*, 1:372; Ari Hoogenboom, *Rutherford B. Hayes: Warrior and President* (Boston: University Press of Kansas, 1914), 57, 94–95, 122; *Chase Papers*, 1:494, 610.

7. Rhode Island manufacturer Nelson Viall, who was born in Plainfield, Conn., in 1827, was a first lieutenant of Rhode Island militia during the war with Mexico. At the start of the Civil War, responding to the call of William Sprague, who was then governor, for troops from Rhode Island, he raised a company and became a captain of infantry from Rhode Island. He worked his way up the ranks to become lieutenant colonel of an African American artillery unit early in 1864. During the final months of the Civil War he was in command of the District of Carrollton in Louisiana. In 1866, Viall was made a brevet brigadier general of volunteers, dating from March 1865. He became the chief of police of Providence, then from 1867 until his death in 1903 was warden of the Rhode Island state prison, earning a national reputation as a prison authority. We do not know if he had any connection to Mary Viall. Eicher and Eicher, *Civil War High Commands*, 544, 760, 822; *New York Times*, May 2, 1903; *Chase Papers*, 1:591, 626.

8. Of the dinner on May 10, Father recorded in his journal: "The conversation was general & pleasant. Sir Fredk. in particular seemed to enjoy himself." Gov. Thomas Swann Jr., of Maryland, Congressman Henry T. Blow of St. Louis, and Congressman John A. Bingham of Ohio were unable to attend. *Chase Papers*, 1:8, 276, 510, 610.

9. English Baptist minister the Reverend Dr. William Brock was the pastor of Bloomsbury Chapel. An active and well-known abolitionist, Brock helped organize the London Freedman's Aid Society. British politician and railroad contractor Sir Samuel Morton Peto helped fund the Baptist chapel in Bloomsbury and one in Regent's Park. Father had met Peto in the fall of 1865, when the Englishman and a delegation of British capitalists were in the U.S. looking at investment possibilities. Daniel Clarke Eddy, *Europa; or, Scenes and Society in England, France, Italy, and Switzerland* (Boston: Ticknor, Reed & Fields, 1859), 117–18; Levi Coffin, *Reminiscences of Levi Coffin, the Reputed President of the Underground Railroad* (Cincinnati: Western Tract Society, [1876]), 667–68; *ODNB*, 43:897–900; *Chase Papers*, 1:600.

10. The E Street Church, a Baptist church completed in 1843, stood on E Street between 6th and 7th streets. *Boyd's Washington and Georgetown Directory*, 218.

11. English political reformer John Bright argued successfully against recognizing the Confederacy in a speech before the British House of Commons in 1863. On William Gladstone's introduction of the government's Reform Bill in March 1866, Bright spoke against

Liberal opponents of the measure. When the government resigned over the bill, Bright energetically promoted the reform cause in addresses to public gatherings. *ODNB*, 7:633; Edward L. Pierce, *Memoir and Letters of Charles Sumner*, 4 vols. (Boston: Roberts Brothers, 1893), 4:147.

12. Father inserted "to both" after he wrote the next sentence.

13. Brothers Peter, William, and George Neff owned a hardware business in Cincinnati. Father had known William Neff since the 1830s. *Nat. Cyc.*, 25:274; *Chase Papers*, 1:114, 125.

14. Henry A. Smythe, a merchant and banker, had become collector of customs at New York earlier in 1866. *Chase Papers*, 1:637.

15. "Sixpence" was sometimes used as a nickname for a person—generally, as in this case, implying constancy and reliability. Massachusetts lawyer Edward Lillie Pierce (b. 1829), Charles Sumner's political acolyte, spent some time in Father's law office in Ohio in the 1850s but left to practice law in Chicago when he thought he might begin to be identified as Father's "parasite." Pierce undertook a political biography of Father, which was never carried out in full form, and the two considered publishing a collection of Father's Senate speeches. During the Civil War, Father made Pierce a special agent of the Treasury superintending the government's relations with freed slaves, first at Fortress Monroe and then in the Sea Islands. Pierce published his observations of those experiences. He served as Boston's collector of internal revenue, 1864–66, and as district attorney for Norfolk and Plymouth counties, 1866–70. He published *A Treatise on American Railroad Law* in 1857 and, later, his *Memoir and Letters of Charles Sumner*. *OED*, 15:575; *DAB*, 14:575–76; *Chase Papers*, 1:238, 266, 277; 2:432–34; 3:118–19, 136–39, 143–46.

16. A banker in Dubuque, Iowa, before the war, Francis Jay Herron attained the rank of major general of volunteers before resigning from the army in June 1865. He was in Louisiana during the latter part of the war and remained there until 1877. *ANB*, 10:676–77.

17. In 1863, Father appointed Texan George W. Brackenridge assistant special agent in the lower Mississippi Valley. *Chase Papers*, 1:521.

18. When ratified in 1868, the Fourteenth Amendment defined citizenship without any preclusion for race, guaranteed everyone "the equal protection of the laws," and made all adult males eligible to vote. The amendment also prohibited anyone from holding federal or state office who had taken an oath to uphold the U.S. Constitution and supported the Confederacy, although Congress could remove that disability. Foner, *Short History of Reconstruction*, 114–15.

19. In May 1866, a grand jury of the federal district court in Virginia indicted Jefferson Davis for treason, but Father would not hold circuit court in states where the civilian justice system had not been restored. As he wrote to President Andrew Johnson in October 1865, "I so much doubt the propriety of holding Circuit Courts of the United States in States which have been declared by the Executive and Legislative Departments of the National Government to be in rebellion & therefore subjected to Martial law, before the complete restoration of their broken relations with the nation & the supercedure of the military by the civil administration, that I am unwilling to hold such courts in such states within my Circuit, which includes Virginia, until Congress shall have had an opportunity to consider and act on the whole subject." Since a "civil Court in a district under Martial law can only act by the sanction and under the supervision of the Military power," he did not think "that it becomes the Justices of the Supreme Court to exercise jurisdiction under such conditions." In 1868, Davis's attorney petitioned for dismissal of the charges against the former Confederate president, arguing that he could only be punished under the provisions of the Fourteenth Amendment. The Supreme Court agreed, dismissing the indictment in 1869. *Chase Papers*, 5:70–71; Hyman, *Reconstruction Justice*, 138–39.

FATHER TO KATE

Washington, June 15, 1866

My dearest Katie,

Your long letter was most welcome / It was very interesting, indeed, and extremely well written. Indeed you and Nettie write such excellent letters that I begin to think that there was a good deal of sense in the remark I once made in answer to some body who wanted to know my opinion on womans-rights, that I was for putting every thing in the hands of the women & letting them govern. Certainly I dont see but you & Nettie are as well qualified to take part in affairs as I was at your age.

Congress at last has proposed its plan of reconstruction. It proposed an amendment of the Constitution (1) defining citizenship & prohibiting the states from abridging personal rights; (2) making representation in Congress substantially in proportion to the number of citizens allowed to vote; (3) excluding certain classes of rebels from office until disability removed by vote of ⅔ds of each house; (4) prohibiting payment of war debt or compensation for slaves.

Congress will now admit Senators & Representatives from such states lately in rebellion as may ratify this amendment; but has yet agreed to no regular plan of admission. Probably a law will be passed providing for admission on ratification & such modifications of state Constitutions & laws as are necessary to conform them to the amendment. There is some expectation that the Legislature of Tennessee will be called together at once & will ratify the amendment without delay: in which case the Senators & Members from that state who can take the oath required by law of non-participation in rebellion (& I believe all can) will be admitted at once. There is a great desire to see these gentlemen in, especially Senator Fowler, & Representatives Stokes & Maynard, before Congress adjourns: and it is now expected that Congress will adjourn about the 15th of July.[1]

For two or three days the weather has been very hot and I have been strongly tempted to seek cooler latitudes; but I hate to leave the Governor here alone in the house. We get along together nicely. I only regret that I cannot be of more use to him.

He tells you I dare say all about the goings on of the establishment—how Mrs Crawford markets—how "oats, peas, beans & barley grow" on the Seaton acres[2]—how we ride evenings—how we sometimes dont—and generally keeps you posted on these matters.

Two evenings since we called at General Schenck's, and passed an hour very pleasantly. The young ladies as you know are very sensible and agreeable talkers. They all enquired very kindly for you.[3]

June 18. To be sure of the Wednesday Steamer letters must be sent today: so I will add a few words, and send this to the Post Office. There is no change here, except that we are all three days older & Thomas & Lois have gone. They went last evening. Poor Lois seemed so sorry to go. She fairly cried, and I was sorry to have go too: for she has been an excellent chamber maid, keeping every thing in perfect order—I gave her a [5], which the poor girl took sobbing. I never knew till Thomas came to say goodbye too that Lois was his wife.

Within the last three days Senator Sumners mother & General Cass & Col Seaton have died.[4] They were very old—each over 80—Gen. Cass, I think the oldest. There are very few living whose lives began in the last century, & when the next Century begins who of those that now take part in the busy scenes will live? It is said somewhere that a man was roused to a sense of the vanity of things earthly, & led to seek for eternal things by reading the 5th Chapter of Genesis, where the account of each patriarch after hundreds of years of life, ends with "And he died!" Well may it excite the most serious reflections. But, good bye, darling. May Heaven bless ye.

Your affectionate father
S P Chase

Library of Congress.

1. When Congress adjourned in July it had not settled how ex-Confederate states would be readmitted to the Union. Tennessee ratified the Fourteenth Amendment, was readmitted as a state, and its legislators were allowed to take their seats in Congress. That established a precedent for the readmission of other states. Slavery opponent Joseph Smith Fowler was elected to the U.S. Senate in 1865 but could not be seated until after Tennessee ratified the amendment on July 19, 1866. When he took his seat on July 24, Fowler became the first senator from a former Confederate state to be admitted to the Senate since the war. William Brickly Stokes achieved the rank of general in the Union Army during the war; he represented Tennessee in the U.S. House of Representatives from 1866 to 1871. Horace Maynard taught mathematics at East Tennessee College before becoming a lawyer and politician. Maynard was elected to Congress in 1866. Foner, *Short History of Reconstruction*, 116–17; *DAB*, 6:564; 12:460–61; *Bio. Dir. U.S. Cong.*, 1870.

2. William W. Seaton, coeditor of the *National Intelligencer* newspaper since 1812 and former five-term mayor of Washington, kept a garden on the square at 5th, 6th, L, and M streets, N.W. The round "Oats, Pease, Beans and Barley Grows" is a children's song that originated in France in the fourteenth century and remains popular in Europe and America to the present day. Traditionally, children sing the refrain while circling around one child: "Oats, pease, beans, and barley grows, / How you, nor I, nor nobody knows. / Oats, pease, beans, and barley grows, / Oats, pease, beans, and barley grows; / How you, nor I, nor nobody knows, / Oats, pease, beans, and barley grows." They then stop circling, and act out the motions of farming while singing the next verse: "Thus the farmer sows his seed, / Stands erect and takes his ease, / Stamps his foot, and claps his hands, / And turns about to view his lands." *Chase Papers*, 1:365, 522; Green, *Washington*, 52, 161–64; William Wells Newell, *Games and Songs of American Children* (New York: Harper & Brothers, 1911), 80–81.

3. A leading Whig in both the Ohio House (1841–43) and the U.S. Congress (1843–51), Robert Cumming Schenck was promoted to major general of volunteers during the war and returned to Congress in 1863. He and his wife, Rennelche W. Smith, had three daughters who were still living at the time of General Schenck's death in 1890. *DAB*, 16:427–28; *New York Times*, Mar. 24, 1890.

4. Relief Jacob Sumner, wife of Boston lawyer Charles Pinckney Sumner, who also died in 1866, died in Boston on June 15. She had nine children, of whom Charles and his twin Matilda were the oldest. Lewis Cass, born in 1782, had been a senator from Michigan, 1845–57, overlapping with Father in that chamber, and U.S. secretary of state, 1857–60. William Winston Seaton, a Virginian, supported the Union but opposed the views of radical abolitionists, arguing instead for gradual emancipation and colonization. *DAB*, 3:562–64; 16:541–42; 18:208; Anna Laurens Dawes, *Charles Sumner* (New York: Dodd, Mead & Co., 1898), 261.

FATHER TO NETTIE

Washington, June 18, 1866

My darling Nettie,

Your last letter was a real treat; though I must say that Katie's which came by the same mail, taken altogether, composition, spelling & penmanship beat your's just a little. Spur up your Pegasus, and make him keep step. Don't be in too great a hurry when you write to write well & correctly. Don't tear your paper. Fold your letters neatly & regularly. Let Pegasus use his wings, but do you use the reins.[1]

I sent both your & Katies letters to Mary Goldsborough to read; having received a note from her making very friendly enquiries for you. She returned the letters Saturday with a note, & she rewards me for sending them by saying "it was so sweet & kind[2] of you & so thoughtful to send me dear Katie & Nettie's letters to read. They are charmingly written & so interesting. I cannot tell you how much I enjoyed them, it seemed like meeting the girls vis-a-vis & having a pleasant chat with them." So you see your letters give pleasure to many.

We had very hot weather last week but yesterday it rained heavily and towards evening became quite cool; and today the temperature is delightful.

Saturday I walked out to Campbell Hospital to see Susan Walker.[3] She was deep in business, finishing off her work for the day. She told me she had taken up her abode at the Hospital, having removed from Mrs Force's on account of the distance. It is a great self denial to live as she does with her tastes & means: but I have no doubt she is far happier than she would be if seeking only her own gratification, or living in society as most do for themselves & friends.

There is a good deal of excitement here about the news from Europe that the proposed Conference is broken off.[4] For my part I don't think Peace Conferences amount to much when differences have become so serious. Ours did not; and yet neither side had armed, as Austria, Prussia & Italy have done.[5] We are all anxious to know when the storm will burst. To me it seems that Prussia & Austria will both get the worst of it. While the two dogs fight, the fox may run away with the bone.[6]

Our Fenian war seems to be over for the present. The Fenians are bitter against the Johnson-Seward proclamation & action: and have some reason.[7]

Santa-Anna is in New Jersey issuing proclamations against Maximilian. He too like the Fenians supposes he is in favor with Johnson & Seward—particularly Seward: and he has a right to suppose so, until it becomes convenient not to let him suppose so any longer.[8]

You see that some changes are being made in the Senate. Gen. Ferry was elected sometime ago in Connecticut over Mr. Foster, & just now Mr.

Patterson has been elected in New Hampshire over Mr. Clark.[9] These changes make the Governor grave and he is inclined to quit his place. I advise against it. He ought to remain where he is, and qualify himself by hard study for the greatest usefulness.

I am thinking of a trip to Oakland this week. Perhaps you don't know that there is such a place. It is quite a favorite mountain resort, about half way between Baltimore & Wheeling. Mr. Garrett asked me to go sometime ago & I promised to think of it, & this morning I have written him on the subject. If I go I shall only be absent a few days, not beyond Monday or Tuesday of next week.[10]

Will you go to Italy? If you do you must see Mr. Powers at Florence; and if it dont cost too much, say not over five hundred dollars, you & Katie must have your busts taken in marble. I will keep them while I live & then each shall have the others[11] / I have been intending to send Jones bust of me to Powers but have kept putting it off.[12]

I dont think of much more to say: but I must add a caution not to forget your Christian character. Travellers for recreation or general observation are too apt to forget it. I know that I am to apt to neglect Sundays & week day's duties when I am on a journey: but when do we more need "the good hand of God" upon us?[13]

Goodbye, my dear child. May God, with his choicest blessings follow my beloved children. I keep the old Brady group in my chamber & it does me good to look at it.[14]

Your affectionate father
S P Chase

Library of Congress.

1. In Ovid's *Metamorphoses*, among other sources of classical myth, the white-winged horse Pegasus had connections to fame and to the Hippocrene spring at Parnassus. Those associations, embellished, enhanced, and recast through the centuries, gave Pegasus a special bond to the Muses and made him the symbolic means by which a writer might hope to reach creative heights. Although Nettie could have known the ancient myth of Pegasus and the later association of the steed with literary genius from a variety of sources, Nathaniel Hawthorne's retelling of the story of Pegasus and Bellerophon in his *Wonder-Book for Girls and Boys* was probably one of the "wonderful magical tales" and "dearly loved romances" by Hawthorne that were familiar to her before she met the author in 1861. In the *Wonder-Book*, which went through a number of printings and editions after its first appearance in Boston in 1851, Hawthorne not only told the original myth but made his fictional narrator yearn to ride Pegasus to make "literary calls" on Longfellow, Melville, and other writers. Nettie probably also knew another Hawthorne story, "A Virtuoso's Collection," from *Mosses from an Old Manse*, in which Hawthorne referred to Pegasus as "hard ridden by many young gentlemen of the day." See the letter written by Nettie and Will Hoyt, Apr. 30, 1871, in this volume; *New York Tribune*, Mar. 8, 1891; Charvat et al., *Centenary Edition*, 7:7, 143–69, 373–76; 10:479–80; Hugo McPherson, *Hawthorne as Myth-Maker: A Study in Imagination* (Toronto: University of Toronto Press, 1969), 13–17, 71–76; Marianne Shapiro, "Perseus and Bellerophon in *Orlando Furioso*," *Modern Philology* 81 (1983): 124–28; Wilfred P. Mustard, "Pegasus as the Poet's Steed," *Modern Language Notes* 23 (1908): 32; Robert J. Clements, "The Cult of the Poet in Renaissance Emblem Literature," *PMLA* 59 (1944): 672–74; *OED*, 11:441; Charles Russell Coulter and Patricia Turner, *Encyclopedia of Ancient Deities* (Jefferson, N.C.: McFarland, 2000), 376.

2. Father originally wrote "so sweet & kind & good," then canceled the "& good."

3. Campbell Hospital, located at the north end of 6th Street in Washington, treated African Americans after the war. Wilhelmus Bogart Bryan, *A History of the National Capital* (New York: Macmillan, 1916), 539.

4. Prussia had readied for war with the Austro-Hungarian Empire in order to annex Schleswig and Holstein. Italians under the leadership of Giuseppe Garibaldi allied with Prussia to force the Austrians to cede Venetia. Throughout the spring of 1866, Britain and other nations attempted to avert a war by diplomatic means, but by June it was clear their efforts had failed. Prussia defeated Austria-Hungary in the ensuing war. Roger Price, *The French Second Empire* (Cambridge: Cambridge University Press, 2001), 305–401; Bruce Waller, *Bismarck*, 2d ed. (Oxford: Blackwell, 1997), 26–31; Otto Pflanze, *Bismarck and the Development of Germany*, vol. 1, *The Period of Unification, 1815–1871* (Princeton, N.J.: Princeton University Press, 1990), 309–10.

5. In February 1861, Father was a delegate to a peace convention called by ex-president John Tyler and the Virginia legislature, with the support of William Seward, in an unsuccessful attempt to avert civil war as Southern states seceded from the Union. *Chase Papers*, 3:xviii; David M. Potter, *The Impending Crisis, 1848–1861*, completed and ed. Don E. Fehrenbacher (New York: Harper & Row, 1976), 545–47; McPherson, *Battle Cry of Freedom*, 256–57.

6. This phrase refers to the Aesop fable, "Two dogs fight over a bone and a third runs away with it," a variation of the fable "The Lion, The Bear and the Fox," in which the lion and the bear fight over a dead fawn and become so exhausted that a fox can take it as they lie and watch. In Father's allusion, France was the fox. Ennis Rees, *Fables from Aesop* (Oxford: Oxford University Press, 1966), 29.

7. The Fenian Brotherhood was an Irish radical nationalist group based in America that aimed to win freedom for Ireland by igniting a war between the United States and Britain. Both President Andrew Johnson and Secretary of State Seward favored an independent Ireland, giving support to the Fenians until June 2, 1866, when a group of 1,500 Fenians crossed into Canada and fought Canadian militia. Johnson issued a proclamation of neutrality, making it clear that the Fenians were operating without federal support. On June 3, Fenians were captured by the U.S. revenue cutter *Michigan* as they attempted to cross the Niagara River. Rising Lake Morrow, "The Negotiation of the Anglo-American Treaty of 1870," *American Historical Review* 39, no. 4 (July 1934): 663–65. William D'Arcy, *The Fenian Movement in the United States: 1858–1886* (Washington, D.C.: Catholic University of America Press, 1947), 157, 159, 162–63; J. Bartlet Brebner, *Canada: A Modern History* (Ann Arbor, Mich.: University of Michigan Press, 1960), 151–52.

8. Antonio López de Santa Anna, the former president of Mexico and general of the Mexican armies during the war with the United States, had met with Seward and was under the impression that the Johnson administration would support him in overthrowing Emperor Maximilian, who had ruled Mexico with support from France since 1864. Santa Anna came to New York in May 1866, receiving positive newspaper attention but hostility from the Mexican minister and no recognition from Seward, who refused to meet Santa Anna or his representatives. Santa Anna continued to make efforts to get the Americans and Mexican nationalist leader Benito Juárez to accept his assistance, but in November 1866 Seward finally ceased to correspond with Santa Anna. In March 1867, the U.S. Navy thwarted Santa Anna's attempt to land in Mexico. Ruth R. Olivera and Liliane Crété, *Life in Mexico under Santa Anna, 1822–1855* (Norman, Okla.: University of Oklahoma Press, 1991), 5–16; "Mexico and Europe," *Living Age*, Aug. 10, 1867, 371–74.

9. Connecticut Republican Orris Sanford Ferry served in the House of Representatives, 1859–61, and as a brigadier general of volunteers, 1862–65, before his election to the U.S. Senate, where he served from 1867 to 1875. Lafayette Sabine Foster was president pro tem of the Senate. James W. Patterson defeated lawyer and soldier Frank Gay Clarke, who served in the House of Representatives, 1863–65 and 1871–75. *DAB*, 6:342–43; *Chase Papers*, 1:332; *Bio. Dir. U.S. Cong.*, 984.

10. An area of high meadows in the mountains of western Maryland along the route of the Baltimore and Ohio Railroad had long been called the Glades. The area's picturesque natural characteristics were a tourist attraction even before the railroad and the Glades Hotel at Oakland, Md., made the locale more accessible. Edward H. Hall, *Appletons'*

*Hand-Book of American Travel. The Southern Tour; being a guide through Maryland, District of
Columbia, Virginia, North Carolina, Georgia and Kentucky . . .* (New York: D. Appleton & Co.,
1866), 17; James D. Dilts, *The Great Road: The Building of the Baltimore and Ohio, the Nation's First Railroad, 1828–1853* (Stanford, Calif.: Stanford University Press, 1993), 31, 240,
283.

    11. The sculptor Hiram Powers was one of the most celebrated artists of his day. He
began his career in Cincinnati before moving in 1835 to Washington, D.C., where he created busts of noted politicians including Andrew Jackson and Daniel Webster. In 1837,
Powers settled in Florence, Italy, and remained there for the rest of his life, gaining ever
more acclaim and wealth. Having sold statues such as his famous "Greek Slave" for more
than $4,000, Powers likely commanded far more than $500 for taking a bust. *DAB*,
15:158–68.

    12. Ohio artist Thomas Dow Jones had modeled a bust of Father commissioned by a
group of Cincinnati citizens in 1858 (see Father to Kate, Apr. 30, 1859, chapter 3 above). In
1876, a bust of Father by Jones was placed in the Supreme Court room of the U.S. Capitol.
Chase Papers, 1:311; Groce and Wallace, *Dictionary of Artists,* 358.

    13. "And by the good hand of our God upon us they brought us a man of understand-
ing." Ezra 8:18.

    14. Probably the photograph of Father, Kate, and Nettie illustrated in this volume. The
well-known Civil War photographer Matthew Brady also photographed Kate visiting General Abercrombie and his staff, which is also in this volume, and took a formal portrait of
Father as secretary of the Treasury. Web Garrison, *Brady's Civil War* (New York: Lyons Press,
2000), 12, 199–200.

FATHER TO NETTIE

Washington June 22, 1866

My darling Nettie,

    This must be a very short letter, the next must atone. Your last from
Ventnor came this morning.[1] You seem to think it not your best; & it
was not; but seemed very good to me hungry as I was for letters from my
children.

    Pretty much all I have to say in addition to what I have put in Katies
letter is that a Splendid mocking bird—splendid in voice I mean came
yesterday—in a big cage—came yesterday in a cage on which was pasted
the direction "Miss Nettie Chase, care of Chief Justice Chase." That was
all. The address was in round hand, which allowed no recognition. I
have a fancy that the bird must have come from Mr Reid who is planting
cotton in Louisiana and is intended as a sort of compensation for your
failure to get one a year ago.

    Mr. Mullett is going to pack up Jones bust of me safely & send it to Mr.
Powers who will put in marble[2] / I must write to Mr Powers.

    Will the War keep you from going to Italy. You remember the Author
of the Roman Exile? I cant; but he is a lawyer now in Italy; very likely at
Florence.[3]

    We suppose here that fighting has begun in the Duchies & probably
also in Italy. Nobody here likes Bismarck or care much about the mere
Austro-Prussian question: but every body sympathizes with Italy: and is

curious to see what Napoleon will do. Somebody writes "il prendra ce qu'il peut."[4] I guess so.

Your always affe. father

S P Chase

Library of Congress.

1. Built on a steep hillside, the seaside town of Ventnor on the Isle of Wight was a popular health resort. Telford Varley, *Isle of Wight* (Cambridge: A. & C. Black, 1924), 132; Aubrey de Selincourt, *Isle of Wight* (London: P. Elek, 1948), 30–31.

2. Born in England in 1834, Alfred Bult Mullett moved to Ohio with his parents as a child. He assisted Cincinnati architect Isaiah Rogers from 1860 to 1865 before serving as acting assistant supervising architect of the U.S. Treasury for a year, and then as supervising architect of the Treasury from 1866 to 1876. *Nat. Cyc.*, 27:452.

3. Guglielmo Gajani, author of *The Roman Exile* (Boston: J. P. Jewett, 1856), is identified on the book's title page as "Professor of Civil and Canon Law, and Representative of the People in the Roman Constituent Assembly in the Year 1849."

4. "He will take what he can." Napoleon III of France, by supporting Italian unification, had put himself in a position that made it difficult to object to Prussia's efforts to unify the states of Germany. However, as indicated by Father's comments in the previous letter, there was some expectation that Napoleon might take advantage of the conflict between Prussia and Austria-Hungary. An 1870 biographical essay published in *Harper's New Monthly Magazine* illustrated that many Americans perceived Prussia's prime minister, Otto Fürst von Bismarck, as an antidemocratic tyrant. David Wetzel, *A Duel of Giants: Bismarck, Napoleon III, and the Origins of the Franco-Prussian War* (Madison, Wis.: University of Wisconsin Press, 2001), 18, 21; Waller, *Bismarck*, 28; S. S. Conant, "Count Otto von Bismarck," *Harper's New Monthly Magazine* 40 (April 1870): 648–61.

FATHER TO NETTIE

Washington, July 2, 1866

My darling Nettie,

Your last letter was your chef d'œuvre.[1] The presentation, a ce que vous en disez,[2] must have been a stupid affair enough; but you succeeded, per force of illustrations, in making the story really interesting. You must write an illustrated book of travels! Moreover your penmanship needed only one thing, junction of letters, to be quite excellent—unique & characteristic to be sure but I would not have it otherwise than that. I would join to that, *junction* & perfect spelling, in which two or three words were defective, not from ignorance but carelessness. I will illustrate what I mean thus, *attitude,* selon moi, *atitude* selon toi.[3] Dont mind—that is, dont be troubled by these small criticisms. Only great paintings oblige the observer to descend to such.

But what were you—what was Katie thinking of when you both wrote such nice long letters, without once mentioning *the Boy.* It was a picture of Eden with the first pair left out. Let us hope that your next will contain so much & so good news of him as to make amends for late omissions.

I sent your letter to Mary Goldsborough who has returned it with much praise & prayers of kind remembrance: and I am going to send it to Jane Auld for her reading & the childrens.

Everybody is talking of Prussia & Austria & Italy, & Napoleon & England. I say Napoleon—for there is at present no France, & I might say Bismarck instead of Prussia only there seems to be a Prussia, threatening to come to life and give the crazy king and his absolute minister[4] some trouble, unless they repent. And is repentance possible for either? Mr. Gladstone expressed my ideas of the rights & wrongs of the situation precisely[5]— Austria wrong in obstinate refusal to cede Venetia & take equivalents, easier obtained & better when obtained for her, without than with war: Austria right, in the regards of the law of Nations and sound political morals— which ought to be the same things—in respect to the Elbe Duchies.

But why talk of these things. I suppose the fight is begun: and the logic of events will not pay much attention to Prussia or Austria either. It will be a good thing if the petty dominations of Germany—which serve principally as Nurseries of husbands & wives for the members of the great Houses, or rather the Houses whose great nations make great—are all broken up—too good a thing, I fear, to happen, for how can the Houses do without the nurseries?

We have our own troubles at home. We all hoped that the President would cease his war on Congress when the Amendment was proposed / But it is not so. The war continues, and grows more & more bitter. The Presidents servants have called a National Convention, and the so called Democrats approve and doubtless there will be a large attendance in Philadelphia in August[6] / It will be just what patronage, with the help of hungry democrats can make it. But it will represent no ideas—nothing but platitudes—and will not have the sympathies of the masses & will fail.

Just now Tennessee is the battle ground of conflict. Gov. Brownlow has called the Legislature to meet on the 4th of July.[7] If it meets it will ratify the amendment and the Senators & Representatives of the State will be at once admitted. So the administration is straining every nerve to prevent the Legislature from coming together, or, if assembled[,] from action. Strange policy this! to profess great anxiety for the readmission of the States to Congress and yet to do every thing possible to prevent them from accepting an amendment admitted to be fair & reasonable, upon the acceptance of which their Senators & Representatives w[ill] be at once admitted.

I have written you only a political letter. Mr. Pike says Mrs P—— was in Paris all the time you were there ignorant of your presence & anxious to see you[8]—We the Governor & I & Grandma,[9] & Mrs Crawford & Albert[10] & the nine dogs—not muses—are all well.

Love Love Love to K & W & for N, from her affectionate [father]

S P Chase

Library of Congress.

    1. Masterpiece.
    2. "Of which you speak."

3. That is, "*attitude* according to me, *atitude* according to you."

4. King Wilhelm of Prussia and Otto von Bismarck.

5. A significant force in Britain's Liberal Party, William Ewart Gladstone became leader of the House of Commons in 1865. He was also chancellor of the exchequer, but resigned with the government after the failure of the Reform Bill. Gladstone resumed his leadership position in the Commons in 1867 and became prime minister after a Liberal victory in parliamentary elections in 1868. *ODNB*, 22:391–94; *The American Cyclopedia* (New York: Thompson & Thompson, 1878), 832.

6. The National Union Convention, also known as the Southern Loyalist Convention, was held August 14–16. Organizers unsuccessfully attempted to organize a political party to bridge the growing gap between Radical Republicans and President Johnson over Reconstruction. Foner, *Short History of Reconstruction*, 118–19.

7. William Gannaway Brownlow was imprisoned by the Confederates for treason, but released and returned to Tennessee in 1863. He was elected governor in 1865. Brownlow called a special session of the Tennessee legislature to meet on July 4, 1866, to ratify the Fourteenth Amendment. E. Meron Coulter, *William G. Brownlow: Fighting Parson of the Southern Highlands* (Chapel Hill, N.C.: University of North Carolina Press, 1937), 309–12; *DAB*, 3:177–78.

8. James Shepherd Pike had returned to the United States in May after serving as U.S. minister to the Netherlands. Father had expected Elizabeth Ellicott Pike to return at the same time as her husband and that she would miss seeing Kate and Nettie in Europe. *Chase Papers*, 1:587; 5:83, 84.

9. Mary Colton Smith.

10. W. Albert Wells.

FATHER TO NETTIE

Beverley, Aug 9, 66

My darling Nettie

Your last date is still July 8, from North Berwick. Katies July 15 from Inverness.[1] I suppose that two or three of your pleasant letters are on the way and will I hope have a more fortunate arrival than Gilpen's hat & wig.[2]

Katie seems to think that I *criticize* too much. But I can't quite agree. Certainly no two girls abroad ever had more appreciative readings than you: and if our admiration of your letters is somewhat stinted in expression it is because I think it not altogether important that you should be entirely satisfied as long as any degree of perfection remains unattained. But I must report *confidentially* what I hinted in my last that your letters are much admired by those who have had the privilege of seeing them or hearing them read. Macte virtute puella—which is being interpreted "Keep on my darling.[3]

That box with its wonderful contents has not yet gladdened my eyes. I expect to find it at Providence next week. Mr. Brown, (our big, goodnatured, obliging Thomas erst of California & now of the New York Custom House) wrote me last week that it would be attended to satisfactorily.

Did you see any accounts of the arrival of the ____ at Belfast? One of the young men who went out on the little craft of 28 tons was Charley Longfellow, son of the Poet. Of course his father had no small anxiety about him. It was allayed by a telegram, which cost him one hundred dollars in gold.[4] Costly consolation that, especially as the telegram could not make one hair white or black. We shall take for granted that you are well from day to day, and may God preserve us from telegrams announcing any ill to either of your dear & precious trio.

Yesterday with a party of ten gentlemen I went a fishing near Norman's Woe immortalized by Longfellows poem of the Wreck of the Hesperus.[5] We tried for cod in the deep sea, but no cod but bite ever to oblige a Chief Justice, nor any other fish, "in the deep bosom of the ocean buried."[6] So we confessed ourselves defeated on that line, & went in near shore & betook ourselves to the ignoble employment of enticing such small fry as inexperienced codlings, pollack, & cunners to swallow our hooks. Our success was entirely disproportioned to our merit; for we captured an indefinite number, fifty or a hundred say. To them we added two fine cod, persuaded from some fishermen, (who had taken the earlier morning; that is from midnight forward,—) by greenback agency, and our skipper with his mate, (who composed our whole crew) made a capital chowder and we had a good time.

It would have amazed you to see our gentlemen transform themselves into fishermen. Some of them in changed apparel would have been hardly recognized by their best friends. Two of our party were older than I, one having come in with the century and one four years later—so you see I passed for a young fellow.

We got back a little after six having been afloat about eight hours. Just as we came in the wind failed, and the gentlemen from Salem six in number had to be sent off in wagons by Mr. Haven & Mr. Rantoul—my present host.[7]

One of our party was General Coggswell, who served creditably in the war.[8] His late experiences will illustrate the way things are now going politically. Some six or eight weeks ago the President nominated for Postmaster of Salem, a worthy citizen of that place, who was confirmed by the Senate. Having thus served the confirmation, he, or rather his Postmaster General acting under his inspiration, considered how the office might be best turned to advantage in promoting the prospects of the Johnson Party in this neighborhood. So they offered it to Gen. Coggswell or rather sent him the Commission, removing the recently appointed incumbent. But the General could not be used, & sent back the Commission with a letter saying that he could not even seem to sacrifice or modify his principles. I am glad to say that so far Johnsonism seems to prosper as little as Tylerism. Though unsuccessful itself however it may be the cause of democratic success: but I hope & trust not.[9]

Mr. R—— is just starting for Boston & this letter must go.

Your ever affectionate father
S P Chase

Library of Congress.

1. A resort town in Haddington County on the east coast of Scotland twenty-six miles from Edinburgh, North Berwick was noted for its sea air, golf course, and nearby Tantallon Castle. Inverness is an ancient port town in northern Scotland located near the Caledonian Canal. In the mid-nineteenth century, it had a population of about 13,000. *Benjie's Guide to Edinburgh and Vicinity Twelfth Edition* (Edinburgh: A. Elliot, n.d.), 96–97; J. Thomas and T. Baldwin, *A Complete Pronouncing Gazeteer, or Geographical Dictionary of the World* (Philadelphia: J. B. Lippincott & Co., 1856), 906.

2. In William Cowper's lively comic poem *The Diverting History of John Gilpin,* first published in England in 1782, Gilpin loses his hat and wig during a ride on a fast horse he cannot control. When he finally comes to a stop, Gilpin puns: "My hat and wig will soon be here, / They are upon the road." William Cowper, *The Diverting History of John Gilpin; Shewing How He Went Farther than He Intended, and Came Safe Home Again* (Newburyport, Mass.: William Charles, 1793), 8; Hugh I'Anson Fausset, *William Cowper* (New York: Harcourt, Brace, 1928), 210–11.

3. In Virgil's *Aeneid* the passage is "Macte nova virtute, puer, sic itur ad astra" (book 9, line 641). A portion of the line, "macte virtute," has commonly been used as a motto. Father retained another word from the original passage, but altered it, changing the masculine "puer," meaning a boy or young man, to the feminine form, "puella," to apply to a young woman. ("Virtute," however, connotes "manliness" or "manhood" as well as bravery or moral excellence.) Virgil's line has been put into English different ways, including "Advance, illustrious youth! increase in fame, . . . This is the way to heaven" (John Dryden, late seventeenth century); "Go on, increase in early valor, boy; / Such is the pathway to the starry heights" (Christopher Pearse Cranch, 1870s); and "Bravo, my boy, bravo, / your newborn courage! That's the path to the stars" (Robert Fagles, early twenty-first century). In a letter to John G. Nicolay in 1863, John Hay lightheartedly translated "macte virtute puer" as "old Italian for 'go in my hearty.'" Arthur Sidgwick, ed., *P. Vergili Maronis: Aeneidos, Liber IX* (Cambridge: Cambridge University Press, 1900), 39; John Dryden, trans., *The Aeneid of Virgil,* ed. Robert Fitzgerald (New York: Macmillan, 1965), 299; Christopher Pearse Cranch, trans., *The Æneid of Virgil* (Boston: Brown and Little, 1879), 381; Robert Fagles, trans., *Virgil: The Aeneid* (New York: Viking, 2006), 287; Burlingame, *At Lincoln's Side,* 45.

4. Charles Longfellow, the adventurous son of the poet Henry Wadsworth Longfellow, crossed the Atlantic during the summer of 1866 on his uncle Thomas G. Appleton's yacht *Alice.* "Editor's Easy Chair," *Harper's New Monthly Magazine* 34 (March 1867): 525; Edward Wagenknecht, *Longfellow: A Full-Length Portrait* (New York: University of California Press, 1955), 271.

5. Norman's Woe is a rocky reef off the coast of Cape Ann, Mass., in Gloucester's outer harbor. The reef is the site of a number of ship wrecks, including the schooner *Favorite* in 1839, which inspired Henry Wadsworth Longfellow to write "Wreck of the Hesperus." Wagenknecht, *Longfellow,* 166–68.

6. The quotation is from the opening scene of Shakespeare's *Richard III,* in Gloucester's "Now is the winter of our discontent" soliloquy.

7. Father was staying with Jane Rantoul's son, attorney Robert Samuel Rantoul, who was collector of customs for Salem, Mass. Father stayed at the Rantouls' beach house August 7–11 that year. Franklin Haven Jr., a banker, was the son of the president of Boston's Merchants Bank. Some of the other members of the fishing party were Samuel Kirkland Lothrop, a Boston minister; J. Vincent Browne, the collector of internal revenue at Salem; and Henry Kemble Oliver, former adjutant general of Massachusetts militia and founder of the state's bureau of statistics and labor. *Chase Papers,* 1:371, 483, 484, 623–24.

8. William Cogswell, an attorney, rose to the rank of brigadier general of volunteers during the Civil War. After the war he practiced law in Salem and became mayor of the town, then a state legislator, state senator, and U.S. congressman. *Bio. Dir. U.S. Cong.,* 804–5.

9. Postmaster General Alexander Williams Randall ardently defended Andrew Johnson. John Tyler, who became president when William Henry Harrison died in 1841, ended up spurning both major political parties, alienating Congress, ignoring the popular will, and isolating his administration. *ANB,* 22:77–79; *DAB,* 15:344–45.

FATHER TO NETTIE

Providence, Aug. 31, 1866

My darling Nettie,

I have just received Katies letter, sent in the diplomatic bag, with Mr. Cleghorn's photograph & papers, & dated London Aug. 10. This is the only letter I have received from either of my precious travellers since yours with the last date of July 28. I presume others are on the way. I have a hunger for your letters.

Katies last is delightful. The account of your researches interested me, but what pleased me most is her praise of you. If you deserve all she says, and I believe you do, I shall have the most delightful of delights in welcoming you home. And next to her account of you is her account of the baby. Dear little Willie! How I long to see him. I expect to be a great favorite of his.

I have just returned from my visit to Cherry Hill. Mr. Waters is the same kind, genial, earnest, happy man that he has always been since I have known him and my visit was a very pleasant one.[1] I have little to add however to the account I gave of it in my letter to Katie.

Day before yesterday I went into Beverly and took up my quarters again with Mrs Rantoul for forty eight hours. Yesterday I dined with Mr. Endicott who had invited Leiut. Gov. Claflin & Mrs Claflin & Mr. Pierce to meet me / The other guests were Mrs Rantoul & Mrs Eastman & Mr. Robert & Mrs Robert Rantoul.[2] Mrs Claflin is one of the loveliest women I have seen—handsome enough and *très avenante.*[3] Mr. Claflin is a very important man in Massachusetts, with great wealth, enormous income & very liberal. They gave me a very kind invitation to their house which I was sorry I could not accept. Mr. Pierce is unchanged. When removed from the Collectorship to which I had him appointed, he was made by the Govt. of Massachusetts District Attorney for the County he lives in, and has a very flattering future before him.

And now darling I must distress you. I enclosed to Claire the little what d'ye-call-it that you sent her in an envelope to Mr. Walker.[4] And not long after received a feeling note from him, acknowledging, on Claires behalf, the kindness, but saying that their little baby has gone to "the happy land," & that[5] the bereavement had proved almost too much for poor Claire, & shadowed all their house. She, however, was getting better when he wrote. My heart ached for them and I know yours and Katies will.

Susan Walker writes me that General Augur is going to take Campbell Hospital for his regiments quarters and that the freedpeople are to be turned out.[6] She is quite sad & indignant. She says she has made several visits to Mrs Smith, & found the old lady very glad to see her. She, Mrs Smith, is quite as well, to all appearances as when you went away.

Governor Sprague is very well & is, now, sitting near me talking over a project of a factory and factory village with a couple of gentlemen from

Maine.[7] (I am writing in his Office) Mrs Sprague is well but I have not seen her yet since my return having come from Beverly this morning, & giving my first moments to you in order to make sure of the steamer to-morrow.

I suppose you see the papers. If you do you must feel pained by the exhibition which Mr. Johnson is now making. The indignation of the country is intense: I mean of course of that country which elected him. Vermont & Maine will vote in a few days next week & the week after, & unless all appearances deceive the majorities against the new Party will be tremendous[8]

I expect to be in Washington next week. Love to dearest Katie & darling Willie & kindest remembrances to Maggie

Your ever affe. father
S P Chase

Library of Congress.

1. Father spent August 17–24 in Providence, R.I., with the Sprague family and visiting textile factories with William. After a day at Beverly, Mass., where he saw Charlotte Eastman, Father went to Cherry Hill to visit Richard P. Waters. He stayed with Waters the nights of August 26–28, but each day his social calls included a visit to the Rantoul house in Beverly, where he saw Lottie Eastman and Jane Rantoul. He stayed overnight at the "Castle," as the Rantoul house was called, on the twenty-ninth and thirtieth, then took trains through Boston to Providence on the thirty-first. *Chase Papers*, 1:493, 625–29.

2. Father dined with Republican businessman William Endicott and his wife, Annie Thorndike Endicott. The other guests were Massachusetts lieutenant governor William Claflin and his second wife, Mary Bucklin Davenport Claflin, who in the 1890s wrote several books drawn on their married life; Edward L. Pierce; Jane Rantoul and Lottie Eastman; and Robert S. Rantoul and his wife, Harriet Charlotte Neal Rantoul. The Rantouls wed in 1858 and had nine children in the course of their marriage. *Chase Papers*, 1:483, 624, 629; *DAB*, 4:111; *Nat. Cyc.*, 41:228.

3. Very pleasing or appealing.

4. Claire Albrecht had married Charles M. Walker; see Father to Kate, Nov. 18, 1863, above.

5. Father repeated this word in the original: "that that."

6. Maj. Gen. Christopher Columbus Augur commanded the Department of Washington, 1863–66, and was transferred west in 1867. *DAB*, 1:427–28.

7. William's company, A. and W. Sprague, purchased lumber land in Maine and built a mill there. Knight, *History of the Sprague Families*, 49–50.

8. On August 28, President Johnson embarked on a speaking tour designed to influence the fall elections. His supporters were nonetheless overwhelmingly defeated at the polls. Vermont ratified the Fourteenth Amendment in October 1866, and Maine in January 1867. Foner, *Short History of Reconstruction*, 118–19.

FATHER TO KATE

Washington, Sep 10, 1866 Monday.

My dear, precious Katie,

I was greatly comforted and gratified on Saturday by receiving a letter from each of my absent children, dated at Paris. There was so long an interval since your preceding letter dated at London that I had become quite impatient.

It is difficult to say any thing satisfactory to myself about the suggestion that Nettie may wish to remain abroad during the coming winter. It is plain that such sojourn may be made very useful to her, if she will go resolutely to work upon a careful & thorough study of the languages, especially of these in what she has already made some progress the French & German. To these I should like to have her add the Spanish & Italian; but I can hardly expect from her what I never accomplished myself. And six months or a year is no great time to give to French & German. As to the painting part of the programme, I confess myself rather indifferent. Nettie has a charming talent for sketching, and I should be glad to have her cultivate that as far as possible; but painting involves too much labor, and time, for a young lady to expect to make great attainment in it who does not expect to consecrate her life to it, like Rosa Bonheur for example.[1] I never knew but one lady, who made much proficiency in the arts and at the same time took her proper part in Society. That was Cora Livingston daughter of the famous—did you ever hear of him?—Edward Livingston of Louisiana.[2]

To me the acquirements which can be most used seem the most valuable. Languages and music & sketching, among accomplishments are in the first rank of these.

After all the question of remaining abroad must be solved by Nettie herself. The thought is certainly not very agreeable to me. It is bad enough to have you away seven months; and it is hard to reconcile myself to the idea of either of you being away for another year. If Nettie remains the winter she will of course wish, and, in that case I should wish too, that she might join you and the Governor next summer. But there is no probability that I shall be with you. What a year may bring forth no one can tell. If I live and remain in my present position it is pretty certain that I shall have little time for travelling any where, except to the places in which I must hold courts. I shall agree to whatever Nettie resolves upon, and do all I can to make the execution of her resolve gratifying to her.

I am glad to hear of Mr. Clay & his happy marriage. If you meet him again remember me kindly to him. Remember me, also, in same manner to Mr Bigelow & Mr Nicolay & Mr. Hay.[3] Mr Hay wrote me sometime ago asking me to send him, as the only requital he would accept for his attention to my request for photographs, copies of what I might say on public affairs. I will write him today or by next steamer and forward a copy of Whitelaw Reids book (which is quite clever) giving an account of his visits South in 1865–6, and containing the only speech I have made since I have been on the bench, which has been printed so as to be fit for reading.[4] Indeed I have made only two other addresses—one at Dartmouth to my brother Alumni last year & one last Spring to the Methodist Centennial Meeting both entirely offhand & never written out by me afterwards.[5]

I came back as I have written Nettie last Thursday Evening. Every thing is well so far as I can observe. Your box containing the picture (of the Hs. of Commons I suppose) and various other articles was opened by Mrs Crawford, & every thing except that picture & a few small articles sent to Providence. Mrs C—— was delighted with her shawl & so were Albert & Cassy with their respective presents. I have not seen [Pauline] nor heard of her;[6] nor have I seen Charlotte[7]

I have only room to add the most astonishing piece of news—Mr. Sumner is going to be married! to Mrs Hooper, daughter in law of my friend! I should not believe it if I had it not from his own hand.[8] Love to all

Most affectionately your father
S P Chase

Library of Congress.

1. The French painter Rosa Bonheur (1822–99) was one of the few female professional artists of her era, and is considered by some the most famous woman artist of the nineteenth century. Bonheur dressed in men's clothes and lived with female partners. In 1872, Father would see Bonheur's famous painting "The Horse Fair" (1853–55) when he toured Alexander T. Stewart's art collection in New York. The painting is now in the Metropolitan Museum of Art. Gretchen van Slyke, "Introduction to the English Edition," in Anna Klumpke, *Rosa Bonheur: The Artist's (Auto)biography* (Ann Arbor, Mich.: University of Michigan Press, 1997), xi, xxvi, xxxi; *Chase Papers,* 1:708.

2. Coralie Livingston Barton (b. 1806) was the daughter of politician and diplomat Edward Livingston and his second wife, Louise Moreau de Lassy. Most contemporary accounts refer to her general brilliance rather than particular artistic skill. Father saw Cora Livingston at least once "in all her splendour" at a social event in Washington when he was a young man there in 1830. In 1872, she made a visit to Washington from Louisiana with two nieces of Nettie's aunt Ruhamah, who had married a Louisianan. Father had undertaken to write an introduction to Edward Livingston's *Code of Reform and Prison Discipline* and consulted Mrs. Barton about that subject during her visit. *Chase Papers,* 1:44, 678, 680, 681, 685, 704; *DAB,* 2:23, 11:309–10; William B. Hatcher, *Edward Livingston: Jeffersonian Republican and Jacksonian Democrat* (University, La.: Louisiana University Press, 1940), 122–23.

3. Diplomat and writer John Bigelow was U.S. minister to France, 1865–66. John G. Nicolay, who had been one of Abraham Lincoln's private secretaries, served as consul at Paris, 1865–69. Nicolay would later become marshal of the Supreme Court, 1872–87, and wrote a ten-volume biography of Lincoln with John M. Hay. Hay, who had also been one of the late president's secretaries (and an admirer of Kate), was secretary to the American legation in Paris, 1865–66. *DAB,* 2:258–59; *ANB,* 10:367–71, 16:412–13.

4. Father wrote to Hay on September 12 and forwarded him a copy of Reid's *After the War.* In the book, Reid printed an address that Father made to African Americans at the Zion Church in Charleston, S.C., when Father and Nettie were there in May 1865. In those remarks he advised his audience to be patient and to demonstrate their readiness to assume the elective franchise, expressing his confidence that they would receive the right to vote. *Chase Papers,* 1:547, 635; 5:47–48, 51, 323.

5. He spoke at Dartmouth's commencement exercises in July 1865. For his address to the Methodist gathering, see his letter to Nettie of April 16 at the beginning of this chapter. *Chase Papers,* 1:591.

6. Apparently Pauline Heckscher.

7. Nettie's aunt, Charlotte Chambers Ludlow Jones.

8. Alice Mason Hooper was the widowed daughter-in-law of Anne Sturgis Hooper and Boston businessman and politician Samuel Hooper, who had been a member of the U.S. House of Representatives since 1861. As a member of the Committee on Ways and Means, Samuel Hooper had been a strong supporter of Father's financial policies during the Civil War. Confirmed fifty-five-year-old bachelor Charles Sumner married twenty-seven-year-old

Alice on Oct. 17, 1866, at King's Chapel in Boston. The couple separated eight months later when Alice began going out socially with another man. The Sumners were divorced in 1873. *DAB,* 9:203; 18:213; *Chase Papers,* 1:316; 3:62–63, 328, 368, 370.

FATHER TO KATE

Washington, Oct 12, 1866

My darling Katie,

Yesterday afternoon, notwithstanding the violence of the storm I went over to Baltimore to attend a public meeting of the American Freedman's Commission of which, by a recent election I was made President.[1] Returning this morning I find that yesterdays mail brought me an unusually rich contribution from the other side. There were two letters from Nettie—one, to be sure, a mere cover for a couple of landscape photographs—and then from you—a dear, long, good letter.

It was a mean thing that your birth day was not commemorated at least by a letter written on it & by due congratulations. I am quite ashamed of that yankee habitude which leads to the neglect of such occasions. I am sure that the neglect does not imply lack of warmest affection; but I quite agree that outward expressions have to the object of love even more value than the inner sentiments and I mean to reform: In the mean time let me assure you that I thought of your birth day and of Netties— (though, shall I confess it? not quite certain which was on the 19th of Augst & which on the 13th of September)—and be both of you assured moreover that your father loves you both dearly, dearly, dearly.[2] Just think of my old mistake 19th for 13th & 13th for 19th!

Today or tomorrow, doubtless, the Governor will have arrived in Liverpool and by Monday he will probably have rejoined you: and I have not the least idea where this letter will find you.

It looked rather discouraging to read the date of your letter "6th Aug.", but it was good enough to make up for its long delay in coming. Where, in the world, can it have been?

Netties letter is dated the 1[3] & 17 Sep. and has not been quite a month on the way. It is a very interesting letter & her sketching, to my unlearned eye, seems admirable. She will, however, make a few mistakes in spelling; though, except the very last letter, she has been for some time remarkably correct. I would not mention this if I did not know how very important accuracy in this particular is.

I was delighted with your photographs. I cant say that I like the curls quite as well as the old style in which I have loved you so long: but they are very pretty nevertheless, and the photographs, and, of course, their original, are very handsome. I took them into your grandmother[3] a moment since, and it may take off the cream of my commendation if I tell you that she said "Is that Katie? It dont look like her. How she has changed?" I left the *new style* with the old lady that she may get acquainted with you in it.

Baron Gerolt has been here since I began this letter. He wants me to attend a meeting of the Heliographic Company this afternoon and to dine with him tomorrow to meet a Mr. La Fevre, an English MP and Mr. Burnley, and I am going to do so.[4] I hope you may meet the Baroness & the young ladies on the Rhine. How suddenly has leaped[5] to equality as a Power with England & France!

Why has not Nettie sent me some photographs of herself? I should like to have a statuette of her in bisque: and if you go to Florence, as, I hope, you will I hope you will carry out the suggestion of my former letter & have Busts of yourself & Nettie made by Powers. The Governor should have one made of himself also. Powers mentioned—in a late letter—I believe though I told you of this that he would be glad to be of any service to you in Florence. He said also that he had heard of the arrival of my cast (Jones') in Paris, but that it had not reached him: I am curious to know what has become of it. I hope it will get to Powers safe; for I want to see how the bust will look in Marble. Of course, Powers cant show his genius in it as if he had taken the bust.

We had a terrific storm yesterday and for two days before. The railroad was so damaged between W. & Baltimore that the trains were suspended for some hours & after they were resumed, & we started at a quarter to three we were over four hours in getting over. All the little streams had overflowed their banks & the overflowed lowlands looked like lakes. In some places the track was [carried] away—or rather one of them. For a long distance the track was under water, & was turned into a [torrent]. In other places where the track was free from overflow torrents rushed along on either side. I never thought the River any thing but a parody till yesterday, but yesterday it did vindicate its title to equality with the "yellow Tibre" of the Eternal City,[6] in its *biggest swell*. When we came back from Baltimore this morning the track which had been most damaged was still impassable for some space & our train was obliged to take the other.

Henry Ward Beecher spoke last night. He made no allusion to his letter. Gen Howard, Judge Russell, of Boston & Judge Bond of Baltimore were the other speakers. The number in attendance was very large considering the Weather.[7]

I will write to Nettie by the next steamer. Dearest love to the darling and to precious little William. I am quite charmed by your accounts of him & wish you wd make him more prominent in your Sketches.

Goodbye, dear, dear [Nettie][8]

S P Chase

Library of Congress.

1. Heavy rain in the Washington-Maryland region on October 10 and 11 caused flooding, property damage, and the loss of several lives. The American Freedmen's Union Commission was an organization of societies aiding former slaves by furnishing teachers, schools, and supplies. As president, Father had little involvement with the organization's

day-to-day operations. *Philadelphia Inquirer,* Oct. 12–13, 1866; *New York Times,* Oct. 14, 1866; *Chase Papers,* 5:278, 280.

2. He originally ended the paragraph here, then came back later to add the next sentence.

3. Mary Colton Smith.

4. George John Shaw Lefevre had traveled in the United States after finishing his degree at Cambridge University in 1853. He made a second, briefer trip to the U.S. in 1866. A member of Parliament since 1863, he sympathized with the Union cause during the Civil War. In politics he was aligned with John Bright and William Gladstone. The secretary of the British legation in Washington, who sometimes acted as chargé d'affaires, was J. Hume Burnley. *ODNB,* 33:163–66; F. M. G. Willson, *A Strong Supporting Cast: The Shaw Lefevres, 1789–1936* (London: Athena Press, 1993), 172, 203; Robin W. Winks, *The Civil War Years: Canada and the United States,* 4th ed. (Montreal: McGill-Queens University Press, 1998), 193; Thomas Wodehouse Legh, Lord Newton, *Lord Lyons: A Record of British Diplomacy,* 2 vols. (London: E. Arnold, 1913), 1:134, 136.

5. Father omitted a word, probably "Prussia" (Gerolt's home country) or "Germany."

6. That is, the Tiber River at Rome.

7. Father chaired a public meeting of the American Freedmen's Union Commission at the Front Street Theater in Baltimore under the auspices of a Baltimore association promoting education of African Americans. The keynote address was by Henry Ward Beecher. In August, in a controversial public letter responding to an invitation to a pro-Johnson convention in Cleveland, Beecher had argued that the Southern states should be restored to the union quickly, even if it meant that white Southerners would reunite with Northern Democrats to dominate national politics. Beecher also said in his letter that there should be no delay in Reconstruction to assure rights to African Americans. "Refusing to admit loyal Senators and Representatives from the South to Congress," he avowed, "will not help the freedmen. It will not secure them the vote. It will not protect them. It will not secure any amendment of our Constitution, however just and wise." The reaction to Beecher's letter was so strong, he had to write a long letter explaining himself to his own congregation in Brooklyn. He declared that he supported the Fourteenth Amendment, had not become a "Johnson man," and had not abandoned the Republican Party, but he would not disavow his letter to the convention committee. Arguing that Andrew Johnson had a good spirit and good intentions, Beecher attempted to advocate a "middle course between the President's and that of Congress." Probably to signal his disagreement with Beecher, Father gave the minister only a perfunctory introduction in the Baltimore meeting. In his address there, Beecher spoke of the importance of education for African Americans and of the responsibility of Christians to assist in that endeavor, but stayed away from the topic of Reconstruction. The other speakers were Gen. Oliver O. Howard, who headed the federal Freedmen's Bureau; Thomas Russell, a superior court judge who was later the collector of customs at Boston and U.S. minister to Venezuela; and Hugh Lennox Bond, a Baltimore judge. Daniel Alexander Payne, African Methodist Episcopal bishop and president of Wilberforce University, gave the opening prayer. *New York Times,* Sept. 1, 10, Oct. 14, 1866; *Baltimore Sun,* Oct. 12, 1866; Paxton Hibben, *Henry Ward Beecher: An American Portrait* (New York: George H. Doran Co., 1927), 199–203; *DAB,* 2:129–35, 431–32; *ANB,* 11:311–12; William T. Davis, *Bench and Bar of the Commonwealth of Massachusetts* (Boston: Boston History Co., 1895; repr., New York: Da Capo Press, 1974), 390; *Chase Papers,* 1:270.

8. He did not write the name clearly; it looks somewhat more like "Nettie" than "Katie."

FATHER TO NETTIE

Washington, Oct 15, 1866.

My darling Nettie,

We had quite a treat this morning. There was the joint production of Willie & Maggie enclosed to Mrs. Smith; Katies own sweet letter to her grandmother; & last but not least your nice charming letter to me. It was delightful to read Katies & Maggie's account of Willie, and of her own improvement physically & yours & your spirited & admirably illustrated descriptions. Your letter is one of your best: though *will* spell[1] some words incorrectly & seem to have a great contempt for commas & their relations, & for capital letters. Mr. Willing & Mr. Wood breakfasted with me this morning and it was very pleasant to see somebody who had seen you. I showed them your sketches in your letter from Berne, &c, & they were greatly pleased with them. For my part I think your sketch of the landscape from the little bridge one of the best things you have done. The view from the Righi is also capital, & the ascent of the Wengen Alps is quite as good. I should have observed the lack of perspective in the base if you had not called my attention to it.

But I notice that Katies letter is dated Sep 30, Baden Baden, while yours is dated Grindelwald Sep 19 and Sep 23, *Lucerne* I suppose though you dont name any "place".[2] This makes your letter a week older than Katies. It is fresher however than your letters have been generally since you have been on the Continent.

I begin to look for you all home now pretty anxiously. After four weeks—sooner by some days indeed I shall cease to write you and expect more & more intently till I see you all. You must let me know on which vessel you take passage & about what time you may be looked for in New York. I shall meet you if possible. By the way why do you never mention what letters of mine you have received. It is rather discouraging to write twice a week, that is by every steamer & not know except semi-semi-occasionally that you ever receive what I write.

Edward has arrived with the horses. Unluckily the alley is in such a bad state that I have been obliged to send him to the livery stable. It may be a fortnight or more before the alley will be repaired. But I make use enough of the horses to keep them from spoiling

Tell the Governor that Baron Gerolt is in quite a fever about the Heliographic Company / We had a meeting two or three days ago—nobody present except Mr. Cooke, the Baron G. & myself, I undertaking to represent the Governor.[3] Knap has been so [busy] in Johnsonism that he has given no attention to the matter.[4] We agreed that Cooke should write to Eggloffstein and authorize him to make arrangements for a Gallery & an outside Agent to get work, so that something may be earned. I hope he will approve.

Tell the Governor too that Cresswell[5] was here today saying that the chance for carrying Maryland is quite good, with almost a certainty of prevent at any rate a Johnson victory. He wants to raise fifteen thousand dollars for the next fortnights work & I gave him letters to New York & Boston & to [*illeg.*] at Providence, to whom I said that as the Governor offered to give $5.000 for the Metropolitan Church if I wanted to subscribe it I thought he might venture to take the responsibility of advancing $1000 towards the Maryland Fund. It may prove a good investment. H. D. Cooke says $5000 shall be raised in Philadelphia.

I suppose you will feel the effect of the Elections even in Europe. In my last I meant to send a slip showing what the Congressional amendment is in order that you may talk intelligently if you talk at all on the subject. I think it now certain that this amendment will become a part of the Constitution. A strong party in favor of it is being already organized in the south: and its ratification by every northern state is now pretty certain. The whole number of states being now 36 the votes of 27 (three fourths) are required for ratification. There are 21 original free states which may be set down as having already ratified or as sure to ratify. This leaves 6 wanting from the late slave states; of these Tennessee has ratified & Missouri will. If Maryland is carried she will make the third. Delaware will probably go the same way as Maryland & will make the fourth. It cannot be doubted I think that two more will be found which will be enough. The rest of the unreconstructed states will doubtless follow. And this great agony will be over. Then will follow universal or at least impartial suffrage.[6]

Pardon this political talk. We are all well except Jet, who is still very sick with little prospect of recovery. Gov Kirk dined with us today. He was in Paris & London on his return from Buenos Ayres & very sorry to miss seeing you.[7] Aunt Charlotte your old Nurse sends her love. I mine to all

Your loving father
SPC.

Library of Congress.

1. So in the original.
2. A popular stop on the nineteenth-century European grand tour, the Swiss alpine region of Righi receives mention in many travel narratives by well-known American writers, including James Fenimore Cooper, Nathaniel Hawthorne, Harriet Beecher Stowe, and Bayard Taylor. Rising to an altitude of 5,905 feet, the Righi summit provides beautiful sunrise and sunset views. Baden-Baden, in the Black Forest region of southwest Germany, was a fashionable spa community based on mineral springs. One of the first Alpine resorts of south central Switzerland, Grindelwald lies at the foot of the Wetterhorn peaks, not far from Lucerne. E. K. Washington, *Echoes of Europe; or, Word Pictures of Travel* (Philadelphia: J. Challen & Son, 1860), 114; Saul B. Cohen, ed., *The Columbia Gazetteer of the World* (New York: Columbia University Press, 1983), 224, 1175, 1798.
3. Apparently, William Sprague bought stock in Egloffstein's venture and intended to give half his purchase to Father. Gerolt later supported Jay Cooke's Northern Pacific Railroad venture. *Chase Papers,* 1:609; Oberholtzer, *Cooke,* 2:164, 240–41, 311.
4. Possibly civil engineer and soldier Joseph Moss Knap, who ran the Fort Pitt foundry in Pittsburgh. *Nat. Cyc.,* 10:351–52.
5. Maryland lawyer and Unionist John Angel James Creswell. *DAB,* 4:541.
6. In late 1866, ten Southern states failed to ratify the Fourteenth Amendment, prompting Congress to pass the Reconstruction Act of 1867, which divided the South into five military districts and forced Southern states to ratify the amendment before they could be readmitted to the Union. Missouri ratified in January 1867. Delaware did not do so until 1901 and Maryland not until 1959. Foner, *Short History of Reconstruction,* 121–22.

7. Robert C. Kirk was U.S. minister to Argentina, 1862–66. Previously he had served as Ohio's lieutenant governor, 1859–61. *Chase Papers,* 5:141–42.

FATHER TO NETTIE

Washington, Oct. 18. 1866.

My darling Nettie,

It was a pleasure as welcome as unanticipated to receive your charming letter from Baden-Baden so soon after the one from "Righi?" which preceded it only three or four days.

I hardly know what to say about your plan of remaining abroad. If I were *perfectly sure* you would be contented and would *continue in good health,* I should not interpose the slightest objection. Nor do I mean to in any case. I shall feel greatly the privation of your society and still more the burden of constant anxiety concerning your health & well being in other respects; but I will not oppose these feelings to any course which approves itself to your judgment as being really the best. I do not feel myself as competent to form a really sound judgment on the whole case as I think you are—so I leave the matter entirely to you. I shall be _very_ glad to see you back again with your sister and the Governor but will not be discontented if you determine to remain and can make an arrangement every way fit & desirable. As to *my* choice of the alternatives, as a matter of feeling & inclination it is, of course "come home"; but as a matter of self improvement it is, "take every thing into consideration & decide for yourself."

At the Freedmens Bureau last evening Gen. Charles Howard told me that information had been just brought in that Mr. Stanton had resigned, should go to Spain & that Gen Sherman would take charge of the War Department temporarily at least.[1] The General said that what he had heard otherwise led him to give credit to this statement. It is probably true—I care very little whether it is true or false. It is a long time since I ceased to regard Mr. Stanton as reliable for any thing except hatred of enemies &, indifference to friends. He is able; harsh; occasionally, but fitfully kind & generous; obstinate & selfwilled yet changeful & capricious; a sincere lover of his country, but prone to sacrifice just interests to private hates or gusts of caprice; meteoric rather than solar. I gave him unreservedly my faith & affection as a friend and he abandoned me for Seward & Weed—Seward & Weed are falling & he joins in the cry against them. If Sherman comes we shall have as true a patriot with a nobler nature; though perhaps with less ability & less sympathy with progress & ideal justice. Sherman never professed friendship for me but I have always found him friendly. Stanton has professed something more than friendship, but it has borne no fruits.[2]

What do you think of all that?

Who do you think has been here for the last thirty six hours? Maria Hawes, née Maria Southgate. She came night before last. Neither her husband nor she sent me any word of her coming; but he telegraphed a Mr. Fisher, (who was Clerk I believe to Major now Col. Febiger), when she left Cincinnati and he met her at the depot & brought her to our house. She is a nice little body; very charming in her manners; & very pleasant and intelligent in her talk. But such a rebel, not a mite converted, nor likely to be. She thinks her husband a noble martyr to his sense of duty, & Jeff. Davis one of the best & most cruelly treated men alive. Well, I would not have her think otherwise than most lovingly of her husband; but I do wish they could both see & feel that desertion of ones flag, abandonment & war upon one's state, & rebellion against one's country & government, with no decent justifying cause, cannot be virtues.[3] She is going back tomorrow night, having come, as she says, only to see her grandmother. She would like, she says, to take the old lady back with her & have her live with her this winter, but she sees she cannot bear the journey. Mrs Smith is very very glad to see Maria & seems happy in her society; but shows no inclination to exchange her present home for one in Kentucky. I don't wonder.

Mrs. Lander is here playing to crowded houses. I have not yet seen her—but mean to call. I had a letter from her, not long ago making particular enquiry for Katie, which I answered.

There is, also, an Opera Troupe here. Two or three evenings since Gen. Beauregard attended the Opera & was received with enthusiastic plaudits—nearly as enthusiastic as would have greeted Davis himself. Ainsi va le monde. Nouveau Président—nouveaux héros![4] Harry Gilmor was here also & he & Beauregard were entertained by Corcoran. Report does not say whether Seward made one of the party.[5]

Mr. Beecher has been explaining away his letter to the Johnson Military Convention, & has come out all right. I doubt, however, whether he can ever regain his old position.

You remember Mr. & Mrs Durant with whom we dined in New Orleans. He has left Louisiana & is now here with his family. They have taken the house next east of that occupied by Dr. Bailey on C. Street. I took Mr. & Mrs D and one of their children with me to ride today: and had a very pleasant time. He is very decided in the opinion that no outspoken friend of the Union, believing in equal rights for all equally devoted to its maintenance, can live comfortably or even safely in New Orleans.[6] The papers of today contain an appeal from a number of the ablest & best men of the South expressing substantially the same opinion in regard to all the non-reconstructed states & urging Congress to take positive measures for reorganization on the basis of equal suffrage & loyal ascendancy in the State Governments. I wish Congress wd. heed this appeal.

Mr. Mullett & his little wife were here last night. She is so sweet & funny—Lavinia Warren was not very much smaller: but she is full of sense and spirit: and loves her husband dearly, &, I suspect, governs him a little. I suspect too that he likes to be governed by her![7] I don't wonder. Mr. Mullett says that Jones Cast of me was very safely packed & directed to Mr. Powers in the care of Mr. Lawrence, our Consul General at Florence. Mr. Powers wrote me that he had heard of it at Paris, but had not received it. I hope you will look after it at Paris if you go there again & also at Florence where I hope you will go.

And now good bye my darling darling. May Heaven's best blessings be upon you & upon each of my dear ones in your party. Love to Katie & Governor; kisses for Willie & kind memories for Maggie.

Your loving father
S.P.C.

Library of Congress.

1. In the fall of 1866, Andrew Johnson attempted to replace Secretary of War Edwin M. Stanton with Gen. William Tecumseh Sherman, who was more sympathetic to the president's Reconstruction policies. Stanton retained his post until February 1868. Charles Henry Howard enlisted in the army in 1861 with his brother, Oliver O. Howard, as a private and retired as a major general. In 1866, Charles Howard was assistant commander of the Freedmen's Bureau—officially the Bureau of Refugees, Freedmen, and Abandoned Lands—and stationed in Washington. At the beginning of the next Congress, the Freedmen's Bureau Act, which gave bureau agents the power to enforce the civil rights of African Americans as well as extending the life of the agency, was adopted over Johnson's veto. In 1867, the Howard brothers, with funding from the Freedmen's Bureau, founded Howard University as a nonsectarian college open to people of both sexes and all races. *DAB*, 9:279; Foner, *Short History of Reconstruction*, 31; Eicher and Eicher, *Civil War High Commands*, 305; James M. Merrill, *William Tecumseh Sherman* (Chicago: Rand McNally, 1971), 311–13.

2. Edwin M. Stanton and Father had been close friends but had severed their personal relationship when Stanton did not support Father's 1860 bid for the Republican nomination for president. Newspaperman and political operative Thurlow Weed organized a well-financed movement for William H. Seward that effectively collapsed the Chase movement. Niven, *Chase*, 212, 438; *DAB*, 19:598–600.

3. Kate's cousin Maria Southgate's husband, James Morrison Hawes, had been a brigadier general in the Confederate service. George L. Febiger was Kate's and Maria's uncle (see appendix).

4. "So goes the world. New president—new hero!" Former Confederate general Pierre G. T. Beauregard served as president of the New Orleans, Jackson, and Mississippi Railway for five years after the war. *DAB*, 2:111–12.

5. Baltimore soldier Harry Gilmor gained some recognition during the war as a Confederate raider leading a small band of guerrilla fighters. His account of his adventures, *Four Years in the Saddle* (New York: Harper, 1866), received favorable notice in the October 1866 issue of the *North American Review*. Banker and philanthropist William Wilson Corcoran, born in 1798, was a Southern sympathizer who spent much of the war in France. He returned to Washington in 1865 and resumed his position as a member of the social elite. In 1868, Corcoran founded the "Louise Home" for upper-class ladies who had fallen upon hard times. *DAB*, 4:440–41; 7:309; Jacob, *Capital Elites*, 61, 210.

6. New Orleans attorney Thomas J. Durant was a Unionist and Lincoln supporter who argued many cases before the Supreme Court during the Reconstruction period. He had been one of the more radical of Louisiana's Unionists, opposed to compromise with more moderate Unionists. He was married to Mary Elizabeth Harper Durant. *DAB*, 5:543–44; *Chase Papers*, 5:8–9.

7. Alfred B. Mullett married Pacific Pearl Myrick Mullett in September 1865; they subsequently had six children. Mercy Lavinia Warren Bump Stratton (1841–1919), better known as "Mrs. Tom Thumb," toured with P. T. Barnum after marrying "General Tom Thumb" or Charles Sherwood Stratton (1838–83) in 1863. *Nat. Cyc.*, 27:452; *Notable American Women*, 3:402.

FATHER TO NETTIE

At Home, [Nov.]¹ 1, 1866

My darling Nettie,

This is my *last letter to*² you in the old world—for this year at least—if as I conclude from *the last from* you you have made up your mind to return with your sister. Oh, how glad I shall be to give you the kiss of welcome. I like to have you happy and to enjoy every opportunity of improvement & recreation: but I like best to have you happy with me & not away from me. Still when separation is best for you, I do not murmur.

That last letter of yours was very interesting, and well illustrated by your clever sketch of "Teutonic felicity."

There is a little writing in it that savored of the Guide Book, but not so decidedly as to make me believe you indebted to it for your inspiration. By the way you must console yourself for these little criticisms of mine, by the reflection that the children of *great* men! are always liable to them! On the 15th of this month it will be just one hundred & seventy five years since Racine wrote from Fontainebleau to his son at the Hague, "Mon cher fils, vous me faites plaisir de me mander des nouvelles: mais prenez garde de ne les pas prendre dans la Gazette de Hollande; car, outre que nous les avons comme vous, vous y pourriez apprendre certain termes qui ne valent rien, comme celui de *recruter* dont vous vous servez au lieu de quoi it faut dire, *faire des recrues.* Mandez moi de nouvelles de vos seurs; il est bon de diversifier un peu et de ne pas vous jeter toujours sur l'Irlande et sur l'Allemagne."³

Now I dare say you will waste a conjecture or two of this sort "Where did father pick up this choice morsel of delicate admonition? Oh, I dare say from some old quotation book, and then he sends it to me as a hint about *guide books,* & *spelling* & *punctuation,* & *more news about sister* & *Willie.* He might be consistent at least and send me something of his own composition." Now, my darling, I shall put your suspicion of the quotation book to utter confusion by calmly informing you that I have been reading "Les Œuvres de Jean Racine (without telling you precisely how much I have read), and found the words I have cited on the 215th page of the [5]th Volume and it occurred to me at once that there was *a moral in them!*

For two or three days past I have been suffering from an excruciating neuralgia in my left under jaw & the two teeth which keep rear guard there. It came on Monday & I went to Dr. Wadsworth.[4] He cut away the gum a little, put in a little creosote & iodine, said he thought I would not suffer much during the night, and dismissed me, tolerably hopeful. Then I took a long walk up Sixth Street to M or whatever other Street bounds Gov Sprague's Square on the north. Coming back the wind was rather chilly. For dinner I swallowed a "hasty plate of Soup"[5] and half a potato & some rice pudding, & came up stairs with evident indications of a night attack of my enemy. Indications too soon fulfilled. I retreated to my bed. He—is neuralgia feminine or masculine? pursued, broke through all my defences, and seized possession. Oh! how I suffered! I turned from side to side continuously: I groaned; I almost laughed; I tried to think; there was no use in trying to think; I tried to imagine it was not so very bad after all; but imagination was not equal to the task; I tried to endure in patience; but patience had ceased to be a virtue. So the night passed—no sleep, no rest, no comfort, nothing but _ache_.[6] I ought to have written that word thus ache.[7] Spread it over the whole page, extend it from side to side of the entire sheet, raise & broaden every letter until the word reaches from top to bottom and from edge to edge, and it will convey some idea of the thing. It lulled a little in the morning & I sent for Dr. W——. He recommended divers things—but said he feared the tooth must come out. He advised, however, that leeches should be applied to the gums: and said he would come again before going to the country and then decide for or against extraction. I thought it no harm to learn what Dr. Hall thought of the matter & so sent for him.[8] The leecher came, and put on the little gourmands who seemed to have a relish for the blood of a Chief Justice! Then Dr. Hall came—advised a poultice for the gum & paregoric to force sleep[9]—and talked as he always does instructively & pleasantly. Whether it was the Doctor's talk or the leeches imbibition the pain diminished sensibly & when three oclock & Dr. Wadsworth came the decision of the main question was postponed till the next Monday. But alas when the Doctors & the leeches had left the field the enemy returned. Frank had staid with me or rather slept on the lounge the first night[10]—Mrs Crawford took the field—I mean the lounge—how these military phrases do run in one's head—the next. With her aid I made a vigorous defence. I plied the gum with cold water, with soft fig poultices, with cotton saturated with laudanum, with camphor, with paregoric with Davis Painkiller &— nothing else that I remember.[11] I bathed my cheek with cold water, clothed it with bags of hot salt, pressed upon it & it upon a jug of hot water, & failed ignomiously. The ache kept its ground. Then I tried a diversion. I called in Paregoric, and took a quantity of it every hour. By its help I procured a short doze of a moment at first, then two or three moments; then a minute, & finally, towards morning,—yesterday morning, I had a doze of a quarter of an hour I should think. I had kept poor

Mrs Crawford pretty busy & I dare say she was well pleased to see the day break. I am sure I was! And this the morning of her daughters wedding.[12] I felt that I had been rather mean in keeping her up so much of the night, but she, who seems never to tire & never to feel that she has done enough, made light of the matter.

Then after awhile came the Doctors & we had another talk & the decision upon extraction was again postponed & they went away; and this time, to my great delight the neuralgia went with them and did not come back. I expected it apprehensively, but it did not come. It was curious. There was a dull pain in the Gum & chin & cheek, but there was no more fierce assault. The battle was over. I felt quite elated in the midst of my fears. But I kept quiet & recumbent. In the evening there was no renewal of the attack. Mr. & Mrs H. H. Cooke[13] came in & came up to my room—(I have been occupying since I came back your sisters room)—and chatted awhile and then they went away & I went to sleep & slept nearly all night and awoke this morning "nearly as good as new."

There I have almost filled my sheet—but console yourself—there is not much else to write about. My home life is monotonous enough & the newspapers will tell the news—the last item of which is sad enough—Fanny Seward dead—so sweet—so young[14]—

Love in most uncommon quantities but distributed as usual from

Your ever loving father
S P Chase

Library of Congress.

1. He apparently wrote "Nov." over "Oct."

2. He underlined "last letter" with one stroke, then underlined "to" separately.

3. The quoted passage is the first paragraph of French dramatist Jean Racine's letter of Sept. 24, 1691, to his son, Jean-Baptiste. Translation: "My dear son, you give me pleasure by sending me news: but take care not to send them from the Gazette of Holland; for, in addition to our having it the same as you, you will learn from it certain wording of no value, such as that of 'to recruit' by which you help yourself instead of what one should say, 'to make recruits.' Send me news of your sisters; it is good to diversify a little and not to fling yourself always toward Ireland and Germany." The passage as Father quoted it truncates one sentence, which in its fuller version reads: "Mandez-moi des nouvelles de vos promenades, et de celles de la santé de vos sœurs" ("send me news of your excursions, and of your sisters' health"). The Chases owned a five-volume edition of Racine's works in French, published in 1826. Jean Racine, *Œuvres Complètes,* ed. Raymond Picard, 2 vols. (Paris: Gallimard, 1951–52), 2:499; *Catalogue of a Most Superb Collection,* item 1140.

4. Possibly Washington dentist H. N. Wadsworth, who published *Wadsworth's Day Book, Ledger, and Dental Recorder: Simplified and Combined for the Use of the Dental Profession* (New York: Clark, Austin, 1851) and received a patent for an "Improved Tooth Brush" in 1860. Hunter, *Washington and Georgetown Directory,* 103; "Patent Claims," *Scientific American,* n.s., 3 (July 2, 1860): 12.

5. In 1846, during the war against Mexico, Gen. Winfield Scott responded to presidential accusations that he was too slow in his prosecution of the war by writing a letter in which he said he had "a fire upon my rear from Washington." Furious, President James K. Polk sent Scott a dismissal letter. Scott answered, beginning, "Your letter of this date, received at about 6 pm, as I sat down to take a hasty plate of soup . . ." The phrase became a recurring jibe throughout Scott's career, earning him the nickname "Marshal Tureen,"

and was featured in numerous political cartoons. *DAB*, 16:505–11; Allan Peskin, *Winfield Scott and the Profession of Arms* (Kent, Ohio: Kent State University Press, 2003), 140–41.

6. Father underlined the word three times.

7. He wrote this word in very large and elongated script.

8. In January 1865, Father consulted Washington physician James C. Hall about retention of urine and rheumatic pain in his back and legs. That may have been the first time Father sought treatment from Hall, who impressed him as "intelligent & self reliant." When Nettie was ill in January 1866 (see the letter of November 27 below), Father summoned Hall to treat her. *Chase Papers*, 1:519, 607–8.

9. The term "paregoric" can simply mean any medicine that alleviates pain, although in this case it could mean a paregoric elixir of opium flavored with aniseed and benzoic acid. *OED*, 11:220.

10. Frank Bronaugh.

11. Invented in 1840, Perry Davis's Painkiller was a popular patent medicine advertised throughout the nineteenth century as a remedy for almost every kind of ailment. Among its ingredients were capsicum, the active ingredient of hot peppers, and opium. Mark Twain, who had been dosed with the painkiller as a child, includes a scene in *The Adventures of Tom Sawyer* wherein Tom gives some of this "fire in liquid form" to a cat, causing it to go crazy and jump out the window. K. Patrick Ober, *Mark Twain and Medicine: "Any Mummery Will Cure"* (Columbia, Mo.: University of Missouri Press, 2003), 56–59, 304.

12. Mrs. Crawford's daughter may have been Miss Anna S. Crawford of Philadelphia, who married Robert J. Ruth of Baltimore. The wedding was in Washington. *Baltimore Sun*, Nov. 3, 1866.

13. Probably Henry D. Cooke and Laura Humphreys Cooke.

14. Born in December 1844, William Seward's daughter Frances Adeline "Fanny" Seward was always introspective and shy, and her health was never strong. She died, probably of tuberculosis, in October 1866. Her mother, Frances Adeline Miller Seward, died in 1865. Fanny was her parents' only daughter. Glyndon G. Van Deusen, *William Henry Seward* (New York: Oxford University Press, 1967), 92, 116, 265, 406, 416–17; *ANB*, 19:676, 680.

FATHER TO NETTIE

Washington Nov. 27, 1866

My darling Nettie,

Your letter & Katies from Dresden came today. Until they came I did not believe you would persist in your purpose of remaining through the winter, and therefore did not write any letter which could not probably reach you before sailing:[1] and I supposed that you would, as the Governor wrote me was probable, return on the Scotia leaving Liverpool on the 17th.[2] So I fear you will have become rather hungry for letters from home before this will reach you.

A wedding card came for you yesterday from New York. A Miss Eva Gurnée is to become Mrs—Somebody—I suppose she was a schoolmate of yours, and hope she is going to be happy.[3]

You are often enquired for and I am often asked to convey messages of kindness to you: but I have a bad memory for such commissions. I must not however forget some of your humble friends. Aunt Charlotte constantly asks for you and always wants me to remember her to Miss Nettie, and so does Marshall. Nor will I omit to tell you that coming through Baltimore yesterday I called at Mr. Albert's to see Mary Goldsborough who is visiting there but failed to find her at home. So today I have a letter from her expressing her disappointment, with many kind expressions of remembrance & interest for you.

I can't say that I am entirely satisfied with your determination to remain; but I do approve and admire your determination to improve yourself in French & German & drawing & am willing to submit to the protracted separation for your sake. I cannot help feeling very anxious about you: left alone as you never were before. I have, however, great confidence in your good sense. You will not omit necessary exercise and you will take every possible care of your health. I don't think you are likely to form any acquaintances which I would not approve, or allow your affections to become engaged to any body while abroad. I hope you will keep constantly in mind your obligation & privilege as a Christian, and avoid all society not of the purest & highest character. Indeed I would advise you to have as little intercourse as possible with English-speaking people. The more you force yourself to talk German & French the better, and the less you read of anything but German & French the better. I believe I will write you in French. Of course the French will be bad, but then you can improve yourself by correcting me. And you may write in French to me.

And you must take special care of your health. A Gentleman who was with me me last night quite alarmed me by saying that Dresden is a very damp place, and that people there are very apt to be troubled with sore throats & lung disorders. You must keep your feet dry & warm & your person well protected; and yet not so very warm as to risk sudden checks of perspiration.[4]

I am very glad to read your account of the motherly character of Mrs Spangenbergh. Give my best respects to her and tell her I shall be very grateful for all her attentions to you and care of you. I hope you will have Carrie Harrington with you, if she is as good a girl as her sister Mary.[5] I would rather you had no companion than a frivolous girl of unsettled principles. I suppose Katie will tell me what you need in the money way, what you have & what you want. There is no reason why you should stint yourself in any thing proper & reasonable. Goodbye darling. I shall be more anxious to hear from you now than ever.

Your loving father
S P Chase

Library of Congress.

1. Dresden was on the Elbe River, in Saxony. In the nineteenth century, the German-speaking states of Europe had no single dominant artistic center. Munich, which reportedly had more than 2,000 artists in residence in 1877; Berlin, which increased in importance during the century; Vienna; and other cities were all centers of activity in the graphic arts. Earlier, Dresden, with an emphasis on Baroque decorative arts, had been called "a German Florence." The picture gallery there, in an ornate building constructed

1847–55, was particularly strong in Baroque, Renaissance, and Old Masters paintings from Spain, Italy, the Low Countries, and Germany. In terms of contemporary art during the nineteenth century, Dresden was home to several influential landscape artists. The city had a well-established art academy, known for its balance of painting and drawing. One member of the academy's faculty, Adrian Ludwig Richter, was a very active book illustrator as well as a painter. Ulrich Finke, *German Painting from Romanticism to Expressionism* (Boulder, Colo.: Westview Press, 1974), 9, 29, 202, 205, 232, 239; Harald Marx and Gregor J. M. Weber, *The Old Masters Picture Gallery in Dresden,* trans. Dorothy Ann Schade-Maurice (Munich: Duetscher Kunstverlag, 1993), 5–7; Kermit S. Champra and Kate H. Champra, *German Painting of the Nineteenth Century* (New Haven, Conn.: Yale University Art Gallery, 1970), 10–12, 45–47; S. G. W. Benjamin, *Contemporary Art in Europe* (New York: Garland Publishing, 1877), 117, 151; Sarah Richards, "'A true Siberia': Art in Service to Commerce in the Dresden Academy and the Meissen Drawing School, 1764–1836," *Journal of Design History* 11 (1998): 109–26.

2. Part of the transatlantic Cunard line from 1862 to 1878, the *Scotia* was an ocean paddle-steamer, the most powerful one built up to that time. Gibbs, *Passenger Liners,* 52.

3. Likely Evelyn Gurnee Scott of New York. She and her husband Edward Padelford Scott had a son, Walter Gurnee Scott, the year after Nettie received this wedding announcement. *New York Times,* Mar. 30, 1895.

4. Nettie had been ill the previous winter. Details are incomplete, but she developed a fever after attending a fancy dress party (for which she was attired "prettily" but not warmly enough, her father thought). She was not incapacitated in the first days of the illness, seeming to have ups and downs, but she had "considerable fever & headache." There is a gap in Father's journal and we do not know the rest of the story or how long Nettie was ill, but one room of the house was turned into a sick room for her. The doctor who first examined her was unsure of the nature of her illness, although in a letter printed in the next chapter, Father characterized it as typhoid fever. See his letters to her of Dec. 12, 1866, Dec. 24, 1866, and Jan. 31, 1867, below; *Chase Papers,* 1:603, 607–8.

5. Carrie and Mary Harrington were likely the daughters of George Harrington, the former assistant secretary of the Treasury who served as U.S. minister to Switzerland, 1865–69. *Nat. Cyc.,* 12:337.

CHRONOLOGY

December 10, 1866	Kate, William, and Willie arrive in Washington, D.C.; Nettie remains in Dresden
late December 1866	William to Providence; Kate follows for New Year's; Willie, recovering from the croup, stays in Washington with Father
January 1867	Father "bravely" receives New Year's callers on his own and begins to host regular receptions; Kate and William return to Washington
February 14, 1867	Kate attends the grand housewarming gala at the Cookes' Ogontz estate outside Philadelphia
February–March 1867	Alice Skinner visiting in Washington
March 1867	William makes a trip to Rhode Island and returns to Washington
April 6, 1867	Kate and Willie sail for France, with Susie Hoyt and her brother Will
June 1867	Father goes to North Carolina to hold his first circuit court in a Southern state
September 1867	Father to New England, New York, and Philadelphia; William is in Rhode Island; Kate and Nettie in Europe travel through Heidelburg and Stuttgart to Paris
September 17, 1867	Father attends dedication of national cemetery at Antietam; he makes a trip to Ohio
October 1867	He holds circuit court in Baltimore; Nettie, Kate, and Willie return to United States by the end of the year

CHAPTER 9

"Mutual Exasperation"

DECEMBER 1866–SEPTEMBER 1867

IN JANUARY 1867, Father wrote Nettie that Congress and President Johnson had reached a state of "mutual exasperation."[1] Though a vast understatement of the problems that arose between Congress and the executive in the postwar years, Father's phrasing does suggest the considerable political anxiety of the time period. His letters of 1866–67 also suggest how he thought about his daughters. He wrote, not so much about society gossip or family news, but of the political news of the day, both at home and abroad. Father's tone also illustrates his assumptions about his daughters' political intelligence. In an age where we often imagine that middle- and upper-class women were seen primarily as mothers or decorative society mavens, Father expected that his girls would be interested in and understand the political news. Indeed a number of women's historians have examined just how politically minded nineteenth-century women could be, and how politics functioned outside the formal halls of government in a way that encompassed the female sphere.[2]

Father's and Nettie's 1865 trip to the ex-Confederacy highlighted the essential problems of reconstructing the nation after the Civil War. Though the problems facing the postwar nation were myriad, most fell into one of two categories: how to readmit the states that had been part of the Confederacy, and what to do with almost four million ex-slaves. The two issues were so divisive that Americans on both sides of the war found compromise almost impossible. Tennessean Andrew Johnson had become president upon Abraham Lincoln's assassination in April 1865. Congressional radicals, with whom Father had considerable sympathy, initially welcomed the Johnson presidency. Lincoln's conciliatory attitude toward former slave owners and secessionists had angered many Northerners, while Johnson had a notorious dislike for the planter elite. The president's hostility, though, did not translate into a desire to support black civil rights or change his white supremacist ideas about who should govern the reconstructed South. Johnson supported a program of readmitting states on their own terms, which in most Southern states translated to forgoing not only suffrage for black men, but the most basic civil rights for all freedpeople.[3]

Many Americans, radical Republicans among them, were outraged at Johnson's approach to Reconstruction. Four years of shockingly violent war did not incline Unionists to conciliatory feelings. Rather, many politicians and citizens wanted the ex-Confederates punished. Though most Northerners were not entirely behind the notion of black civil rights, they were willing to support these rights if it irritated those whom they felt had provoked the war and, in their eyes, had caused the deaths of more than 618,000 Americans. Also, an important minority of Americans had believed strongly in rights for African Americans before the war (Father among them). Abolitionists' and antislavery advocates' numbers had swelled during the war, in part because 180,000 black soldiers had strengthened army ranks and helped turn the tide of the war to the Union after 1862.[4] Thus many Americans saw this postwar period as an opportunity to remake the South, ending the nation's history as "half slave, half free," and feared that Johnson's Reconstruction plan would land the country back where it had been before the war. Father concurred with these worries, in part because the 1865 Southern trip he had taken with Nettie convinced him that black Americans were loyal to the Union and deserved full citizenship. He worried that Johnson's Reconstruction plan would abandon potential black voters to the control of their old masters.[5]

Father's Reconstruction-era letters to his daughters clearly illustrate where his interest lay in this national drama, particularly with regard to the Fourteenth Amendment. The proposed amendment became the symbolic dividing line between the presidential and congressional Reconstruction plans. By the end of 1866, ten Southern states had failed to ratify the amendment, which called for black civil rights and black male suffrage and barred ex-Confederate officials from state and national political office.[6] Father worried that the amendment might go too far, particularly in barring ex-Confederates from office, but he believed the amendment ought to be ratified by the Southern states. He urged Johnson to adopt "universal suffrage with universal amnesty," but to no avail.[7] Congress forced the issue, and ratification of the amendment became a primary condition for a state's readmission into the Union by mid-1866. Nonetheless, the amendment continued to be a bone of contention between factions until it became law in 1868.

The "mutual exasperation" felt on the national political level during 1866 and 1867 mirrored the personal politics between Kate and William Sprague. The marriage, which had begun to sour seemingly minutes after the honeymoon, continued to deteriorate after baby Willie's birth. In October 1866, newspapers reported a rumor from Providence that the couple would divorce. "Domestic infelicity or infidelity" was cited as the cause. Father deemed the report a "scandalous libel," an "outrage" that was "as devoid of truth as of decency," but William, who had left for Europe to escort Kate home, was not available to refute the rumor. Father had recently used Jacob W. Schuckers, who had been his secretary at the Treasury Department, to feed his views on Reconstruction and the Supreme Court to the press. When John Russell Young, the managing editor of the *New York Tribune,* volunteered to rebut the story, Father asked Schuckers to furnish Young with information and suggestions. The refutation that appeared in the *Tribune* dismissed the rumor as the work of William's political opponents, chiefly Democrats who had never accepted his early and constant support of the Union cause. Young's newspaper, lamenting that the pillory was no longer in use, declared that "jail for a term of years" would be suitable punishment for the "prurient creatures" who instigated such "scandals on the private lives of public men."[8]

The Spragues managed a marital rapprochement while Kate was abroad, though the peace did not last long after the couple was once again faced with the day-to-day reality of life together. William continued to spend much of his time in Providence, at his mother's house, leaving Kate and Willie in Washington, D.C., with Father. William had tried to quit drinking while Kate was abroad, or at least that was what he told her in his letters, but it appears that he was drinking again in 1867. When William was too sick to come down to breakfast in the morning or unable to make it to the dinner table, Father believed, or pretended to believe, that his son-in-law suffered from a stomach disorder. In his letters to Nettie, Father paired mentions of William's "dyspepsia" with discussion of his marital excellence. "No woman could have a kinder more indulgent husband than he has been to Katie," Father wrote, adding: "Sometimes I feel she don't feel it quite enough." This about a woman who was undoubtedly the victim of what today we would recognize as domestic abuse.[9]

Though Father meant well, greatly loved his daughters, and wanted the best for them, perhaps his blindness about Kate's marriage represented his deeper parental inadequacies. Little in his background prepared him for the emotive tenor of the mid-nineteenth century, leaving him underprepared to meet his daughters' needs. To his credit, though, Father shared with his daughters a "mutual exasperation" about his fathering difficulties. His weaknesses were failures of personality, not will, and no father was happier than he when his daughters came home from their travels.

1. Father to Nettie, Jan. 24, 1867, below.
2. For example, see Robert Dinkin, *Before Equal Suffrage: Women in Partisan Politics from Colonial Times to 1920* (Westport, Conn.: Greenwood Press, 1995); Rebecca Edwards, *Angels*

in the Machinery: Gender and American Party Politics from the Civil War to the Progressive Era (New York: Oxford University Press, 1997); Nancy Isenberg, *Sex and Citizenship in Antebellum America* (Chapel Hill, N.C.: University of North Carolina Press, 1998); Jo Freeman, *A Room at a Time: How Women Encountered Party Politics* (Lanham, Md.: Rowman & Littlefield, 2000); Allgor, *Parlor Politics;* Melanie Sue Gustafson, *Women and the Republican Party, 1854–1924* (Urbana, Ill.: University of Illinois Press, 2001); Lamphier, *Kate Chase and William Sprague.*

3. Brooks D. Simpson, *The Reconstruction Presidents* (Lawrence, Kans.: University of Kansas Press, 1998), 67–71; Foner, *Short History of Reconstruction,* 84–85.

4. McPherson, *Ordeal by Fire,* 350–55; Peter Kolchin, *American Slavery, 1619–1887* (New York: Hill & Wang, 1993), 203–7.

5. Niven, *Chase,* 397–98.

6. While not directly providing for black male suffrage, the amendment did say that a state's representation could be limited based on the number of male citizens denied suffrage. Thus states that limited voting on the basis of race lost political power. Women's rights advocates certainly saw the Fourteenth Amendment as a male suffrage bill, particularly because it introduced into the Constitution the word *male* in relationship to voting rights for the first time. Foner, *Short History of Reconstruction,* 114–17; Ellen Carol DuBois, *Feminism and Suffrage: The Emergence of an Independent Women's Movement in America, 1848–1869* (Ithaca, N.Y.: Cornell University Press, 1978), 58–62.

7. However much Father believed that ex-slaves would make as good or better voters than white Northerners, he thought that only states had the right to determine who could and could not vote. Niven, *Chase,* 408–9.

8. Father to Schuckers, Oct. 16, 1866 (Chase Papers, LC); *New York Tribune,* Oct. 31, 1866; *Macon Daily Telegraph,* Oct. 5, 1866; *Chase Papers,* 5:124–29.

9. Father to Nettie, Jan. 1, 1867, below; Lamphier, *Kate Chase and William Sprague,* 88–89, 145–46, 181–83.

FATHER TO NETTIE

Washington, December 12, 1866
Wednesday.

My darling Nettie,

It was a joyous meeting when Katie and her Governor and little Willie made their appearance Monday Morning / The only draw back was that you were not with us. But then just after they came your second letter to me arrived; and it was so pleasant and cheerful that it made us all feel as if you *were* with us after all. It was a delight to *see* Katie & Willie & the Governor [so] well & in such good spirits and it was an equal delight to read your own assurances of your health & contentment and pleasant Surroundings.

By the way I must tell you that I was yesterday Evening at Baron Gerolts, where you were kindly enquired for. The Baroness and her two unmarried daughters are now at home, having arrived a few days ago from Bremen. This however is only introductory to something else / As we talked of you and your temporary residence in Dresden the Baron exclaimed: Oh, I know Madame Spangenbergh. She was a very handsome young lady and I often danced with her." He spoke also of her daughter, whom he had seen and seemed much pleased to hear of the family, and begged me to convey to [her] through you his kind remembrances. If there is no mistake of identity your kind hostess will be pleased to hear this. The Baron said that Herr Spangenbergh after his marriage to his handsome acquaintance went abroad (to Mexico I think) and died there or shortly after his return to Fatherland. I had never seen so much of the Gerolts as I saw last evening. They are a very pleasant folk. Dr. Rosing who has succeeded Schleiden was there.[1]

From Baron Gerolts I went to Sumner's / Mrs Sumner was out; but Sumner was surrounded with gentlemen from North Carolina & Massachusetts. The North Carolinians, among whom were Mr. Holden, Mr Johnson's provisional Governor, Mr Pool who was elected Senator by the Legislature organized under Mr. Johnson's auspices and several more notables had called to consult the Senator on the subject of loyal State Government in N.C.[2] They were all satisfied that the Experiment had failed & were anxious that Congress should interpose by an enabling act authorizing the people black & white to vote for members of a Convention, who might form a state Constitution of Republican Government.

I left this letter unfinished till now that I might add any thing if any thing of interest should occur. But I find nothing to add. We are all well. The boy is in excellent condition, and seems to take to his Grandpa very decidedly. Katie is very well. The Governor is well too and has been making a little Speech on Woman's suffrage, which seemed to me very good.[3]

Some people who are anxious to defeat loyal black suffrage endeavor to put its friends in an inconsistent position by propositions for Woman suffrage: but with little success actual or probable.

You must be very careful of your health, particularly in the point of keeping your feet dry and warm & your rooms well ventilated, without exposing yourself to draft / You had typhoid last winter and it sometimes returns the next winter. Hence the more reason for care & thoughtfulness on your part

When you write tell me what letters you receive from me by their dates & let me see that you reply to them.

Most affectionately

S P Chase

Library of Congress.

1. Rudolph Schleiden had served as the Hanseatic Republic's minister to Washington and welcomed the Chase sisters during their European travels. Johannes Rosing was the chargé d'affaires of the Hanseatic legation, which had its office in New York rather than Washington. The Hanseatic Republic, which consisted of the "free cities" of Hamburg, Bremen, and Lübeck, was already feeling the pressure of Prussian expansion. The Hanse cities joined Prussia in a North German Confederation and, in 1868, closed their separate legation in the United States. *Chase Papers*, 1:703; *New York Times*, Aug. 23, 28, Nov. 16, Dec. 21, 1866, June 24, 1867, Sept. 26, 1868.

2. William Woods Holden, a Democratic newspaper editor in Raleigh, N.C., became a Republican after the war. Andrew Johnson appointed him provisional governor in May 1865, but Holden lost the election in November. North Carolina lawyer and state senator John Pool had supported the Union during the war and was elected to the U.S. Senate in 1865. However, Pool was denied his seat when his state refused to ratify the Fourteenth Amendment. Congress having made ratification a condition of readmission, Pool and Holden organized the North Carolina Republican Party. Holden supported the amendment and on Jan. 1, 1867, gave a speech advocating unrestricted suffrage for blacks. With Pool's aid he ran successfully for governor in 1868. After the readmission of North Carolina, Pool served in the U.S. Senate. *DAB*, 9:138–39; *ANB*, 17:665–66.

3. The Senate was considering a bill to regulate voting and extend the suffrage to African American men in the District of Columbia. An effort to derail the measure by attaching an amendment that would give women the right to vote in the district elicited a long address on December 12 by Senator B. Gratz Brown of Missouri. "I stand for universal suffrage," Brown declared, "and as a matter of fundamental principle do not recognize the right of society to limit it on any ground of race, color, or sex." Voting was, he said, "intrinsically a natural right." William spoke after Brown, and according to a Georgia newspaper the senator from Rhode Island also "took ground in favor of universal suffrage." William's speech concentrated on differences between an "aristocratic" South and a "democratic" North, and on the president's efforts "in the interest of a class, in opposition to the privileges and highest welfare of the great mass of the people." He declared himself in favor of female suffrage, though apparently not at that particular juncture: "When it is necessary that women shall vote for the support of liberty and equality I shall be ready to cast my vote in their favor. The black man's vote is necessary to this at this time." William joined the majority of the Senate in voting down the amendment, 37 to 9. *Congressional Globe*, 39th Cong., 2d sess., 1866, 76, 81–82; *Macon Weekly Telegraph*, Dec. 17, 1866; *Journal of the Senate of the United States of America, Being the Second Session of the Thirty-Ninth Congress* (Washington, D.C.: Government Printing Office, 1867), 32.

FATHER TO NETTIE

Washington, Dec. 24, 1866

My darling Nettie,

We have had no letter from you for two weeks, and I am quite anxious about you: for it seems to me impossible that you have not written, if you have not been ill. So my only relief is to blame the Mails, and I hope that all the blame is due to them. It takes away a good deal of my satisfaction in your opportunities of improvement to have you so far, that in case of sickness none of us can be near you. It is some consolation to know that you are among friends, who have shown every disposition to be kind to you: and that Madame Spangenbergh is so motherly & benevolent.

There is very little of new or interesting here outside of our family circle. Dear little Willie has had a bad turn of croup & has been quite ill. This has been a great grief to all of us. The dear little fellow is not very patient and he has suffered a great deal. At first Katie sent for Dr. Hall who gave him a little calomel. He seemed to get better, but the next day was worse again. Then Katie sent for Dr. Pope a homœpathic physician who has a great reputation I find in Washington[1] / *He* thought and of course

Katie thought that it was the calomel; but I, like a good judge, reserve my opinion. The baby, at any rate, had a hard time, but last night began to improve, and is still improving this morning. I hope we may now regard him as fairly convalescent. The Governor is in Providence & Christmas seems likely to be dull with us. I wish I had more of the German in me then I should know what to buy & what to give & what to do to make every body happy. I want to, but don't know how. I never learned & fear I never shall.

On the evening of the 22d. some of the New Englanders here—mostly of the Congregational church, had a supper in commemoration of Forefathers Day. I was present half an hour and found every thing very pleasant. The supper was abundant and the guests all seemed in good humor. One table was covered with the dishes of lang syne in Yankeedom—such as rye & Indian bread—hasty pudding & milk, shell barks—called now hickory nuts, popped corn, black walnuts in substitution for butter nuts, and two pumpkin pies on one of which were the words, in sugar frosting, Landing at Plymouth 1620 & on the other Negro Suffrage 1866. I suppose that Manhood suffrage is a logical result of the principles of civil & religious liberty, but I doubt whether the Pilgrims were *very* zealous for any other civil & religious liberties than their own. The quakers did not think they were, nor did the negroes & much less the Indians of that day.[2]

Congress has taken a long holiday, from last Thursday to Thursday of next week. I hinted to the Judges that they should do likewise but they would not take the hint.[3] I wanted to attend a Meeting of Delegates for the Alpha Delta Phi Societies in New York where they are to have a session on the 26th, & the Wedding of Jennie Cameron which is to take place on the 27th; but I am cut off from both.[4]

Mrs Eames gave a very agreeable party Saturday Evening, where I passed an hour or two pleasantly after leaving "the Forefathers".[5] Quite a number of your old acquaintants were there & the enquiries for you were very kind. I asked Miss Goddard, if they did not miss Admiral Dahlgren who has been ordered to the South Pacific. She said she was very glad he was gone. She liked him as well as she could have liked any body her mother married, but she liked him best farthest away. A new version of the old saying "le plus loin le plus cher."[6] Goodbye darling. May our Heavenly Father watch over you in love.

Yours most affectionately
S P Chase

Library of Congress.

1. Probably Washington physician Gustavus W. Pope. *Boyd's Washington and Georgetown Directory*, 125.

2. Celebrated on December 22 during the nineteenth century, Forefathers' Day commemorated the supposed date of the Pilgrims' landing at Plymouth Rock. The importance of Forefathers' Day receded after the Civil War, when Thanksgiving—a holiday that previously had not been connected to the Massachusetts origin legend—evolved from a regional religious observance into a Pilgrim-themed national holiday incorporating many of the rites associated with Forefathers' Day. Ann Ihry Abrams, *The Pilgrims and Pocahontas: Rival Myths of American Origin* (Boulder, Colo.: Westview Press, 1999), 9–10, 42; John Seelye, *Memory's Nation: The Place of Plymouth Rock* (Chapel Hill, N.C.: University of North Carolina Press, 1998), 146.

3. In addition to Father, the members of the Supreme Court at this time were Nathan Clifford, David Davis, Stephen J. Field, Samuel F. Miller, Noah H. Swayne, and James M. Wayne. *Chase Papers*, 1:225, 424, 513, 517, 519, 601.

4. Father was a member of the Alpha Delta Phi fraternity. The organization was founded at Hamilton College in 1832, and the various regional chapters began holding conventions starting in 1836. Simon Cameron's daughter Virginia Rolette Cameron, who had been one of the party when Kate and Nettie visited Fortress Monroe in July 1861, married Wayne MacVeagh of Pennsylvania in 1866. *The Alpha Delta Phi, 1832–1882* (Boston: Alpha Delta Phi, 1882), xxv, 56–57, 260; Erwin Stanley Bradley, *Simon Cameron, Lincoln's Secretary of War: A Political Biography* (Philadelphia: University of Pennsylvania Press, 1966), 51.

5. Frances Campbell Eames, known for her wit and fine parties, was the wife of Charles Eames, a Harvard graduate, newspaperman, and lawyer. Their home at the corner of 14th and H streets was one of the hubs of Washington society. Collections of the Association for the Preservation of the Historic Congressional Cemetery, *Interments in the Historic Congressional Cemetery* (Washington, D.C.: Turk, Tracy and Larry, 2003); *DAB*, 5:592–93; Ellet, *Court Circles*, 500–501; Burlingame and Ettlinger, *Inside Lincoln's White House*, 6, 273.

6. "The more distant, the more dear." Adm. John Adolphus Bernard Dahlgren married his second wife, Madeleine Vinton Goddard, a wealthy Ohio-born widow with two children, in the summer of 1865. Not long after his marriage, Dahlgren was ordered to command the South Pacific Squadron, which he did from 1866 to 1868. An author who wrote under the pen names "Corinne" and "Cornelia," Madeleine founded the Washington Literary Society in 1873. She was the daughter of Samuel Finley Vinton, who was a Whig congressman from Ohio when Father entered the Senate in 1849. Romaine Goddard was her daughter from her first marriage. *DAB*, 5:29–31; Robert J. Schneller Jr., *A Quest for Glory: A Biography of Rear Admiral John A. Dahlgren* (Annapolis, Md.: Naval Institute Press, 1996), 322, 329, 357; *Chase Papers*, 1:209; 2:57–59, 232.

FATHER TO KATE

Washington, Jany 4, 1867.

My dearest Katie,

Your thoughtful and affectionate letter of New Years came yesterday. I wish I had time to give you as good a one in return, but I have not.

I am glad you went to Providence / Your first duty is to your husband. That duty unperformed or carelessly performed there is no chance of happiness in the married relation. I cant tell you how much joy it gives me to see you possessed of your husbands entire confidence & affection. No joy exceeds it and hardly any satisfaction except that which flows from the conviction that you deserve it. I hope that henceforth you will find less and less enjoyment in the society-whirl & more & more in making *home* attractive to husband & child.[1]

Little Willie came down this morning very cheerful and almost well. I suppose indeed that he is quite well, except that his mouth is still a little sore, though getting better every day. The little fellow was quite grave this morning, as if he was trying to unravel some mystery. You have indeed a treasure in Maggie. Nothing can surpass her watchfulness & devotion

I got along bravely on New Years. The table was set in the dining room with coffee & Sherry & cold water for drinks and some chicken salad for eatables. On a side table I had some "Sunshine."[2] I directed Marshall who attended the door to say to every one that Gov & Mrs Sprague were in Providence but that the Chief Justice was at home. Some did not come in, but left cards—Most however paid their respects to me—perhaps two hundred & fifty—quite enough. They all seemed quite content with the treatment they received; and on the whole I was glad that I did not shut the house[3]

Every thing seems to go on well so far as the housekeeping is concerned. Your grandmother took a bad cold just about the time you went away, and has not been much down stairs. She is not at all seriously ill however.

I am myself pretty well; with no greater amount of aches than common.

Yesterday I had a letter from Nettie, in a much more cheerful tone than her last / The same mail brought one from you[4] which I enclose with this.

Sir Fred. Bruce and Mr. Antrobus[5] were out in a red sleigh yesterday & paid me the honor of a call. Sir Frederick was agreeable as usual and enquired particularly for you & the Governor

And now the Coupee has come to take me to the Capitol. It is so wet & sloppy that I dont like to walk.

With kindest regards to Mrs Sprague & Miss Almira & best love to your Governor

Your loving father
S P Chase

Historical Society of Pennsylvania.

1. Kate and William had marital trouble before she left for Europe, though they were briefly reconciled through letters while she was abroad and when he joined the sisters in Germany and Switzerland. The Spragues returned to the Washington house they shared with Father on December 10, but William soon after left for his mother's home in Providence, in spite of the fact that his son was ill. The family remained apart for Christmas. Kate left Willie with Father and Maggie for her trip to Providence, but sometime probably before January 22 returned to Washington, where she stayed until the fall, when she went to Germany to accompany Nettie home. Because the Thirty-ninth and Fortieth Congresses were in session, William split his time between Rhode Island and Washington that winter and spring. Father to Nettie, Jan. 24, 1867, below; Lamphier, *Kate Chase and William Sprague*, 88–91.

2. A bottled beverage shipped to Father by Thomas H. Yeatman of Cincinnati, who later sent bottled water from Michigan. *Chase Papers*, 5:122; Nettie and Will Hoyt to Father, Apr. 30, 1871, below.

3. New Year's Day receptions were common among Washington's political and social elite. Phelps, *Kate Chase*, 113, 193; *Chase Papers*, 1:512, 601, 645.

4. He probably meant to write "for you."

5. Probably painter, poet, and journalist John Antrobus. Born in Warwickshire, Eng., he lived in Montgomery, Ala., and New Orleans before the Civil War. After the war he lived in Chicago and Washington, D.C., before settling in Detroit. Groce and Wallace, *Dictionary of Artists*, 12.

FATHER TO NETTIE

Washington, Jany 17, 1867.

My darling Nettie

I have received two of your always welcome letters within the last week. The first was without a date except December—the second was the 26th: the day after Christmas.

You say in your last that I have only to tell you what to do or omit and your greatest pleasure will be to comply with my wishes. Now I am going to put you at once to the test. I do want to have you write a plain good hand, with the letters joined and no *long* lines drawn through your ts, and shorter legs to your gs, and shorter horizontals at the end of many of your letters. And then I want your spelling right—it is pretty nearly so—and your points and capitals rightly made & placed. Just let me give you some specimens of what I mean

Your long looked for letter came last night, the &c[1]

Do you take? Katie when of your age wrote nearly as carelessly as you do: but she has greatly improved, though she still lacks plainness and legibility, of which you may say very fairly that *I* ought not to complain.

I have always thought a great deal about neat penmanship, and accuracy in punctuation, use of capitals & arrangement of sentences / And in most of these particulars I am tolerably correct, though I must confess to a sad deterioration in the first, as I have become more and more immersed in business. I think one good rule is never to allow letters to go above or below the next line to that on which they are written: and if possible avoid any interference by letters on one line with letters on another. This fault and the failure to connect your letters with each other and the queer legs of your gs & ys and the long horizontals in termination of letters & words & in crossing of ts can be corrected. And I really think it worth your while to correct them.

Now do you know that I hate to write this because I fear it may annoy you; and I don't want to imagine tears starting into those dear eyes of yours with father too far off to kiss them away.

My ambition for you is the same as yours for yourself that you may be a true christian and an accomplished woman. You won't be an old maid and you need not flatter yourself that you will. You will share the common lot but I hope it will be made uncommon by a sweet christian spirit.

I am pleased that you make so good progress in your German; but I hope you do not neglect your French. The latter is the more important language by far: and you must insist on your teacher's dealing candidly with you, and pointing out small faults as well as large. The French is so idiomatic & has so many peculiar turns that it is hard to master. It will be a good exercise—a very good exercise to read a page of familiar French & then write it without looking at what you have read, & then compare, & then try it again. A daily exercise of this sort, if only of two or three sentences will greatly improve you. You will find it equally useful to write English the same way; and on the comparison note every error in punctuation, use of capitals &c.

My first reception took place last night. It was not very largely attended. No ladies came except Mrs Jordan.[2] Few comparatively knew it would take place. Four of the Judges came, nearly all the Ohio Members, a General or two, (*principally* Gen. Sickles & Gen Tom Smith,)[3] a lot of lawyers, a number of distinguished strangers, pretty much all the South American diplomats, &c in all say a hundred or more. The next time I expect a crowd: but don't want one. The people seemed to enjoy themselves, though I gave them no great things to eat or drink

The baby has got almost quite well. He is a dear little fellow. Strange to say, especially when one remembers the gentle & even tempers of pa & ma, he has a will of his own; and yet he is not obstinate. It is nice to see with what a grace he submits when he finds he can't help himself.

We still have sleighing—a wonder for Washington. And we have bought two cows; I one not thinking that the Sprague branch was buying, & the Sprague branch one not thinking that I was buying. So we have plenty of milk. Please send me *your* German photograph & Madame S——s In my next I will send you some

Most affectionately your father
S P Chase

Library of Congress.

1. He wrote this line in imitation of what he considered to be the quirks of her handwriting, with some letters elongated horizontally and, in particular, very long crosses on the t's.

2. Likely Augusta Woodbury Jordan. Her husband, Ohioan Edward Jordan, was solicitor of the U.S. Treasury, 1861–69. Their daughter Emily, born in 1858, was educated at Vassar and, as the widow of Henry Clay Folger, an executive of the Standard Oil Company, founded the Folger Shakespeare Library in Washington. *Chase Papers,* 2:74; *ANB,* 8:167–68.

3. Daniel Edgar Sickles, a congressman from New York, 1857–61, was a major general in the Civil War and lost a leg at Gettysburg. In 1859, Sickles shot and killed his wife's lover but won acquittal from a charge of murder on the grounds that a man had a right to use violence to control his wife. The incident did little to affect Sickles's political or social standing with the elites of Washington. Thomas Kilby Smith had been Father's law student in the 1840s. He rose to the rank of major general of volunteers during the war. Hendrick Hartog, *Man and Wife in America* (Cambridge, Mass.: Harvard University Press, 2000), 218–40; *DAB,* 17:150–51; *Chase Papers,* 1:187.

FATHER TO NETTIE

Washington, Jany 24, 1867.

My darling Nettie,

I sent you last week a rather critical letter. This shall be one of talk news & nothings. Only I must remind you that you were to be particular in writing so that I receive a letter every week: for if I do not I cannot help feeling uneasy about my darling away off in Dresden. How far that away off seems!

And first I must tell you about the baby—that baby of babies before whom all other babies hide their diminished heads. But first of all this moral reflection, How wisely it is ordered that every family thinks its own baby the best baby in the world: What security it gives to the little one & what assurance of care & tender nurture. But our baby!—_Our_ baby grows more interesting & knowing day by day. He knows perfectly how to say *dinner*—to be sure he says it in rather a drawl way *deenar* but he knows, the little rogue, what it means, and insists on his rights and like other folks wants them given in the most extended sense. He has a proper regard for his own dignity. If he considers himself as at all slighted he gets mad as quick as any body you ever saw. But he is politic too: as soon as he is convinced that he can make nothing by anger he comes out of it at once & tries conciliation. See what a diplomatist he is going to be! He is quite well now except that the teething period is not quite over and he is still troubled a little by that process. His mother dresses him up *en prince*—& he is *facile* princeps to her.[1]

Katie is very well. I cannot tell you how thankful I am that her health seems so fully established. She is stouter than ever, & yet not stout. She is handsomer than ever. So far this winter she has not gone out much—but I suppose she will go now; for[2]

Sarah & Susie Hoyt are with us looking ever more charming than they did last winter. Almost the first thing they both said after they came was "how I wish Nettie was here! The party doesnt seem complete without her." They only came night before last, under the charge of their brother Will. We were at the Presidents dining and so they had to entertain themselves till we came back. Last evening they were quite the ornaments of my reception. Mr. Vallé was quite devoted to them as were also two other foreigners—*nouveaux venus*[3]—travelling for information— the Vicomte de Chabrol & the Baron Mackay[4]—Of course they had, also, their full share of American admiration: but young gentlemen were scarce last night: for Mrs & General Grant gave a party & all the world was there.

But I must leave the girls & tell you about the Governor—our Governor. He is pretty well this winter, but suffers still a great deal from dyspepsia.[5] Last night he felt so badly that he could not come down. He takes more to *the boy* than to any thing or any body else. No woman could have a kinder or more indulgent husband than he has been to Katie. Sometimes I fear she don't feel it quite enough; though I know that she loves him truly & is proud of him.

So far I had written before breakfast this bright Thursday morning and, now, just after breakfast I resume. We had nice birds, nice sliced potatoes, nice rolls, nice every thing, and if we had only had nice Nettie there would have been nothing to desire, except better health for the Governor who came down looking quite ill, & soon went up stairs again, having eaten almost nothing.

But I must tell you a little about the Presidents dinner. Since Mr. Pierce's time the old Presidential fashion of giving dinners to the Diplomats, to the Supreme Court, to Senators & Representatives has been discontinued. Mr. Buchanan dined such as he liked.[6] Mr. Lincoln tried two or three dinners & gave it up. Mr. Johnson has resumed the old practice. Last week he gave a dinner to the Members of the Corps diplomatique. This week it was to the Supreme Court, and to a number of the Senators. Unfortunately the relations between the Congress & the President have become such & the mutual exasperation is such that a number of Senators & Representatives will not accept the Presidents invitations. I thought it my duty to accept and I found the dinner agreeable. Mrs Patterson the Presidents daughter, who presides at the White House was my *partie*. On her left was Mr. Seward & on my right Judge Clifford. So there was no lack of talk. The whole number of guests was about thirty. And here I must break off for it is near time to go to the Capitol: only saying that the White House has been completely renovated under the tasteful supervision of Mrs Patterson, & is now an elegant mansion fit for a gentleman to live in.[7]

Most affy your father
S P Chase

Katie has just recd. your letter dated Jany 9—*My* last date was Dec. 26. I suppose another is on the way—Yours to Katie is charming & does me a great deal of good by its assurances that you are so well.

Library of Congress.

1. Using French, and then drawing ultimately from Latin, Father declared that Kate dressed Willie as a prince and the baby was unquestionably foremost in his mother's attention.

2. Apparently he was interrupted and forgot to finish the sentence.

3. New arrivals.

4. The Vicomte de Chabrol and another French traveler were visiting schools in the United States to learn about American elementary education. In November 1866, a New York newspaper listed Baron Mackay as a member of a party traveling from Scotland.

He was evidently Eric Mackay, who was Lord Reay of the Scottish peerage and also a baronet. *Flake's Bulletin,* Oct. 11, 1866; *New York Times,* Nov. 23, 1866; George E. Cokayne, *The Complete Peerage of England, Scotland, Ireland, Great Britain and the United Kingdom,* 12 vols. (London: St. Catherine Press, 1910; repr., Stroud, Eng.: Sutton, 2000), 10:757.

5. The family used "dyspepsia" to refer to the effects of William's alcoholism. While Kate was abroad in 1866, her husband tried to quit drinking but failed. After the 1880s, William suffered from what was likely alcohol-induced dementia. Lamphier, *Kate Chase and William Sprague,* 84–85, 229–30.

6. Franklin Pierce's wife, Jane Appleton Pierce, was a reluctant first lady and White House hostess, in part because her son was killed in a train derailment while the family was en route to Washington for the president's inauguration. Consequently the Pierce White House was begun in mourning, and the Pierces remained socially withdrawn throughout his administration. Harriet Lane, the niece of bachelor James Buchanan, organized large state dinners at the White House and acted as her uncle's official hostess until she married in 1866. *DAB,* 3:207–14; 14:576–80; Peacock, *Famous American Belles,* 161–74.

7. Andrew Johnson's wife, Eliza McCardle Johnson, suffered from chronic illness, possibly tuberculosis, for much of her adult life, and made only two public appearances as first lady. Their daughter Martha, who married Tennessee politician David T. Patterson, acted as the president's first lady. The White House was vandalized during Mary Lincoln's long mourning period after her husband's assassination. Congress appropriated $30,000 for repairs, which Martha J. Patterson supervised. *Nat. Cyc.,* 12:217; Annie Commire, ed., *Women in World History: A Biographical Encyclopedia,* 17 vols. (Detroit: Yorkin Publications, 1999–2002), 8:241.

FATHER TO NETTIE

Washington, January 31, 1867

Darling Nettie,

A few words on the last day of the first month of the New Year and then perhaps a few more tomorrow before my scribbling sets off on its long journey to my dear sweet child who has my heart with her all the time.

Katie is very well, though the Governor insists that late hours are impairing somewhat her well being / The two Hoyts are here and being very pretty and agreeable are much admired, & like other folks like to be much upon the theatre of success.[1] So when there is a German coming off or on they *must* go and Katie must go with them: and they seldom come home before three & sometimes not before four in the morning.[2]

Thursday Morning.[3] So far had I written yesterday when I was interrupted. I was going on to express a pretty unfavorable opinion of the German & late hours, but I believe I will leave it to inference.

I hear the patter of small feet over head. It is Master William Jr trotting about in the Nursery. I am writing in my library or office. Master William occupies with Maggie the room directly above, which I occupied last winter as a sleeping room. It has been enlarged by the addition of the small room adjoining which was then used for trunks &c and I have taken the room in which you were during the last half or three quarters of your illness. Master William is a great boy. He has quite recovered from his croup & fever & is now in a fair way to do well if he escapes the danger of candy & the like.

There goes the first bell & I must hurry for I must finish in the next ten minutes to make sure of the mail.

Do you know that I am having Jones bust put in marble for you at Florence by Powers. I wish you could see it *before* completed: But that cannot be and I can only hope that it will please you when done.

There is a gentleman here making a new picture of me for Mr. Jay Cooke who wants it for his new house. His name is Coggeswell & he seems rather clever.[4] I hope he will succeed for there has never yet been painted a good picture of me—the fault, I know, mainly of the subject, for there is nothing *peculiar* about my face.

Mrs Pike has come to Washington & her husband has taken rooms near us. May Pike is with them. You remember them I presume / May is very smart & extremely well informed / Mrs P—— is ditto and withal one of my best friends.

Master Willie just comes in and Maggie makes him say as well as he can L-o-v-e to Aunt Nettie. He gets along nicely with Auntie but boggles at the rest. Now he goes down stairs—"by—by Willie".

The court goes on as usual. I get very tired of leaving the house a few minutes before eleven every day in the week—six to go to the Capitol & the other to go to Church / This week my time has been so occupied that I have done very little. Thursday I dont remember what besides the court except a call & talk with Gov. Orr of South Carolina on reconstruction. He says they are trying to arrange a counter proposition to that of Congress—admitting most of its features except dis franchisement, & adding by way of State action a law allowing impartial Suffrage. North Carolina is to take the initiative in this. I wish them good progress, but don't hope for much from any thing except a ratification of the amendment.[5]

Tuesday I dined with Mr. [Dorf] of New York & then called on Mrs Eastman at Dr. Parkers & then went to Mr. Wetmore's to an Ohio party.[6]

Wednesday was my reception and then I went with Katie & the girls to Mrs Morgans ball where the whole world was.[7]

Yesterday I hoped to have for work: but Mr Evarts came to dinner[8] & in the evening a number of other gentlemen.

Today I have begun with this scrawl to you. Then I go to the Capitol— then work for an hour or two *in sitting* to Mr. Coggeswell rather dull & unprofitable—then I hope a little time for court work.

I send you by this mail Frank Leslies illustrated Guar paper & a Freedmans Report where you will find something of mine.[9]

Most affectionately your father
S P Chase

Library of Congress.

1. Sarah and Susie Hoyt.

2. In the United States by the middle part of the nineteenth century, a "German" was a dancing party or cotillion. Originally the term meant a particular dance that featured complicated steps and figures. It was extended to apply to the group of dances called quadrilles, then became the name for a ball or dancing party. *OED*, 3:996; 6:469; Sir William A. Craigie and James R. Hulbert, eds., *A Dictionary of American English on Historical Principles*, 4 vols. (Chicago: University of Chicago Press, 1938–44), 2:1113, 1114.

3. Jan. 31, 1867, was a Thursday, which would seem to indicate that Father began this letter on Wednesday, January 30.

4. William F. Cogswell (b. 1819), a self-taught portraitist who worked in New York, Washington, and St. Louis, is best known for his portrait of Abraham Lincoln. In 1867–68, he worked on a painting of Ulysses S. Grant and his family. According to the Catalog of American Portraits, the U.S. Supreme Court owns two versions of Cogswell's oil portrait of Father, one dated 1867 and a smaller one dated 1868. Groce and Wallace, *Dictionary of Artists*, 136; *New York Times*, Jan. 6, 1868.

5. James Lawrence Orr had been a member of the Confederate Senate but made accommodations to the reality of Southern defeat. As the first governor of South Carolina elected after the war, he favored limited suffrage and other limited rights for former slaves and aligned himself with forces working for a "New South" in which a combination of industrialization and small farms would lessen the gap between poor and rich Southerners. However, Orr recommended rejection of the Fourteenth Amendment, though state constitutional conventions in his state and North Carolina guaranteed civil and political rights to freedmen. South Carolina was the only state in which blacks came to dominate the state legislature in the 1870s. *ANB*, 16:768–69; Foner, *Short History of Reconstruction*, 97–98, 118, 137–38, 149, 151.

6. A medical doctor and ordained Presbyterian minister, Peter Parker served as a missionary in East Asia in the 1830s and founded the Medical Missionary Society. In the 1850s he assisted the U.S. legation in China and continued his hospital work there. After returning to the U.S. in 1857, he lived in Washington. He was married to Harriet Colby Webster, the sister of Emeline Colby Webster Lindsly. Harriet and Emeline, who were distantly related to Daniel Webster, were nieces of Dr. Thomas Sewall, and possibly through that connection related to Charlotte Sewall Eastman. Father was well acquainted with James C. Wetmore, the agent for the state of Ohio in Washington and one of a contingent of Ohioans in the national capital. *ANB*, 17:40–42; Charles M. Wiltse and Harold D. Moser et al., eds., *The Papers of Daniel Webster*, 14 vols. (Hanover, N.H.: University Press of New England, 1974–89), *Correspondence*, 5:22; 6:31; Kelly and Burrage, *Dictionary of American Medical Biography*, 1096; *Chase Papers*, 1:388, 477, 479, 532, 600, 637, 674.

7. Possibly Eliza Waterman Morgan, wife of Edwin Denison Morgan, a wealthy New York merchant and Republican senator. *ANB*, 15:825–26.

8. One of the preeminent lawyers of his generation, William Maxwell Evarts was a strong antislavery advocate before the Civil War and a founder of the Republican Party in New York in the 1850s. Considered a leading candidate for the chief justiceship when Lincoln appointed Father instead, Evarts argued cases before the Supreme Court and later became attorney general in Andrew Johnson's cabinet. Evarts and his wife were both New Englanders by birth, and Father visited them at their farm at Windsor, Vt., in July 1866. *ANB*, 7:626–28; *Chase Papers*, 1:519, 618–19; 5:122.

9. Possibly *The American Freedman*, a monthly journal of the American Freedmen's Union Commission. The journal reported the commission's progress in providing relief and education to freed people. The November 1866 edition contained a letter from Father that thanked the organization for electing him their president and emphasized the importance of the commission's work. In 1855, Henry Carter, an immigrant from England who had become an engraver for a number of illustrated newspapers in New York, launched *Frank Leslie's Illustrated Newspaper*. A weekly publication that combined news with pictures made from woodcut engravings, the newspaper became extremely popular during the 1860s. *New York Tribune*, Jan. 11, 1880; Budd Leslie Gambee Jr., *Frank Leslie and His Illustrated Newspaper, 1855–60* (Ann Arbor, Mich.: University of Michigan Department of Library Science, 1964), 3–9.

FATHER TO NETTIE

Washington, Feb. 15. 1867.

My darling Nettie

I had another charming letter from you this week. You had the advantage in the account of your discussion with the Russian which the *man* had in painting the fight with the lion. The Lion doubted whether a Lion Painter would have given the victory to the man.[1] But I shall take your version, & give you the credit of having the best of the discussion.

I have sent to Cincinnati for some copies of Mr. Reid's book, and will send you one as soon as they come. I am sure it will interest you.

Katie has gone to Philadelphia to attend Jay Cooke's great house warming. Mr. Corwine has just told me that he left her there last evening at nine, & that the Cookes' outdid all past possibilities of American splendor.[2] Oh how I hope you will retain your simplicity of tastes! I dont want you to be dowdy or even plain—but simple while elegant—Not expensive beyond our moderate means, but at the same time not parsimonious. Katie will return tomorrow I suppose, & Alice Skinner will probably arrive this evening or possibly not till tomorrow to spend some days with us.

I am delighted to hear your account of your health & improvement. You speak more of German than French: but you must not forget that French will be use for you fifty times where German will be once.

Congress is coming to the end of its life: but the New Congress will meet under the new law on the same day that the Old dies. Le roi est mort—vive le roi.[3] And Congress just now is our king.

But I am very busy, and scribbling only that I may save the mail of tomorrow and save you the disappointment of not receiving your weekly letter.

Goodbye darling darling. May Heaven Watch over you & make you all that you need to be for this worlds happiness[4] & that of the next. So prays

Your fond father
S P Chase

Miss Nettie Chase

Library of Congress.

1. The story went back to Aesop's fable of "The Man and the Lion Traveling Together." In the nineteenth century, black abolitionists and their supporters used the allegory to counter those who claimed that blacks were inferior to whites. Chaucer had alluded to the fable in *Canterbury Tales* to suggest that depictions of women by male writers could not be considered impartial. Patrick Rael, *Black Identity and Black Protest in the Antebellum North* (Chapel Hill, N.C.: University of North Carolina Press, 2002), 1, 300; Olivia Temple and Robert Temple, trans., *The Complete Fables: Aesop* (New York: Penguin, 1998), 47.

2. Father had known attorney Richard M. Corwine in Ohio in the 1850s, before Corwine moved to Washington. According to the invitations, the Cookes' housewarming party for their newly finished house, Ogontz, was the evening of February 14. The party ran from 6 P.M. to midnight and featured music and dancing. *Chase Papers*, 1:266, 710; Oberholtzer, *Cooke*, 2:451–52.

3. "The king is dead. Long live the king." The second session of the Thirty-ninth Congress adjourned Mar. 3, 1867, and the first session of the Fortieth Congress began on March 4. *Bio. Dir. U.S. Cong.*, 183.

4. Father and Nettie were surely both aware that in his *Confessions*, Saint Augustine wrote of the need to give up the pursuit of "this world's happiness" (*felicitate terrena*) to satisfy one's spiritual quest. Augustine, *Confessions*, trans. F. J. Sheed, intro. by Peter Brown (Indianapolis: Hackett Publishing Co., 1993), 139; Augustine, *Confessions*, ed. James J. O'Donnell, 3 vols. (Oxford: Oxford University Press, 1992), 1:96.

FATHER TO NETTIE

Washn. March 23, 67

Darling Nettie,

Your last letter gave us a deal of pleasure. Alice has several which had already come to Jenny Jewett, who had returned them, with very pleasing compliments to the writer. In fact, we all agree that nothing is wanting, except that I and your sister *would like perfect* spelling and punctuation. In spelling I am happy to say that your last *was perfect*. At least I remember no defect.

The other day—last Monday—I was dining at Baron Gerolt. There I met Mrs Freeman of the British Legation a new comer; a very decent woman, as Bishop Chase used to say, meaning thereby all that is charming & becoming.[1] Well, Mrs Eastman talked about your friends the Campbells. She had met them, I think, both at the Hague and at Dresden, and spoke of them in the most agreeable terms. Since then Mrs Campbell has come herself, and confirmed by her person, & her manners Mrs Freeman's Report. Her sister Mrs Root? of New York is with her and they are both to dine with us on Monday. According to Mrs Campbells account you have been very gay this winter. I suppose she means that you have always seemed happy when in Society; for you cannot have been very gay in our Washington sense, going out only once a week. She says too that you have made excellent progress in your German, and that you talk freely & without minding a few mistakes, which are inevitable to all who begin talking in a new language. I am glad of this; but you must be very careful in observation & learn to correct yourself by what others say / It is very well to have some friend point out mistakes occasionally— though too much criticism rather tends to discouragement I think.

There, at this moment, as I judge from voices sitting here at my library table are Katie & Willie with the Senator looking on and putting a word in occasionally, going down stairs to breakfast. Willie under Mama's superintendence is attempting the feat of walking down, clinging to the bannister. There! down he goes in a little tumble, and there is a little cry; and soothing tones & caresses from Mama & all is well again. They have gone down & I must follow.

And now breakfast is over, and I am again in the little library: and, oh! horror here comes a gentleman all the way from Knoxville & ten to one he wants to be a Register under the Bankrupt law:[2] and—there goes the bell, and I am afraid that another is coming. No it was not an applicant— since writing "applicant" two or three or persons have been in & I am quite confused—it was a Minister wanting aid for a college in Tennessee. Then came two applicants; and a gentleman who wanted to explain that his signature to a recommendation meant nothing; and Senator Sherman, my good friend who is going to Europe on the 13th April. And now the talk is over till the next one calls.

You wonder at the reason of my being so pestered with calls; and such calls And you must know that it has pleased Congress to put on me the duty of nominating to the District Judges one or more Registers in Bankruptcy for each Congressional District—say three hundred & fifty or sixty in the United States—Of course this excites many wishes & leads to many applications all of which in the first instance were addressed to me. And many come to present their applications in person, & many friends come to support them.

We have had snow and rain with a very few sunshiny days for the last three months. I never knew such a winter in Washington. Professor Agassiz says this year is a Cosmic Winter—the winter of our System as well as the winter of our planet.[3] I Dont know what he means; but, I suppose, something [brittle].

The Governor has been in Rhode Island. He came back last night: and is looking very well. The baby grows in sense & grace daily: he is really a sweet child. His occasional bursts of temper are like April Storms—soon come—soon gone. I hear his little tramp in the nursery over my head at the moment. Mr. Baumgras has painted a very pretty miniature of him which Katie will doubtless bring & show you.[4]

You know that Powers is copying Jones' bust of me for you, in Florence. I hope you will see him & it & that you will like it. Katie hopes that you will be able to meet her in Paris. If not she will come directly for you, & then you will all go to Italy.[5] She talks of returning as early as July or August: and I hope she will, for I shall long to see you.

Goodbye, darling. All blessings attend you.

Your Affe. father
S P Chase

Library of Congress.

1. Mrs. Freeman was the wife of a member of the British legation in Washington. She and Nettie went to dinner and the theater together in January 1870. *Philadelphia Inquirer,* Jan. 24, June 7, 1870; *Chase Papers,* 1:648.

2. A newly passed federal law put bankruptcy cases in the hands of U.S. district courts and authorized Father, as chief justice, to nominate at least one individual in each congressional district to act as register for bankruptcy. Father objected to this addition to his work burden. On March 21 a bill was introduced into Congress to repeal that part of the law, but it died in committee. *Chase Papers*, 5:149–50.

3. Swiss-American geologist and Harvard professor Jean Louis Rodolphe Agassiz (1807–73) is considered one of the founders of the modern American scientific tradition. In the 1830s and 1840s, Agassiz posited that weather was not only cyclical year by year, but in long periods of time, and that Europe had once been colder and covered with glacial ice. *DAB*, 1:114–22; Edmund Blair Bolles, *The Ice Finders: How a Poet, a Professor and a Politician Discovered the Ice Age* (Washington, D.C.: Counterpoint, 1999), 117–19, 211.

4. Peter Baumgras, a Bavarian-born artist who immigrated to the United States in the 1850s after studying at Dusseldorf and Munich. He painted the last portrait of Abraham Lincoln but was known for his still-life paintings as well as his portraits and had painted miniatures to support himself even as a student in Germany. From 1864 to 1872 he taught drawing at the Columbia Institution for the Instruction of the Deaf, Dumb, and Blind, a forerunner of Gallaudet University, and he later taught at the University of Illinois. *Nat. Cyc.*, 10:365; Peter Hastings Falk et al., eds., *Who Was Who in American Art, 1564–1975: 400 Years of Artists in America*, rev. ed., 3 vols. (Madison, Conn.: Sound View Press, 1999), 1:239; Waldo S. Pratt, *A Forgotten American Portrait-Painter: Peter Baumgras, 1827–1903* (Hartford, Conn.: privately printed, 1937).

5. Kate sailed from New York on April 6 on the steamship *Europe*, bound for the ports of Brest and Le Havre in France. Although the newspaper listing of passenger departures did not list Willie, he was probably with her, and it seems likely that the unnamed "servant" who did appear in the list was his nursemaid, Maggie. Also aboard the *Europe* were Susan Sprague Hoyt and her brother, William S. Hoyt. *New York Times*, Apr. 7, 1867.

FATHER TO NETTIE

Philadelphia, Sep. 12, 1867

My precious child,

Your very agreeable letter from Heidelburg and Stuttgart found me, last Saturday, at Providence, just starting on a ride from P—— to the Farm[1] with Gov. S——. It was of course impossible for me to answer so that my letter will meet you in Paris on arrival; but you will find other letters there, which, I hope, will be equally agreeable. You will find some from me—one enclosing a draft for F2167.50 part of your $600 and I presume another from Mr. Cooke enclosing the balance, not included through misapprehension in the first draft; and I now enclose the *second* of the F2167.50 series that you may use it, if by any accident the *first* of the same amount has miscarried. You know of course that these bills are in triplicate for security & that payment of any one, whether first, second or third discharges all.[2] I have still the third. If by any accident the bill shall not be paid, it must be protested *immediately* for nonpayment, & notice sent to Mr[3] Riggs & Co. or the money will be lost. A days delay in protest & notice is often fatal. This is the rule for all bills.

I also enclose the second of a series of Fcs 442.00, of which I sent the first to Katie by the last Steamer. This is to pay for an Optical instrument

& some photographic views purchased for me, by her direction, by Mr. Frs. Colton our Consul at Venice.[4] Mr. Colton wrote me about the purchase & the price, & said that the instrument had been forwarded to New York to the address of Senator Sprague. I take it for granted that every thing is right; but as nothing has yet been heard of the arrival of the box and no bill of lading has been forwarded I have thought it best to send the bills endorsed to Mr. Colton to Katie in order that she may forward them, if there be no mistake in the matter, to Mr. Colton. What makes me the more cautious is that neither you nor Katie have mentioned the purchase, which I supposed had been made to replace your alethoscope which I sent to the Soldiers Fair at Cincinnati.[5]

I cannot send you a sample glove as you suggest. Those which Katie bought last year were about right only a little too short at the wrists. My number, I believe, is 8½. I would like to have you buy me, also, a nice but not extravagant dressing case. I want the articles in it good & the whole for use & not for show.[6]

In my last letter I told you that if the $600 should prove insufficient you must call or ask for *enough more* to make *enough*, being, of course, not very unreasonable in your idea of *enough*.

I have become altogether confused in my idea of your birth days. As we were riding down to the Farm last Saturday the Governor said that his birth day came on the 12th & Katies on the 13 of September & now you write on the 18th Aug that you celebrated Katies birthday. This then must have been on the 13th August, and then your birthday must come on the 19th of September a week hence & will be celebrated in Paris.[7] I shall set the Governor down as mistaken therefore, unless better informed, especially as in your letter you speak of being nearly twenty. Katie twenty seven. Nettie twenty—to think of so many years so soon past: and how much more rapidly the equal numbers to come if God continues your lives will float away, and that in all human probability before the half of the shortest number has gone, I shall be no more on earth! "Lord teach us to number our days that we may apply our hearts unto wisdom."[8] My longing for both of you is most earnest that you may lay up your treasures in Heaven.

While in New England I saw a lady whose face was like that of an angel. She is a widow—the mother of a numerous family—highly accomplished & exceedingly intelligent. Long years ago she had the misfortune, if indeed it was a misfortune to lose one of her lower limbs, amputated at the thigh, & has ever since walked on crutches. Her circumstances are easy, & she dedicates herself to the care of her family & to doing good. She says she does not know what it is to be unhappy, so perfect is her trust & confidence in God her Savior. She cannot sing with Cowper, she says, "Where is the blessedness I knew," for since she began to love & obey God, she has never known aught but blessedness.[9] Is not that beautiful.

Love to Katie & all the rest.

Your affectionate father
S P Chase

I am at the Continental today.[10] Tomorrow I go to Washington & next week, I expect, to Ohio.[11]

Library of Congress.

1. Sprague Farm, or Canonchet, in Rhode Island. Father had been in New England, including the Boston area, earlier in the month. One event during the trip was a "brilliant reception" given in his honor by William Claflin at Newton, Mass., and attended by "numerous notabilities and a large concourse of friends." *Chase Papers*, 5:173; *Philadelphia Inquirer,* Sept. 10, 1867.

2. He was sending money in the form of bank drafts payable in francs.

3. Father first wrote "Mr," then altered it illegibly, possibly to "Messrs." George Washington Riggs and his half-brother, Elisha Riggs, founded the Washington-based international private banking firm of Riggs and Company in 1848. *DAB*, 15:603–4.

4. Francis C. Colton, a U.S. consular official at Venice, 1866–69. *The American Yearbook and National Register for 1869* (Hartford, Conn.: O. D. Case & Co., 1869), 82, 88; Carrie Westlake Whitney, *Kansas City, Missouri: Its History and Its People, 1800–1909* (Kansas City, Mo.: S. J. Clarke Pub. Co., 1908), 271–72.

5. Carlo Ponti, an optician, instrument maker, and photographer of Venice, garnered the Grand Prize of the London Exposition of 1862 with his invention, the alethoscope (or megalethoscope). The device magnified pictures, but Ponti, who had published albums of his photographs of buildings and street scenes of Venice and northern Italy, also designed the alethoscope to hold double-image photographic prints that, depending on the direction of the light, could depict a daylight or a nighttime view of a scene. Soldiers' fairs and sanitary fairs were popular during and after the Civil War as fund-raising bazaars for disabled veterans or war monuments. Philanthropic women's organizations erected booths, vying with each other over the magnificence of their booths' decorations and the amount of money they raised by selling donated and handmade items. These fairs often had music, dancing, and food. Cincinnati had such events throughout the Civil War years. International Center of Photography, *Encyclopedia of Photography* (New York: Routledge, 1984), 402; Turner Browne and Elaine Partnow, *Macmillan Biographical Encyclopedia of Photographic Artists and Innovators* (New York: Macmillan, 1983), 487; *History of Cincinnati and Hamilton County, Ohio: Their Past and Present* (Cincinnati: S. B. Nelson Co., 1894), 361–62; Robert Rydell, *All the World's a Fair* (Chicago: University of Chicago Press, 1984), 10; Charles J. Stille, *History of the United States Sanitary Commission* (Philadelphia: Hurd and Houghton, 1866), 192–93.

6. A man's dressing case was a small piece of luggage, often of morocco leather, containing toilet utensils. *OED*, 4:1046.

7. Kate's birthday was August 13, Nettie's September 19.

8. Psalms 90:12.

9. One of the sixty-seven Olney Hymns composed by William Cowper between 1771 and 1773 in collaboration with John Newton, "Walking with God" contains the line "Where is the blessedness I knew, When first I saw the Lord?" H. S. Milford, ed., *The Complete Poetical Works of William Cowper* (Oxford: Henry Frowde, Oxford University Press, 1907), 433.

10. Like the Willard Hotel in Washington, the Continental Hotel on the corner of Chestnut and South 9th streets in Philadelphia was a favorite stop for politicians. A meeting at the Continental launched Father's campaign for the 1868 Democratic presidential nomination. *Chase Papers*, 5:230–31.

11. Father apparently went to Philadelphia to visit Jay Cooke. The *Philadelphia Inquirer* reported that after his arrival in the city from New York on September 11 he went to "the residence of a friend." The paper also noted that "his visit has no political significance

whatever." On the seventeenth, with many other dignitaries, he attended a great dedication ceremony for the national cemetery at the Antietam battlefield. He did go to Ohio later in the month, voting in the election there, seeing his niece Jane Auld, and arriving back in Washington on the morning of October 14. He then almost immediately went to Baltimore for circuit court and, in his ruling in the case *In re Turner*, overturned a Maryland apprenticeship system that discriminated against blacks. Kate, Nettie, and Willie returned to the United States later in the year. *Philadelphia Inquirer*, Sept. 12, 18, Oct. 15, 1867; Macon *Georgia Weekly Telegraph*, Sept. 27, 1867; *Chase Papers*, 5:185–86.

CHRONOLOGY

March–May 1868	Andrew Johnson's impeachment trial
July 1868	Kate in New York City for Democratic convention; Nettie visits Minnesota
August 1868	Father travels to Parkersburg, W.Va., for circuit court
September 1868	Father and Nettie visit Albany and Troy, N.Y.
October 1868	Kate at Narragansett; Father and Nettie vacation in Maine
Late November– early December 1868	Father holds circuit court in Richmond; Kate with William on business trip to Georgia and South Carolina
March–April 1869	William makes speeches in Senate
April 1869	Father on circuit to Baltimore; Kate and Nettie go to Aiken, S.C.
May–June 1869	Father on circuit in Virginia, South Carolina, and North Carolina; Kate and Nettie summer in Rhode Island
August 1869	Father on circuit in West Virginia
September 1869	Nettie and Father travel from Rhode Island to visit Cookes outside Philadelphia
October 1869	Father and Nettie move out of house at 6th and E streets; Kate's daughter Ethel born in Rhode Island
Fall 1869– Spring 1870	Father sits with Supreme Court in Washington
June–August 1870	Father makes visits to Philadelphia and New York, then travels with Nettie to Ohio, Illinois, and Minnesota
August 1870	Father suffers a stroke en route home through New York State, goes to Canonchet to recuperate
January–February 1871	Father and Nettie in New York, where Kate joins them for part of the time

CHAPTER 10

"Girls *Are* Nice"

MAY 1868–OCTOBER 1870

IN NOVEMBER 1869, Kate gave birth to her second baby, a girl she named Ethel. Eliza Whipple, who had attended the birth, wrote both Father and Nettie that Kate and the baby were doing well. Father rejoiced at the news. He congratulated Kate on her accomplishment, writing: "And I am glad that the baby is a girl. For my part I like girls rather better than boys," though he thought that "a brother apiece" for his daughters might have been all right. "But *girls* are *nice*," he exuberantly added, leaving Kate little doubt her father had ever regretted her sex.[1]

Indeed, Father's and Kate's correspondence from 1868 makes clear just how much he depended on her political acumen. In May, the Senate reached a verdict in President Andrew Johnson's impeachment proceeding. As chief justice, Father presided over the trial. Though he had no vote in the matter, except in the case of a tie, he believed "the whole business seems wrong" for suggesting "that Congress is above the Constitution."[2] Kate and Nettie sat in the Senate's gallery seats during much of the trial, no doubt forming opinions they could share with their father over dinner. Kate's husband, William, now a senator for Rhode Island, did not favor acquittal as Father, Kate, and Nettie did. This difference of opinion, which found Kate taking sides with her father against her husband, led to a family quarrel, though Father tried mightily to remain above the fray. Thus the opening letters of this section find Kate in Rhode Island and New York, after having quarreled with her husband. William eventually voted Andrew Johnson guilty of eleven counts of high crimes or misdemeanors, though the Senate did acquit the president by a slim margin.[3]

Father's insistence that the impeachment trial be a judicial, rather than partisan, event had scuttled any chances he may have had at gaining the Republican presidential nomination that year. Republicans denounced him as a traitor to their cause and by March began accusing him of courting the Democratic Party.[4] Too, the immense popularity of Ulysses S. Grant made the war hero's nomination almost a foregone conclusion. With the focus on Grant, who was moderate on Reconstruction questions, the party also adopted "new shibboleths of republican faith" that Father said he "could not frame my lips to pronounce."[5] During the spring he refused to rule out the possibility that his old party, the Democrats, might adopt a platform that aligned with his principles, and he would not close the door to the prospect of a Democratic nomination if it should be offered. The chances of a suitable platform were slim and the possibility of wresting a nomination from the competing Democratic machines even slimmer. "My private judgment," he confided to Jacob Schuckers in June, "is that the talk about me will come to nothing." The Democratic Party "is not democratic enough yet."[6] Nevertheless, Schuckers and other of his supporters made preparations, and Kate worked as hard as anyone to try to get him the nomination. When the Democrats' national convention met in New York early in July, it was Kate who acted as her father's de facto campaign manager. She established informal Chase headquarters in her suite at the Fifth Avenue Hotel and also worked from Edwin Hoyt's residence on Fifth Avenue. One of Father's old friends who saw her in action called her "a Magnificent woman" and boasted: "With her shrewdness & force, & with ninety days time, I could have you nominated by acclamation & elected by an overwhelming majority."[7] Unfortunately Kate did not have ninety days, and all her efforts failed to garner more than 4 votes for her father out of a possible 317. On the twenty-second ballot Horatio Seymour received all the convention votes. In the fall, after the party took a bruising in state elections, some Democrats considered dumping Seymour and substituting someone else, such as the chief justice, as the party's nominee for the presidency. Father refused to have his name considered for such a gambit. Seymour remained on the ticket and lost badly to Grant in the election—as probably any Democratic nominee would have.[8]

While Kate labored in the thick of politics, twenty-year-old Nettie took a trip out west. Her letter from Minnesota breathes fresh air into the family correspondence, providing a bright contrast to Kate's and Father's letters. In 1868, Minnesota was very much the frontier, a wild place still recovering from the 1862 Sioux revolt, in which insurgent Dakota bands killed nearly five hundred white emigrants. Nettie's comments on the wretchedness of the Indians reflect the destruction of a peaceful interethnic relationship, fueled by white Americans' imposition of cultural conformity. This shift in relations had spelled disaster for Minnesota's native people.[9] In Minnesota, Nettie visited members of her mother's extended family who had relocated there after the Civil War. She illustrated her letter of July 21, providing evocative pencil drawings of the falls of Minnehaha and Native American dwellings. From Minnesota, Nettie traveled to Rhode Island, where she spent the remainder of the summer with her sister.

In the spring of 1869 Kate's husband made a series of well-publicized Senate speeches in which he accused fellow legislators, the press, Rhode

Island soldiers, and American women of corruption and immorality. In one speech he attacked Americans who traveled to Europe and returned "to inculcate the immoralities that they have seen upon their own society."[10] His comments figured as public attacks on his own wife, and a deep marital rift opened between William and Kate, as Father's letters to Kate attest. Father counseled Kate to act with patience and submission. Others were not so understanding of William's newfound oratorical abilities. Senator Joseph Abbott, for example, attempted to defend two of the men impugned by William. William called Abbott a "mongrel puppy dog" obedient to the Senate's powerful "mastiffs." Mutual public insults followed, but Charles Sumner and John Sherman averted possible bloodshed by arranging a truce between the two factions.[11] Some people admired William for what they perceived as his honesty and bravery against the forces of corruption. One night workingmen serenaded "Little Rhody" and took up the cry "Sprague for President," but little came of the movement.[12]

Exultant at what he perceived as his senatorial success, William crossed a moral boundary. In early May he moved one of his paramours into the 6th and E street house. Father discovered the arrangement after William had left on a trip for New York, and he wrote his son-in-law a letter of mild reproach, asking if it was perhaps "a little risky" to install "a very fine looking Englishwoman" on the household's staff when no woman of the family was in the house.[13] A few months later Father and Nettie moved out of the house they had shared with the Spragues. They moved to a rented house on I Street. Father purchased Edgewood, an estate a couple of miles north of the Capitol, but it required extensive renovation before he could move there. However nice Father found girls, he was beginning to have second thoughts about his son-in-law. In February 1871, a bill to increase the chief justice's salary to $10,500 failed in the Senate by one vote—William Sprague's.[14]

During the summer of 1870, Nettie and Father took a long trip, seeing friends and family in Ohio and Illinois and spending time in Minnesota. On the journey home, on a train between Niagara Falls and New York City, Father suffered a mild stroke. Nettie took her father to the Hoffman House hotel in New York and sent word to her sister. Kate and William came to New York at once, and a week later moved Father to Canonchet to convalesce under the direction of John G. Perry, a New York physician who also saw patients in Rhode Island. Under Perry's care Father followed a regimen based on a restricted, bland diet and moderate exercise. Nettie went to Narragansett also, and by December both she and her father were restless and ready to move on before the weather grew any colder. "I shall remain here until the Doctor tells me what better to do," Father wrote to his friend Richard C. Parsons, the marshal of the Supreme Court, but Father and Nettie made plans for a stay of several weeks in New York City after Christmas. Kate joined them there for part of the time. Father's reason for the visit was to allow him access to Dr. Perry, but the stay in New York in January and February 1871 also involved planning for the upcoming nuptials of Nettie and Will Hoyt. Not until March was Father ready to return to Washington and resume his place with the Supreme Court.[15]

1. Father to Kate, Nov. 7, 1869, below.
2. *Chase Papers*, 5:207–9.
3. Foner, *Short History of Reconstruction*, 142–44; McPherson, *Ordeal by Fire*, 530–33.
4. In his newspaper, Theodore Tilton, for example, blasted Father for appearing to step away from the Republican Party. See "A Folded Banner," *Independent*, Apr. 16, 1868; *Chase Papers*, 5:210–11.
5. *Chase Papers*, 5:210; Benedict, "Salmon P. Chase," 464, 478.
6. Father to Schuckers, June 6, 1868 (Chase Papers, LC); Benedict, "Salmon P. Chase," 479.
7. Hamilton Smith to Father, July 5, 1868, *Chase Papers*, 5:254–55.
8. *Chase Papers*, 5:283–84; Coleman, *Election of 1868*, 382.
9. Gary Clayton Anderson, *Kinsmen of Another Kind: Dakota-White Relations in the Upper Mississippi Valley, 1650–1862* (Lincoln, Neb.: University of Nebraska Press, 1984), ix, 280.
10. *Congressional Globe*, 41st Cong., 1st sess., 1869, 361; see Father to Kate, Apr. 15, 1869, below.
11. Father to Kate, Apr. 29, 1869, below.
12. Belden and Belden, *So Fell the Angels*, 233–35; Father to Kate, Apr. 15, 1869, below.
13. Father to William, May 2, 1869 (Chase Papers, LC); see Father to Kate, May 4, 1869, below.
14. The vote took Father by surprise. The only explanation he could come up with was that perhaps William opposed having the Supreme Court justices' salaries linked in the bill to other federal judges' pay. *Chase Papers*, 5:342; Father to Richard C. Parsons, Feb. 17, 1871 (Chase Papers, LC).
15. Father to Nettie, [Sept. 19], Oct. 15, 1870, below; Richard C. Parsons, Dec. 15, 26, 1870, Feb. 13, 1871, Father to Hiram Barney, Dec. 6, 1870, to Henry C. Cabell, Dec. 6, to John G. Perry, Dec. 18, to Hamilton Smith, Dec. 26, to Elizabeth Wirt Goldsborough, Jan. 10, 1871, to Henry D. Cooke, Jan. 31, to P. E. Jones, Feb. 24, to Henry Clark, Mar. 22 (Chase Papers, LC); *Chase Papers*, 1:662.

FATHER TO KATE

Washington, May 10, 1868.
My dear dear Katie,

I am ashamed that your affectionate letter has remained so long unanswered; but you know how prone I am to procrastination, and what excuses—(not sufficient however I admit)—I have lately had for it.

But my duties connected with the Impeachment are nearly over, and I *will* write you a few words today:[1]

The Governor tells me that you will probably leave Narragansett very soon.[2] He is anxious about you, and talks of going south with you as soon as the trial is ended. If he does go I will and go at once; so if you incline that way and wish Nettie to go with you please write her immediately and come home.

I was dreadfully frightened about your cold, and very uneasy about your going north when you did. The Governor says you have found the Narragansett air too bracing and his uneasiness increases mine. You *must* take care of yourself.

How I wish you would take a different view of your social duties, & cease exposing yourself, by attending those wretched night parties. You could do so, I think, & lose nothing in any respect.

Most of all I long to see you an earnest christian woman—not only religious but happy in religion. I realize painfully how far short I come of my own ideal; but I am not on that account the less desirous that you should excel where I fail. One thing I am sure of that true faith in Christ is the only thing on earth really worth having; and the only thing that we can carry from earth.

How I do love you my darling! My whole heart seems to go towards you while I write and tears come into my eyes. How wrong it is for those who love not to express their love. I remember how often you have felt hurt by my apparent indifference to what interested you: and I feel sorry that I ever occasioned any such feelings to you. I see now in your husband something of that which I blame on myself. But I know how strong my love really was, and I know how strong his is. And I am very glad that, while you have sometimes forgotten that the happiness of a wife is most certainly secured by loving submission & loving tact, you, generally, conquer by sweetness. I never saw him so much affected as by the difference that occurred between you just before you went away. He was almost unmanned—moved to tears. I have not thought it best to refer to it; but try to make my society pleasant for him & hope I succeed. You must *love away all his reserve*—and help yourself to do so by reflecting how generous, self sacrificing & indulgent a husband he has been to you. How few husbands would consent to such absences, & be at once so liberal & thoughtful. If he were only a true Christian he would be nearly perfect.

The final question on the impeachment is ordered for Tuesday—day after tomorrow, and it is probable that it will then be taken. My own judgment & feeling favors acquittal; but I have no vote & do not know how the Senators will vote.[3] It seems to be that there is very little balance of probability either way. It is not impossible that something may occur to postpone the question a day or two. It will require parts of two days probably to complete the vote when begun. The question is to be taken on each article and it may be that some articles will be divided. The form of the question to be put by me on each article to each Senator is "Mr Senator ——— How say you? Is Andrew Johnson President of the United States guilty or not guilty of a high misdemeanor as charged in this article?": and each Senator must rise in his place & answer "guilty" or "not guilty." It will take about half a minute for each Senator & there are fifty four Senators—say 25 minutes to each article & there are 11 articles, making with the time required for reading about 6 hours. Shan't I be tired?[4]

Goodbye my darling—kisses & dear love for Willie—don't let him forget grandpa.

Your affectionate father
S P Chase

Library of Congress.

1. The House of Representatives had presented the Senate with articles of impeachment of President Andrew Johnson early in March. The primary charge was violation of the Tenure of Office Act by replacing Secretary of War Edwin Stanton without the Senate's consent. As chief justice, it was Father's duty under the Constitution to preside over the Senate's impeachment proceedings. In his efforts to make the trial a judicial rather than a political process, Father clashed with congressional radicals. He doubted the propriety of the proceedings, which he believed were more irresponsible and subversive of the Constitution than Johnson's Reconstruction policies. *Chase Papers,* 1:xlvix, 641–42; 5:189–91; Niven, *Chase,* 421–22.

2. Kate had been in Washington for much of the trial but left for Narragansett in early May. Reports that she did so because of her inability to compel her husband to vote as her father wished are probably incorrect. Lamphier, *Kate Chase and William Sprague,* 94; Belden and Belden, *So Fell the Angels,* 190.

3. There was no precedent for the impeachment trial of a president. Article 1 of the Constitution specifies only that the chief justice "shall preside." Although some people argued that the chief justice could vote on any question that might arise during the proceedings, Father maintained that his role as presiding officer was the same as that of the vice president when presiding over the Senate and that therefore he had, according to the Constitution, "no vote, unless they be equally divided." He did believe, though, that he had that tie-breaking vote and was alarmed when his friend Charles Sumner tried, ultimately without success, to deprive him of that power. *Chase Papers,* 5:195, 199.

4. Though Father may have preferred that his son-in-law vote for acquittal, for reasons of his own William cast a guilty vote. The Senate's final vote was one short of the necessary two-thirds majority needed to convict the president. Niven, *Chase,* 425; *Trial of Andrew Johnson, President of the United States, Before the Senate of the United States, on Impeachment by the House of Representatives for High Crimes and Misdemeanors,* 3 vols. (Washington, D.C.: F. & J. Rives and Geo. Bailey, 1868), 2:482–98.

KATE TO FATHER

94. Fifth Avenue[1]
New York. 2 July /68

Dearest Father,

Your dear loving letter came this morning—Don't pray worry your-self about me—I feel perfectly well, & don't cough at all—The perfect quiet & rest, I find here, is perfectly delightful to me. Mr. Hoyt's family are all at Astoria but one or the other of its members come in to see me every day[2]—Amasa is here & working with all his might. The young men are the life of this movement[3]—Things look a good deal clearer, & A. insists that *he* "will know to-night which way the cat will jump"—The point now is to select *the* man to be spokesman in the convention—Governor Seymour, Mr. Van Buren, insists,—Gov S—— is the guest of Mr. Van B—is perfectly sincere in his intention under no circumstances to be a Candidate—He would like to be permanent President of the Convention, but thinks it would be discourteous to the Inst, & Gov. Bigler, or Mr. Richardson of Ill—— are talked of, nothing is settled, however, as to that.[4] Mr. Belmont has bought out a German, & goes into the Convention as a Delegate.[5]

Mr. Hunter, Col Cabell, Bradley Johnson, & Gilmer, have been sent for to-day[6]—It is thought they would be useful—*Edgerton* of Ills. is as bitter as gall, & swears he would not vote for you under any circumstances[7]—this from Mr. H—— Smith[8]—but such men are very rare. The popular voice here is all one way, most singularly enthusiastic. I have been afraid they would get up a popular demonstration prematurely, & give undue offense to the Western delegates. The Pendleton men are very fractious. I enclose a P—— Green-back[9]—I think of spending Sunday at Narragansett, with dear little Willie. I shall be obliged to go back to Washington & shall return with the Governor, when he comes from R.I—

I am glad to hear of Nettie & her safe arrival in Cinti. I wrote her there.

I am glad you are not going to be greatly disappointed if the nomination is not for you—I should like to see this bright jewell added to your crown of earthly distinction, & *I believe it will* be. But we can love & be very happy & just as proud of you with-out it. Will the *Country* do as well[10]

Devotedly your daughter

Katie

On monogrammed stationery with a multicolor crest bearing a rampant lion above four suspended rings containing the letters K-A-T-E. Historical Society of Pennsylvania.

1. Though some sources have assumed that 94 Fifth Avenue was the address for the Fifth Avenue Hotel, where Kate did have a suite of rooms during the Democratic convention, this address was actually the home of Edwin Hoyt, father of Sarah, Susan, and Will Hoyt. The hotel, standing at 190 Fifth Avenue, served as convention headquarters for many candidates and delegates, including the Ohio delegates. The convention was held at the newly completed Tammany Hall, on 14th Street off Union Square. Wilson, *Trow's New York City Directory, For . . . 1871*, 577; *New York Times*, July 1, 3, 5, 1868; Burrows and Wallace, *Gotham*, 995; Coleman, *Election of 1868*, 189.

2. The Hoyt family owned a residence in Astoria, across the East River from Manhattan. Nettie and Will to Father, Mar. 28, 1871, below.

3. William's brother Amasa helped organize a "committee of one hundred" in support of Father's nomination. Though the committee accomplished little, as a Rhode Island nominating delegate Amasa did work closely with Kate. Coleman, *Election of 1868*, 131–32; Lamphier, *Kate Chase and William Sprague*, 100.

4. Democratic politician and financial adviser John Dash Van Buren acted as Father's campaign manager during the 1868 convention. Former New York governor Horatio Seymour acted as the president of the convention. The Democrats also chose him as their presidential candidate. Seymour believed his acceptance to be the single greatest mistake he ever made. William Bigler was a former governor and senator from Pennsylvania. Former representative and senator William A. Richardson was the chairman of the Illinois delegation. *Appletons'*, 7:229; Niven, *Chase*, 428–32; *DAB*, 2:264; 17:6–9; Coleman, *Election of 1868*, 199; *Bio. Dir. U.S. Cong.*, 1737.

5. Diplomat and New York banker August Belmont had been U.S. minister to Austria, 1844–50, and to the Netherlands, 1853–57. As the chairman of the Democratic National Executive Committee, Belmont gave the convention's opening speech, accusing the

Republican Party of bringing "evils upon the country." *New York Times,* July 1, 5, 1868; *DAB,* 2:169–70.

6. Henry Coalter Cabell was a former Confederate colonel related by marriage to William Wirt, Father's old mentor. Former Confederate brigadier general Bradley Tyler Johnson practiced law in Richmond and later was a member of Virginia's state senate. In 1873, Johnson compiled for publication reports of Father's circuit court decisions. Attorney John H. Gilmer, also of Virginia, had been a state senator. *Chase Papers,* 5:129, 247–48, 368–69; *DAB,* 10:91; Johnson, *Reports of Cases.*

7. Probably Joseph Ketchum Edgerton, a former congressman from Indiana, not Illinois. *Chase Papers,* 5:247–48.

8. Father's old friend Hamilton Smith. Writing to Father a few days after this letter from Kate, Smith was unsettled and exasperated by convention intrigue and the intense summer weather ("I am heated almost to the boiling point," he wrote, "& so nervous that my writing will be almost as indistinct as yours"). Smith had found almost no one to be trusted, but proclaimed Kate's abilities (see Father's letter of July 7, below). *Chase Papers,* 5:254–56; Father to Kate, Apr. 19, 1851, in chapter 1.

9. Ohioan George Hunt Pendleton, once a peace Democrat and member of Congress, was reputed to be the Democratic presidential nominee of choice of Western delegates. Some called him "Young Greenbacks" due to his support for the redemption of Civil War bonds with paper money. Father was himself closely associated with the legal-tender currency, had been dubbed "Old Greenbacks" and "General Greenbacks" during the war, and had seen his visage appear on mock representations of currency as well as the actual one-dollar greenback bill. *DAB,* 14:419–20; *Chase Papers,* 1:illus.; 4:246 and illus.; 5:248.

10. Father and the Democrats had not come to agreement on platform issues, especially in regard to Reconstruction issues. He seemed reserved about his chances to obtain the nomination and had declared his "intention to support the nominees of the Convention, if the platform is such that I can honorably accept it," although in the early days of July he found himself almost "unwilling . . . to make any pledge whatever." *Chase Papers,* 5:248–49, 253–54.

KATE TO FATHER

New York.
5 July 1868.

Dearest Father.

I have just enclosed & addressed a letter from Mr. H—— Smith, who poor man is so overpowered by the heat he finds it hard to endure[1]— Day before yesterday, yesterday & to-day have been as hot as weather can well be, too hot by far, for the warm work on hand here—You will be sorry perhaps, to learn that I did not go to the country, as I had intended—but I really could not make up my mind, to leave just now. I am so comfortably established, & as I have to go to Washington again, in any event, I decided to postpone the visit to the boy—Dear little fellow, I do long very much to see him.

There is a noble work being done here by your friends—& whether success or failure crowns their efforts, they will be always proud to have had a hand in it—I will not enter into details, but every thing, as far as developed looks well—only New York—friends inside that close corporation say, their action is cautious, those outside call it *timid.*[2]

I am so glad that it does not fall to you to bear the burden & heat, & I love to think of you quietly at home, perhaps enjoying a game of Croquet or ten-pins—

Lovingly your child
Katie

On stationery with a monogrammed crest of the superimposed letters K, C, and S. Historical Society of Pennsylvania.

1. Hamilton Smith wrote Father, on Kate's monogrammed stationery, news of the New York and Indiana delegations. He also confessed nervousness about the convention. *Chase Papers,* 5:254–55.

2. Smith also was unsure what to make of the New York politicians. "These New Yorkers possibly may be trusted," he offered warily, "but nobody will trust them." The Tammany Society and the Manhattan Club were rumored to have reserved a large number of tickets for "ladies . . . and general comers" in an effort to thwart Western delegations. Pendleton supporters threatened to move the convention to a local opera house if the Tammany politicians had their way. Samuel Tilden, who chaired the New York delegation, refused to declare support for Father or anyone else, saying only that they were "ready to go for anyone but Pendleton." Ibid.; *New York Times,* July 1, 2, 1868.

KATE TO FATHER

94. Fifth Avenue
New York. 7. June[1] 1868.

Dearest Father,

I telegraphed you this morning, to put you on your guard against Col. F. A. Aikin who is too indiscreet to be trusted by you in any way[2]—He has been missing since yesterday quite early in the day, & now, past noon has just appeared, still a good deal under the effects of his late intemperance—He has done no good, while pretending to be authorized by you, & to have your entire confidence. I telegraph you because, the idea struck me that, finding he was not trusted & consulted by your friends, he might possibly have gone to Washington to obtain some reserved & additional authority from you direct—But he has turned up, & is now before the Committee to have his accounts of moneys received to defray the expenses of the "Head-Quarters." The Comte. thought it best your letter of "July 3." should not be delivered to him, & propose to return it to you.[3] There is an idea that the two points telegraphed you this morning by J. P. Tucker,[4] in the platform, might be used as points you would not accept— Judge Thurman (who has been put into the Convention in exchange for a delegate with-drawn,) it was suspected, would rise & instance these two as points you would not concede, a trap of course, & Mr. Sweitzer & others wanted to be prepared for such a move—hence the dispatch— The excitement here is intense—The outside pressure is very great,—& "chase" is the pass word in the throng gathered about Tamany Hall: Pendleton & Johnson have already been put in nomination but no balloting has as yet begun[5] / There are various opinions about the duration of

the Convention—The feeling improves every hour & there is a growing
confidence every where that you will Ultimately be the choice—There
are snares & pitfalls every where—Oh if the Convention would only have
the *Courage* to do right

Affectionately & ambitiously for Country—the Democracy, & its No-
blest Patriot & Statesman

Your daughter
K. C. Sprague.

P.S.

Your friends suggest that as soon as you see the Platform, which of
course you will see it to night in the Press you send such a telegram as
may be advisable & *necessary* to be read in *open Convention* addressed to
James C; Kennedy Esqr.[6]

94. Fifth Avenue—
Mr. Kennedy is so well know by all the prominent men of the New York
Delegation, & so entirely commands their confidence that no question
will arise as to its Authenticity

K. C. S.

or to any one else outside of the Convention, if you think best—

On stationery with the KCS monogram. Historical Society of Pennsylvania.

1. July, not June, as is obvious from the letter's contents.

2. Along with William's brother Amasa, Frederick A. Aiken, editor of the *Washington Constitutional Union,* had helped to organize the "committee of one hundred." Father
valued the opinions of Aiken, who served as one of his unofficial campaign managers and
had established a Chase headquarters across the street from Tammany Hall. One observer
described Aiken as "Mrs. Sprague's master of ceremonies" because he brought so many
politicians to her rooms at the Fifth Avenue Hotel. Coleman, *Election of 1868,* 131–32, 215;
Aiken to Father, June 26, 1868 (Chase Papers, LC); *Chase Papers,* 5:251–52; Benjamin Perley Poore, *Perley's Reminiscences of Sixty Years in the National Metropolis* (Philadelphia: Hub-
bard Bros., 1886), 2:238.

3. Alexander Long, a Cincinnati attorney and politician with whom Father had recently revived an acquaintance, was a delegate to the convention and wrote to Father from
New York on July 3 to state that it was "of the utmost importance that some one should
hold authority from you to say that you will abide by the action of the convention and support its nominees." Long sent his request to Washington with a messenger who would wait
for a reply: "You can give it any date you prefer and should it become necessary to make it
public the letter to which it is intended to be a reply we can prepare." In his response,
which he dated July 1, Father said that he would support the outcome of the Democratic
convention unless its platform was one "to which I cannot yield my assent without disregard of my settled convictions of duty and of the whole tenor of my public life." Writing
to John D. Van Buren, probably on July 4, Father explained that he could not give the
"unconditional pledge" sought by Long that would bind him in advance to support a candidate and a platform yet to be decided upon. On reflection, Father informed Van Buren,
he wanted to retract even the qualified statement he had made to Long. *Chase Papers,*
1:201; 5:201–2, 250, 253–54.

4. Josiah Prentice Tucker, the husband of Kate's cousin Hannah Whipple, had attended the organizational meeting at the Continental Hotel in Philadelphia in June that
called for the formation of the "committee of one hundred." *Chase Papers,* 5:230–31.

5. State conventions in Tennessee and North Carolina endorsed Andrew Johnson for
the nomination as early as February. The delegations from those states and six other
Southern states provided Johnson with almost all of the 65 votes he received in the first

ballot of the national convention, second to Pendleton's 105 votes. Johnson's support evaporated over the next several ballots. Coleman, *Election of 1868*, 164, 208.

6. James Charles Kennedy, a medical doctor and Democratic politician from Clermont County, Ohio. *Chase Papers*, 5:251.

FATHER TO KATE

Washington, July 7, 1868.

Dearest Katie,

Your telegram about F.A.A. has just come & surprised me greatly. There must be some mistake: for I have just received a telegram signed "Aiken" giving an account of the 6th ballot. "Pendleton 122½; Hancock 47—two highest—name of Chief Justice not yet presented—all going well."[1] I trust your informant was mistaken about him: but I shall be careful.

I also had a telegram signed J. P. Tucker giving the platform so far as adopted relating to debt & suffrage and asking if acceptable;[2] to which I answered "Not prepared to say till I have seen the whole. Shall be gratified personally if friends will agree not to have my name presented to the Convention."

My telegrams to you & to Prentice were sent to the Office not more than ten minutes ago.

I am glad that my name was not presented at first, & shall be better pleased if it is not presented at all.[3] You know how little I have desired a nomination and how averse I have been to making any efforts to secure it. I have feared all along that it could not be tendered to me on any platform which would allow any hope of considerable accessions from the republicans; and without that hope any other person might as well be nominated as I. And I am entirely satisfied with the opportunities of usefulness which my present position afford.

I can accept well enough the platform so far as Prentice sent it to me. But I can't say that I like it, nor do I suppose that any body will like it. Every body will take, as every body will construe it. So I did not think it best to reply categorically to his telegram. Besides I thought that if any thing of the sort was thought necessary to be sent to me, it would come from Col. Van Buren & Mr. Long, one, or both of them, who have authority to represent me more fully than any other persons: and are perfectly well informed as to my views.

Another telegram from "Aiken" has just come "Convention has adjourned no nomination made—carried our point in gaining time."

You will get this therefore before the Convention meets. I wish a few of my most discreet friends could & would consult together—Say Col Van Buren, Mr. Long, Mr. Kennedy Amasa Sprague, Mr. Smith, Mr. Cisco,[4] and any others that these might select and act for me. I shall be entirely willing to be disposed of by them. But I must say that I think it will be much better not to have my name go before the Convention at all unless it goes upon such a demand as will ensure its acceptance by the necessary vote. Unless nominated now it is my fixed purpose to have nothing more to do with political life. I cannot think of any exigency that can arise in which I can forego this purpose. And I shall feel much more contented with the memory of the movement in my favor—so spontaneous & so remarkable though without results—than I shall with the reflection that I was made a candidate before a Convention & defeated.

If I vote at all this fall I shall in all probability vote for the democratic nominees.[5] No matter how the Convention goes, the manifestation of so great a sentiment in my favor, without asking any modification of my views on the questions of suffrage & debt—good faith to the laboring masses white or black & good faith to the National Creditors—this manifestation I say proves a vast advance in the sentiments of the party especially of its younger & more progressive wing; and if I were a little younger & unembarrassed by the gown I should like nothing better than to lead this wing to ascendancy & the party to glorious victory. With such an element in it the party seems to me worth more than the Republican Party as now constituted.

Mr. Barlow wrote to a friend here who showed me his letter today, that you were to have an interview with Mr McLean, my old friend today:[6] and Mr Hamilton Smith writes with great admiration of your abilities.[7] I am afraid my darling, that you are acting too much the politician. Have a care. Don't do or say anything which may not be proclaimed on the housetops. I am so anxious about you that I cannot help wishing you were in Narragansett or here where I take all things very quietly & play croquet nearly every evening, & sleep as soundly as the heat will let me every night.

Most affectionately

Your father,
S P Chase

Mrs Kate C. Sprague

Historical Society of Pennsylvania.

1. Convention balloting began on July 7. The count of the sixth ballot as reported by Frederick Aiken was correct. Maj. Gen. Winfield Scott Hancock, esteemed as a hero of Gettysburg, was the candidate of choice of a "Soldiers' and Sailors' Convention" that was meeting in New York at the same time as the Democratic national convention. In the national convention, by the eighteenth ballot Hancock's candidacy peaked at 144½ votes. His supporters threw their votes to Horatio Seymour on the final ballot. Coleman, *Election of 1868*, 166–75, 191–93, 382; *DAB*, 8:221–22.

2. Father's position on the platform called for universal manhood suffrage, but left implementation to the states in an effort to gain Democrats' favor. While he supported "honest payment of the public debt," he did not specify whether debts and war bonds should be paid in gold or paper currency. Warden, *Chase,* 706; Coleman, *Election of 1868,* 138–39; *Chase Papers,* 5:259.

3. Father's name did not appear in the balloting until the twelfth round, on July 8. He never received more than four votes. Coleman, *Election of 1868,* 382.

4. Wall Street banker John J. Cisco. He was former assistant treasurer at New York. Conflicts over choosing a replacement for Cisco when he left that position in 1864 precip-

itated Father's departure from Lincoln's cabinet. *New York Times,* Mar. 24, 1884; *Chase Papers,* 1:312, 466–71.

5. The convention finally nominated Horatio Seymour, with Francis Blair Jr. as his running mate. The presence of Blair, whom Father "personally detested and politically scorned," on the ticket ensured that Father would not support the Democratic candidates. Niven, *Chase,* 432; *Chase Papers,* 5:261.

6. Samuel L. M. Barlow was a New York attorney. Pendleton's supporters had evicted Washington McLean, a prominent Ohio Democrat and publisher of the *Cincinnati Enquirer,* from the state's delegation at the convention. *Chase Papers,* 1:213; 5:254–55, 259.

7. "What a Magnificent woman Kate has become," Smith wrote Father on July 5. "With her shrewdness & force, & with ninety days time, I could have you nominated by acclamation & elected by an overwhelming majority." *Chase Papers,* 5:255.

FATHER TO KATE

Washn July 10, 1868.

My dear Katie,

Are you not heartily tired of New York. I am of receiving telegrams from it.

Do you see Mr. Van Buren. I think that he & Mr. Cisco are my best & most judicious & reliable friends there. Mr. V.B. is the best posted & understand best how, & what & when to do. Please see him & give him all the information you can, & let Mr. S——[1] furnish him a list of all my friends that will be useful, if it be not already too late. I *must* refer all enquiries about platform &c &c to him.

Affectionately,
S. P. Chase

Have written him by this mail

Historical Society of Pennsylvania.

1. Possibly Hamilton Smith, who was part of the important Chase cadre in New York for the convention; but this reference could well be to Jacob W. Schuckers, an Ohioan who had been one of the Treasury clerks working directly under the secretary of the Treasury when Father held that position. Schuckers graduated from Albany Law School in 1865. In the months and weeks prior to the 1868 Democratic convention, he made himself useful to Father, especially in the collection and dissemination of political information. As indicated by Kate in the next letter, Schuckers was in New York during the convention. Following Father's death, Kate favored him to write a biography of Father (see the epilogue). *Chase Papers,* 1:501; 3:xxv–xxvi; Coleman, *Election of 1868,* 107, 121, 134, 216, 222.

KATE TO FATHER

New York—10 June[1] 1868

My dearest Father,

You have been most cruelly deceived & shamefully used by the man whom you trusted implicitly, & the *Country* must suffer for his duplicity. I would not write you yesterday, in the excitement of the result of the action of the Convention, & until I had carefully gone over in my mind all the circumstances that had come under my knowledge of the action of Mr. Van Buren. When I get comfortably settled at Narragansett, I will write out a full & detailed history of my *knowledge* of this matter that can not fail to convince you of his bad faith. Nothing more would be needed, than that since the result of the Nomination was announced Mr. Van Buren though constantly at the Manhattan Club, next door has not been near me, & has passed both Mr. Kennedy & Mr. Schuckers this morning without a recognition[2] / Had Mr. Kennedy had the authority to act for you, you would have been as certainly nominated on the wave of the en-thusiasm created in the Convention by the ½ vote cast by California day before yesterday, as any thing could be[3]—Mr. Van Buren's telegraph to you, "to answer no questions in regard to the Platform, was the block he put in the way of your Nomination—& when at the critical juncture he was at last found, (for he has scarcely been seen in the Convention) he refused to take the responsibility of speaking for you, & said he was not authorized. At 3½ P.M. when I finally saw him, he said he would divide the responsibility with Mr. Long—*but took no action,* & *the* moment had gone by—Had I received my letter at the hour it was due, or any time before 3½ P.M—I believe all would have been different. Mr. Kennedy & Mr. Long were both true as steel, but neither of them were equal (or so situated as to be equal) to the combinations against them. Mr. Tilden & Mr. Kernan have done this work[4] & Mr. Van Buren has been *their tool*—This is my honest belief; but I will mite it out carefully[5]—So dear Father in the future, be guided by the advice of some of those who are devoted to you, but who are more suspicious than your own noble heart will allow you to be—

With all this *you personally* can have nothing to regret. Your friends have worked noble—& the universal disappointment to-day is amaz-ing—Not a flag floats nor, is the semblance of rejoicing visible anywhere.

Your name is a watch word with the people, & they have been out-raged & deceived—

I am perfectly well, & go to the Country to kiss Willie & see the Gov-ernor. I may return, & think I shall, to Washington with the Governor, then I hope we can capture you & take to Narragansett.[6] Mr. Cisco, is as true as tried steel, Mr. Long has gone home broken hearted. You can form no conception of the depression here

Your devoted
Katie

Library of Congress.

1. July.
2. The Manhattan Club, which stood at 96 Fifth Avenue, counted among its members most of New York City's leading Democrats, who met there to select nominees. Wilson, *Trow's New York City Directory, For* . . . *1873,* 19; Coleman, *Election of 1868,* 149, 162.
3. On July 8, during the twelfth roll call, California cast one-half vote for Father. That half-vote was repeated on the next four ballots, but Father's campaign managers were unable to take advantage of this show of support. The plan had been for him to have his name brought forward late in the balloting, and Father believed that he would have been

nominated on the twenty-second or twenty-third ballot if things had gone as planned. Coleman, *Election of 1868,* 227–30; *Chase Papers,* 5:270.

4. Kate originally wrote "Mr. Tilden and Mr. Belmont," but crossed out Belmont's name with a single stroke and replaced it with Kernan's. It was New York delegate Francis Kernan who helped to begin the convention stampede for Seymour on the twenty-second ballot, thus forestalling hopes of a late movement for Father. As a leading New York Democrat, Samuel Jones Tilden commanded the largest block of delegates and had been sympathetic to the Chase movement. Coleman, *Election of 1868,* 240–42, 382; Niven, *Chase,* 430; *DAB,* 10:356; 18:537–41; *Bio. Dir. U.S. Cong.,* 1406.

5. On the last day of balloting, Tilden, Kernan, and the rest of the New York delegation voted for Seymour. Father wrote Van Buren, "I was told that Seymour was for himself before the Convention met; but would not believe it. I thought *you could not be* deceived & I knew you would not deceive." Coleman, *Election of 1868,* 239–40; Father to Van Buren, July 10, 1868 (Chase Papers, LC).

6. Father left for Narragansett on July 17, went back to Washington briefly, and returned to Narragansett the evening of July 25. Father to Henry W. Hilliard, July 17, 1868, and to Gerrit Smith, July 26 (Chase Papers, LC); Father to Jay Cooke, July 15, 1868 (Chase Papers, HSP).

NETTIE TO FATHER

Frontenac
July 21st. 1868

My own dear Father.

I am in love with Minnesota[1]—We have just returned from a most perfect trip to St Paul and vicinity, I say perfect because my enjoyment of it was without a drawback. Do you know I think that I have inherited a soupçon of the old pioneer spirit, for when I feel myself beyond civilization, a kind of wild delight comes over me, my Indian wakes and gives a warwhoop. Do you remember Burnet McLean? a son of the General's, he went with us on our expedition and was a great comfort to me, for he is even more venturesome than I am, and Jep is rather lasy—lasy, but so goodnatured and thoughtful[2]—So he and Anna stayed in the inns, and Burnet and I tramped and explored to my hearts content[3]—St Paul is an exceedingly pretty town, the good taste that was displayed everywhere astonished and delighted me, even the little frame cottages are pretty and varied in their architecture—and some of the larger houses are beautiful. They use a light grey building stone, which is quarried in the neighborhood, and which is very effective, particularly when rough hewn.[4] Some of the churches too are as pretty as any I ever saw, and on one or two of them the ivy is already quite well grown. Of course our first excursion was to Ft Snelling, and the falls of Minnehaha[5]— The latter were rather larger than I had expected, but quite as romantic— We followed the stream through thicket and marsh to its mouth in the Missisippi, and the scene was well worth the exertion—I sketched it on the back of a note book with the end of a burnt match, as both pencil and paper were wanting—But most beautiful of all are the Dalles of St Croix[6]—There we saw Indians, and a more degraded looking set of wretches I never beheld[7]—Their wigwams are made of strips of birchbark wrapped over a frame of rough branches, and seem very comfortless— From the Dalles we drove from sunset until dawn in an open wagon across the country to Still Water—Such a drive! It was perfectly delightful! first we had the sunset, clear, bright, red, and gold, then the moon, but it was rather young and went to bed early—but the Aurora took its place, and illuminated the whole northern sky—We stopped at midnight at a farm house demi inn and roused up the people, & the woman soon had a hot supper ready for us. It was rather jolly waiting in the kitchen by the fire, for the night was quite fresh—the farmer's wife was a busy bustling little woman. She told us she had a Sister living in the *West*. I suppose she considers Minnesota as the East. after supper we drove on until Sunrise. Was it not complete! Sunset moon Aurora and Sunrise!

They are very anxious that I should return in December to see the winter here, Will you let me come? Israel guaranties me a return escort.[8] They wear moccasins, the lake is all frozen over, and the air they say is perfectly delicious—Northern lights nearly every night and sometimes four suns & four moons. I should so like it, I think then that I should be satisfied. I should only care to stay through December. Please dont think that I am erratic and please dont say no—

I received the letter you sent me last night / I liked the envelope best of all

Do you think this is a very gushing letter?

Lovingly ever and ever
Nettie

I will write once more before I leave

On monogrammed stationery with a crest of the letters JRC superimposed on a rampant lion. Endorsed by Jacob W. Schuckers: "Miss Chase." Library of Congress.

1. Nettie had connections to Minnesota through her extended Ludlow clan. Israel Ludlow Garrard (b. 1825), a son of Nettie's great aunt Sarah Bella Ludlow by her first marriage, built a lodge at Frontenac. Located about fifty miles southeast of St. Paul on the Lake Pepin portion of the Mississippi River, Frontenac was described in the early 1870s as "a favorite resort of invalids and sportsmen." Israel Garrard's lodge there served as a creative retreat for Henry Ward Beecher, John La Farge, and other artists and writers in the 1870s and 1880s. Nathaniel Collins McLean, mentioned in this letter as "the General," also moved to Minnesota in the postwar period, in his case to farm. He was a son of John McLean, Sarah Bella Ludlow's second husband, by John's first marriage, and so Nathaniel C. McLean and Israel L. Garrard were stepbrothers. A Harvard-trained lawyer who had served as a U.S. general during the war, Nathaniel was seven to ten years older than Israel.

Garrard, also educated at Harvard Law School (in his case after Bethany College), and also an officer rising to the rank of general during the war, had been a Free Soil newspaper editor—and a political ally of Father—in Ohio in the late 1840s. Federal Writers' Project, Works Project Administration, *Minnesota: A State Guide*, rev. ed. (New York: Hastings House, 1954), 301; Adolph von Steinwehr, *The Centennial Gazetteer of the United States* (Philadelphia: J. C. McCurdy & Co., 1873), 342; Eicher and Eicher, *Civil War High Commands*, 250, 381–82; *Chase Papers*, 1:196, 207, 217, 226; 2:193, 213, 223.

2. Nathaniel C. McLean's son Burnet was a grandson of John McLean, and his other grandfather, Judge Jacob Burnet, had also been a prominent figure in the Cincinnati area in an earlier day. "Jep" was Israel Garrard's brother, Jeptha Dudley Garrard Jr. As sons of Sarah Bella Ludlow, the Garrards were Nettie's mother's cousins. Jep, born in Cincinnati in 1836, educated at Yale and in law school at Cincinnati, was a patent attorney. Like his brother and their stepbrother Nathaniel, he had been a Federal army officer during the Civil War. Jep attended Kate's wedding in 1863. Burnet McLean's parents married in 1838, so he was probably somewhat younger than Jeptha. *Appletons'*, 4:144; *Chase Papers*, 1:413; 4:181–82; Eicher and Eicher, *Civil War High Commands*, 250.

3. Jep Garrard had married Anna Knapp in October 1864. *Who Was Who*, 1:441.

4. Founded in 1841 on the banks of the Mississippi River, St. Paul became the capital of Minnesota in 1858. Both limestone and granite were quarried in Minnesota and used in buildings there and elsewhere. Carol Brink, *The Twin Cities* (New York: Macmillan, 1961), 16, 57–58; Federal Writers' Project, *Minnesota*, 98–100, 301.

5. Situated on the bluffs at the confluence of the Minnesota and Mississippi rivers, Fort Snelling predates Minneapolis and St. Paul. Built in the 1820s, the fort was named after its first commander, Josiah Snelling, and remained an active military base until 1946. Minnehaha Creek runs through present-day Minneapolis, and the Falls of Minnehaha, immortalized in Longfellow's *Song of Hiawatha* (1855), are not too far from Fort Snelling. Brink, *Twin Cities*, 13–16, 28, 122–24; Federal Writers' Project, *Minnesota*, 46, 141, 192–93.

6. The St. Croix River and the Mississippi join below St. Paul. The Dalles are a series of igneous rock ledges in the gorge of the St. Croix. Federal Writers' Project, *Minnesota*, 453–54.

7. By the nineteenth century, Dakota Sioux people lived in the area surrounding the confluence of the Mississippi and Minnesota rivers. After the 1862 Sioux uprising, the U.S. government imprisoned hundreds of women and children at Fort Snelling. By 1868, many of the area's Sioux had been dispersed to the Dakota and Nebraska territories. William E. Lass, *Minnesota: A History*, 2d ed. (New York: W. W. Norton and Co., 1998), 130–33.

8. Probably Israel Garrard, since Nettie referred to his brother Jep by first name. It is possible, though, that this reference is to Nettie's uncle, Israel Ludlow.

FATHER TO KATE

Parkersburg, Aug. 9. 1868.

My darling child.

Letters come slowly from Narragansett to Parkersburg.[1] Yours of the 4th only reached me last night.

I am very sorry for your loss of the horse and don't wonder that the Governor was greatly provoked. The men deserved dismissal if the loss was through their carelessness, especially if they had been drinking to excess & driving too hard. But I fear you will have difficulty in replacing Edward.

Your letter makes me fear that you and your husband had some unpleasant words about his prompt action. It was quite natural doubtless that you should feel hurt by his sudden action in a matter which so nearly concerned your own comfort: but if you did I hope you suppressed any external manifestation of it as far as possible. You must reflect, my darling, that there can be but one head to a family, and that while a husband will always find the happiness of both increased by mutual counsels, yet that it is the wife's part when the husband chooses to act, in any matter upon his own judgment without asking hers, to acquiesce cheerfully and affectionately. This is a part of her marriage vow: and the best way, by all odds, to obtain & retain the confidence, affection, & consultation of her husband. Remember how cheerfully & beautifully Mrs Hamilton Smith yielded to her husband and how he devoted himself to her.[2] Few wives ever had a more indulgent husband, and a husband to be more justly proud of than you. You love & honor him I know; but sometimes you complain when he thinks it unreasonable & contend with him when duty & prudence require submission. You can conquer only by love & submission—not by argument & pertinacity. An end gained by pertinacity is really lost.

But here I am sermonizing away, & I fear you are impatient. But remember, my child, that it is your father who loves you beyond expression, and longs to see you perfect in every wifely & christian duty.

I think it *not impossible* that Judge Jackson & his daughter, a sweet little girl, of sixteen, something of an invalid and a little deaf, but very cheery, bright, & pleasant may come with me.[3] I am sure you will like her and the Governor will like the Judge. He knows all about these oil regions. I say not impossible, though it is hardly probable. It would be impossible for any one to be more kind to me than the whole family have been, & I want you to be as kind to them if they come.

Would you like to have Herbert come with me? I will bring him if you wish. He can drive & do almost every thing; but would not like I suppose to be considered exactly as a coachman. He is with me here as my servant & if you dont want him will return to Washington. He has [no] wages, being under half pay as messenger at the request of the Judges whom he attended last winter.[4] I shall not take him east, if you do not want him. Telegraph me if you do, if you get this on Wednesday. I expect to start on my return Thursday afternoon at 4.30. When I shall reach Nt.[5] will depend on the roads.

A letter from Nettie dated Frontenac, Aug. 2d came night before last. She said she should write again before leaving. If only again I infer she would leave within ten or twelve days after the 21st—say 31st July or 3d Aug. If this inference is correct she is already with you or will be when I return. How glad I shall be to see her. Goodbye. Make the usual distribution of kisses, love, remembrances. Tell Willie to be a good boy. Try to make him know something of Christ.

Most affectionately your father
S P Chase

Historical Society of Pennsylvania.

1. In a letter to Kate on August 6, Father described a fatiguing journey from Washington through Baltimore to Parkersburg, W.V., to hold circuit court. The trip took him from Monday evening, August 3, to the afternoon of Wednesday the fifth, with only about two and a half hours' sleep in a hotel at Grafton, W.V., in the predawn hours of Wednesday. The journey was prolonged because of a "great break" in railroad connections between Ellicott's Mills, Md., and Grafton that required Father to make that leg of the trip by horse-drawn "omnibus." The coach, which encountered delays along the road, was stuffed with passengers, including squalling babies, and had four additional passengers riding on top. *Chase Papers*, 5:271–72.

2. Hamilton Smith and Louise Rudd of Springfield, Ky., had married in 1846. She was his second wife. *Chase Papers*, 1:575; 2:55.

3. In 1861, Lincoln appointed John Jay Jackson Jr. the U.S. district court judge for West Virginia. Jackson had married Carrie C. Glime in 1847, with whom he had two children, Lily Irene, who became an artist, and her brother Benjamin Vinton Jackson. The Jacksons hosted Father in their Parkersburg mansion during his stay for the circuit court session. Judge Jackson invited Father to accompany the family to Oakland in the Maryland Glades, but Father suggested that the judge, Mrs. Jackson, and their daughter go with him to Narragansett instead. *Nat. Cyc.*, 11:521; *Chase Papers*, 5:272.

4. Father's servant on the trip to West Virginia was Ananias Herbert, an African American. *Chase Papers*, 5:275.

5. Narragansett.

FATHER TO KATE

Washington Sep. 29, 1868.

My dearest Katie,

We came home last night only eight hours & ten minutes from New York. Prescott Smith has really worked a great reform.[1]

Enclosed are some letters for you which I found here.

It was a great comfort to leave you and the Governor so well—him apparently better contented & happier & you prettier & more lovely as well as more happy than I ever saw either of you.

And our journey homewards including the side trip to Albany was very pleasant. The Parkers & Pruyns seem to like Nettie so much that it made me like them.

Old Mr. Corning made us go to Troy with him to look at his & Mr. Berdans Iron Works. He & Mr. Griswold, the Repn. candidate for Governor, are engaged in the manufacture of Bessemer steel, & I was curious to witness the process. Unfortunately an accident had occurred & the works were not in operation. But we saw the process of casting Railroad bars from the beginning in the puddling furnace to the end. And then we saw Mr. Berdan's big wheel: only think of it, 60 feet in diameter; some fifteen [*illeg.*] breadth of rim; & 180 feet, circumference. I believe the Governor has some idea of building one & if so he should see Mr. Berdan, & then he has such a fine barn.[2]

We went out to Mr. Hoyts Sunday and attended Church with them in the afternoon. It rained too hard to go in the morning. What a lovely place theirs is: but Mr. Hoyt is as full of projects of improvement as you are.[3]

I wish I could get the Hazard place next you: and think that $20.000 would be safe there. Try your wits & judgment[4]

Give my best—very best love—to your excellent husband: and take the same to yourself. I will try to be worthy of yours. And dear little Willie how my heart yearns towards him.

Nettie is commencing housekeeping bravely. Marshall was still here & every thing in perfect order. He was dismissed as you directed; but I could not help feeling sorry for him; he seems so grieved & mortified.

Your affe. father
S P Chase

Mrs K. C. Sprague

Library of Congress.

1. William Prescott Smith was master of transportation for the Baltimore and Ohio Railroad and was known for the efficiency he brought to the New York and Washington rail lines. The week before Father wrote this letter, he and Nettie had been in Albany and Troy, N.Y. While in Albany they stayed with John Van Schaick Lansing Pruyn, a lawyer and railroad financier. They also visited lawyer and Democratic politician Amasa Junius Parker. In 1865, Pruyn married Anna Fenn Parker, daughter of Amasa and Harriet Parker. *Chase Papers*, 5:278–80, 156, 157, 369; *DAB*, 14:214–15; 15:253–54; *Appletons'*, 5:130; *New York Times*, Oct. 20, 1872.

2. Erastus Corning, a former Democratic congressman and four-time mayor of Albany, and John A. Griswold, former mayor of Troy, were prominent iron manufacturers who jointly owned Rensselaer Iron Works. Griswold was one of the men responsible for the 1865 introduction of the Bessemer steel-manufacturing process to the U.S. In 1851, Henry Burden, owner of Burden Iron Works, constructed what at the time was the second-largest water wheel in the world. Sixty feet in diameter and twenty-two feet wide, it carried thirty-six buckets, each six feet deep. The wheel had a 482-horsepower capacity. The Chases' friend Helen Burden McDowell, wife of Gen. Irvin McDowell, was Henry Burden's daughter. *DAB*, 4:446–47; Irene D. Neu, *Erastus Corning: Merchant and Financier, 1794–1872* (Ithaca, N.Y.: Cornell University Press, 1960), 32–39; A. J. Weise, *History of the City of Troy* (Troy, N.Y.: E. Green, 1876), 169–70, 262; Daniel J. Walkowitz, *Worker City, Company Town: Iron and Cotton Worker Protest in Troy and Cohoes, New York, 1855–84* (Urbana, Ill.: University of Illinois Press, 1978), 23–26; F. R. J. Sweeny, *The Burden Water-Wheel*, Society for Industrial Archeology Occasional Publication No. 2 (Washington, D.C.: Society for Industrial Archeology, 1973), 3–7; *Baltimore Sun*, Dec. 14, 1891.

3. Nettie and Father probably visited the Hoyts' place in Astoria.

4. The Hazards were a large and prosperous Rhode Island family who made much of their fortune in woolen manufacturing. Several members of the family lived in the vicinity of Narragansett. Peter J. Coleman, *The Transformation of Rhode Island, 1790–1866* (Providence, R.I.: Brown University Press, 1963), 95, 179–81; *Chase Papers*, 1:587–90.

KATE TO FATHER

Canonchet
Narragansett
5 October. 1868.

My dear Father,

After having seen my husband once more in his office, I came back to-day, & feel as though my occupation were gone[1]—The Governor has so

far recovered, that Dr. Perry says it is now only as a precautionary measure that he urges him still to use his crutches / The doctor came back
yesterday morning took off the bandages & boot, put the leg into a hot
bath & then left it free to work its own cure, by exercise & judicious
use[2]—The Governor went up to Providence yesterday, on a Boat sent
down to the Ferry for his use,—& we all went as escort, to see him safe
there—Doctor Perry returns to New York to-night, & will come once
more to see his convalescent patients Governor, & Mr. Coates. I asked the
Doctor, what he thought of your symptoms described as accurately as I
could give them[3] / He said it would be entirely impossible without seeing
you, & examining for himself to say any thing satisfactory. That the ir-
regular action of your heart was probably due to indigestion caused from
a want of sufficient physical exercise in proportion to the mental labor
you perform—But he might be entirely mistaken & the disturbance be
after all,—functional. He would very much like to see you. Can you not
go on to New York, before the Supreme-Court meets? I will meet you there
if you like, or Doctor Perry would perhaps go on to Washington to see
you if you preferred—I will arrange this with him, (if you will express
your desire,) the next time he comes—I must go to New York, before
many days to do some fall shopping, & do not think I shall be able to
resist running on to Washington to see how you are getting on, & to admire Nettie at the head of affairs. I am delighted to hear that she is doing
so well; I hope she will learn to like the responsibility, & then it will rest
easily upon her. We had really a very pleasant visit from Mr. Schuckers.
He improved greatly in health while here, & left us jubilant over the prospects of his machine.[4] I really think he needed the rest he found, he
looked very feeble, when he came, & should never again expose himself,
to the trying heat in Washington. Have you abandoned the Savannah trip,
or have you it still in prospect.[5] Please let me know as soon as possible, as
I may set off to call upon you any day—I write to Nettie by the same post—

Affectionately your daughter
Kate C. Sprague

On monogrammed stationery bearing an ornate letter S and the words *Canonchet* and *Narragansett*. Library of Congress.

1. William had broken his leg and Kate acted as his nurse. This dependency created
one of the couple's happy periods. When his leg healed their marital discord resumed.
Lamphier, *Kate Chase and William Sprague*, 106.
2. John Gardner Perry (1839–1926), a native of Boston educated at Harvard College
and Harvard Medical School, practiced medicine and surgery in New York City for many
years. Father later became one of his patients. *New York Times*, Dec. 3, 1926; *Chase Papers*,
1:662, 688.
3. Father and Nettie had recently been to Passamaquoddy Bay and the St. Croix River
in Maine. Father was "not at all well" during the trip and probably talked to Kate about it
at Narragansett. Father to Jane Auld, Oct. 8, 1868 (Chase Papers, LC).
4. Jacob Schuckers had become involved in a New York company that made mowing
and harvesting machines. Father had also invested in the company. In 1870, Schuckers

patented a "Harvester-rake," a horse-drawn farm implement that raked cut hay into windrows or piles. *Chase Papers*, 1:501; 5:124–25, 128.

    5. Father was expecting to go to Savannah, Ga., for circuit court. Apparently he did not make that trip. Late in November and early in December he was in Richmond for circuit court, hearing arguments pertaining to the potential trial of Jefferson Davis. *Daily Columbus (Ga.) Enquirer*, Nov. 4, 1868; *New York Times*, Oct. 20, Dec. 5, 1868; *Chase Papers*, 5:286–87.

FATHER TO KATE

Washington, Apl. 15, 1869

My dearest Katie,

I was very glad to receive your letter and to note the indications in it of a more tranquil mind than you carried from Washington. You have been sorely tried, my precious child; but much of your trial is as you acknowledge brought upon you & continued by yourself, and all is allowed to a wise & kind Father in Heaven who intends, I trust, to ensure your best happiness by it. Trust Him & love Him & follow Christ. I have great faith in the power of a truly Christian woman to overcome the greatest difficulties.[1]

Have you written to the Governor? I hope you have and in the best spirit. He went to New York the evening after you left, and only returned day before yesterday morning. Since then he has been so busy with his speeches & letters & I so busy with my records & opinions & the business of the Court that we have seen very little of each other, only meeting at table. The Court adjourned today, and I hope to have opportunities of conference with him before the week ends. I have no great expectation of benefit from what I can say: but what I can I will do. You can do more than any body else. Naturally you say "Must I do all?" It is hard to be loving & affectionate, when met by unkind words and unkind acts." I know it is; but I know too that she who thus acts will have her reward. There will come after a while a sweet internal serenity which will make duty easy & almost certainly ensure a return of love & affection.

The Governor's speeches have attracted great attention throughout the country. I have not considered what he proposes sufficiently to have any definite opinion as the merits of it; but undoubtedly he has gained a very prominent position; and, if your old mutuality of affection can be restored, you will be happier than ever; for, if I am not mistaken, you have been always ambitious for him. But, with his new position new responsibilities will come. How I wish you could be at his side bearing all things, believing all things, hoping all things, a real helpmeet.[2]

Tonight I am to have quite a company / The members of the Academy of Sciences are to call—Agassiz, Pierce, & Co—& I have invited a number to meet them. My heart is not much in it; but I will try to make myself agreeable.[3]

I have Netties letter today with the picture of the house and the story of Willie & mudpies & the garden & strawberries. How I wish I could be with you. Tell Nettie that I will allow her any amount of money to spend on black ink, nice paper & good pens. I could with difficulty read her letter, the ink was so pale. Give my best love to her and dear little Willie. Either you or Nettie must write me every day, if only the briefest letters.

I began this expecting to be very short and *here I am!*

> Most lovingly your father
> S P Chase

Historical Society of Pennsylvania.

1. In the spring of 1869, Kate's husband made a series of the strangest speeches ever heard in the Senate. Although his remarks centered on national financial policy, William attacked fellow senators, lawyers, corruption in government, Gen. Ambrose Burnside, and American women. "Americans who travel abroad mix and mingle in that filth and come home here to inculcate the immoralities that they have seen upon their own society," he proclaimed on March 30. Responding to reports about him in the newspapers, William declared "that my words and courage do not rest on wine or whisky, or any other stimulant, but upon knowledge of the shrinkage of property and the loss of virtue going on around me. . . . I utter no words that are not deeply considered. . . . Let those who think I am 'crazed' study as I have done for three years past; let them examine without prejudice, patiently as I have done, into our exact situation." *Congressional Globe,* 41st Cong., 1st sess., 1869, 64–66, 156–59, 242–46, 358–62, 475, 614–20; *Chase Papers,* 5:298.

2. The day after Father wrote this letter, an article appeared in the *New York Herald* that referred to William Sprague as "a grand reformer" and presidential candidate. That same day the *Herald* recorded that "workingmen and mechanics of Washington" had gathered on several recent occasions in front of the Sprague-Chase house to serenade Sprague and cry "Sprague for President." The movement came to nothing. *New York Herald,* Apr. 16, 1869; Emily Edson Briggs, *The Olivia Letters: Being Some History of Washington City for Forty Years as Told by the Letters of a Newspaper Correspondent* (New York: Neale Pub. Co., 1906), 112–16; Lamphier, *Kate Chase and William Sprague,* 111–17.

3. Agassiz was foreign secretary of the National Academy of Science. Benjamin Pierce, a mathematician and astronomer who, like Agassiz, taught at Harvard, was superintendent of the U.S. Coast Survey beginning in 1869. He was one of the founders of the academy. Father interacted with scientists in his capacity as chancellor of the Smithsonian Institution beginning in November 1868. *DAB,* 14:393–97; Rexmond C. Cochrane, *The National Academy of Sciences: The First Hundred Years, 1863–1963* (Washington, D.C.: National Academy of Sciences, 1978), 634–37; *Chase Papers,* 5:144, 300; Father to Nettie, Mar. 23, 1867, above.

FATHER TO KATE

> Washn. Apl. 17, 1869.

My darling Katie,

My heart is full of sympathy for you my precious child: but I pray earnestly & hope humbly that out of this great trial may come true peace for you.

I have not yet seen the Governor; there has been no opportunity. Have you written him? You can do far more than I, probably. I do not know how he will receive my unasked interference. But I shall try, & try before I go to bed tonight if I find the least opportunity.

Let me entreat you to indulge no hard thoughts of him. You have both erred greatly; and each *ought* to do all that is possible towards reconciliation. If he won't you must my darling. Humble your pride—yield even when you know you have the right on your side—remember the sacred obligation of your marriage vow—read it over & pray for strength & affection to keep it *fully*, in spirit as well as in act.

I have asked Mr. Schuckers to collect your Screw Money.[1] I wish now you had written a kind note to your husband asking him to collect it for you; for any little may now help to heal the breach: and it would certainly please him, I think, to attend to your matters as usual.[2]

I have sent Nettie a hundred dollars, which must be for your joint use. My account is considerably overdrawn but I hope to be able to make it good on the 1st of May.[3]

I enclose a note from the Post Office—your letter to Mr. Ward. It came to me just as it it.[4] You forgot to put a stamp on it, & I am rather glad, for I don't want to have you write anything to any body of the Male Variety of the human Species.[5]

Your affectionate father
S P Chase

Mrs K. C. Sprague

Historical Society of Pennsylvania.

1. Kate owned four shares of stock in the American Screw Company, which had paid a dividend of ten dollars per share on March 31. Father to Kate, Apr. 8, 1869 (Chase Papers, HSP).

2. Kate and Nettie had gone to Aiken, S.C. Kate had been with William on a trip to the South, including South Carolina, in late November and early December. On that trip, William initiated the purchase of a canal for industrial water power and other property in Columbia, S.C., as well as two large tracts of land on Cumberland Island near the Georgia-Florida line. At a dinner in Charleston he heaped praise on a cotton mill in Augusta, Ga., and spoke strongly in favor of industrial investment in the South. His remarks were publicized and praised by newspapers in several states. He was called the "great Yankee millionaire," yet according to a correspondent of the *New York Times* in Columbia, "Gov. Sprague is no carpet-bagger." *New York Times*, Dec. 23, 26, 1868, Jan. 10, 11, 14, 15, 1869; *Flake's Bulletin* (Galveston, Tex.), Jan. 2, 9, 1869; *Georgia Weekly Telegraph*, Jan. 8, 1869; *Morning Bulletin* (Little Rock, Ark.), Jan. 8, 1869; *Daily Columbus Enquirer* (Columbus, Ga.), Jan. 9, Feb. 19, 1869; *Macon Weekly Telegraph*, Feb. 12, 1869; *Houston Union*, Jan. 20, 1869; Henry W. Hilliard to Father, Dec. 5, 1868 (Hilliard Papers, Duke University).

3. On April 8, having received bills from a shopping excursion they had made to New York, Father wrote to Kate: "I am out of Money for the present but hope for some in a few days." "You must be economical," he reminded Nettie when he sent the check for $100 on April 9, "& let Katie have what she wants of your money." Early in the year he had written to Jay Cooke about obtaining loans, pledging more than $100,000 in stocks and bonds as collateral. Father to Jay Cooke, Jan. 11, 1869 (misdated 1868), and to Kate, Apr. 8 (Chase Papers, HSP); to Nettie, Apr. 9, 1869 (Chase Papers, LC).

4. So written, but he evidently meant "as it is."

5. There were two men named Ward with clear connections to the family at this time, and neither is an obvious candidate for the "Mr. Ward" to whom Kate addressed a letter. Samuel Ward (b. 1814), a New York financier and lobbyist, had been involved with Tilden and Van Buren during the 1868 Democratic convention. James Wilson Ward (b. 1803), was

one of Father's friends from his college days (addressed by Father as "Brother Ward" as late as 1870). *Chase Papers,* 1:21; 5:245, 333; *DAB,* 19:439.

FATHER TO KATE

Baltimore, Apl. 18, 1869

My dearest Katie,

I came over this morning & having a moment or two before Judge Giles will come give them to you.[1]

Last night or Yesterday I could not see the Governor to any advantage. He had some body about him all the time. This morning before he was up, I went into his room, & told him I wanted to have a talk with him before he went north, & would come over to Washington if he could not stop over a train in Baltimore. He was in very good temper, & said he would stop in Baltimore; & seemed gratified that I had called.[2]

Since writing what precedes I have been hearing a cause & it is now past 3 and I must close or I shall lose the mail.

I shall do the best I can darling: but it really seems to me that the case is one for womans tact guided by enduring love and patience rather than for any other one even a father. I think your husband was a man whom any woman might be proud to win & is a man whom any woman might be proud to retain, or if temporarily alienated to regain. You can do it with God's help & grace.

Most affy your father
S P Chase

Always dearest love to Nettie & Willie

Historical Society of Pennsylvania.

1. William Fell Giles, who had served one term in Congress as a Democrat in the 1840s, was the U.S. district judge for Maryland, 1853–79. He and Father together made up the U.S. circuit court for Maryland. *Bio. Dir. U.S. Cong.,* 1060; *Chase Papers,* 1:522–24, 531.

2. It appears that Father did not speak to William until early May; see Father to Kate, May 4, 1869, below.

FATHER TO KATE

Washington, Ap. 26, 1869.

My dear child,

I was disappointed coming home, Saturday that I found no letter from you. I do not know whether you have written to your husband or not; nor whether you have had any letter from him since the letter in which you said he had not written you.

When I returned the affair in the Senate which has made so much noise—more here of course than anywhere else—had just occurred—the day before. The attack on the Governor was a meanly concerted affair. When he replied the Senate went again into Executive Session, & then Abbott asked leave to make a personal explanation. The Governor said that if leave was given he should claim the right of replying in full, & the Senate refused to open its doors. The Governor then left the Chamber not supposing that anything more would be said of a personal nature. Abbott must have known this fact; and yet when the Senate shortly afterwards changed its mine[1] & opened the doors to give him a chance to say his say, he charged the Governor with having skulked out of the Senate. This was entirely untrue, and he must have known it. It was intended, probably, to force the Governor to take the offensive in a personal assault.[2]

The Governor very properly has taken no notice of the matter. Mr. Sumner & Mr. Sherman have been here this morning as I suppose with a view to compose the affair with what result I do not know.

The Governor does not consult me at all in his matters; and I do not feel myself at liberty to obtrude unasked counsels: though I would not hesitate to volunteer, if I had any reason to believe that good would come of it. I fear the contrary.

Since I came back I have seen very little of him, He is visited a great deal & is almost constantly engaged. The newspaper men are, of course, eager to get something for their papers; and a great many want to see the man whose speeches have made such a stir. Besides callers he has ever so many letters. Mr. Halsted of New Jersey has been with him about two weeks giving him a great deal of aid in various ways.[3]

He does not seem as cordial towards me as formerly; but it may be that I am more sensitive to his natural reserve & abruptness.

I am anxious for a good opportunity for a frank conversation, and must have one before I leave for Richmond next Saturday or Monday.

A letter from Nettie this morning mentions Mr. Charles Leary as staying with you for a day or two, and being your escort to Graniteville.[4] Does she mean that Mr. L—— is your guest? I hope not.[5]

You cannot be too careful, my child. I have learned more of the slanderous propensities of men within the last few years than I ever knew before. Only this morning I received a most abominable note from New York. I seldom read these anonymous libels, but I read enough of this to find that it was full of the most detestable abuse of you & the Governor not sparing either me or our innocent Nettie. Of course I at once destroyed it. For Heaven's sake, for my sake, for your own sake avoid all possibility of occasion for evil eyes & evil tongues.

Your devoted father
S: P: Chase

Historical Society of Pennsylvania.

1. So in the original.

2. In his April 8 speech, William defamed both Rhode Island senator William Anthony, with whom he was engaged in a political power struggle, and Ambrose Burnside, Rhode Islander and Civil War general. Two weeks later senators Joseph Carter Abbott of North Carolina and James Warren Nye of Nevada gave speeches defending Anthony and Burnside. William left the Senate chamber, though whether he did so to avoid confrontation or to get a gun remains unclear. Charles Sumner and John Sherman arranged a truce to avert a scandal. *Congressional Globe*, 41st Cong., 1st sess., 1869, 614–20, 744–45, 776–77; *New York Herald*, Apr. 27, 1869.

3. William Halstead, born in 1794, had been a congressman from New Jersey and a U.S. district attorney. Halstead was in Washington by April 9 assisting William with the "new & really heavy work" of preparing his speeches for publication and handling the load of correspondence he was receiving. Jacob Schuckers was also helping and took the speeches to New York to be printed. Five of William's speeches appeared in print, with titles reflecting the subjects of the debates when he gave them: *The Financial Condition* (speech of March 15), two called *The Civil Tenure Act* (March 17 and 24), *The National Currency* (March 30), and *The Tax Bill* (April 8). The complete set also appeared under the title *National Affairs: Speeches of William Sprague, in the Senate of the United States, March 15, 17, 24, and 30, and April 8, 1869.* Father to Nettie, Apr. 9, 1869, Father to William, May 2, 1869 (Chase Papers, LC); *New York Herald*, Apr. 23, 1869; *Bio. Dir. U.S. Cong.*, 1118.

4. Graniteville was a small mill town just west of Aiken, S.C. The Graniteville Manufacturing Company made textiles there. P. F. Henderson, *A Short History of Aiken and Aiken County* (Columbia, S.C.: R. L. Bryan Co., 1951), 20–24.

5. The object of Father's concern may have been Charles C. Leary, one of Arthur Leary's brothers. Born about 1842, Charles was a New York City merchant, shipowner, and businessman. During the Civil War, Arthur Leary named one of his company's propeller steamships the *Charles C. Leary*. Later, Arthur, Charles, and their sister Annie were among the wealthy socialites who regularly summered at Newport, R.I. *New York Times*, Dec. 24, 1865, May 23, 1890, Mar. 9, 1893, Aug. 28, 1895, July 23, 1896, Dec. 15, 16, 1898; Lewis Leary, "More Letters from the *Quaker City*," *American Literature* 42 (1970): 197; Wilson, *Trow's New York City Directory, For . . . 1864*, 500; *Baltimore Sun*, Nov. 23, 1864.

FATHER TO KATE

Washn. Apl. 29, 1869.

My dear Katie,

Your last letter came yesterday. I have only time now for a few words.

My hope and belief is that all will come out right: but you must use all your tact and discretion guided by a sincere affection & duty.

Yesterday the Governor mentioned your last letter to him at table. It was the first time and he had some of his friends with them. He seemed much gratified by something you had said; but not exactly satisfied with some of your criticisms. What pleased him I don't know; but one thing he did not like was your disapproval of the Mastiff & puppy story.[1]

Sometime afterwards he showed me a line or two written on a slip cut from the Margin of a newspaper, and asked me if I knew the hand. It so happened that I did not, nor did I recognize the initials—"C.E.R" if I remember. But the writer was very impertinent, and it angered him that it should have been sent to you. And I am sorry that you sent it to him.

By the way I think the dog & pup story has turned out very well & has had a good effect. I only hope now that the Governor will say nothing more of a personal nature. He says he shall not—that what he has said was said on purpose & has effected its object—and that no more of the same sort will be needed.[2]

I shall send some more money in a day or two. I am trying to pay the Governors advances for Nettie. I have paid over $6000 & a little more than $3000 remains to be paid. I want to get it down to $2000 this month & this keeps me short.[3]

But patience & courage, & above all trust in God, & shaping all words & acts by His Will!

Most affectionately
S P Chase

Historical Society of Pennsylvania.

1. William answered Abbott's rebuttal by calling him "a mongrel puppy dog" controlled by the wealthy "mastiffs" of the Senate. Abbott then reportedly threatened to shoot William and hired "thugs" to menace him. Nye explained that Abbott had only wanted to "spank little Spraguey, spank him and send him to bed." *Congressional Globe*, 41st Cong., 1st sess., 1869, 744, 745, 766; *New York Herald*, Apr. 27, 1869.

2. Father wrote to Jacob Schuckers, who had returned to New York: "*I* think that our Governor came out of the Abbott scrape very well. At first I was sorry he got into it; but on the whole I think it was best that he did. The Governor has undergone, of course, some sharp criticism; but he is the brighter for the rubbing." Father to Schuckers, Apr. 30, 1869 (Chase Papers, HSP); see also Father to James Kelly, Apr. 30, 1869 (Chase Papers, LC).

3. William had advanced funds for Nettie's stay in Europe, which Father was paying back with interest. A few days after writing this letter he sent William a check for $1,204.40 to bring the balance to an even $2,000. Father to William, May 2, 1869 (Chase Papers, LC).

FATHER TO KATE

Richmond, May 4, 69
My darling Katie.

Your letter by express came to me here by mail from Washington this morning.[1] I read it with profound interest and the deepest sympathy for you. It is my firm faith that you have only to carry out the purpose you express, with patience and perseverance, to win a happy issue. Trust God, have faith in Christ, accuse no one but yourself, cherish every wifely sentiment whether now reciprocated or not, have no disguises with your husband, let your conduct be as the day, and all will come right. God is trying you severely now. I you[2] take the trial as a loving child of God it will make you better & happier, & bring you nearer to Him where perfect safety is. Don't rebel, or let any impatience [be] suffered in your thoughts. Make all happy around you. Make Willie happy, & Nettie, and the domestics. Overcome your own temper, and be transparently truthful.

What I wrote you was in warning not in distrust. You have very little idea what dreadful things are said; and you cannot be too careful. On the other hand let no despairing or even despondent thoughts find lodgment in your soul.

My advice to you is not to criticize your husbands public action even in your thoughts. Of course you say nothing to outsiders except all you can say honestly in agreement & approval. But you may write something else to him, which will do harm rather than good. He cannot take criticism from you now patiently. Let him take his own course without any words but cheer & support. His own judgment will correct what may prove erroneous.[3]

As I wrote you he seemed gratified by something you had written; but I found afterwards that there was some admonition in the letter which he did not like, though he said nothing from which I could infer any thing more than this.

He went to New York last Friday by the noon train, and before he went I had a conversation with him.[4] I found him under some excitement. He said he had been sincerely anxious to have peace & good will restored; but could not do any thing which was not misinterpreted by you, and that you seemed all the time to be wanting to make up a case against him or defend yourself against him. That very morning, he said that, having missed some things for several days, he had gone into your room & found the small trunk or box in which they & other things—papers I understood—were & packages taken out of it which [& been] sealed up and one in particular which contained your letters from Col Crosby broken open & the letters taken away.[5] He then spoke of your coming into his room when you thought he was asleep, & searching his pockets. This matter you had explained to me, & I tried to make the same explanation to him but what had just occurred made it impossible to get a hearing. He then went on to say that he could not be controlled by you &[6]

Incomplete. Library of Congress.

1. Father had left Washington the day before to hold circuit court in Virginia, South Carolina, and North Carolina during May and June. *Chase Papers*, 5:303.

2. So written. He meant "If you."

3. Father soon learned that William had ordered the dismissal of a member of the household staff and her replacement with "a very fine looking Englishwoman." When he found out, Father wrote to William that the woman "appears very well & seems to understand her business. But is it not a little risky to bring such a woman into the house while there are no other women here?" Father did not mention the woman to Kate. He moved out of the house that fall. Among the seven women Kate named in her 1881 divorce petition accusing her husband of infidelity was one "Harriet Brown, in the year 1869 at Washington." Father to William, May 2, 1869 (Chase Papers, LC); Father to Kate, Oct. 1, 1869, below; *New York Times*, Dec. 20, 1881; Lamphier, *Kate Chase and William Sprague*, 118.

4. May 4 was a Tuesday. The previous Friday was April 30.

5. Possibly John Schuyler Crosby, born 1839, consul to Florence, 1876–82, and Montana territorial governor, 1882–84. Known as a sporting man and adventurer, Crosby married Gen. Stephen Van Rensselaer's daughter, Harriet, in 1863. He became a Union of-

ficer during the Civil War, remained in the army until 1870, and from March 1869 until
late 1870 served with Gen. Philip Sheridan in the West with the rank of lieutenant colonel.
There is no evidence as to the nature of Crosby's and Kate's relationship. *DAB*, 4:568–69.
    6. The remainder of the letter is missing.

FATHER TO NETTIE

Richmond, May 4, 1869

My dear Nettie,

Hurrah for the mails! Your letter of the 1st, postmarked 2d, has just
reached me—only two days and a few hours on the road. That's some improvement.

Yes; your letter is neat. I notice no mistakes in spelling; there is a little
& very little interlineation; only punctuation is disregarded. Now can't
you take some pains about that? The rules are few & simple & easily remembered. It is the practice only that is difficult. You say you love me & I
have no doubt of it. I am sure that I love you & thats why I want you perfect in these apparently small but really important matters. Perfection will
cost you labor & pains—more perhaps than many other girls; but can't
you pay the price for my gratification & your own internal satisfaction?

You need never be afraid of boring me with your views of public affairs or of any questions whatever. I thought what you wrote in your last
letter very sensible.

I am not at all sure that the particular views which the Governor just
now thinks most important & practicable will turn out to be so: but I
think he is doing much to attract public attention to public matters in
new aspects; showing unexpected power & resources; & may be safely left
to find his own way & correct his own errors, if any. A man is only a grown
child: and as the child will instinctively pick himself up when he falls &
keep out of the pond when he has once tumbled in, so the man will retrieve his own mishaps & amend his own mistake. Advice is sometimes,
doubtless, very good; especially when one asks for it, & the adviser loves
the advised.

I came here yesterday morning & went to work at once as you will see
by the papers; and now I have my hands full. I hope to dispose of what
I now have subd.[1] this week: but new cases may detain me all next week.
I will consider your suggestion of taking Aiken in my way to Charleston;
but as I must be there as soon as possible after getting through here I
hardly think it will be best.[2]

I am glad & sorry that Sue is going to be married. I sincerely hope
that Mr. Hoyts objections have no solid foundations & will not be carried
so far as they were in Sarah's case.[3]

I don't object at all to your Swedish notion. Who knows that you will
not become an apostle of Scandinavian unity.[4] All I ask is that you do

well what you do at all, & not skim things; for except of milk what is skimmed is not usually cream.

I hope you got the $200 I sent you. By the way your affairs continue to thrive. You have now in my hands

$7000 Philadelphia & Erie R.R. bonds, &

5000 Warren & Franklin R.R. bonds, &

_5000_ United States Pacific R.R. bonds, in all

17000 on which the interest (7% on the first $12.000 & 6% on the last 5000) amounts $1140 a year. Set off against this the road tax, in your 15 acres, of about $.200; but I will try to pay this for you. I have paid the Governor $1204 & odd cents for your last year in Europe leaving $2000 still to be paid.

> Most affy your father
> S P Chase

I am glad to see that you are determined to take every thing in the best spirit. A cheerful heart doeth good like a medicine and she that ruleth her spirit is better than *she* that taketh a city.[5]

Library of Congress.

1. Possibly "subscribed," to mean "undertaken."

2. Father probably did not go to Aiken, and on May 15 he learned that William expected to go there after a trip to Memphis and escort Kate home. Why Kate and Nettie chose Aiken as a destination in the spring of 1869 remains a mystery. Aiken, in the western part of the state, is not too far from Augusta, Ga., which Kate had visited with William on his Southern trip some months earlier. Father knew William Wilson Corcoran, whose granddaughter would marry into one of Aiken's leading families. Also, Henry William Ravenel, an Aiken botanist, was in Washington and visited the Senate chamber in March 1869. He may have met Kate there. Also, William S. Hoyt, whom Nettie married in 1871, visited Aiken at least once in his life. Certainly a May 1869 article in a widely read popular magazine which touted Aiken's benefits as a health resort suggests that Aiken had become a popular destination for elite travelers from the northeast. Father to Kate, May 15, 1869 (Chase Papers, HSP); Henry W. Hilliard to Father, Dec. 5, 1868 (Hilliard Papers, Duke University); Henderson, *Short History of Aiken*, 6, 33; Harry W. Smith, *Life and Sport in Aiken* (New York: Derrydale Press, 1935), 5, 14; Robinson Childs, *The Private Journal of Henry William Ravenel, 1859–1887* (Columbia, S.C.: University of South Carolina Press, 1947), 60, 333; *Chase Papers*, 1:232; 4:68–69; "Southern Life and Scenery in Aiken," *Frank Leslie's Illustrated Magazine*, May 22, 1869.

3. Susan Hoyt married Charles G. Francklyn in August. Her sister Sarah had married J. Bowers Lee in January 1869. See appendix; *Representative Men and Old Families of Rhode Island*, 1:416.

4. Nettie did not travel to Sweden during Father's lifetime. In the 1860s a pan-Scandinavian movement gained some popularity in Sweden. The conservative movement sought to return Finland to Sweden's control and thus turn Sweden's path toward Russia. The movement foundered in the 1880s as Sweden became increasingly pro-German. Kurt Samuelsson, *From Great Power to Welfare State: Three Hundred Years of Swedish Social Revolution* (London: Allen & Unwin, 1968), 142–44.

5. Father paraphrased two passages of the Bible: "A merry heart doeth good like a medicine: but a broken spirit drieth the bones" (Proverbs 17:22), and "He that is slow to anger is better than the mighty; and he that ruleth his spirit than he that taketh a city" (Proverbs 16:32).

FATHER TO KATE

Philadelphia, Sep. 15, '69.

My dearest Katie,

We had a very pleasant journey from Narragansett to New York, and no very unusually unpleasant experiences in getting from the Steamer to the Ferry boat. Our hackman did well—our express-man very badly—besides keeping for himself a couple of dollars I had given him to buy "compartment" tickets on the Railroad he was so long in getting our baggage from one Pier to the other that we just escaped missing the train.

Once in the cars, however on the Jersey side all went smoothly enough. The train was stopped to let us get off at Germantown—a great favor—where Mr. Cooke was waiting for us with a carriage to take us to Ogontz. By this kindness we were saved the depot in Phila & some miles of driving and some hours of journeying. Our reception was most cordial, & so far our visit has been a most pleasant one.[1]

The Church near Ogontz has been greatly enlarged & has an excellent rector. It will suit you that it is all of stone. Some months ago Mr. Cooke & Mr. Moorhead offered to build a parsonage & pay for the ground &c if the Congregation would pay for enlarging the Church &c. The offer was accepted & the result is the Enlargement; the Parsonage with two or three acres I believe of ground; & a fine Hall (a separate building for meetings of all sorts connected with the Parish, for lectures &c &c. I know of nothing more complete in the Church way or that would suit you better.[2]

I need say nothing of the House: you know all about it. The grounds are greatly improved, & undergoing constant improvement.

I suppose the Governor is in Maine, [&] trust that he will meet great success in all his objects including the fishing.[3]

Day before yesterday Mr. Cooke & I went a fishing. We took the cars from Camden down the Peninsula of New Jersey towards Cape May, stopping at Cape May Court House with a Mr Beesly—(one of the quiet, good, efficient, kindly sort of men—a rare sort)—who unites in himself the capacities of Manufacturer Farmer, Fisherman, & Representative in the Legislature. Yesterday Morning we went out with him in his boat to the fishing grounds, where we fished & fished & fished all day from eight oclock in the morning till six in the afternoon, catching altogether two hundred fish all with the hook, of which Mr. Cooke caught 84 & I 68 & Mr. Beesly the rest, besides attending to our lines, baiting my hook, taking off my fish &c &c. I just missed catching two prodigious fellows; but was very well pleased on the whole with my share of the work / Our fish were of several kinds poggies, most, next goodies; then blue fish, mackerel, flying fish, a couple of sharks &c &c. I hope the Governors success will exceed ours.[4]

This Morning (as well as yesterday) I was up at five and we returned by the 7 A.M. train to Phila. We have not yet been out to Ogontz & I have not seen Nettie.

It was a great delight to me to see the restoration of the old affection between you & your husband. God grant that it may never be interrupted again. How happy it seemed to make you both. It was wrong in you to leave me to be informed by others that you expect to be a mother again in October.[5] I cannot help being very anxious about you; but trust that our Heavenly Father, whose Mercies have ever exceeded our *ingratitude*, will give you safety and blessedness in your experience, and give us all love and obedience to Himself.

I wish you would write Nettie about the part of the *old* furniture you desire to retain. That in my Library rooms you know belongs to the Government. Keep what you please of the rest except the silver (not much) the pictures & the bust.[6] It is painful to separate, but it will be little of separation after all, & doubtless is for the best.[7]

Most tenderly & affectionately your father
S P Chase

Historical Society of Pennsylvania.

1. Kate and Nettie returned to Narragansett, from Aiken, in May and spent the summer in Rhode Island. Father visited them there during the summer before traveling to Parkersburg, W.V., to hold circuit court in August. He was back in Narragansett in early September, then he and Nettie traveled by train and ship to New York City. From there they took a ferry to New Jersey and another train to Philadelphia to stay with Jay Cooke at Ogontz. Father to Jay Cooke, Sept. 4, 9, 1869 (Chase Papers, HSP); *Chase Papers*, 5:303, 312–13, 316–17.

2. Cooke's brother-in-law and business partner, Philadelphia railroad financier William G. Moorhead, had, like Cooke, an estate at Chelten Hills. Cooke was a major contributor to the nearby St. Paul's Episcopal Church, where the Reverend Robert J. Parvin was rector. Oberholtzer, *Cooke*, 1:140–42; 2:447, 484–85; undated letter from Nettie to Kate following the one of Nov. 27, 1861, in chapter 4, above.

3. Part of A. and W. Sprague's holdings consisted of the Kennebec Land and Lumber Company in Maine. William often had business in Maine. *Latham v. Chaffee* (7 Fed. Rep. 520), 5–7.

4. Thomas Beesley, a Republican, was a member of the New Jersey legislature. The "pogy" is the Atlantic menhaden, and "goodies" is another name for the kind of croaker better known as the "spot." *Chase Papers*, 5:316–17.

5. We do not know by what means Father learned that Kate was pregnant or how recently he had received the news. Though some of Kate's biographers have accused her of hiding her condition, it is likely that she hoped he would notice on his own, or, as Father seems to intimate in this letter, sought to protect him from the anxiety her pregnancies caused him. Thomas Belden suggested that William must have learned of Kate's pregnancy months earlier and surmised that the child was not his, which Belden presumed was the incitement for William's comments about immorality in his Senate speeches of March and April 1869. Belden rested that supposition on William's absences from the Senate in January and February, when, Belden thought, William "must have" made a trip to the South that he alluded to in his speeches. In fact, William made that Southern visit in November and December, not in mid-January or after as Belden supposed. William and Kate were together at least once in January, on a trip to Maine to see the operations of the Kennebec Land and Water Power Company, which contradicts the assumption that the two of them must have been apart when the baby was conceived. Although in later years William some-

times made inconsistent accusations that he was the father of none of Kate's children except Willie, he does not appear to have made any actual allegation about the paternity of Ethel, the child born in 1869. We have found no evidence that Kate was unfaithful to her husband early in that year. Lamphier, *Kate Chase and William Sprague,* 109, 119, 195, 283–84; Belden and Belden, *So Fell the Angels,* 228, 239–40, 291, 381; Sokoloff, *Kate Chase,* 180; Thomas Belden, "William Sprague: The Story of an American Tragedy" (M.A. thesis, George Washington University, 1949), 52; *New York Times,* Dec. 23, 1868, Jan. 31, 1869; Henry W. Hilliard to Father, Dec. 5, 1868 (Hilliard Papers, Duke University).

    6. Father or someone else put a jagged vertical line in the left margin alongside the first three sentences of the paragraph.

    7. In early October Father and Nettie moved out of the house at 6th and E streets. They took up residence in a house at 1827 I Street that Father rented for a year from Anna P. Hoover. Kate had been considering making improvements to the house at 6th and E, which according to Father's journal was "undergong refitment" by January 1870. Lamphier, *Kate Chase and William Sprague,* 118; *Chase Papers,* 1:647; 5:318, 340, 341; Father to Hoover, Sept. 27, Oct. 26, Dec. 9, 1870 (Chase Papers, LC); Father to Kate, Nov. 17, 1868 (Chase Papers, HSP).

FATHER TO KATE

Washington, Oct. 1, 1869

My darling child,

    I was very glad to get your last letter yesterday: for my anxiety about you had become great. If you will only think what your concern about little Willie is, and add almost as much more to that you will have a good idea of mine about you.

    God send you comfort & safety in your approaching trial. How I wish I could be assured that in all trials your faith in Christ & in God through Christ is such as to make your heart cheerful & confident.

    I will write the Governor; though I have had no answer to former letters,—not, however, perhaps, really requiring a reply—that I don't know exactly how it will be taken. I wish I could feel him loving me and trusting me. But his nature is reserved; and he has been always in the habit, as I have been myself, of acting on his own judgment & saying little of his matters to any body. If he could only feel towards me as a Son how glad I should be.

    As a wife your duty is clear—not to expect him to change his nature—not to complain if he is reticent, or to feel like complaining—but "to love, honor, cherish & obey", and this cheerfully, heartily & perseveringly asking God's blessing, and God's blessing will come.

    I am sorry—very sorry—to part even so far as to have a separate house in the same city; but I really think it will be for the best. You know how I like comparatively early hours & regularity; and you are late & irregular / This to be sure is not much,—and I could easily conform, & would if you and the Governor really felt any need of me.

    But Nettie naturally feels that she wants a house of her own, or rather that her father should have a house & that she should be at the head of it.

And I think I ought to gratify her. You presided over my house some five years and did it admirably. I rather shall like to have her try her hand.

The worst is that we find no house near yours: and shall probably have to go over to I St, beyond Mr. Thorntons.[1] Nothing however is yet definitely settled. Fortunately the street cars abridge distances.

I must close now. I will write soon again. Write as often as you can. Love to your husband & little Willie. God bless you all.

Most affy

your father
S P Chase

Mrs K. C. Sprague

Historical Society of Pennsylvania.

1. Edward Thornton, who had held several diplomatic posts in Latin America, became the British minister to the United States in 1867. He was made knight commander of the Order of the Bath in 1870. *ODNB*, 54:628–30.

FATHER TO KATE

Washington, Nov. 7, 1869

My darling child,

A letter from Eliza to Nettie last night gave us a great deal of pleasure. It was the first particular account of the baby we have had.[1] In her note to me Eliza comforted me by the assurance that you are doing as well as could be expected, and I had the same from the Governor: though both charged you with some imprudence, from which I was delighted to learn you had escaped without serious consequences. But neither seemed to think it worth while to say much of baby. Now that defect in our information is supplied. And I congratulate you on being the mother of such a dear pretty little one. And I am glad that the baby is a girl. For my part I like girls rather better than boys though I would— I believe—have put up with one—perhaps two—for the sake of having a brother apiece for you and Nettie. But *girls* are *nice*. And it will be so good for Willie to have a little sister.

And now will come your additional responsibility. It is a great thing to have the charge of a little mortal, & to know that the character of all its life here below depends so largely on the direction given to the setting out. How much more to have the charge of young *immortals,* with all the influence which mothers necessarily possess. Let these things, my dear child, draw you close and closer to the Savior.

There is nothing new to tell you here. Our goings on are pretty much the same from day to day. Yesterday I varied the monotony a trifle by going out to my new purchase,[2] after the conference was over, about half past four. It was a bleak November afternoon. I thought of you and the Governor as we (Parsons & I) rode by the old Rhode Island Camping ground. The trees where Ballou lay with his regiment were almost bare / Wind & frost have dealt roughly with the foliage[3]

Parsons, always inclined to flatter, professed himself delighted with my place.[4] But indeed it did look beautiful: except so bare & worn. The prospect of the Capitol & the Potomac beyond and the hills is splendid—nothing can be finer. If I were only able to get it up & put in order—that is if I had ten thousand dollars to spare—I really believe I would spend more than half the winter there. It is not too far for a good walk, for I tried it the other day with Mr. Hilliard.[5] We walked out on the new railroad track till we came very near the house, & returned, in little more than an hour & a half.[6] It is certainly less than an hour walk either way. But no more of this. Good bye darling. I am half inclined to run on to Narragansett just to kiss you and the baby. Don't be *imprudent* again.

Your Affe. father
S P Chase

Mrs K. C. Sprague

Library of Congress.

1. Kate gave birth to her second child, a girl she named Ethel, at Canonchet. Eliza was Kate's and Nettie's cousin, Eliza C. Whipple. Phelps, *Kate Chase*, 228.

2. In September Father had purchased Edgewood, a large brick house on forty acres of land two and a quarter miles north of the Capitol building. The house was in the District of Columbia, but outside the boundary of the city of Washington at that time. Father, Kate, and Nettie were all involved in extensive renovations and new construction on the $22,000 house, and Father did not move there until 1871. He sold a good deal of his Cincinnati property to purchase and upgrade Edgewood and to acquire adjacent land. Niven, *Chase*, 443–44; Sokoloff, *Kate Chase*, 185; *Chase Papers*, 5:320, 332–33, 341–42; Father to Alfred B. Mullett, Dec. 9, 1870, Father to Richard C. Parsons, Dec. 8, 9, 1870, Feb. 8, 1871 (Chase Papers, LC); Father to Flamen Ball, Oct. 4, 1869 (Chase Papers, Cincinnati Historical Society Library, Cincinnati Museum Center).

3. In 1861, the First Rhode Island Regiment camped on a ridge near Edgewood and Glenwood Cemetery. Kate and William had ridden around the area during the early stages of their courtship. Maj. Sullivan Ballou, who had once been a Rhode Island legislator, briefly served in the Second Rhode Island Infantry. On July 21, 1861, he was killed at the First Battle of Bull Run. Sokoloff, *Kate Chase*, 185; Belden and Belden, *So Fell the Angels*, 44; *Washington Evening Star*, July 5, 1861; *Chase Papers*, 5:320.

4. Father's friend Richard C. Parsons, who at this time was marshal of the Supreme Court, helped oversee the work at Edgewood and tended to some other business affairs for Father. *Chase Papers*, 5:320, 340–42.

5. Henry W. Hilliard of Augusta, Ga., an attorney and former college professor of literature, had come to Washington with a delegation that called on President Ulysses S. Grant from the Southern Commercial Convention, a recent conference in Louisville, Ky. A political maverick, in the late 1840s and early 1850s Hilliard served in the U.S. House of Representatives as a Whig from Alabama. During that period he felt strong doubts about slavery and the war with Mexico but supported Southern sectional interests. He initially opposed secession, then raised a military unit for the Confederacy. His tenure in Congress had overlapped with the beginning of Father's term in the Senate. Though their

acquaintance then had been "very slight," Father opened a correspondence with Hilliard about Reconstruction policy in the spring of 1868, and they had remained in touch. *ANB*, 10:815–17; *Chase Papers*, 5:211–13; Henry W. Hilliard to Father, Dec. 5, 1868 (Hilliard Papers, Duke University); *Galveston Tri-Weekly News*, Oct. 15, 1869; *Flake's Bulletin*, Nov. 6, 1869.

6. A branch of the Baltimore and Ohio Railroad constructed in 1869 ran past Edgewood on its way to Washington. John F. Stover, *History of the Baltimore and Ohio Railroad* (West Lafayette, Ind.: Purdue University Press, 1987), 114, 142–43; *Chase Papers*, 5:320.

FATHER TO NETTIE

Narragansett June[1] 19, 1870

My dear child,

I am not well enough to write a note worth the reading.[2] But such as I can give, you want, for your birthday.

So I will pray God to bless you evermore. This is the best wish I can form for you.

Devotedly your father,
S. P. Chase

Miss Nettie Chase.

Library of Congress.

1. The month should be September, not June, a fact made obvious by the reference to Nettie's birthday, the Narragansett dateline, and Father's handwriting, which shows the effect of his stroke.

2. Father had spent the winter of 1869–70 sitting with the Supreme Court. In June he made trips to Philadelphia and New York, where he consulted a physician, Dr. Alonzo Clark, who thought his heart trouble and palpitations were "not serious." Clark, who was on the faculty of the College of Physicians and Surgeons of New York, was more concerned about diabetes, and apparently at the doctor's request Father started monitoring his output of urine. He may have stayed in New York for a few days of treatment under Clark's supervision, then returned to Washington, finished writing his court opinions from the last sessions, and on June 23 left for Ohio with Nettie and his attendant, William Joice (see the letter of October 15, below). After a stay at Gibraltar, Jay Cooke's summer retreat in the Lake Erie islands, they made a stop in Toledo early in July to see their relatives the Walbridges, then traveled to Champaign County, Ill., where Nettie's Uncle Dun, James Dunlop Ludlow, lived with his family. Father and Nettie then went to Minnesota, where they stayed until early August. On their homeward journey, Father suffered a sudden onset of paralysis on the evening of August 16 aboard a train between Niagara Falls and New York City. As he later informed Richard Parsons, by the time he arrived in New York his "right side from the toe to the scalp was sensibly affected so that I could scarcely speak intelligibly." For a week he and Nettie stayed in a New York hotel. Alonzo Clark and William Alexander Hammond, a neurologist and former surgeon general of the army, examined him and said that effects of the stroke were "unusually moderate." Kate and William removed Father to Canonchet, where he convalesced until December. Doctors did not allow him to write or dictate letters until the twenty-fourth or twenty-fifth of September. Eugene L. Didier, a thirty-two-year-old writer from Baltimore who was deputy marshal of the Supreme Court, went to Rhode Island to act as his secretary for a few weeks in September and October, then Jacob Schuckers took up that function until early the next year. *Chase Papers*, 1:645–60, 662; 5:336–40; *ANB*, 6:583–84; Kelly and Burrage, *Dictionary of American Medical Biography*, 227.

FATHER TO NETTIE

Oct. 15.

My dear Child:—

I suppose when this reaches you, you will be in New York, I will, there-fore, say nothing about the house until I see you.

Last night I suffered a good deal with pains in my chest, but slept on the whole pretty well, and am this morning much better.[1] I have walked already in the house about 20 minutes, and breakfasted and am going out to take a walk with William as soon as I finish this letter.[2] It is now twenty minutes past ten.

The children are well and so is Katie. The baby grows in grace and beauty day by day and I look soon to see her walking and talking. Willie improves continually.

The Governor, as long as Katie was absent, was very constant in his at-tendance, coming down every night. Since he went up on Wednesday morning, he has not returned but we expect him to-night as usual. His place is well supplied by Katie.

I am still kept on my short diet, but I suppose it is best for me.[3] Please bring me a bottle of cologne and a *good modern Arithmetic.*

Give my best regards to Susie Francklyn. I hope her little one is im-proving constantly.[4] My best regards also, to Mr. Hoyt.

I shall write to Dr. Perry by this mail.[5]

Your affectionate Father,
S. P. Chase

Miss Chase (See next page)
P.S. to Miss Chase's letter of the 15.

So far I had written this morning and sent it by mail; but as the Gover-nor is going over to night I thought it best to rewrite what I have written, and send it by him.

Since writing in the morning, I have taken a walk, and, also, a dose of Rochelle Salts. The former was rather hard, coming as it did about the same time. I had, also, ridden to Wakefield with your sister. And, on the whole, was rather weak. I hope, however, that it will go off without serious results. I have taken a bit of a nap, and am now refreshed and better.

Your affectionate Father
S. P. Chase

Letterbook copy by Eugene L. Didier. Library of Congress.

1. Though recovering from his stroke at Kate's Narragansett house, Father continued to suffer chest pains at night and partial paralysis. His right leg dragged, but doctors in-sisted that he exercise. Father to John G. Perry, Oct. 5, 8, 10, 15, 1870 (Chase Papers, LC); *Chase Papers,* 5:339.
2. William Joice, an African American employed as a messenger of the Supreme Court, was Father's driver and personal attendant. He often traveled with the chief justice.

Mentioned only infrequently in letters or in Father's diary, Joice had accompanied Father and Nettie on their trip around the Southern coast in 1865 and was with them on the journey to Ohio and Minnesota in the summer of 1870. *Chase Papers,* 1:578, 587, 655, 657, 663, 664, 665.

3. Father subsisted primarily on a diet of beef broth, bread, soft boiled eggs, and black tea. Father to John G. Perry, Oct. 5, 10, 1870 (Chase Papers, LC); *Chase Papers,* 1:661.

4. Susan Hoyt Francklyn and Charles G. Francklyn had two children, Gilbert and Doris. *New York Times,* Apr. 7, 1932.

5. Father wrote New York doctor John G. Perry twice that day. In his first note he described his diet and chest pains, while in his second letter he described the difficulties he was experiencing enduring the pain of his illness. Father to Perry, Oct. 15, 1870, two letters (Chase Papers, LC).

CHRONOLOGY

March 23, 1871	Nettie (age twenty-four) marries William S. Hoyt in Washington, D.C.
April 1871	Nettie and Will depart from New York for the British Isles and Europe
May 1871	Kate takes her children on a visit to Albany; Father in Washington
June 1871	Kate in Washington, New York, and Narragansett; Father goes to springs at St. Louis, Mich.
July–mid-September 1871	Father at Bethesda Springs, Waukesha, Wisc.
August 1871	*New York Herald* suggests Father as presidential prospect
October 1871	Father and Kate visit Nettie in New York, shopping there and in Philadelphia for furnishings for Edgewood
December 1871	Father visits Nettie in Astoria, N.Y.
January 14, 1872	Nettie's first child, daughter Janet, is born
February 2, 1872	Kate's third child and second daughter, Portia, is born
March 1872	Father visits Nettie in Astoria
April 1872	Kate holds reception for Father in Washington
May 1872	Nettie and Will have residences in New York City and Pelham, N.Y.; Father hosts dinner at Edgewood for visiting Japanese diplomats
June–September 1872	Father spends the summer in different locations in New England; returns to Washington in October for Supreme Court term
late November–early December 1872	Father visits Pelham and New York City; Kate and her family are in Rhode Island
April 1873	Nettie's son Edwin is born
May 1873	Father travels to Nettie's and Will's Manhattan residence, where at the age of sixty-five he suffers a stroke and dies; Kate is thirty-two, Nettie, twenty-five

CHAPTER 11

"Take Care of Yourself"

MARCH 1871 – APRIL 1873

FATHER STRUGGLED to recover from the effects of his stroke of August 1870. He did not attend the fall 1870 session of the Supreme Court, staying instead at Narragansett, where he took walks and recuperated as best he could. In January 1871, he went to New York, then in March to Washington, D.C., where he resumed his seat with the court. "My hand writing, however," he wrote to Gerrit Smith, "shews that I am not well physically, though much better than I was, and growing better from month to month. Intellectually my mind seems clear enough, but incompetent to much thoroughness of investigation, especially where protracted & continuous attention is required." The ravages of the paralytic attack were obvious to those around him. He had begun to lose weight even before the stroke, and by the summer of 1871 he was carrying as little as 145 pounds on his six-foot-two-inch frame.[1] Yet until Horace Greeley won the Liberal Republican nomination in the spring of 1872, some of the chief justice's admirers hoped that he would be strong enough, both physically and politically, to receive the presidential nomination.[2]

He needed assistance with his correspondence following the stroke, and the position of secretary was filled first by Eugene L. Didier, then by Jacob W. Schuckers on an interim basis, followed by David Demarest Lloyd. Interestingly enough, all either were or became writers, at least avocationally. Schuckers had been one of the Treasury clerks working directly under Father during the Civil War. He graduated from law school in 1865. In addition to writing *The Life and Public Services of Salmon Portland Chase* (1874), he later wrote and spoke on politics and monetary issues. Didier, who was in his early thirties when he worked for the chief justice, came from Baltimore, where he had founded a short-lived literary magazine. He later wrote biographies of Edgar Allan Poe and Elizabeth Patterson Bonaparte.[3] Lloyd was the brother of Henry Demarest Lloyd, who later garnered fame as a muckraking journalist exposing corporate and political misdeeds. D. D. Lloyd wrote for newspapers, too, and also became a playwright (see the notes to the first letter in this chapter). Father's private secretary in this period was paid through a clerkship made possible by the Bankruptcy Act of 1867, which gave the chief justice the job of naming registers in bankruptcy throughout the country. In March 1873, Robert Bruce Warden succeeded Lloyd as the chief justice's secretary.[4]

For months after the stroke, Father dictated rather than wrote almost all of his correspondence. In some cases Didier even signed letters on his behalf. Gradually Father resumed penning many of his own letters, but even late in 1872 he remarked that writing letters was arduous for him (see the letter of December 15 to Nettie). And his handwriting, never acclaimed for its legibility, took on a jerky, almost spastic quality. Lloyd later put the best possible face on his employer's handwriting from before the illness, calling it "peculiarly elastic, delicate, and almost fanciful." After the paralysis, as Lloyd aptly described it, the script was "shorn of its curves," "condensed and minute."[5]

But other, happier changes came too. On March 23, 1871, an illustrious audience that included Vice President Schuyler Colfax, other dignitaries, and "nearly all the distinguished ladies of fashion" of New York filled St. John's Church, across Lafayette Square from the White House, to witness what the *New York Times* called "one of the most brilliant weddings which ever occurred in Washington." After a quiet courtship, Nettie Chase married William Sprague Hoyt, a New York businessman and the son of one of William Sprague's cousins. Sprague himself, however, had no official part in the rite: Kate was escorted into the church by the new groom, the pair of them preceding Nettie and her father. Newspapers described the bride's gown of "white illusion, looped with natural orange flowers," and her sister's attire of "rib-green silk, with a court-train, and over-dress and shawl of elegant point lace." After the ceremony, crowds choked the streets around the Sprague residence at 6th and E, where the Marine Band entertained a "brilliant reception" attended by President Grant, the justices of the Supreme Court, Gen. William Tecumseh Sherman, Secretary of State Hamilton Fish, and members of the Joint High Commission negotiating a treaty between the United States and Great Britain. The event, observed the *Times*, demonstrated "how refinement and wealth make a fine art of entertaining. Every part of the programme at the house, as at the church, was fulfilled with perfect freedom from confusion and mistakes, and not a single event occurred to mar the brightness of the day." John Hay chirped that Will Hoyt was "a very nice fellow" with "no end of cash," and Nettie was "a very nice girl" with "no end of talent."[6]

Early in April the newly married couple embarked for Liverpool to begin a long honeymoon in Europe, after which they settled into domestic life in Astoria and New York City. Astoria, which in 1870 became a ward of the newly incorporated Long Island City, was a "beautiful village . . . filled with elegant dwelling houses and villas." From there Will, who was in his father's dry goods mercantile firm called Hoyt, Spragues and Co., could cross the East River by ferry to reach his place of business at 107 Franklin Street in Manhattan.[7] And for the first time in many years Father had neither of his daughters residing with him. While he and Nettie had lived in a rented house on I Street in Washington, he had initiated renovations at Edgewood, the house and acreage outside the city that he purchased in 1869. He asked Edward Clark, the architect of the Capitol, to design a new barn for the place. A new, state-of-the-art facility for extracting gas from coal provided the means of illuminating the house at night. With time, improvements would include a new well and alterations to the approach road. In 1871, the chief justice took up residence in the house, which had a large garden and fruit trees tended by hired hands.[8]

Kate, who stayed sometimes in the Washington residence at 6th and E and sometimes at the Narragansett estate, also traveled to visit friends or relatives. Father made visits to Narragansett, to Astoria, and, beginning in 1872, to the suburban residence that Nettie and Will established at Pelham, New York. And he tried to walk his way back to full health. He walked in Narragansett in the aftermath of the stroke, sometimes covering four to six miles on a jaunt. Living at Edgewood, he walked to the Supreme Court chambers in the Capitol building, to Rock Creek Church, around the property with Lloyd, to visit neighbors, or, if nothing farther afield offered itself, up and down the portico of the house.[9] He followed a bland diet prescribed by Dr. John G. Perry of New York and drank water bottled at what were considered to be the most beneficial springs. Eaton Rapids water sent by an old acquaintance late in 1870 interested him in Michigan's curative waters, and in the spring of the following year he journeyed to that state, then found his way to Waukesha, Wisconsin, where he spent the latter part of the summer.[10] Waukesha's Bethesda Springs were reputed to "work wonders in cases of prostration from disorders from the liver and kidneys," and he believed that his "own troubles" came "in great part, from disorders of these organs."[11] After his return east he continued to drink therapeutic water bottled at Bethesda Springs and Rockbridge Alum Springs in Virginia. But full health and vigor still eluded him, and his doctor closely monitored his urine and his bowel function, concerned in particular about diabetes.[12]

In their correspondence, members of the family often distinguished the three Williams by calling Nettie's husband "Will," Kate's husband "the Governor," and Kate's son "Willie." Nettie's first child, a girl, was born on January 14, 1872. "Let her name be Janet Ralston," Father advised, "after her mother, grandmother, & great grandmother; or name her after Wills mother." Nettie followed the suggestion and named the child Janet.[13] A couple of weeks after the baby's birth, Kate's third child, a daughter named Portia, was born.[14] In the spring of 1873, Nettie and Will had a son they called Edwin after his Hoyt grandfather. The baby's other grandsire, who unknown to everyone had only weeks to live, gently overruled Nettie's wish that the infant have his name. Instead he urged that the little one be called something he "would like when grown." Nettie compromised, naming the child Edwin Chase Hoyt.[15]

1. To Smith, Apr. 20, 1871, and to Richard C. Parsons, Aug. 9, [1871] (Chase Papers, LC); Warden, *Chase*, 725, 741; Schuckers, *Chase*, 620–21; and see photo facing *Chase Papers,* 5:169.

2. In April 1872, Kate hosted a reception in Washington in an effort to show that her father was still robust. *Chase Papers*, 1:677, 679; 5:355–60; Blue, *Chase*, 316–17.

3. *ANB*, 6:583–84. Schuckers also became involved in business ventures that involved hay-mowing equipment and, apparently, a button machine. Father to Schuckers, May 17, 1871 (Chase Papers, HSP); Father to Schuckers, June 24, 1872 (Chase Papers, LC); *Chase Papers*, 1:501; 5:124–25, 128.

4. Father to John G. Nicolay, Mar. 24, 1873 (Lincoln Papers, LC); Warden, *Chase*, 769; *Chase Papers*, 1:646.

5. *Chase Papers*, 5:xxiii–xxiv, xxvi.

6. Belden and Belden, *So Fell the Angels*, 259; *New York Times*, Mar. 24, 1871; *Washington Evening Star*, Mar. 23, 24, 1871.

7. *History of Queens County New York, with Illustrations, Portraits, & Sketches of Prominent Families and Individuals* (New York: W. W. Munsell and Co., 1882), 259, 279, 314; Wilson, *Trow's New York City Directory, For . . . 1871*, 577; Wilson, *Trow's New York City Directory, For . . . 1875*, 620–21.

8. *Chase Papers*, 1:665–66, 705, 710; 5:320, 341–42. For Nettie's drawing of the house, which no longer stands, see the illustrations between pp. 168 and 169 of *Chase Papers*, vol. 5.

9. Schuckers, *Chase*, 620, 622; *Chase Papers*, 1:663–75, 679, 703, 705.

10. See Father to Nettie, June 5, 1871, and Kate to Father, Aug. 29, 1871.

11. Father to Richard C. Parsons, Aug. 9, [1871] (Chase Papers, LC). For contemporary chemical and medical assessments of the waters of Waukesha, Wisconsin, and St. Louis, Michigan, see Robley Dunglison, *A Dictionary of Medical Science* (Philadelphia: Lea Brothers & Co., 1874), 655, 1123; and A. N. Bell, *Climatology and Mineral Waters of the United States* (New York: Wood, 1885), 177–78.

12. *Chase Papers*, 1:665, 666, 675, 687, 688–90, 696–97, 701, 704–7.

13. Janet Ralston Hoyt died in 1947. Father to Nettie, Jan. 23, 1872 (Chase Papers, LC); *New York Times*, June 5, 1947.

14. Alice Hunt Sokoloff, citing a birth date given on Portia's death certificate, asserted that Kate's third child was Katherine (called Kitty), and that Portia was the fourth and last child. Other biographers, including Mary Merwin Phelps, who in researching her book interviewed friends, relatives, and acquaintances of Kate, concurred in naming Portia as the third child and Katherine as the fourth. In addition, when Kate referred to those two daughters, she tended to name Portia first, then Kitty. Newspaper sources that state or imply Portia's and Kitty's relative ages are contradictory, although at least one published version of Kate's divorce petition in 1880 stated the sequence as Willie, Ethel, Kitty, then Portia. Sokoloff, *Kate Chase*, 194, 200, 304; Phelps, *Kate Chase*, 237, 241; Ross, *Proud Kate*, 225, 230; Belden and Belden, *So Fell the Angels*, 262, 286; Lamphier, *Kate Chase and William Sprague*, 285; *Baltimore Sun*, Dec. 20, 1880, May 13, 1899; *Minneapolis Journal*, Oct. 1, 1897; Lexington, Ky., *Morning Herald*, Oct. 4, 1897; *Grand Forks Daily Herald*, Oct. 3, 1897; *Macon Telegraph*, Oct. 17, 1897.

15. He attended Columbia University, became a New York attorney, and died in 1954. Father to Nettie, Apr. 12, [1873], below; *New York Times*, Oct. 22, 1954.

NETTIE AND WILL HOYT TO FATHER

Astoria March 28th[1]

My own dear dear Father—

Your dear letter came today, and I can not tell you what a pleasure it gave me—It was so sweet, and like you—the girls *did* find time for a short account of their doings I am so glad that they enjoyed themselves so much[2]—but poor Sister must have been thoroughly used up—and she _was_ so good through it all. The children she writes are improving, dear bairnies how I should like to see them! I shall always remember baby's Hight, Hight, bullaye boy—! in church,—and shall have the pleasure of reminding her of it when she grows to be a dignified Miss—although she bids fair now to be a regular witch.[3] We are getting on very nicely here / I wrote to Sister about our ménage this morning, and how Miss Fenn sent us out—an excellent person no doubt but it _is_ rather inconvenient to have a house maid who can not hear a word—

Passing thro' the hall this morning I was present at the following—

(Will) Is there any lamp oil in the house?

House maid paying no attention to his presense, he repeats—

(House maid finally becoming cognizant of his vicinity—eh Sir?

Will putting on full lung power) _Is! there! any! oil! in! the! house!!!_

House maid placidly. Oh yes Sir I shut them all down—

Will becoming excited Kerosene!! Lamp oil!! Oil!! Oil!! Lamp!! for the _Lamp_!! Oil!!!!—

House maid pleasantly—yes Sir because it was getting dark Sir—

Will), weak & in despair—What an ass that woman is[4]—

Nettie has omitted to mention one of the most charming peculiarities of this singular woman, viz. her manner of ascertaining whether it will be proper for her to enter a room—Ordinary mortals knock at ones door, but _this_ creature, knowing that any calls of "Come in" would never reach _her_ consciousness, gently opens the door & peeks carefully through the crack—whereupon she uses her discretion about an entrée. We should probably have always remained in blissful ignorance of this little idiosyncracy, had it not been that I accidentally caught her in the act.[5] We go in town to dine with Susy Francklyn Thursday, and on Saturday dine with Minnie.[6] Do urge the Govenor to come on with Sister—as I say—although I long to have you, I would not for the world have you attempt it, unless you were sure that it would not do you harm.

Will you please ask Mr Lloyd to send me six cards and to direct cards to Jane Auld[7] I wrote to Alice this morning so they will only think it some delay and I for[got] too the Toledo people—I think that I sent cards to Aunt Eliza but am not entirely sure[8]—

Good night—my own dear Will sends love and I send more than I have room to write

Lovingly
Nettie

By the way please direct letters to Astoria L.I. care of Will as it delays them to send them to town as we do not send in every day

Library of Congress.

1. Although no year appears in the dateline, the references to a young daughter of Kate of the right age to be the "baby" who piped up "in church," the circumstance of that child attending a rite at which her grandfather, the recipient of the letter, would also have been present, the mention of "cards" to be sent to distant relatives, and the seeming newness to Nettie (and her father) of the employees and routines of the Hoyt household in Astoria together indicate that Nettie and her new husband composed this joint letter five days after their wedding in Washington on Mar. 23, 1871.

2. Likely Will Hoyt's sisters, Sarah and Susan.

3. Seventeen-month-old Ethel Chase Sprague.

4. The letter to this point is in Nettie's hand. Will Hoyt wrote the portion beginning with the next sentence.

5. Will ceased writing here and Nettie completed the letter.

6. Minnie Vail had been a bridesmaid at Nettie's and Will's wedding. *New York Times,* Mar. 24, 1871.

7. David Demarest Lloyd (1851–89), who generally went by Demarest rather than David, had passed the entrance exams for New York University at the age of twelve and wrote for the *New York Tribune* at nineteen. He was Father's private secretary, 1871–72. In the latter year, when he assisted his brother, writer and reformer Henry Demarest Lloyd, in an attempt to organize a Free Trade splinter from the Liberal Republican Party, a newspaper described him as "a good-looking, fair-skinned, brown-haired boy, of affable, dignified, and confident address." Along with assisting Father with correspondence, he kept memoranda titled "Farm Notes" that recorded some of the work activity at Edgewood in the spring of 1872 (Chase Papers, LC). Later Lloyd again wrote for newspapers and was the author of four plays. William Dean Howells declared that Lloyd's first play, called *For Congress,* "is keeping a play of Mark Twain's and mine off the boards." After Lloyd's death, William Winter commemorated him in verse as "A brave and gentle soul, a noble mind." Caro Lloyd, *Henry Demarest Lloyd, 1847–1903: A Biography,* 2 vols. (New York: Putnam, 1912), 1:14, 19–20, 33–34, 49, 72–73, 139–40; W. J. Burke and Will D. Howe, *American Authors and Books: 1640 to the Present Day,* 3d ed., rev. by Irving Weiss and Anne Weiss (New York: Crown Publishers, 1972), 384.

8. That is, Alice Auld; the family of Nettie's late aunt, Helen Chase Walbridge; and Eliza Whipple.

NETTIE AND WILL HOYT TO FATHER

Conway Wales
April 30th. '71—

I was so ever so much disappointed my dearest Father, to find no letters at Carnarvon, Thoroughly disappointed, although Will said that there was not more than one chance in ten that I would find any—as unless letters were posted four days after we sailed they would not reach us until we travelled up to the Chester budget—but I wanted and longed for my home news so much that it made me sanguine of finding something—now I am so anxious to reach Chester that posting seems too slow—so our man drives back the horses & wagon from here, and we go back by rail—for the rail road runs into this queer, quaint little town, directly under one of the most beautiful ruined castles I have ever seen, and strangely incongruous it seems, for the railway bridge is swung across the river to the castle walls, and they have aped the old architecture in bran new white stone, so side by side they stand, the old and the new—it looks brazen and pushing, that railway bridge, and jars upon the melancholy dignity of the old ruin[1]

What cares the nineteenth century Progress, for Edward's victories or Llewellyn's raids—and what can these old walls have to do with the bustling present[2]—It is, as I say, incongruous. There is a high wall about this little town, with eight towers besides the castle, so it is [thouroughly] picturesque surrounded as it is with fine hills, and on the borders of the river Conway

We were at church this morning—where we had an excellent sermon from a fine earnest faced young curate—fortunately for us he preached in English, although he gave his text in English & Welsh—A week ago in Barmouth where I wrote you from, they had only a welsh church[3]—Do you remember Mary, a welsh housemaid we had once in Columbus, and who afterwards died, poor thing? So many of the women here, remind me of her[4]—they are a pleasant civil people as far as our experience goes, and many of the women are pretty. good straight features, and once in a while we see a perfect complection—Since Barmouth we have been to several pretty places with unpro[nounceable] names—It is extraordinary the amount of consonants they collect together & put into one word— You could never gain the least idea of the pronunciation from the spelling or of the spelling from the pronunciation—At Badgelleth we took a guide & ponies and made the ascent of Mt Snowdon[5]—I enclose a leaf relating our sad experiences there, with that exception our chief excitements have been sketching, and photographing and jogging along welsh highways behind our steeds who have *not* proven themselves to be Bucephalus's—plutôt Rosinantes[6]—eating fresh eggs and mutton Chops for breakfast, and no end of beer and bread & cheese & butter for lunch, and spring lamb for dinner—Will smokes his cigar, I finish up my sketches, Will reads out loud, I continue to sketch. We breakfast at nine lunch at two and dine at seven—I shall very soon have news of you now dear Father / I pray God you are growing continually better, do you still think of Michigan[7] my dear dear love to all

Devotedly
Nettie

Nettie seems to have left me but a small share of the news,[8] as she has given it all up to last night, & today our chief & almost only occupation has been sketching & photographing in the Castle, & a charming subject

it is—better than any ruins I ever saw—I regret so much not having had
any opportunity yet of giving my negatives to be printed, as I know a
good many of them would interest you, on account of a certain subject
I have introduced whenever she would sit for me—Our last few days
in Wales have been something of what we had hoped for, & we are
far better able to appreciate the bright blue skies, after our ten days of
clouds & rain—Tomorrow we go to Chester by rail & shall probably leave
for London on Friday—Our stay there will be very short, as the Midnight
Sun will not wait for us in the North, & in default of Iceland we must at
least be there in time[9]—If Paris were not now in this fearful state of tur-
moil, we should go there directly from London & then down to Spain
for about three weeks, but of course that is quite impossible,[10] so that we
shall go at once to Dresden, reaching there about the fifteenth or twentieth of May—As Nettie has told you, we are very anxious to find our letters at Chester tomorrow night, as it seems a long time since that day we
left you on the steamer—I join most sincerely with Nettie in the hope
that you have since then been growing continually stronger—& with
kind remembrances to all believe me most sincerely Yours

W S Hoyt

We ascend Snowdon[11]

Joyful start, blue sky, lasily sailing
white clouds, green fields, skipping
lambs, birds singing, hedges in blossom,
streamlets dancing, simply perfect in short.
We reach the mountain, a fog arises and grows thicker and thicker,
mountain grows steeper and steeper, wind whistles chilly, our John
Thomas wishes sotto voce that he "was safe at home with a whole skin"[12]
general discomfort and no view fog covering every thing.

The fog changes to a violent hail storm, I err—the fog continues and a violent hail storm is added to it, wet exhausted and bruised, we reach the summit at last and find a little hut where we dry our dripping garments. Guides pronounce it dangerous to descend the same side of the mountain we came up, so we go down on the other side take a fly[13] & drive fourteen miles to our hotel this is the "last drop About ten P.M. we reach a haven at last—
Advice to those about to ascend Snodon
Dont

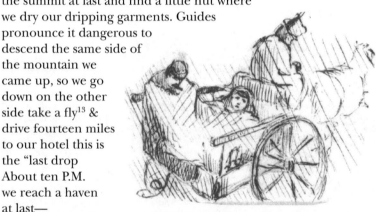

Library of Congress.

1. Both Conway (or Conwy) on the north coast of Wales and Carnarvon (Caernarfon) to the west had imposing castles that dated from the late thirteenth century, when Edward I of England solidified his control over Wales. In the 1820s the foot of a suspension bridge, designed by the noted engineer Thomas Telford, impinged on the walls and obliterated the river entrance of the fortress at Conway. Two decades later Robert Stephenson built a railroad bridge alongside Telford's span. Crenellated stone support towers of both bridges mimicked the architecture of the castle. Stephenson's bridge enclosed the railway in unadorned rectangular metal tubes. Michael Senior, *Portrait of North Wales* (London: Hale, 1973), 65–67, 70, 157–58; Derrick Beckett, *Telford's Britain* (Newton Abbot: David & Charles, 1987), 108–9, 166; Derrick Beckett, *Stephenson's Britain* (Newton Abbot: David & Charles, 1984), 139–45; Ifor Rowlands, "The Edwardian Conquest and Its Military Consolidation," in *Edward I and Wales,* ed. Trevor Herbert and Gareth Elwyn Jones (Cardiff: University of Wales Press, 1988), 50–53.

2. Edward, who became king of England in 1272, and the Welsh prince Llywelyn ap Gruffudd had a long history of conflict beginning in the 1250s. Over many years Llywelyn consolidated his power in different parts of Wales, variously allied himself with or fought against powerful barons and members of his own family, and made significant incursions

into English-controlled areas. At the apogee of Llywelyn's influence, the English conceded him most of Wales as his principality. His refusal to maintain allegiance to English authority brought on invasions of his homeland in 1277 and 1282, during the second of which he was killed. *ODNB*, 17:809–10, 813, 815; 34:185–91.

3. In the nineteenth century such prominent Britons as Tennyson, Shelley, Wordsworth, and John Ruskin visited Barmouth, on Cardigan Bay along the western coast of Wales. Senior, *Portrait*, 217.

4. Mary Richards, born in Wales about 1835, worked in the Chases' household in Columbus before the family moved to Washington. 1860 census, Franklin County, Ohio, Columbus Ward 2, 86.

5. A mass of peaks constitutes the picturesque Snowdon, highest mountain in Wales and long a popular attraction. The Watkin path, one of several routes to the top, began above the town of Beddgelert south of the mountain. Nettie and Will, as she notes later in the letter, descended on the opposite side, probably by the easily traversed Llanberis path. According to a description based on a period photograph, in the 1870s "a sort of shanty town of huts, rather like old changing sheds at a decrepit seaside," occupied the summit. Senior, *Portrait*, 106–7, 109–10, 118; Showell Styles, *The Mountains of North Wales* (London: Gollancz, 1973), 80–85, 88.

6. *Plutôt* means "rather" or "on the whole" in French; that is, the horses were more like Don Quixote's emaciated horse, Rosinante, than Alexander the Great's spirited steed, Bucephalus. Since Nettie was familiar with the works of Nathaniel Hawthorne, she probably knew Hawthorne's story "A Virtuoso's Collection," from *Mosses from an Old Manse* (1846), in which Bucephalus and Rosinante stand side-by-side in a collection of creatures from literature. Charvat et al., *Centenary Edition*, 10:478.

7. The previous December, Thomas H. Yeatman, a Cincinnati businessman and politician who had been a Treasury agent during the Civil War, sent Father a supply of Eaton Rapids Magnetic Water from a spring in Michigan. Father began drinking the water as part of his recuperative regimen. As shown by his letter to Nettie of June 5, 1871, and Kate's to him of August 29 (both below), he had decided to visit the Michigan springs. *Chase Papers*, 1:190–91, 662; 5:318.

8. Will wrote this postscript.

9. In the early stages of planning for the wedding trip, Will was "strongly inclined for Iceland." Father to Richard C. Parsons, Feb. 13, 1871 (Chase Papers, LC).

10. France went to war with Prussia in 1870, and the rule of Napoleon III came to an end in the autumn of that year when the emperor capitulated to the victorious Prussians. The city of Paris endured a terrible siege, and after an armistice ended the war, republicans and socialists in Paris who feared the country would fall back into monarchy proclaimed the Commune. From March until May 1871, when after bloody fighting the city was finally taken by troops of the French government, Paris was controlled by a revolutionary council. Sophie Guichard, *Paris 1871, la Commune* (Paris: Berg, 2006), 133–37; Geoffrey Wawro, *The Franco-Prussian War: The German Conquest of France in 1870–1871* (Cambridge: Cambridge University Press, 2003), 247–48, 276–84, 295–98.

11. This account of their trip up the mountain begins on a new page, in Nettie's handwriting and illustrated with her sketches.

12. Apparently a reference to their guide; Nettie may have been alluding to Maj. Gen. John Thomas, who in March 1776 led American troops up Dorchester Heights in a maneuver that forced the British to withdraw from Boston. Robert Middlekauff, *The Glorious Cause: The American Revolution, 1763–1789* (New York: Oxford University Press, 1982), 310–11.

13. A lightweight horse-drawn vehicle available for hire. *OED*, 5:1115.

FATHER TO NETTIE

Washington, May 22, 1871

Darling Nettie,

Two letters have come from you since my last was written—the first *sketching* your trip to Snowden to our great amusement and gratification,

& the other written from Chester on your return from Wales.[1] Katie read the first before leaving. I sent the other to her by the Governor, who took the children to her in New York on Saturday night, with the full approbation of Master Will[2] who seemed rather too happy to get away from Washington and us. The Governor only spent Sunday in New York, coming back last night & breakfasting with Col. Latham & myself this morning. Katie takes the children with her to Albany tomorrow & will pass a week there with the Pruyns after which she will take them to Narragansett.

I, as you see from the date, still linger in Washington. So far the weather has been rather coolish and very pleasant, and I am greatly interested at Edgewood. Perhaps you dont know that Katie recommended & I adopted quite a change in the plans for the reconstruction of the house, by taking the first floor above ground—the kitchen still occupying the basement—of the addition for the dining room, and taking the backroom (northwest) of the Old [Home] for butlers pantry, linen closet & back stairs. This is a great improvement: giving a very fine dining room (25 x 24) with a nice outlook front & north and much more convenient back stairs than our original plan. Now there seems little left to be desired. The portico or Verandah will be up this week: and the whole may be completed in the course of eight weeks. But I don't expect to stay here for that. On the contrary I mean to be off by the first of next week and leave the finishing in the hands of Mr. Clark. Where I shall go I leave to the decision of Dr. Bliss who is cogitating upon the subject.[3] In my next I expect to give you my summer programme pretty definitely. My health seems so much improved that I shall take any that Dr. Bliss prescribes whether in Europe Asia or America; with hardly a choice, except that Europe will give me the earliest sight of you. I hope however that if I go to Europe I may be fortunate enough to go out with the Cookes or some friends equally agreeable.

On Saturday I called at Mrs Patterson's and Mrs Admiral Goldsboroughs &, at both places you were kindly enquired for.[4] At Mrs P—— I met Mrs Aulick with her Secretary of the Navy: and also Mrs Senator Stockton. For the first time, I believe, I was presented to Mrs Aulick and found her very agreeable. She talks very well indeed and very sensibly. Mrs S—— was complaining of indisposition but looking quite well.[5] Mrs P——'s place was looking beautifully in its May dress and her strawberries and cream were very nice. At the Admiral's I was received with their usual exuberant welcome—all the pleasanter because I am sure they both like me and are always really glad to see me. They both pressed me to come again & spend a day with them before leaving town—and I half promised—Perhaps I will—The Admiral promised me some chickens of the Brahmin herd.[6] By the way tell Will he must not forget his promise of chickens though I cannot now remember the name of the variety.

Judge Field goes to California in about four weeks.[7] I believe Mrs F—— does not accompany him, but will go East somewhere possibly to

Narragansett, where the Governor informs me that New York Company will open the New House on Tower Hill about the 1st of July.[8] By the way I understand that a steamer is to ply to & fro between N—— and Newport this summer.

Mrs Bailey, Fanny, & Marcel were here last evening at the same time with Judge Field. They still hold their idea of establishing themselves at Florence next fall and staying for a year or two—I mean the female part of the family, Marcel is doing very well here. Fred, you know, on the death of his second wife, went abroad to join the French & has not, I believe, been heard from since[9]

I enclose a letter I presume from [Romaine whom] I should like to see—Love—best love to Will of which take too your share

Your loving father
S. P. Chase

Mrs J. R. C. Hoyt

Library of Congress.

1. The first letter is that of April 30 just above; we have not located the second one.
2. Willie Sprague.
3. D. W. Bliss was Father's physician in Washington in this period, and Father signed a letter to him as "Truly your friend." In July 1871, the Medical Association of the District of Columbia, which at the time admitted only allopathic physicians to membership and prohibited consultations with homeopathic physicians, African American doctors, or female practitioners, expelled Bliss for protesting those restrictions and consulting with a colleague who had been refused membership because he served on the district's new board of health, which included a homeopath. Bliss then cofounded a more inclusive medical organization. Immediately after his expulsion from the society, President Grant appointed him to the board of health, where Bliss worked not only with homeopathic doctors but also closely with the educator and attorney John Mercer Langston, whose mother had been a Virginia slave. In July 1881, Secretary of War Robert Todd Lincoln summoned Bliss after Charles Guiteau shot President James Garfield, the Chases' old friend, in a Washington railroad depot. Bliss put himself in charge of the president's care until Garfield died of infection two and a half months after the shooting. Bliss's management of Garfield's treatment was controversial, and in that instance he generally rebuffed the advice of other physicians, including homeopaths. Bliss had been a military surgeon during the Civil War, earning Walt Whitman's praise in *Specimen Days. New York Times,* July 10, 13, 1871, July 4, 5, 1881, May 5, July 6, 1888; Ira Rutkow, *James A. Garfield* (New York: Times Books, 2006), 85–86, 91–96, 101–2, 122–27, 131–35; James C. Clark, *The Murder of James A. Garfield: The President's Last Days and the Trial and Execution of His Assassin* (Jefferson, N.C.: McFarland, 1993), 61, 73–77, 94–99, 112–15, 145; John Mercer Langston, *From the Virginia Plantation to the National Capitol* (Hartford, Conn., 1894; repr., New York: Kraus Reprint, 1969), 318–34; Father to Bliss, Aug. 10, 1871 (Chase Papers, LC).
4. Elizabeth Pearson Patterson, the widow of a naval officer, lived at Brentwood, an estate in the District of Columbia once owned by her grandfather, Robert Brent. Brentwood was close enough to Edgewood for Father to call there on a walk in January 1872. *Chase Papers,* 1:667.
5. The following year Mary Isabelle Ogston Aulick, a widow, and George M. Robeson, the secretary of the navy since June 1869, married. Sarah Marks Stockton was the wife of John Potter Stockton of New Jersey, which was also Robeson's home state. Controversy tinged the political careers of both men: Stockton for his first election to the Senate, which was by a plurality rather than a majority of the state legislature and was set aside by the Senate in 1866, and Robeson for his administration of the Navy Department. *DAB*, 16:31; 18:44–45.

6. Brahma chickens, a numerous variety in the United States, were raised primarily for their meat. R. B. Sando, *American Poultry Culture: A Complete Hand Book of Practical and Profitable Poultry Keeping for the Great Army of Beginners and Small Breeders* (New York: Outing Publishing Co., 1909), 88.

7. Stephen Johnson Field, a brother of the prominent attorney David Dudley Field, was born in Connecticut in 1816 and grew up in western Massachusetts. He moved to California in 1849, won election to the state's supreme court in 1857, and became its chief justice in 1858. In 1863, Abraham Lincoln appointed him an associate justice of the U.S. Supreme Court. Field's circuit duties took him back to the West Coast annually. Sue Virginia Swearingen had married him in 1859. *ANB*, 7:893–96.

8. Tower Hill, the highest prominence inland from Narragansett Pier, was near Canonchet. The hotel that opened there in 1871 had a wide piazza running the length of the building on the ground floor, gas lighting in each room, and electric bells to summon the staff. Guests could also rent individual cottages on the hotel grounds. Two years after its completion the Tower Hill House was touted as "one of the finest hotels in the country." Watson, *Narragansett Pier,* 67–71; *A Sketch of Narragansett Pier: Its Past, Present and Future* (Wakefield, R.I.: Narragansett Times, 1888); Bacon, *Narragansett Bay,* 223–24.

9. Father had known Gamaliel and Margaret Bailey's sons—Marcellus, who was the same age as Kate, and Frederick, a year younger—since they were boys. They were their parents' eldest offspring. During the Civil War, Marcellus served as an officer in different regiments of African American soldiers, with the secretary of the Treasury keeping a watchful eye over his career advancement. He left the army in 1866. Frederick W. Bailey entered West Point in the summer of 1861 and upon graduation four years later became an infantry officer. He rose to the rank of captain, but was without an assignment in 1869 and was honorably discharged at his request in November 1870. In Europe he joined the cause of Italian nationalism, which had long interested his parents. He died in 1878. Harrold, *Bailey,* 42, 55, 71, 214; Heitman, *Historical Register,* 1:181–82; *Chase Papers,* 1:514, 593; 2:299, 300.

FATHER TO NETTIE

Washington June 5, 1871

Dearest Nettie,

Another week has passed and still no letter from you or Will. This is the third I have written since receiving one. True, Katie returned from Albany last Friday, and said that she had received a short letter from you dated London & Dora Moorhead told me Sunday Evening that her brother Will mentioned in his letter to her that you & your Will were to dine with him at Richmond.[1] So the anxiety I had begun to feel about you was measurably relieved; but I felt the want of a letter hardly the less.

Tomorrow Katie leaves for New York and Narragansett. If Dr. Bliss had advised it I should have gone with her; but he has not yet returned from Southbend or if he has, arrived only this evening & I have not yet seen him. I may see him tomorrow. Whatever he advises I shall do my impression is that he will advise the Michigan Springs and the probability is that I shall leave in that direction day after tomorrow (Wednesday) Morning.[2] At any rate my next letter will inform you of my whereabouts. In the meantime letters directed to Washington will be promptly forwarded.

This morning Albert & Bessie left for Narragansett.[3] When Katie & Col Latham go tomorrow I shall be left alone—but shall still have

[Nusby] and Mr. Lloyd with me, and York and Annie. Turner will as usual be in charge of the house. So you see the appearances indicate a general clearing out for the summer

Mr. Corcoran's health has unexpectedly & greatly improved. For two or three days past he has been wheeled into the garden and has taken the fresh air. Every body is thankful[4]

The event of this week is the departure of Capt[.] Hall and his staunch little Polaris for the Artic regions[.] We—that is Katie & I, with Gov. & Mrs Cooke and their little boys Pitt & Jay,[5] and Dora Moorhead—went down to the Navy Yard to bid him goodbye. His little ship is a marvel of compactness, convenience & strength. His officers and crew are all picked men. Buddington, the second in command, is familiar with the region & its dangers and trials.[6] Morton, another of his officers, was, you probably remember, with Dr. Kane, and saw the open Polar Sea.[7] Capt. Hall remembers, with unmerited gratitude, the early interest which I took in his original enterprise, more than ten years ago, and took leave of me with more than ordinary feeling; which was even more than reciprocated.[8] God grant that he may return successful to his[9] highest hopes.

Leaving Capt Hall we made a short call on Mrs Goldsborough. and I am to take dinner with them when they take their lunch tomorrow

But I must close. It is time to get ready for bed, So with ever so much love for you and your dear husband I remain

Your affectionate father
S P Chase

Mrs Janet R. C. Hoyt

Library of Congress.

1. Richmond, on the Surrey side of the Thames, had been the location of Henry VII's royal palace, demolished in the eighteenth century, and of the 2,000-acre Richmond Park laid out in the reign of Charles I. Hotels and residences built in the 1700s marked the locale as a fashionable gathering place, which it remained through much of the nineteenth century. Dora Moorhead and her brother William E. C. Moorhead had been at Gibraltar, Jay Cooke's summer residence at Put-in-Bay, Ohio, when Father and Nettie visited in the summer of 1870. Dora and Will were the daughter and the son of Sarah Cooke Moorhead, Jay Cooke's and Henry Cooke's sister, and William G. Moorhead. In 1869, the younger William Moorhead had accompanied an inspection party sent by the Cookes to view the prospective route of the Northern Pacific Railroad. He obtained a position in a branch of the Cooke family's banking firm that opened in London early in 1871. Christopher Trent, *Greater London: Its Growth and Development through Two Thousand Years* (London: Phoenix House, 1965), 116, 118, 131, 149–50, 228, 235; Oberholtzer, *Cooke*, 1:40, 101–2; 2:113–15, 124, 202, 206–7; *Chase Papers*, 1:654–57.

2. On June 7, Father hoped to leave that day or the next for St. Louis, Mich., and arrive there the following week. Mineral springs in central Michigan, which quickly became resort spots with hotels for health-seeking visitors, had first opened in 1869. That year a well sunk at St. Louis, in Gratiot County, in search of salt-bearing water yielded instead an alkaline water that was soon claimed to have healthful magnetic properties. By 1873, St. Louis would offer visitors a bath house supervised by a resident physician and four hotels with room for several thousand guests. Other locales experienced a similar rapid development, including Eaton Rapids, from which Father had received a shipment of water sent by Thomas Yeatman in 1870. By 1873 that town had seven hotels, each associated with a mineral well. Father's interest in St. Louis springs may have come from a suggestion by

Gen. Joseph Hooker. Father to Joseph Hooker, November 29, 1870; Father to Jacob W. Schuckers, June 7, 1871 (Chase Papers, LC); Charles Richard Tuttle, comp., *General History of the State of Michigan* (Detroit: R.D.S. Tyler & Co., 1873), 658–63; A. N. Bell, *Climatology and Mineral Waters of the United States* (New York: Wood, 1885), 176–77.

3. W. Albert Wells and, apparently, another employee named Bessie.

4. W. W. Corcoran was in ailing health through much of the spring, apparently from infection associated with erysipelas. His condition attracted considerable notice, including a recipe for a home remedy supplied by First Lady Julia Dent Grant. Corcoran's country estate, Harewood, was not far from Edgewood, and in February 1873 Father made Corcoran a gift of radishes from Edgewood's gardens. [W. W. Corcoran], *A Grandfather's Legacy; Containing a Sketch of his Life* (Washington, D.C.: H. Polkinhorn, 1879), 339–49, 417; Goode, *Capital Losses*, 76, 348.

5. Henry D. Cooke was the territorial governor of the District of Columbia, 1871–73. *Chase Papers*, 1:532.

6. The *Polaris*, formerly the steam tug *Periwinkle*, had been fitted out at the Washington Navy Yard to meet Arctic conditions and carry a government-sponsored attempt by Charles Francis Hall to reach the North Pole. The expedition left Washington on June 10. On August 30, the explorers attained a latitude of 82° 11', farther north than any previous ship had reached. Turned back by ice, they found meager winter shelter along the coast of Greenland. Hall died in November 1871 after an apparent stroke, although some questions about his death were never resolved. Command of the vessel fell to the master of the *Polaris*, Sidney O. Budington (or Buddington). He had commanded a ship on an earlier exploration by Hall, but on the *Polaris* there had been friction between the two, and between Hall and others, including the medical officer. Discipline eroded under Budington, who abandoned the damaged ship. The remnants of the expedition, separated by a storm, were rescued in 1873. An official inquiry documented the expedition's troubles but took no action against Budington. Chauncey C. Loomis, *Weird and Tragic Shores: The Story of Charles Francis Hall, Explorer* (New York: Knopf, 1971), 248, 255, 257, 260, 265–68, 273–330, 344–53; *DAB*, 8:120–21; *Appletons'*, 7:40.

7. William Morton, an Irish-born Navy yeoman with considerable experience, was second mate of the *Polaris*. He had been steward and personal aide to the acclaimed Arctic explorer Elisha Kent Kane. Returning to Kane's ship *Advance* from a scouting trip in 1854, Morton reported that he had seen water free of ice above 81° latitude. That report lent credence to an erroneous theory that the northern polar region was covered by open sea. Father, and likely Kate and Nettie, met Morton after Kane's death in 1857. The explorer's remains were transported with great ceremony from New Orleans to Philadelphia, and Father as governor of Ohio played a role in the tribute in Columbus. For a while afterward, Morton served as the costumed narrator of a traveling "Panorama of Dr. Kane's Arctic Voyage." George W. Corner, *Doctor Kane of the Arctic Seas* (Philadelphia: Temple University Press, 1972), 119–20, 126, 165–67, 275; Loomis, *Weird and Tragic Shores*, 252–53, 257; *ANB*, 12:368–69; *Chase Papers*, 1:274–75.

8. Hall lacked scientific training or military experience but proved an energetic recruiter of political and financial backing. A native of New Hampshire, he had arrived in Cincinnati in 1849, fell into the business of making seals to emboss documents, then by the late 1850s published newspapers that promoted Arctic exploration, balloon flight, the trans-Atlantic telegraphic cable, and similar endeavors. When Hall first sought to organize his own Arctic expeditions in the late 1850s, Father signed a petition of support, and on other occasions also the explorer sought his patronage. Loomis, *Weird and Tragic Shores*, 27–37, 46–47, 148, 158, 233, 235–43; *DAB*, 8:120–21.

9. Father wrote "his his," at the break of a line in the manuscript.

KATE TO FATHER

Narragansett 29. Aug. 1871.

Dearest Father

I have just had your last letter enclosing Circulars &c from the Springs which I send at once to Dr. Perry[1]—Mr. Coates whom you will remember as our nearest winter neighbor, has a bachelor brother who was prostrated a month or two since by an illness which in many of its outward manifestations was much like your attack, & it occurred to me that the Dr. would recommend for him some of the water bottled & drank here.[2] If he does, I will write & ask you to have a case sent to him—

Two letters have come for you within a day or two, which I enclose. I have had another very charming letter from dear Nettie a Birthday greeting.[3] I was so pleased that she remembered to think of me on that day. I fear I am a good deal of a child about such things yet, though the yearning for love is hardly one of the childish things one would wish to put away—Enclosed in Nettie's letter was a Photograph of herself & Will taken together, which I think excellent, better than the one of Nettie alone you send, I would send it out to you, on the supposition you had not seen it, but it came to me so badly crushed that I took it off the card, & pasted it into my Album—Mr. Throop[4] sent me his Photograph of a large group taken at St. Louis in which you are both distinguished and distinguishable, but not flattered & I confess that neither from closely scanning your face as presented in full, & in profile on Mr. Throop's coat sleeve, could I make up my mind that you had grown handsomer under the magic of these magnetic waters. There is a Mineral Spring some-where in the Swiss Mountains, where—(the guide book assures one—) the effect is to "make one enamored of oneself—Is this the effect at Bathsheba?[5]

I have a letter too from Mrs Hamilton Smith from "Durham," saying they were ready now to come to me—But she gave me no address but Durham, & the Post mark consisted of two or three letters & the date & threw no light on their whereabouts[6]—The Governor said it was in Mass. & I sent my letter there, but have had no reply, & fear I am not right in the direction—Tomorrow I shall try telegraphing—

You say nothing in your letter about the death (& circumstances attending it of Mrs. Jay Cooke. I am anxious to have your advise in regard to my writing to Mr. Cooke. I have thought of him & his family very often since I read of their bereavement.[7]

You will probably have seen (still I cut it out and send it you) an article in the N.Y. Herald, advocating a Mutual friend of ours for the next Presidency[8]—If you meet him in your travels, advise him not to make too many speeches, or attend too many celebrations of one sort or another, but to devote all his energies for a while to getting quite well, that he may yet live a long while to gladden the hearts of his children & if need be serve his Country—

My little curly-headed girl[9] came to me to-day, with the paper-weight containing your Photograph (& which I always keep on the table before me, though Willie claims you gave it to him—) & said "I want Grandpa Chase to pum, (read come)—I hurrah for Bubnor Sprague, & I hurrah for Chase—" Her sentence was a little less connected but that was what she intended—When I tell you that after mashing her "Poupet's" nose the other day, she came to me to "wipe the tears from sorrow's Eyes" you will not wonder that her little tongue is so ready—She is only twenty-two months old, & she has many of Mother Goose's Melodies, as well as such Epics as "Good bye John", & "Up in a Balloon" quite pat[10]—Willie has been made proud & happy by having received from his Aunt Nettie a miniature mitrailleuse which I have the honor to be saluted by most every morning before I am up & find ready cocked & elevated for the purpose, at night, at the foot of Willies bed,—beside my own[11]—

I am at the End of my sheet, & it is growing late. I am *angling* a little for better terms for your site on Narragansett Height—I will attend to it you may depend[12]—

Devotedly
Katie

Please remember me to Mr. Schuckers. Perhaps I will go with you to Peterboro, if you will let me know just when you will be there[13]—

1. Father liked the St. Louis springs well enough, but not the area's summer climate, which he thought was conducive to fevers and ague. Falling victim to what he characterized as a relatively mild version of such an ailment (treated with quinine), he left Michigan in the latter part of July. Traveling to Waukesha, Wis., west of Milwaukee, he expected to stay there one day but found the Bethesda Springs so appealing that he fell into a regimen of "simple diet & open air exercise" and lingered until at least the second week of September. Perhaps the circulars he had sent were copies of Richard Dunbar's tract, *Dunbar's Wonderful Discovery! The Waukesha Bethesda Mineral Water of Waukesha, Wisconsin: Directions for Using It,* published in 1871. Father to Gerrit Smith, Sept. 1 and 9, and to Henry D. Cooke, Sept. 1, 1871 (Chase Papers, LC); to Whitelaw Reid, Sept. 1, 1871 (Reid Papers, LC); Lillian Krueger, "Waukesha, 'The Saratoga of the West,'" *Wisconsin Magazine of History* 24 (1941): 394–424.

2. A mineral spring, "according to the neighboring inhabitants possessing wonderful virtue," was located in the hills inland from Narragansett Beach. Watson, *Narragansett Pier,* 68.

3. Kate had turned thirty-one on August 13.

4. Perhaps New York attorney Montgomery Hunt Throop, who revised that state's law statutes and compiled other legal works. *DAB,* 18:511–12.

5. Kate likely meant "Bethesda," the name Dunbar gave to the Waukesha springs as he began to develop them in the late 1860s. The name is shared by a church and its neighborhood in Waukesha County. Krueger, "Waukesha," 395; Robert E. Gard and L. G. Corden, *The Romance of Wisconsin Place Names* (New York: October House, 1968), 11.

6. Probably Durham, N.H., Hamilton Smith's native town. George Thomas Chapman, *Sketches of the Alumni of Dartmouth College* (Cambridge, Mass.: Riverside Press, 1867), 250.

7. Dorothea Elizabeth Allen Cooke had succumbed to heart disease on July 22. The previous month her husband had taken her to recuperate at their summer home in the Lake Erie islands, but when she failed to improve he brought her back, much of the way by private rail car, to Ogontz, where she died. Oberholtzer, *Cooke,* 2:293; *New York Times,* July 24, 1871.

8. On August 24, James Gordon Bennett's *New York Herald,* having a few days earlier mockingly declared Horace Greeley's hopes for an alternative Republican presidential nomination dead, proposed Father as a "new departure of the democratic party," the only chance to unseat the incumbent, Ulysses Grant, in the 1872 presidential election. Touting

the importance of the votes of Southern blacks and moderates, the newspaper reminded its readers that the *Herald* had supported a Chase candidacy in 1868, only to watch as the Democratic convention, "after coquetting with him as a doubting damsel dallies with a new lover, or as a cat plays with a mouse, cruelly sacrificed him." The chief justice could provide the Democratic Party with "a new man . . . completely detaching the party from its dead men and dead issues." *New York Herald,* Aug. 21, 24, 1871; *Chase Papers,* 5:312.

9. Ethel.

10. "Up in a Balloon," a popular song written by G. W. Hunt, first appeared in England in 1868. Mrs. Agnes Power wrote a set of lyrics especially for women, and the work became part of the repertoire of several performers. In 1869, Henry B. Farnie wrote American lyrics for the song. Though not as well documented, "Good Bye John" was also the title of at least one song, composed by J. B. Kimball and published by Henry De Marsan in New York early in the 1860s. Michael Kilgarriff, comp., *Sing Us One of the Old Songs: A Guide to Popular Song, 1860–1920* (Oxford: Oxford University Press, 1998), 95, 268, 434, 458, 506, 556.

11. The Montigny *mitrailleuse* was an early model of a machine gun first employed by the French, although not very effectively, in the Franco-Prussian War of 1870. John Ellis, *The Social History of the Machine Gun* (New York: Pantheon Books, 1975), 63–64; Roger Ford, *The Grim Reaper: The Machine-Gun and Machine-Gunners* (London: Sidgwick & Jackson, 1996), 8–10.

12. Canonchet was on a low ridge of land inland from the beach. Behind it, on somewhat higher ground that included Tower Hill and was called Narragansett Heights, a land development company laid out building sites for summer homes and "villas." Watson, *Narragansett Pier,* 67–69; Bacon, *Narragansett Bay,* 223.

13. For almost thirty years Father had maintained a relationship of warm camaraderie with the noted abolitionist and reformer Gerrit Smith, who lived in Peterboro, Madison County, N.Y. Father hoped to take in Peterboro on his return from the Midwest and thought that Smith might persuade Kate to rendezvous with him there. *ANB,* 20:187–88; *Chase Papers,* 2:96–99; 5:269–71, 278–80, 367; Father to Smith, Sept. 1, 4, and 9, 1871 (Chase Papers, LC).

FATHER TO NETTIE

Washington, Oct. 14, 1871

Dearest Nettie,

We arrived here, safe & sound, yesterday evening. As prearranged we spent one whole day and parts of two others in Philadelphia looking at carpets &c. I was very much taken with some wood carpets, which imitate such rooms as Mr. Hoyt's billiard room in a great variety of styles and at an expense quite moderate as compared with that incurred by rice: but oil cloth was finally determined on on the score of beauty & cost. And we selected a carpet for the dining room which I think rather prettier than the one we saw at Sloans, tho I believe the cost $2.50 per yard was a little more.[1] This leaves very little to be done in the way of selection—hardly any thing indeed except a stair carpet perhaps and a carpet for one of the chambers. Today we have been at Edgewood with Susan Walker & by appointment met Mr. Clark there. The house looks well—solid & substantial & large without show or pretension. I should like I confess a little more beauty and ornament, but am content. The library and the bedroom above are ready for occupancy, pa[pe]red & furnished complete. Both are really handsome rooms & look as if one might take genuine comfort in both, in one for the mind & in the other for the body. The dining room will all be finished in about a week—& then there will be two rooms to comfort the body in; though, on the whole I think the mind & the body ought to go halves in the dining room. It will take two or three weeks to finish the whole, and then I hope that you & Will will come & see me.

[I] have lost the bathing tub with one of my bath towels and some other things. Will you have them replaced & sent me by Adams & Co Express. [The] towel was bot at Stewarts & cost six dollars[2]—you know where the bath tub can be procured.

I left a Volume of Penna. Reports at Mr. Hoyt's.[3] Please send it also by Adams Express, each article in separate packages

Love to Will & best regards to Mr. Hoyt & kind remembrances to Miss Fenne.

I hope your cold & Wills ailments are gone

Mo. affy. yr. father
S P Chase

Library of Congress.

1. The carpet store of William and John Sloane occupied 649, 651, and 655 Broadway in Manhattan, and the firm played a significant role in the wholesale and retail carpet trade into the 1890s. Wilson, *Trow's New York City Directory, For . . . 1872*, 1068; John S. Ewing and Nancy P. Norton, *Broadlooms and Businessmen: A History of the Bigelow-Sanford Carpet Company* (Cambridge, Mass.: Harvard University Press, 1955), 65, 93–95, 136, 141, 143, 149, 164, 196, 218.

2. At the time, Alexander T. Stewart's dry goods firm had locations at 272 and 784 Broadway in New York. In December 1872, Father dined at Stewart's "magnificent" new house. Wilson, *Trow's New York City Directory, For . . . 1872*, 1107; *Chase Papers*, 1:708.

3. Probably a volume of the *Reports of Cases Adjudged in the Supreme Court of Pennsylvania*, which Father may have consulted in connection with the Pennsylvania College Cases. The Supreme Court heard arguments in that group of three cases, which asked whether the state of Pennsylvania had violated the contract clause in the merger of two colleges, in January 1872. John William Wallace, *Cases Argued and Adjudged in the Supreme Court of the United States*, vol. 13 (Washington, D.C.: W. H. & O. H. Morrison, 1872), 190–222; Fairman, *Reconstruction and Reunion*, 1349.

NETTIE TO FATHER

Saturday
Jan 6th 1872

Dearest Father,

Your very welcome note told me that you had safely reached Washington but not that you had gone directly out to Edgewood,[1] that Jennie Sister's maid told us for Annie the nurse had an accident to her foot & Sister wrote for her maid. The busy little legs of Miss Ethel & Willie require some one to follow them about but of course you have seen Sister & the bairns by this time

We are leading a very quiet humdrum sort of a life. but I rather like it, Aunt Charlotte & I read sew walk & drive during the day & in the evening Will comes home and he generally reads to us until bed time.[2]

We are reading now Lord Bantum an english satire on the existing state of things—and yet not an illnatured satire either, recognizing the good where ever it is to be found—a book calculated to do good I think although the subject does not bring it so immediately under our own experiences as did the author's first work "Ginx's baby"—still, I think the Lord B—— would please you[3]

I do hope yr wintering in the country will be as pleasant to you as mine, thus far has been to me—How does it promise so far? Pray do not be too indifferent as to how yr meals are cooked, and do write to me exactly how it all agrees with you—Will told me to tell you that the advertisement Mrs Clements spoke of was a package belonging to a Mrs Warden & that it did not answer the description of yr lost property in the least—I am so sorry that both of yr Astoria trips should have been so unlucky

Did you receive any calls New Years? we of course had none. Sister went in town early in the morning with the children and I did not see her again I suppose she went on to Washington Thursday—

Aunt Charlotte & Will both send love and with a good night kiss

I am yr ever loving daughter
Nettie

On monogrammed stationery with interlocked JRCH crest. Library of Congress.

1. Father had visited Astoria and returned to Washington and Edgewood on December 27. Father to Hiram Barney, Jan. 4, 1872 (Barney Papers, Huntington Library).

2. Charlotte Chambers Ludlow Jones was no doubt visiting in anticipation of the birth of Nettie's baby.

3. English politician and writer John Edward Jenkins, who had been educated in Canada and the United States, achieved far greater popular success with his first satire, *Ginx's Baby; his Birth and Other Misfortunes,* which he published anonymously in 1870, than he did with a number of subsequent works. The book, which centered on competition over the religious education of a child, was followed by *Lord Bantam,* a political satire, in 1871. *ODNB,* 29:956.

FATHER TO NETTIE

Washington, (Edgewood)
Feb. 4, 1872

Dearest Nettie,

Your letter was made doubly welcome by the fact that you wrote it yourself, and yet I could not help regretting the effort you made when I found that it was written in bed, and that even with a pencil it gave you so much labor. How sick you must have been, dear child. I have not realized how much you must have suffered.[1]

If you were only as much favored in this respect as Katie! It seems almost a luxury to her to have children. On Friday morning—the day your letter is dated—I went into the city to attend Court not dreaming of the tidings that awaited me. At the door of our reception room in the

Capitol Prentice Tucker met me with the news that Katie had given birth to my fourth grandchild![2] I was the more surprised because Katie had been at Edgewood Thursday Evening, and, of course, less than twelve hours had elapsed since she left my house before the baby was born. Eliza Whipple told me yesterday that she had written a full account of all particulars to you. I have not been in town today, not feeling very well, and Alice Walbridge and a young Mr Comstock who came out with her last evening, wishing to go.[3] So I put them in care of Mr Lloyd and remained at home myself. Mr. Lloyd brought me your letter and I am answering it even though I shall not be able to mail until tomorrow

Lily Walbridge is staying with me at present. She is a sweet girl and a great acquisition. I mean to keep her as long as I can / Alice talks of going to Japan as a teacher. The Japanese government is making arrangements for a corps of lady teachers & Alice is quite taken with the idea of being one of them. Prof Henry, who has been consulted by Mr. Mori, the Japanese Minister & who gives employment to Alice as a copyist, rather favors the notion. I should not be surprised however if young Mr. Comstock proves a serious obstacle.[4]

The snow fell heavily night before last, & yesterday: The ground is covered. The two ashes in front of the house were resplendent this morning in the sunlight. I wish you could see it—though the prospect here is not to be compared with that you enjoy. Still we think it very fine.

I have had quite a revolution in my household. Cassie and Mrs Hardin could not get on together; so I concluded to give up Mrs H—— and this involved, as [I] found, the necessity of parting with Mr Hardin took[5] and, of course, Fanny went with them.[6] Now I have colored servants altogether, three for the place, William & a young nephew of his for the house, Cassie for Chambermaid & general overlooker & a cook.[7] We get along with these pretty well. Last night our gas, to our great comfort, worked well; and I have hopes that all will go right for the future.[8] Nothing remains now, but to put up the mirrors & pictures (all here) and I shall be as well fixed as my means & present leanings permit. Did I mention in my last that I have at last received the clock case. The works had preceded it but are not put up yet. It is a quaint affair & reminds me of a little old woman without hoops.

Excuse my writing. It looks to me rather worse than usual

Love to Will and Aunt Charlotte—tell both to write—and kisses for little Nettie

Most affectionately your father
S P Chase

Library of Congress.

1. Will Hoyt's first news of the birth of the baby Janet on January 14, a telegram from New York, said nothing of a difficult labor or delivery, although he did refer to the size of the ten-pound newborn. His initial report was that the new mother was "doing well." Subsequent word from Will gave Father to understand that Nettie was not recovering as quickly as

she might, and Father advised her not to exert herself. *Chase Papers,* 1:668; Father to Nettie, Jan. 23, 1872 (Chase Papers, LC).

2. By inference, Kate's baby was born on Friday, Feb. 2, 1872. According to most biographers, this child was Portia (see the chapter introduction).

3. Nettie's and Kate's cousin Alice Walbridge called frequently at Edgewood during January and February 1872. Since sometime in the previous year she had been employed as a clerk in the Smithsonian Institution, of which Joseph Henry was secretary and Father the chancellor. She left that position in March 1873. *Chase Papers,* 1:665, 667, 668, 671, 672; 5:145, 300; Employees File (Smithsonian Institution Archives); Joseph Henry, letter of recommendation, Feb. 18, 1873 (Smithsonian Institution Archives, Outgoing Correspondence, Office of the Secretary); Alice Walbridge to Henry, Mar. 15, 1873 (Smithsonian Institution Archives, Incoming Correspondence, Office of the Secretary).

4. Education was one object of interest to the Iwakura embassy, a party of Japanese diplomats who arrived in the United States in December 1871. Japan later adopted a system of universal education, with David Murray, a professor at Rutgers College, advising the government on teacher training. Mori Arinori (1847–89) was chargé d'affaires of the Japanese legation in Washington but sometimes used the title "minister resident." Mori had studied in the United States and England. His brash manner and advocacy of rapid westernization for Japan sometimes put him in conflict with members of the Iwakura mission. Sidney Devere Brown and Akiko Hirota, trans., *The Diary of Kido Takayoshi,* 3 vols. (Tokyo: University of Tokyo Press, 1983–86), 1:xviii, xx–xxi, xxiii, 133, 167, 181; Charles Lanman, *The Japanese in America* (Tokyo: Japan Advertiser Press, 1926), 41–42.

5. So in the original, although he must have meant "too."

6. The Hardins (also written Harden, Harding) had been in Father's employ and worked at Edgewood since 1870. Fanny, who was probably a housemaid and whose last name is not known, was the lowest-paid member of the staff at Edgewood, earning six dollars per month. At twenty-five dollars a month, Mr. Hardin was the highest paid employee, and his wife's wages were ten dollars. *Chase Papers,* 1:663, 665, 667; financial memoranda in 1872 journal (Chase Papers, HSP).

7. At the time, the three outdoor workers were probably Henry Williams, William Waters, and Robert Warren. Williams had more decision-making authority than the others, sold Edgewood's produce, and became the operator of the estate's new gas-making apparatus. Waters and Warren, who each made twelve dollars at the beginning of the year and fifteen dollars by April, left or were discharged early in the spring of 1872, to be replaced by William Chase (who had no evident relationship to his employer) and John Pendleton. During the spring and summer, Henry Williams's regular monthly wages were thirty dollars, Chase's twenty, and Pendleton's eighteen. William Joice's nephew has not been identified. The cook, generally referred to in the records by her function rather than her name, may have been named Catherine White. She and Cassie Vaudry both received eight dollars per month in wages at the beginning of 1872 and ten dollars by April, when the cook left her position at Edgewood. *Chase Papers,* 1:667, 674, 676; "Farm Notes," 1872 (Chase Papers, LC); financial memoranda, 1872 journal (Chase Papers, HSP).

8. The new gashouse at Edgewood extracted gas from coal and stored it in a tank within a cistern of water for use in illuminating the residence. The system was initially plagued by leaks in the cistern, and during January Father had called on the expertise of U.S. Navy engineers to solve the problem. *Chase Papers,* 1:664–66, 670.

FATHER TO NETTIE

Edgewood, Mar. 8, 1872

My darling Nettie,

We have just breakfasted, Mr Lloyd, Cousin[1] & Eliza Whipple & I, and it is now 9 o'clock, & I give a few moments to you before making ready to go into the City.

I can hardly tell you how much your last gratified me. That you have been again out of doors is a most welcome proof of your convalescence:

and I hope you will be very careful to do nothing to retard it. I am so thankful that you have such a kind & thoughtful husband. You can never love him enough, & he seems more like an own son than a son merely in law. Give my warmest love to him

With great pleasure do I look forward to seeing you. I hoped to come this week, but the Court will sit in conference tomorrow & probably on Monday also, and I expect to be retained here on Tuesday. On Wednesday or Thursday I expect, if alive & well enough, to come to you.

We have had very cold & snowy weather for the past six days. The only pleasant day in March so far, was the first. My farm work goes on slowly of course; but I hope to have something to show you when you come in April or May.[2]

The Japanese are all the rage just now. Last Thursday they held a reception for the judges At the Arlington. I went of course. Three of them besides their secretaries received us. Mr. Mori, the chargè, was also with them. They stood,—first, Iwakura, an oldish, short, man, with an intelligent face; next a privy Counsellor of the Mikado; & next the minister of Finance[3]

Must break off abruptly.

> Most affy your father
> S: P: Chase

Library of Congress.

1. Probably Lillie Walbridge.

2. Although no real farmer, Father did put his Edgewood property to more than ornamental use. In March 1872, the garden contained, or would receive for cultivation in the coming weeks, potatoes, parsnips, turnips, carrots, onions, asparagus, cabbage, lettuce, eggplant, tomatoes, corn, okra, squash, cucumbers, melons, various beans, strawberries, and blackberries. Some of the vegetables were started in hothouses or protected beds; the property had grapevines, an orchard, and fields or meadows of hay, clover, oats, and grass. About the time he wrote this letter, the three men who did the outdoor labor were busy manuring, cutting and removing brush and wood, filling hollows, and trying to establish the regular generation of illuminating gas for the house. Father also had them plant a variety of hardwood trees later in the spring. "Farm Notes," 1872 (Chase Papers, LC).

3. The Iwakura mission, which visited several European nations as well as the United States, gathered information about forms of government, commerce, and other subjects and hoped to negotiate new treaties. The group, which stayed at the Arlington Hotel on Vermont Avenue and some nearby buildings, consisted of five associate ambassadors, several secretaries, and others. The embassy took the name of its senior diplomat, Iwakura Tomomi (b. 1825), a noble who played an important role in the Meiji Restoration and was a deputy chancellor in the imperial government. The other associate ambassadors at the reception for the Supreme Court were Kido Takayoshi (b. 1833), a member of the imperial council, and Okubo Toshimichi (b. 1830), who had been appointed minister of finance a few months before the group's departure for the United States. They had worked cooperatively in the restoration of the emperor to direct rule in 1868 and the dismantling of the feudal system in 1871. The highest-ranking secretaries of the Iwakura embassy were Tanabe Yasukazu, Ga Noriyuki, Shioda Atsunobu, and Fukuchi Gen'ichiro. Father entertained several of the Japanese diplomats, the president and Mrs. Grant, Kate, and others at dinner at Edgewood on May 25. Brown and Akiko Hirota, *Diary of Kido*, 1:xv, 3, 64; 2: xvii–xviii, xxi, xxiv–xxv, xxvi, 68, 133, 168; Lanman, *Japanese in America*, 8, 37–41; *Chase Papers*, 1:683–84.

FATHER TO NETTIE

601 E St[1] Mar 20.

Dearest Nettie

A letter addressed to Prentice at Boston will be sure to reach him—
J. Prentice Tucker, Boston Mass / I don't know the Street, and it is of no
consequence

I reached Washn at 5—dined at Katie's—& went straight home,
taking Lily with me & found all well.[2] The China has come safe. The
Bible will be sent you tomorrow or next day by Express (Adams).

Love Will! It would be strange if I did not. He is every way worthy of it;
and then he is so judiciously kind to you & thoughtful of your every want

I look forward to your visit eagerly / But the March winds are I fear
too blustry

In haste,

Your always affe father
S P Chase

Library of Congress.

1. Kate had a room available for her father's use in the house at 6th and E, although
he generally tried to return to Edgewood after evening events in Washington. Father to
Nettie, Jan. 23, 1872 (Chase Papers, LC).
2. He had been to see Nettie. Despite the personal nature of his visit, "three gentlemen found their way" to Astoria from Manhattan to see him about politics. *Chase Papers,*
5:352–54.

FATHER TO NETTIE

Edgewood, May 20, 1872

My darling Nettie,

How careless you are! You have not even mentioned whether you received your mothers Bible, which I sent by Express or not?

As to the dinner set I should not mind about adding a hundred dollars to the price if I could get a *satisfactory* set. The bill for the one I have
is $150.00 and I think there was one expected, which seemed to me very
pretty, priced at $230 to $240.

I am quite in earnest about going to Europe: and should like to be
fully posted by those who have Experience, as Will has, as to best state-
room &c, &c. I go, if at all, to attend the Prison Discipline Conference at
London,[1] and several of the Lines give round tickets, the White Star at
$125 gold; the Inman at $120.00; the National at $100 Currency / The
Cunard has not yet agreed to give round trip tickets.[2]

Lily leaves me this week. I shall miss her much—She & Carrie Moulton[3] & Alice were with me yesterday. All well at corner of E & 6th.

Love to Will & kisses for Janet Jr. How does Pelham, & the house in town.[4]

Do you ever see Dr. Perry. I want to have his advice before going

Most affy. your father

S. P. Chase

If I go to England I want to leave Washn by the 18th[5] & New York about the 20th June.

Library of Congress.

1. The International Penitentiary Congress, which considered issues relating to prisons, reformatories, and punishment, convened in London in July 1872. Father was writing an introduction for a new edition of Edward Livingston's *A Code of Reform and Prison Discipline* brought out by the National Prison Association in anticipation of the meeting. Father did not attend the London conference. *Chase Papers,* 1:681–82, 684–85, 687; 5:361, 362.

2. The Cunard company advertised one-way cabin passage from New York to Britain at $80 to $130 in gold. The fare to Liverpool on the weekly trips of the White Star Line was comparable, $80 gold, and cost $75 in gold on the semiweekly departures of the Royal Mail steamers of the Inman company (each of those lines offered steerage passage at $30 currency). The National line, with departures for Liverpool every week and directly to London every two weeks, posted fares of $65 to $75 in currency for cabins ($28 for steerage). *New York Times,* May 20, 1872.

3. Caroline Chase Moulton, born in Randolph, Vt., in 1817 and later a resident of Keene, N.H., addressed Father as "Cousin." She was a great-granddaughter of one of his aunts, Alice Chase Cotton. Carrie Moulton solicited the chief justice's help in finding government employment in Washington and took a position with the Agriculture Department. *The Illustrated Historical Souvenir of Randolph, Vermont* (Randolph, Vt.: Nickerson & Cox, 1895), 76; William H. Child, *History of the Town of Cornish New Hampshire with Genealogical Record, 1763–1910,* 2 vols. (Concord, N.H.: Rumford Press, [1911?]), 2:62; *Chase Papers,* 1:663; Moulton to Father, Oct. 14, 1868, and "Family Memoranda" (Chase Papers, LC).

4. Nettie and Will were making a transition from the Manhattan residence of Will's father, at 94 Fifth Avenue, and the Hoyt family's suburban house in Astoria to residences of their own, on 33d Street near Fifth Avenue in Manhattan and at Pelham, on Long Island Sound between Westchester and New Rochelle. In 1875, a promotional tract boasted that Pelham had "many of New York's wealthiest and most prominent citizens" as summer residents. Pelham could be reached from Manhattan by two rail connections: on the main line of the New York, New Haven, and Hartford Railroad, the Pelhamville station was fifteen miles from Grand Central Station, while the Pelham Manor stop on the Harlem River Branch Railroad was ten miles from a dock on the Harlem River at Morrisania. From that landing, steamboats of the Morrisania Steamboat Company plied the East River as far down as Fulton Market, and Astoria was a regular stop several times during the day. After visiting Nettie and Will Hoyt in Pelham later in 1872, Father departed for New York from New Rochelle, where the two rail lines met and which may have been closer to the Hoyts' house than the stops in Pelham proper. Nettie's letter of "Sunday evening," below; *Homes on the Sound for New York Business Men* (New York: George L. Catlin, 1875), 17–18, 23–26, 34, 37–38; Scharf, *History of Westchester County,* 1:520, 708; Wilson, *Trow's New York City Directory, For . . . 1873,* 576; *Chase Papers,* 1:688, 701.

5. Father first wrote "17," then changed it to "18."

FATHER TO NETTIE

Washington, Decr. 15, 1872

My darling Nettie

Not a word from you or Will since I came from New York![1] "Nor from you, Sir!" you may rejoin, or might have rejoined before receiving this. I confess my delinquency, but it is palliated on my part by the difficulty I find in writing & the length of time I am obliged to give to a letter.

However I do the best I can: nobody can do more.

Your sister writes that she will not be in Washington before the 10th of January & of course cannot join the contemplated Christmas party at Edgewood. And I begin to fear that the road will not be completed so as to give you a tolerable approach in time to make your visit there an agreeable one. It is in a very bad condition at present. I am in the City at Katies, and do not propose to go out unless you will come & prefer staying there to staying here. I can make you quite comfortable except as to the road. The house is open and all the servants are with me there or here. Pray write me immediately whether you will prefer? I can, with perfect convenience receive you here. The governor will not come till the 10th January till which time both houses will be kept by me & you can take your choice. You will be nearer those who love you in town than in Country. If the absence of Katie and the children makes you incline to postpone your visit later in the winter I will acquiesce without grumbling. Only let me know at once.

The Court has ordered a recess from Friday next till the Monday after New Years,—sixteen days—which will give me quite a rest.

Mr. & Mr. Bridge were here today but I had not returned from Church & did not see them. Carrie Moulton told me that Mrs B—— enquired very kindly after you.[2]

Col Parsons as you know has been elected to Congress from Cleveland & has resigned the Marshalship. Mr. Nicolay was elected in his place. The Court would not give me the man I preferred Mr. Schley; but Mr. N—— was my second choice, & worthy to be first. So I am almost satisfied.[3]

I took Carrie and Amy out to Edgewood yesterday.[4] A week or two of fine weather are needed to put the road into fair condition. My barn or stable is nearly finished, to the great comfort of my cows & horses. While I was examining their quarters, Mr. Sumner & Mr. Hooper made their appearance. Both looked very well, though neither is so in reality. Mr. S—— had by no means forgotten you.

But I must stop. Goodbye. Love to Will & kisses for little Jennie.[5]

I must not omit to advise you to attend Prof. Tyndalls lectures. They are really wonderful. Get seats where you can *see* well—nearly or quite in front of the Speaker & not very far off so that you can observe the experiments.[6]

Most affectionately your father
S. P. Chase

Library of Congress.

1. Father had gone to Pelham and New York City the latter part of November. Greeted on the morning of the thirtieth with the news that Horace Greeley had died, he

stayed in New York to serve as a pallbearer at Greeley's funeral, then returned to Washington on December 5. He had spent the entire summer of 1872, during the Supreme Court's recess, away from the capital city. In June, although ill with fever and chills, he stayed in New York for a few days, where he saw Dr. Perry, and then he went on to Narragansett. There Nettie, Will, and baby Janet made a visit. Father was not in good health, but he recovered well enough to go to Boston under William Sprague's escort for the World's Peace Jubilee, a music festival, and he stayed on to visit friends in the area. He spent much of August, and into September, with J. Prentice Tucker's family at a cottage in New Hampshire. During September he returned to Rhode Island, then went to Pelham for a few days. After a trip to Philadelphia in October he returned to Washington for the court's new term. *Chase Papers,* 1:687–709.

  2. Later in the month Horatio and Charlotte Marshall Bridge were among the guests at Christmas dinner at Edgewood. The Bridges had lived in the same hotel as the Chases when Father, Kate, and Nettie moved to Washington in 1861. Horatio Bridge was a native of Maine and a Bowdoin College classmate of Nathaniel Hawthorne, and it was the Bridges who introduced Nettie to the author whose stories she loved. Horatio Bridge was chief of the U.S. Navy's Bureau of Provisions and Clothing from 1854 until 1869 and continued to hold positions in the navy's clothing and pay divisions until his retirement in 1873. Charlotte Marshall Bridge was originally from Boston. *Chase Papers,* 1:320, 710; Nettie's recollections in *New York Tribune,* Mar. 8, 1891; Charvat et al., *Centenary Edition,* 15:5, 37–41; 16:166.

  3. Richard C. Parsons served a single term in Congress. He had been marshal of the Supreme Court since the position was created in 1867. While in that office he had been involved in a congressional lobbying scheme with Charles T. Sherman, a federal judge in Ohio who was a brother of John Sherman and Gen. William Tecumseh Sherman. When the court filled the marshal's position vacated by Parsons, Father was the only justice to favor Frederick Schley of Maryland, a former newspaper editor and collector of internal revenue who likely had a connection to Mary Goldsborough's mother, Margaret Schley Goldsborough. John G. Nicolay served as marshal for almost fifteen years. *Chase Papers,* 1:644, 709; Fairman, *Reconstruction and Reunion,* 85, 836, 1451; *Bio. Dir. U.S. Cong.,* 1614; *Biographical Directory of the Federal Judiciary, 1789–2000* (Lanham, Md.: Bernan Press, 2001), 759; *DAB,* 17:84; Williams and McKinsey, *Frederick County,* 1:251; 2:1241.

  4. In October, Father had made arrangements and paid the expenses for his grandniece Amy Auld to travel from Ohio to Washington. Father to Amy Auld, Oct. 19 and 25, 1872 (Chase Papers, LC).

  5. Nettie's daughter Janet.

  6. John Tyndall, superintendent of the Royal Institution in England, was an ardent popularizer of science. On his tour of seven U.S. cities from October 1872 to February 1873, he delivered thirty-five lectures on the subject of light, complementing an accessible, "colloquial" style with demonstrations using a brilliant carbon arc lamp and other apparatus. Despite opposition in some quarters to Tyndall's religious views, which doubted the efficacy of prayer, audiences crowded his lectures and the *Tribune* printed each of the talks he gave in New York. Father attended a lecture by the scientist on the evening of December 7 at Lincoln Hall in Washington. Katherine Russell Sopka, "John Tyndall: International Populariser of Science," in *John Tyndall: Essays on a Natural Philosopher,* ed. W. H. Brock, N. D. McMillan, and R. C. Mollan (Dublin: Royal Dublin Society, 1981), 193–203; Gillispie, *Dictionary of Scientific Biography,* 13:521–24; Warden, *Chase,* 753–54.

NETTIE TO FATHER

Sunday evening[1]
4, Thirty Third Street West.[2]

Dearest Father.

I searched Will's pockets after he returned from Oswego & there found my letter and what was more an invitation to dinner to a young man from a lady who did not know the y m's address & to whom Will had promised safe deliverance of the invitation / I do not often trust to such a doubtful conveyance but I have been out of stamps lately & when he posts them down town he stamps them. I have been entirely quiet lately & know very little of the world that buzzes around me every one else however has been very gay it seems—Yesterday Mrs Rice Gertrude Stevens that was lunched with me & we went for a sleighride[3] afterwards in the park where we broke down but managed to patch up matters enough to reach home—Will had had bob runners as they call them put on my Victoria[4] this sort of arrangement you know & they were not securely enough attached but it is an excessively comfortable arrangement as carriages are always so much more comfortable than sleighs—Have you had good sleighing in Washington? Little Janet is well again but the dr advises that she should be kept in the house until April so we are going to have the back 3rd. Story room as a play room as the sun comes in there all the afternoon & try to keep it both ventilated & warm—I cant say that I quite like the idea as I have great faith in the open air—but after having seen baby once so ill, I should never have courage to disobey his directions and would far rather see her cheeks a little pale than run the slightest risk of another of those dreadful attacks—

The Francklyn & Lee children have both been ill from croup & bronchitis but not nearly so sick as Janet.[5] this winter has been most trying—yesterday was warm and thawing for example & today bitter cold with a biting cutting wind / I was thankful that you are in warmer latitudes.

I must go now & help Will cook tea he is already at his oysters. With love to all

Always lovingly dear Father
Nettie

On monogrammed stationery with JRCH crest and printed street address. Library of Congress.

1. This letter and the next one are undated. Their contents imply that Nettie wrote them in the early months of 1873.

2. A city directory printed in 1872 listed Will Hoyt's residence as "L.I."—Long Island—meaning, in Will's case, Astoria. However, the next year's directory gave his house address as 4 West Thirty-Third Street, which was just west of Fifth Avenue. Wilson, *Trow's New York City Directory, For . . . 1873*, 577; Wilson, *Trow's New York City Directory, For . . . 1874*, 621.

3. Nettie inserted this word in place of "drive."

4. A light carriage with a folding top. *OED*, 19:608.

5. Nettie's sister-in-law, Susan S. Hoyt Francklyn, and her husband, Charles Francklyn, had two children who survived infancy, Charles Gilbert Francklyn and Doris Francklyn, and two others who died while very young. Will Hoyt's other sister, Sarah, and J. Bowers Lee had two daughters, Alice and Marion. *Representative Men and Old Families of Rhode Island*, 1:416.

NETTIE TO FATHER

Sunday

4, Thirty Third Street West.

Dearest Father

Is it not odd how the old proverb troubles never come Singly seems constantly to verify it self—the name of my small troubles lately has certainly been legion.[1] Of course little Janet's sickness has been the only real unhappiness but I really have been dreadfully bothered—One after another of my servants have been Sick—The doctor advised my getting a new nurse, but Miss baby did not approve of the proceedings at all & for a fortnight refused to have any thing to do with her at night or at meal time and then to cap the climax poor Parsons gave over to lust utterly & disappeared for a week's spree. Will says we will not think of taking him back again so now I am hunting up another butler—Voila mes maux[2] do you not sympathize with me?

A few nights ago we were awaked by a violent ringing at the door which proved to be the telegraph boy—I was awfully frightened or rather startled & aprehensive of every thing, but the telegram was from Aunt Charlotte—saying she would stop with me en route for Paris—She arrived the next day having travelled day & night from New Orleans— the cause of her sudden start was a telegram from her niece Fanny Jones saying "sick, come" & date from Caens France, since then she Aunt Charlotte has telegraphed three times to Fanny, the Mitchells whom she believes Fanny to be with and the banker's where Fanny cashed her drafts (she had no letter of credit)—and received no answer / She sailed yesterday in the German line in great anxiety about the poor girl, Aunt Kate arrived at the last moment & went with her[3]—It was a sad start—

What a terrible time they are having in Washington with their investigations! and how all these frauds every where shake trust.[4]

With dear love to all

Ever lovingly

Nettie

On monogrammed stationery with JRCH crest and printed street address. Library of Congress.

1. "And he asked him, what is thy name? and he answered, saying, My name is Legion: for we are many" (Mark 5:9). The origins of the proverb, "Joys never come in pairs; troubles never come singly," have been attributed to China. A similar notion appears in Act 4, Scene 5, of *Hamlet:* "When sorrows come, they come not single spies / But in battalions." Burton Stevenson, comp., *The Home Book of Proverbs, Maxims and Familiar Phrases* (New York: Macmillan Co., 1948), 1275.

2. "Those are my hardships."

3. The arrival of Catherine Ludlow Baker Whiteman, "Aunt Kate," to serve as companion on the trip argues that the Aunt Charlotte rushing to Paris was Charlotte Chambers

Ludlow Jones, Catherine's sister. Presumably Charlotte was visiting their sister Ruhamah or perhaps some of their Kenner relatives when her niece's telegram summoned her from New Orleans. It seems less likely that the Aunt Charlotte who rushed from New Orleans was Charlotte Riske Kenner, whose first marriage had been to a man named Jones (see the appendix). Nettie's use of "Aunt Charlotte" without a surname implies that she meant Charlotte Jones.

4. The Crédit Mobilier scandal first came to public notice in September 1872 with accusations that members of Congress had been bribed with shares of stock in the corporation responsible for construction of the Union Pacific Railroad. In December a select committee of the House of Representatives began hearings that were initially closed but were opened to the public the following month. Another committee opened investigations, and the full House considered the matter during February, when the Senate also held committee hearings. The complex and confusing inquiries resulted in the censure of only two members of the House, Oakes Ames and James Brooks. Father had had some familiarity with both of them in the past. The Senate considered expelling his New Hampshire acquaintance, James W. Patterson, but let the matter drop as Patterson's term expired early in March 1873. Maury Klein, *Union Pacific: Birth of a Railroad, 1862–1893* (Garden City, N.Y.: Doubleday, 1987), 291–99; *Chase Papers*, 1:122, 503.

FATHER TO NETTIE

Washington, Apl. [12], 1872[1]

My darling Nettie

Your letter was written I suppose last Saturday, for that is its date, but I only received it this morning. I went to Richmond last week Friday and returned only yesterday. The weather there was delightful. Peach trees and pear trees were in full bloom & the trees generally had begun to put forth their foliage. Vegetation seemed about in advance of vegetation here, as here it is in advance of vegetation in New York. And the kindness of my reception! I was the guest of Gen and Mrs Johnson[2] who omitted nothing they could think of to render my stay pleasant. Gen J—— is engaged in preparing for the press a volume embodying my judicial administration in my circuit and my employment was aiding his revision of my decisions. So I was not altogether idle.[3] I could & would have done more and enjoyed more, if I had been in better health but I did very well for an invalid

Dont trouble yourself about your lady guests. Invite them it best suits you.[4] I shall not come to New York for ten days yet, & perhaps not for a week later; and then if it is not entirely convenient for you to receive me I can easily find lodgings at the Hotel. I cannot stop at any rate more than a day or two—just to look in upon you & to make the acquaintance of my new Grandson. By the way I am of Will's mind about the name, only I should give the first son the father's name—next to his I should take the paternal grandfather's, especially if one which the child would like when grown. And Edwin is just such a name. So, pet, I must vote against you.[5]

I had a letter from Mary Parker announcing her engagement. It was so kind of her to make me a sharer of her joy, I have thanked & congratulated her as well as I could[6]

I am quite prepared to admire your baby / Katie says he is splendid. Your letters make me a little afraid for your own health. Take care [of] yourself. Goodnight—It is eleven o'clock & I must go to bed: Love to Will & kisses for the little ones

Your loving father
S P Chase

Library of Congress.

1. The reference to Nettie's baby son, Edwin, confirms that Father wrote this letter in 1873, not 1872. He wrote over the day of the month, apparently to change it from "11" to "12."

2. Bradley T. Johnson and his wife, Jane Saunders Johnson. *DAB,* 10:91.

3. Under an 1866 statute, the circuit assigned to the chief justice included Maryland, Virginia, West Virginia, and the Carolinas. Bradley Johnson, a Virginia attorney, wished to publish decisions of cases from that circuit to confirm the validity of everyday legal processes, such as deeds, contracts, and court proceedings, that had continued under Confederate authority during the Civil War. By the winter of 1872–73, that question appeared to have been settled. Johnson wrote of Father's visit to Richmond in April 1873 to go over his compilation of the circuit court decisions: "The manuscript of this volume was then submitted to him for revision, and he went over the whole of it with the reporter, making such corrections as he deemed necessary. They were generally merely verbal, and in the main consisted of softening the language or expressions used in alluding to the war." That "softening" included the substitution of "civil war" for "insurrection" and "rebellion," and the alteration of "rebels" and "insurgents" to "belligerents"—verbal changes that could suggest legal and constitutional distinctions of great concern to Johnson and others. Johnson hoped to have another conversation with Father in Washington to discuss additional material for the book, but that meeting did not come about. When the volume appeared in print in 1876, its title page noted that it had been "Revised and Corrected by the Chief Justice." Johnson, *Reports of Cases,* iii–v; Hyman, *Reconstruction Justice,* 103, 119; *Chase Papers,* 5:14, 133–34, 311.

4. So written.

5. Nettie and Will named the recent arrival, their second child, Edwin Chase Hoyt. *New York Times,* Oct. 22, 1954.

6. Amasa J. Parker's daughter Mary wed Erastus Corning Jr. in the spring of 1873. *Chase Papers,* 5:369.

Epilogue

I.

The chief justice sat with the Supreme Court for the remainder of the 1873 spring term, but his energy was failing. In mid-April he made the only dissent in the Myra Bradwell case, opposing his fellow justices' rebuff of a woman's attempt to gain admission to the Illinois bar, yet he was unable to write an opinion to articulate his reasons for supporting Bradwell's claim under the Fourteenth Amendment. He attended the final day of the term but allowed Justice Nathan Clifford to preside. On May 3, 1873, he left Washington for New York, expecting to visit first Nettie, then Kate in Rhode Island.

He had also elected to get medical care from Charles Sumner's doctor, Charles Éduard Brown-Séquard. Sumner put faith in the bold, reassuring diagnoses and decisive prescriptions of treatment Brown-Séquard had given him since 1858, when the physician first began to treat the Massachusetts senator for complex, lingering effects of the brutal caning Sumner had received from Preston Brooks two years earlier. By the 1870s Brown-Séquard, a peripatetic and audacious experimenter in physiology, saw very few patients, but they included, in addition to Sumner, Louis Agassiz. In the spring of 1873, Brown-Séquard was based in New York, although Father, who spoke with Sumner just before leaving Washington, expected to catch up with the doctor in Boston, where Brown-Séquard lectured. The chief justice planned to stay with his niece, Alice Stebbins, and her family during his visit to Boston, and he thought that afterward he would travel to Colorado for general recuperation. By his own admission he was in poor shape: in one of his last letters, to Richard C. Parsons from New York on May 5, he confessed that "I am too much of an invalid to be more than a cipher. Sometimes I feel as if I were dead, though alive." Two months earlier he had been unsure of the physical cause of his problems, thinking it was perhaps heart trouble, perhaps "debility proceeding from a torpid liver & deficient Circulation." Brown-Séquard—on the basis of what, if any, examination is unclear—considered the problem to be "morbid states" of the brain.[1]

He never got to Boston. At Nettie's and Will's residence on West Thirty-Third Street in New York, when William Joice came in on the morning of May 6 to open the curtains and rouse his sleeping employer, he found that Father had suffered a massive stroke. The Hoyts summoned medical assistance, including John Perry, but there was nothing the doctors could do. The stricken man remained unconscious until midmorning on the seventh, when Nettie, Kate, and both of their husbands were present as he expired.

There were funeral services in both New York and the District of Columbia, where, perhaps because it had been discovered that the embalming process had failed, the body was placed in a chapel vault in Oak Hill Cemetery on May 12 and soon buried in a plot owned by Henry D. Cooke. Reflecting the deceased statesman's Protestant eclecticism, the last church service he attended was Presbyterian, the New York memorial service was in the Episcopal Church of St. George, and a Methodist pastor presided at the Washington funeral. Vice President Henry Wilson attended the service in New York, where the official pallbearers included Gen. William Tecumseh Sherman, Hamilton Fish, Gerrit Smith, and William M. Evarts. In Washington, the body lay in state in the Supreme Court chamber, and President Grant, members of his cabinet, and other dignitaries attended the funeral service in the Senate chamber. Official buildings in Washington were closed and draped in mourning, and flags were at half-staff as the procession of an estimated eighty carriages made its way to the cemetery.[2]

The rites were not at an end. In 1886 there was a large ceremony in Cincinnati when Father's remains were brought from Washington for interment in Spring Grove Cemetery, and in 1923, William Howard Taft, then chief justice, spoke at the dedication of a grave monument provided by the American Bar Association.[3]

Just as there was no single observance to mark his passing, so was there competition almost from the moment of his death over who would shape his legacy. In the last months of Father's life, an Ohioan, Robert Bruce Warden, received—to his own satisfaction, at least—sanction to write a biography of the statesman. Born in Kentucky in 1824, Warden had studied and practiced law in Cincinnati and won election as a common pleas judge there in 1851. He received an appointment to the state's supreme court in 1855, but did not retain the seat when it was filled by election a few months later. In addition to compiling a volume of the printed reports of the Ohio Supreme Court before joining that court, he produced a mixed group of writings that included *Arvoirlich: A Romantic Tragedy in Five Acts* (1857), *A Voter's Version of the Life and Character of Stephen Arnold Douglas* (1860), *A Familiar Forensic View of Man and Law* (1860)—which one reviewer thought was "somewhat too diffuse and artificial in its style"—and a memoir of a son killed in battle, *Ernest and the*

Flag He Followed.[4] In Washington in December 1872, Warden revived an old, not particularly intimate, acquaintance with Father. He had been urged by someone to write a biography of the chief justice, and in a verbose letter to Father on January 13, 1873, the recipient's sixty-fifth birthday, Warden declared his intention to undertake such a work. "Should you pursue the purpose you indicate," Father replied, "I shall be happy to afford you all the aid—not much—in my power." He offered Warden the clerkship under the Bankruptcy Act by which he kept a secretary, a position D. D. Lloyd would vacate in March, and though Warden later claimed that he was "affronted" by the offer of such a lowly job, he accepted. The post gave Warden a desk in the Sprague house at 6th and E streets, access to papers of interest to him as a biographer, and the prospect of a room at Edgewood to work in during the chief justice's expected absence in the summer.[5]

Warden considered himself Father's authorized biographer, "in effect, his literary executor," even though the chief justice, when pressed by Charles Sumner about Warden's qualifications, had given a limited answer, saying that he thought Warden's intended work would be aimed at a local audience in Ohio and that the author seemed suited to that task. After Father's unexpected death Warden never occupied the promised room at Edgewood and instead found himself frozen out by "illwill" on the part of the family, especially Kate, and scorned in print by the *New York Herald*. Soon his rival in the contest to write a Chase biography would be Jacob W. Schuckers, whose modest career writing about financial policy still lay ahead of him. But Schuckers, an 1865 graduate of Albany Law School, had the advantages of long, loyal service as Father's clerical assistant, as a Treasury clerk during the Civil War and on a fill-in basis thereafter, and Kate's active sponsorship.[6]

The race ended, effectively, in a tie. Both biographies, Warden's *An Account of the Private Life and Public Services of Salmon Portland Chase* and Schuckers's *The Life and Public Services of Salmon Portland Chase*, appeared in 1874. Both were thick, seemingly authoritative tomes. Warden's liberal use of texts from his subject's papers, particularly diaries, has pleased historians. But Schuckers also larded his drier, more modestly toned biography with extracts of documents. Warden's work was more appealing, though, to anyone interested in a harsh assessment of Kate Chase or what passed for a knowingly cynical interpretation of her father. Warden made his book part of the polemic over the Chase biographies and gave himself a place in his narrative. He depicted himself as an innocent wronged by a Jacob Schuckers who stole documents and by a cunning Kate Chase Sprague who tried to block publication of Warden's work and control her dead father's image. Warden's biography of Father and a subsequent work written to answer critics, *An Appeal by the Author of the "Best Abused Book of the Period"* (Washington, D.C., 1876), were the only

narratives of the dispute, and to that extent Warden won much of the
battle over legacy. One need not question that Kate was distressed by
Warden's biographical approach, which he claimed would reveal the private man, and by the uses to which the idiosyncratic author might put
her father's papers. There is no basis for the claim, however, that she
was obsessively jealous of the affection her father showed, in his private
journals, for his first wife, Kitty, Kate's mother's predecessor.[7] There is
much to distrust about Warden's use of materials in his possession: for
example, he chose to ignore an oral account of personal political history
he heard from the chief justice himself and gave no clear explanation of
his manipulation of text from the journal record of Kitty's last illness and
death—a document that has not been located since Warden used it.[8]

Moreover, by thrusting himself into his book, Warden gave it a peculiar, contradictory perspective. He referred to Father as "our hero"
throughout, but adopted a cynical stance toward his subject. As *The Nation* observed in November 1874, Warden's disgust with "the eagerness of
biographers to exalt their subject" had evidently made him "determined
to degrade his." While scorning outright Warden's "confused manner"
of writing, which turned important political narrative into "a tangled
mass of names" and compelled the reader to consult Schuckers's book
for clarification, *The Nation* had little in the way of effusive praise for
Schuckers's creation. Neither book, the reviewer felt, did much to illumi-
nate the person behind the public Salmon P. Chase.[9]

It was unusual for two hefty biographies, each claiming a form of legitimacy, to appear the year following a nineteenth-century American
statesman's death, and the competition between the biographers caused
an equally unusual bifurcation of the subject's papers. There are smaller
groups of Father's papers, but the two large collections are at the Library
of Congress and the Historical Society of Pennsylvania. Late in the nineteenth century the historian Albert Bushnell Hart labored to reclaim
from various hands much of the material Warden had used, and it became the core of the Library of Congress collection, while papers that
Schuckers and Kate had gathered for Schuckers's biography ended up in
Philadelphia at the historical society. The matter of legacy would never
be straightforward.[10]

II.

Few of Kate's acquaintances questioned her lifelong devotion to her father. Indeed, many thought that his death rendered her life hollow and
even meaningless. The letters in this volume illustrate how Kate's relationship with her father was more ambivalent, more fraught with tension
and disappointment than any outsider could perceive. Indeed, Kate's

post-1873 behavior strongly suggests that she found a kind of freedom in her father's death; the freedom, for example, to separate from William and eventually divorce him. For a few years in the late 1870s she took a lover, finding the love and acceptance in his arms that she never received from either her father or husband. The affair created an infamous public scandal that would turn her life into a Gilded Age morality tale that illustrated what happened to ladies who strayed from the path of respectability.[11]

Kate was pregnant with her fourth and last child when her father died in 1873. In the months after her daughter was born, President Ulysses S. Grant offered his friend, New York senator Roscoe Conkling, the chief justiceship. Conkling, who was the party boss of a powerful Republican political machine in New York, turned down the sumptuous offer, understanding that the highest court in the land was a political dead end. Years later people would charge that Kate had urged Roscoe to reject Grant's offer, but no good evidence suggests the two were involved with each other before late 1876. Rather, Roscoe employed the good political sense that would gradually bring him to Kate's attention.

Roscoe Conkling was at the height of his power in 1876. Commonly known as "the Adonis of the Senate," he had brilliant red-gold hair, a lock of which curled artfully at his forehead, blue eyes, and "the finest torso in public life," gained by the gentlemanly art of pugilism.[12] He ran New York politics from his Senate seat and had the ear of the president. He was tall, elegant, handsome, kind to ladies, temperate, and politically astute— in short he had all the characteristics that Kate found lacking in her husband. A Republican, Roscoe favored antislavery and women's rights and was intimate with the nation's most powerful men. He was married, but his wife, Julia, seldom left Utica, New York, where she lived in a house she did not share with her husband. For Kate, Roscoe combined the best of her father's attributes without her father's difficulty in expressing affection. The pair seemed made for each other, much to the shocked delight of Washington gossips.

The affair exploded on the public scene during the summer of 1879. William arrived at the couple's Rhode Island mansion unexpectedly, only to discover that Roscoe was among Kate's houseguests. Drunk, the irate husband demanded Kate's lover leave the house, then later followed Roscoe into town and threatened him with a shotgun. The witnesses to the scene were too numerous for the affair to remain a private matter. Newspapers carried daily stories about the threatened lover, cuckolded husband, and unfaithful wife, each day bringing new revelations to the titillating scandal. William took the children from Kate, and then used them to lure her back to their house, where he kept her prisoner for more than two weeks. Kate escaped, making a hasty exit out the back door and into a waiting carriage that hied off for parts still unknown.

When Kate finally emerged from hiding she initiated divorce proceedings against her husband. In her divorce petition she accused William of violating his marital vows, and she had names and dates to bolster her claims. She also made it clear that she had been the victim of both mental and physical spousal abuse. William was an alcoholic and prone to violent rages. He isolated Kate, refused to support her and his four children, threatened her, beat her, and on one notable occasion attempted to kill her. He also appears to have sexually preyed upon female household servants, had a long running affair with a woman who had had his child before he married Kate, and been a frequent visitor to a number of brothels. Kate's and William's relationship had been a hideous parody of nineteenth-century standards of companionate marital bliss, and Father failed to recognize this reality, counseling Kate again and again with words that held her responsible for the wreck that was her marriage.[13]

Kate and Roscoe continued their relationship after the summer of 1879. Kate went so far as to appear incognito at the Republican presidential convention held in Chicago in June 1880. The affair required complete and utter secrecy that year, given Kate's pending divorce suit and Conkling's ultimately unsuccessful efforts to salvage his political career. Kate continued her politicking on her lover's behalf into 1881, particularly after James A. Garfield's assassination made Conkling's one-time political lieutenant Chester Arthur president. Unfortunately, her artful letters could not remove the tarnish from Roscoe Conkling's public life. He resigned from the Senate in 1881 and retired to a private law practice in New York City. The strain of secrecy and failure no doubt contributed to the end of Kate and Roscoe's affair, for the two saw no more of each other after 1882.

The divorce, granted in May of that year, gave William custody of Willie and Kate custody of the three girls. Technically the grounds for the divorce was nonsupport by William. It was a plausible enough charge, for the great financial panic precipitated by the collapse of Jay Cooke's railroad financing schemes in September 1873 had forced the A. and W. Sprague company, which had assets of more than $19 million before the panic, into trusteeship. The Hoyts' enterprises suffered a similar fate, and in 1874 Will Hoyt's company, Hoyt and Francklyn, brought suit against the Sprague firm. Other setbacks and a depression in cotton manufacturing hindered any recovery of the Sprague fortune. The divorce settlement granted Kate's request that she be allowed to abandon her married name and be known again as Kate Chase.[14]

William remarried in 1883, to Inez Weed Calvert, a widow of dubious moral background twenty-three years his junior. In 1885, Willie married Inez's younger sister Avice. The groom was nineteen and the bride fifteen. The marriage was brief, and when Avice announced her pregnancy,

Willie left Rhode Island and his young wife. Evidently the baby was not his. Willie drifted through a series of jobs; alcoholism and his dysfunctional past kept him from emotional or economic stability. He committed suicide in Seattle in 1890.[15]

Ethel, Portia, and Kitty remained with their mother after the divorce. From 1883 to 1887 the four lived near Paris, though Kate returned briefly in 1886 to arrange the transfer of her father's remains from Washington to the family plot in Cincinnati's Spring Grove Cemetery. Ethel took up acting for a period in 1887 and appeared on the stage in several cities. A newspaper story that described her fast-paced horseback rides in the vicinity of Edgewood called her the "most accomplished, most daring horsewoman" in Washington, "a lithe, womanly figure, with the brightest of eyes and a shock of curly, black hair." She married Dr. Frank Donaldson. They had one child, whom they named Chase. Ethel eventually became a journalist in San Francisco. Portia worked for a time as a clerk for the U.S. Treasury, the department her grandfather had once headed. In 1897, she initiated a brief reunion with her father, and she later lived, at least for a time, at Narragansett Pier. She married twice but never had children. Kitty, who was developmentally disabled, lived with her mother, then later with Portia. She died young, perhaps of consumption.[16] In 1909 Canonchet burned to the ground, leaving William and Inez essentially homeless. They moved to Paris, where, during World War I, their apartment was used as a convalescent hospital. William died in 1915 at eighty-five years of age. He was the last of the Civil War governors.[17]

Kate did not live to see the twentieth century. In July 1899, she succumbed to the effects of either liver or kidney disease. Washington society had shunned her in her later years, but her passing was national news as Americans reminded themselves of her story.[18] But Kate and her sister had become estranged long before. A short time after Kate's death, Nettie responded to a letter from one of her Ludlow relatives.

> I feel as if an unhappy chapter of my life has been closed. What grieved me beyond everything, more than any injustice to me, was the way Kate (although she did not realise the harm she was doing) injured our father's memory.
>
> The unjust & grossly exaggerated criticisms of his great desire for "the presidency" came all through her intrigues with second rate politicians during the latter part of his life. And since his death it was very very hard for me to have her beg money in his name. However that is all over now. Poor soul, her life was certainly a tragic one.[19]

Whatever discomfort Nettie felt at Kate's involvement in politics on their father's behalf, there can be little doubt that he chose his own political course. The divide that developed between the sisters after their father's death was not solely about political ambition. The financial collapses set in motion by the panic of 1873 opened a huge rift between the Hoyt and Sprague clans. Not only did the extended families face off in court over the various firms' assets, Kate and Nettie were at odds over the disposition of Edgewood. Kate finally bought Nettie's share of the property, but the differences between them were never reconciled.[20]

III.

Nettie and Will Hoyt had more children: a son, Franklin Chase Hoyt, who became a judge and a pioneer in the juvenile justice system in New York City, and daughters they named Placidia and Beatrix.[21] Nettie also continued her involvement in art, most notably as a promoter of arts education and professional development. In 1877, Candace Wheeler and others in New York formed the Society of Decorative Art to enlist "the sympathy and interest of the influential class of New York women" in furnishing the instruction and gallery space necessary for women to achieve commercial success in the decorative arts. Nettie had become acquainted with Wheeler years before in Dresden, where they had both studied art and where Wheeler, who was married, acted as a matron for the younger American women. When Nettie created a tapestry and sent it to the Society of Decorative Art, Wheeler, who became a leading designer and promoter of textile art, thought the work a remarkable step in the development of needlework as a medium for original American art. Wheeler and Nettie found their friendship renewed by their common involvement in the decorative arts.[22]

In the mid-1880s, Nettie involved herself in the new Industrial Education Association, which promoted industrial arts training in schools and reformatories. She established the "Pelham Industry" in Westchester County, an institution to provide "young persons of both sexes instruction in the decorative and industrial arts." Its students could learn drawing, design, cabinetry and carpentry, wood carving, sewing, embroidery, tapestry making, upholstering, brassworking, and leatherworking, honing their skills by crafting items for sale. In the winter of 1885, Nettie organized a New York City fund-raising benefit for the school that featured a salon performance by some of high society's most prominent amateur actors.[23]

Members of that affluent New York society began more and more to pass their summers in "cottages" near Southampton along the southern edge of eastern Long Island. There in 1890, Nettie took the first steps to form a summer art school at Shinnecock Hills. Formal instruction was the means by which American artists hoped to compete with Europeans, and women were particularly admonished to master technique if they hoped to be taken seriously as artists. Nettie saw qualities of light and landscape that would make Long Island a fine location for outdoor painting. Recognizing that her plan was "ambitious," she recruited the president of the Society of American Artists, William Merritt Chase—an Indianan of no close relation to Nettie's family—to head the Shinnecock school. Philanthropists Samuel L. Parrish, who provided land, and Annie Porter, the wife of a Pittsburgh locomotive manufacturer, were also involved in the school, which held its first session in the summer of 1891. Within two summers it had an enrollment of 150 men and women. Chase established his summer studio on Long Island, promoted the school, and served as its chief instructor in residence. Nettie organized an art club of thirty female students. Their building served as a social center for what was soon called the Art Village, and Nettie's daughter Janet entered into some of the theatrical entertainments the artists staged to amuse themselves during the evening. Even after the summer school ceased to function, the Art Village endured.[24]

At the same time that Nettie got the art school under way, the area's summer residents also founded a golf course at Shinnecock Hills. The first incorporated golf club in the United States, it boasted a clubhouse designed by Stanford White, who was also the architect of the house and studio used by William M. Chase. Nettie and her husband were involved in the new club, as they were also in starting the Westchester Country Club. Moreover, their daughter Beatrix, who learned the game at the Shinnecock Club, emerged as a teenager in 1896 to win the women's national golf championship, taking the Cox Silver Cup that was offered for the first time that year as a trophy of the women's championship. Captivating public attention with her youthful style and energy, "Little Miss Hoyt," as the *New York Times* dubbed her in one headline, was "the Sprite of the Downs"—referring to her home course at Shinnecock, which was laid out over low rolling hills or "downs." She won the championship match on a course founded "by women for women" at Morristown, New Jersey, where her grandmother, Belle Ludlow Chase, had gone to fight her tuberculosis in the middle of the century. Beatrix Hoyt won the women's title the two succeeding years also, and the attention she drew as a young sensation in the 1890s helped bring public notice to women's golf.[25]

Will Hoyt died in 1905. Nettie survived him by twenty years and died in 1925 at Thomasville, Georgia, where she and Candace Wheeler liked to spend the winter in neighboring houses. Beatrix, who studied painting and made sculptures after quitting competitive golf, and Placidia, the wife of an Episcopal minister, also lived at Thomasville.[26]

1. *Chase Papers*, 5:368–70; Schuckers, *Chase*, 622–23; Warden, *Chase*, 799–805; David Donald, *Charles Sumner and the Coming of the Civil War* (New York: Knopf, 1960), 337–42; David Donald, *Charles Sumner and the Rights of Man* (New York: Knopf, 1970), 266, 567–68;

Gillispie, *Dictionary of Scientific Biography*, 2:524–26; J. M. D. Olmsted, *Charles-Éduard Brown-Séquard: A Nineteenth Century Neurologist and Endocrinologist* (Baltimore, Md.: Johns Hopkins Press, 1946), 120, 128–29, 139; Alice Skinner Stebbins to Father, May 6, 1873 (Chase Papers, LC). It is not certain what physician Alice Stebbins meant when she referred to the prospect of her uncle seeing "our magnetic doctor" in Boston.

2. Schuckers, *Chase*, 624–25; *New York Times*, May 11–13, 1873; Oberholtzer, *Cooke*, 2:415.

3. Blue, *Chase*, 392; *New York Times*, Oct. 15, 1886, May 31, 1923.

4. *DAB*, 19:444; S. Austin Allibone, *A Critical Dictionary of English Literature and British and American Authors Living and Deceased: From the Earliest Accounts to the Latter Half of the Nineteenth Century*, 3 vols. (Philadelphia: J. B. Lippincott, 1870–71), 3:2579; Coyle, *Ohio Authors*, 668; Warden, *Chase*, 531, 738, 743–49.

5. Warden, *Chase*, 741, 753–54, 756–66, 769–70, 802–5.

6. Warden, *Chase*, 803, 806–7; *Chase Papers*, 1:501, 534; 3:xxv–xxviii; 5:61–62; John Foster Kirk, *A Supplement to Allibone's Critical Dictionary of English Literature and British and American Authors*, 2 vols. (Philadelphia: J. B. Lippincott Co., 1891), 2:1322.

7. See Belden and Belden, *So Fell the Angels*, 266–83. The Beldens adopted Warden's interpretation of the controversy, which fit well with their construct of a grotesquely ambitious Kate Chase. But the Beldens simply erred in concluding that a locked diary Warden made much of was Father's journal relating to Kitty Garniss Chase. To the Beldens, the lock was implicit evidence of the deeply private aspect of that journal and made a visceral reaction to that document by Kate more plausible—Warden, after all, wrote that he was "almost prostrated by the sense of the responsibility" he felt on receiving the locked diary (Warden, *Chase*, 772). In fact, however, that "locked diary," which according to Warden contained tremendous "revelations," was not the journal about Kitty but one from 1862, when Father was secretary of the Treasury (*Chase Papers*, 1:lvii, lxv–lxvi). Warden did have access to Father's journal recording Kitty's demise, but that document was not central to Kate's probably very sound objections to Warden and his biographical enterprise. Frederick Blue, in "Kate's Paper Chase: The Race to Publish the First Biography of Salmon P. Chase," *Old Northwest* 8 (1982–83): 353–63, accepted Warden's account of the controversy and also implicitly followed the Beldens' speculations about Kate.

8. Warden, *Chase*, 804; *Chase Papers*, 1:lvii–lx, 81–94.

9. *Nation* 19, no. 488 (Nov. 5, 1874): 302–3.

10. *Chase Papers*, 1:liv–lv.

11. For Kate's story after her father's death, see Lamphier, *Kate Chase and William Sprague*, 131–258.

12. Ibid., 131.

13. For Father's position on divorce, see ibid., 204–5.

14. Belden and Belden, *So Fell the Angels*, 327; Lamphier, *Kate Chase and William Sprague*, 128–29.

15. Lamphier, *Kate Chase and William Sprague*, 222–23, 232–35.

16. Ibid., 224–25, 240, 247; *New York Times*, Aug. 17, 1899, Dec. 20, 1936; *Baltimore Sun*, Aug. 17, 1899; *Macon Telegraph*, Nov. 12, 1888; *Bismarck Daily Tribune*, Sept. 20, 1889; *Philadelphia Inquirer*, Oct. 28, 1890; *Kansas City Star*, Dec. 25, 1890; *Minneapolis Journal*, Oct. 1, 1897; *Grand Forks Daily Herald*, Oct. 3, 1897; *Columbus (Ga.) Enquirer-Sun*, Aug. 1, 1899.

17. Lamphier, *Kate Chase and William Sprague*, 244–46.

18. *Kansas City Star*, July 31, Aug. 2, 3, 1899; *Minneapolis Journal*, July 31; *San Jose (Calif.) Evening News*, July 31; *Baltimore Sun*, Aug. 1, 2; *Charlotte Daily Observer*, Aug. 1, 3; *Columbus (Ga.) Enquirer-Sun*, Aug. 1; *New York Times*, Aug. 1; *Philadelphia Inquirer*, Aug. 1; *Omaha World-Herald*, Aug. 1, 6; *Washington Post*, Aug. 1; *Columbia (S.C.) State*, Aug. 4; *Duluth News Tribune*, Aug. 4; *Dallas Morning News*, Aug. 9.

19. Nettie to "Aunt Annie," Aug. 17, 1899, typescript, Ludlow-Dunlop-Chambers Collection, American Heritage Collection, University of Wyoming. "Annie" is certainly a misreading of "Ammie," the family's name for Nettie's aunt Ruhamah Ludlow Hunt. The transcriber also misread "Shinnecock Hills" in the dateline of Nettie's letter as "Shammrock Hills."

20. Lamphier, *Kate Chase and William Sprague*, 230.

21. Walter I. Trattner, ed., *Biographical Dictionary of Social Welfare in America* (New York: Greenwood Press, 1986), 411–13; *ANB*, 11:373–74.

22. Candace Wheeler, *Yesterdays in a Busy Life* (New York: Harper, 1918), 197–201, 222–23; Candace Wheeler, *The Development of Embroidery in America* (New York: Harper & Brothers, 1921), 109–12, 115, 117; Anthea Callen, *Women Artists of the Arts and Crafts Movement, 1870–1914* (New York: Pantheon Books, 1979), 129–32; *ANB*, 23:131–33.

23. *New York Times*, Jan. 18, May 23, 1885; Scharf, *History of Westchester County*, 1:708.

24. Keith L. Bryant, *William Merritt Chase: A Genteel Bohemian* (Columbia, Mo.: University of Missouri Press, 1991), 149–53; John Gilmer Speed, "An Artist's Summer Vacation," *Harper's New Monthly Magazine* 82 (1893): 3–14; "Women in Art," a series of articles by Gleeson White, Susan M. Ketcham, and William M. Chase in *The Ladies' Home Journal* 8, no. 12 (Nov. 1891): 10; 9, no. 1 (Dec. 1891): 37; *New York Times*, June 26, 1892, Aug. 6, 1893, June 9, 1895; Kirsten Swinth, *Painting Professionals: Women Artists and the Development of Modern American Art, 1870–1930* (Chapel Hill, N.C.: University of North Carolina Press, 2001), 3–5, 8, 14–19; W. Stewart Wallace, comp., *A Dictionary of North American Authors Deceased before 1950* (Toronto: Ryerson Press, 1951), 345; *Nat. Cyc.*, 13:445.

25. Richard J. Moss, *Golf and the American Country Club* (Urbana, Ill.: University of Illinois Press, 2001), 24–27, 69–71, and illus. following p. 76; *ANB*, 11:373–74; *New York Times*, Oct. 1, 7, 10, 11, 1896, Oct. 3, 1897 (magazine, p. 2); Bryant, *William Merritt Chase*, 150.

26. *New York Times*, Apr. 29, 1905, Nov. 20, 1925; Wheeler, *Yesterdays*, 7–12, 18, 223; *ANB*, 11:374.

Appendix

THE FAMILY EXTENDED

This collective biographical sketch identifies members of the extended family who are mentioned in the letters in this volume. Their names are highlighted in small capitals, and we have tried to include the names by which the Chases themselves, in their correspondence, referred to their relatives (AUNT CHARLOTTE, for example). People not mentioned in the correspondence may appear in this appendix, but without their names highlighted and usually lacking much biographical information. We have not attempted to tell the full story, or name all the members, of every family unit.

To keep the annotation to this sketch manageable, we have generally not cited information that can be easily found by referring to the person's name in the indexes of the five volumes of *The Salmon P. Chase Papers;* nor have we cited the compilation of vital dates, the "Family Memoranda," that Chase inscribed over time in an undated memorandum book now in his papers at the Library of Congress (see reel 43, beginning frame 882, of the Chase Papers microfilm edition; the family record is on pp. 13–14 and 93–96 of the memorandum book).

I.

Salmon P. Chase was twenty-six in March 1834 when he married CATHARINE JANE (KITTY) GARNISS (August 1811–December 1, 1835). The eminent clergyman Lyman Beecher, then president of Lane Theological Seminary, performed the ceremony in the Cincinnati residence of Kitty's parents. On their first acquaintance in 1831, Chase had considered Kitty "an affected and shallow girl," but he soon found her "beautiful" and agreeably bookish.[1] She died from complications after giving birth to a baby girl whom Chase insisted on naming CATHARINE JANE (November 16, 1835–February 6, 1840) as a memorial to Kitty. He did this despite the strong wish of his mother-in-law, AMELIA GARNISS (d. 1864), for the baby to have her name. As the child grew, she was called Kate rather than Kitty. The first of Chase's children, she died of scarlet fever at the age of four.

At the time of Kitty's death she and Chase lived with her parents. Chase's papers depict Amelia Garniss and her husband, businessman JOHN P. GARNISS (d. 1867), the co-owner of a steam ferry company on the Ohio River, as obstinate and difficult. Within months of Kitty's death, Chase wrote that "every day's experience teaches me that I cannot longer expect to harmonize" with the Garnisses;

"our views, feelings, habits of thought are all too dissimilar—too opposite I may say to allow a residence under the same roof." Despite his early recruitment of his sister Helen to act as housekeeper of an independent residence, however, he and his young daughter continued to live with the Garnisses at least through 1837. During the 1840s, John and Amelia Garniss moved to New York City. Harboring the notion that his partner in the ferry business, Cincinnati businessman and bank director Samuel Wiggins, had "swindled" him, Garniss held his son-in-law to an ancient pledge of filial devotion and harried Chase to find some means of winning his acrimonious claim against Wiggins.[2] While the Garnisses had no actual kinship to the Kate Chase of this volume (the successor in name to their granddaughter), when she attended boarding school in New York in the early 1850s they played a near-familial role. Judging from references in Chase's letters of September 6, 1853, and July 5, 1854, John Garniss sometimes called himself Kate's "Uncle John."

Although Kitty Garniss Chase seems to have had no siblings by birth, her parents adopted—how formally is not clear—Cordelia Picket, who styled herself as Chase's and his daughters' COUSIN DELIA. She married, by the early 1840s, DAVID AUSTEN, originally of Staten Island, who ran his family's auction house and subsequently had a kerosene business. Delia died by mid-1861. One of their children was JOHN GARNISS AUSTEN.[3]

On September 26, 1839, about six weeks before the bride's eighteenth birthday, Chase married Cincinnati native ELIZA ANN SMITH (November 12, 1821–September 29, 1845). Chase had known the presiding minister, Henry Van Dyke Johns, the Episcopal pastor of St. Paul's Church, ten years earlier in Washington, and this was a double wedding, in which Chase wed Eliza—LIZZIE— and his sister Helen married the Reverend Henry B. Walbridge. Lizzie was one of eight children of Edmund Curtis Smith Sr. (1790–1833).[4] She and Chase had three children. The first, born on August 13, 1840, six months after the death of Chase's adored little daughter of the same name, was the KATE of this volume. Her father carefully inscribed her name in his record of family events as "Catharine Jane Chase, 2nd." Two other girls, both namesakes of their mother, died in infancy: Lizzie (May 30–August 30, 1842) and Lizzie "2nd" (June 16, 1843–July 24, 1844).

A few days after the death of Lizzie Smith Chase of consumption in 1845, Chase wrote an anguished letter to a friend: "I have no wife, my little Kate has no mother, and we are desolate."[5] Since most of her mother's brothers and sisters died young, Kate had few surviving Smith relatives. Her grandmother, Lizzie's mother MARY COLTON SMITH, evaded the tuberculosis that devastated her family and died of a hemorrhage in the fall of 1867. For a time Chase acted as guardian of Lizzie's younger siblings, Edmund Curtis Smith Jr. (1823–47) and CAROLINE A. SMITH (1829–52). He sent Caroline to boarding school in Louisville soon after Lizzie Chase's death. Caroline married George L. Febiger, a Cincinnati grocery merchant, and they evidently had a daughter, but Carrie died of consumption in October 1852, not long after the single reference to her in a letter in this volume as AUNT CARRIE.[6] Kate's cousin MARIA J. SOUTHGATE (b. 1836), the daughter of her mother's older sister Jane and James Southgate of Covington, Kentucky, married JAMES MORRISON HAWES (1824–89), also a Kentuckian, in February 1857. A professional soldier trained at West Point, Hawes served with the U.S. Army on the frontier, joined the Confederate service during the Civil War and advanced to the rank of brigadier general, and then became a hardware merchant in Covington.[7] Another of Lizzie's sisters, Maria—who died of tuberculosis in 1836 and for whom Maria J. Southgate was probably named—also married a Southgate. Her husband was the HENRY H. SOUTHGATE (1807–55) whose death Chase reported in a letter of April 13, 1855 (above in this volume).[8]

If Chase and Kate had few relatives from the Garniss and Smith connections, they united with a large and significant Cincinnati clan upon Chase's marriage to SARAH BELLA DUNLOP LUDLOW (April 20, 1820–January 13, 1852), known familiarly as BELLE. Chase's friend Charles Petit McIlvaine, the Episcopal bishop of Ohio, performed the marriage on November 6, 1846, at the Cincinnati home of the bride's aunt, SARAH BELLA LUDLOW MCLEAN (1802–82), known to the Chases as "Aunt McLean," and her husband JOHN MCLEAN (1785–1861), an associate justice of the United States Supreme Court.[9]

Chase's relationship with the prosperous Ludlow family dated as far back as 1839, when he undertook to act as attorney for the heirs of Belle's grandfather, Israel Ludlow. One of the original proprietors of Cincinnati, Ludlow had bequeathed his descendants a rich, if complicated, legacy of land titles and property holdings. The Ludlows also had strong connections to two other families, Chambers and Dunlop. Indeed, those ties were doubled, for Belle Chase's parents, James Chambers Ludlow and Josephine Dunlop Ludlow, were first cousins. Their mothers—that is, Belle's two grandmothers, Charlotte Chambers Ludlow and Sarah Bella Chambers Dunlop—were sisters. The use of Chambers and Dunlop as middle names by Ludlows of Belle's generation testifies to the dynastic links, as do first names that recurred through the allied clans.

Belle's parents had both died before she, the oldest of their eight children, married Chase. Seven months before they married, in April 1846, he became the guardian of four of Belle's younger brothers and sisters.[10] The youngest of Belle's siblings, her brother ISRAEL (1840–73) and sister JOSEPHINE (JOSIE, JOSEY) LUDLOW (1838–66), were actually quite close to Kate Chase in age. It seems likely that Josephine, like Belle, died of tuberculosis.[11] Educated in Andover, Massachusetts, and at Antioch College in Yellow Springs, Ohio, Israel enthusiastically enlisted as a private at the beginning of the Civil War, but his siblings asked their brother-in-law, the new secretary of the Treasury, to obtain a commission for the young man. He became a Federal artillery officer, was wounded and captured at Chickamauga in September 1863, and spent several months confined to Libby Prison at Richmond. After the war he read law and practiced in Cincinnati before moving to Texas for his health.[12]

The distinctive name of the next oldest sibling, RUHAMAH (1833–1913)— known affectionately as AMMIE or "Ham"—was a legacy of the Chambers family.[13] A relative described her, when she began "going a good deal into society" at about the age of twenty, as "an uncommonly handsome fine looking girl." She married Randall Hunt, a professor of law and subsequently president of the University of Louisiana, who opposed secession and remained loyal to the Union during the Civil War even if he did not take a leadership role among Louisiana's Unionists. In November 1860, Ruhamah wrote to Chase in the hope that he could somehow ameliorate the sectional crisis, and his reply served as a position paper outlining his views on the problems facing the country.[14]

Belle's brother BENJAMIN CHAMBERS LUDLOW (1831–98) graduated from the University of Pennsylvania with a medical degree. During the Civil War he began service as an officer of Missouri cavalry, then called on Chase for help in advancing himself to a staff position under Joseph Hooker. He became inspector of artillery under George Meade and subsequently chief of cavalry for Benjamin F. Butler, receiving the brevet rank of brigadier general of volunteers in the fall of 1864. He remained in the army until August 1865 and, like his brother Israel, later became a resident of Texas.[15]

The AUNT KATE of this volume was Belle's sister CATHERINE LUDLOW (1828–1905). At the time of Chase's and Belle's marriage, Kate Ludlow was a boarding student at D. S. Burnet's Hygeia Female Atheneum near Cincinnati. In 1850 she accompanied Belle on visits to hydropathic institutions in Northampton, Massachusetts, and Morris County, New Jersey. Late in that year Kate married an unidentified MR. BAKER. His death was probably the terrible "visitation" that caused her grief mentioned by Chase in his letter of March 9, 1853, printed above in this volume. She was widowed again: her second husband, Kentucky-born Cincinnati commission merchant LEWIS (OR LOUIS) WHITEMAN (1796–1862), a widower to whom she was likely married by May 1860, died in February 1862.[16]

The oldest of the brothers, JAMES DUNLOP LUDLOW (1822–86), who generally went by his middle name (sometimes shortened to DUN), escorted the ailing Belle on some of her travels in search of improved health in 1850–51, when her husband was caught up in politics and the Senate. Earlier, Dun had invested with apparently indifferent results in a lumber business and a grist mill in Lafayette, Indiana. After 1853 he found greater success developing lands along the route of the Illinois Central Railroad in Champaign County, Illinois, where he married and raised a family.[17]

CHARLOTTE CHAMBERS LUDLOW—AUNT CHARLOTTE in these pages—was evidently the sister closest in age to Belle. Named for her paternal grandmother, she married CHARLES A. JONES (c. 1815–51), who wrote essays and verse for publication while living in Cincinnati before he commenced the practice of law in New Orleans.[18] Their son Ludlow ("Lud" or "Luddy") added a Welsh prefix to his surname to become LUDLOW AP-JONES (b. 1844). Graduating from Harvard College with an A.M. degree in 1865, he became an attorney in Cincinnati. His sister JOSEPHINE (JOSIE) JONES, "a year older than Nettie" according to Chase's letter to Kate of January 7, 1852, was by that reckoning born about 1846. The next child, a boy named Charley, died late in 1850.[19] We do not know the fate of the child who was born close enough to Charles A. Jones's death in July 1851 to be the "baby" referred to in Chase's letter of January 7, 1852.

Chase's and Belle's contributions to this sprawling clan were two daughters: the NETTIE of this volume, born on September 19, 1847, and named Janet Ralston Chase after her father's mother, and JOSEPHINE LUDLOW CHASE (July 3, 1849–July 28, 1850), named for her maternal grandmother and called both JOSEY and ZOE. Seemingly never very robust, little Zoe was the baby sister mentioned in letters in this volume, her death described in Belle's letter to Kate of August 29, 1850.

An even larger web of Ludlows and allied kin also figures in this volume. AUNT ADELA LUDLOW was Helen Adela Slacum Ludlow (1807–72), a native of

Virginia and the widow of another Israel Ludlow—this one Israel L. Ludlow, Belle's father's brother, who died in 1846. Adela's daughter, the COUSIN LOUISA mentioned in letters from late 1851 and early 1852, was the Mrs. Louisa Goodloe whose pending marriage to a Virginian Chase mentioned in his letter to Kate of September 15, 1854. During the Civil War the death of her husband, a man named Mitchell, left her stranded in Richmond, prompting Adela Ludlow to ask Chase to arrange authorization for Louisa's return north through military lines.[20]

To distinguish Charlotte Dunlop Clarkson, Belle's mother's sister, from other Charlottes in the clan, she bore the label AUNT CLARKSON. Appropriately, her husband Charles S. Clarkson—not the only Uncle Charles in the family paired with an Aunt Charlotte—was UNCLE CLARKSON. A former army paymaster originally from Boone County, in northern Kentucky not far from Cincinnati, he consulted Chase about legal matters in the early 1840s and aspired unsuccessfully to the postmastership at Cincinnati. He had business or other interests in Missouri by the late 1840s, and the Clarksons came to reside at least part of the time in St. Louis County.[21]

Although mentioned in the letters only as MISS CLOPPER rather than by any term of kinship, Caroline Chambers Clopper (c. 1800–1875) was a daughter of Rebecca Chambers Clopper of Chambersburg, Pennsylvania, and by that connection was related to Belle. She moved west with members of her family in the 1820s and remained in the Cincinnati area, where the Cloppers acquired adjacent properties called Rose Cottage and Beechwood, about a third of a mile from their Ludlow relatives' home seat at Ludlow Station. Caroline, who as a teenager had been educated at a Moravian young ladies' seminary in Bethlehem, Pennsylvania, worked as a governess and taught school, and in 1851, after Belle Chase returned to Ohio from Texas, she played a role in Belle's care. She also became Nettie's governess and teacher in Clifton and at the Ludlow and Clopper properties around Cumminsville for some months following Belle's death early in 1852.[22]

Belle's (and little Nettie's) visit to Texas in the winter of 1850–51 was the product of marriage connections between the interlaced Ludlow-Chambers-Dunlop clans and the Kenner family of Louisiana. After the death of Belle's grandfather Israel in 1804, her grandmother Charlotte Chambers Ludlow married a clergyman, David Riske. They evidently had at least three daughters: one named Ruhamah, who married William Butler Kenner of Louisiana; Charlotte, AUNT CHARLOTTE KENNER in the family's correspondence, who in the mid-1840s married Kenner's brother, GEORGE R. KENNER (1812–52); and another daughter, whose widowhood Chase alluded to in his letter to Kate of October 8, 1853. A member of a prominent planting family, George Kenner moved to Matagorda County, Texas, as it became a sugar-growing area.[23] He called his property, on Caney Creek in an area along the Gulf Coast naturally suited to growing cane, "Oakland" after his family's home plantation in Louisiana. Apparently the extended family found means of accommodating the contradiction posed by some of its members' ownership of slaves and Chase's prominence in free soil politics. Once when Adela Ludlow paid a call in January 1848, Chase "told Belle to speak to her about Texas slaves." Such a direct confrontation of the issue was unusual, perhaps unique, the existence of the Kenners' slaves receiving little notice in the family's correspondence. Charlotte Kenner may not have been the most adamant proponent of slavery in any case: when a series of house burglaries plagued

Clifton, Ohio, in 1852, it was Charlotte and her daughter Emily, on a visit to their Ohio relatives, who went to the empty Chase residence with a servant named Shadrach and, finding the other silver already in the protection of other family members, brought away an inscribed pitcher presented to Chase in 1845 for his efforts to assist Samuel Watson, a fugitive slave. Charlotte and Emily deemed the pitcher "the most valuable article in your possession, from its being a testimonial of regard and gratitude, from an oppressed people whom you have benefited." After her husband's death that year, Charlotte put the plantation up for sale and transferred ownership of its enslaved labor force to a Kenner brother-in-law to settle a debt.[24]

Charlotte Riske had the surname Jones when she wed George Kenner, and the COUSIN EMILY or EMMIE JONES associated with her in the correspondence must have been a daughter from the previous marriage. Emily had a sister, Georgine, whose death in 1852, along with that of George Kenner, still affected Charlotte Kenner when Chase wrote to Kate on October 8, 1853.[25] Ruhamah and William Butler Kenner had a daughter named Josephine, the JOSIE KENNER mentioned in the family's correspondence during the early 1850s as one of Kate's schoolmates in New York. BELLE KENNER, also a student at Henrietta Haines's school and who died unexpectedly in New York in 1852, was probably her sister. Their siblings Charlotte (LOTTIE) Kenner, MARY Minor Kenner, and Frederic BUTLER Kenner, all likely younger than Belle and Josephine, are mentioned in Belle Chase's letter to Kate of December 11, 1850.[26] In terms of generations within the family, Charlotte Riske Jones Kenner and Ruhamah Riske Kenner were Belle Chase's aunts (half-aunts, actually) and Nettie's great aunts, but some of their children were evidently younger than Kate Chase.

Belle Chase's connection to the Collins family of Hillsboro, Ohio, came by way of her mother and the Dunlop branch. One of her mother's sisters, Jane Catherine Dunlop, married Caspar W. Wever, an engineer for the National Road. She is mentioned once in this volume as AUNT WEVER. One of their daughters married Dr. C. C. Sams of Hillsboro, and afterward another daughter, CATHARINE (1818–1911), married WILLIAM OLIVER COLLINS (1809–80), a Hillsboro attorney and businessman. After Belle died, it was with her cousin Catharine that Chase placed young Nettie to stay, particularly from November 1853 to September 1855. During that period Chase was to pay Catharine Collins three dollars a week for Nettie's board, plus her expenses for clothing. Kate, too, stayed in Hillsboro for a time in 1855, and both she and Nettie visited the Collins household when their father was occupied by the Ohio election of 1857. Significantly, Catharine Collins gave Nettie what were very likely her first lessons in drawing, as well as some instruction in French. In 1854, Mrs. Collins expressed the "pleasure" she derived from having Nettie in her home. Just as the Collinses were effectively Nettie's foster parents for a couple of years, her presence in their household helped fill a void created by the death of a daughter, Mary Collins, at the age of six. Catharine Collins wrote Chase "of the solace to my heart" given by Nettie "since the death of my own sweet, darling Mary."[27] Nevertheless, in correspondence between Chase, Kate, and Nettie, the Collinses were referred to as "Mr." (later "Col.") and "Mrs.," only occasionally receiving fictive reference as Nettie's "uncle" and "aunt" (as in Chase's letter of August 10, 1860). Perhaps Nettie avoided using the term "cousin" for Mrs. Collins because it would have implied membership in the same generation. When Kate Ludlow (who like Belle was Catharine Collins's first cousin) penned the letter of September 29, 1850, on young Nettie's behalf, she did refer to Mrs. Collins as "our Cousin."

In his letter to Kate of March 23, 1855, Chase called the Collins's daughter JOSEPHINE (JOSIE) COLLINS (d. 1916) Nettie's "little cousin." Josie, according to a young Nettie Chase, "is a year younger than me" (see Nettie's letter of April 1, 1854). The oldest child in the Collins family was a son, CASPAR WEVER COLLINS (1844–65), who like Nettie received drawing lessons from his mother. When William O. Collins, concluding a term as a state senator, raised a cavalry regiment during the Civil War, it was deployed not against the Confederates, but to the West to protect the overland mail route. Caspar, still in his teens, accompanied his father as a volunteer clerk and draftsman. Receiving a lieutenant's commission in June 1863, Caspar remained in the West in the spring of 1865 when his father was mustered out of the service. In July of that year the younger Collins was killed in a dramatic clash with Native Americans on the North Platte River. His father already having left behind a Fort Collins in Colorado, Caspar's first name, with an inadvertent misspelling that became permanent, was given to the place where he had died: Casper, Wyoming.[28]

II.

Kate and Nettie never knew their paternal grandparents, Ithamar (1762–1817) and Jannette (or Janet) Ralston Chase (1773–1832) of Cornish, New Hampshire. Salmon Portland Chase, born in 1808, was one of ten children to survive early childhood. The firstborn of his siblings, his sister Hannah Ralston Chase Whipple (1792–1850), does not appear in the letters in this volume, but her husband and widower, JOHN WHIPPLE (1789–1857), an attorney, local official, and businessman, does.[29] They resided near Hopkinton and later at Concord, New Hampshire, and had six children, two of whom, ELIZA CHASE WHIPPLE and HANNAH RALSTON WHIPPLE, had close relationships with Chase, Nettie, and Kate. Hannah and Eliza generally appear in the letters by their first names unadorned by titles, although Chase referred to Eliza Whipple as AUNT ELIZA in some correspondence addressed to Nettie. This practice may indicate that, as in the case of Catharine Collins, the age difference between Nettie and Eliza was sufficient to place Eliza out of range for comfortable address as "cousin." If so, circumstances were different for Kate, for Eliza appears at least once in a letter from Chase to Kate as COUSIN ELIZA. Too, Eliza was so much a part of her sister's household that she may well have been the person whom Hannah called, in a letter to Chase, "Auntie." In that case, her fictive role as Nettie's "Aunt Eliza" could have been, in part, an artifact of her relationship with Hannah's children.[30]

Before Kate and Nettie were even born, for more than two years during the period 1838–40, Eliza lived in Chase's household in Cincinnati. During part of that time her cousin Jenny Skinner and their aunt Helen Chase also resided with the widowed Chase and his young child (the first Kate). In May 1839 it was a note to Eliza, left on the parlor table where its misspellings caught his eye, that first brought Eliza's seventeen-year-old friend, Lizzie Smith, to Chase's attention.

Later that year the widower married his niece's young friend, Eliza later recalling Lizzie with fondness as "my girl aunt." Back in Concord, Eliza taught school briefly, was treasurer of the Soldiers' Aid Society, a local women's relief organization, during the Civil War, and spent much of her time in the household of her sister Hannah, who in 1857 married JOSIAH PRENTICE TUCKER.[31] During the war Tucker had customhouse positions in Boston and New Orleans, afterward evidently splitting his time between Boston and New Hampshire. In 1868 he worked actively in the unsuccessful movement to secure the Democratic presidential nomination for Chase.

Another tie connected the Chases and the Whipples. In July 1842, Frances Mary ("Frank") Smith, an older sister of Kate's mother, married Boston merchant John L. Whipple, who was apparently a nephew of John Whipple of New Hampshire. Frances, afflicted with the tuberculosis that felled so many of her family at a young age, died less than a year after her marriage. Chase and her husband had some correspondence thereafter, but John L. Whipple, who remarried in 1844, seems not to have retained any overt kinship status for Nettie and Kate—in other words, they and their father do not seem to have called him "uncle." The same holds true for the senior John Whipple following the death of Hannah Chase Whipple in 1850. He was likely the "Mr. Whipple" meant by Chase in his letters to Kate in July 1854.[32]

Chase's oldest brother, Alexander Ralston Chase (1797–1847), died too early to play any role in Kate's and Nettie's correspondence, and his wife, Stella King Chase, either died also or simply faded from view. However, their daughter, whose married name was JANE CHASE AULD (b. 1824 or 1825), intermittently appeared in Chase's correspondence over many years, if sometimes in unhappy circumstances. Alexander Chase suffered from health problems, including alcoholism, and never established himself financially. Even before his death Jane's family was often separated, her father in search of a livelihood, her mother boarding with relatives, Jane herself posted with Alexander's brothers in succession. In the spring of 1843, with Lizzie Chase ailing from tuberculosis, Jane lived with Chase and Lizzie in Cincinnati, and Chase found his niece to be a "solitary & reserved" member of the household.[33] She married, but her husband, Robert Auld, died a few years into their marriage, leaving Jane with three daughters, Jane (JENNIE), ALICE, and AMY, all of whom must have been born between the later 1840s and the early 1850s. Chase provided financial assistance to the little family, and as indicated in his letter to Kate of April 13, 1855, Jane Auld obtained employment in the school in Clifton, the Cincinnati suburb dominated by Chase's influential friends. Her position there evidently did not last, however, for later in the 1850s and in the 1860s she resided elsewhere in Ohio, seemingly never far from financial hardship. When the 1860 census was taken, Jane and her daughters Jennie (age 12) and Alice (age 9) were listed as members of the Chase household in Columbus.[34] Jennie died late in 1864 or early in 1865 after a difficult illness. Alice and Amy Auld were among the nieces who made extended visits to Chase in Washington during the last years of his life. In his will he set aside $6,000 for the Aulds, Jane to receive seven percent interest from the money during her life and her daughters, if they survived her, to divide the principal between them upon her death. In 1874 Amy married Edward Yerbury Goldsborough, a Maryland attorney and younger brother of Chase's friend Mary Goldsborough.[35]

Like Alexander Chase, Chase's sister Abigail Corbet Chase (1799–1838) and their brother Dudley Heber Chase (1801–20), who died after going to sea as a teenager, played no direct role in Kate's and Nettie's lives. With her husband, ISAAC COLBY (1793–1866), a physician and antislavery advocate, Abigail had moved from New Hampshire to Cincinnati early in the 1830s, not long after Chase went there. Abigail, who had taught school in New England and was described by a niece as "a great scholar" adept at Latin, Greek, French, German, and Italian, had six children with Dr. Colby, but they all died at an early age.[36]

AUNT JANE, Chase's sister Janette Logan Chase Skinner (1803–56?), lived in Lockport, New York, with her husband Josiah K. Skinner, a physician and native of Vermont. Letters in this volume mention four of the Skinners' seven offspring, the oldest of whom were significantly older than Kate Chase. Presuming that the order in which Chase listed them in his "Family Memoranda" may reflect their birth sequence, the eldest was Kate's and Nettie's COUSIN BELLE, Isabel R. D. Skinner. Like her cousin Eliza Whipple, Belle Skinner may have made a sojourn to Cincinnati as a schoolgirl. She married GEORGE WALBRIDGE (d. 1861) and lived with him in Toledo, evidently forming a link to another family connected to the Chases (see below). JANETTE SKINNER had her mother's first name, but went by JENNY rather than Jane. She too made an extended stay in Chase's household in Cincinnati, where she attended school in 1839. In 1852, she married J. J. L. C. ("Jack") Jewett, the MR. JEWETT of the letter written by a teenaged Nettie Chase on August 26, 1865. In that letter Nettie also discussed the Jewetts' young twin daughters, BELLE and DAISY. Jenny and Jack, who had other children as well, lived in Buffalo, New York, until unspecified business difficulties may have displaced them.[37]

Next in Chase's sequence stood JAMES RALSTON SKINNER (1830–93), closely associated with the Chase household for a number of years. Known initially as James but soon calling himself by his middle name, Ralston moved to Cincinnati from Lockport during the late 1840s. Through the 1850s he read law, tended to various tasks in Chase's law office, and acted as a property manager and general factotum for his often-absent uncle. It was he who noted Nettie's energetic little tabletop "Mazurka" in 1848. His involvement with Chase's business and legal affairs bringing him into contact with the Ludlow estate, he developed close relationships with some members of that family. Indeed his decision to stop using his first name parallels that of his good friend, Belle Chase's brother James Dunlop Ludlow. In 1857, Skinner married Louisa Wiggins, a daughter of Samuel Wiggins. During the Civil War Skinner worked in the office of the second comptroller in Washington, then joined the army as a judge advocate and major of volunteers, attaining with his uncle's influence a position on the staff of Maj. Gen. William S. Rosecrans.[38]

Before the war, however, Skinner had suffered depression and delusional episodes. Early in 1863, home on leave after the ferocious battle at Stones River, he suffered a nervous collapse that an extended rest under Dunlop Ludlow's watchful eye could not cure. Skinner entered the Pennsylvania Hospital in Philadelphia but was unable to recover sufficiently to resume service with the army. Thought by his wife to be "much improved" by September 1865, he nonetheless does not appear in the correspondence in this volume after 1862.[39]

The fourth and youngest of the Skinner offspring mentioned in the letters in this volume, ALICE (ALLIE), attended Kate's wedding in November 1863 and afterward accompanied Nettie in the wedding party to Rhode Island. According to Chase, Alice at that time "took the palm of admiration from every body. She is as sweet as she can be." By mid-1872 she had married Henry Stebbins of Boston. Perhaps the last letter Chase ever wrote was one to Alice Stebbins, who had suggested that he come to Boston for medical treatment.[40]

Alice Skinner bore the name of her (and Nettie's and Kate's) AUNT ALICE, Chase's sister closest to him in age. Never married, her intention to wed Josiah Skinner's brother dashed by his death shortly before the wedding, ALICE JONES CHASE (1805–59) provided live-in help to her brother's household from time to time, for example during the interval, from late 1845 into 1846, between Lizzie Chase's death and Chase's marriage to Belle. Alice was with the family again in Columbus in February 1859, when on her return from an evening lecture at the Episcopal church she collapsed from a stroke in the dooryard of the house. She died during the night despite the ministrations of two physicians.[41]

After chafing under the tutelage of their uncle Philander Chase at Kenyon College in Ohio, Chase's younger brother EDWARD ITHAMAR CHASE (1810–62) settled upon a career in law and lighted, as had their sister Jane, in Lockport, New York. There Kate's and Nettie's UNCLE EDWARD was a lawyer and, from 1861 until his death the next year, United States marshal for the northern district of New York. He appears in this volume only through the role that he and his wife Mary Eliza played in assisting the daughters of his and Chase's brothers Alexander and William.

The youngest of the brothers, William Frederick Chase (1813–52), died in St. Louis too early to figure in the correspondence in this volume. Like Edward, he married a woman named Mary, the former Mary Gillespie of St. Louis. William, troubled and irresponsible, died indigent.[42] His widow was the AUNT MARY who, as Chase mentioned in his letter of August 4, 1853, moved to Lockport to live under Edward's benefaction. With her were two daughters, Kate's and Nettie's cousins MISSOURI, who died of consumption in 1859, and VIRGINIA, who married William H. Shook (b. 1832) and lived with him in Kentucky and Indiana.[43]

Under the scrutiny of her sister Abigail, Helen Maria Chase (1815–64), the youngest of Chase's brothers and sisters, studied Latin and other subjects as a girl in New England, then moved to Cincinnati with Abigail and her husband early in the 1830s. AUNT HELEN acted as Chase's housekeeper off and on before her marriage in 1839 to Henry B. Walbridge, who became an Episcopal minister in Toledo. Before the spring of 1862, Helen suffered a stroke that left her with a residual lameness on the right side of her body, despite her use of an exercise "machine" prescribed by a physician in New York to strengthen her leg. She died late in 1864. Of Helen's children mentioned in the letters in this volume, MARY must have succumbed to the advanced tuberculosis that Chase noted in his letter of April 22, 1855, when she was seventeen. Also as noted in that letter, a baby boy had died earlier that year. We know that in 1867 Lillie Walbridge (rendered consistently by her Uncle Salmon as LILY) acted as her father's housekeeper and that her sister ALICE attended Kemper Hall, an Episcopal school for young women recently established in Kenosha, Wisconsin. DUDLEY was a clerk in the Custom House in New York during the Civil War and later worked as a commission merchant in Chicago.[44]

Their brother W. HUNT WALBRIDGE (born c. 1845) caused Chase some embarrassment during the war. In 1862, Hunt enlisted for three months' service with a company of "the first boys of Toledo," but even the conditions at Camp Chase, Ohio, well removed from the hardships of battle and life on the march, revealed to him his "utter inability to sustain the hardship of a soldiers life." Yet after a well-placed word from Kate landed him an easy posting as a clerk on the staff of the general who superintended military railroads in that district of Ohio, Hunt boldly determined upon a military career and importuned his influential uncle for an appointment to West Point. Within six months of his arrival at the academy, however, Hunt amassed enough demerits to require his dismissal. Chase appealed personally to Abraham Lincoln, who along with the secretary of war was willing to intervene. However, Hunt's transgressions, unspecified in his uncle's correspondence with the Walbridges, proved to be such that the law forbade his reinstatement. Hunt, who pleaded that he had "never been really designedly bad," subsequently failed to retain business positions in Detroit and Toledo. When he continued to entreat for assistance in obtaining a position, Chase patiently replied that he could not give him a satisfactory recommendation and that Hunt must reform his ways.[45]

III.

The final extensions of the family came by way of Kate's and Nettie's own marriages, and they in fact wed into two families that were already interrelated. On November 12, 1863, Kate married WILLIAM SPRAGUE (1830–1915) of Rhode Island. William's father, Amasa Sprague Sr., had died in 1843. William's mother, Fanny Morgan Sprague (b. 1805), appears in letters in this volume as MRS. SPRAGUE. She comes across in the correspondence as something of a cipher, more of a location to be visited in Providence than a person with distinctive traits. A shoemaker's daughter, she had married William's father in 1824. William's brother, also named AMASA SPRAGUE (1828–1902), lived in Cranston, Rhode Island, the original base of the family's cotton printing operations. Amasa's wife, Mary, died in 1864. William and his brother had two sisters. One of them, ALMIRA SPRAGUE, married Thomas Arthur Doyle, a Providence politician, in 1869. The other sister, Mary Ann, married first John E. Nichols and subsequently Frank W. Latham. Mary Ann's daughter, Ida Nichols, was a bridesmaid at Kate's wedding. In 1864 and 1865, Ida sometimes visited Kate and Nettie. Ida abruptly and without fanfare married Philip Tillinghast in 1866, and the couple immediately left on a trip to Europe under Mary Ann's escort. The hasty marriage and quick departure implied scandal, and even the flawed William Sprague referred to Philip Tillinghast as "dissolute." The Tillinghasts were not permanently out of favor, however, since Chase recorded in his journal that the couple came to dinner at Narragansett in June 1872.[46]

Through Kate's and William's courtship and marriage, Nettie became acquainted with two sisters, SARAH and SUSIE Hoyt. Born in 1844 and 1845, respectively, the Hoyt sisters were slightly older than Nettie. They were daughters of William's first cousin, Susan Sprague Hoyt, who was born about 1822 and died in 1853. Sarah and Susie had two younger brothers, one of whom, WILLIAM

SPRAGUE HOYT (1847–1905), became Nettie's husband on March 23, 1871. Sarah Hoyt married J. Bowers LEE in January 1869. In August of that year, Susie, whose proper name was Susan S. Hoyt, became SUSIE FRANCKLYN when she and Englishman Charles G. Francklyn, a nephew of Sir Edward Cunard of the trans-atlantic steamship company, married. Both sisters continued to reside in New York. The Hoyt siblings' father, Edwin Hoyt (1804–74) was the MR. HOYT mentioned in letters in this volume. A native of Stamford, Connecticut, he began his career as a clerk in a New York business, became a successful commission merchant in the dry goods trade, and weathered the Panic of 1837 to attain renewed prosperity. In 1858, he joined members of the Sprague family to form Hoyt, Spragues, and Co. Described as an energetic and self-reliant businessman, on his death he was commended for his "unswerving rectitude and integrity," and prominent dry goods merchants paid homage at his Presbyterian funeral service. He has been characterized as "one of the most quiet and modest of men." That diffidence may account for the fact that little of Edwin Hoyt as a person comes through in the letters in this volume.[47]

1. *Chase Papers*, 1:82.

2. Chase to Helen Chase, Apr. 24, 1836, Helen to Chase, Dec. 20, 21, 1837, John Garniss to Chase, May 27, Oct. 2, 1854, Aug. 1, 1855 (Chase Papers, HSP); Chase to David Austen, Mar. 16, 1867 (Chase Papers, LC).

3. Cordelia Austen to Chase, Nov. 2, 1846, John G. Austen to Chase, July 7, 1862 (Chase Papers, LC); *The New-York City Directory, for 1852–1853* (New York: John Doggett Jr., 1852), 34–35.

4. Eliza Chase Whipple memorandum of recollections, [ca. 1873] (Chase Papers, HSP); interment record, Spring Grove Cemetery, Cincinnati.

5. To Charles D. Cleveland, Oct. 1, 1845. *Chase Papers*, 2:121–22.

6. Interment records, Spring Grove Cemetery, Cincinnati; 1850 census, Hamilton Co., Ohio, Cincinnati Ward 2, 143; Chase to Febiger, June 17, 1862 (Chase Papers, HSP). For Carrie's schooling in Kentucky, see her letters to Chase, November 1845 to March 1846 (Chase Papers, LC). Lizzie Chase's father, Edmund C. Smith Sr., like several of his offspring, died of tuberculosis (interment records, Spring Grove Cemetery, Cincinnati).

7. Jon L. Wakelyn, *Biographical Dictionary of the Confederacy* (Westport, Conn.: Greenwood Press, 1977), 221–22.

8. Interment records, Spring Grove Cemetery, Cincinnati.

9. Just over a month before the wedding ceremony in their home, the McLeans lost the only child they had together, a baby boy named Ludlow who died in October 1846 at ten months of age. Before marrying McLean in 1843, Sarah Bella Ludlow was the widow of Jeptha Garrard. She had children by that marriage who survived to adulthood. John McLean had also been married before and had children from his first marriage. *Chase Papers*, 1:51, 106, 110, 179, 188, 207, 217, 413; *ANB*, 15:143; interment records, Spring Grove Cemetery, Cincinnati.

10. The four were Israel, Josephine, Ruhamah, and Catherine. Statement of account with Catherine Ludlow Baker, Feb. 10, 1852, or after, in legal papers, Chase Papers, LC.

11. Israel Ludlow to Chase, Feb. 26, 1866 (Chase Papers, LC).

12. Robson, *Biographical Encyclopædia*, 629; James Dunlop Ludlow to Chase, May 25, June 27, 1861, Catharine Ludlow Whiteman to Chase, June 13, 1861 (Chase Papers, LC).

13. The name can be traced at least as far as Ruhamah Chambers, a daughter of Benjamin Chambers, the founder of Chambersburg, Pa. Paul Swain Havens, *Chambersburg, Frontier Town, 1740–1794: A Bicentennial Narrative of the Origin and Growth of Chambersburg and Franklin County in Pennsylvania* (Chambersburg, Pa.: Craft Press, 1975), 41.

14. Emily Jones to Chase, Mar. 2, 1853 (Chase Papers, LC); *Chase Papers*, 3:37–40, 223, 323.

15. *Appletons'*, 7:169–70; Heitman, *Historical Register*, 1:646; Robson, *Biographical Encyclopædia*, 629; Benjamin C. Ludlow to Chase, Oct. 31, 1862 (Chase Papers, LC).

16. Catherine Ludlow to Chase, Sept. 29, 1850, James Dunlop Ludlow to same, Dec. 26, 1850, May 30, 1860, March 4, 1862, and statement of account with Catherine, Feb. 10, 1852, or after (Chase Papers, LC); interment records, Spring Grove Cemetery, Cincinnati. For Burnet's school, see Chase to Kate, July 22, 1850, in chapter 1.

17. Ludlow to Chase, Oct. 8, 1847, Apr. 30, 1848, Feb. 6, Apr. 11, 1850, Apr. 16, 1862, Oct. 5, 1868 (Chase Papers, LC); J. S. Lothrop, comp., *J. S. Lothrop's Champaign County Directory, 1870–1, with History of the Same, and of Each Township Therein* (Chicago: Rand, McNally and Co., 1871), 390–93.

18. Coyle, *Ohio Authors*, 343.

19. James Dunlop Ludlow to Chase, Dec. 26, 1850 (Chase Papers, LC).

20. Interment record, Spring Grove Cemetery, Cincinnati; Ruth V. McKee, *Ludlows in America in the 17th, 18th, and 19th Centuries* (Minneapolis: Surname Sources, 1989), 36; Chase to Helen A. Ludlow, Chase to Ambrose Burnside, both June 4, 1863 (Telegrams sent, 1850–74, General Records of the Department of the Treasury, Record Group 56, National Archives); Chase to Edwin M. Stanton, June 4, 1863 (Chase Papers, HSP).

21. Charles S. Clarkson to Chase, Dec. 8, 1842, Mar. 15, 1848, Oct. 7, 1858, Charlotte C. Clarkson to Chase, June 19, 1861 (Chase Papers, LC).

22. Clopper, *American Family*, 21, 25, 42, 58–59, 104–5, 212, 231, 283, 418–19, 422–23, 446, 570; Charlotte Ludlow Jones to Chase, Mar. 9, May 26, 1852, and C. C. Clopper to Chase, June 30, 1852 (Chase Papers, LC).

23. Clopper, *American Family*, 98–99; Stanley Clisby Arthur, *Old Families of Louisiana* (New Orleans, La.: Harmanson, 1931), 159; Craig A. Bauer, *A Leader among Peers: The Life and Times of Duncan Farrar Kenner* (Lafayette, La.: University of Southwestern Louisiana, 1993), 17–18, 33–34; Junann J. Stieghorst, *Bay City and Matagorda County: A History* (Austin, Tex.: Pemberton Press, 1965), 3, 17; Glenn R. Conrad, gen. ed., *A Dictionary of Louisiana Biography*, 2 vols. (New Orleans, La.: Louisiana Historical Association, 1988), 1:460.

24. *Chase Papers*, 1:172, 195; Emily Jones to Chase, May 26, Dec. 13, 1852, Mar. 2, 1853 (Chase Papers, LC).

25. Emily Jones to Chase, May 26, 1852 (Chase Papers, LC).

26. Arthur, *Old Families*, 159.

27. Catharine Collins to Chase, Sept. 21, 1854, Aug. 25, Dec. 11, 1855 (Chase Papers, LC); Chase to Kate, Aug. 10, 1855 (Chase Papers, HSP); Spring, *Caspar Collins*, 53–56. Although the available sources spell her mother's middle name "Catherine," Mrs. Collins signed herself "Catharine."

28. Spring, *Caspar Collins*, 50, 68, 96; see also Chase's letter to Kate of Sept. 4, 1865, above in this volume. Spring's book reproduces some of Caspar's sketches—less skilled, it would seem, than Nettie's work—of Western scenes.

29. Lyford, *History of Concord*, 1:395, 664; 2:969, 972.

30. Hannah Whipple Tucker to Chase, Sept. 23, 1872 (Chase Papers, LC).

31. Eliza Chase Whipple to Chase, Aug. 31, 1857, to [Jacob W. Schuckers], June 27, [1873], and memorandum of recollections, [1873] (Chase Papers, HSP); Lyford, *History of Concord*, 1:496; 2:1173, 1250; John Whipple to Chase, July 16, 1840 (Chase Papers, LC); *Chase Papers*, 1:119.

32. John Whipple (Concord) to Chase, July 16, 1840, Sept. 1, 1842, Chase to Lewis Tappan, Sept. 24, 1842, John L. Whipple (Boston) to Chase, Nov. 15, 1842 (with note from Frances to Lizzie), May 8, 1844, Apr. 29, Oct. 11, Nov. 28, 1845 (Chase Papers, LC).

33. *Chase Papers*, 1:163; Alexander Ralston Chase to Chase, Nov. 9, 1836, July 1840, June 11, 1846 (Chase Papers, LC).

34. 1860 census, Franklin County, Ohio, Columbus Ward 2, 86; *Lathrop's Columbus Directory* (Columbus, OH, [1860]), 3.

35. Chase's assistance to the Aulds included, in 1863, $1,000 he received from his brother Edward's widow in repayment of an old loan. Chase placed the money with Jay Cooke for investment in Jane Auld's behalf. *Chase Papers*, 4:240; *New York Times*, May 22, 1873; Williams and McKinsey, *Frederick County*, 2:1241–42.

36. Eliza Whipple to [Jacob W. Schuckers], June 27, [1873] (Chase Papers, HSP); see also *Chase Papers*, 2:33–36.

37. Isabel Skinner to Chase, May 16, 1836, Jan. 19, 1837, Jenny Jewett to Chase, May 18, 1859, June 22, 1863, Chase to Jenny, Mar. 28, 1867 (Chase Papers, LC).

38. W. P. Anderson, *Anderson Family Records* (Cincinnati: W. F. Schaefer & Co., 1936), 156–57; Carrie A. Smith to Chase, Dec. 3, 1845, Chase to Ralston Skinner, Jan. 8, Feb. 27,

1850, Ralston Skinner to Chase, Dec. 18, 1848, Oct. 4, 1852, Mar. 16, 1857, Oct. 4, Nov. 26, 1858, June 21, 1862 (Chase Papers, LC).

39. *Chase Papers,* 1:511–12, 595–96, 696; Ralston Skinner to Chase, June 24, 1850, Nov. 15, 1862, Jan. 14, Mar. 27, Aug. 22, Sept. 5, 1863, July 9, 29, 1864, James Dunlop Ludlow to Chase, June 5, 11, Oct. 1, 1863 (Chase Papers, LC); Chase to Laura Wiggins, May 23, 1863, Chase to Ralston Skinner, Sept. 12, 1863, Chase to Louisa Skinner, Jan. 10, 1865, Charles A. Dana to Chase, Feb. 13, 1865 (Chase Papers, HSP); Heitman, *Historical Register,* 1:890.

40. Chase to Belle Walbridge, May 4, 1864 (Chase Papers, HSP); Alice Skinner to Chase, Nov. 22, 1863, and as Alice Nora Stebbins, May 6, 1873 (Chase Papers, LC); *Chase Papers,* 5:370.

41. Chase recorded the incident in his journal: *Chase Papers,* 1:310–11. For Alice's betrothal, Eliza Whipple to [Jacob W. Schuckers], June 27, [1873] (Chase Papers, HSP).

42. Niven, *Chase,* 72.

43. William Shook was evidently dead or absent for some reason by 1870. Virginia Shook to Chase, Dec. 14, 1862, Jan. 20, 1867, William H. Shook to Chase, Apr. 29, 1863, Chase to Virginia Shook, Mar. 31, 1870 (Chase Papers, LC).

44. W. Hunt Walbridge to Chase, Mar. 4, Oct. 30, 1862, Henry B. Walbridge to Chase, June 5, Sept. 22, 1862, May 21, 1863, Dec. 4, 1867 (Chase Papers, LC); Harold Ezra Wagner, *The Episcopal Church in Wisconsin, 1847–1947: A History of the Diocese of Milwaukee* (Milwaukee, Wis.: Diocese of Milwaukee, 1947), 169–70.

45. W. Hunt Walbridge to Chase, Mar. 4, June 17, Aug. 26, Oct. 30, 1862, Dec. 7, 1863, Feb. 17, 1864, Henry B. Walbridge to Chase, Dec. 4, 1867, Chase to W. Hunt Walbridge, June 20, 1870 (Chase Papers, LC); Chase to Henry B. Walbridge, July 9, 1862, July 11, 1864, Chase to W. Hunt Walbridge, Feb. 18, 1864, Apr. 14, 1865, Chase to Helen Chase Walbridge, Jan. 22, Feb. 11, 1864 (Chase Papers, HSP).

46. Warren Vincent Sprague, *Sprague Families in America* (Rutland, Vt.: Tuttle Co., 1913), 299, 389, 416; Oliver Payson Fuller, *The History of Warwick, Rhode Island* (Providence, R.I.: Angell, Burlingame & Co., 1875), 255–56; Knight, *History of the Sprague Families,* 9, 17–20; *Representative Men and Old Families of Rhode Island,* 1:416; Lamphier, *Kate Chase and William Sprague,* 67, 73, 275; *Chase Papers,* 1:499, 501, 512, 515, 590, 692; 4:432; William to Kate, May 22, 1866 (Brown University Library).

47. David W. Hoyt, *A Genealogical History of the Hoyt, Haight, and Hight Families* (Boston, 1871; repr., Somersworth, N.H.: New England History Press, 1984), 469–70; *Representative Men and Old Families of Rhode Island,* 1:416; Edwin Hoyt's obituary and funeral notice, *New York Times,* May 16 and 19, 1874.

Bibliography

The works in this list are cited in shortened form throughout the book. Works with special abbreviations are listed first. Books and articles in the main listing of the bibliography are cited in the notes by author's last name and a shortened form of the title.

ABBREVIATIONS

ANB   *American National Biography.* Edited by John Arthur Garraty and Mark C. Carnes. 24 vols. New York: Oxford University Press, 1999.

Bio. Dir. U.S. Cong.   *Biographical Directory of the United States Congress, 1774–1989.* Edited by Bruce A. Ragsdale and Kathryn Allamong Jacob. Bicentennial Edition. Washington, D.C.: General Publications Office, 1989.

Chase Papers   *The Salmon P. Chase Papers.* John Niven, James P. McClure, Leigh Johnsen, et al., eds. 5 vols. Kent, Ohio: Kent State University Press, 1993–98.

DAB   *Dictionary of American Biography.* American Council of Learned Societies. 20 vols. Supplement, 10 vols. New York: Charles Scribner's Sons, 1928–96.

Nat. Cyc.   *The National Cyclopaedia of American Biography.* 63 vols. New York: J. T. White, 1891–1984.

ODNB   *Oxford Dictionary of National Biography.* Edited by H. C. G. Matthew and Brian Howard Harrison. 60 vols. Oxford: Oxford University Press, 2004.

OED   *The Oxford English Dictionary.* Edited by J. A. Simpson and E. S. C. Weiner. 2d ed. 20 vols. Oxford: Oxford University Press, 1989.

OR   *The War of the Rebellion: A Compilation of the Official Records of the Union and Confederate Armies.* 128 vols. Washington, D.C.: Government Printing Office, 1880–1901.

WORKS CITED BY AUTHOR AND TITLE

Allgor, Catherine. *Parlor Politics: In Which the Ladies of Washington Help Build a City and a Government.* Charlottesville, Va.: University Press of Virginia, 2000.

Appletons' Cyclopædia of American Biography. Edited by James Grant Wilson and John Fiske. 6 vols. New York: D. Appleton & Co., 1887–89.

Ashmead, Henry Graham. *History of Delaware County, Pennsylvania.* Philadelphia: Everts, 1884.

Bacon, Edgar Mayhew. *Narragansett Bay: Its Historic and Romantic Associations and Picturesque Setting.* New York: Putnam, 1904.

Beale, Howard K., ed. *Diary of Gideon Welles, Secretary of the Navy under Lincoln and Johnson.* 3 vols. New York: W. W. Norton, 1960.

Beckman, Elizabeth. *An In-depth Study of the Cincinnati Silversmiths, Jewelers, Watch and Clockmakers Through 1850.* Cincinnati: B.B. & Co., 1975.

Belden, Thomas Graham, and Marva Robins Belden. *So Fell the Angels.* Boston: Little, Brown, 1956.

Benedict, Michael Les. "Salmon P. Chase and Constitutional Politics." *Law and Social Inquiry* 22 (1997): 459–500.

Blue, Frederick J. *Salmon P. Chase : A Life in Politics.* Kent, Ohio: Kent State University Press, 1987.

Boyd, William H. *Boyd's Washington and Georgetown Directory.* Washington, D.C.: Boyd and Waite, 1860.

Brooke Hall Female Seminary. *Catalogue of the Teachers and Pupils of Brooke Hall Female Seminary.* Media, Pa., 1872–73.

Burlingame, Michael, ed. *At Lincoln's Side: John Hay's Civil War Correspondence and Selected Writings.* Carbondale, Ill.: Southern Illinois University Press, 2000.

Burlingame, Michael, and John R. T. Ettlinger. *Inside Lincoln's White House: The Complete Civil War Diary of John Hay.* Carbondale, Ill.: Southern Illinois University Press, 1997.

Burrows, Edwin G., and Mike Wallace. *Gotham: A History of New York City to 1898.* New York: Oxford University Press, 1999.

Catalogue of a Most Superb Collection of Extremely Rare and Elaborate Furniture . . . Formed by the Late Hon. Salmon Portland Chase. New York: Alexander Press, 1900.

Chambrun, Clara Longworth de. *The Making of Nicholas Longworth: Annals of an American Family.* New York: R. Long & R. R. Smith, 1933.

Charvat, William, et al., eds. *The Centenary Edition of the Works of Nathaniel Hawthorne.* 23 vols. Columbus, Ohio: Ohio State University Press, 1962–97.

Clemmer, Mary. *Ten Years in Washington: or, Inside Life and Scenes in Our National Capital as a Woman Sees Them.* Hartford, Conn.: Hartford Publishing Co., 1883.

Clopper, Edward Nicholas. *An American Family: Its Ups and Downs through Eight Generations in New Amersterdam, New York, Pennsylvania, Maryland, Ohio, and Texas, from 1650 to 1880.* Cincinnati, Ohio: privately printed, 1950.

Coleman, Charles H. *The Election of 1868: The Democratic Effort to Regain Control.* New York: Columbia University, 1933.

Coyle, William. *Ohio Authors and Their Books: Biographical Data and Selective Bibliographies for Ohio Authors, Native and Resident, 1796–1950.* Cleveland: World Publishing Co., 1962.

Denney, Robert E. *The Civil War Years: A Day-by-Day Chronicle of the Life of a Nation.* New York: Sterling Publishing Co., 1992.

Donald, David. *Lincoln.* New York: Simon & Schuster, 1995.

Eicher, John H., and David J. Eicher. *Civil War High Commands.* Stanford, Calif.: Stanford University Press, 2001.

Ellet, Elizabeth Fries. *The Court Circles of the Republic, or, the Beauties and Celebrities of the Nation.* Sketches by Mrs. R. E. Mack. Hartford, Conn.: Hartford Publishing Co., 1869.

Fairman, Charles. *Reconstruction and Reunion, 1863–88, Part One.* Vol. 6 of Paul A. Freund, gen. ed., *The Oliver Wendell Holmes Devise History of the Supreme Court of the United States.* New York: Macmillan, 1971.

Farnham, Christie Anne. *The Education of the Southern Belle: Higher Education and Student Socialization in the Antebellum South.* New York: New York University Press, 1994.

Fisher, Richard Swainson. *A New and Complete Statistical Gazetteer of the United States of America, Founded on and Compiled from Official Federal and State Returns, and the Seventh National Census.* New York: J. H. Colton, 1853.

Foner, Eric. *Free Soil, Free Labor, Free Men: The Ideology of the Republican Party before the Civil War.* New York: Oxford University Press, 1970.

———. *A Short History of Reconstruction, 1863–1877.* New York: Harper & Row, 1990.

Gibbs, Charles Robert Vernon. *Passenger Liners of the Western Ocean: A Record of the North Atlantic Steam and Motor Passenger Vessels from 1838 to the Present Day.* London: Staples Press, 1952.

Gienapp, William E. *The Origins of the Republican Party, 1852–1856.* New York: Oxford University Press, 1987.

Gillispie, Charles Coulston, ed., *Dictionary of Scientific Biography.* 18 vols. New York: Scribner, 1970–1990.

Goode, James M. *Capital Losses: A Cultural History of Washington's Destroyed Buildings.* 2d ed. Washington, D.C.: Smithsonian Books, 2003.

Goss, Charles Frederic, ed. *Cincinnati: The Queen City, 1788–1912.* 4 vols. Chicago: S. J. Clarke Publishing Co., 1912.

Green, Constance McLaughlin. *Washington: Village and Capital, 1800–1878.* Princeton, N.J.: Princeton University Press, 1962.

Groce, George C., and David H. Wallace. *The New-York Historical Society's Dictionary of Artists in America, 1564–1860.* New Haven, Conn.: Yale University Press, 1957.

Harrold, Stanley. *Gamaliel Bailey and Antislavery Union.* Kent, Ohio: Kent State University Press, 1986.

Hart, Albert Bushnell. *Salmon Portland Chase.* Boston: Houghton, Mifflin, 1899.

Heitman, Francis B. *Historical Register and Dictionary of the United States Army, from Its Organization, September 29, 1789, to March 2, 1903.* 2 vols. Washington, D.C.: Government Printing Office, 1903.

Herr, Pamela, and Mary Lee Spence, eds. *The Letters of Jessie Benton Frémont.* Urbana, Ill.: University of Illinois Press, 1993.

Howells, William Dean. *Years of My Youth and Three Essays.* Edited by David J. Nordloh. Bloomington, Ind.: Indiana University Press, 1975.

Hunter, Alfred. *The Washington and Georgetown Directory, Strangers' Guide-Book for Washington, and Congressional and Clerks' Register.* Washington, D.C.: Kirkwood & McGill, 1853.

Huntington, E. B. *A Genealogical Memoir of the Huntington Family in this Country.* Stamford, Conn.: E. B. Huntington, 1863.

Hyman, Harold M. *The Reconstruction Justice of Salmon P. Chase: In Re Turner and Texas v. White.* Lawrence, Kans.: University Press of Kansas, 1997.

Jabour, Anya. *Marriage in the Early Republic: Elizabeth and William Wirt and the Companionate Ideal.* Baltimore, Md.: Johns Hopkins University Press, 1998.

Jacob, Kathryn Allamong. *Capital Elites: High Society in Washington, D.C., after the Civil War.* Washington, D.C.: Smithsonian Institution Press, 1995.

Joblin, Maurice, & Co. *Cincinnati Past and Present: Or, Its Industrial History as Exhibited in the Life-Labors of Its Leading Men.* Cincinnati: Elm Street Print. Co., 1872.

Johnson, Bradley Tyler, ed. *Reports of Cases Decided by Chief Justice Chase in the Circuit Court of the United States Fourth Circuit.* New York: Diossy, 1876. Reprint, with introduction by Ferne B. Hyman and Harold M. Hyman, New York: Da Capo Press, 1972.

Keckley, Elizabeth. *Behind the Scenes.* Edited by Frances Smith Foster. Chicago: Lakeside Press, R. R. Donnelly & Sons, 1998.

Kelly, Howard A., and Walter L. Burrage. *Dictionary of American Medical Biography: Lives of Eminent Physicians of the United States and Canada, from the Earliest Times.* New York: D. Appleton & Co., 1928.

Knight, Benjamin. *History of the Sprague Families in Rhode Island, Cotton Manufacturers and Calico Printers, from William I to William IV.* Santa Cruz, Calif.: H. Coffin, 1881.

Lamphier, Peg A. *Kate Chase and William Sprague: Politics and Gender in a Civil War Marriage.* Lincoln, Neb.: University of Nebraska Press, 2003.

Larson, Henrietta Melia. *Jay Cooke, Private Banker.* Cambridge, Mass.: Harvard University Press, 1936.

Long, E. B., with Barbara Long. *The Civil War Day by Day: An Almanac, 1861–1865.* Garden City, N.Y.: Doubleday, 1971.

Lyford, James O., ed. *History of Concord, New Hampshire: From the Original Grant in Seventeen Hundred and Twenty-Five to the Opening of the Twentieth Century.* 2 vols. Concord, N.H.: Rumford Press, 1903.

Lystra, Karen. *Searching the Heart: Women, Men, and Romantic Love in Nineteenth-Century America.* New York: Oxford University Press, 1989.

Lytle, William M., and Forrest Robert Holdcamper, comp. *Merchant Steam Vessels of the United States, 1790–1868.* Revised and edited by C. Bradford Mitchell. Staten Island, N.Y.: Steamship Historical Society of America, 1975.

Maizlish, Stephen E. "Salmon P. Chase: The Roots of Ambition and the Origins of Reform." *Journal of the Early Republic* 18 (1998): 47–70.

Maxwell, Sidney Denise. *The Suburbs of Cincinnati.* Cincinnati: G.E. Stevens & Co., 1870. Reprint, New York: Arno Press, 1974.

McCulloch, Hugh. *Men and Measures of Half a Century: Sketches and Comments.* New York: C. Scribner's Sons, 1889.

McPherson, James M. *Battle Cry of Freedom: The Civil War Era.* New York: Oxford University Press, 1988.

———. *Ordeal by Fire: The Civil War and Reconstruction.* New York: Knopf, 1982.

Miers, Earl Schenck, ed. *Lincoln Day by Day: A Chronology, 1809–1865.* 3 vols. Washington, D.C.: Lincoln Sesquicentennial Commission, 1960.

Niven, John. *Salmon P. Chase: A Biography.* New York: Oxford University Press, 1995.

Notable American Women, 1607–1950: A Biographical Dictionary. By Edward T. James, Janet Wilson James, and Paul S. Boyer. 3 vols. Cambridge, Mass.: Belknap Press of Harvard University Press, 1971.

Oberholtzer, Ellis Paxson. *Jay Cooke: Financier of the Civil War.* 2 vols. Philadelphia: G. W. Jacobs & Co., 1907.

Peacock, Virginia Tatnall. *Famous American Belles of the Nineteenth Century.* Philadelphia: J. P. Lippincott Co., 1901.

Phelps, Mary Merwin. *Kate Chase, Dominant Daughter: The Life Story of a Brilliant Woman and Her Famous Father.* New York: Thomas Y. Crowell Co., 1935.

Reid, Whitelaw. *After the War: A Southern Tour. May 1, 1865, to May 1, 1866.* New York: Moore, Wilstach & Baldwin, 1866.

Representative Men and Old Families of Rhode Island: Genealogical Records and Historical Sketches of Prominent and Representative Citizens and of Many of the Old Families. 3 vols. Chicago: J.H. Beers & Co., 1908.

Rix, Guy S. *History and Genealogy of the Eastman Family of America.* 2 vols. Concord, N.H.: I. C. Evans, 1901.

Robson, Charles, ed. *The Biographical Encyclopædia of Ohio of the Nineteenth Century.* Cincinnati: Galaxy Pub. Co., 1876.

Rose, Willie Lee. *Rehearsal for Reconstruction: The Port Royal Experiment.* Indianapolis, Ind.: Bobbs-Merrill, 1964.

Ross, Ishbel. *Proud Kate: Portrait of an Ambitious Woman.* New York: Harper, 1953.

Rothman, Ellen K. *Hands and Hearts: A History of Courtship in America.* New York: Basic Books, 1984.

Scharf, J. Thomas. *History of Westchester County, New York.* 2 vols. Philadelphia: L. E. Preston & Co., 1886.

Schlesinger, Arthur Meier, Sr., ed. "Salmon Portland Chase: Undergraduate and Pedagogue." *Ohio Archaeological and Historical Quarterly* 28 (1919): 119–61.

Schuckers, Jacob W. *The Life and Public Services of Salmon Portland Chase.* New York: D. Appleton, 1874.

Schurz, Carl. *The Reminiscences of Carl Schurz.* 3 vols. New York: McClure Co., 1907.

Simpson, Brooks D., LeRoy P. Graf, and John Muldowny. *Advice after Appomattox: Letters to Andrew Johnson, 1865–1866: Special Volume No. I of the Papers of Andrew Johnson.* Knoxville, Tenn.: University of Tennessee Press, 1987.

Slotten, Hugh Richard. *Patronage, Practice, and the Culture of American Science: Alexander Dallas Bache and the U.S. Coast Survey.* Cambridge: Cambridge University Press, 1994.

Smith, George. *History of Delaware County, Pennsylvania.* Philadelphia: H. B. Ashmead, 1862.

Smith, John. *Harper's Statistical Gazetteer of the World.* New York: Harper & Brothers, 1855.

Sokoloff, Alice. *Kate Chase for the Defense.* New York: Dodd, Mead, 1971.

Spring, Agnes Wright. *Caspar Collins: The Life and Exploits of an Indian Fighter of the Sixties.* New York: Columbia University Press, 1927.

Stowe, Harriet Beecher. *Men of Our Times; or Leading Patriots of the Day. Being Narratives of the Lives and Deeds of Statesmen, Generals, and Orators.* Hartford, Conn.: Hartford Publishing Co., 1868.

Thompson, James H. *The History of the County of Highland, in the State of Ohio, From its First Creation and Organization, to July 4th, 1876.* Hillsboro, Ohio: Hillsboro Gazette, 1878.

Ward, Peter. *Courtship, Love, and Marriage in Nineteenth-Century English Canada.* Montreal: McGill-Queen's University Press, 1990.

Warden, Robert B. *An Account of the Private Life and Public Services of Salmon Portland Chase.* Cincinnati: Wilstach, Baldwin & Co., 1874.

Watson, Irving. *Narragansett Pier as a Fashionable Watering Place, and Summer Residence. The Standard Guide Book for 1873.* Providence, R.I.: A. Crawford Greene, 1873.

Wheeler, William Ogden, comp. *The Ogden Family in America: Elizabethtown Branch.* Edited by Lawrence Van Alstyne and Charles Burr Ogden. Philadelphia: J. B. Lippincott Co., 1907.

Who Was Who in America. Chicago: Marquis-Who's Who, 1942– .

Williams, C. S. *Williams' Columbus Directory, City Guide, and Business Mirror. Volume 1. 1856–'57.* Columbus, Ohio: J. H. Riley & Co., 1856.

———. *Williams' Columbus Directory, City Guide, and Business Mirror. Volume 2. 1858–'59.* Columbus, Ohio: J. H. Riley & Co., 1858.

Williams, T. J. C., and Folger McKinsey. *History of Frederick County, Maryland.* 2 vols. Frederick, Md.: L. R. Titsworth & Co., 1910. Reprint, Baltimore, Md.: Regional Pub. Co., 1967.

Wilson, H., comp. *Trow's New York City Directory, For the Year Ending May 1, 1862.* New York: J. F. Trow, 1861.

———. *Trow's New York City Directory, For the Year Ending May 1, 1863.* New York: J. F. Trow, 1862.

———. *Trow's New York City Directory, For the Year Ending May 1, 1864.* New York: J. F. Trow, 1863.

———. *Trow's New York City Directory, For the Year Ending May 1, 1865.* New York: J. F. Trow, 1864.

———. *Trow's New York City Directory, For the Year Ending May 1, 1871.* New York: J. F. Trow, 1870.

———. *Trow's New York City Directory, For the Year Ending May 1, 1872.* New York: J. F. Trow, 1871.

———. *Trow's New York City Directory, For the Year Ending May 1, 1873.* New York: J. F. Trow, 1872.

———. *Trow's New York City Directory, For the Year Ending May 1, 1874.* New York: J. F. Trow, 1873.

———. *Trow's New York City Directory, For the Year Ending May 1, 1875.* New York: J. F. Trow, 1874.

Works Projects Administration Writers' Program. *Cincinnati: A Guide to the Queen City and Its Neighbors.* Cincinnati: Wiesen-Hart Press, 1943.

Index